S0-BDT-615

COMPENSATION

George T. Milkovich
Cornell University

Jerry M. Newman
State University of New York–Buffalo

With the assistance of Carolyn Milkovich

Boston Burr Ridge, IL Dubuque, IA Madison, WI New York San Francisco St. Louis
Bangkok Bogotá Caracas Lisbon London Madrid
Mexico City Milan New Delhi Seoul Singapore Sydney Taipei Toronto

Irwin/McGraw-Hill

A Division of The **McGraw-Hill** *Companies*

COMPENSATION

This book is printed on acid-free paper.

4 5 6 7 8 9 0 DOC/DOC 3 2 1 0

ISBN 0-256-25965-8

Vice president and editorial director: *Michael W. Junior*
Publisher: *Craig S. Beytien*
Senior sponsoring editor: *John E. Biernat*
Developmental editor: *Christine Scheid*
Marketing manager: *Kenyetta Giles*
Senior project manager: *Pat Frederickson*
Production associate: *Debra R. Benson*
Freelance design coordinator: *Gino Cieslik*
Supplement coordinator: *Rose M. Range*
Compositor: *GAC Shepard Poorman Communications*
Typeface: 10/12 Times Roman
Printer: *R. R. Donnelley & Sons Company*

Library of Congress Cataloging-in-Publication Data

Milkovich, George T.
Compensation / George T. Milkovich, Jerry M. Newman ; with the assistance of Carolyn Milkovich. — 6th ed.
p. cm.
ISBN 0-256-26906-8
1. Compensation management. I. Newman, Jerry M. II. Milkovich, Carolyn. III. Title.
HF5549.5.C67M54 1999
6658.3′2—dc21

http://www.mhhe.com

Preface

When the supertanker Exxon Valdez ran aground in Prince Edward Sound, fast action was required to rescue the Alaskan wildlife from the spreading oil. For $20 an hour, local members of an Inuit tribe were hired to care for stranded whales, cleaning and feeding them until they could be released. When these temporary, high-pay jobs were no longer available, the Inuits went back to their usual occupation—hunting the whales. *Money matters.*

It matters what you pay for. Many years ago, when Green Giant discovered too many insect parts in the pea pack from one of its plants, it designed a bonus plan that paid people for insect parts. Green Giant got what it paid for: insect parts. Innovative Green Giant employees brought insect parts from home to add to the peas right before they removed them and collected the bonus.

And speaking of bugs . . . a well-known west coast software house designed a bonus plan that paid software engineers to find bugs in software code. Plan designers failed to realize that the people who found the bugs were the very same ones who wrote the buggy software code in the first place. Engineers joked about "writing me a sport-ute."

And it matters how you pay. Motorola trashed its old-fashioned pay system that employees said guaranteed a raise every six months if you were still breathing. They replaced it with a system that paid for learning new skills and working in teams. Sounded good. Wasn't. Employees resented those team members who went off for six weeks of training at full pay, while remaining team members picked up their work. Motorola was forced to trash its new-fashioned system, too.

We live in interesting times. Economic and social pressures are forcing managers to reexamine how people get paid and what difference it makes. Traditional approaches to compensation are being questioned and rejected. But what is being achieved by all this experimentation and change? We have lots of fads and fashions, but is it all folderol? Where are the results?

In this book, we strive to cull the beliefs from facts, wishful thinking from demonstrable results, and paid pundits' opinions from scholarly research. Yet when all is said and done, managing compensation is an art. Like any art, not everything that can be learned can be taught.

ABOUT THIS BOOK

This book is based on the strategic choices in managing compensation. We introduce these choices in the compensation model in Chapter 1 and use the model as an integrating framework throughout the book. Major compensation issues are discussed in the context of current theory, research, and practice. The practices illustrate new developments as well as established approaches to compensation decisions.

This book also provides an opportunity for you to develop decision-making skills through real-life "Your Turn" exercises that apply the concepts and techniques discussed in each chapter. A workbook with a more extensive case and computer applications is also available directly from the authors (telephone 607-257-3859; fax 607-257-6639). Completing these exercises will help you develop skills readily transferable to future jobs and assignments.

But caveat emptor! One manager recently told us that she searched for this book in her local Walden Bookstore. The store personnel finally found the listing in their information system—under fiction!

WHAT'S NEW

All chapters of this edition have been completely revised. A new chapter (2) tells how to craft a compensation strategy and examines the research on strategic perspectives applied to compensation. New chapters on performance-based pay dig into all forms of variable pay such as profit sharing, gain sharing, and team-based approaches. Person-based plans are contrasted with job-based plans, including recent developments in skill and competency approaches. The increased use of market pricing, broadbanding, and total compensation is also discussed. Employee benefits, always changing and always important, are treated in two chapters. We have always used international examples in every section; this edition includes a chapter on international compensation.

Try out our Cybercomps, which are new this edition—short exercises that help you learn where to find some of the tremendous information available on the web.

Research and surveys about compensation are burgeoning. We have included the best and most relevant of it, along with a reader's guide on how to be an informed consumer of this material.

ACKNOWLEDGMENTS

In addition to our Walden shopper, many people have contributed to our understanding of compensation and to the preparation of this textbook. We owe a special, continuing debt of gratitude to our students. In the classroom, they motivate and challenge us, and as returning seasoned managers, they try mightily to keep our work relevant.

Jack Barry *Motorola*
Roberta Bixhorn *TRW*
John Bronson *Pepsico*
Michael Carey *Johnson & Johnson*
Clifton Chang *Johnson & Johnson China*
John Cross *KLA Instruments*
Larry Drake *Graphic Controls*
Dennis Donovan *General Electric*
Andrew Doyle *Toshiba Japan*
Sally Fanning *Praxair*
Alejandro Fernandez *Petroleos de Venezuela*
Richard Frings *Johnson & Johnson*
Steve Gross *W.W. Mercer*
Michael Guthman *Hewitt*
Lada Hruba *Bristol Meyers Squibb*
Steve Kane *Baxter*
Ann Killian *TRW*
Dae-Ki Kim *Yukong, Korea*
Tae-Jin Kim *Yukong, Korea*
Sharon Knight *Phillip Morris*
Doug McKenna *Microsoft*
Harvey Minkoff *TRW*
Yvonne Moore *Medtronic*
David Ness *Medtronic*
Bob Ochsner *Hay*
Nelson Olmedillo *Hay*
Sandra O'Neal *Towers Perrin*
Robert Obler *Johnson & Johnson*
Larry Phillips *Citicorp*
Susan Podlogar *Johnson & Johnson*
Walt Read *consultant*
Tom Ruddy *Xerox*
Robert Rusek *Lucent Technologies*
Richard Thier *Xerox*
Josie Tsao *IBM*
Robert White *TRW China*

Our universities, Cornell and Buffalo, provide forums for the interchange of ideas among students, experienced managers, and academic colleagues. We value this interchange. Other academic colleagues also provided helpful comments on this edition of the book. We particularly thank

Ronald Ash *University of Kansas*

David Balkin *University of Colorado at Boulder*

Lubica Bajzikova *Comenius University, Bratislava*

Melissa Barringer *University of Massachusetts*

Kay Bartol *University of Maryland*

Matt Bloom *University of Notre Dame*

Renae Broderick *Cornell University*

Barry Gerhart *Vanderbilt*

Luis Gomez-Mejia *Arizona State University*

Greg Hundley *University of Oregon*

Jiri Kamenicek *Charles University, Prague*

Frank Krzystofiak *SUNY Buffalo*

Ed Montemayer *Michigan State University*

Michael Moore *Michigan State University*

Janez Prasnikar *University of Ljubljana*

Yoko Sano *Keio University*

Donald Schwab *University of Wisconsin*

Susan Schwochau *University of Iowa*

Michael Sturman *Louisiana State University*

Jan Tichy *Cornell University*

Theresa Welbourne *Cornell University*

Nada Zupan *University of Ljubljana*

Brief Contents

Contents

PART I

Internal Consistency: Determining the Structure

3 Defining Consistency 51

4 Job Analysis 81

5 Evaluating Work: Job Evaluation 107

PART VI

Managing the System

CHAPTER 1

The Pay Model

Chapter Outline

A friend of ours writes that she is in the touring company of the musical *Cats.* In the company are two performers called *swings* who sit backstage during each performance. Each swing must learn five different lead roles in the show. During the performance, the swing sits next to a rack with five different costumes and makeup for each of the five roles. Our friend, who has a lead in the show, once hurt her shoulder during a dance number. She signaled to someone offstage, and by the time she finished her number, the swing was dressed, in makeup, and out on stage for the next scene.

Our friend is paid $2,000 per week for playing one of the cats in the show. She is expected to do a certain number of performances and a certain number of rehearsals per week. She gets paid for the job she does. The swing gets paid $2,500 per week, whether she performs 20 shows that week or none. She is paid for knowing the five roles, whether she plays them or not.

Think of all the other employees, in addition to the performers, required to put on a performance of *Cats.* Electricians, trombonists, choreographers, dressers, janitors, nurses, vocal coaches, accountants, stagehands, payroll supervisors, ushers, lighting technicians, ticket sellers—the list goes on. Consider the array of wages paid to these employees. Why does the swing get paid more than other performers? Why does the performer get paid more (or less) than the trombonist? Why does the *Cats* trombonist get paid more (or less) than the trombonist in a regional orchestra? How are these decisions made, and who is involved in making them? Whether it's our own or someone else's, compensation questions engage our attention.

Does the compensation received by all the people connected with *Cats* matter? Increasingly, employers believe that how people are paid can be a source of competitive advantage. Pay systems affect people's behaviors at work. They affect an organization's success.

COMPENSATION: TRANSLATION PLEASE?

Taken literally, compensation means to counterbalance, to offset, to make up for. It implies an exchange. However, it does not mean the same thing in every country. In the United States, we equate compensation with wages and benefits given in exchange for effort or work. In China, the traditional characters for compensation are based on the signs for logs and water; compensation provides the necessities in life. In today's China, however, the reforms of the last decade have led to use of a new word, *Dai Yu,* which refers to how you are treated or taken care of. When people talk about compensation, they ask each other "How about the 'dai yu' in your company" rather than asking about the wages. So the benefits part of total compensation is very important. Another very popular question related to compensation is to ask "how about the performance of your company?" which indicates how tightly the employees' *dai yu* is tied to the firm performance.

Compensation in Japanese is *kyuyo,* which is made up of two Chinese characters (*kyu* and *yo*), both meaning "giving something". *Kyu* is an honorific used to indicate that the person doing the giving is someone of high rank, such as a feudal lord, an emperor, or a Samurai leader. Traditionally, compensation is thought of as something given by one's superior. Today, business consultants in Japan try to substitute the word *hou-syu,* which means reward, and has no associations with notions of superiors. The many allowances which are part of Japanese compensation systems translate as *teate*, which means "taking care of something" or "dealing with something". *Teate* is regarded as compensation which takes care of employees' financial needs. This concept is consistent with the fact that family allowance, housing allowance, and comuting allowance are common in japanese companies.

In the Czech language, the word for salary is *plat*, from *platno*, which means linen or canvas. Tenth century currency in the region was shaped like linen scarves. The bigger the scarf, the more it was worth. From platno comes a verb *platit*, meaning to pay, be worth.[1] So compensation translates into different meanings among countries and even varies over time.

Society Views

Perceptions of compensation differ *within* countries as well.[2] Some in society may see pay differences as a measure of justice. For example, a comparison of earnings of women with those of men highlights what many consider inequities in pay decisions. The gender pay gap in the United States, after adjustment for differences in education, experience, and occupation, narrowed from 36 percent in 1980 to 12 percent in 1997. Neverthless, it persists and always to the benefit of males.[3]

Union leaders sometimes identify differences in compensation among countries as a cause of loss of U.S. jobs to less developed economies. Production workers in Mexico earn less than a tenth of production workers in the United States.[4] However, as Exhibit 1.1 reveals, U.S. average labor costs for manufacturing jobs are now less than those paid in Japan ($21.04) and Germany ($31.87). And *consumers* who seek the highest quality at the lowest costs may not believe that higher labor costs are to their benefit. *Voters* may see compensation, pensions, and health care for public employees as the cause of increased taxes. Public *policymakers* and legislators may view changes in average pay as guides for adjusting eligibility for social services (medical assistance, food stamps, and the like).

Stockholders' Views

To stockholders, executive pay is of special interest. In the United States, stock options are commonly believed to tie pay of executives to the financial performance of the company. Unfortunately, practice often falls short of that objective. For example,

---

[1]Participants in an international compensation seminar at Cornell University provided the information on various meanings of compensation.

[2]G. T. Milkovich and M. Bloom, "Rethinking International Compensation: From National Cultures to Markets and Strategic Flexibility," *Compensation and Benefits Review,* January 1998, pp. 1–10.

[3]Francine D. Blau and Lawrence M. Kahn, "Swimming Upstream:Trends in the Gender Wage Differentials," *Journal of Labor Economics* 15, no. 1 (1997), pp. 1–42; Fran D. Blau, Marianne A. Farber, and Ann E. Winkler, *The Economics of Women, Men, and Work,* 3rd ed. (New York: Simon & Schuster, 1998).

[4]C. Sparks and M. Greiner, "U.S. and Foreign Productivity and Unit Labor Costs," *Monthly Labor Review,* February 1997, pp. 26–35.

EXHIBIT 1.1 Germany and Japan Beat the United States—in Labor Costs
Hourly Compensation Costs in U.S. Dollars for Production Workers in Manufacturing

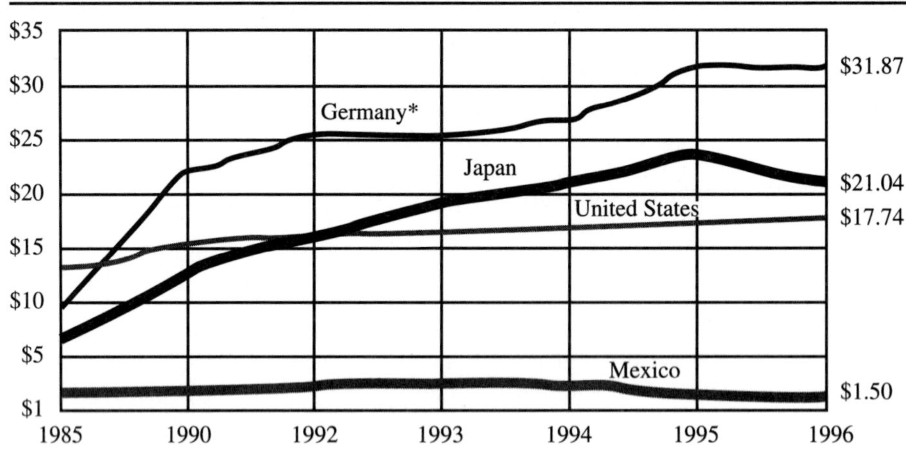

*Former West Germany
Source: Bureau of Labor Statistics **(http://stats.bls/gov/news.release.ichcc.t02.htm)**

the CEO and chairman of Grand Casinos Inc., Lyle Berman, received a grant of one million shares of company stock in 1996, at a time when the stock price was $32. However, problems with a project drove the stock price down to around $13 a share. Did Mr. Berman's pay take a beating commensurate with the company's poor financial performance? Not at all. While ordinary investors lost over 59 percent of their investment, the board of directors simply repriced Mr. Berman's options at a price *below* the new low price. So a subsequent rise in stock price—to a level still well below the original $32 value—increased his net worth by over $2 million.

The former CEO of Apple Computer, Gil Amelio, did even better. Huge stock grants were used to hire him to turn around the still-ailing computer company; unfortunately, he was unable to do so. (Perhaps he was distracted by managing Aero Ventures, a company he owned, whose airplanes were rented by Apple executives.) Nevertheless, when the board finally fired him, the stock market reacted positively to the news and Apple stock value increased—thereby permitting the unsuccessful CEO to profit from his own firing! As one disgruntled shareholder wrote, "If Gil Amelio had run the company with the skill he'd used to negotiate his remarkable pay package, he'd still be considered a 'turnaround artist,' and my stock wouldn't be trading near its all-time low."[5]

Executive pay practices are typically unique to each country, since regulatory requirements that vary among countries determine the attractiveness of various approaches. Stock options are most heavily used (and occasionally abused) in the United States.

[5]Anne Faircloth, "Apple's Bonus Babies Irk a Shareholder," *Fortune,* March 3, 1997, p. 105. Brian J. Hall and Jeffery Liebman, *Are CEOs Really Paid Like Bureaucrats?* (Boston, MA: NBER #6213, October 1997). Those readers interested in the inside details on CEO pay should look at *The Crystal Report,* a periodic newsletter published by Graef Crystal. E-mail graefc@ix.netcom.com, or check their website, www.crystalreport.com.

Employees

In contrast to the perspective of society and stockholders, *employees* may see compensation as an exchange for services rendered or as a reward for a job well done. Compensation to some reflects the value of their personal skills and abilities, or the return for the education and training they have acquired. Benefits such as medical insurance, pensions, or wellness programs help protect employees and their dependents. The pay individuals receive for the work they perform is usually the major source of personal income and financial security, and hence a vital determinant of an individual's economic and social well-being.

Rather than an exchange or a return, some employees in large state-owned companies in Russia and China believe their pay is an entitlement: their just due, regardless of their own performance or that of their employer's. They are not yet able to shrug off the past for the freedom and uncertainties of the market-based economies. Political leaders in these countries often regulate wage increases to ensure stability of the workforce.[6]

Managers

Managers also have a stake in compensation: it directly influences their success in two ways. First, it is a *major expense.* Competitive pressures, both internationally and domestically, force managers to consider the affordability of their compensation decisions. Studies show that in many enterprises labor costs account for more than 50 percent of total costs. Among some industries, such as service or public employment, this figure is even higher. Even within an industry (e.g., automotive manufacturing, financial services), labor costs as a percent of total costs vary among individual firms. Firms that vary their pay policies do so because they believe that compensation decisions can be a source of competitive advantage.[7]

In addition to treating pay as a expense, a manager also treats compensation as a possible *influence on employee work attitudes and behaviors and their organization performance.* The way people are paid affects the quality of their work; their focus on customer needs; their willingness to be flexible and learn new skills, to suggest innovations and improvements; and even their interests in unions or legal action against their employer. This potential to influence employees' work attitudes and behaviors, and subsequently the productivity and effectiveness of the organization, is another reason why many believe that pay decisions can become a source of competitive advantage.[8]

These contrasting perspectives of compensation—**societal, stockholder, employee,** and **managerial,** each with different stakes in compensation decisions—can account for the relevance of the topic. But these perspectives can also cause confusion

---

[6]Li Hua Wang, "Research in Pay Determination Policies in China: What We Know and What We Do Not Know," (CAHRS Working Paper: Ithaca, NY, 1998).

[7]*Industry Total Labor Cost Studies* (Philadelphia: The Hay Group, 1997); J. E. Triplett, *An Essay on Labor Costs* (Washington, D.C.: Office of Research and Evaluation, U.S. Bureau of Labor Statistics, 1997).

[8]B. E. Becker and Mark Huselid, "High Performance Work Systems and Firm Performance: A Synthesis of Research and Management Implications," in *Research in Personnel and Human Resources,* ed. G. Ferris (Greenwich, CT: JAI Press, 1998).

unless everyone is talking about the same thing. So let's define what we mean by compensation. Compensation, or pay (the words are used interchangeably in this book), is defined in the following terms:

Compensation refers to all forms of financial returns and tangible services and benefits employees receive as part of an employment relationship.

FORMS OF PAY

Exhibit 1.2 shows the variety of returns people may receive from work. Financial returns are part of total compensation. However, nonfinancial, relational returns (security, personal status, opportunity to belong, challenging work and so on) are important, too. Nevertheless, this book will focus on those aspects of compensation included on the left side of the exhibit.

Total compensation includes pay received directly as cash (e.g., base wages, merit increases, incentives, cost of living adjustments) or indirectly through benefits and services (e.g., pensions, health insurance, paid time off). Programs that distribute compensation to employees can be designed in an unlimited number of ways, and a single employer typically uses more than one program. The major categories of compensation include base wage, merit pay, short-and long-term incentives, and employee benefits and services.

Base Wage

Base wage is the basic cash compensation that an employer pays for the work performed. Base wage tends to reflect the value of the work or skills and generally ignores differences attributable to individual employees. For example, the base wage for machine operators may be $12 an hour, but some individual operators may receive more because of their experience and/or performance. Some pay systems set base wage as a function of the skill or education an employee possesses; this is common for engineers and scientists. Periodic adjustments to base wages may be made on the basis of changes in the overall cost of living or inflation, changes in what other employers are paying for the same work, or changes in experience/performance/skill of employees.

A distinction is often made in the United States between salary and wage, with *salary* referring to pay for those workers who are exempt from regulations of the Fair Labor Standards Act, and hence do not receive overtime pay.[9] Managers and professionals usually fit this category. We refer to such employees at *exempts*. Their pay would be calculated at an annual or monthly rate rather than hourly, because hours worked do not need to be recorded.

[9] U.S. Department of Labor Employment Standards Administration, Wage and Hour division.

EXHIBIT 1.2 Total Returns in Exchange for Work

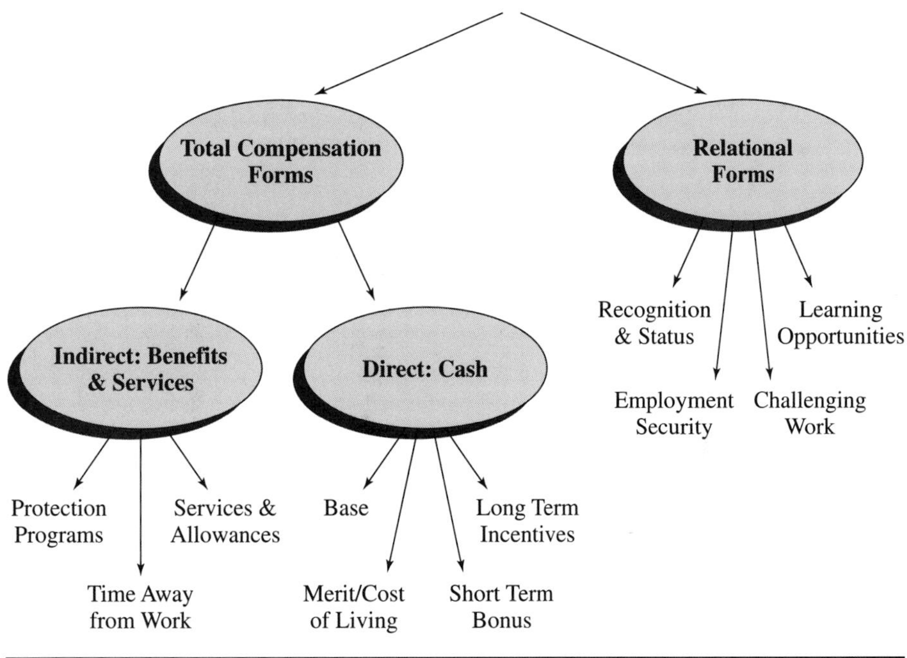

In contrast, workers who are covered by overtime and reporting provisions of the Fair Labor Standards Act—*nonexempts*—usually have their pay calculated at an hourly rate referred to as a *wage.* Some employers, such as Hewlett-Packard and IBM, label all base pay as salary in an attempt to support a management philosophy that all employees are working as a team, rather than being divided into salaried and wage earners.[10]

Merit

Merit pay recognizes past work behaviors and accomplishments. Given as increments to the base pay, merit programs typically vary with performance. Thus, outstanding performers may receive a 6 to 7 percent merit increase 12 months after their last increase, whereas a satisfactory performer may receive, say, a 4 to 5 percent increase after 12 or 15 months. According to surveys, 90 percent of U.S. firms use merit pay.[11]

---

[10]*Employee Buy-In to Total Quality,* Report 974 (New York: Conference Board, 1991); *Hewlett-Packard Personnel Policies and Guidelines.*

[11]Robert Heneman, *Merit Pay: Linking Pay Increases to Performance Ratings* (Reading, MA.: Addison–Wesley,1992); Robert Bretz, Jr., George Milkovich, and Walter Read, "The Current State of Performance Appraisal Research and Practice: Concerns, Directions, and Implications," *Journal of Management,* 1992.

Incentives

Incentives also tie pay directly to performance. Sometimes referred to as variable compensation, incentives may be long or short term, and can be tied to the performance of an individual employee, a team of employees, a total business unit, or some combination of individual, team, and unit. Performance objectives may be defined as cost savings, volume produced, quality standards met, revenues, return on investments, or increased profits; the possibilities are endless.

Short-term incentives usually use very specific performance standards. For example, at Prax Air's Chemicals and Plastics Division, for every quarter that an 8 percent return on capital target is met or exceeded, bonus days of pay are awarded. A 9.6 percent return on capital means two extra days of pay for every participating employee for that quarter. Twenty percent return on capital means 8.5 extra days of pay.

Long-term incentives are intended to focus employee efforts on multiyear results. Top managers or professionals are often offered stock ownership or bonuses to focus on long–term organizational objectives such as return on investment, market share, return on net assets, and the like.[12] Coca-Cola grants shares of stock to selected "Key Contributors" who make outstanding contributions to the firm's success. Microsoft, Pepsi, Wal-Mart and Procter and Gamble offer stock options to all their employees. These companies believe that having a stake in the company supports a culture of ownership: Employees will behave like owners.[13]

Incentives and merit pay differ. Although both may influence performance, incentives do so by offering pay to influence future behavior. Merit, on the other hand, recognizes outstanding past performance. The distinction is a matter of timing.

Incentive systems are offered prior to the actual performance. For example, an auto sales agent knows the commission on a Cadillac versus that on a Chevy prior to making the sale. Gainsharing plans also specify the possible pay before the performance. Corning employees at their Blacksburg, Virginia, facility know the amount of the bonus they will receive if their plant exceeds its financial goals. Merit pay, on the other hand, typically is not communicated beforehand.

Perhaps the most important distinction is that merit pay usually adds into and permanently increases base pay, whereas incentives are one–time payments and do not have a permanent effect on labor costs. When performance declines, incentive pay automatically declines, too.

---

[12]M. C. Jensen and K. J. Murphy, "CEO Incentives: It's Not How Much You Pay, But How," *Harvard Business Review,* May–June 1990, pp. 138–53; Graef Crystal, *In Search of Excess* (New York: W. W. Norton, 1991); "Overview of CEO and Director Compensation," *Compensation Briefs,* October 1994 (Washington, D.C.: Peat Marwick); J. D. Bloedorn and P. T. Chingos, "Executive Pay and Company Performance," *ACA Journal,* Autumn 1994, pp. 70–79.

[13]Some believe greater stock ownership motivates performance; others argue that the link between individual job behaviors and the vagaries of the stock market are tenuous at best. J. L. Pierce, S. A. Rubenfeld, and S. Morgan, "Employee Ownership: A Conceptual Model of Process and Effects," *Academy of Management Review 16,* no. 1 (1991), pp. 121–44; D. Kruse and J. Blasi, "Employee Ownership, Employee Attributes and Firm Performance," National Bureau of Economic Research paper 5277, 1996.

Benefits and Services

Employee benefits include time away from work (vacations, jury duty), services (drug counseling, financial planning, cafeteria), and protection (medical care, life insurance, and pensions). Because the cost of providing these services and benefits has been rising (for example, employers pay nearly half the nation's health care bills, and health care expenditures have been increasing at annual rates in excess of 15 percent), they are an increasingly important form of pay.[14] In a recent Gallup poll, people claimed they would require $5,000 more in extra pay to choose a job without pension, health care, and life insurance.

Services and benefits vary widely from country to country. For example, in response to shortages and high costs in Korea, Yukong Petroleum and the Hyundai shipyards include housing (dormitories and apartments) and transportation allowances in their pay package. Japanese companies provide similar allowances, plus they offer a family allowance based on number of dependents (though this latter practice is declining). Almost all companies with operations in China discover that housing, transportation, and fixed allowances are crucial for attracting and retaining talented employees. And in the United Kingdom, it is not only whether a car is provided, managers also care about the make and model of the car.[15]

In addition to these four pay forms that make up the total compensation package, nonfinancial returns also affect employees' behavior. Exhibit 1.2 shows these relational forms to include recognition and status, employment security, challenging work, and opportunities to learn. Other relational forms might include personal satisfaction from successfully facing new challenges, working with great co-workers, and the like. Relational forms undoubtedly are an important part of the total returns people receive from their work. Such factors may be thought of as part of an organization's "total reward system" and are often coordinated with compensation. So while this book is about compensation, let's not forget that compensation is only one of many factors affecting people's decisions. Even an offer of better wages, an expense account, and a company car couldn't compete with the alternative rewards songwriter Roger Miller's hero found in his job in this popular song from the 1960s:

> Got a letter just this morning, it was postmarked Omaha
> It was typed and neatly written offering me a better job,
> Better job and higher wages, expenses paid, and a car.
> But I'm on TV here locally, and I can't quit, I'm a star.
>
> I come on TV a grinnin', wearin' pistols and a hat,
> It's a kiddie show and I'm the hero of the younger set.
> I'm the number one attraction in every supermarket parking lot.
> I'm the king of Kansas City. No thanks, Omaha, thanks a lot.
>
> (refrain)
> Kansas City Star, that's what I are . . .

[14]See Employee Benefits Research Institute's website at http://www.ebri.org. See also the EBRI's *Fundamentals of Employee Benefits,* (Washington, D.C.: EBRI, 1997).

[15]See D. J. B. Mitchell, "Employee Benefits in Europe and the United States" in *Research Frontiers in IR and HR,* ed. D. Lewin (Madison, WI: IRRA, 1996), pp. 587–625.

Expected Costs and Present Value of a Stream of Earnings

Up to this point we have treated compensation as something paid or received at a moment in time. But compensation decisions have a temporal effect. Think about the manager who makes you a job offer—say $30,000. Assume you stay with the firm 5 years and receive an annual increase of 7 percent in each of those 5 years. You will be earning $39,324 in 5 years. The expected cost commitment of the decision to hire you turns out to be $224,279 ($30,000 base compounded by 7 percent for 5 years, plus benefits equal to 30 percent of base). So the decision to hire you implies a commitment of at least a quarter of a million dollars from your employer.

Few students, even accounting/finance majors, evaluate competing job offers in terms of present value of a stream of future earnings. A present value perspective shifts the choice from comparing today's initial offers to consideration of future bonuses, merit increases, and promotions. Andersen Consulting, for example, convinces some students every year that their relatively low starting offers will be overcome by larger future pay increases. In effect, Andersen is selling the present value of the stream of earnings. But few students apply those same financial skills to calculate the future increases required to offset the lower initial offers.

So compensation can be treated as a stream of future earnings or costs. It can include nonfinancial returns as part of a total reward system. And it can take several forms: cash, benefits, and services. Our pay model serves as both a framework for examining current pay systems and a guide for must of this book.

A PAY MODEL

The pay model shown in Exhibit 1.3 contains three basic building blocks: (1) the strategic policies that form the foundation of the compensation system, (2) the techniques of compensation, and (3) the compensation objectives.

Compensation Objectives

Pay systems are designed and managed to achieve certain objectives. The basic objectives, shown at the right side of the model, include efficiency, equity, and compliance with laws and regulations.

The *efficiency* objective can be stated more specifically: (1) improving performance, quality, delighting customers, and (2) controlling labor costs. Compensation objectives at Hewlett-Packard and Medtronic are contrasted in Exhibit 1.4. They emphasize performance, business success, and market responsiveness.

Equity is fundamental to pay systems. Statements such as "fair treatment for all employees" or "a fair day's pay for a fair day's work" reflect a concern for equity. In Hewlett-Packard's objectives, this is reflected in "ensure fair treatment" and "be open and understandable."

Thus, the equity objective attempts to ensure fair pay treatment for all participants in the employment relationships. The equity objective focuses on designing pay systems that recognize both employee *contributions* (e.g., offering higher pay for greater performance or greater experience or training) and employee *needs* (e.g., providing a fair wage as well as fair procedures).

Exhibit 1.3 The Pay Model

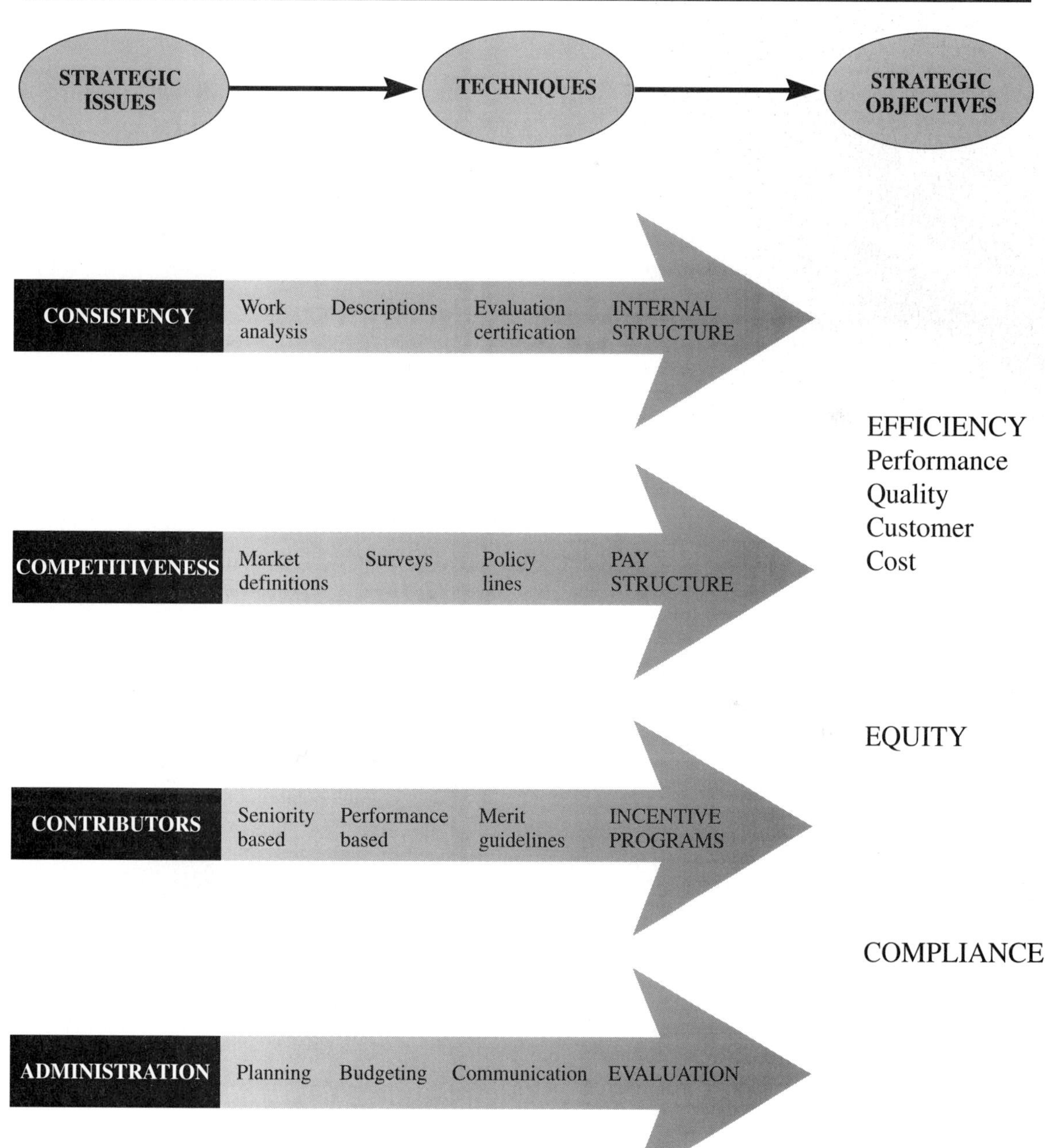

Exhibit 1.4 Comparison of Pay System Objectives

Pay Objectives at Medtronic and Hewlett-Packard

Medtronic	*Hewlett-Packard*
• Support objectives and increased complexity of business • Minimize increases in fixed costs • Emphasize performance through variable pay and stock • Competitiveness aligned with financial performance: 50th percentile performance paid at 50th percentile of market, 75th percentile performance paid at 75th percentile of market	• Help H-P continue to attract creative and enthusiastic people who contribute to its success • Pay among the leaders • Reflect sustained relative contribution of unit, division, and H-P • Be open and understandable • Ensure fair treatment • Be innovative, competitive, and equitable

Procedural equity is concerned with the processes used to make decisions about pay.[16] It suggests that *the way* a pay decision is made may be as important to employees as *the results* of the decision.

Compliance as a pay objective involves conforming to various federal and state compensation laws and regulations. As these laws and regulations change, pay systems may need to be adjusted to ensure continued compliance.

There are probably as many statements of pay objectives as there are employers. In fact, highly diversified firms such as TRW and General Electric, which compete in multiple lines of businesses, may have different pay objectives for different business units. Objectives at Medtronic and Hewlett-Packard emphasize high-quality and innovative performance (productivity), competitiveness (costs), ability to attract and retain quality people (productivity), and equity (employee communications, openness, and simplicity).

Objectives serve several purposes. First, they guide the design of the pay system. Consider the employer whose objective is to reward outstanding performance. That objective will determine the pay policy (e.g., pay for performance) as well as the elements of pay plans (e g., merit and/or incentives).

Another employer's objectives may be to develop a flexible, continuously learning work force. This employer believes that flexibility is increased through job design, training, and team-building techniques. A pay system that is consistent with this employer's objectives may have a policy of paying salaries that at least equal those of competitors and that recognize increased skills or knowledge. This system would be very different from the one in our first example. So, different objectives guide the design of different pay systems.

Objectives also serve as the standards for judging the success of the pay system. If the objective is to attract and retain a highly competent staff, yet skilled employees are

[16]Marcia P. Miceli, "Justice and Pay System Satisfaction" in *Justice in the Workplace: Approaching Fairness in Human Resource Management* (Lawrence Erlbaum Associates, 1993).

leaving to take higher paying jobs at other employers, the system may not be performing effectively. Although there may be many nonpay reasons for turnover, objectives provide standards for evaluating the effectiveness of a pay system.

Four Strategic Policies

Every employer must address the policy decisions shown on the left side of the pay model: (1) internal consistency, (2) external competitiveness, (3) employee contributions, and (4) administration of the pay system. These policies form the building blocks, the foundation on which pay systems are built. These policies also serve as guidelines for managing pay in ways that accomplish the system's objectives.

Internal Consistency. Internal consistency refers to comparisons among jobs or skill levels *inside* a single organization. Jobs and skills are compared in terms of their relative contributions to the organization's objectives. How, for example, does the work of the word processor compare with the work of the computer operator, the programmer, and the software engineer? Does one contribute to satisfying customers and shareholders more than the others? Does one require more skill or experience than another? Internal consistency becomes a factor in determining the pay rates both for employees doing equal work and for those doing dissimilar work. In fact, determining what is an appropriate difference in pay for people performing different work is one of the key challenges facing managers.

Internal consistency policies affect all three compensation objectives. Pay relationships within the organization affect employee decisions to stay with the organization, to become more flexible by investing in additional training, or to seek greater responsibility. By motivating employees to choose increased training and greater responsibility in dealing with customers, pay relationships indirectly affect the efficiency of the work force and hence the effectiveness of the total organization.

External Competitiveness. External competitiveness refers to how an employer positions its pay relative to what competitors are paying. How much do we wish to pay accountants in comparison to what other employers would pay them? Employers have several policy options. Recall that Medtronic's policy is to pay competitively in the market based on its financial performance versus the financial performance of its competitors, while Hewlett-Packard's policy is to pay among the leaders.

Increasingly, organizations claim their pay systems are market driven. However, "market driven" gets translated into practice in different ways. Some employers may set their pay levels higher than their competition, hoping to attract the best applicants. Of course, this assumes that someone is able to identify and hire the "best" from the pool of applicants.

Medtronic sets its base pay to match its competitors but offers bigger bonuses for achieving better performance. Plus it offers stock options to employees to promote a culture of ownership. The assumption is that owners will pay closer attention to the business. Yet another employer may offer lower base pay but greater opportunity to work overtime or better benefits. Or pay and benefits may be lower, but job security may be higher.

The policy regarding external competitiveness has a twofold effect on objectives: (1) to ensure that the pay is sufficient to attract and retain employees—if employees do not perceive their pay as competitive in comparison to what other organizations are offering for similar work, they may be more likely to leave—and (2) to control labor costs so that the organization's prices of products or services can remain competitive. So external competitiveness directly affects both efficiency and equity. And it must do so in a way that complies with relevant legislation.

Employee Contributions. The policy on employee contributions refers to the relative emphasis placed on performance. Should one programmer be paid differently from another if one has better performance and/or greater seniority? Or should all employees share in the organization's financial successes (and failures) via profit sharing? Perhaps more productive teams of employees should be paid more than less productive teams.

The degree of emphasis to be placed on performance and/or seniority is an important policy since it directly affects employees' attitudes and work behaviors. Employers with strong pay for performance policies are more likely to place greater emphasis on incentive and merit schemes as part of their pay systems. Medtronic seeks to celebrate growth and development. And it emphasizes stock options and sharing the success of corporate performance with the employees. Hewlett-Packard emphasizes performance at the unit, division, and companywide level.

Administration. Policy regarding administration of the pay system is the last building block in our model. While it is possible to design a system that incorporates internal consistency, external competitiveness, and employee contributions, the system will not achieve its objectives unless it is managed properly.

The greatest system design in the world is useless without competent management. Managers must plan the elements of pay included in the system (e.g., base pay, short-term and long-term incentives), communicate with employees, and judge whether the system is achieving its objectives.

Are we able to attract skilled workers? Can we keep them? Do our employees feel our system is fair? Do they understand how their pay is determined? How do the better performing firms, with better financial returns and a larger share of the market, pay their employees? Are the systems used by these firms different from those used by less successful firms? How do our labor costs compare to our competitors"?

Such information is necessary to tune or redesign the system, to adjust to changes, and to highlight potential areas for further investigation. Hewlett-Packard's objectives include a plan designed to be "open and understandable." Medtronic hopes to promote fairness.

Pay Techniques

The remaining portion of the pay model in Exhibit 1.3 shows the pay techniques. The exhibit provides only an overview since techniques are the topic of much of the rest of the book. Techniques tie the four basic policies to the pay objectives. *Internal consistency* is typically established through a sequence that starts with analysis of the work done. Information about the person and/or the job is collected, organized, and evaluated. Based on these evaluations, a structure of the work is designed.

This structure depicts relationships among jobs and skills or competencies inside an organization. It is based on the relative importance of the work in achieving the organization's objectives. The goal is to establish a structure that supports the organization's objectives and is internally equitable. In turn, equity of the pay system affects employee attitudes and behaviors as well as the organization's regulatory compliance.

External competitiveness is established by setting the organization's pay level in comparison with what competitors pay for similar work. The pay level is determined by defining the relevant labor markets in which the employer competes, conducting surveys to find out what other employers pay, and using that information in conjunction with the organization's policy decisions to generate a pay structure. The pay structure influences how efficiently the organization is able to attract and retain a competent work force and to control its labor costs.

The relative emphasis on *employee contributions* is established through performance and/or seniority-based increases, incentive plans, and stock options and other performance-based approaches. Increasingly, organizations in the United States and around the globe are using some form of incentive plans to share their success with employees. In addition to managing costs, these practices are all intended to affect employee attitudes and behaviors, in particular the decisions to join the organization, to stay, and to perform effectively.

Uncounted variations in pay techniques exist; many are examined in this book. Surveys report differences in compensation policies and techniques among firms. Indeed, most consultant firms have web pages in which they report their survey results. You can obtain updated information on various practices by simply surfing the web.

The American Compensation Association **http://www.acaonline.org** provides information on their compensation-related journals and special publications, as well as short courses aimed at practitioners. The Society of Human Resource Managers **http://www.shrm.org** also offers compensation-related information as well as more general HRM. information. Their *student services* section offers guidance on finding jobs in HR. Both sites are good sources of information for people interested in careers in HRM. The Employee Benefits Research Institute (EBRI) includes links to other benefits sources on its website at **http://www.ebri.org.** The appendix to Chapter 18 describes many additional compensation web sites. The appendix is followed by HR-related website information prepared by research librarians at the Catherwood Library at Cornell University.

BOOK PLAN

Compensation is such a broad and compelling topic that several books could be devoted to it. The focus of this book will be on the design and management of compensation systems. To aid in understanding how and why pay systems work, a pay model has been presented. This model, which emphasizes the key strategic policies, techniques, and objectives of pay systems, also provides the structure for much of the book.

The next chapter (2) discusses how to formulate and implement a compensation strategy. We analyze what it means to be strategic about how people are paid and how compensation can help achieve and sustain an organization's competitive advantage.

The pay model plays a central role in formulating and implementing an organization's pay strategy. The pay model identifies four basic policy decisions that are the core of the pay strategy. After we discuss strategy, the next sections of the book examine each in detail. The first, internal consistency (Chapters 3 through 6), examines pay relationships within a single organization. The next section (Chapters 7 and 8) examines external competitiveness—the competitive pay relationships among organizations—and analyzes the influence of market-driven forces.

Once the compensation rates and structures are established, other issues emerge. How much should we pay each individual employee? How much and how often should a person's pay be increased and on what basis—experience, seniority, or performance? Should pay increases be contingent on the organization and/or the employee's performance? How should the organization share its successes (or failures) with employees? Stock awards, profit sharing, bonuses, merit pay? These are examples of employee contributions, the third building block in the model (Chapters 9 through 11).

After that, we cover employee services and benefits (Chapters 12 and 13). Next, we cover systems tailored for *special groups*—sales representatives, executives, contract workers, unions (Chapters 14 and 15) as well as more detail on compensation systems around the world (Chapter 16). The government's role in compensation is examined in Chapter 17. We conclude with managing the compensation system (Chapter 18) which includes planning, budgeting, evaluating, and communicating.

Even though the book is divided into sections that reflect the pay model, that does not mean that pay policies and decisions are discrete. All the policy decisions are interrelated. Together, they influence employee behaviors and organization performance and can be a source of competitive advantage.

Throughout the book our intention is to examine alternative approaches. We believe that rarely is there a single correct approach; rather, alternative approaches exist or can be designed. The one most likely to be effective depends on the circumstances. We hope that this book will help you become better informed about these options and how to design new ones. Whether as an employee, a manager, or an interested member of society, you should be able to assess effectiveness and equity of pay systems.

CAVEAT EMPTOR—BE AN INFORMED CONSUMER

> Ever since I was a boy I have wished to write a discourse on Compensation; for it seemed to me that life was ahead of theory and the people knew more than was taught.
>
> —paraphrased from Ralph Waldo Emerson[17]

[17]Ralph Waldo Emerson, "Compensation," *The Riverside Essays,* Vol. 1 (New York: Houghton Mifflin, 1904).

Our understanding of compensation management grows as research evidence accumulates. Nevertheless, evidence needs to be evaluated to determine its quality, relevance, and information value. Managers need to be informed consumers. Belief is a poor substitute for informed judgment.

So your challenge is to become an informed consumer of compensation information. How-to-do-it-advice abounds, best-practices prescriptions are plentiful, and academic journals are packed with pay-related theory and research. So we end the chapter with a brief consumer's guide that includes three questions.

1. Does the Research Measure Anything Useful?

How useful are the variables used in the study? How well are they measured? For example, many studies purport to measure organization performance. However, performance may be accounting measures such as return on assets or cash flow, financial measures such as earnings per share or total shareholder return, operational measures such as scrap rates or defect indicators, or qualitative measures such as customer satisfaction. It may even be the opinions of compensation managers, as in: How effective is your gain-sharing plan? (Answer choices are highly effective, effective, some, disappointing, not very effective.) So the informed consumer must ask, Does this research measure anything important?

2. Does the Study Separate Correlation from Causation?

Correlation does not mean causation. For example, many studies investigate the relationship between the use of performance-based pay and performance. Just because the observed use of gain-sharing plans is related to improved performance does not mean it caused the improvement. Other factors may be involved. Perhaps new technology, reengineering, improved marketing, or the general expansion of the local economy underlie the results.

Once we are confident that our variables are accurately defined and measured, we must be sure that they are actually related. Most often this is addressed through the use of statistical analyses. The correlation coefficient is a common measure of association and indicates how changes in one variable are related to changes in another. Many research studies use a statistical analysis known as regression analysis. One output from a regression analysis is the R^2. The R^2 is much like a correlation in that it tells us what percentage of the variation is accounted for by the variables we are using to predict or explain. For example, one study includes a regression analysis of the change in CEO pay due to change in company performance. The resulting R^2 of between 0.8 percent and 4.5 percent indicates that only a very small amount of change in CEO pay is *related to* changes in company performance.

Note that *relation* is not necessarily *causation*. For example, just because a manufacturing plant initiates a new incentive plan and the facility's performance improves, we cannot conclude that the incentive plan caused the improved performance. The two changes are associated or related, but causation is a tough link to make.

Too often, case studies or consultant surveys are presented as studies that reveal cause and effect. They are not. Case studies are descriptive accounts whose value and limitations must be recognized. Just because the best-performing companies are using a practice does not mean the practice is causing the performance. IBM for a long time pursued a full-employment policy. Clearly, that policy did not cause the value of IBM stock to increase or improve IBM's profitability.

However, compensation research often attempts to answer questions of causality. Does the use of performance-based pay *lead to* greater customer satisfaction, improved quality, and better company performance? Causality is one of the most difficult questions to answer and continues to be an important and sometimes perplexing problem for researchers.

3. Are There Alternative Explanations?

Consider a hypothetical study that attempts to assess the impact of a performance-based pay initiative. The researchers measure performance by assessing quality, productivity, customer satisfaction, employee satisfaction, and the facility's performance. The final step is to see if future periods' performance improves over this period's. If it does, can we safely assume that it was the incentive pay that caused performance? Or is it equally likely that the improved performance has alternative explanations, such as the fluctuation in the value of currency, or perhaps a change in executive leadership in the facility? In this case, causality evidence seems week.

If the researchers had measured the performance indicators several years prior to and after installing the plan, then the evidence of causality is only a bit stronger. Further, if the researchers repeated this process in other facilities and the results are similar, then the preponderance of evidence is stronger. Clearly, the organization is doing something right, and incentive pay *may* be part of it.

The best way to establish causation is to account for these competing explanations, either statistically or through control groups. The point is that alternative explanations often exist. And if they do, they need to be accounted for to establish causality. Our experience suggests that it is very difficult to disentangle the effects of pay plans to clearly establish causality. However, it is possible to look at the overall pattern of evidence to make judgments about the effects of pay.

SUMMARY

The model presented in this chapter provides a structure for understanding compensation systems. The three main components of the model include the objectives of the pay system, the policy decisions that provide the system's foundation, and the techniques that link policies and objectives. The following sections of the book examine in turn each of the four policy decisions—internal consistency, external competitiveness, employee contributions, and administration—as well as the techniques, new directions, and related research.

Two questions should constantly be in the minds of managers and readers of this text. First, Why do it this way? There is rarely one correct way to design a system or pay an individual. Organizations, people, and circumstances are too varied. But a well-trained manager can select or design a suitable approach.

Second, So what? What does this technique do for us? How does it help achieve our organization goals? If good answers are not apparent, there is no point to the technique. Adapting the pay system to meet the needs of the employees and to help achieve the goals of the organization is what this book is all about.

The basic premise of this book is that compensation systems do have a profound impact. Yet too often, traditional pay systems seem to have been designed in response to some historical but long-forgotten problem. The practices continue, but the logic underlying them is not always clear or even relevant.

Review Questions

1. How do differing perspectives affect our perceptions of compensation?
2. What is your definition of compensation? What "returns" from working would you exclude in your perspective? Compare your definition to the different perspectives discussed in the chapter.
3. How does the pay model help organize one's thinking about compensation?
4. What can a pay system do for an organization? For an employee?
5. Under what circumstances would one of the four basic pay policies be emphasized relative to the others? Try to think of a separate example for each basic pay policy.
6. Answer the three questions in *Caveat Emptor* for any study or business article that tells you how to pay people.

YOUR TURN

To Pay or Not to Pay—Ah, There's the Rub: Glamorous Internships

Greg Petouvis, a junior at Cornell University, worked for the Equal Employment Opportunity Commission in Washington, D.C., during a recent summer. The job included performing site compliance visits at several companies, interviewing people who filed discrimination complaints, determining if complaints had merit, and settling disputes. The work was very similar to that done by full-time EEOC field analysts. In fact, the agency manager reported that Petouvis was one of the top field analysts.

But no pay. Not even a housing allowance for living in Washington, D.C., during two and one-half summer months.

Another Cornell student, Erica Volini, worked that same summer for Andersen Consulting on project teams with three different Andersen client companies. She earned over $500 per week plus benefits and a housing allowance.

Hope Wagner, from the University of Nebraska, worked in media relations for a professional sports team this summer. She drafted news releases, filed clippings, and worked on a 75-page media guide.

She took home plenty of team souvenirs—coffee mugs, key chains, T-shirts—but not one cent.

The giant chip maker Intel pays undergraduate interns between $450 and $750 a week and tosses in a free rental car during the summer.* General Motors doesn't provide the car, but it does pay $450 to $600 a week, paid vacation days, round-trip travel, plus it provides health insurance. "The Late Show with David Letterman" pays nothing, yet claims to receive over 800 applications for 30 unpaid summer intern positions.

So what's the deal?

1. What do employers receive from summer interns? What returns do students get from the opportunities?
2. Should summer interns be paid? If so, how much? How would you recommend an employer decide the answers to both these questions?
3. What added information would you like to have before you make your recommendations? How would you use this information?

*Sources: *America's Top Internships* and *The Internship Bible,* part of the Princeton Review series published by Random House.

Chapter 2 Strategic Perspectives

Chapter Outline

You probably think you can skip this chapter. After all, what can be so challenging about forming and implementing a compensation strategy? Need a strategy? Just pay whatever the market rate is.

But a dose of reality quickly reveals that employers cannot behave so simply. As noted in the last chapter, companies like Medtronic and Hewlett-Packard compete very differently for very similar talent. If we add Microsoft to this comparison, we see yet another strategic perspective.

As Exhibit 2.1 shows, Microsoft, like Hewlett-Packard and Medtronic, emphasizes employee performance and commitment, but achieves it very differently. Microsoft, almost cult-like, calls for its employees to "put some skin in the game," as they say. Microsoft employees often take a cut in their base pay to join the company (Microsoft's competitive position is to lag competitors in base pay). The relatively low base is offset by an aggressive emphasis on performance and success sharing (Microsoft far exceeds competitors in incentives plus value of stock options). Hence, Microsoft's strategic perspective on compensation is revealed in the *relative* importance of different pay forms (less base, greater incentives and options). Medtronic also uses stock options and incentives tied to performance, but covers a smaller portion of its workforce than does Microsoft. Hewlett-Packard focuses on base pay, merit pay, and profit sharing to meet competitors' practices. The three companies have very different perspectives on total compensation.

The simple "let the market decide our compensation strategy" doesn't work internationally either. In many nations, markets do not operate as in the United States and do not even exist in some regions. In China and some Eastern European countries, markets for labor are just emerging. In Japan and some South American countries, there is very little movement of people among companies, so letting the market decide does not apply.[1]

The point is that a strategic perspective on compensation is more complex than it first appears. So we suggest that you continue to read the chapter.

STRATEGIC PERSPECTIVES

Because pay matters so much to most of us, it is sometimes too easy to become fixated on techniques: Examining and evaluating techniques becomes the end in itself. Questions such as "*What* does this technique do for (to) us?" or, "*How does it help* achieve our objectives?" or, "*Why bother* with this technique?" are not asked. So before proceeding to the particulars, let us consider what it means to look at pay as a potential source of competitive advantage—how pay can support the business strategy and adapt to external pressures. You should know how to develop a compensation strategy after completing this chapter. More importantly, you should also know why you would bother doing so. Train yourself to ask the *"so what"* question as you read this book. Once you do, you will be prepared to shine when your employer asks if your proposal makes sense.

[1]*Capital Choices: Changing the Way America Invests in Industry: A Research Report* (Washington, D.C.: Council on Competitiveness, 1996); Groves, "China's Evolving Managerial Labor Market," *Journal of Political Economy* 103, no. 5 (1995), pp. 873–91; R. Boisot and J. Child, "From Fiefs to Clans to Network Capitalism: Explaining China's Emerging Economic Order, *Administrative Science Quarterly* 41 (1996), pp. 600–28.

Exhibit 2.1 Strategic Perspectives Toward Total Compensation

	Microsoft (MS)	Hewlett-Packard (HP)	Medtronic
Objectives	¥ Support the business objectives ¥ Support recruiting, motivation, and retention of MS-caliber talent ¥ Preserve MS core values	¥ Continue to attract creative and enthusiastic people ¥ Ensure fair treatment ¥ Reflect sustained relative contribution	¥ Support business missions and strategies ¥ Signal core values ¥ Attract, retain, motivate top people
Internal Consistency	¥ Integral part of MS culture ¥ Support MS performance-driven culture ¥ Business/technology-based organization design structure	¥ Reflect HP Way ¥ Support crossfunction ¥ Support HP careers ¥ Long-term commitment	¥ Reflect business objectives ¥ Align with job and work performed
Externally Competitive	¥ Lead in *total* compensation ¥ Lag in base pay ¥ Lead with bonuses, stock options	¥ Pay among leaders ¥ Integral part of HP Way	¥ Aligned with Medtronic financial performance ¥ 50th percentile performance paid at 50th percentile of market, 75th percentile performance paid at 75th percentile of market.
Employee Contributions	¥ Bonuses and options based on individual performance	¥ Merit increase and profit sharing ¥ Based on individual performance	¥ Support performance and ownership culture ¥ Emphasize performance-based bonuses, stock options, and ownership
Administration	¥ Open, transparent communications ¥ Centralized administration ¥ Software supported	¥ Open communications	¥ Simple, clearly understood ¥ Administrative ease ¥ Open, employee choice

SUPPORT BUSINESS STRATEGY

A currently popular theory found in almost every textbook and consultant's report tells managers to tailor their pay systems to support the organization's strategic conditions. The rationale is based on contingency notions. That is, differences in a firm's strategy should be supported by corresponding differences in its human resource strategy, including compensation. The underlying premise is that the greater the alignment, or *fit,* between the organization and the compensation system, the more effective the organization.[2]

As Exhibit 2.2 depicts, compensation systems can be designed to support the organization's business strategy and to adapt to the social, competitive, and regulatory pressures in the environment. The ultimate purpose is to gain and sustain competitive advantage.[3]

It then follows that when business strategies change, pay systems need to change. A classic example is IBM's strategic and cultural transformation. IBM's emphasis on internal consistency (well-developed job evaluation plan, clear hierarchy for decision making, policy of no layoffs) had served well when the company dominated the market for huge mainframe computers, where profit margins were high. But it did not provide the flexibility to react to the rapid changes in the computer industry in the late 1980s. A redesigned IBM now emphasizes cost control (incentive pay), greater risk taking, and an increased focus on customers (market product and service leadership). IBM changed its pay system to support its changed business strategy.[4]

If the basic premise of a strategic perspective is to align the compensation system to the business strategy, then different business strategies will translate into different compensation approaches. Exhibit 2.3 illustrates compensation systems tailored to three different strategies.[5]

---

[2]Henry Mintzberg, "Five Tips for Strategy," in *The Strategy Process: Concepts and Contexts*, ed. Henry Mintzberg and James Brian Quinn (Englewood Cliffs, NJ: Prentice-Hall, 1992); J. E. Delery and D. H. Doty, "Models of Theorizing in Strategic Human Resource Management," *Academy of Management Journal* 39, no. 4, pp. 802–35; Lee Dyer and T. Reeves, "Human Resource Strategies and Firm Performance: What do we Know and Where do we Need to Go?" *International Journal of Human Resource Management* 6, no. 3 (1995), pp. 656–70; Helen L. DeCieri and Peter Dowling, "Theoretical and Empirical Developments in Strategic International HRM," in *Research and Theory in Strategic HRM: An Agenda for the Twenty-First Century,* ed. Pat Wright et al (Greenwich, CT: JAI Press, 1999); L. R. Gomez-Mejia and D. B. Balkin, *Compensation, Organization Strategy, and Firm Performance* (Cincinnati: Southwestern, 1992); R. Schuster and P. K. Zingheim, *The New Pay: Linking Employee Strategy and Organization Performance* (New York: Lexington Books, 1992). Ediberto F. Montemayer, "Aligning Pay Systems with Market Strategy," *ACA Journal,* Winter 1994, pp. 44–53.

[4]Jill Kanin-Lovers and Sharon E. Parr, "Developing a Total Compensation Approach," in *Compensation Guide 1996*, ed. W. A. Caldwell (Boston: Warren, Gorham & Lamont), pp. 2.1–2.12. Also see H. A. Thompson, "Supporting Sears' Turnaround with Compensation," *ACA Journal,* 1997, pp. 8–12.

[5]M. Porter, "What is Strategy?" *Harvard Business Review*, November–December 1996, pp. 61–78; J. Jackson, "Why Being Different Pays," *Financial Times*, June 23, 1997, p. B1; M. Treacy and F. Wiersma, *The Discipline of Market Leaders* (Reading, MA: Addison-Wesley, 1997).

EXHIBIT 2.2 Strategic Perspective: an Illustration

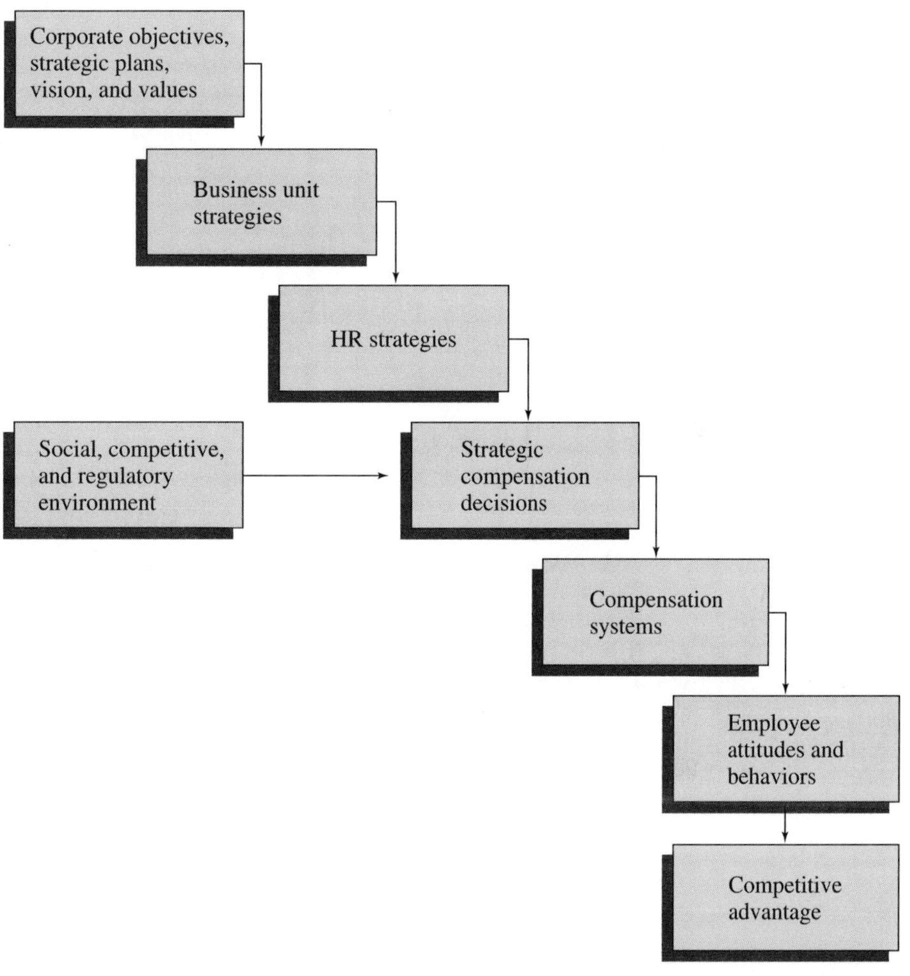

The innovator stresses risk taking by placing less emphasis on assessing and evaluating skills and jobs and greater emphasis on incentives to encourage innovations in new production processes that can shorten design-to-customer time. The cost leader's efficiency-focused strategy stresses doing more with less by minimizing costs, encouraging productivity increases, and specifying in greater detail exactly how jobs should

EXHIBIT 2.3 Tailor the Compensation System to the Strategy

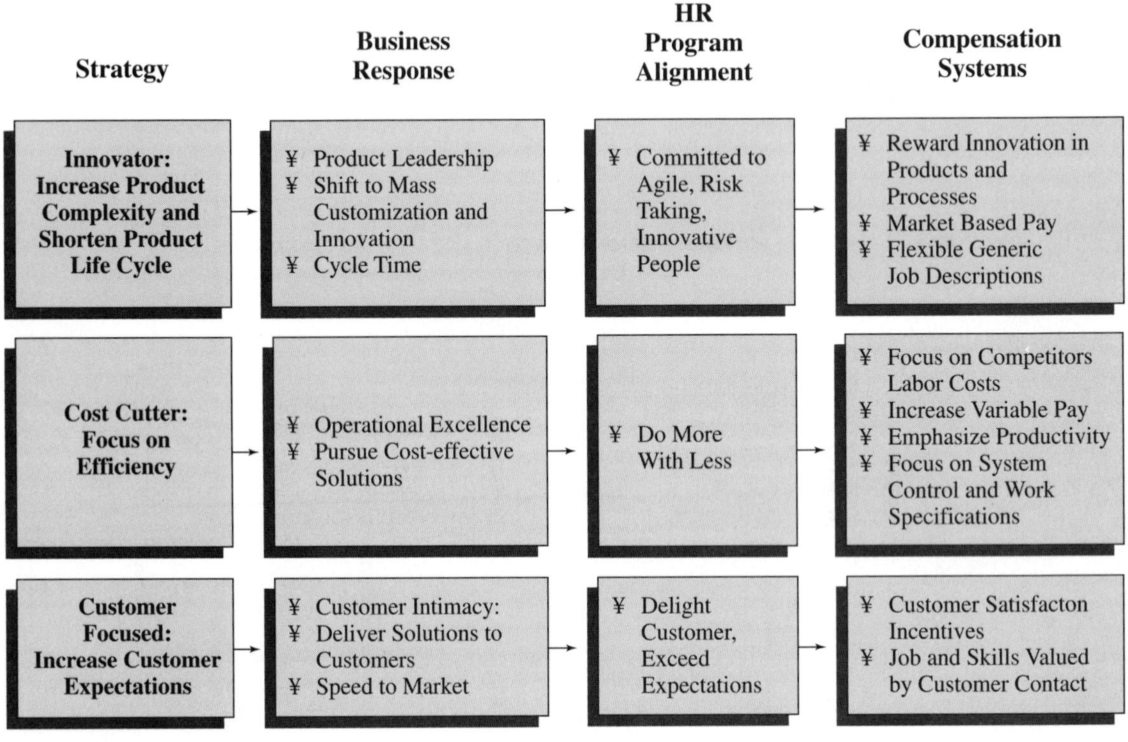

be performed. The customer-focused business strategy stresses delighting customers and bases employee pay on how well they do this. Different business strategies require different compensation approaches. One size does not fit all.[6]

WHICH PAY DECISIONS ARE STRATEGIC?

Strategy refers to the fundamental directions that an organization has chosen. An organization defines its strategy through the tradeoffs it makes in choosing what (and what not) to do. Exhibit 2.4 relates these strategic choices to the quest for competitive advantage. At the corporate level, the fundamental strategic choice is, *What business should we be in?* At the business unit level, the choice shifts to *How do we gain and sustain competitive advantage? How do we win in those businesses?* At the functional/systems level the strategic choice is, *How should total compensation help gain and sustain competitive advantage?*

[6]V. Pucik, N. Tichy, and C. Barnett, eds., *Globalizing Management: Creating and Leading the Competitive Organization* (Wiley, 1992), L. R. Gomez-Mejia, "Structure and Process of Diversification, Compensation Strategy, and Firm Performance," *Strategic Management Journal,* October 1992.

EXHIBIT 2.4 Strategic Choices

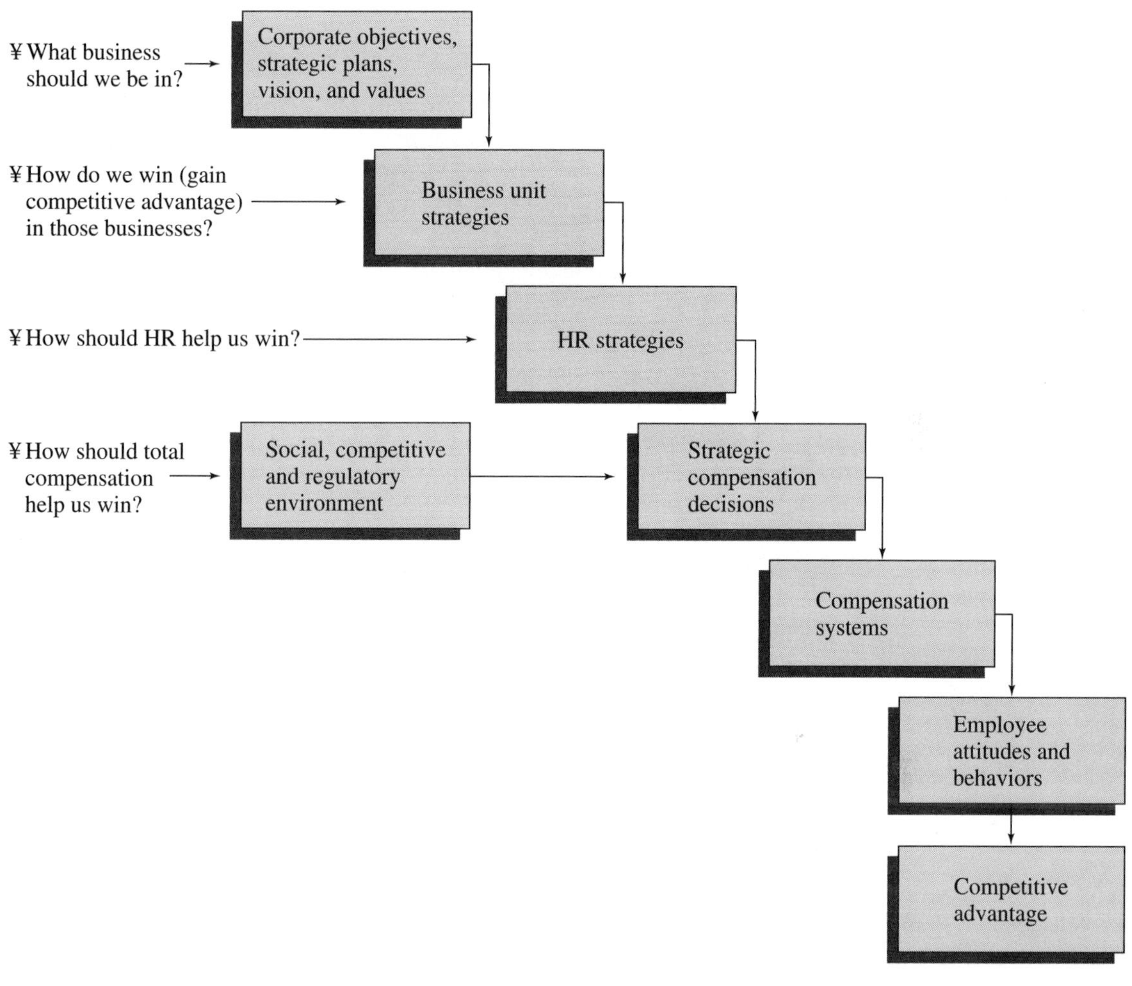

A strategic perspective toward compensation focuses on the set of compensation choices that help the organization gain and sustain competitive advantage.

The competitive advantage of Starbucks is apparent with the first sip of their specialty drink mocha valencia. What started out as a Seattle seller of coffee beans has, through strategic decisions, grown to a familiar chain of coffeehouses stretching across

North America.[7] Along the way, Starbucks managers have designed a pay system to support this change in fundamental direction (from coffee bean importer to trendy coffee houses) and growth (over 1,000 of them).

Using our pay model, the strategic compensation decisions facing Starbucks managers can be considered in terms of the objectives and the four basic policies.

1. Objectives: *How should compensation support the business strategy and be adaptive to the cultural and regulatory pressures in the environment?* (Starbucks objectives: Grow by making employees feel valued. Recognize that every dollar earned passes through employees' hands. Use pay and perquisites to help gain employee loyalty and become difficult to imitate.)
2. Consistency: *How differently should the different types and levels of skills and work be paid within the organization?* (Starbucks: Deemphasize differences. Use egalitarian pay structures with employees as "partners.")
3. Competitiveness: *How should our total compensation be positioned against our competitors?* (Starbucks: Pay just slightly above other fast-food employers, which is a low-wage industry.)
4. Contributions: *Should pay increases be based on individual and/or team performance, on experience and/or continuous learning, or improved skills, on changes in cost of living, on personal needs (housing, transportation, health services), and/or on each business unit's performance?* (Starbucks: Provide health insurance and stock options, called bean stocks, for all employees including part-timers—even though most are relatively young and healthy, and few stay long enough to earn stock options.)
5. Administration: *How open and transparent should the bases for pay decisions be to all employees? Who should be involved in designing and managing the system?* (Starbucks: As members of the Starbucks "family," our employees realize what is best for them. Partners can and do get involved.)

The decisions underlying *these five issues, taken together as a pattern, form an organization's compensation strategy.*

Articulated versus Emergent Strategies

All organizations that pay people have a compensation strategy. Some may have written, or articulated, compensation strategies for all to see and understand. Others may not even realize they have a compensation strategy. Ask a manager of these organizations what the compensation strategy is, and you may get a strange look. "We do whatever it takes" will be a pragmatic response. These organizations do have a compensation strategy; it is simply unstated, or emergent. The strategy emerges from the pay decisions that they have made. Emergent compensation strategy is inferred from compensation practices.[8]

---

[7]Howard Schultz and Dori Jones Yang, *How Starbucks Built a Company One Cup at a Time* (New York: Hyperion 1997).

[8]H. Mintzberg, "Crafting Strategy," *Harvard Business Review*, July-August 1970, pp. 66–75; G. Hoefstede, *Culture's Consequences: International Differences in Work Relationships and Values* (Thousand Oaks, CA: Sage Publications, 1980).

The point is that all organizations make the five strategic decisions discussed earlier. Some do it in a systematic way, others do it very pragmatically—as ad hoc responses to pressures from the economic, social, and regulatory context in which the organization operates.

STEPS TO FORMULATE A TOTAL COMPENSATION STRATEGY

Developing a compensation strategy involves four simple steps. As Exhibits 2.4 and 2.5 reveal, the steps are familiar to any manager.

1. *Assess total compensation implications of cultural values, global competitive pressures, employee needs, and organization strategy,*
2. *Fit compensation decisions with the organization strategy and environmental context,*
3. *Design a compensation system which translates strategy into practice, and*
4. *Reassess the fit.*

While the steps are simple, executing them is complex. The process really becomes an art; experience and insight play major roles.

Exhibit 2.5 Key Steps to Formulate a Total Compensation Strategy

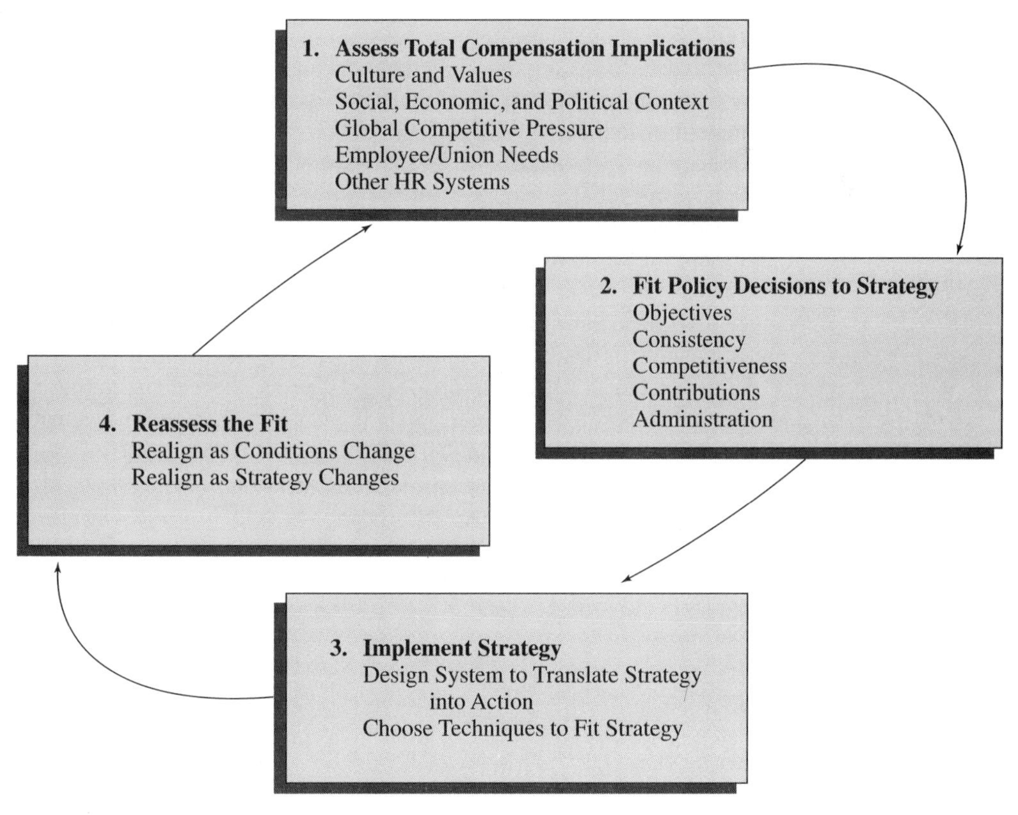

Step 1: Assess Total Compensation Implications

This first step requires an understanding of the industry in which the organization operates and how it plans to compete in that industry. We have already discussed examples of fitting different compensation strategies with different business strategies in Exhibit 2.3 using the three business strategies of cost-cutter, customer centered, and innovator.

Cultural Values. The values underlying an employer's treatment of its employees are reflected in the pay system.[9] Some employers articulate their philosophies. AT&T's and Medtronic's statements of values are shown in Exhibit 2.6. These philosophies guide their pay systems.

Medtronic value number 5 recognizes employees' worth by allowing "personal satisfaction in work accomplished, security, advancement opportunity, and means to share in the company success." Its compensation strategy fits this value by including incentives and stock options to share the company success and job progressions for "advancement opportunities."

Social, Economic, and Political Context. In Exhibit 2.5, the environmental context also affects compensation choices. Context refers to a wide range of pressures, including competitive pressures from product and labor markets, legal and regulatory requirements, cultural differences, changing work force demographics, values and expectations, and the like. In the case of Starbucks, business is very people intensive. Consequently, Starbucks managers expect that an increasingly diverse work force and increasingly diverse forms of pay (child care, chemical dependency counselling, educational reimbursements, employee assistance programs) may add value and be difficult for competitors to imitate.[10]

If Starbucks goes global, it will find that work force diversity takes on a whole new meaning in a global business. Cultural norms about minorities' and women's work roles and pay differ and may be at odds with Starbucks' corporate policies. Different regions of the world may require different approaches to pay.

Governments are major players in the management of compensation. Hence, government relations (read, lobbying) to influence laws and regulations may be part of compensation strategies. In the United States, managers probably will not sit by passively while Congress considers whether to impose taxes on benefits paid to employees. Similarly, as Starbucks enters the European Union, its social contract becomes a matter of interest for the Starbucks leadership. So, from a strategic perspective, managers of compensation may need to try to shape the environment as well as be shaped by it.

---

[9]M. Bloom and G. Milkovich, "Strategic Perspectives on International Compensation and Reward Systems," in *Research and Theory in Strategic HRM: An Agenda for the Twenty-First Century,* ed. Pat Wright et al (Greenwich, CT: JAI Press, 1999); D. D. McKenna and J. J. McHenry, *Microsoft's Maniacal Work Ethic* (Redmond, WA: Microsoft, 1996); A. Sorge, "Strategic Fit and Societal Effect: Cross National Comparisons of Technology, Organization, and HR," *Organization Studies* 1991, pp. 1–2.

[10]Howard Schultz and Dori Jones Yang, *How Starbucks Built a Company One Cup at a Time* (New York: Hyperion, 1997).

Exhibit 2.6 Comparison of AT&T and Medtronic Mission and Values

Medtronic Values

Medtronic's mission imparts stability and provides a firm foundation for the company's growth. Written more than 30 years ago, our mission statement gives purpose to our work, describes the values we live by, and is the motivation behind every action we take.

1. To contribute to human welfare by application of biomedical engineering in the research, design, manufacture, and sale of instruments or appliances that alleviate pain, restore health, and extend life.
2. To direct our growth in the areas of biomedical engineering where we display maximum strength and ability; to gather people and facilities that tend to augment these areas; to continuously build on these areas through education and knowledge assimilation; to avoid participation in areas where we cannot make unique and worthy contributions.
3. To strive without reserve for the greatest possible reliability and quality in our products; to be the unsurpassed standard of comparison and to be recognized as a company of dedication, honesty, integrity, and service.
4. To make a fair profit on current operations to meet our obligations, sustain our growth, and reach our goals.
5. To recognize the personal worth of employees by providing an employment framework that allows personal satisfaction in work accomplished, security, advancement opportunity, and means to share in the company's success.
6. To maintain good citizenship as a company.

AT&T Values

Help the Customer Succeed	*Continuous Improvement*	*People*	*Integrity*	*Profit*
To support customers' success, each of us will •Interact with customers as a partner •Know our customers' business •Anticipate what is required for our customers' success •Identify and know our value to our customer •Develop creative/innovative ways to serve our customer •Be responsive and flexible in providing quality products and services to our customers •Provide value-added solutions •Provide unconditional customer satisfaction	**In the uncompromising pursuit of quality, we will make decisions based on data and will continuously** •Measure and improve customer satisfaction •Improve the "value add" we provide our customers •Analyze and simplify our business process •Promote change as an opportunity to improve •Promote continuous learning •Evaluate our operations and perform only that which has value for the customer •Recognize no limits to improvement	**Each of us is important in determining the success of AT&T. Therefore, each of us** •Is empowered and expected to act •Will treat each other with respect and dignity •Is expected to grow and achieve •Shares responsibility for the success of our customers and company	**Integrity and a high standard of ethics are fundamental in our business, community, and interpersonal relationship; therefore, each of us will** •Make and keep commitments •Operate at the highest ethical standards •Act in a forthright and honest manner •Conform to the spirit and letter of the laws that govern our worldwide operations	**Sustained profitability is the ultimate measure of how well we serve our customers and is necessary to** •Be a reliable partner and foster beneficial relationships with our Customers Investors Communities Vendors •Execute long-term plans •Provide opportunity for personal growth and reward

Exhibit 2.7 International Comparisons of Pay and Hours Worked

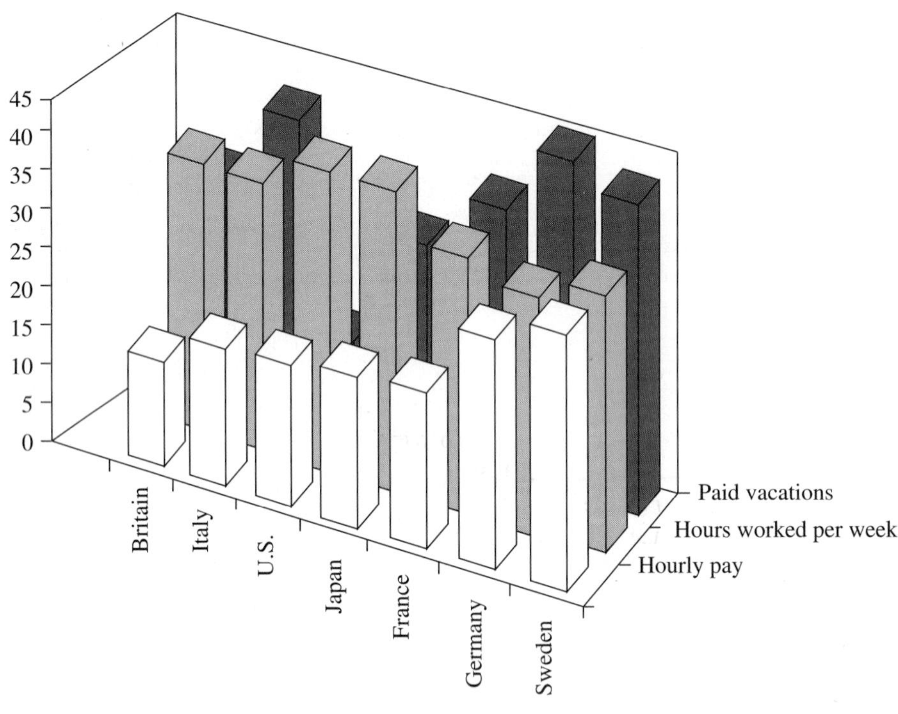

Global Competitive Pressure. Assessing international competitive pressure is increasingly important when developing a compensation strategy. However, comparing pay between countries is often not the whole story, as Exhibit 2.7 illustrates. In comparison to Germany, the United States has relatively lower hourly labor costs ($16.17 versus $25.95), a longer work week (40 versus 37.6 hours), fewer vacation days (23 versus 42 days per year), and a longer work year (1,847 versus 1,499 hours). These data provide some of the reasons BMW built a new facility in South Carolina rather than Dusseldorf, Germany.[11]

Differences in the actual pay systems among international competitors also influence pay strategies. Exhibit 2.8 describes Toshiba's pay system for its managers. Several items in the exhibit stand out. First, note that bonuses make up about 37 percent of a Toshiba manager's pay. Because they are paid out twice a year rather than in a biweekly paycheck, the use of bonuses offers a cash flow advantage to Toshiba. In addition,

[11]C. Sparks and M. Greiner, "U.S. and Foreign Productivity and Unit Labor Costs," *Monthly Labor Review* 120 (1997), pp. 226–35.

EXHIBIT 2.8 Toshiba's Managerial Compensation Plan

Pay Elements	*Based on*	*Annual Amount*	*(%)*
1. Core salary	• Performance • Ability • Length of service	¥4,440,000	62.8%
2. Position and rank	• Performance	2,280,000	
	Subtotal	**6,720,000**	
3. Bonus* (Example)		3,980,000	37.2
Total		**¥10,700,000**	100%

*Paid twice a year (June and December).

bonuses are not added into the employee's base pay, so they do not become fixed costs. While a common misperception is that Japanese pay systems are based solely on seniority, notice that Toshiba's managers' pay depends on educational level (ability), experience (i.e., seniority), and performance.[12] The "so what" question is that no longer do managers simply face domestic competitors; they must become knowledgeable in how their global competitors compete with pay, too.

More than 1,200 experts from 12 different countries were asked how organizations should use human resources to achieve competitive advantage in the 21st century.[13] Some of the results are summarized in Exhibit 2.9. The percentages refer to the amount of agreement among experts. In the United States, 87 percent of the experts agreed that "rewarding employees for customer service" was the top priority for achieving competitive advantage. Of the Germans, 96 percent judged that "identifying high potential employees early" was the highest priority; 85 percent of the Japanese agreed that "communicating business directions, problems, and plans" is a key action; and the Italian experts couldn't agree on the priorities.

In the United States, four of the six actions the experts agreed upon were pay related (reward employees for customer service, reward employees for business/productivity gains, reward employees for innovation and creativity, implement pay systems promoting sharing). Clearly, U.S. experts see pay as having strategic value in achieving competitive advantage. Japanese experts agreed that only three actions were critical for competitive advantage, and one was pay related: focus on merit pay philosophy and individual performance. Germans agreed on the largest number of actions, 11, and 4 of these were pay related.

Although consensus exists among international experts that pay systems are critical for achieving competitive advantage, significant cross-cultural differences exist

[12]Often bonus payments are distributed around major holidays, much as the end-of-year bonus in western companies. Yoko Sano, *HRM Practices in the Japanese Companies,* 1993.

[13]Based on data from an IBM/TPF&C study, 1992. Half the experts were corporate executives, one-fourth were consultants, and one-fourth academics.

Exhibit 2.9 International Perspectives on Competitive Advantage

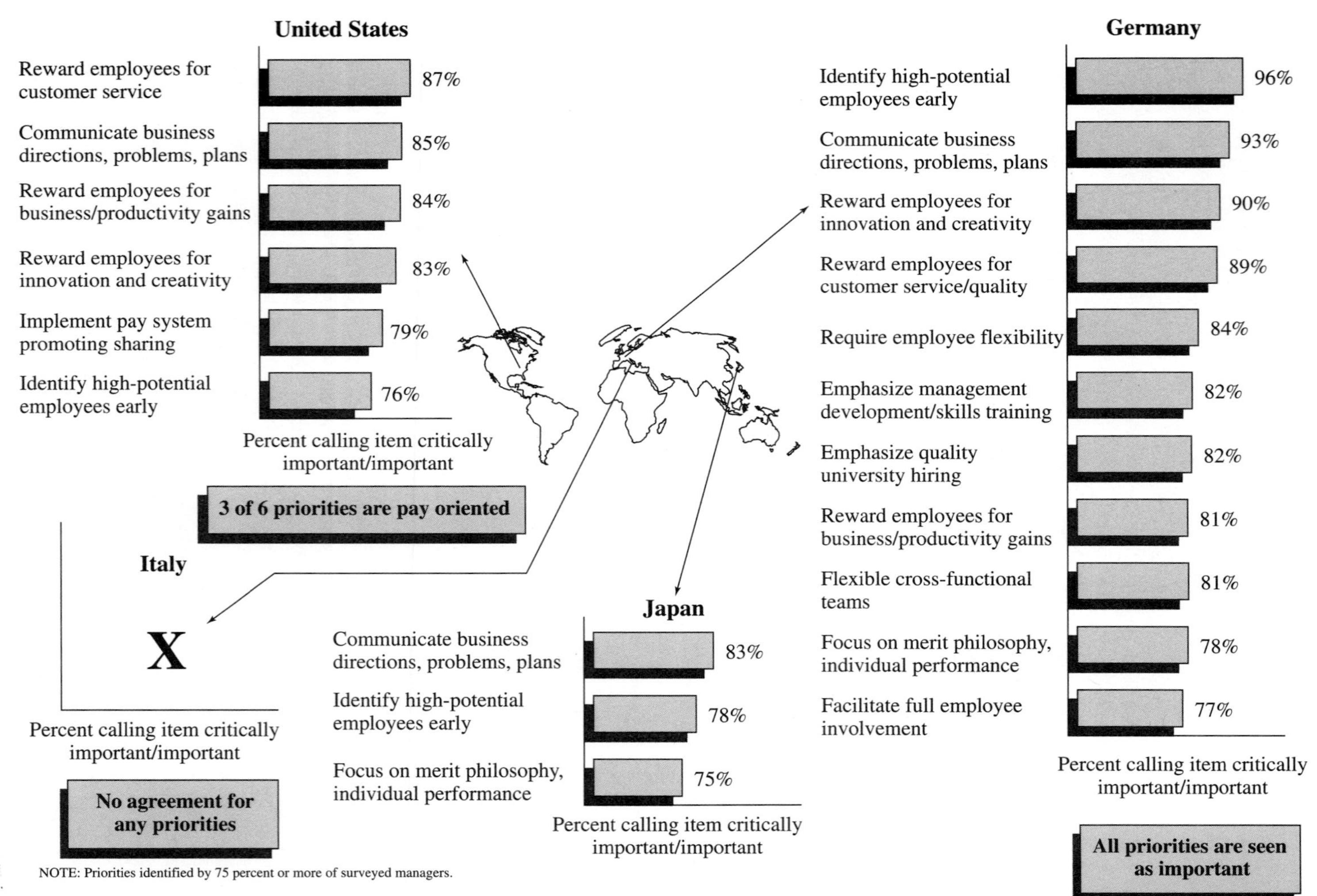

NOTE: Priorities identified by 75 percent or more of surveyed managers.

over the types of pay programs that are significant. The Japanese, for example, are moving from seniority-based pay toward individual merit pay, whereas U.S. experts are moving toward more team- and group-based approaches.

The leaders of companies across the world, not only in the United States, believe that how people are paid can help achieve and sustain competitive advantage. Seventy-eight percent of top executives at over 2,000 companies from 23 different countries stated that "performance-based pay is one of the top concerns for implementing their business strategies."[14] Yet only about 30 percent consider their current compensation systems designed to support their company's business strategies.

Employee Needs—Flexible Compensation Systems. The simple fact that employees differ is too easily and too often overlooked in formulating a compensation strategy. Individual employees join the organization, make investment decisions, design new products, assemble components, and judge the quality of results. Individual employees receive the pay. A major limitation of contemporary pay systems is the degree to which individual attitudes and preferences are ignored: Older, highly paid workers may wish to defer taxes by putting their pay into retirement funds, while younger employees may have high cash needs to buy a house, support a family, or finance an education. Dual career couples who are overinsured medically may prefer to use more of their combined pay for child care, automobile insurance, financial counseling, or other benefits. Employees who have young children or dependent parents may desire dependent care coverage.[15]

Perhaps it is time to consider letting employees specify their own pay form. Unlimited choice would meet with disapproval from the U.S. Internal Revenue Service and would be a challenge to administer.[16] However, pay systems can be designed to encourage some employee choices. Flexible benefit plans are examples, and increasing numbers of employers are adopting them.[17] A very few organizations allow employees the opportunity to trade cash received from incentives for stock options. These organizations believe that allowing employees their choice adds value and is difficult to imitate—it is a source of competitive advantage. Whether this belief is correct remains to be studied.

---

[14]*Competing in a Global Economy* (Bethesda, MD: Watson Wyatt Worldwide, 1998); Jiing-Lih Farh, Rodger W. Griffeth, and David B. Balkin, "Effects of Choice of Pay Plans on Satisfaction, Goal Setting, and Performance," *Journal of Organizational Behavior* 12 (1991), pp. 55–62; Dan Cable and Tim Judge, "Pay Preferences and Job Search Decisions: A Person-Organization Fit Perspective," *Personnel Psychology,* Summer 1994, pp.317–48.

[15]R. D. Bretz, R. A. Ash, and G. F. Dreher, "Do People Make the Place? An Examination of the Attraction-Selection-Attrition Hypotheses," *Personnel Psychology* 42 (1989), pp. 561–81; B. Gerhart and G. Milkovich, "Employee Compensation" in M. Dunnette and L. Hough, ed. *Handbook of Industrial and Organization Psychology* 3 (Palo Alto, California: Consulting Psychologists Press, 1992).

[16]Melissa Barringer and George Milkovich, "Employee Health Insurance Decisions in a Flexible Benefit Environment," *Human Resource Management* 35 (1996), pp. 293–315.

[17]Most of the leading consulting firms also publish yearly surveys of pay practices of firms, for example, Towers Perrin, *Benchmarking Employee Compensation Practices*; Hewitt Associates, *Benchmarking Best Practices*; Hay Associates, *Annual Employee Compensation Survey of Practice*, Mercer, *Global Survey*.

Unions. Pay strategies also need to be adapted to the nature of the union-management relationship.[18] Strategies for dealing with unions vary widely. The federal government formed a joint labor-management committee to examine how to strengthen the relationship between pay and performance for federal workers. At the other extreme, Caterpillar started hiring new, nonunion employees five months into a strike by the United Auto Workers. Between these extremes, hundreds of union contracts are negotiated each year with little fanfare or rancor.

Stripping out the heavily unionized public sector, U.S. union membership among private sector workers is now just under 10 percent of the U.S. workforce. Even so, union influence on the design and administration of pay systems is significant. Union preferences for different forms of pay (e.g., cost of living adjustments, improved health care) and their concern with job security affect pay system design.

Internationally, the role of unions in determining pay varies greatly[19] In Europe, unions are major players and must be considered in any strategic pay decisions. The point is, however, that recognizing union interests is part of assessing environmental pressures when formulating compensation strategies.

Role of Pay in Overall HR Strategy: On the Point, Support, Change Agent. The pay system is just one of many HR systems that make up the HR strategy and the pay strategy in the organization; strategy is also partially influenced by how it fits with the other HR systems in the organization. A highly centralized and confidential pay system, controlled by a few people in a corporate unit, will not operate effectively in a highly decentralized and open organization.

The importance of fit between pay programs and other HR management processes can be illustrated with examples of recruiting, hiring, and promoting. The pay linked with a job offer or a promotion must be sufficient to induce acceptance. Some employers do not maintain significant pay differences among various skill levels and levels of responsibility. Lack of adequate differences in pay diminishes the incentive for employees to take the training required to become more skilled or to accept the promotion to supervisor. The situation is reversed for many engineering and research jobs, where the pay for managerial positions induces people to leave engineering and research positions.

---

[18]D. C. Johnson, "On Pay Day, Union Jobs Stack Up Very Well," *New York Times*, August 31, 1997, p. B1; Henry Farber and Alan B. Krueger, "Union Membership in the United States: The Decline Continues," in *Employee Representation: Alternatives and Future Directions,* ed. Bruce E. Kaufman and Morris M. Kleiner (Madison, WI: Industrial Relations Research Association, 1993), pp. 135–68; E. Applebaum and Rosemary Batt, *The New American Workplace* (Ithaca, NY: ILR Press, 1994); T. A. Kochan and P. Osterman, *The Mutual Gains Enterprise: Forging a Winning Partnership among Labor, Management, and Government* (Cambridge: Harvard Business School Press, 1994).

[19]Richard B. Freeman and Lawrence F. Katz, ed. *Differences and Changes in Wage Structures* (Chicago: University of Chicago Press, 1995); K. Murphy, "Paying People in Europe," *International HR Journal*, Winter 1997, pp. 23–28; A. Hegewisch, C. Brewster, and J. Koubek, "Different Roads: Changes in Industrial and Employee Relations in the Czech Republic and East Germany since 1989," *Industrial Relations Journal* 27 (1996), pp. 50–65; and R. Bronstein, "Labour Law Reform in Latin America: Between State Protection and Flexibility," *International Labour Law Review*, Spring 1997.

In sum, assessing the compensation implications of a series of factors including the organization's business strategy, its culture and values, the environmental context, global competitive pressures, employee needs, unions, and how pay fits with other HR systems is all necessary to better formulate a compensation strategy that "fits."

In the overall HR strategy, pay can be *on the point* playing the lead role, it can be a *supporting player,* or it can be an *agent of change.* In any of these roles, compensation is part of the total HR approach.

Steps 2, 3, and 4: A Total Compensation Strategy

The compensation strategy is formulated in the five decisions outlined in the pay model: set objectives, and specify four policies on consistency, competitiveness, contributions, and administration. This is the **Step 2** in developing a compensation strategy. It involves making compensation decisions that fit the organization's business strategy and environment context (See Exhibit 2.3). As we have already noted, compensation decisions support different business strategies—making the right compensation decisions based on how the organization decides to compete. Exhibit 2.2 compares the compensation strategies followed by Medtronic, Microsoft, and Hewlett-Packard.

The rest of the book discusses these compensation decisions in detail. It is important to realize, however, that *the decisions made on these five issues together form the compensation strategy.*

Step 3 in the strategy is to implement it through the design of the compensation system. The compensation system translates the strategy into practice.

Step 4, reassess and realign, closes the loop. It recognizes that the compensation strategy must change to fit changing conditions. To insure this, periodic reassessing of the fit is needed.

SOURCE OF COMPETITIVE ADVANTAGE: TWO TESTS

Designing and implementing a pay strategy that is a source of competitive advantage is easier said than done. Not all compensation decisions are strategic nor a source of competitive advantage. Two tests determine if a pay strategy is a source of advantage: (1) Does it add value? and (2) Is it difficult to imitate?[20] These are high hurdles to overcome.

Adding Value

Pay decisions add value by helping to attract and retain critical talent, control costs and motivate people to continue to learn and improve performance. Decisions about some pay techniques probably do not add value and thus are not strategic, nor do they

---

[20] J. Barney, "Firm Resources and Sustained Competitive Advantage," *Journal of Management* 17 (1997), pp. 99–120; P. M. Wright, G. C. McMahan, and A. McWilliams, "Human Resources and Sustained Competitive Advantage: A Resource-Based Perspective," *International Journal of Human Resource Management* 5 (1994), pp. 301–26.

seem to provide any advantage. Examples probably include which job evaluation plan, how many levels in the performance evaluation rating scales, or whether or not to provide dental insurance.

Difficult to Imitate

If the pay plan is relatively simple for any competitor to copy, then how can it possibly be a source of advantage? The answer, according to the strategic perspective, is that the real sustained advantage comes from (1) the way the organization's business strategy and compensation systems fit together, (2) the fit among compensation and other HR activities, and (3) how the systems are implemented.

In 1995, Southwest Airlines pilots agreed to a 10-year contract that provided no wage increases for the first 5 years. In the second 5 years, the pilots agreed to receive stock options plus 3 percent annual wage increases. This strategy added value by linking the financial interests of the pilots with those of the Southwest stockholders (both benefit if share value increases). It also helped secure Southwest's competitive advantage as a low-cost provider of frequent, no-frills flights. This strategy is difficult for competing airlines to imitate.

However, it has also turned out to be difficult for Southwest to sustain. During the past few years, U.S. airlines have been financially successful. Passenger load rates are at all-time highs, fuel costs are stable, and profits are up. However, pay for pilots at other airlines exceeds Southwest's. Southwest pilots recently called in sick en masse as a protest to the "no wage increase" policy. Additionally, Southwest is experiencing problems recruiting pilots.

So the initial "we can make this happen" spirit that contributed to the success of Southwest may be fraying. Changing external pressures (improving customer demand, pilot shortages, etc.) are working against Southwest's original compensation strategy, changing it from a source of advantage to a source of disadvantage. A real difficulty in any strategy is deciding when to sustain it and when to adjust it—"when to hold 'em, when to fold 'em."

FORMING/IMPLEMENTING STRATEGY: *AND*, NOT *OR*

Some suggest that the real advantage is in *how the strategy gets implemented* rather than in the formulation of the strategy.[21] Clearly, if pay is to be strategic, then advantage can spring from both how it is *formulated and* how it is *implemented.*

Focusing on winning solely by superior implementation means adopting the "cost cutter" approach—doing more with less. However, another key to the strategic perspective is to innovate—to risk being different. This applies to compensation strategy

[21]J. Pfeffer, "When it Comes to 'Best Practices', Why do Smart Organizations Occasionally do Dumb Things?" *Organizational Dynamics* 25 (1997), pp. 33–44; and J. Pfeffer, *Competitive Advantage through People* (Cambridge: Harvard Business School Press, 1994); R. Kanigel, *The One Best Way: Frederick Winslow Taylor and the Enigma of Efficiency* (New York: Viking Press, 1997).

as well as business strategy. An organization can rely on superior implementation to win (being more efficient) and/or by innovating (seeking new approaches to pay).

BASIC ISSUE: DOES "FIT" PAY OFF?

The basic underlying premise of any strategic perspective is that if managers align pay decisions with the organization's strategy and values, are responsive to employees and union relations, and are globally competitive, then the organization is more likely to achieve competitive advantage.[22]

Socioeconomic/ political environment	→	Organization strategy	→	HR/compensation policies	→	Competitive advantage

Up to this point we have stressed that the business strategy leads to the compensation plan. The challenge is to design the "fit" among the environment, business strategy, and pay plan. The better the fit, the greater the competitive advantage.

Now let's turn this perspective on its head.

"Best Practices"

There are those who believe that (1) a set of best pay practices exists, and (2) these practices *should* be applied *independent* of the situation.[23] They challenge the "match-the-business-strategy" view. Does better fit between business strategy and compensation plans really yield better performance? Or is there a set of best practices that yields better performance with almost any business strategy? The latter perspective can be depicted as:

Socioeconomic/ political environment	→	HR/compensation policies	→	Organization strategy	→	Competitive advantage

[22]Wright, McMahan, and McWilliams, "Human Resources and Sustained Competitive Advantage;" T. Jackson, *Inside Intel: Andy Grove and The Rise of the World's Most Powerful Chip Company* (New York: Dutton, 1997); Andrew S. Grove, *Only the Paranoid Survive* (New York: Doubleday, 1996).

[23]P. Cappelli and H. Singh, "Integrating Strategic HR and Strategic Management," Chapter 5, in *Research Frontiers in IR and HR, Industrial and Labor Relations Review*, 1993; P. Wright and G. C. McMahan, "Theoretical Perspectives for Strategic Human Resource Management," *Journal of Management* 18, no. 2 (1992), pp. 295–320; T. Kochan and P. Osterman, *The Mutual Gains Enterprise* (Cambridge: Harvard Business School Press, 1994); J. R. Schuster and P. K. Zingheim, *The New Pay* (New York: Lexington Books, 1992); J. Pfeffer, "Pitfalls on the Road to Measurement: the Dangerous Liaison of HR with Ideas of Accounting and Finance," *Human Resource Management* 36, no. 3 (Fall 1997), pp. 357–65; J. Pfeffer, "Seven Practices of Successful Organizations," *California Management Review* 49, no.2 (1998), pp. 96–124.

The underlying premise here is that adopting the best pay practices will allow the employer to gain preferential access to superior human resource talent and competencies (i.e., valued assets). These superior human resources will in turn influence the strategy the organization adopts and be the source of its competitive advantage. This resource-based approach takes literally the oft-heard refrain from corporate public relations: Human resources are our most important asset. This may appear to be a chicken-egg discussion: Which comes first, the HR/compensation policies or the business strategy? Yet the answer is critical in the design of a pay plan.

If best practices do exist, what are they? It depends on who you ask. Exhibit 2.10 summarizes two different views. Under the "new pay," employee pay is based primarily on market rates; pay increases depend on performance (not cost of living or seniority increases), and the employment relationship is uncertain, less secure. The logic is that the implicit contract is a partnership in which successes (and risks) are shared.

The competing view, "*high commitment*," prescribes high base pay, sharing performance successes only (not risks), guaranteeing employment security, promoting from within, and the like. These practices are believed to attract and retain a highly committed workforce, which will become the source of competitive advantage. Some political leaders in advanced industrial countries argue that public policies should support high-wage, higher-skilled jobs via laws and tax incentives. Such an approach would encourage less labor-intensive technologies (e.g., Hewlett-Packard, Exxon, Merck) over more labor-intensive operations such as Wal-Mart and McDonald's.

SO WHAT MATTERS MOST?

It would be nice to be able to say which compensation strategy best fits each situation, or which list of best practices truly represents the best. Unfortunately, little research has directly examined the competing views. However, there is some recent research that gets us beyond the theories and rhetoric.[24]

One study examined eight years of data from 180 U.S. companies.[25] The authors reported that while differences in relative pay levels (external competitiveness) existed among these companies, these differences were *not* related to their subsequent financial performance. However, differences in the percent of bonuses and the percentage of people eligible for stock options *were* related to future financial success of the organizations. It appears that it is not *how much* you pay, but *how* you pay, that matters.

---

[24]R. D. Bretz, R. A. Ash, and G. F. Dreher, "Do People Make the Place? An Examination of the Attraction-Selection Attrition-Hypothesis," *Personnel Psychology* 42 (1989), pp. 561–81; B. Gerhart and G. Milkovich, "Employee Compensation" in M. Dunnette and L. Hough, ed. *Handbook of Industrial and Organization Psychology* 3 (Palo Alto, California: Consulting Psychologists Press, 1992). A. S. Blinder, ed., *Paying for Productivity* (Washington, DC: Brookings Institute, 1990); B. Gerhart, C. Trevor, and M. E. Graham, "New Directions in Compensation Research" in *Research in Personnel and Human Resource Management*, ed. G. R. Ferris (Greenwich, CT: JAI Press 1996).

[25]B. Gerhart and G. Milkovich, "Organization Differences in Managerial Compensation and Financial Performance," *Academy of Management Journal* 33 (1990), pp. 663–91; K. Murphy and M. Jensen, "It's Not How Much, But How You Pay," *Harvard Business Review,* 1993.

EXHIBIT 2.10 Best Practices Options

*The New Pay**	*High Commitment†*
• External market-sensitive-based pay, not internal consistency • Variable performance-based pay, not annual increases • Risk-sharing partnership, not entitlement • Flexible opportunities to contribute, not jobs • Lateral promotions, not career path • Employability, not job security • Teams, not individual contributors	• High wages: You get what you pay for • Guarantee employment security • Apply incentives; share gains, not risks • Employee ownership • Participation and empowerment • Teams, not individuals, are base units • Smaller pay differences • Promotion from within • Selective recruiting • Enterprisewide information sharing • Training, cross-training, and skill development are crucial • Symbolic egalitarianism adds value • Long-term perspective matters • Measurement matters

*Source: J.R. Schuster, *The New Pay;* E. Lawler, *New Pay.*
†Source: Pfeffer, *Competitive Advantage through People.*

Another study not only found similar results, it also reported that the relative effect of the compensation strategy on a firm's performance was equal to the impact of *all other aspects of the HR system* (high involvement, teams, training programs, etc.) *combined.*[26] These findings are near and dear to the hearts of many of our compensation cronies.

Other studies also tend to confirm that compensation strategies can have effects on organization performance.[27] What still remains an open question is *whether fit matters.* Do compensation systems that are aligned with both the business, strategic, and environmental context and other HR systems having greater effects? Much of the research suggests that compensation strategies have impact, whether or not they are aligned.

One set of studies that focuses on specific U.S. industries including auto, steel, and telecommunications reports that high performance work systems (which include gainsharing and competitive pay levels plus training, teams, participation) *all acting together*

[26]Brian Becker and Mark Huselid, "High Performance Work Systems and Firm Performance: A Synthesis of Research and Managerial Implications," in *Research in Personnel and Human Resource Management*, ed. G. R. Ferris (Greenwich, CT: JAI Press, 1997).

[27]Stroh, J. Brett, Baumann and Reilly, "Agency Theory and Variable Pay Compensation Strategies," *Academy of Management Journal* 393 (1996), pp. 751–67; M. Bloom and G. Milkovich, "Issues in Managerial Compensation Research," in *Trends in Organization Behavior*, ed. G. L. Cooper and D. M. Rousseau (New York: Wiley, 1996).

are more effective that any single pay program.[28] Other compensation researchers emphasize fitting pay strategies to organization strategies and environmental conditions.[29]

Further supporting the perspective that HR systems are interconnected, two researchers found relationships between compensation system design and employment security.[30] They report fewer layoffs and less downsizing in companies that have more performance-based (variable) pay strategies. The logic underlying their findings is that managers are less likely to lay employees off in bad times because labor costs are controlled through lower pay (fewer performance incentives) rather than lower head count.

Still Maybe after All These Years

We believe that the preponderance of recent evidence supports the view that compensation strategies influence employee behaviors and organization performance. We also believe that the debate on how much fit matters is still unresolved. Hence, taking a strategic perspective on pay remains a theory to be more fully studied.

Caution and more evidence are required to interpret and apply many of these studies. *It may be that organizations that are successful* (higher profits, greater market share and revenues and appreciated stock values) *are better able to offer incentives and stock sharing*. A colleague's study reveals that profit sharing and stock options are related to firm performance only when the organization is performing well.[31] When there is success to share, success sharing seems to work. However, when the organization's performance is relatively weaker, these compensation plans have *no* effect. So rather than pay systems affecting employee behavior and organization performance, perhaps the reverse occurs: employee behaviors and organization performance cause changes in the pay systems.

SO WHAT'S THE DEAL?

Throughout this chapter, whether through strategic perspectives or finding the best practices, compensation and people have been treated almost mechanically, like ingredients in a recipe. If only the right fit or the one right way or the right recipe can be found, then

---

[28]S. A. Snell and J. W. Dean, Jr. "Strategic Compensation for Integrated Manufacturing: The Moderating Effects of Job and Organizational Inertia," *Academy of Management Journal* 37 (1994), pp. 1109–14.

[29]Gomez-Mejia and Balkin, *Compensation, Organization Strategys, and Firm Performance;* Montemayer, "Aligning Pay Systems with Market Strategy," *ACA Journal*, Winter 1994, pp. 44–53; J. P. MacDuffie, "Human Resource Bundles and Manufacturing Performance: Organizational Logic and Flexible Production Systems in the World Auto Industry," *Industrial and Labor Relations Review* 48 (1995), pp. 197–221; J. B. Arthur, "Effects of Human Resource Systems on Manufacturing Performance and Turnover," *Academy of Management Journal* 37 (1994), pp. 670–87; and R. Batt, "From Bureaucracy to Enterprise? The Changing Jobs and Careers of Managers in Telecommunications Service," in P. Osterman, ed. *The Changing Jobs and Careers of Professional, Technical, and Managerial Workers* (Oxford: University Press, 1997).

[30]B. Gerhart and C. O. Trevor, "Employment Variability under Different Managerial Compensation Systems," *Academy of Management Journal* 39, no. 6 (1996), pp. 1692–1712. Also see R. Gibbons, "Incentives and Careers in Organizations" (Working paper, Johnson Graduate School of Management, Cornell University, 1997).

[31]J. Abowd, "Does Performance Based Managerial Compensation Affect Corporate Performance?" *Industrial and Labor Relations Review* 435 (1990), pp. 52S–73S.

people will respond and organizations will succeed. However, it cannot be overemphasized that it is the relationship with employees that is strategic.

In the first pages of the book, we noted that compensation can be described as a return received *in exchange* for people's efforts and ideas given at their workplace. *Exchange as part of the relationship* is key. For most people, many of the terms and conditions of their employment exchanges are left unstated, forming an implicit contract, *the deal.*[32]

An **implicit employment contract** is an unwritten understanding between employers and employees over their reciprocal obligations and returns; employees contribute toward achieving the goals of the employer in exchange for returns given by the employer and valued by the employee.

Compensation is an important part of this implicit employment relationship. Unanticipated changes in compensation often breach this implicit understanding. Introducing more incentives in place of annual pay increases, or raising the deductibles on health care insurance may breach the implicit contract and therefore have a negative influence on employee behavior.

Transactional and Relational Returns

Recall the total returns exhibit shown in the previous chapter (Exhibit 1.2). Returns take transactional and relational forms in the implicit employment deal.[33] These implicit deals signal the organization's compensation strategy. Some are more transactional, emphasizing the cash and benefits forms, others may be more relational, emphasizing more socio-psychological returns.

Exhibit 2.11 lays out a grid with transactional forms on one axis and relational forms on the other. It is possible to categorize compensation strategies in terms of their emphasis on transactional returns, relational returns, or both.

Organizations that pay low compensation and offer low relational forms of returns are called "commodity". They view labor as a commodity, like any other input into the production process. In the United States, perhaps migrant workers operate with this type of deal.

---

[32] I. R. Macneil, "Relational Contracts: What We Do and Do Not Know," *Wisconsin Law Review*, 1985, pp. 483–525; D. M. Rousseau and J. M. McLean Parks, "The Contracts of Individuals and Organizations," in *Research in Organization Behavior*, L. L. Cummings and B. M. Staw (Greenwich, CT: JAI Press); A. S. Tsui, J. L. Pearce, L. W. Porter, and J. P. Hite, "Choice of Employee-Organization Relationships," in *Research in Personnel and Human Resource Management*, ed. G. R. Ferris (Greenwich, CT: JAI Press, 1995); Kenneth L. Deavers, "Outsourcing: A Corporate Competitiveness Strategy, Not a Search for Low Wages," *Journal of Labor Research* XVIII, 4 (Fall 1997), pp. 503–19; and Marvin H. Kosters, "New Employment Relationships and the Labor Market," *Journal of Labor Research* XVIII, no. 4 (Fall 1997), pp. 551–59.

[33] D. M. Rousseau, *Psychological Contracts in Organizations* (Thousand Oaks, CA: Sage Publishers, 1995); I.R. Macneil, *The New Social Contracts* (New Haven, CT: Yale University Press, 1980); I. R. Macneil, "Relational Contracts."

Exhibit 2.11 Framework for Analyzing Different "Deals"

Transactional	Relational: Low	Relational: High
High	High Pay—Low Commitment Hired Guns (Solomon Brothers)	High Pay—High Commitment Cult-like (Microsoft)
Low	Low Pay—Low Commitment Workers as Commodity (Employers of Migrant Farm Workers)	Low Pay—High Commitment Family (Starbucks)

Organizations that offer both high compensation and high relational forms of returns seem to be cult-like. Microsoft, Hewlett-Packard, and Toyota are examples. The strong belief in and commitment to the organization shows in the words and actions of employees: "Being at the center of technology, having an impact on the work, working with smart people, the sheer volume of opportunities, shipping winning products, beating competition."[34]

Some organizations offer a family relationship: high relational forms with lesser transactional forms of returns. Starbucks may be an example; one writer calls them the "touchy-feely coffee company."[35]

Finally, there are the "hired guns,"—all transactional, "show-me-the-cash" relationships. Perhaps brokerage houses or auto dealerships in the United States are examples.

While labeling these companies is fun, and even convenient for describing different deals, it may be misleading. Caution is required. For example, the Starbucks CEO states that he pays above his competitors and offers health insurance and "bean stock" to Starbuck partners/employees. Yet Starbucks' turnover rate is about 60 percent, so most "partners" do not stay in the family very long. Our point is that analyzing compensation strategies in terms of an exchange or implicit relationship highlights the fact that it is the relationship with employees that is strategic. Compensation is an important part, albeit not the only part, of the employment relationship.

---

[34]McKenna and McHenry, "Microsoft's Work Ethic."

[35]R. Thomkins, "Touchy-Feely Coffee Company," *Financial Times*, October 9, 1997, p. 14.

Go to Towers Perrin's website (**http://www.towersperrin.com,** then either *News* or *Hot Topics*) to read about its Workplace Index. The Workplace Index survey of 2,500 U.S. employees, which includes measures of security, alignment, customer focus, and efficiencies, reveals that while workers believe they are contributing to their companies' record performance, they doubt that their hard work is being fully recognized or rewarded.

1. Compare 1995 data to current data. What's the deal?
2. Are these results important for managing compensation?
3. Consider the four types of deals depicted in Exhibit 2.12. Do the website data focus on all four types, or only on the high transactional/high relational types?

Summary

A strategic perspective on compensation takes the position that how employees are compensated can be a source of sustainable competitive advantage. Two alternative approaches are highlighted—contingent business strategy/environmental context approach, and the best practices approach. The contingent approach presumes that one size does not fit all. The art of managing compensation strategically involves fitting the compensation system to the different business and environmental conditions.

In contrast, the best practices approach assumes that there exists one best way. So the focus is not so much a question of what the best strategy is, but how to best implement the system.

A four-step process for forming and implementing a compensation strategy includes (1) assessing conditions, (2) deciding on the best strategic choices following the pay model (objectives, consistency, competitiveness, contributions, and administration), (3) implementing the strategy through the design of the pay system, and subsequently (4) reassessing the fit.

Recent studies have begun to research what really does matter, but the answer is still fuzzy. More research is required before an answer emerges.

Finally, an essential point is that the deal—the employment relationship—includes both transactional and relational forms of compensation. While in this book we tend to focus more on the transactional forms, the relational forms matter, too. It is the total deal, the relationship with people, that makes an organization successful.

Review Questions

1. Select a company with which you are familiar. Or, analyze the approach your college uses to pay teaching assistants and/or faculty. Infer its compensation strategy using the five issues (objectives, consistency, competitiveness, employee considerations, and administration). How does your company compare to

Microsoft? To Starbucks? What business strategy does it seem to "fit" (i.e., cost cutter, customer centered, innovator, or something else)?

2. Contrast the essential differences between the strategic business-based and best practice perspectives.
3. Reread the culture/values statements of AT&T and Medtronic in Exhibit 2.6. Discuss how, if at all, those values might be reflected in a compensation system. Are these values consistent with "let the market decide"?
4. Two tests for any source of competitive advantage are "adds value" and "difficult to imitate." Discuss whether these two tests are difficult to pass. Can compensation really be a source of competitive advantage?
5. Set up a debate over the following proposition: Best practices is superior to the business-based approach when designing a compensation system.
6. So what is the deal between your instructor and the college? Is it more like hired gun, commodity, family, or cult-like? Discuss if it would make any difference in teaching effectiveness if the deal were changed. What would you recommend and why?

YOUR TURN

WHAT'S MY STRATEGY?

Consider the Medtronic, Hewlett-Packard, and Microsoft compensation strategies depicted back in Exhibit 2.1. Do they meet the tests of "adds value" and "difficult to imitate?" On the face of it, these strategies seem easy to copy (or at least to articulate). But determining which one best fits an organization's business strategy and culture and the external pressures it faces may make the strategy more difficult to truly imitate. It is the relationships, the fit, or the way a pay system works with other aspects of the organization that make it difficult to imitate and adds value. It is not the techniques themselves, but their interrelationships that make a strategic perspective successful.

Spend some time looking at the websites for each of these three companies. Look at their annual reports. What can you infer about each company's business strategy and its organization culture? Consider the industry in which each company operates. What are the external pressures each company is facing?

After you have a sense of what each company is like, decide whether you think each company's compensation strategy fits its business strategy, organization culture, and external pressures. How would you change it?

EXHIBIT I.1 The Pay Model

STRATEGIC ISSUES → TECHNIQUES → STRATEGIC OBJECTIVES

STRATEGIC ISSUES	TECHNIQUES				STRATEGIC OBJECTIVES
CONSISTENCY	Work analysis	Descriptions	Evaluation certification	INTERNAL STRUCTURE	EFFICIENCY Performance Quality Customer Cost
COMPETITIVENESS	Market definitions	Surveys	Policy lines	PAY STRUCTURE	
CONTRIBUTORS	Seniority based	Performance based	Merit guidelines	INCENTIVE PROGRAMS	EQUITY
ADMINISTRATION	Planning	Budgeting	Communication	EVALUATION	COMPLIANCE

Internal Consistency: Determining the Structure

Exxon employs a chief executive officer, chemical engineers, plant managers, nurses, market analysts, laboratory technicians, financial planners, hydraulic mechanics, accountants, guards, oil tanker captains, sailors, and word processors. How is pay determined for all these different types of work? Is the financial planner worth more than the accountant, or the mechanic more than the word processor? How much more? What procedures are used to set pay rates and who does it? Should the potential consequences of errors in the job, such as the disastrous Alaskan oil spill blamed on the captain of the *Exxon Valdez,* be considered in setting pay? How important are the characteristics of the employees—their competencies, knowledge, skills, or experience? How important are the characteristics of the work, the conditions under which it is done, or the value of what is produced? What about the employer's financial condition, or employee and union preferences?

Beyond understanding how pay is determined for different types of work, there are other critical questions in compensation management. Does how we pay employees make a difference? Why do we pay the financial planner more than the accountant or the mechanic more than a word processor? Does the compensation system support Exxon's business strategy? Does its compensation system help Exxon attract and retain the talent it needs? Do the procedures used to set pay support the way the work is organized and performed, such as the use of semiautonomous work teams in Exxon's Baytown, Texas, refineries? Or are the procedures bureaucratic burdens that hinder focusing on customers, employee flexibility, and teamwork? Does it matter whether employees are paid based on the jobs they perform versus the skills or competencies they possess?

So two basic questions lie at the core of compensation management: (1) How is pay determined for the wide variety of work performed in organizations? (2) How does pay affect employees' attitudes and work behaviors and subsequently the success of the organization?

These questions are examined within the framework introduced in Chapter 1 and shown again in ExhibitI.1. This part of the book examines the framework's first strategic policy issue, internal consistency. The focus of these chapters is within the organization. In Chapter 3, the policy of internal consistency—what affects it and what is affected by it—is considered. Chapter 4 discusses how to assess the similarities and differences in work content. Chapters 5 and 6 scrutinize job-based, skill-based, and competency-based approaches for determining internal pay structures.

CHAPTER

Defining Consistency

Chapter Outline

For the kingdom of heaven is like a householder who went out early in the morning to hire laborers for his vineyard. And having agreed with the laborers for a denarius a day, he sent them into his vineyard. And about the third hour, he went out and saw others standing . . . idle; and he said to them, "Go you also into the vineyard, and I will give you whatever is just." And again he went out about the vineyard, and about the ninth hour, and did as before. . . . But about the eleventh hour he went out and found others . . . and he said to them, "Go you also into the vineyard." When evening came, the owner said to his steward, "Call the laborers, and pay them their wages, beginning from the last even to the first." When the first in their turn came . . . they also received each his denarius. . . . They began to murmur against the householder, saying, "These last have worked a single hour, and thou hast put them on a level with us, who have borne the burden of the day's heat." But answering them, he said, "Friend, I do thee no injustice; take what is thine and go."[1]

Matthew's parable raises age-old questions about internal consistency and pay structures within a single organization.[2] Clearly, the laborers in the vineyard felt that those "who have borne the burden of the day's heat" should be paid more, perhaps because they had contributed more to the householder's economic benefit. According to the laborers, "fair pay" should be based on two criteria: the value of contributions and the time worked. Perhaps the householder was using a third criterion: an individual's needs without regard to differences in the work performed.[3]

Matthew doesn't tell us how the work in the vineyard was organized. Perhaps the laborers had organized into teams, with some members pruning the vines and others pulling weeds or tying the vines. Maybe pruning requires more judgment than tying. Pay structures in contemporary compensation plans are typically designed by assessing how the work is organized and performed, its relative value, and the skills and knowledge required to perform it. This is done through procedures acceptable to the parties involved. If the procedures used or the resulting pay structure is unacceptable to managers or employees, they'll probably murmur, too. Is pruning more valuable than tying? Today, murmuring may translate into turnover, unwillingness to try new technology, and maybe even a lack of concern about the quality of the grapes in the vineyard or the customer satisfaction with them.

This chapter examines the policy of internal consistency in pay structures and its consequences for employees' behaviors and the organization's success.

COMPENSATION STRATEGY: INTERNAL CONSISTENCY

Internal consistency, our first pay policy in a strategic approach, addresses the relationships inside the organization. How do the responsibilities and pay of a vine fastener, pruner, or weeder relate to each other? How do they relate to the responsibilities

---

[1]Matthew 20: 1–16.

[2]For an excellent history of the different standards for pay, see N. Arnold Tolles, *Origins of Modern Wage Theories* (Englewood Cliffs, NJ: Prentice Hall, 1964).

[3]Several Japanese firms still base a small portion of a worker's pay on the number of dependents. In the early 1900s, workers who were "family men" received a pay supplement in some U.S. firms as well.

and pay of the cook, the wine steward, or the accountant employed in the same household? The relationships among different jobs inside an organization make up its internal structure.[4] A policy on internal consistency addresses the logic and consistency underlying these relationships.

Internal consistency, often called internal equity, refers to the relationship between the pay structure and the design of the organization and the work. It focuses attention on the importance of designing a pay structure that *supports the workflow*, is *fair to employees*, and *directs their behaviors* toward organization objectives.

Exhibit 3.1 shows a structure for an engineering and scientific job cluster at a division of Lockheed, a large defense contractor. The structure includes six levels that range from entry to consultant. You can see the relationships among the jobs in the descriptions of each level of work.

Deciding how much to pay the six levels creates a pay structure.

Pay structure refers to the array of pay rates for different work or skills within a single organization. It focuses attention on the *number of levels*, *differentials* in pay between the levels, and the *criteria* used to determine those pay differences.

Supports Work Flow

Work flow refers to the process by which goods and services are delivered to the customer. The challenge is to design a pay structure that supports the efficient flow of that work.[5] For example, most drug companies base the size of their sales force on the number of physicians to be called on per day and the number of working days per year. Astra-Merck, a joint venture between the U.S. drug manufacturer Merck and the Swedish drug company Astra, decided to take a nontraditional approach to organizing sales and marketing.

Astra-Merck's analysis indicated that the ability of physicians to choose specific drugs was being undermined by managed care programs and government regulations that control access to products for their members. So rather than asking sales representatives to call solely on physicians, Astra-Merck created sales teams consisting of account executives, customer representatives, and medical information scientists. Such a cross-functional team responsible for a distinct geographic area (rather than a list of physicians) provides a more responsive and flexible approach to selling products. The

---

[4]E. E. Lawler, *Strategic Pay: Aligning Organizational Strategies and Pay Systems* (San Francisco: Jossey-Bass Publishers, 1990).

[5]S. G. Cohen and D. E. Bailey, "What Makes Teams Work: Group Effectiveness Research From The Shop Floor To Executive Suite," *Journal of Management* 23 (1997), pp. 239–291; A. Weiss, "Incentives And Worker Behavior: Some Evidence," in *Incentives, Cooperation, and Risk Sharing*, ed. H. R. Nalbantian (Totowa, NJ: Rowman & Littlefield, 1987), pp. 137–150.

EXHIBIT 3.1 Engineering Structure at Lockheed

Entry Level

Engineer
Limited use of basic principles and concepts. Develops solutions to limited problems. Closely supervised.

Senior Engineer
Full use of standard principles and concepts. Provides solutions to a variety of problems. Under general supervision.

Systems Engineer
Wide applications of principles and concepts, plus working knowledge of other related disciplines. Provides solutions to a wide variety of difficult problems. Solutions are imaginative, thorough, and practicable. Works under only very general direction.

Lead Engineer
Applies extensive expertise as a generalist or specialist. Develops solutions to complex problems that require the regular use of ingenuity and creativity. Work is performed without appreciable direction. Exercises considerable latitude in determining technical objectives of assignment.

Advisor Engineer
Applies advanced principles, theories and concepts. Contributes to the development of new principles and concepts. Works on unusually complex problems and provides solutions that are highly innovative and ingenious. Works under consultative direction toward predetermined long-range goals. Assignments are often self-initiated.

Consultant Engineer
Exhibits an exceptional degree of ingenuity, creativity, and resourcefulness. Applies and/or develops highly advanced technologies, scientific principles, theories, and concepts. Develops information that extends the existing boundaries of knowledge in a given field. Often acts independently to uncover and resolve problems associated with the development and implementation of operational programs.

Recognized Authority

teams can keep customers apprised of regulations and cover drugs for a wider range of medical conditions than could individuals. One team even translated into Russian a brochure explaining a course of treatment for a physician whose patient population included recent immigrants to the United States. Such a response would have been beyond the resources of a single sales representative. (Of course, the recommended treatment did include an Astra-Merck product.)

To support this new work flow based on teams, Astra-Merck designed a new compensation structure. The pay differences between account executives, customer representatives, and medical information scientists were a major issue. Just as they had been for the vineyard owner described in the bible, just as they are for the engineers at Lockheed.

Supports Fairness

An internally consistent pay structure is more likely to be judged fair if it is based on the work and the skills required to perform the work and if people have an opportunity to be involved in some way in determining the pay structure.[6]

Two sources of fairness are important: the *procedures* for determining the pay structure, called *procedural justice;* and the *actual results* of those procedures, which is the pay structure itself, called *distributive justice.*

Suppose you are given a ticket for speeding. *Procedural justice* refers to the process by which a decision is reached: the right to an attorney, the right to an impartial judge, and the right to receive a copy of the arresting officer's statement. *Distributive justice* refers to the fairness of the decision: guilty. Researchers report that employees' perceptions of procedural fairness significantly influence their acceptance of the results; employees and managers are more willing to accept low pay if they believe the way this result was obtained was fair. This research also strongly suggests that pay procedures are more likely to be perceived as fair (1) if they are consistently applied to all employees, (2) if employee participation and/or representation is included, (3) if appeals procedures are available, and (4) if the data used are accurate.

Applied to internal structures, procedural justice addresses how the design and administration decisions are made, and whether procedures are applied in a consistent manner. Distributive justice addresses the actual internal pay differences among employees—whether they are judged to be reasonable.

Directs Behavior toward Organization Objectives

Internal pay structures influence employees' behavior. Again, the challenge is to design the structures so they direct people's efforts toward organization objectives. The criteria or rationale on which the structure is based ought to make clear the relationship between each job and the organization's objectives.[7] This is an example of "line-of-sight." The more employees can "see" or understand links between their work and the organization's objectives, the more likely the structure will direct their behavior toward those objectives. Internal consistency in pay structures helps create that line-of-sight.

---

[6]Marcia P. Miceli and and Paul Mulvey, "Satisfaction with Pay Systems: Antecedents and Consequences." paper presented at National Academy of Management meetings, San Diego, 1998.

[7]D. I. Levine, "What Do Wages Buy?" *Administrative Science Quarterly* 38 (1993), pp. 462–483; P. Milgrom and J. Roberts, "An Economic Approach to Influence Activities in Organizations," *American Journal of Sociology* 94 (1988), pp. S154–S179.

WHAT SHAPES INTERNAL STRUCTURES?

The major factors that shape internal structures are shown in Exhibit 3.2. The *external* factors include cultural norms and customs, the economic conditions in which the organization operates, and laws and regulations. *Organization* factors include the technology used, which, to a large extent, affects the organization design and the flow of work; the organization strategy, which tells us how the organization is going to compete; and HR policies, including compensation policies, which the pay structures are designed to support. Exhibit 3.2 also includes employee acceptance and costs, since the expected consequences of these structures also affect their design.

Exactly how these factors interact is not well understood. No single theory accounts for all factors. Rather, a number of theories emphasize certain factors over others, and many ignore competing factors. As we discuss the factors that influence pay structures, we will also look at various theories.

External Factors: Cultures and Customs

Culture is the mental programming for processing information that people share in common.[8] Such shared mindsets may form a judgment of what is fair.

Historians tell us that in 14th century western Europe, the church endorsed a "just wage" doctrine, a structure of wages that supported the existing class structure in the society.[9] The doctrine was an effort to end the economic and social chaos resulting from the death of one-third of the population from bubonic plague. The shortage of workers that resulted from the devastation led nobles and landholders to bid up the wages for surviving craftspeople. By allowing the church to determine wages, market forces such as labor scarcity were explicitly denied as appropriate determinants of pay structures.

Even today, as we enter the 21st century, cultural factors shape the pay structures used in organizations around the world. In the Slovak Republic in central Europe, we visited an entire government agency devoted to maintaining a 15–level pay structure required in all Slovak companies (but not foreign ones). The detailed procedures manuals and job descriptions filled a number of shelves. People dissatisfied with the pay rate for their jobs could appeal to this agency. Not surprisingly, few did.

In China, too, the government dictates that state-owned enterprises use a universal structure. Eight levels exist for industrial workers, 16 levels for technicians and engineers, and 26 for government administrators. Government agencies regulate and monitor compliance. However, reform plans are trying to increase differentials and get rid of the "iron rice bowl"—the practice of paying all workers the same without regard to performance.[10]

---

[8]G. Hoefstede, *Culture's Consequences: International Differences in Work Relationships and Values* (Thousand Oaks, CA: Sage Publications, 1980); M. Bloom and G. Milkovich, "Strategic Perspectives on International Compensation and Reward Systems" in *Research and Theory in Strategic HRM: An Agenda for the Twenty-First Century,* ed. Pat Wright et al (Greenwich, CT: JAI Press, 1999).

[9]N. Arnold Tolles, *Origins of Modern Wage Theories* (Englewood Cliffs, NJ: Prentice Hall, 1964).

[10]Duanxu Wang, "Intraorganizational Pay Differentials in the Chinese Context" (Working paper, Hong Kong University of Science and Technology).

Exhibit 3.2 What Shapes Internal Structures?

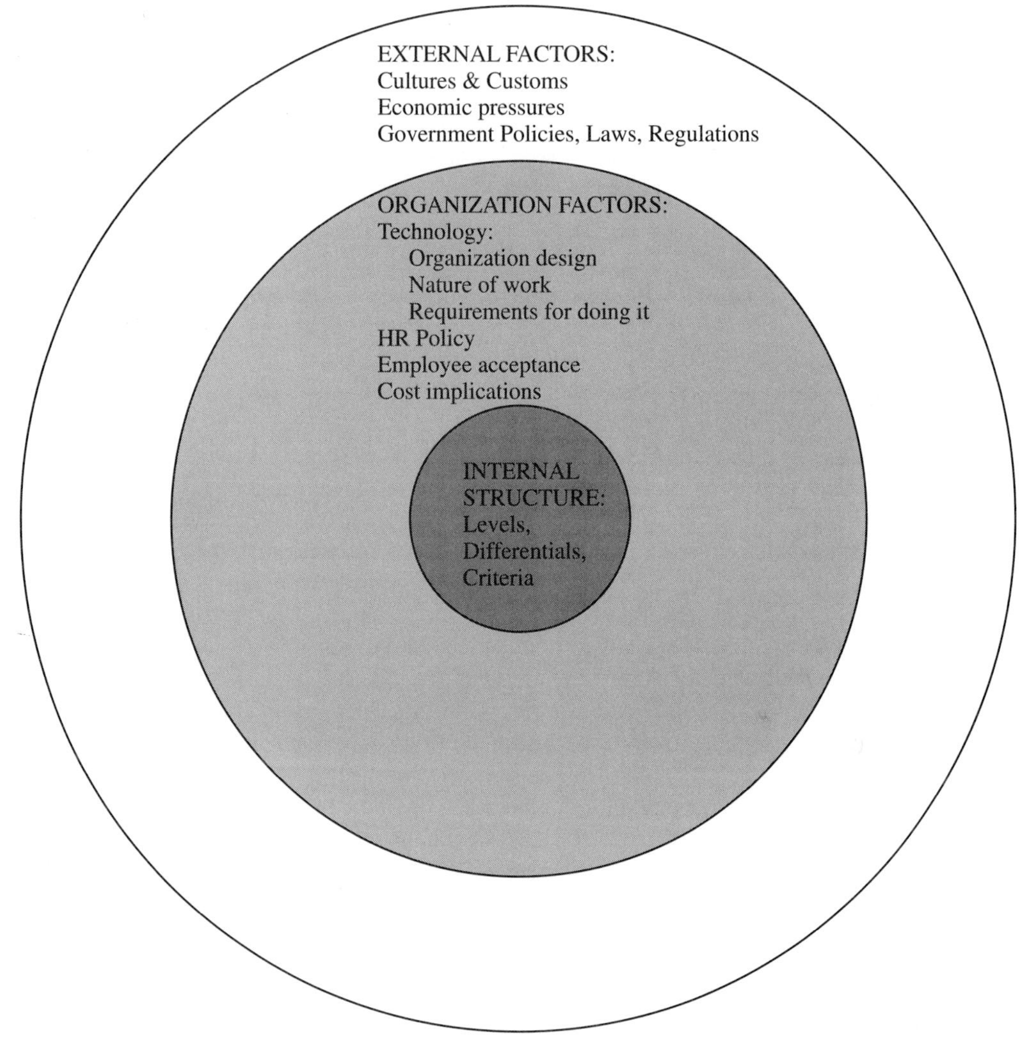

Societal judgments about the fairness of pay structures do change in response to other pressures. For example, many traditional Japanese employers place heavy emphasis on seniority in their internal pay structures. But pressures from global competitors plus an aging workforce have made Japan's traditional age-based pay structures very expensive. Consequently, many Japanese employers are changing their systems. This change is particularly irksome to us; as we have grown older, we seem to more fully appreciate the wisdom of paying on age.

External Factors: Market Pressures

Adam Smith was an early advocate of letting economic market forces influence pay structures. Smith ascribed to human resources both an exchange value and a use value. *Exchange value* is whatever wage the employer and the employee agree on. *Use value* reflects the values of the goods or services labor produces. New technologies associated with the Industrial Revolution increased the use value of labor.

However, Karl Marx countered with his notion of *surplus value.* He accused capitalistic economic systems of basing pay structures on exchange value, with employers unfairly pocketing the surplus created by the difference between what owners were willing to pay workers and what owners earned from workers' efforts. He urged workers to overthrow capitalistic systems in order to reap the benefits of their labor and become owners themselves.[11] In some sense, broad-based stock ownership by employees, a pay technique that is growing in popularity, is following Marx's suggestion.

These early theorists concentrated on the supply of labor to explain pay structures. But in the face of rising wages in the last half of the 19th century, new theories began to examine the demand for labor. One of the best-known theories, the *marginal productivity theory*, says that employers do in fact pay use value.[12] Unless an employee can produce a value equal to the value received in wages, it will not be worthwhile for the employer to hire that worker.

Accordingly, pay differences among the job levels reflect differences in use value associated with different jobs. The marginalists assert that one job is paid more or less than another because of differences in relative productivity of the job and/or differences in consumer valuation of the output. Hence, differences in productivity provide a rationale for the internal pay structure. These views underlie many contemporary compensation practices.

External Factors: Government Policies, Laws, and Regulations

In the United States, equal employment legislation forbids pay systems that discriminate on the basis of gender, race, religion, or national origin. The Equal Pay Act and the Civil Rights Act require "equal pay for equal work," with work defined as equal if it requires equal skill, equal effort, equal responsibility, and is performed under equal working conditions. So an employer may set any number of levels, with differentials

[11]C. Tucker, ed., *The Marx-Engels Reader* (New York: W. W. Norton, 1978).

[12]Allan M. Cartter, *Theory of Wages and Employment* (Burr Ridge, IL: Richard D. Irwin, 1959).

of any size, as long as the criteria for setting them are not gender, race, religion, or national origin. While this may seem obvious, it has not always been so, as we shall discuss in Chapter 17 on pay discrimination.

Much pay-related legislation attempts to regulate economic forces to achieve societal welfare objectives. A contemporary U.S. example is "living wage."[13] A number of U.S. cities require minimum hourly wage rates well above the federal minimum of $5.15 per hour. Sometimes these living wage rates apply to city employees only; sometimes they apply to employers who receive assistance from the city above a specified amount. Baltimore's living wage is $7.10 per hour. Boston requires a wage matched to the poverty level for a family of four. Los Angeles's minimum is $7.25 per hour if health coverage and holidays are included, and $8.50 per hour if they are not. The anticipated outcome of such legislation is a flatter, more compressed structure of wage rates in society.

Slovenian regulations require an 11-to-1 ratio between the top managers' pay and the average pay of the organization workforce. However, a general manager told us that it was impossible to recruit and retain talented sales and finance managers within these pay regulations. So how does he manage? He conceded that he has established accounts for these managers in an Austrian bank, thereby circumventing the law.

As we have already stated, most developed countries have some sort of legal standard regulating pay structures. Whatever they are, organizations operating within those countries must reckon with them.

Organization Factors: Strategy

You have already read in the last chapter how organization strategies influence internal pay structures. Different business strategies may require different pay structures to support them. Pay structures that are not aligned with the organization strategy may become obstacles to the organization's success.

Organization Factors: Design of Work

The *technology* employed is another critical organization factor influencing the design of pay structures.[14] Technology used in producing goods and services influences the *organizational design*, its functional specialties, work teams, and departments. It influences the *work* to be performed and the *skills* required to perform it.

A case in point is the difference in the number of levels in the engineering pay structures at Lockheed, with six levels for engineering alone—versus GE Plastics, with five levels for all managerial/professional/technical employees. The technology required to produce military hardware differs from that used to manufacture plastics. Defense contract work is more labor intensive (more than 50 percent of operating expenses are labor costs) than is plastics (less than 20 percent); hence, different structures emerge.

---

[13]Lawrence B. Glickman, *A Living Wage* (Ithaca, NY: Cornell University Press, 1997).

[14]P. Milgrom and J. Roberts. *Economics, Organization, and Management* (Englewood Cliffs, NJ: Prentice Hall, 1992).

Organization Factors: HR Policies

The organization's *human resource policies* are another influence on pay structures. Most organizations use promotions as an incentive to induce employees to apply for higher-level positions (e.g., machinists to first-line supervisors).[15] In other organizations, offering "titles" is considered a sufficient inducement, and little or no pay differential is offered.[16] If pay differentials are designated as a key mechanism to encourage employees to accept greater responsibilities and/or learn new skills, then the pay structure must be designed to facilitate that policy. Higher pay is required for higher-level jobs to encourage employees to undertake the necessary training and gain the required experience and skills to perform these jobs.

Internal Labor Markets: Combining External and Internal Forces

Internal labor markets combine both external and organizational factors. As depicted in Exhibit 3.3, internal labor markets refer to the rules and procedures that allocate employees among different jobs within a single organization.[17] Individuals tend to be recruited and hired only for specific entry-level jobs (an engineer would be hired right out of college; a senior engineer would have a few years' experience) and are later allocated (promoted or transferred) to other jobs. Because the employer competes in the external market for people to fill these entry jobs, their pay is tied to the external market. It must be high enough to attract a qualified pool of applicants. In contrast, pay for nonentry jobs (those staffed internally via transfer and promotions) is more heavily influenced by the organization's internal factors such as culture, norms, and/or contribution to the organization's success. External factors are dominant influences on pay for entry jobs, but the differentials for nonentry jobs tend to reflect the organization's internal factors.

Employee Acceptance: A Key Factor

A classic article on pay structures asserts that employees desire "fair" compensation.[18] Employees judge the fairness of their pay through comparisons with the compensation paid others for work related in some fashion to their own. Accordingly, an important factor influencing the internal pay structure is its *acceptability to the employees involved.*[19]

---

[15]Paul Schumann, Dennis Ahlburg, and Christine B. Mahoney, "The Effects of Human Capital and Job Characteristics on Pay," *The Journal of Human Resources* XXIX, no. 2, pp. 481–503.

[16]A. Kohn, *Punished by Rewards: The Trouble with Gold Stars, Incentive Plans, A's, Praise and Other Bribes* (Boston, MA: Houghton Mifflin Co. 1993); Jerald Greenberg and Suzy N. Ornstein, "High Status Job Titles as Compensation for Underpayment: A Test of Equity Theory," *Journal of Applied Psychology* 68, no. 2 (1983), pp. 285–97.

[17]Thomas A. Mahoney, "Organizational Hierarchy and Position Worth," *Academy of Management Journal*, December 1979, pp. 726–37.

[18]E. Robert Livernash, "The Internal Wage Structure," in *New Concepts in Wage Determination,* ed. G. W. Taylor and F. C. Pierson (New York: McGraw-Hill, 1957), pp. 143–72.

[19]H. G. Heneman, III, "Pay Satisfaction," in *Research in Personnel and Human Resource Management,* Vol. 3, ed. K. M. Rowland & G. R. Ferris (Greenwich, CT: JAI Press, 1985).

EXHIBIT 3.3 ILLUSTRATION OF AN INTERNAL LABOR MARKET

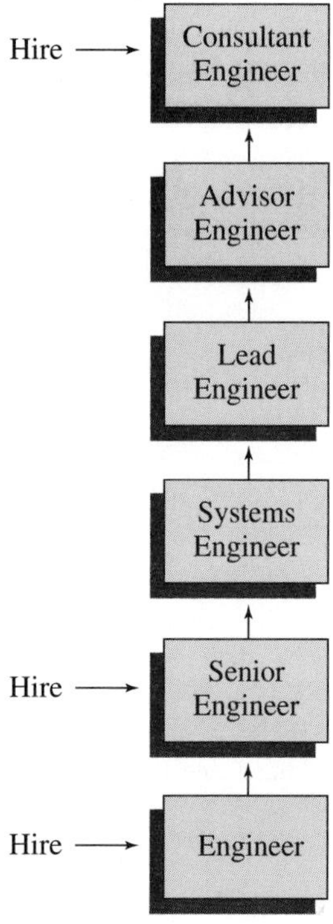

At one point in time, some pay structures may have reflected very rational economic and social purposes such as competitive pressures, technology, and the differences in the work performed. But changes in pay structures may arise in response to changing economic pressures such as skill shortages. Over time, the distorted differences in pay became accepted as equitable and customary; efforts to change them are resisted as destructive of social relationships.[20] Thus, the pay structures established for organizational and economic reasons may be maintained for cultural or other reasons until another economic jolt overcomes the cultural resistance. Then new norms are formed around the new structure.

[20]Robert Folger and Mary Konovsky, "Effects of Procedural and Distributive Justice on Reactions to Pay Raise Decisions," *Academy of Management Journal,* March 1989, pp. 115–30; Jerald Greenberg, "Looking Fair vs. Being Fair: Managing Impressions of Organizational Justice," in *Research in Organizational Behavior,* vol. 12, ed. B. M. Staw and L. L. Cummings (Greenwich, CT: JAI Press, 1990).

EXHIBIT 3.4 Managerial/Professional Levels at General Electric Plastics (GEP)

Level	*Description*
Executive	Provides vision, leadership, and innovation to major business segments or functions of GEP
Director	Directs a significant functional area or smaller business segment
Leadership	Individual contributors leading projects or programs with broad scope and impact, or managers leading functional components with broad scope and impact
Technical/ managerial	Individual contributors managing projects or programs with defined scope and responsibility, or first tier management of a specialty area
Professional	Supervisors and individual contributors working on tasks, activities, and/or less complex, shorter duration projects

STRUCTURES VARY

An internal pay structure is defined by (1) number of *levels* of work, (2) the pay *differentials* between the levels, and (3) the *criteria* used to determine those levels and differentials. These are the factors that a manager may vary to design a structure that supports the work flow, is fair, and directs employee behaviors toward objectives.

Levels

One feature of any pay structure is its hierarchical nature: the number of levels and reporting relationships. Because pay structures typically reflect the organization design and the flow of the work, some are more hierarchical with multiple levels; others are flat with few levels.[21] For example, in comparison to Lockheed's six levels for a single job group (Exhibit 3.1), GE Plastics uses five broad levels, described in Exhibit 3.4, to cover all professional and executive work. GE Plastics would probably fit the Lockheed structure into two or three levels.

Differentials

The pay differences among levels are referred to as differentials. Pay structures typically pay more for work that requires more qualifications to perform, is performed under less desirable working conditions, and/or whose input is more valued.[22] Exhibit 3.5 shows the differentials attached to Lockheed's engineering structure.

[21] C. W. Hill, M. A. Hitt, and R. E. Hoskisson, "Cooperative Versus Competitive Structures In Related And Unrelated Diversified Firms," *Organization Science,* 1992, pp. 501–521.

[22] D. M. Cowherd and D. I. Levine, "Product Quality and Pay Equity between Lower-Level Employees and Top Management: An Investigation of Distributive Justice Theory," *Administrative Science Quarterly* 37 (1992), pp. 302–20; M. Bloom and G. Milkovich, "Money, Managers, and Metamorphosis," in *Trends in Organizational Behavior,* 3rd ed., ed. D. Rousseau and C. Cooper (New York: John Wiley & Sons, 1996).

Exhibit 3.5 Engineering Pay Structure at Lockheed

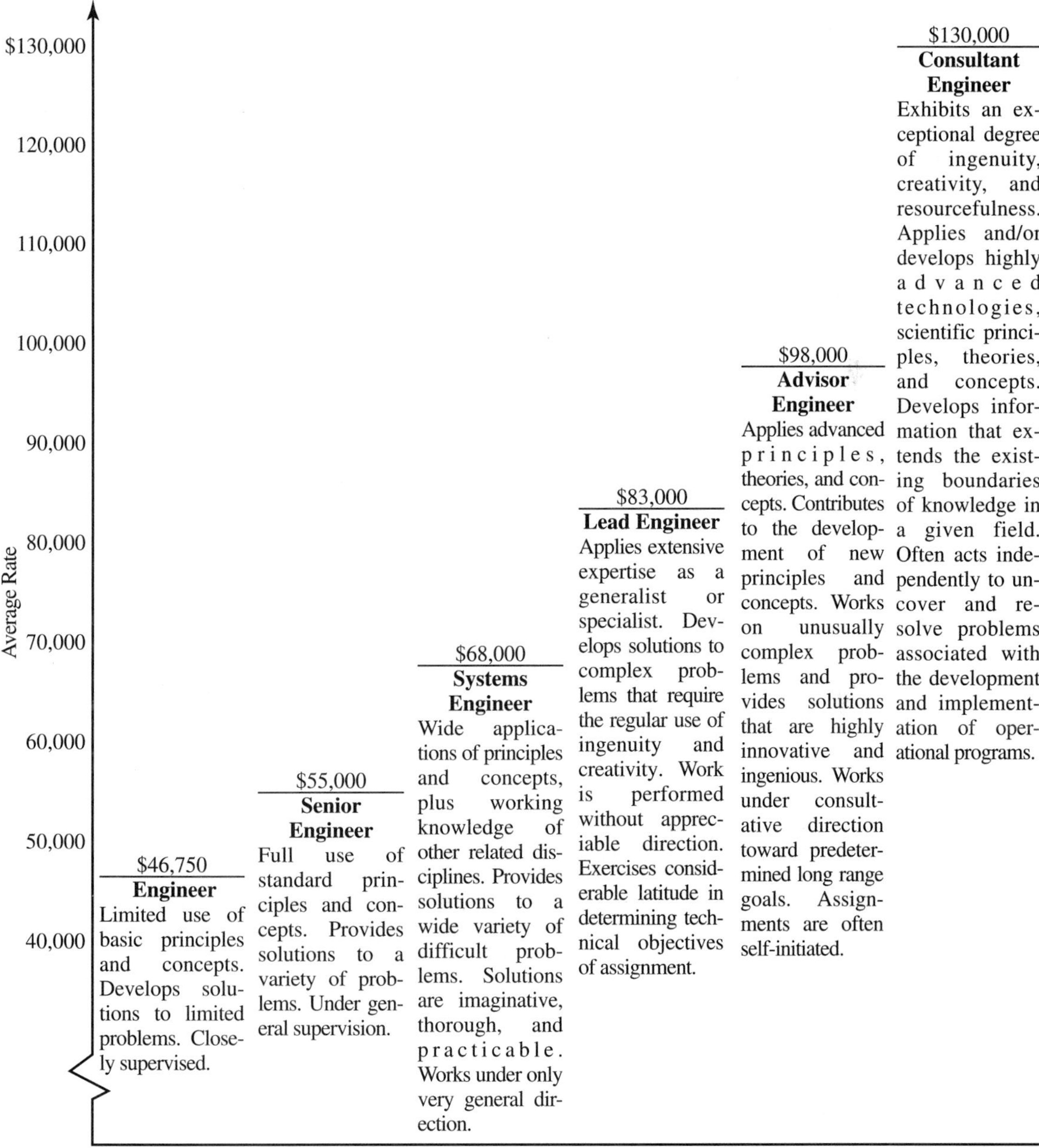

Pay differentials of particular interest in managing compensation include those between adjacent levels in a career path, between supervisors and subordinates, or between union and nonunion employees, and between executives and regular employees.

Criteria: Job- or Person-Based

The criteria used to determine the number of levels and size of the pay differentials can be categorized as either *job-based* or *person-based.* A job-based structure looks at the work content—what tasks are done, what behaviors are expected, what results are expected. Person-based structures shift the focus to the employee: the *skills or knowledge* the employee possesses, whether or not they are used on the particular job the employee is doing, or the *competencies* an employee is assumed to possess.[23]

While this theoretical division into person-based and job-based criteria is convenient, the two categories are not necessarily discrete. In the real world, it is hard to describe a job without reference to the jobholder's behavior. Conversely, it is hard to define job-related knowledge or competencies without referring to work content. As we shall see in later chapters, both criteria require similar decisions. However, they begin with different perspectives. The criterion chosen can influence employee behaviors by describing what is required (i.e., promotion to high level of responsibility, certification of skills/competencies, and/or improved performance) to get higher pay in the structure. The engineering structure at Lockheed (Exhibit 3.1) uses the work performed as the criterion. GE Plastics (Exhibit 3.4) uses the competencies that are required at each level of work.

STRATEGIC CHOICES AMONG STRUCTURE OPTIONS

The basic premise underlying the strategic approach is that fit matters. So the belief is that pay structures tailored to be consistent with the organization, to support the way the work gets done, and to fit the organization's business strategy will be more likely to lead to success. Misaligned structures become obstacles. They may motivate employee behavior that is inconsistent with the organization's strategy.

But what does it mean to fit or tailor the pay structure to be internally consistent? Two strategic choices are involved: (1) how tailored to organization design and work flow to make the structure, and (2) how to distribute pay throughout the levels in the structure.

Tailored versus Loosely Coupled

A low-cost, customer-focused business strategy such as followed by McDonald's or Wal-Mart may be supported by a closely tailored structure. Jobs are well defined with detailed tasks or steps to follow. You can go into a McDonald's in Cleveland, Prague, or

[23]E. E. Lawler III, "From Job-Based to Competency-Based Organizations," *Journal of Organization Behavior* 15 (1994), pp. 3–15.

Shanghai and find they all are very similar. Their pay structures are, too. The customer representative and the food preparation jobs are very well defined in order to eliminate variance in how they are performed. There is little overlap between what the customer representative does and what the food preparer does. The amount of ketchup that goes on the burger is premeasured, even the keys on the cash register are labeled with menu items rather than prices. And the differences in pay among jobs are relatively small.

In contrast to McDonald's, Microsoft's business strategy requires constant product innovation and short product design-to-market cycle times. Companies like Microsoft need to be very agile, constantly innovating and adapting. Their software engineers may work on several teams developing several products at the same time. The roles each engineer assumes may vary in a single day. Microsoft's pay system needs to accommodate this flexibility. Hence, their pay structures need to be more loosely coupled to the organization in order to facilitate constant change.

Egalitarian versus Hierarchical

Pay structures can range from egalitarian at one extreme to hierarchical at the other. Egalitarian structures have fewer levels and smaller differentials between adjacent levels and between the highest and lowest paid workers.

Exhibit 3.6 shows some variations on structures. Structure A has eight different levels, with relatively small differentials in comparison to structure B, which has only

EXHIBIT 3.6 Which Structure Has the Greatest Impact on Performance? On Fairness?

STRUCTURE A Layered	STRUCTURE B Delayered
Chief Engineer	Chief Engineer
Engineering Manager	
Consulting Engineer	Engineering Manager
Senior Lead Engineer	
Lead Engineer	Consulting Engineer
Senior Engineer	Systems Engineer
Engineer	
Engineer Trainee	Associate Engineer

five levels. Structure A is hierarchical in comparison to the egalitarian structure of B; the multiple levels typically include detailed descriptions of work done at that level and delineate who is responsible for what. Hierarchical structures are consistent with a belief in the motivational effects of frequent promotions. Hierarchies support the recognition of differences in employee skills, responsibilities, and contributions to the organization.[24]

Structure B can also be characterized as "delayered." Several levels of responsibility and supervision are removed so that all employees at all levels become responsible for a broader range of tasks, but also have greater freedom to determine how best to accomplish what is expected of them. An egalitarian structure implies a belief that all workers should be treated equally, that more equal treatment will improve employee satisfaction, aid work team unit, and therefore affect workers' performance.[25]

While it is hard to be against anything called egalitarian, if we instead use the word "averagism," as Chinese workers do when describing the pay system in state-owned enterprises, some of the possible drawbacks of this approach become clear: Equal treatment can result in more knowledgeable employees with more responsible jobs being unrecognized and unrewarded, which may cause them to leave the organization. They may physically leave for another job, or they may simply slack off or tune out and refuse to do anything that is not specifically required of them. Their change in behavior will lower overall performance. So a case can be made for both egalitarian and hierarchical structures.

Exhibit 3.7 clarifies the differences between egalitarian and hierarchical structures. Keep in mind, though, that the choice is not either/or. Rather, the differences are a matter of degree. So levels can range from many to few, differentials can be large or small, and the criteria can be based on the job, the person, or some combination of the two.

Two categories of differentials are of particular interest in hierarchical versus egalitarian or delayered structures. The first is the differential between CEO pay and the pay of the average employee in the same company. The second is the overall distribution of pay within the workforce.

CEO Differentials. Interest in pay differences between top executives and other employees is not new. Plato declared in *The Laws* that society was strongest when the richest earned a maximum of four times the lowest pay. Aristotle favored a five-times limit. In 1942 President Franklin Roosevelt proposed a maximum wage: a 100 percent tax on all income above 10 times the minimum wage.[26]

CEO differentials vary among countries. Exhibit 3.8 shows some international comparisons. Comparing the average pay for a manufacturing employee with average CEO pay, the ratio in the United States is 27 to one, but only 11 to one in Germany and Japan. The ratio in the United States is the highest among industrialized countries

---

[24]Elliot Jaques, "In Praise of Hierarchies," *Harvard Business Review,* January-February 1990.

[25]R. D. Bretz and S. L. Thomas, "Perceived Equity, Motivation, and Final-offer Arbitration in Major League Baseball," *Journal of Applied Psychology* 77 (1992), pp. 280–287.

[26]Paul Glover, "Fair Pay Forum," *Hour Town,* Feb-March 1997, p. 1.

EXHIBIT 3.7 Strategy: Hierarchical vs Egalitarian

	Hierarchical	**Egalitarian**
Levels	Many	Fewer
Differentials	Large	Small
Criteria	Person or Job	Person or Job
Supports:	Close Fit	Loose Fit
Work Organization	Individual Performers	Teams
Fairness	Fairness	Fairness
Behaviors	Opportunities for promotion	Cooperation

and is growing larger. A large part of the gap is attributable to the widespread use of stock options for executive pay in the United States and the unprecedented increase in stock market value in the mid-1990s.[27] Note, however, that Exhibit 3.8 does not include options which would further increase the size of the differentials.

Every April, like tulips, stories about the outlandish differentials in the U.S. corporations appear in the business press. The most famous example is Michael Eisner, the CEO of Disney, who was paid $750,000 in base salary for 1997. However, he exercised $565 million in stock options. Mr. Eisner said he needed to sell the options to pay the taxes on his $9.9 million bonus. Apparently he had not had enough taxes withheld from his paycheck.

The Eisner pay package stands in sharp contract to that earned by Disney employees who perform as Mickey or Minnie Mouse. Mickey, Minnie, Pluto, Goofy, and even Snow White are all represented by the Teamsters and earn between $9 and $15 an hour, compared to Mr. Eisner's $1,210 an hour. (If we assume Mr. Eisner works 24 hours a day, 7 days a week, 52 weeks a year.)

The AFL-CIO is counting on information on CEO differentials to rally support for the union movement. Their website at **http:ww.aflcio.org** contains CEO pay for a number of utility companies. Website visitors are invited to compare their pay to what the CEO of their company makes. Exhibit 3.9 shows the nature of the comparisons made.

Visit the website and check out the differentials. Select a company for which *you* will be the compensation manager. Prepare a brief report recommending how the company should explain information available on the web to employees (whose average salary is $32,000), customers, and regulators.

[27]Kevin J. Murphy, "Recent Trends in Executive Compensation" (paper prepared for the Board of Governors of the Federal Reserve System, Washington, DC, October 23, 1997); G. S. Crystal, *In Search of Excess: The Overcompensation of American Executives* (New York: Norton, 1991); D. C. Bok, *The Cost of Talent: How Executives and Professionals Are Paid and How It Affects America* (New York: Free Press, 1993).

EXHIBIT 3.8 Pay through the Ranks

Manufacturing Employee	White-collar Employee	Manager	CEO
Germany $36,857	Britain $74,761	Italy $219,573	United States $717,237
Canada $34,263	France $62,279	France $190,354	France $479,772
Japan $34,263	Germany $59,916	Japan $185,437	Italy $463,009
Italy $31,537	Italy $58,263	Britain $162,190	Britain $439,441
France $30,019	United States $57,675	United States $159,575	Canada $416,066
United States $27,606	Canada $47,231	Germany $145,627	Germany $390,933
Britain $26,084	Japan $40,990	Canada $132,877	Japan $390,723

Yet egalitarian structures can cause problems, too. For example, Ben and Jerry's Homemade, a purveyor of premium ice cream, tried to maintain a ratio of only 7-to-1 between its highest paid and lowest paid employee. (When the company started, the spread was an Aristotelean 5-to-1.) The relatively narrow differential reflected the company's philosophy that the prosperity of its production workers and its management should be closely linked. The narrow spread also generated a great deal of free,

Exhibit 3.9 The AFL–CIO's Paywatch Website

Intro | Home | Runaway CEO Pay | The OverBoard Room
The CEO and You | What You Can Do | BackTalk

How You Compare to Your CEO

You would have to work 55 years to equal T. Milton Honea's 1996 compensation.

You better get working, because you can't take a vacation until 2052 A.D.

T. Milton Honea's compensation could support 55 workers earning your salary.

show me how others compare

Above values calculated with your entered compensation of $40,000

favorable publicity. However, it eventually became a barrier to recruiting. Ben and Jerry's was forced to abandon this policy to hire an accounting manager and a new CEO. However, without the presence of the quirky founders Ben Cohen and Jerry Greenfield, the company floundered; its profit levels slipped, and in 1997 they even lost money. (They have regained profitability since then.) Additionally, Ben and Jerry never publicized the fact that their own stock ownership increased their total compensation to much more than the 7 to 1 ratio. Just like the Slovenian managers, they found a way to deal with economic reality. The Slovenian general manager established accounts outside the country; Ben and Jerry's changed their policy.

Earnings Distribution. If we assume that an organization has a compensation budget of x amount to distribute among its employees, there are a number of ways to do so. The compensation budget can be divided by the number of employees to give everyone the same amount. The Moosewood restaurant in Ithaca, New York, adopts this approach. But few organizations in the world are that egalitarian. In most, pay varies among employees.

Researchers use a statistic called the *gini coefficient* to describe any distribution of pay. A gini of zero means everyone is paid the identical wage. The higher the gini coefficient (maximum =1), the greater the pay differentials among the levels.[28]

Compare structures A and B in Exhibit 3.6 again. Both of them have the same salary at the top of the structure and at the bottom of the structure. However, the salaries in B are less uniformly distributed in the structure; B would have a higher gini.

In Exhibit 3.10, structure B would have an even higher gini, since the pay differentials are even higher at the top than the comparison structure. Some economists recommend structures with high ginis, as we shall see in the next section.

WHAT THE RESEARCH TELLS US

Before managers recommend which pay structure is best for their organizations, we hope they will not only look at the factors in their organization, such as work flow, what is fair, and how to motivate employee behavior, but also look to research for guidance.

Both economists and psychologists have something to tell us about the effects of various structures.

Equity Theory

The equity theory model shown in Exhibit 3.11 suggests that employees judge equity on the basis of comparisons between the work, qualifications, and pay for job A versus the work, qualifications, and pay for job B, and those for their own job.[29] However, very little research addresses the question of what specific factors influence employees' perceptions of the equity or fairness of the *pay structure,* as opposed to the equity or fairness of the *pay.*[30] Consequently, equity theory could support both egalitarian and hierarchical structures.

Tournament Theory

Economists, on the other hand, have focused more directly on the motivational effects of structures. Specifically, they say that in a comparison of structures A and B in Exhibit 3.10, structure B would have a more positive effect on performance than would

[28]D. Donaldson and J. A. Weymark, "A Single-Parameter Generalization of the Gini Indices of Inequality," *Journal of Economic Theory* 22 (1980), pp. 67–86.

[29]E. E. Lawler, *Pay and Organizational Effectiveness: A Psychological View* (NY: McGraw-Hill, 1971); T. A. Mahoney, *Compensation and Reward Perspectives* (Homewood, IL: Richard D. Irwin, 1979).

[30]H. G. Heneman, III, "Pay Satisfaction," in *Research in Personnel and Human Resource Management* Vol. 3, ed. K. M. Rowland & G. R. Ferris (Greenwich, CT: JAI Press, 1985).

EXHIBIT 3.10 Which Structure Has the Greatest Impact on Performance? On Fairness?

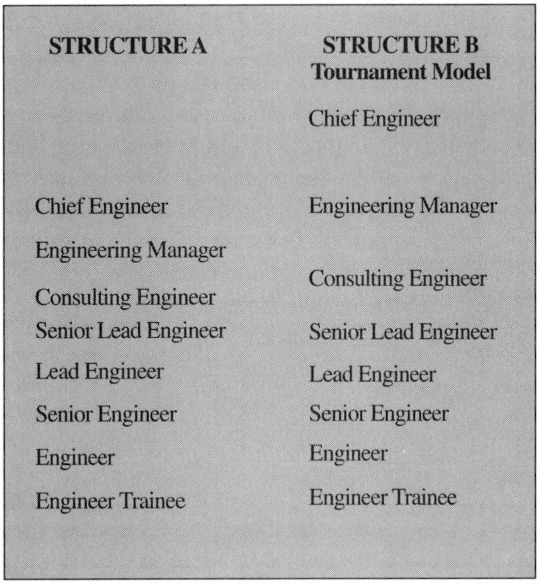

STRUCTURE A	STRUCTURE B Tournament Model
	Chief Engineer
Chief Engineer	Engineering Manager
Engineering Manager	
	Consulting Engineer
Consulting Engineer	
Senior Lead Engineer	Senior Lead Engineer
Lead Engineer	Lead Engineer
Senior Engineer	Senior Engineer
Engineer	Engineer
Engineer Trainee	Engineer Trainee

EXHIBIT 3.11 Perceived Equity of a Pay Structure

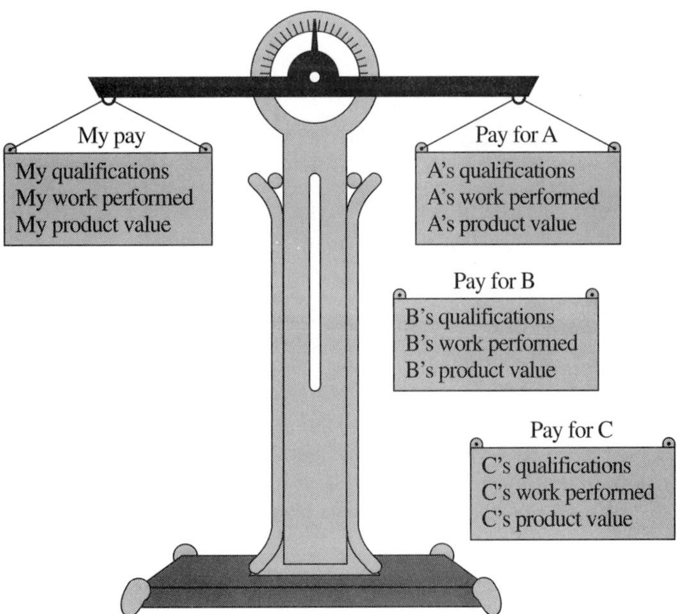

structure A. Indeed, the pay distribution in structure B has positive effects on the performance of people at *all levels* in the structure, they say. These studies view pay structures as a tournament.[31]

Suppose that structure A in Exhibit 3.10 includes 10 engineering managers at the second-to-the-top level, each making $70,000, and each competing for five chief engineer positions, where the pay is $85,000. A tournament model says that in structure B, where the chief engineers are instead paid $95,000, everyone will work even harder. Rather than making engineering managers resentful of the big bucks paid to the chief engineers, the greater differential will motivate all employees at all levels in the structure to try to be the "winner," or get promoted to the next level.

Developing this argument, economists point out that the main outcome affected by individuals' performance is whether or not they get promoted to the next level—for instance which engineering managers get the chief engineer positions.[32] Because the pay for the chief engineers is set before candidates agree to take the job, that pay has little motivational effect on people already in that job. Instead, the pay offered to the chief engineers motivates those at lower levels in the organization.[33] They are motivated to come to work and do their best in order to stay in contention for promotion to the chief engineer position. The pay for chief engineers should be set with its motivational effects on people at lower levels in mind.

It then follows that, within limits, the bigger the prize for getting to the next level, the greater the motivational impact the structure will have. According to the tournament model, employees in structure B will work harder than employees in structure A.

Some research supports tournament theory. Raising the total prize money by $100,000 in the Professional Golf Association tournament lowered each player's score, on average, by 1.1 strokes over 72 holes.[34] And the closer the players got to the top prize, the more their scores were lowered. An Australian study concluded that effort increases and absenteeism is reduced when firms give larger raises upon promotion.[35]

Tournament models can even account for CEO pay in the United States versus Japan.[36] Because Japanese CEOs are appointed much later in their careers than are their U.S. counterparts, a Japanese firm will have a lot of information about a CEO

---

[31]B. E. Becker and M. A. Huselid, "The Incentive Effects of Tournament Compensation Systems," *Administrative Science Quarterly* 37 (1992), pp. 336–50; E. Lazear and S. Rosen, "Rank-Order Tournaments As Optimum Labor Contracts," *Journal of Political Economy* 89 (1981), pp. 841–864.

[32]E. P. Lazear, *Personnel Economics* (Cambridge, MA: The MIT Press, 1995).

[33]R. D. Bretz and S. L. Thomas, "Perceived Equity, Motivation, and Final-offer Arbitration in Major League Baseball," *Journal of Applied Psychology* 77 (1992), pp. 280–287.

[34]R. G. Ehrenberg and M. L. Bognanno, "The Incentive Effects of Tournaments Revisited: Evidence from the European PGA Tour," *Industrial and Labor Relations Review* 43 (1990), pp. 74–S–88–S.

[35]E. P. Lazear, *Personnel Economics* (Cambridge, MA: The MIT Press, 1995).

[36]Arne L. Kalleberg and James R. Lincoln, "The Structure of Earnings Inequality in the United States and Japan," *American Journal of Sociology,* vol. 94, supplement S121–S153; Vladimir Pucik, "Revolution or Evolution: The Transformation of Japanese Personnel Practices" (Working paper, Center for Advanced Human Resource Studies, Cornell University); Takao Kato and Mark Rockel, "Experiences, Credentials, and Compensation in the Japanese and U.S. Managerial Labor Markets: New Evidence from Micro Data," *Journal of the Japanese and International Economies* 6 (1992), pp. 30–51.

candidate before a decision is made. The selection is a relatively safe bet. On the other hand, decisions in the United States are made earlier in a person's career, from among CEO candidates who may have worked for a number of companies. So a company choosing a CEO will not have as much information about a candidate before making a decision. Consequently, the possibility of error is greater, for both the company and losing candidates. Chance plays a bigger role in the decision.

From a candidate's perspective, this has a negative effect on motivation. If the probability of superior performance winning a promotion is reduced because decision makers don't accurately perceive superior performance, then the likelihood of hard work paying off is reduced. People will only stay in contention for promotion if the money associated with the promotion, the premium, is sufficiently large. Tournament theorists claim that U.S. firms must offset the effort-reducing effects of chance by paying much larger CEO salaries. Only large salaries can motivate people to continue to strive for promotion despite the uncertainty of their efforts leading to promotion.

Testing the Theories

But most work is not a round of golf, nor does it lead towards the company presidency. A problem with much of the research on internal structures is that it does not fit the real world of work. Virtually all the research that supports hierarchical structures is in situations where individual performance matters most (auto racing, bowling, golf tournaments), or at best where the demands for cooperation among a small group of individuals are relatively low (professors, stockbrokers).

Baseball provides a setting where both individual players' performance and the cooperative efforts of the entire team make a difference.[37] Using eight years of data on major league baseball, one researcher found that the average team gini was .62, with a range of .81 (hierarchical; very large differentials among players) to .19 (egalitarian; practically identical salaries). He concluded that internal structures had a sizeable effect on players' performance, over and above the effects of player talent, age, and experience. The greater the difference between a player's pay and the maximum pay on the team, the lower the individual performance, particularly for those players who were near the bottom of the pay structure.

So if identical players earning the same salary went to two teams, one with a high maximum salary and the other with only a moderate maximum salary, would the second player perform better? This is not the prediction of tournament theory. So you decide—is your workplace like a round of golf or a baseball game?

Institutional Model: Copy Others

Some organizations, just as some people, ignore the question of strategy altogether. Instead, they take the path of least resistance: They simply copy what others are doing.

---

[37]Matthew C. Bloom, "The Performance Effects of Pay Structures on Individuals and Organizations," (Working paper, University of Notre Dame, 1998).

By extension, pay structures are sometimes adopted because they mimic "accepted practice" rather than because they fit differences in organization design or work flow.[38]

While there is little empirical research that addresses the issue, it is not uncommon for executives to bring back "the answers" discovered at the latest conference. Surveys that benchmark the practices of the best companies facilitate others' copying those practices. Recent examples of such behaviors include the rush to delayer, to emphasize teams, deemphasize individual contributions, and to shift to a competency-based pay system, often with little regard to whether any of these practices make sense for the organization or its employees.[39]

WHICH STRUCTURE FITS BEST?

In practice, the decision about which structure best fits a particular business strategy probably lies in our original definition of internal alignment and consistency: *An internally consistent structure supports the work flow, is fair to employees, and directs their behavior toward organization objectives.* The bottom part of Exhibit 3.7 summarizes the effects attributed to egalitarian and hierarchical structures.

How the work is organized. Work can be organized around teams, with all members on a team making roughly the same pay. Or it can be organized around individuals, with pay differences celebrated as a way to motivate performance. The pay structure should support the underlying organization structure. In organizations where work is highly interdependent and involves a larger group of people, the competition among workers for the higher pay fostered by hierarchical structures may work against organization performance.[40]

Fair to employees. George Meany, an early 20th century U.S. labor leader, is famous for his reaction to proposed pay innovations: "Tell me how much pay we will get, and I will tell you if I like it." Hierarchical structures evoke the same response. If I am at the top of the structure, I am probably persuaded that my high pay is an important signal to suppliers and customers that the company is doing well. If I am lower in the structure, I am probably less persuaded that the company ties its pay to employee performance—at least, not *my* performance.[41]

Little is known about the impact that pay ratios have on people's behaviors or an organization's success. Historical documents show that Meriwether Lewis received $40 a month plus food and uniform allowances for his leadership during the

---

[38]L. G. Zucker, "Institutional Theories of Organization," *American Review of Sociology* 13 (1987), pp. 443–64; and D. Wazeter, "Determinants and Consequences of Pay Structures" (Ph.D. dissertation, Cornell University, 1991).

[39]Harry Levinson, "Why the Behemoths Fell: Psychological Roots of Corporate Failure," *American Psychologist* 49, no. 5 (1994), pp. 428–36.

[40]R. H. Frank and P. J. Cook, *The Winner-Take-All Society* (New York: Penguin Books, 1995); T. A. Kochan and P. Osterman, *The Mutual Gains Enterprise: Forging a Winning Partnership Among Labor, Management, and Government.* (Boston, MA: Harvard Business School Press, 1994).

[41]R. L. Heneman, *Merit Pay: Linking Pay Increases to Performance Ratings* (Reading, Mass.: Addison-Wesley Pub. Co, 1992); H. H. Meyer, "The Pay-For-Performance Dilemma," *Organization Science* 33 (1975), pp. 39–50.

1804-1806 exploration of the western half of what would become the United States, compared to $30 a month for Lieutenant Clark, $8 a month for sergeants, $7 for corporals, and $5 for privates. A ratio of 8 to 1. Would a larger (or smaller) ratio have made any difference to the success of their expedition, or their collective display of what President Jefferson described as "undaunted courage?"[42] The fact is that we just do not know.

Directs behavior toward organization objectives. More hierarchical structures tend to reduce cooperative behavior. However, they may be appropriate where individual behavior is closely tied to organizational outcomes (e.g., a talented surgeon, a big-name movie star).

A conflict between a hierarchical structure with sizeable differentials in a setting that requires cooperation may produce lower individual and organizational performance.

Compare the television program ER, which originally began with no stars and lots of talented actors and actresses, with the program Seinfeld, which began with a huge star and a small ensemble of talented actors and actress. As the Seinfeld show became a hit and the formerly supporting ensemble members became more famous, the size of the differential between their pay and Jerry Seinfeld's pay was renegotiated. The point is that in any organization, the pay structure needs to be designed in a way that directs employee efforts toward organization objectives and avoids becoming a counterproductive obstacle.[43]

CONSEQUENCES OF CONSISTENCY

But why worry about internal consistency at all? Why not simply pay employees whatever it takes to get them to take a job and to show up for work every day? Why not let the internal pay structure depend completely on external market forces and what others are paying?

The answer can be found in several situations. The first is strategic competitive advantage. If there is a competitive advantage in the way you pay people, then you want to be different. As discussed in Chapter 2, you want to be difficult to imitate.

The second situation is unique jobs that reflect organization idiosyncracies. For example, John D. Rummell is employed by the National Aeronautics and Space Administration (NASA) as a planetary protection specialist. His job is to see that neither Mars nor Earth (nor any other planets) are inadvertently contaminated in the course of planetary exploration. No other employer in this world (or any other) has a planetary protection specialist on the payroll. How does NASA determine the appropriate pay for Mr. Rummell? To the extent that they can, they compare his skills/knowledge/experience/responsibilities with requirements for other NASA jobs. So the existing internal pay structure provides a basis for arriving at a rate for unique jobs.[44]

---

[42]Stephen Ambrose, *Undaunted Courage* (New York: Simon & Schuster, 1995).

[43]J. W. Harder, "Equity Theory Versus Expectancy Theory: The Case of Major League Baseball Free Agents," *Journal of Applied Psychology* 76 (1991), pp. 458–464.

[44]Previous editions of this textbook have used an example of a unique job taken from Cornell University's School of Veterinary Medicine. Former students have expressed great affection for the "Cornell cows." However, in light of a changing environment, we are trying to moove from the agrarian to the aquarian.

Another reason is that some organizations are basing pay structures on the skills or competencies employees possess rather than the jobs they perform. Yet competitive market data are not available from other organizations who use the same approach to price such skills/competencies as "process leader." Other, more common illustrations may be found under titles such as administrative assistant, team leader, or associate. The specific tasks vary with the technologies employed, the manner in which the work is designed, the skills and experiences of the particular incumbent, and so on.

It is also possible that some jobs or skills are valued by a specific organization more or less than the rates reflected for that job in the market. For example, top-notch compensation specialists or accountants may have greater value to a compensation or accounting consulting firm than to heavy manufacturing companies. The consulting firm may pay higher-than-market rates for the greater contribution of the particular job to organization goals. Some genetics and engineering professors are leaving academia to design products for biotech firms—and become eligible for bonuses and stock options that universities cannot match.

The practical question is, Does any of this really matter? Recall the dimensions of internal pay structures. What difference does the number of levels, the size of pay differentials between levels, and the criteria (job versus person) make to the compensation system goals of efficiency, equity, and compliance? Exhibit 3.12 suggests some of the consequences of the internal pay structures.

Efficiency: Competitive Advantage

Why manage the pay structure? Because it has the potential to lead to better organization performance. If the structure does not motivate employees to help achieve the organization's objectives, then it is a candidate for redesign.

Internal pay structures imply future rewards. We have already pointed out that the size of the pay differentials between the entry level in the structure and the highest level may induce employees to undertake the training and obtain the experience required for promotions. According to this view, a hardware design engineering job should pay more than a programming job. Without that pay difference, individuals are less likely to go through the education (and forgo earnings while in school) required to become an engineer. Similar logic can be applied to differentials between team leaders and team members, which encourage employees to undertake more responsibilities. Pay differentials within organizations induce employees to remain with the organization, increase their experience and training, cooperate with co-workers, and seek greater responsibility.[45]

Equity

Several writers argue that employees' attitudes about the fairness of the pay structure affect their work behaviors. Livernash, for example, asserts that departures from an

---

[45]Edward Lazear, "Labor Economics and Psychology of Organization," *Journal of Economic Perspectives* 5 (1991), pp. 89–110; David Wazeter, "Determinants and Consequences of Pay Structures."

EXHIBIT 3.12 Some Consequences of an Internally Consistent Structure

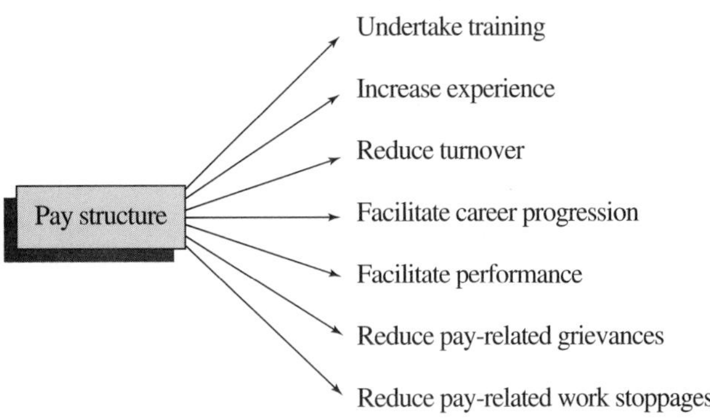

acceptable wage structure will occasion turnover, grievances, and diminished motivation.[46] Jaques argues that if fair differentials among jobs are not paid, individuals may harbor ill will toward the employer, resist change, change employment if possible, become depressed, and "lack that zest and enthusiasm which makes for high efficiency and personal satisfaction in work."[47]

Others, including labor unions, have long held the belief that more egalitarian pay structures support team workers, high commitment to the organization, and improved performance. Studies have reported that the greater the wage differences, the more likely employees will vote for unions, and that smaller differences in wages between hourly employees and managers were related to greater product quality.[48]

Compliance

Certainly, all internal pay structures need to comply with government laws and regulations. In many countries this includes legislation in support of nondiscriminatory pay for women and minorities. The regulatory influences on compensation management are examined in Chapter 17. At this point, it is enough to recognize that the design and

[46]E. Robert Livernash, "The Internal Wage Structure," in *New Concepts in Wage Determination,* ed. G. W. Taylor and F. C. Pierson (New York: McGraw-Hill, 1957), pp. 143–72.

[47]Elliot Jaques, "In Praise of Hierarchies," *Harvard Business Review,* January-February 1990; T. Zenger, "Why Do Employers Only Reward Extreme Performance? Examining the Relationships among Performance, Pay, and Turnover," *Administrative Science Quarterly* 37 (1992), pp. 198–219.

[48]J. Giacobbe-Miller, D. Miller, and V. Victorov, "A Comparison of Russian and U.S. Pay Allocation Decisions, Distributive Justice Judgments, and Productivity under Different Pay Conditions" (Amherst, MA: Working paper, 1998); William Dickens, Douglas Wholey, and James Robinson,"Correlates of Union Support in NLRB Elections," *Industrial Relations* 26 (1987); pp. 240–52, D. M. Cowherd and David Levine, "Product Quality and Pay Equity between Lower-Level Employees and Top Management," *Administrative Science Quarterly* 37 (1992), pp. 302–20.

administration of pay structures must comply with the regulations of the countries in which the organization operates.

What is the appropriate number of levels, the size of the differentials, and the criteria to advance employees through a structure? We believe the answers lie in understanding the factors discussed in this chapter: the organization's strategic intent, the norms and customs of the culture, the economic circumstances, and, perhaps most importantly, the nature of the work and employees. For example, narrow, egalitarian structures may be related to improving satisfaction and performance when the technology and the nature of the work requires cooperation and teamwork compared to more independent and autonomous situations. On the other hand, it is not difficult to think of examples in which very large pay differentials exist within highly successful teams (e.g., Michael Jordan and the Chicago Bulls basketball team). We believe that aligning the pay structures to fit the organization and the surrounding conditions is more likely to lead to competitive advantage for the organization and a sense of fair treatment for employees.

Summary

This chapter discusses what is meant by the strategic policy regarding internal consistency and how it affects employees, managers, and employers. *Internal consistency* refers to the pay relationships among jobs/skills/competencies within a single organization. Although the potential consequences of internal pay structures are vital to organizations and individuals, little guidance has emerged from research concerning employee perceptions of internal pay structures.

Pay structures—the array of pay rates for different jobs within an organization—are shaped by societal, economic, organizational, and other factors. Employees judge a structure to be equitable on the basis of comparisons. The ratio of a job's relative pay to its relative requirements, work performed, and value of that performance is compared to the ratio for other jobs in the structure. Congruent ratios are believed to be equitable. Acceptance by employees of the relative pay differentials is the key test of an equitable pay structure.

Keep the goals of the entire compensation system in mind in thinking about internal pay structures. There is widespread belief and considerable research that differences in pay structures influence employees' attitudes and work behaviors and therefore the success of organizations. However, research to date offers conflicting advice regarding what the appropriate structure is in different situations.

Review Questions

1. Why is internal consistency an important policy issue for the compensation system?
2. Discuss the factors that influence internal pay structures. Based on your own experience, which ones do you think are the most important?

3. How would you go about trying to manage employees' impressions of the pay structure? Is this potentially destructive manipulation?
4. What is the "just wage" doctrine? Can you think of any present-day applications?
5. What employee behaviors are more egalitarian versus more hierarchical structures likely to affect?

YOUR TURN

SO YOU WANT TO LEAD THE ORCHESTRA!

Peter Drucker calls orchestras an example of an organization design that will become increasingly popular in the 21st century, in that it employs skilled and talented people, joined together as a team to create products and services. (Drucker may hear what he wants to hear. In spite of his confidence in orchestral teamwork, jokes like the following are common among orchestra members. *Q. Why do so many people take an instant dislike to the viola? A. It saves time.*)

Job descriptions for orchestras look simple: play the music. *(Q. How is lightning like a keyboardist's fingers? A. Neither strikes the same place twice.)* Violins play violin parts, trumpets play trumpet parts. Yet one study reported that orchestra players' job satisfaction ranks below prison guards. However, they were more satisfied than operating room nurses and hockey players.

Exhibit 3.13 shows the pay structure for a regional chamber orchestra. *(Q. How can you make a clarinet sound like a French horn? A. Play all the wrong notes.)* The pay covers six full orchestra concerts, one Caroling by Candlelight event, three Sunday Chamber Series Concerts, several Arts in Education elementary school concerts, two engagements for a flute quartet, and one Ring in the Holidays brass event as well as the regularly scheduled rehearsals. *(Q. How can you tell when a trombonist is playing out of tune? A. When the slide is moving.)* The figures do not include the 27 cents per mile travel pay provided to out-of-town musicians.

1. Describe the orchestra's pay structure in terms of levels, differentials, and job- or person-based.
2. Discuss what factors may explain the structure. Why does violinist I receive more than the oboist and trombonist? Why does the principal trumpet player earn more than the principal cellist and clarinetist but less than the principal viola and flute players? What explains these differences? Does the relative supply versus the demand for violinists compare to the supply versus the demand for trombonists? Is it that violins play more notes?
3. How well do equity and tournament models apply?

EXHIBIT 3.13 Orchestra Compensation Schedule

Instrument	*Fee*
Violin, Concertmaster	$5,245
Principal Bass and Conductor	$3,815
Principal Viola	$3,790
Principal Flute	$3,265
Principal Trumpet	$3,185
Principal Cello	$3,145
Principal Clarinet	$3,120
Trumpet	$2,745
Principal Oboe	$2,720
Principal Violin II	$2,625
Principal Horn	$2,550
Keyboard I	$2,530
Cello	$2,430
Principal Percussion	$2,295
Violin I	$2,180
Cello	$2,170
Principal Bassoon	$2,125
Violin I	$2,020
Violin I	$1,870
Violin I	$1,870
Violin I	$1,870
Violin II	$1,870
Violin II	$1,870
Viola	$1,870
Violin II	$1,485
Viola	$1,665
Oboe	$1,660
Trombone	$1,615
Viola	$1,530
Violin II/Viola	$1,340
Cello	$1,230
Clarinet	$1,165
Horn	$1,165
Flute	$1,095
Keyboard II	$1,045
Bassoon	$950
Violin II	$885

Chapter 4 Job Analysis

Chapter Outline

"The End of the Job," trumpets the cover story of *Fortune,* a leading business magazine.[1] The story informs us that, "Jobs as a way of organizing work. . . is a social artifact that has outlived its usefulness." If organizations expect to be successful, they need to "get rid of jobs" and "redesign to get the best out of the de-jobbed worker." If we no longer can expect to hold jobs, then can we at least hold a position? Unfortunately, no. Positions may be "too fixed." Roles? Nope. Too unitary, single-purposed. Skills and competencies then? Guess again; they will become obsolete.

Fortune tells us that the post-job workers will likely be self-employed contract workers hired to work on projects or teams. Intel and Microsoft are suggested as examples of companies that design work around projects. People will work on six to ten projects, maybe for different employers at one time. However, the United Parcel Service strikers in the summer of 1997 enjoyed widespread public support thanks in part to their catchy slogan, "Part-time work won't work." The union for the popular brown-uniformed UPS workers wanted full-time *jobs* with UPS, not multiple projects with multiple employers.

The reality at Microsoft is not the same as *Fortune*'s pundits report, either. Walk into Microsoft's lobby in Redmond, Washington, and you will find five volumes of *job* vacancies (over 300 pages of them). Look at Microsoft's web page (http:www.// microsoft.com). Microsoft is eager to hire employees who will work for no one but Microsoft. The hours worked by Microsoft software engineers are legendary.[2] They may be working on 6 to 10 projects at once, but for different employers at one time? Not in the Microsoft model.

Nevertheless, the concept of work is changing, with fluid organizations that require constant adaptation no longer the exception. Sophisticated office equipment and computer software means clerical support employees don't need to worry about their spelling; however, they do need to know how to maintain the local area networks that link their machines and how to send E-mail attachments to Dublin and Caracas. Librarians who used to recommend and shelve books and provide guidance for research projects now show patrons how to run computerized searches to access a world full of resources in order to locate reams of information. Retiring auto assembly workers who were hired right out of high school are replaced by people trained to operate high-tech machinery and work well in teams. Exhibit 4.1 emphasizes the changes.

Yet, while there have been considerable changes in the way work is done, using a job as a way to organize and group tasks and responsibilities has not yet disappeared. A recent survey of over 200 organizations sponsored by the American Compensation Association found that more than 80 percent still use conventional job analysis programs and the majority still use conventional job evaluation programs.[3] Organizations continue to recognize that if pay is to be based on the work performed, a systematic way is needed to *assess what work is performed,* and more importantly, *its similarities and differences*.

---

[1]William Bridges, "The End of the Job," *Fortune,* September 19, 1994, pp. 62–68.

[2]D. D. McKenna and J. J. McHenry, *Microsoft's Maniacal Work Ethic* (Redmond, WA: Microsoft, 1996).

[3]*Raising the Bar: Using Competencies to Enhance Employee Performance* (Scottsdale, AZ: American Compensation Association, 1996).

EXHIBIT 4.1 Work Design

FROM

Occupants
of
Fixed Jobs
with
Defined
Tasks
and Duties

TO

Owners
of
Fluid
Assignments
with
Responsibility
for Results

SIMILARITIES AND DIFFERENCES FORM THE INTERNAL STRUCTURE

The constantly changing nature of work presents a major challenge to managing people. The work a person does is a major determinant of pay. Consequently, some way is needed to assess work and describe its differences and similarities in comparison to other work in the same organization. But how do you assess something that is changing? If you answered, "very carefully," you have been watching the Comedy Channel too much.

Recall the Lockheed engineering structure example in the previous chapter. When Lockheed changed its marketing and product development strategy, it also redesigned its internal organization structure. The previous six levels of engineering work were collapsed by merging the systems engineer with the lead engineer and the entry engineer with the senior engineer. Each distinct level in the structure corresponds with a major difference in the complexity of the work and the knowledge required to perform it.

Lockheed made these changes in order to remove obstacles to cross-functional cooperation and to permit its engineers to work more efficiently. Now, Lockheed managers need to decide if the differences among the new levels in their engineering structure are important enough to pay differently. If so, how much should these differences be? Assessing similarities and differences in work and deciding if these work differences justify pay differences is an important component of compensation.

STRUCTURES BASED ON JOBS OR PEOPLE

Managers are experimenting with a variety of responses to the challenge of constantly changing work. Some are *measuring loose*. Work is described in more general, generic terms and a wider variety of tasks are grouped together for pay purposes. The result is a delayered structure that allows employees to move among a wider range of tasks without having to adjust pay with each move.[4]

[4]Peter Leblanc, "Pay for Work: Reviving an Old Idea for the New Customer Focus," *Compensation and Benefits Review*, July/August 1994, pp. 5–10.

EXHIBIT 4.2 Many Ways to Build An Internal Structure

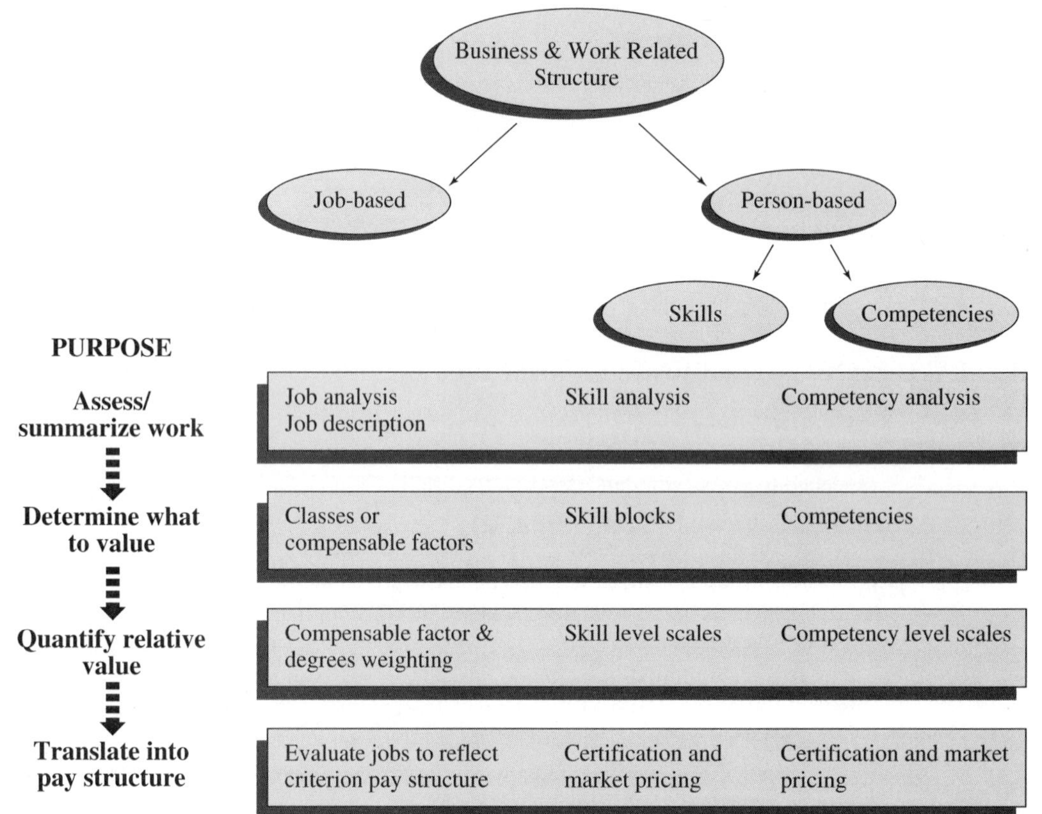

Others are switching from job-based to person-based approaches.[5] Rather than analyzing the tasks that make up a job, they analyze the skills or competencies a person must possess to perform the work. However, some way is still needed to document the differences and similarities in these skills and competencies.

JOB-BASED APPROACH: MOST COMMON

Exhibit 4.2 outlines the process for constructing an internal structure using alternative criteria. The process starts with looking at a person at work. Job-based structures look at the tasks and accountabilities; skill- and competency-based structures look at the

[5]Barbara J. Dewey, "Changing to Skill-Based Pay: Disarming the Transition Landmines," *Compensation and Benefits Review,* January–February 1994, pp. 38–43; Gordon Betcherman and Anil Verma, "Followup to the New Technology Survey," paper presented to the Canadian Industrial Relations Research Association, June 1993.

EXHIBIT 4.3 Determining the Internal Job Structure

Internal relationships within the organization →	**Job analysis** →	**Job descriptions** →	**Job evaluation** →	**Job structure**
	Collecting information about the nature of specific jobs	Summary reports that identify, define, and describe the job as it is actually performed	Comparison of jobs within an organization	An ordering of jobs based on their content or relative value

Some Major Issues in Job Analysis

- Why collect information?
- What information is needed?
- How to collect information?
- Who should be involved?
- How useful are the results?

person. However, the underlying process is the same: (1) design the work based on technology and/or customers' needs; (2) collect and analyze information, (3) summarize the information, and (4) evaluate the information.

Job content, determined through job analysis, is still the most common approach for creating an internal structure. If the structure is to be based on jobs, then we begin by examining the actual work performed.

Job analysis is the systematic process of collecting relevant, work-related information related to the nature of a specific job.

The basic premise underlying job analysis is that jobs are more likely to be described, differentiated, and valued fairly if accurate information about them is available.[6] Exhibits 4.2 and 4.3 show that job analysis provides the underlying information for preparing job descriptions and evaluating jobs. Job analysis is a prerequisite for job-based pay structures. It is the input for describing and valuing work.

Exhibit 4.3 also identifies the major decisions in designing a job analysis: (1) Why are we collecting job information? (2) What information do we need? (3) How should we collect it? (4) Who should be involved? (5) How useful are the results?

[6] Particularly valuable sources of information on job analysis definitions and methods are U.S. Department of Labor, Manpower Administration, *Handbook for Analyzing Jobs* (Washington, DC: U.S. Government Printing Office, 1972); Robert J. Harvey, "Job Analysis," in *Handbook of Industrial and Organizational Psychology,* vol. 2, ed. M. D. Dunnette and L. Hough (Palo Alto, CA: Consulting Psychologists Press, 1991), pp. 72–157.

Why Perform Job Analysis?

Historically, job analysis has been considered the cornerstone of personnel administration. Potential uses for job analysis have been suggested for every major personnel function.[7] Often the type of job analysis data needed varies by function. For example, job analysis identifies the skills and experience required to perform the work, which clarifies hiring and promotion standards. Training programs may be designed with job analysis data; jobs may be redesigned based on it. In performance evaluation, both employees and supervisors look to the required behaviors and results expected in a job to help assess performance.

Although job analysis is not legally required, it provides managers a work-related rationale for pay differences. Employees who understand this rationale can better direct their behavior toward organization objectives. Job analysis data also help managers defend their decisions when challenged.

There are two critical uses for job analysis in compensation: (1) to establish similarities and differences in the content of the jobs, and (2) to help establish an internally equitable job structure. If jobs have equal content, then in all likelihood the pay established for them will be equal. If, on the other hand, the job content differs, then those differences, along with the market rates paid by competitors, are part of the rationale for paying jobs differently.

The key issue for compensation decision makers is still to ensure that the data collected serve the purpose of making decisions and are acceptable to the employees involved. As the flowchart in Exhibit 4.3 indicates, collecting job information is only an interim step, not an end in itself.

JOB ANALYSIS PROCEDURES

Exhibit 4.4 summarizes some job analysis terms and their relationship to each other. Job analysis usually collects information about specific tasks or behaviors. A group of tasks performed by one person makes up a position. Identical positions make a job, and broadly similar jobs combine into an occupation.[8]

The U.S. federal government, one of the biggest users of job analysis data, suggests that analysts follow the procedures shown in Exhibit 4.5. Their step-by-step approach includes developing preliminary information, conducting the interviews, and then using the information to create and verify job descriptions.

What Job Information Should Be Collected?

A typical analysis starts with a review of information already collected in order to develop a framework for further analysis. Job titles, major duties, and work flow information may

---

[7]Most human resource management texts discuss these multiple uses of job analysis information. See, for example, chapter 3 in G. Milkovich and J. Boudreau, *Human Resource Management* (Burr Ridge, IL: Irwin, 1997).

[8]E. J. McCormick, "Job and Task Analysis," in *Handbook of Industrial and Organizational Psychology,* ed. M. D. Dunnette (Chicago: Rand McNally, 1976), pp. 651–96; E. J. McCormick, *Job Analysis: Methods and Applications* (New York: AMACOM, 1979).

Exhibit 4.4 Job Analysis Terminology

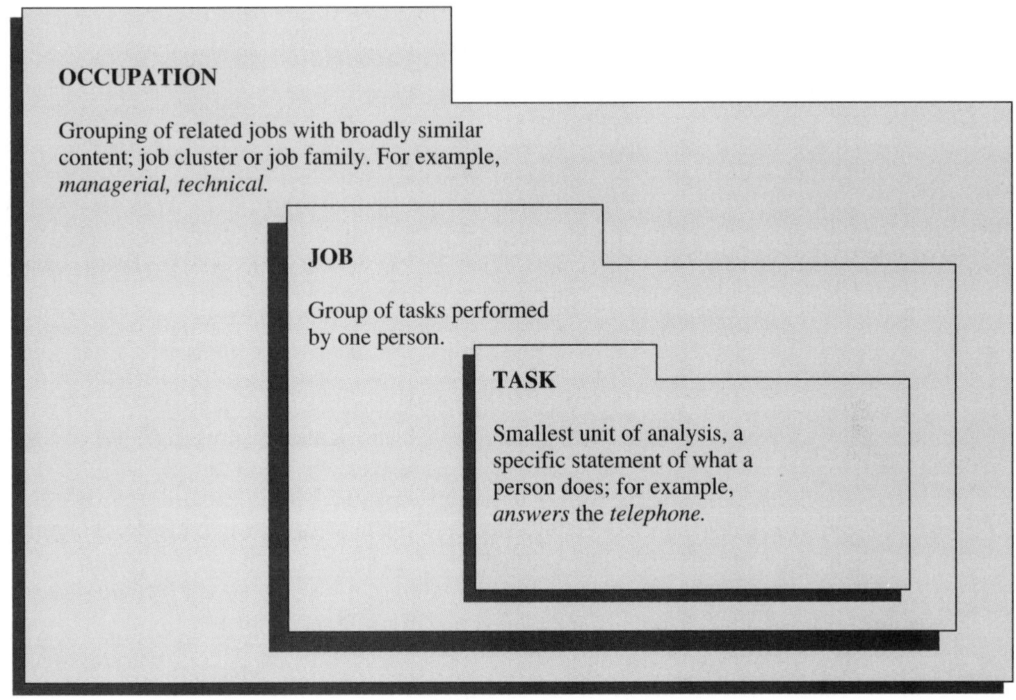

already exist. However, they may no longer be accurate. So the analyst must be prepared to clarify existing information, too.

Generally, a good job analysis collects sufficient information to adequately identify, define, and describe a job. Exhibit 4.6 lists some of the information that is usually collected.

Identifying a Job. Job titles, departments, the number of people who hold the job, and whether it is exempt from the Fair Labor Standards Act are examples of information that identifies a job.

While a job title may seem pretty straightforward, it may not be. An observer of the U.S. banking system commented that "every employee over 25 seems to be a vice president." Deliberate or not, sometimes titles mislead. In a discussion on HRNet, an internet discussion group on a wide variety of HR issues, R. J. Harvey notes that: "Many of the problems that have been attributed to job descriptions can be traced straight back to the mistakes made by the HR officer who assigned the job title in question to the given collection of positions. Often, the positions that share a job title (and description) are FAR too heterogeneous in what they do, or in what they produce, to be lumped together."

Exhibit 4.5 General Procedures for Conventional Job Analysis

Step	*Things to Remember or Do*
1. Develop preliminary job information	*a.* Review existing documents in order to develop an initial "big-picture" familiarity with the job: its main mission, its major duties or functions, work flow patterns. *b.* Prepare a preliminary list of duties which will serve as a framework for conducting the interviews. *c.* Make a note of major items that are unclear or ambiguous or that need to be clarified during the data-gathering process.
2. Conduct initial tour of work site	*a.* The initial tour is designed to familiarize the job analyst with the work layout, the tools and equipment that are used, the general conditions of the workplace, and the mechanics associated with the end-to-end performance of major duties. *b.* The initial tour is particularly helpful in those jobs where a first-hand view of a complicated or unfamiliar piece of equipment saves the interviewee the thousand words required to describe the unfamiliar or technical. *c.* For continuity, it is recommended that the first level supervisor-interviewee be designated the guide for the job-site observations.
3. Conduct interviews	*a.* It is recommended that the first interview be conducted with the first-level supervisor who is considered to be in a better position than the jobholders to provide an overview of the job and how the major duties fit together. *b.* For scheduling purposes, it is recommended that no more than two interviews be conducted per day, each interview lasting no more than three hours.
Notes on selection of interviewees	*a.* The interviewees are considered subject matter experts by virtue of the fact that they perform the job (in the case of job incumbents) or are responsible for getting the job done (in the case of first-level supervisors). *b.* The job incumbent to be interviewed should represent the *typical* employee who is knowledgeable about the job (*not* the trainee who is just learning the ropes *nor* the outstanding member of the work unit). *c.* Whenever feasible, the interviewees should be selected with a view towards obtaining an appropriate race/sex mix.

Describing a Job. This is the heart of job analysis. The U.S. Department of Labor's (DOL) work on job analysis over 20 years ago may still be the strongest single influence on job analysis as practiced in the United States. The DOL's *Handbook for Analyzing Jobs* suggests two categories of data: the actual work performed (job content), and the knowledge and/or experience required by an employee to do a job (worker characteristics).

Exhibit 4.5 ***(concluded)***

Step	*Things to Remember or Do*
4. Conduct second tour of work site	*a.* The second tour of the work site is designed to clarify, confirm, and otherwise refine the information developed in the interviews. *b.* As in the initial tour, it is recommended that the same first-level supervisor-interviewee conduct the second walk through.
5. Consolidate job information	*a.* The consolidation phase of the job study involves piecing together into one coherent and comprehensive job description the data obtained from several sources: supervisor, jobholders, on-site tours, and written materials about the job. *b.* Past experience indicates that one minute of consolidation is required for every minute of interviewing. For planning purposes, at least five hours should be set aside for the consolidation phase. *c.* A subject matter expert should be accessible as a resource person to the job analyst during the consolidation phase. The supervisor-interviewee fills this role. *d.* Check your initial preliminary list of duties and questions—all must be answered or confirmed.
6. Verify job description	*a.* The verification phase involves bringing all the interviewees together for the purpose of determining if the consolidated job description is accurate and complete. *b.* The verification process is conducted in a group setting. Typed or legibly written copies of the job description (narrative description of the work setting *and* list of task statements) are distributed to the first-level supervisor and the job incumbent interviewees. *c.* Line by line, the job analyst goes through the entire job description and makes notes of any omissions, ambiguities, or needed clarifications. *d.* Collect all materials at the end of the verification meeting.

The DOL's functional job analysis (FJA) is still widely used in the public sector. It relates what the employee does to the goals and objectives of the organization. Although few private sector employers use FJA, all job analysis practices reflect its influence.

Data Related to Job. *Job content data involve the elemental tasks or units of work, with emphasis on the purpose of each task.* An excerpt from a job analysis questionnaire that collects task data is shown in Exhibit 4.7. The inventory describes the job aspect of "Communication" in terms of actual tasks, for example, "read technical publications" and "consult with co-workers." The inventory takes eight items to cover "obtain technical information" and another seven for "exchange technical information." In fact, the task inventory from which the exhibit is excerpted contains

Exhibit 4.6 Typical Data Collected for Job Analysis

Data Related to Job	
Job content/context factors	*Work characteristics*
Tasks	Risk or exposure
Activities	Constraints
Performance criteria	Choices
Critical incidents	Conflicting demands
Working conditions	
Roles (e.g., negotiator, monitor, leader)	
Data Related to Employee	
Employee characteristics	*Internal relationships*
Professional/technical knowledge	Boss & other superiors
Prior experience	Peers
Manual skills	Subordinates
Verbal skills	
Written skills	
Quantitative skills	*External relationships*
Mechanical skills	Suppliers
Conceptual skills	Customers
Managerial skills	Regulatory
Bargaining skills	Consultants
Leadership skills	Professional/industry
Consulting skills	Community
Interpersonal skills	Union/employee group

250 items and covers only systems and analyst jobs. New task-based questions need to be designed for each new set of jobs.

The other distinguishing characteristic of the inventory in the exhibit is the emphasis on the *objective* of the task; for example, "read technical publications *to keep current on industry*" and "consult with co-workers *to exchange ideas and techniques.*" Task data reveal the actual work performed and its purpose or outcome.

Data Related to People. *Jobs can be described by the behaviors that are expected of the people working in the job.* Exhibit 4.8 shows how "Communications" can be described with verbs (e.g., negotiating, persuading). The exhibit is from the Position Analysis Questionnaire (PAQ),[9] which groups work information into seven basic

[9]Much of the developmental and early applications of the PAQ was done in the 1960s and 1970s. See, for example, McCormick, *Job Analysis*; McCormick, "Job and Task Analysis"; McCormick et al., *A Study of Job Characteristics and Job Dimensions as Based on the Position Analysis Questionnaire* (West Lafayette, IN: Occupational Research Center, Purdue University, 1969). The PAQ is distributed by the University Book Store, 360 West State St., West Lafayette, IN 47906. For more recent discussions, see PAQ Newsletters.

Exhibit 4.7 Communications: Task-Based Data

1. Mark the circle in the "Do This" column for tasks that you currently perform.
2. At the end of the task list, write in any unlisted tasks that you currently perform.
3. Rate each task that you perform for relative time spent by marking the appropriate circle in the "Time Spent" column.

Please use a No. 2 pencil and fill all circles completely.

Time spent in current position: 1 Very small amount, 2 Much below average, 3 Below average, 4 Slightly below average, 5 About average, 6 Slightly above average, 7 Above average, 8 Much above average, 9 Very large amount

PERFORM COMMUNICATIONS ACTIVITIES	Do This	Time spent in current position
Obtain technical information		
421. Read technical publications about competitive products.	○	①②③④⑤⑥⑦⑧⑨
422. Read technical publications to keep current on industry.	○	①②③④⑤⑥⑦⑧⑨
423. Attend required, recommended, or job-related courses and/or seminars.	○	①②③④⑤⑥⑦⑧⑨
424. Study existing operating systems/programs to gain/maintain familiarity with them.	○	①②③④⑤⑥⑦⑧⑨
425. Perform literature searches necessary to the development of products.	○	①②③④⑤⑥⑦⑧⑨
426. Communicate with system software group to see how their recent changes impact current projects.	○	①②③④⑤⑥⑦⑧⑨
427. Study and evaluate state-of-the-art techniques to remain competitive and/or lead the field.	○	①②③④⑤⑥⑦⑧⑨
428. Attend industry standards meetings.	○	①②③④⑤⑥⑦⑧⑨
Exchange technical information		
429. Interface with coders to verify that the software design is being implemented as specified.	○	①②③④⑤⑥⑦⑧⑨
4301. Consult with co-workers to exchange ideas and techniques.	○	①②③④⑤⑥⑦⑧⑨
431. Consult with members of other technical groups within the company to exchange new ideas and techniques.	○	①②③④⑤⑥⑦⑧⑨
432. Interface with support consultants or organizations to clarify software design or courseware content.	○	①②③④⑤⑥⑦⑧⑨
433. Attend meetings to review project status.	○	①②③④⑤⑥⑦⑧⑨
434. Attend team meetings to review implementation strategies.	○	①②③④⑤⑥⑦⑧⑨
435. Discuss department plans and objectives with manager.	○	①②③④⑤⑥⑦⑧⑨

factors: information input, mental processes, work output, relationships with other persons, job context, other job characteristics, and general dimensions. Similarities and differences among jobs are described in terms of these seven factors, rather than in terms of specific aspects unique to each job.[10] The communications behavior in Exhibit 4.8 is part of the "relationships with other persons" factor.

The entire PAQ consists of 194 items. Its developers claim these items are sufficient to analyze any job. However, you can see by the exhibit that the reading level is quite high. A large proportion of employees need help to get through the whole thing. In addition, many employers believe that the information provided by the PAQ is too general for pay purposes.

However appealing it may be to rationalize job analysis as the foundation of all HR decisions, collecting all of this information for so many different purposes is very expensive. In addition, the resulting information may be too generalized for any single purpose, including compensation. If the information is to be used for multiple purposes, the analyst must be sure that the information collected is accurate and sufficient for each use. Trying to be all things to all people often results in being nothing to everyone.

Americans with Disabilities Act

In addition to sections that identify, describe, and define the job, the Americans with Disabilities Act (ADA) requires that essential *elements* of a job—those that cannot be reassigned to other workers—must be specified for jobs covered by the legislation. If a job applicant can perform these essential elements, it is assumed that the applicant can perform the job. After that, reasonable accommodations must be made to enable an otherwise qualified handicapped person to perform those elements.

The difficulty of specifying essential elements varies with the discretion in the job. Note that the law does not require any particular kind of analysis. However, many employers have modified the format of their job descriptions to specifically call out the essential elements.

Settlements of complaints filed under the law seem to target blanket exclusions that ignore the individual in hiring and job assignments. For example, in 1997 the metropolitan government of Nashville, Tennessee, and Davidson County settled a lawsuit by agreeing to hire an applicant for an emergency medical technician–paramedic position even though the applicant was deaf in one ear.

Although the applicant had been working part-time as a paramedic in the state for over six years, Nashville applied an absolute medical/physical standard that automatically excluded him because of his hearing loss. His successful lawsuit forced the government to base hiring decisions on an individualized assessment of a candidate's physical condition.

Our experience suggests that this ADA requirement is not well reflected in job analysis practice yet. A lack of compliance places an organization at risk.

[10] R. C. Mecham, E. J. McCormick, and P. R. Jeanneret, *Technical Manual for the Position Analysis Questionnaire (PAQ) System* (Logan, UT: PAQ Services, 1977).

Exhibit 4.8 Communications: Behavioral-Based Data (from the Position Analysis Questionnaire)

Section 4 Relationships with Other Persons

This section deals with different aspects of interaction between people involved in various kinds of work.

Code Importance to this Job (1)
N Does not apply
1 Very minor
2 Low
3 Average
4 High
5 Extreme

4.1 Communications

Rate the following in terms of how important the activity is to the completion of the job. Some jobs may involve several or all of the items in this section.

4.1.1 Oral (communicating by speaking)

99 ____ Advising (dealing with individuals in order to counsel and/or guide them with regard to problems that may be resolved by legal, financial, scientific, technical, clinical, spiritual, and/or other professional principles)

100 ____ Negotiating (dealing with others in order to reach an agreement or solution, for example, labor bargaining, diplomatic relations, etc.)

101 ____ Persuading (dealing with others in order to influence them toward some action or point of view, for example, selling, political campaigning, etc.)

102 ____ Instructing (the teaching of knowledge or skills, in either an informal or a formal manner, to others, for example, a public school teacher, a machinist teaching an apprentice, etc.)

103 ____ Interviewing (conducting interviews directed toward some specific objective, for example, interviewing job applicants, census taking, etc.)

104 ____ Routine information exchange: job related (the giving and/or receiving of *job-related* information of a routine nature, for example, ticket agent, taxicab dispatcher, receptionist, etc.)

105 ____ Nonroutine information exchange (the giving and/or receiving of *job-related* information of a nonroutine or unusual nature, for example, professional committee meetings, engineers discussing new product design, etc.)

106 ____ Public speaking (making speeches or formal presentations before relatively large audiences, for example, political addresses, radio/TV broadcasting, delivering a sermon, etc.)

4.1.2 Written (communicating by written/printed material)

107 ____ Writing (for example, writing or dictating letters, reports, etc., writing copy for ads, writing newspaper articles, etc.; do *not* include transcribing activities described in item 4.3, but only activities in which the incumbent creates the written material)

Source: E. J. McCormick, P. R. Jeanneret, and R. C. Mecham, *Position Analysis Questionnaire,* copyright © 1969 by Purdue Research Foundation, West Lafayette, IN 47907. Reprinted with permission.

Level of Analysis

The job analysis terms defined in Exhibit 4.4 are arranged in a hierarchy. The level in this hierarchy where one begins an analysis may influence the decision of whether the work is similar or dissimilar. At the occupation level, bookkeepers, tellers, and accounting clerks are considered to be similar; yet at the job level, these three are considered dissimilar. An analogy might be looking at two grains of salt under a microscope versus looking at them as part of a serving of french fries. If job data suggest that jobs are similar, then the jobs must be paid equally; if jobs are different, they can be paid differently. In practice, many employers are finding it difficult to justify the time and expense of collecting detailed information. They may collect just job-level data and argue that more detailed information is not necessary to determine wages. However, the ADA's "essential elements" for hiring and promotion decisions seem to require more detail than is required for pay decisions.

Many managers are increasing their organization's flexibility by adopting broad, *generic descriptions* that cover a large number of related tasks akin to the occupation level in Exhibit 4.4. Two employees working in the same broadly defined jobs may be doing entirely different sets of related tasks. But for pay purposes, they are doing work of equal value. Employees working in very broadly defined jobs can easily be switched to other tasks that fall within the broad range of the same job, without the bureaucratic burden of making job transfer requests and wage adjustments. Thus, employees can more easily be matched to changes in the work flow.

Still, a countervailing view deserves consideration. More specific distinctions among jobs represent career paths to employees. Titles may represent promotional opportunities, recognition, and rewards. Reducing the number of levels in a structure may also reduce opportunities for recognition and advancement. Reducing titles or labeling all employees as "associates" may signal an egalitarian culture. But it sacrifices a sense of advancement and opportunity.[11]

HOW CAN THE INFORMATION BE COLLECTED?

Conventional Methods: Interviews

The most common way to collect job information is to ask the people who are doing a job to fill out a questionnaire. Sometimes an analyst will interview the job holders and their supervisors to be sure they understand the questions and that the information is correct. By always asking the same questions in the same order, a uniform response format is more likely. This approach requires considerable involvement of employees and supervisors, which increases their understanding of the process, pro-

[11]V. L. Huber, S. Crandall, and G. B. Northcraft, "A Rose by Any Other Name Is Not as Sweet: Effects of Job Titles and Upgrade Requests on Job Evaluation and Wage Decisions" (unpublished manuscript, University of Washington, 1992).

vides an opportunity to clarify their work relationships and expectations, and increases the likelihood that the results of the analysis will be acceptable.[12]

Exhibit 4.9 shows part of a job analysis questionnaire used in a structured interview. Questions range from "Give an example of a particularly difficult problem that you face in your work. Why does it occur? How often does it occur? What special skills and/or resources are needed to solve this difficult problem?" to "What is the nature of any contact you have with individuals or companies in countries other than the United States? What percent of time is spent dealing with non-U.S. individuals or companies?"

These examples are drawn from the "Complexity of Duties" section of a job analysis questionnaire used by 3M. Other sections of the questionnaire are Skills/Knowledge Applied (19 to choose from), Impact this Job Has on 3M's Business, and Working Conditions. It concludes by asking respondents how well they feel the questionnaire has captured their particular job.

The advantage of conventional data collection is that the involvement of employees increases their understanding of the process. However, the results are only as good as the people involved. If important aspects of a job are omitted, or if the job holders themselves either do not realize or are unable to express the importance of certain aspects, the resulting job descriptions will also be faulty. If you look at the number of jobs in an organization, you can see the difficulty in expecting a single analyst to understand all the different types of work and the importance of certain job aspects. Different people have different perceptions, which may result in differences in interpretation or emphasis. The whole process is open to bias and favoritism.[13]

As a result of this potential subjectivity, as well as the huge amount of time the process takes, conventional methods have given way to more quantitative (and systematic) data collection.

Quantitative Methods: Questionnaires

A quantitative job analysis is simply a questionnaire that lists a number of possible tasks or behaviors, called an *inventory.* Exhibits 4.7 and 4.8 are excerpts from quantitative inventories. A questionnaire typically asks jobholders to assess each item in the inventory for whether or not that particular item is part of their job. If it is, they are asked to rate how important it is, and the amount of job time spent on it. The results can be machine scored similar to a multiple choice test (only there are no wrong answers), and the results can be used to develop a profile of the job. If more than one person is doing a particular job, results of several people in the job can be compared or averaged to develop the profile. Exhibit 4.10 compares profiles for a number of software jobs—programmer aide, associate programmer, senior programming analyst, and

---

[12]G. R. Schmidt and J. L. Sulzer, "Defining the Criticality of Job Content: A Survey of Job Analysis Procedures," paper presented at the Annual Conference of the Society for Industrial and Organizational Psychology, Boston, April 1989.

[13]E. E. Lawler, *Pay and Organizational Effectiveness: A Psychological View* (NY: McGraw-Hill, 1971).

Exhibit 4.9 3M's Structured Interview Questionnaire

I. Job Overview

Job Summary

What is the main purpose of your job? (Why does it exist and what does the work contribute to 3M?)
Examples: To provide secretarial support in our department by performing office and administrative duties.
To purchase goods and services that meet specifications at the least cost.
To perform systems analysis involved in the development, installation, and maintenance of computer applications.

Hint: It may help to list the duties first before answering this question.

Duties and Responsibilities

What are your jobs main duties and responsibilities? (These are the major work activities that usually take up a significant amount of your work time and occur regularly as you perform your work.)

In the spaces below, list your job's five most important or most frequent duties. Then, in the boxes, estimate the percentage of the time you spend on each day.	Percentage of Time Spent (Total may be less than but not more than 100%)
1.	
2.	

II. Skills/Knowledge Applied

Formal Training or Education

What is the level of formal training/education that is needed to start doing your job?
Example: High School, 2 Year Vo-Tech in Data Processing. Bachelor of Science in Chemistry.
In some jobs, a combination of education and job-related experience can substitute for academic degrees.
Example: Bachelors Degree in Accounting or completion of 2 years of general business plus 3–4 years work experience in an accounting field.

What additional training, certification program, or licensing requirement is needed in order to start doing your job?

Experience

Months: Years: None

Skills/Competencies

What important skills, competencies, or abilities are needed to do the work that you do? (Please give examples for each skill are you identify.)

A. Coordinating Skills (such as scheduling activities, organizing/maintaining records)
Are coordinating skills required? ☐ Yes ☐ No If yes, give examples of specific skills needed
Example
B. Administrative Skills (such as monitoring

III. Complexity of Duties

Structure and Variation of Work

How processes and tasks within your work are determined, and how you do them are important to understanding your work at 3M. Describe the work flow in your job. Think of the major focus of your job or think of the work activities on which you spend the most time.

1. From whom/where (title, not person) do you receive work?
2. What processes or tasks do you perform to complete it?

Problem Solving and Analysis

3.
Give an example of a particularly difficult problem that you face in your work.
Why does it occur?
How often does it occur?
What special skills and/or resources are needed to solve this difficult problem?

VI. General Comments

General Comments

What percentage of your job duties do you feel was captured in this questionnaire?
☐ 0–25% ☐ 26–50% ☐ 51–75% ☐ 76–100%
What aspect of your job was not covered adequately by this questionnaire?

EXHIBIT 4.10 Comparison of Duty Profiles for Software Jobs

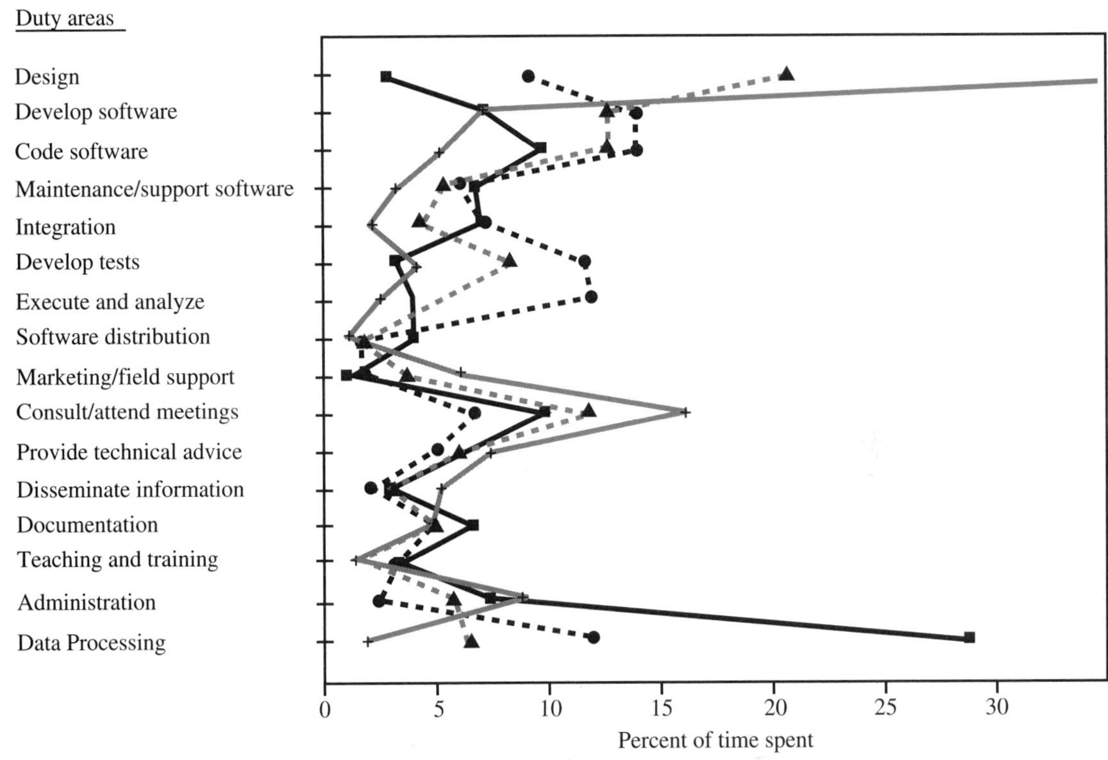

consultant. The chart also shows the number of employees in each job. While it may be interesting to compare responsibilities among jobs, this information is probably more useful for staffing or work design decisions rather than pay decisions.

Some consulting firms have developed quantitative inventories they can tailor to the needs of a specific organization or to a specific family of jobs, such as data/information processing jobs. Many organizations find it practical and cost effective to modify these existing inventories rather than to develop their own analysis from ground zero.

However, turning the analysis over to a consulting shop does not mean the organization and its employees are not heavily involved in the process, both as sources of information, and as consumers who want to be sure the results are useful.

WHO IS INVOLVED IN JOB ANALYSIS?

The third step of Exhibit 4.5 is to conduct interviews. The two issues here are, who collects the information, and who provides it.

Who Collects the Information?

Collecting job analysis information can be an onerous, thankless task. No matter how good a job you do, you are going to face challenges from other employees. Who needs it? Although organizations frequently assign the task of collecting the data to a new employee, justifying the assignment on the grounds that it will help the new employee become familiar with the jobs of the company, the analysis is better done by someone thoroughly familiar with the organization and its jobs.

Who Provides the Information?

The decision on the source of the data (job holders, supervisors, and/or analyst) hinges on how to ensure consistent, accurate, and acceptable data.[14] Expertise about the work resides with the job holders and the supervisors; hence, they are the principle sources. For key managerial/professional jobs, supervisors "two levels above" have also been suggested as valuable sources since they may have a more cosmic view of how jobs fit in the overall organization. In other instances, subordinates and employees in other jobs that interface with the job under study are also involved.

The number of incumbents per job from which to collect data probably varies with the stability of the job. An ill-defined or changing job will require either the involvement of more respondents or a more careful selection of respondents. Obviously, the more people involved, the more time-consuming and expensive the process.

How to Resolve Discrepancies? What happens if the supervisor and the employees present different pictures of the job? While supervisors, in theory, ought to know the jobs well, they may not, particularly if jobs are changing or ill-defined in the first place. People actually working in a job may change it. They may find ways to do things more efficiently, or they may not have realized that certain tasks were supposed to be part of their job. The crossfire from differing perspectives on the nature of a job indicates why conducting a job analysis can be a dangerous place for a brand-new HR employee.

3M had an interesting problem when they collected job information from a group of engineers. The engineers listed a number of responsibilities that they viewed as part of their jobs; however, the manager realized that those responsibilities actually belonged to a higher level of work. The engineers had enlarged their jobs beyond what they were being paid to do. No one wanted to tell this highly productive group of employees to throttle back and slack off. So 3M looked for ways to recognize and reward these engineers rather than bureaucratize them.

---

[14]Robert Harvey, "Incumbent vs. Superior Perception of Jobs," Presentation at SIOP Conference, Miami, FL, 1990.

What should the manager do if employees and their supervisors do not agree on what is part of the job? The answer is to collect more data. Enough data are required to ensure *consistent, accurate,* and *acceptable* results. In general, the more unique the job, the more sources of data will be required. Discussing discrepancies with everyone, then asking both employees and supervisors to sign off on the proposed analysis helps ensure agreement, or at least understanding, of the results.

Top Management Support Is Critical. In addition to involvement by analysts, job holders and their supervisors, support of top management is absolutely essential. They must be alerted to the cost of a thorough job analysis, its time-consuming nature, and the fact that changes may result after it is completed. For example, jobs may be combined, pay rates may be adjusted. If top management is not willing to carry through, or at least seriously weigh, any changes suggested by job analysis, the process is probably not worth the bother and expense.

JOB DESCRIPTIONS

The data collected during the interview is translated onto a summary job description sheet (Steps 4 and 5 in Exhibit 4.5). Exhibit 4.11, a partial description of a nursing job, shows its relationship to the categories of data collected: data to identify, define, and describe a job. The job description is the end point of job analysis and the beginning point for other HR activities, including, as we shall see in the next chapter, job evaluation, and the eventual determination of the pay for that work.

The job description provides a word picture of the job. Exhibit 4.12, a description of a nurse's job 100 years ago, paints a vivid picture of changing expectations.

Describing Managerial/Professional Jobs

In addition to defining and describing the job, descriptions of *managerial* jobs require further explanations of the dimensions, nature and scope, and accountability of the job. One difficulty is the expectation that an individual manager will influence the job. Therefore, the format for describing managerial jobs must be adjusted to adequately capture the relationship between the job, the person performing it, and the organization objectives—how the job fits into the organization, the results expected, and what the person performing brings to the job. Someone with strong information systems and computer expertise performing the compensation manager's job will probably shape it differently, based on this expertise, than someone with strong negotiation and/or counseling expertise.

Results versus Task-based Descriptions. Many employers use results-oriented job descriptions rather than task-oriented ones, particularly for managerial and professional work. The results-oriented description focuses on outcomes (e.g., solves problems that have been stated and defined), whereas the task-based approach describes the job in greater detail (e.g., encodes, tests, debugs and installs operating programs and procedures).

Exhibit 4.11 Contemporary Job Description for Registered Nurse

Job Title

Registered Nurse

Job Summary

Accountable for the complete spectrum of patient care from admission through transfer or discharge through the nursing process of assessment, planning, implementation, and evaluation. Each R.N. has primary authority to fulfill responsibility for the nursing process on the assigned shift and for projecting future needs of the patient/family. Directs and guides patient teaching and activities for ancillary personnel while maintaining standard of professional nursing.

Relationships

Reports to: Head Nurse or Charge Nurse.
Supervises: Responsible for the care delivered by L.P.N.'s, nursing assistants, orderlies, and transcribers.
Works with: Ancillary Care Departments.
External relationships: Physicians, patients, patients' families.

Qualifications

Education: Graduate of an accredited school of nursing.
Work experience: Critical care requires one year of recent medical/surgical experience (special care nursing preferred), medical/surgical experience (new graduates may be considered for noncharge positions).
License or registration requirements: Current R.N. license or permit in the State of Minnesota.
Physical requirements:
A. Ability to bend, reach, or assist to transfer up to 50 pounds.
B. Ability to stand and/or walk 80 percent of 8-hour shift.
C. Visual and hearing acuity to perform job-related functions.

Essential Responsibilities

1. Assesses physical, emotional, and psycho-social dimensions of patients.
   Standard: Provides a written assessment of patient within one hour of admission and at least once a shift. Communicates this assessment to other patient care providers in accordance with hospital policies.
2. Formulates a written plan of care for patients from admission through discharge.
   Standard: Develops short and long term goals within 24 hours of admission. Reviews and updates care plans each shift based on ongoing assessment.
3. Implements plan of care.
   Standard: Demonstrates skill in performing common nursing procedures in accordance with but not limited to the established written R.N. skills inventory specific to assigned area. Completes patient care activities in an organized and timely fashion, reassessing priorities appropriately.

Note: Additional responsibilities omitted from exhibit.

EXHIBIT 4.12 Job Description for Nurse 100 Years Ago

In addition to caring for your 50 patients each nurse will follow these regulations:

1. Daily sweep and mop the floors of your ward, dust the patient's furniture and window sills.
2. Maintain an even temperature in your ward by bringing in a scuttle of coal for the day's business.
3. Light is important to observe the patient's condition. Therefore, each day, fill kerosene lamps, clean chimneys, and trim wicks. Wash the windows once a week.
4. The nurse's notes are important in aiding the physician's work. Make your pens carefully, you may whittle nibs to your individual taste.
5. Each nurse on day duty will report every day at 7 A.M. and leave at 8 P.M. except on the Sabbath on which day you will be off from 12:00 noon to 2:00 P.M.
6. Graduate nurses in good standing with the director of nurses will be given an evening off each week for courting purposes, or two evenings a week if you go regularly to church.
7. Each nurse should lay aside from each pay day a goodly sum of her earnings for her benefits during her declining years, so that she will not become a burden. For example, if you earn $30 a month you should set aside $15.
8. Any nurse who smokes, uses liquor in any form, gets her hair done at a beauty shop, or frequents dance halls will give the director good reason to suspect her worth, intentions, and integrity.
9. The nurse who performs her labors and serves her patients and doctors faithfully and without fault for a period of five years will be given an increase by the hospital administration of five cents a day, provided there are no hospital debts that are outstanding.

Verify

The final step in the job analysis process is to verify the accuracy of the resulting job descriptions (Step 6 in Exhibit 4.5). The verification brings together all the interviewees as well as their supervisors to determine if the proposed job description is accurate and complete. The description is discussed, line by line, with the analyst, making notes of any omissions, ambiguities, or needed clarifications.

Many companies post a sample of job openings on their websites. Compare the job postings from several companies. How complete a job description is included with the posting? Are "essential elements" listed? Are job titles specific or generic? Can you get any sense of a company's culture from its job postings? This website: **http://a2z.lycos.com/Business_and_Investing/Corporate_Home_Pages_A2Z/U.S./** includes links to many company websites.

http://www.groupweb.com/opening/jobs.htm is one of many forums for job hunters on the Web.

For small companies, links to fast-growing private companies can be found at: **http./www.inc.com/500/about.html.**

IS JOB ANALYSIS A NECESSARY TECHNIQUE OR AN OBSTACLE?

HRNet, the world's largest internet discussion group related to HR issues, provoked one of its largest number of responses ever to the query, "What good is job analysis?" Some felt that managers have no basis for making defensible, work-related decisions without it. Others called the process a bureaucratic boondoggle.

A large part of the disagreement centers on the issue of *flexibility.* Many organizations today are trying to become more competitive by reducing their costs. Using fewer employees to do a wider variety of tasks and jobs is part of that cost reduction strategy. Streamlining job analysis and reducing the number of different jobs can reduce costs by making work assignments more fluid.

Generic descriptions that cover a larger number of related tasks (e.g., "associate") can provide flexibility in moving people among tasks without adjusting pay. Employees may be more easily matched to changes in the work flow; the importance of flexibility in behavior is made clear to employees.

Traditional job analysis that makes fine distinctions among levels of jobs has been accused of reinforcing rigidity in the organization. Employees may refuse to do certain tasks that are not specifically called out in their job descriptions. It should be noted, however, that this problem mainly arises where employee relations are already poor. In unionized settings, union members may "work to the rules" (i.e., not do anything that is not specifically listed in their job description) as a technique to put pressure on management. Where work relationships are poor, a detailed job description can get used as a "weapon" by both managers and employees.[15]

On the other hand, the hierarchies and distinctions among jobs may also represent career paths and opportunities. Changing jobs often means a promotion and/or recognition of performance, not to mention a fatter paycheck. Reducing the number of jobs reduces these opportunities for recognition and advancement. Also, generic descriptions leave employers open to challenges from employees who feel they have greater responsibilities than other employees who are being paid the same.

Some companies who have delayered are "relayering." Johnson & Johnson (J&J) corporate HR, for example, wanted to reduce the number of levels in the pay structure as part of an effort to become more agile. However, J&J Japan successfully resisted this, arguing that fewer levels reduced the opportunity to recognize valued employees through promotions (even with small pay increases). J&J China, in an effort to cut turnover from around 25 percent a year, also relayered—from 7 levels to 28.

JUDGING JOB ANALYSIS

Beyond beliefs about its usefulness, or lack thereof, for satisfying both employees and employers, there are several ways to judge job analysis.

---

[15]S. G. Cohen and D. E. Bailey, "What Makes Teams Work: Group Effectiveness Research from the Shop Floor to Executive Suite," *Journal of Management* 23 (1997), pp. 239–291.

Reliability

If you measure something tomorrow and get the same results you get today, or if I measure and get the same result you did, the measurement is considered to be reliable. This doesn't mean it is right—only that *repeated measures* give the same result. Reliability is a measure of the *consistency of results* among various analysts or various methods or various sources of data or over time.

Research on employee and supervisor agreement on the reliability of job analysis information is mixed.[16] For instance, experience may change an employee's perceptions about a job since the employee may have found new ways to do it, or added new tasks to the job. The supervisor may not realize the extent of change. In such cases, the job the employee is actually doing may not be the same job originally assigned by the supervisor. Obviously, the way to increase reliability in a job analysis is to reduce sources of variance. Quantitative job analysis helps reduce variance. But we need to be sure that we do not eliminate the richness or the nuances of a job while eliminating the variance.

Validity

Does the analysis create an accurate portrait of the work? There is almost no way of showing statistically the extent to which an analysis is accurate, particularly for complex jobs. Consequently, validity examines convergence of results among sources of data and methods. However, a signoff on the results does not guarantee their accuracy. In fact, it may only mean everyone was sick to death of the process and wanted to get rid of the analyst so they could get back to work.

Acceptability

If jobholders and managers are dissatisfied with the initial data collected and the process, they are not likely to buy into the resulting job structure nor the pay rates that are eventually attached to that structure. Conventional job analysis is not well accepted because of its potential for subjectivity and favoritism. One writer says, "We all know the classic procedures. One (worker) watched and noted the actions of another . . . at work on (the) job. The actions of both are biased and the resulting information varied with the wind, especially the political wind."[17] But the acceptability of quantitative job

---

[16]V. L. Huber and S. R. Crandall, "Job Measurement: A Social-Cognitive Decision Perspective," in *Research in Personnel and Human Resources Management* 12, ed. Gerald R. Ferris (Greenwich, CT: JAI Press, 1994), pp. 223–69.

[17]E. M. Ramras, "Discussion," in *Proceedings of Division of Military Psychology Symposium: Collecting, Analyzing, and Reporting Information Describing Jobs and Occupations,* 77th Annual Convention of the American Psychological Association, Lackland Air Force Base, TX, September 1969, pp. 75–76.

analysis is also mixed. Even after four years in development, one application ran into such severe problems that managers refused to use it.[18]

Practicality

Practicality refers to the usefulness of the information collected. For pay purposes, job analysis provides work-related information to help determine how much to pay for a job—it helps determine if the job is similar or different from other jobs. If job analysis does this in a reliable (consistent), valid (accurate), and acceptable (cost effective) way, then the technique is of practical use.

As we have noted, some see job analysis information useful for multiple purposes, such as hiring and training. But multiple purposes may require more detail or more behavioral information than is required to assess pay. The practical utility of all-encompassing quantitative job analysis plans, with their relatively complex procedures and analysis, remains in doubt. Some advocates get so taken with their statistics and computers that they ignore the role that human judgment must continue to play in job analysis. As Dunnette states, "I wish to emphasize the central role played in all these procedures by human judgment. I know of no methodology, statistical technique or objective measurements that can negate the importance of, nor supplement, rational judgment."[19]

A JUDGMENT CALL

In the face of all the difficulties, time, expense, and dissatisfaction, why on earth would you as a manager recommend that your employer bother with job analysis? Because work-related information is needed to determine pay, and differences in work determine pay differences. There is no satisfactory substitute that can ensure the resulting pay structure will be work related or will provide reliable, accurate data to make and explain pay decisions.

If work information is required, then the real issue should be, How much detail is needed to make these pay decisions? The answer is: Enough to help set individual employees' pay, encourage continuous learning, increase the experience and skill of the workforce, and minimize the risk of pay-related grievances. The risk of omitting this detail is dissatisfied employees who file lawsuits or complain about management's inability

[18]Gomez-Mejia et al., "A Comparison of the Practical Utility of Traditional, Statistical, and Hybrid Job Evaluation Approaches." Ronald A. Ash and Edward L. Levine, "A Framework for Evaluating Job Analysis Methods," *Personnel* 57, no. 6 (November–December 1980), pp. 53–59; E. L. Levine, R. A. Ash, and N. Bennett, "Exploratory Comparative Study of Four Job Analysis Methods," *Journal of Applied Psychology* 65 (1980), pp. 524–35; R. A. Ash, E. L. Levine, and F. Sistrunk, "The Role of Jobs and Job Based Methods in Personnel and Human Resources Management," *Research in Personnel and Human Resources Management* 1 (1983), pp. 45–84; Edward L. Levine, Ronald A. Ash, Hardy Hall, and Frank Sistrunk, "Evaluation of Job Analysis Methods by Experienced Job Analysts," *Academy of Management Journal* 26, no. 2 (1983), pp. 339–48.

[19]M. D. Dunnette, L. M. Hough, and R. L. Rosse, "Task and Job Taxonomies as a Basis for Identifying Labor Supply Sources and Evaluating Employment Qualifications," in *Affirmative Action Planning,* ed. George T. Milkovich and Lee Dyer (New York: Human Resource Planning Society, 1979), pp. 37–51.

to justify their decisions. The response to inadequate analysis ought not to be to dump the analysis; rather, the response should be more useful analysis.

Summary

Encouraging employee behaviors that help achieve an organization's objectives and foster a sense of fairness among employees are two hallmarks of a useful internal pay structure. One of the first strategic pay decisions is how much to align a pay structure internally compared to aligning it to external market forces. Do not be misled. The issue is not achieving internal consistency versus alignment with external market forces. Rather, the strategic decision focuses on sustaining the optimal balance of internally consistent and externally responsive pay structures that help the organization achieve its mission. Both are required. This section of the book is about one of the first decisions you face in designing pay systems: how much to emphasize pay structures that are internally consistent with the work performed, the organization's structure, and its strategies. Whatever the choice, it needs to support (and be supported by) the organization's overall human resource strategy.

Next, managers must decide whether job and/or individual employee characteristics will be the basic unit of analysis supporting the pay structure. This is followed by deciding what data will be collected, what method(s) will be used to collect it, and who should be involved in the process.

A key test of an effective and equitable pay structure is acceptance of results by managers and employees. The best way to ensure acceptance of job analysis results is to involve employees as well as supervisors in the process. At the minimum, all employees should be informed of purposes and progress of the activity.

If almost everyone agrees about the importance of job analysis for equitable compensation, does that mean everyone does it? Of course not. Unfortunately, job analysis can be tedious and time-consuming. Often the job is given to newly hired compensation analysts, ostensibly to help them learn the organization, but perhaps there's also a hint of "rites of passage" in such assignments.

Alternatives to job-based structures such as skill-based or competency-based systems are being experimented with in many firms. The premise is that basing structures on these other criteria will encourage employees to become more flexible, and fewer workers will be required for the same level of output. Nevertheless, job content remains the conventional criterion for structures.

Review Questions

1. Job analysis has been considered the cornerstone of human resource management. Precisely how does it support managers making pay decisions?
2. What does job analysis have to do with internal consistency?
3. Describe the major decisions involved in job analysis.

4. Distinguish between task and behavioral data.
5. What is the critical advantage of quantitative approaches over conventional approaches to job analysis?
6. How would you decide whether to use job-based or person-based structures?
7. Why do many managers say that job analysis is a colossal waste of their time and the time of their employees? Are they right?

YOUR TURN

JOB ANALYSIS

1. Use the job analysis questionnaire in Exhibit 4.9 to describe a specific job you presently hold or have held in the past. This can be a part-time job or volunteer work for which you were not paid. Be sure to put your name on the questionnaire.
2. After you have completed the questionnaire, pick a teammate (or the instructor will assign one) and exchange completed questionnaires with your teammate.
3. Write a job description for your teammate's job. Does the questionnaire give you sufficient information? Is there additional information that would be helpful?
4. Exchange descriptions. Critique the job descriptions written by your teammate. Does it adequately capture all the important job aspects? Does it indicate which aspects are most important?
5. Save the description. We will examine it again in a later case.

Chapter 5 Evaluating Work: Job Evaluation

Chapter Outline

As soon as my daughter turned 14, she absolutely refused to go shopping with me. At first I thought it was because I like to hum along with the mall music. But she says it is because I embarrass her when I interrogate the assistant store manager about how he is paid—more precisely, how his pay compares to that of the stock clerks, the manager, and regional managers. My daughter claims I do this everywhere I go. *Compensationitis,* she calls it. And I know it's contagious, because a colleague of mine grills his seatmates on airplanes. He's learned the pay rates for captains who pilot Boeing 747 jets versus those who pilot the 101A Airbus for American Airlines.

Reporters often catch compensationitis, too, particularly when writing about other people's salaries. For example, gossip columnist Liz Hodgson reported that extras on movie director Steven Spielberg's film *Amistad* won a massive pay raise after complaining they should have been classified as singers.[1] The black actors, playing West African slaves being transported to the United States in the true story of a slave uprising in 1839, were originally paid just $79 a day, the union minimum. But they protested that they should have received $447, the singers' rate, because they had to learn and rehearse traditional tribal songs. Spielberg's DreamWorks SKG company worked out a deal with the Screen Actors Guild for extra pay totaling $250,000.

How does any organization go about valuing work? The next time you go to the supermarket, check out the different types of work there: store manager, produce manager, front-end manager, deli workers, butchers, stock clerks, checkout people, bakers—the list is long, and the work surprisingly diverse. If you managed a supermarket how would you value work? Specifically, what techniques would you use, and would the technique really matter? But be careful—compensationitis is contagious, and it can embarrass your friends.

This chapter and the next one discuss techniques used to value work. Both chapters focus on "how to"—the specific steps involved. Job evaluation techniques are discussed in this chapter. Person-based techniques, both skill-based and competency-based, are in the next chapter. The objective of all the techniques is an internally consistent pay structure. Ultimately, the pay structure helps the organization sustain its competitive advantage by influencing employee behaviors.

JOB-BASED STRUCTURES: JOB EVALUATION

An exhibit from the previous chapter orients us to the process of valuing work. Exhibit 4.2 contrasts job-based and person-based structures. Notice that no matter the approach, some method for valuing is required. Job-based structures use job evaluation.

Exhibit 5.1 shows how job evaluation fits into the process of determining the internal job structure. The process begins with job analysis, where the information on jobs is collected. Job descriptions summarize the information and serve as input for the evaluation.

[1]Liz Hodgson, "Spielberg Raises Slave Wages," *South China Morning Post,* April 30, 1997, p. 16.

EXHIBIT 5.1 Determining an Internally Consistent Job Structure

Internal consistency: Work relationships within the organization → **Job analysis** → **Job description** → **Job evaluation** → **Job structure**

Some Major Decisions in Job Evaluation

- Establish purpose of evaluation.
- Decide whether to use single or multiple plans.
- Choose among alternative approaches.
- Obtain involvement of relevant stakeholders.
- Evaluate plan's usefulness.

Job evaluation is the process of systematically determining the relative worth of jobs to create a job structure for the organization. The evaluation is based on a combination of job content, skills required, value to the organization, organizational culture and the external market.

The potential to blend both internal forces and external market forces is both a strength and a challenge to job evaluation.

CONTENT, VALUE, AND EXTERNAL MARKET LINKS: DEFINING JOB EVALUATION

Content and Value

Perspectives differ on whether job evaluation is based on job content or job value. A structure based on job *content* refers to the skills required for the job, its duties, and its responsibilities. A structure based on job *value* refers to the relative contribution of the job to the organization's goals. Job value may also refer to the job's value in the external market, or to some other set of rates that have been agreed upon through collective bargaining or other negotiation process.

Not surprisingly, a structure based on content may differ from one based on value. Not only may the content be described and valued differently by different observers, but the value added by the same work may be more (or less) in one organization than in another. The value added by a compensation specialist to a firm whose earnings are generated through sales of manufactured goods or engineering expertise may differ from the value added by that specialist to a consulting firm whose revenues come through the sale of compensation expertise. The skills are similar, yet their relative value to each organization's objectives differs.

Linking Content with the External Market

Some see job evaluation as a process to link job content with external market rates. Aspects of job content (e.g., skills required and customer contacts) take on value based on their relationship to market wages. Because higher skill levels or willingness to work more closely with customers usually commands higher wages in the labor market, then skill level and nature of customer contacts become useful criteria for establishing differences among jobs.

If some aspect of job content, such as working conditions, is not related to wages paid in the external labor market, then that aspect is excluded in the job evaluation. In this perspective, the value of job content is based on what it can command in the external market; it has no intrinsic value.[2]

But not everyone agrees. A developer of the Hay job-evaluation plan (perhaps the plan most widely used by large corporations), states that the "measures are independent of the market and encourage rational determination of the basis for pricing job content."[3] Hay claims that job evaluation establishes the relative value of jobs based on their content, independent of a link to the market.

"Measure for Measure" versus "Much Ado about Nothing"

Researchers, too, have their own perspective on job evaluation. Some believe that job evaluation takes on the trappings of measurement (objective, numerical, generalizable, documented, and reliable). If it is a measurement instrument, then job evaluation can be judged according to technical standards. Just as with employment tests, the reliability and validity of job evaluation plans can be compared.

Those involved in actually making pay decisions have a different view. They see job evaluation as a process to help gain acceptance of pay differences among jobs—an administrative procedure through which the parties become involved and committed. It invites give and take—an exchange of views. Employees, union representatives, and managers can haggle over the relative worth of jobs—"the rules of the game." As in sports contests, we are more willing to accept the results if we believe the rules are fair.[4] Consensus building often requires active participation by all those involved.

So the perspectives on job evaluation vary. Exhibit 5.2 summarizes the assumptions that underlie the perspectives. Some say the content of jobs has intrinsic value which the evaluation will uncover; others say the only fair measure of job value is found in the external market. So while some say job evaluation is just and fair, others say it is "just fair." One writer goes so far as to say that "beneath the superficial

---

[2]Donald P. Schwab, "Job Evaluation and Pay Setting: Concepts and Practices," in *Comparable Worth: Issues and Alternatives,* ed. E. Robert Livernash (Washington, DC: Equal Employment Advisory Council, 1980), pp. 49–77.

[3]Alvin O. Bellak, "Comparable Worth: A Practitioner's View," in *Comparable Worth: Issue for the 80's,* vol. 1 (Washington, DC: U.S. Civil Rights Commission, 1985).

[4]Robert Folger and Mary Konovsky, "Effects of Procedural and Distributive Justice on Reactions to Pay Raise Decisions," *Academy of Management Journal,* March 1989, pp. 115–30.

EXHIBIT 5.2 Aspects of Job Evaluation

Job evaluation is:	*Assumption*
A measure of job content	Content has innate value outside of external market.
A measure of relative value	Relevant groups can reach consensus on relative value.
Link with external market	Job worth cannot be specified without external market information.
Measurement device	Honing instruments will provide objective measures.
Negotiation	Puts face of rationality to a social/political process. Establishes rules of the game. Invites participation.

orderliness of job evaluation techniques and findings, there is much that smacks of chaos."[5] We try to capture all these perspectives in this chapter.[6]

MAJOR DECISIONS

The major job evaluation decisions are depicted in Exhibit 5.1. They are: (1) establish the purpose(s), (2) decide on single versus multiple plans, (3) choose among alternative methods, (4) obtain involvement of relevant stakeholders, and (5) evaluate the usefulness of the results.

Establish the Purpose

Job evaluation is part of the process for establishing an internally consistent pay structure. Recall from Chapter 2 that an internally consistent pay structure supports the work flow, is fair to employees, and directs their behavior toward organization objectives.

Support Work Flow. The job evaluation process supports work flow by integrating each job's pay with its relative contributions to the organization and setting pay for new, unique, or changing jobs.

Fair to Employees. Job evaluation can reduce disputes and grievances over pay differences among jobs by establishing a workable, agreed-upon structure that reduces the role that chance, favoritism, and bias may play in setting pay.

---

[5]M. S. Viteles, "A Psychologist looks at Job Evaluation," *Personnel* 17 (1941), pp. 165–176.

[6]Vandra Huber and S. Crandall, "Job Measurement: A Social-Cognitive Decision Perspective" in *Research in Personnel and Human Resources Management,* vol. 12, ed. Gerald R. Ferris (Greenwich, CT: JAI Press, 1994).

Directs Behavior toward Organization Objectives. Job evaluation calls out to employees what it is about their work that the organization values; what supports the organization's strategy and its success. It can also help employees adapt to organization changes by improving their understanding of what is valued and why that may change.

While no one has studied the effects of job evaluation on any of these objectives, if the purpose of the evaluation is not called out, it becomes too easy to get lost in complex procedures and bureaucracy. Establishing the objectives can help insure that the evaluation actually is the rational and systematic process it was meant to be.

Single versus Multiple Plans

Rarely will an employer evaluate all jobs in the organization at one time. More typically, related groups of jobs, for example, production, engineering, or marketing, will receive attention. Many employers design different evaluation plans for different types of work. They do so because they believe that the work content is too diverse to be adequately evaluated by one plan. For example, production jobs may vary in terms of working conditions, manipulative skills, and knowledge of statistical quality control required. But engineering and marketing jobs do not vary on these factors, nor are those factors particularly important in engineering or marketing work. Rather, other factors such as technical knowledge and skills and the contacts with customers may be relevant. Consequently, a single plan may not be acceptable to employees in such diverse jobs.

Rather than using either universal factors or entirely unique factors for each type of work, some employers, notably Hewlett-Packard, use a core set of common factors and another set of factors unique to particular occupational or functional areas (finance, manufacturing, software and systems, sales). Their experience suggests that unique factors tailored to different job families are more likely to be acceptable to employees and managers and are easier to verify as work related than generalized universal factors.

Choose among Methods

Ranking, classification, and point method are the most common job evaluation methods, though uncounted variations exist. Exhibit 5.3 compares the methods. They all begin by assuming that an accurate job analysis has been translated into useful job descriptions.

RANKING

Ranking simply orders the job descriptions from highest to lowest based on a global definition of relative value or contribution to the organization's success. Ranking is the simplest, fastest, easiest to understand and explain to employees, and the least expensive method, at least initially. However, it can create problems that require difficult and potentially expensive solutions.

Two ways of ranking are common: alternation ranking and paired comparison. *Alternation ranking* orders job descriptions alternately at each extreme. Exhibit 5.4 illustrates the method. Agreement is reached among evaluators on which jobs are the most

EXHIBIT 5.3 Comparison of Job Evaluation Methods

	Advantage	*Disadvantage*
Ranking	Fast, simple, easy to explain.	Cumbersome as number of jobs increases. Basis for comparisons is not called out.
Classification	Can group a wide range of work together in one system.	Descriptions may leave too much room for manipulation.
Point	Compensable factors call out basis for comparisons. Compensable factors communicate what is valued.	Can become bureaucratic and rule-bound.

EXHIBIT 5.4 Alternation Ranking

Jobs *Title*	**Rank** *Most Valued*
Shear operator	Master welder
Electrician	Electrician
Punch press operator	
Master welder	
Grinder	
Receiving clerk	Receiving clerk
	Least Valued

and least valuable, then the next most and least valued, and so on, until all the jobs have been ordered. In the exhibit, evaluators agreed that the job of master welder was the most valued of the six jobs and that receiving clerk was the least valued. Then they selected most and least valued from the four remaining jobs on the list.

The *paired comparison* method uses a matrix to compare all possible pairs of jobs. In Exhibit 5.5, starting at the top left cell and moving to the right, each pair of jobs is compared, and the higher-ranked job is entered in the cell. For example, of the

Exhibit 5.5 Paired Comparison Ranking

	Electrician	Punch press operator	Master welder	Grinder	Receiving clerk
Shear operator	Electrician	Shear operator	Master welder	Shear operator	Shear operator
Electrician		Electrician	Master welder	Electrician	Electrician
Punch press operator			Master welder	Punch press operator	Punch press operator
Master welder				Master welder	Master welder
Grinder					Grinder

Total favorable comparisons:	*Resulting ranks:*
Shear Operator: 3	Master welder
Electrician: 4	Electrician
Punch press operator: 2	Shear operator
Master welder: 5	Punch press operator
Grinder: 1	Grinder
Receiving clerk: 0	Receiving clerk

shear operator and the electrician, the electrician is ranked higher. Moving to the right to compare the shear operator and the punch press operator, the shear operator is ranked higher. When all comparisons have been completed, the job most frequently judged "more valuable" becomes the highest ranked job, and so on.

Alternation ranking and paired comparison methods may be more reliable (produce similar results consistently) than simple ranking. Nevertheless, ranking has drawbacks. The criteria or factors on which the jobs are ranked are usually so poorly defined, if they are specified at all, that the evaluations can become subjective opinions that are difficult, if not impossible, to explain and justify in work-related terms.

Further, evaluator(s) using this method must be knowledgeable about every single job under study. The numbers alone turn what should be a simple task into a formidable one—50 jobs require 1,225 comparisons; and as organizations change, it is difficult to remain knowledgeable about all jobs. Some organizations try to overcome this difficulty by ranking jobs within single departments and merging the results. However, even though the ranking appears simple, fast, and inexpensive, in the long run, the results are difficult to defend, and costly solutions may be required to overcome the problems created.

CLASSIFICATION

Picture a bookcase with many shelves. Each shelf is labeled with a paragraph describing the kinds of books on that shelf and, perhaps, one or two representative titles. This same approach describes the classification system of job evaluation. Job descriptions are slotted into a series of classes that cover the range of jobs. Class descriptions are the labels that serve as the standard for comparing job descriptions. Each class is described in such a way that it captures sufficient work detail, yet is general enough to cause little difficulty in slotting each job onto its appropriate "shelf" or class.

The classes may be described further by including titles of benchmark jobs that fall into each class. A benchmark job has the following characteristics:

- Its contents are well known, and relatively stable over time.
- The job is common across a number of different employers. It is not unique to a particular employer.

Writing class descriptions can be troublesome when jobs from several occupations or job families are covered by a single plan. Although greater specificity of class definition improves the reliability of evaluation, it also limits the variety of jobs that can easily be classified. For example, class definitions written with sales jobs in mind may make it difficult to slot office or administrative jobs and vice versa. You can see the difficulty by examining the class definitions from the federal government's 18-class evaluation system (see Exhibit 5.6). The vagueness of the descriptions seems to leave a lot of room for "judgment." Including titles of benchmark jobs for each class helps make the descriptions more concrete.

In practice, the job descriptions not only are compared to the standard class descriptions and benchmark jobs but also to each other, to ensure that jobs within each class are more similar to each other than to adjacent classes. The final result is a series of classes with a number of jobs in each. The jobs within each class are considered to be equal (similar) work and will be paid equally. Jobs in different classes should be dissimilar and may have different pay rates.

O*Net, the Occupational Information Network, is the U.S. Department of Labor's database that identifies and describes occupations; worker knowledges, skills, and abilities; and workplace requirements for jobs across the country in all sectors of the economy. For more information, visit their site: **http://www.doleta.gov/programs onet/**

How could public sector agencies use this information? Go to an occupation of interest to you. Compare the information offered by the Department of Labor to the job opening descriptions you looked at for specific companies (Chapter 4 Cybercomp). Why are they different? What purpose does each serve?

Go to the FAQ (frequently asked questions) section to see how this information fits the government's General Schedule.

Exhibit 5.6 Examples of General Schedule Descriptions for the Federal Government's Job Classification Method

Grade-General Schedule 1 includes all classes of positions the duties of which are to be performed, under immediate supervision, with little or no latitude for the exercise of independent judgment, (1) the simplest routine work in office, business, or fiscal operations, or (2) elementary work of a subordinate technical character in a professional, scientific, or technical field.

Grade-General Schedule 9 includes all classes of positions the duties of which are (1) to perform, under general supervision, very difficult and responsible work along lines requiring special technical, supervisory, or administrative experience which has (A) demonstrated capacity for sound independent work, (B) thorough and fundamental knowledge of a special and complex subject matter, or of the profession, art, or science involved, and (C) considerable latitude for the exercise of independent judgment; (2) with considerable latitude for the exercise of independent judgment, to perform moderately difficult and responsible work, requiring (A) professional, scientific, or technical training equivalent to that represented by graduation from a college or university of recognized standing, and (B) considerable additional professional, scientific, or technical training or experience which has demonstrated capacity for sound independent work; or (3) to perform other work of equal importance, difficulty, and responsibility, and requiring comparable qualifications.

Grade-General Schedule 13 includes all classes of positions the duties of which are (1) to perform, under administrative direction, with wide latitude for the exercise of independent judgment work of unusual difficulty and responsibility along special technical, supervisory, or administrative lines, requiring extended specialized, supervisory, or administrative training and experience which has demonstrated leadership and marked attainments; (2) to serve as assistant head of a major organization involving work of comparable level within a bureau; (3) to perform, under administrative direction, with wide latitude for the exercise of independent judgment, work of unusual difficulty and responsibility requiring extended professional, scientific, or technical training and experience which has demonstrated leadership and marked attainments in professional, scientific, or technical research, practice, or administration; or (4) to perform other work of equal importance, difficulty, and responsibility, and requiring comparable qualifications.

The Federal Government's General Schedule

A reporter for the *Wall Street Journal* once compiled a list of the ten most unusual U.S. government jobs. He included Smokey Bear's manager, a Supreme Court seamstress (job responsibility: keeping the Supremes in stitches), a gold stacker, condom tester, currency reconstructor, and Air Force art curator.

In order to set the pay for these jobs, the government's General Schedule uses 18 classes, called grades, distinguished by level of difficulty of work. A factor evaluation system provides nine factors (Exhibit 5.7) to be considered when writing the class descriptions. The general class descriptions are written to capture the varying emphasis on these factors.[7]

Most jobs are in 15 grades; the top 3 have been combined into a "supergrade" that covers senior executives. Employees in these top three grades are eligible for bonuses and special stipends based on performance. Collapsing the top three classes into one supergrade makes it easier to move people at this level among different agencies in order to best use their skills and meet different agency needs.

[7]Steven W. Hays and T. Zane Reeves, *Personnel Management in the Public Sector* (Boston: Allyn and Bacon, 1984); *Modernizing Federal Classification: An Opportunity for Excellence* (Washington, DC: National Academy of Public Administration, 1991).

EXHIBIT 5.7 Factor Evaluation System: Nine Factors with Subfactors

Knowledge required by the position
1. Nature or kind of knowledge and skills needed.
2. How the knowledge and skills are used in doing the work.

Supervisory controls
1. How the work is assigned.
2. The employee's responsibility for carrying out the work.
3. How the work is reviewed.

Guidelines
1. The nature of guidelines for performing the work.
2. The judgment needed to apply the guidelines or develop new guides.

Complexity
1. The nature of the assignment.
2. The difficulty in identifying what needs to be done.
3. The difficulty and originality involved in performing the work.

Scope and effect
1. The purpose of the work.
2. The impact of the work product or service.

Personal contacts

Purpose of contacts

Physical demands

Work environment

Many states and other governmental units use variations of the classification system, too.[8] In addition, classification is applied to a wide variety of private sector jobs. High-technology and defense-related businesses have frequently developed four to six job classes for engineers. However, the differences among classes in this setting are often more related to experience or "years-since-degree" than to differences in work done by engineers.

POINT METHOD

Point methods have three common characteristics: (1) compensable factors, with (2) factor degrees numerically scaled, and (3) weights reflecting the relative importance of each factor.[9] Each job's relative value, and hence its location in the pay structure, is determined by the total points assigned to it.

Point plans are the most commonly used approach to establish pay structures in the United States. They represent a significant change from ranking and classification methods in that they make explicit the criteria for evaluating jobs: compensable factors. Compensable factors are defined on the basis of the strategic direction of the

[8]See, for example, H. G. Doggett, *Advancing Managerial Excellence: A Report on Improving the Performance Management and Recognition System* (Washington, DC: Office of Personnel Management, 1994).

[9]Factor comparison, another method of job evaluation, bears some similarities to the point method in that compensable factors are clearly defined and the external market is linked to the job evaluation results. However, factor comparison is used by less than 10 percent of employers who use job evaluation. The method's complexity makes it difficult to explain to employees and managers, which limits its usefulness.

Exhibit 5.8 The Point Plan Process

Step One: Conduct Job Analysis

- A representative sample of benchmark jobs
- The content of these jobs is basis for compensable factors

Step Two: Determine Compensable Factors

- Based on the work performed (what is done)
- Based on strategy and values of the organization (what is valued)
- Acceptable to those affected by resulting pay structure (what is acceptable)

Step Three: Scale the Factors

- Use examples to anchor

Step Four: Weight the Factors

- Can reflect judgment of organization leaders, committee
- Can reflect a negotiated structure
- Can reflect a market-based structure

Step Five: Apply to Nonbenchmark Jobs

business and how the work contributes to that strategy. The factors are then scaled to reflect the degree to which they are present in each job and weighted to reflect their overall importance to the organization. Points are then attached to each factor weight. The total points for each job determines its position in the job structure.

Exhibit 5.8 lists the steps involved in the design of a point plan.

- Conduct job analysis.
- Determine compensable factors.
- Scale the factors.
- Weight the factors according to importance.
- Communicate the plan and train users; prepare manual.
- Apply to nonbenchmark jobs.

The end product of this design process is an evaluation plan that helps develop and explain the pay structure.

Conduct Job Analysis

Just as with ranking and classification, point plans begin with job analysis. Typically a representative sample of jobs, that is, benchmark jobs, is drawn for analysis. The content of these jobs serves as the basis for defining, scaling, and weighting the compensable factors.

Determine Compensable Factors

Compensable factors play a pivotal role in the point plan. These factors reflect how work adds value to the organization. They flow from the work itself and the strategic direction of the business.

Compensable factors are those characteristics in the work that the organization values, that help it pursue its strategy and achieve its objectives.

To select compensable factors, an organization asks itself, What is it about the work that adds value? One company chose decision making as a compensable factor. As shown in Exhibit 5.9, the definition of decision making is three-dimensional: (1) the risk and complexity (hence the availability of guidelines to assist in making the decisions), (2) the impact of the decisions, and (3) the time that must pass before the impact is evident.

In effect, this firm determined that its competitive advantage depends on decisions employees make in their work. And the relative value of the decisions depends on their risk, their complexity, and their impact on the company. Hence, this firm is signaling to all employees that jobs will be valued based on the nature of the decisions required by employees in those jobs. Jobs that require riskier decisions with greater impact have a higher relative worth than jobs that require fewer decisions of relatively little consequence.

To be useful, compensable factors should be

- Based on the work performed.
- Based on the strategy and values of the organization.
- Acceptable to the stakeholders affected by the resulting pay structure.

Based on the Work Itself. Employees are the experts in the work actually done in any organization. Hence, it is important to seek their answers to what should be valued in the work itself. Some form of documentation (i.e., job descriptions, job analysis, employee and/or supervisory focus groups) must support the choice of factors. Work-related documentation helps gain acceptance by employees and managers, is easier to understand, and can withstand a variety of challenges to the pay structure. For example, managers may argue that the salaries of their employees are too low in comparison to those of other employees, or that the salary offered to a job candidate is too low. Union leaders may face questions from members about why one job is paid differently from another. Allegations of pay discrimination may be raised. Employees, line managers, union leaders, and compensation managers must understand and be able to explain why work is paid differently or the same. Differences in factors that are obviously based on the work itself provide that rationale. Properly selected factors may even diminish the likelihood of the challenges arising.

Based on the Strategy and Values of the Organization. The leadership of any organization is the best source of information on where the business should be going and how it is going to get there. Clearly, their input into factors in the work that help create value is crucial. So if the business strategy involves providing innovative, high quality products and services designed in collaboration with customers and suppliers, then jobs with greater responsibilities for product innovation and customer contacts should

EXHIBIT 5.9 Example of Compensable Factor Definition: Decision Making

Compensable Factor Definition: Evaluates the extent of required decision making and the beneficial or detrimental effect such decisions would have on the profitability of the organization.
Consideration is given to the:

- Risk and complexity of required decision making
- Impact such action would have on the company

What type of guidelines are available for making decisions?

_____ 1. Few decisions are required; work is performed according to standard procedures and/or detailed instructions.

_____ 2. Decisions are made within an established framework of clearly defined procedures. Incumbent is only required to recognize and follow the prescribed course of action.

_____ 3. Guidelines are available in the form of clearly defined procedures and standard practices. Incumbent must exercise some judgment in selecting the appropriate procedure.

_____ 4. Guidelines are available in the form of some standard practices, well-established precedent, and reference materials and company policy. Decisions require a moderate level of judgment and analysis of the appropriate course of action.

_____ 5. Some guidelines are available in the form of broad precedent, related practices and general methods of the field. Decisions require a high level of judgment and/or modification of a standard course of action to address the issue at hand.

_____ 6. Few guidelines are available. The incumbent may consult with technical experts and review relevant professional publications. Decisions require innovation and creativity. The only limitation on course of action is company strategy and policy.

What is the impact of decisions made by the position?

_____ 1. Inappropriate decisions, recommendations or errors would normally cause minor delays and cost increments. Deficiencies will not affect the completion of programs or projects important to the organization.

_____ 2. Inappropriate decisions, recommendations or errors will normally cause moderate delays and additional allocation of funds and resources within the immediate work unit. Deficiencies will not affect the attainment of the organization's objectives.

_____ 3. Inappropriate decisions, recommendations or errors would normally cause considerable delays and reallocation of funds and resources. Deficiencies will affect scheduling and project completion in other work units and, unless adjustments are made, could affect attainment of objectives of a major business segment of the company.

_____ 4. Inappropriate decisions, recommendations or errors would normally affect critical programs or attainment of short-term goals for a major business segment of the company.

_____ 5. Inappropriate decisions, recommendations or errors would affect attainment of objectives for the company and would normally affect long-term growth and public image.

The effectiveness of the majority of the position's decisions can be measured within:

_____ 1. One day.
_____ 2. One week.
_____ 3. One month.
_____ 4. Six months.
_____ 5. One year.
_____ 6. More than a year.

Source: Jill Kanin-Lovers, "The Role of Computers in Job Evaluations: A Case in Point," *Journal of Compensation and Benefits* (New York: Warren Gorham and Lamont, 1985).

Exhibit 5.10 Compensable Factor Definition: Multinational Responsibilities

This factor concerns the multinational scope of the job. Multinational responsibilities are defined as line or functional managerial activities in one or several countries.

1. The multinational responsibilities of the job can best be described as:

A. Approving major policy and strategic plans.
B. Formulating, proposing, and monitoring implementation of policy and plans.
C. Acting as a consultant in project design and implementation phases.
D. Providing procedural guidance and information on well-defined topics.
E. Not applicable.

2. Indicate the percentage of time spent on multinational issues:

A. > 50%
B. 25–49%
C. 10–24%
D. < 10%

3. The number of countries (other than your unit location) for which the position currently has operational or functional responsibility:

A. More than 10 countries
B. 5 to 10 countries
C. 1 to 4 countries
D. Not applicable

probably be highly valued, and these factors will be compensable. Or if the business strategy is more Wal-Mart-like, "providing goods and services to delight customers at the lowest cost and greatest convenience possible," then compensable factors might include impact on cost containment, customer relations, and so on. The point is that compensable factors need to reinforce the organization's culture and values as well as its business direction and the nature of the work.

Changes in the organization or its strategic directions may require that the compensable factors also change. For example, both 3M and TRW include international responsibilities, as shown in Exhibit 5.10, as a factor in their managerial job-evaluation plans. The factor is defined in terms of the type of responsibility, the percent of time devoted to international issues, and the number of countries covered. In both firms, strategic business plans call for increased emphasis on international operations. Consequently, the compensable factors include international responsibilities as well.

By the same token, factors may be eliminated if they no longer support the business strategy. The railway company Burlington Northern revised its job evaluation plan to omit the factor number of subordinates supervised. Although many plans include a similar factor, Burlington Northern decided that a factor that values increases to staff runs counter to the organization's objective of reducing the work force size. Major shifts in the business strategy are not daily occurrences, but when they do occur, compensable factors should be reexamined to ensure they are consistent with the new directions.

Acceptable to the Stakeholders. Acceptance of the pay structure by managers and employees is critical. This is also true of compensable factors used to slot jobs into the pay structure. To achieve acceptance of the factors, all the relevant parties' viewpoints need to be considered.

Acceptability of factors may be a function of tradition, too. For example, people who work in hospitals, nursing homes, and child care centers make the point that responsibility for people is used less often, and valued lower, than responsibility for property.[10] This may be a carryover from the days when nursing and child care service were provided by family members, usually women, without reimbursement. People now doing these jobs for pay say that properly valuing a factor for people responsibility would raise their wages. So a frequently asked question is, acceptable to whom? The answer ought to be to the stakeholders: employees, union, and, perhaps, market competitors.

Adapting Factors from Existing Plans. Although a wide variety of factors are used in standard existing plans, the factors tend to fall into four generic groups: skills required, effort required, responsibility, and working conditions. These four were used more than 50 years ago in the National Electrical Manufacturers Association (NEMA) plan and are also included in the Equal Pay Act (1963) to define equal work.

Many of the early points plans, such as those of National Metal Trades Association (NMTA) and NEMA, and the Steel Plan, were developed for nonexempt manufacturing and/or office jobs. Since then, point plans have also been applied to managerial and professional jobs. The Hay Guide Chart—Profile Method of Position, used by 5,000 employers worldwide (130 of the 500 largest U.S. corporations), is perhaps the most widely used. The classic three Hay factors—know-how, problem solving, and accountability—and an example of the guide charts are included in the Appendix.

How Many Factors? A remaining issue to consider is how many factors should be included in the plan. Some factors may have overlapping definitions or may fail to account for anything unique in the criterion chosen. In fact, the NEMA plan explicitly states that the compensable factor experience should be correlated with education. One writer calls this the "illusion of validity"—we want to believe that the factors are capturing divergent aspects of the job, and that both are important.[11]

Another problem is called the "law of small numbers."[12] If even one job in our benchmark sample has a certain characteristic, we tend to use that factor for the entire work domain. Unpleasant working conditions is a common example. If even one job has it, it must be a compensable factor.

---

[10]M. K. Mount and R. A. Ellis, "Investigation of Bias in Job Evaluation Ratings of Comparable Worth Study Participants," *Personnel Psychology* 40 (1987), pp. 85–96; H. Remick, *Strategies for Creating Sound, Bias-Free Job Evaluation Plans.* Paper presented at the I.R.C. Colloquium, Atlanta, GA, September 1978.

[11]D. F. Harding, J. M. Madden, and K. Colson, "Analysis of a Job Evaluation System," *Journal of Applied Psychology* 44 (1960), pp. 354–57.

[12]R. Nisbett, D. Krantz, C. Jepson, and A. Kunda, "The Use of Statistical Heuristics in Everyday Intuition," *Psychological Review* 90 (1983), pp. 339–63.

Once a factor is part of the system, others are likely to say their job has it, too. For example, clerical staff may decide that ringing telephones or leaky toner cartridges constitute unpleasant/hazardous conditions.

In one plan, senior manager refused to accept a job evaluation plan unless the factor working conditions was included. The compensation specialist, a recent college graduate, demonstrated through statistical analysis that working conditions did not vary enough among 90 percent of the jobs under study to have a meaningful effect on the resulting pay structure; statistically, working conditions did not affect the results. The manager rejected these data, pointing out that the new graduate had never worked in the other 10 percent of the jobs, which were in the plant's foundry. The manager knew that working conditions were important to the foundry employees. To get the plan and pay decisions based on it accepted, the plan was redesigned to include working conditions.

In one study, a 21-factor plan produced the same job structure that could be generated using only 7 of the factors. Further, the jobs could be correctly slotted into classes using only 3 factors. Yet the company decided to keep the 21-factor plan because it was "accepted and doing the job."

Research as far back as the 1940s demonstrates that the skills dimension explains 90 percent or more of the variance in job evaluation results; three factors generally account for 98 to 99 percent of variance.[13] However, we have already noted that factors are often included to ensure the plan's acceptance.

Scale the Factors

Once the factors are chosen, scales reflecting the different degrees within each factor are constructed. Each degree may also be anchored by the typical skills, tasks, and behaviors taken from the benchmark jobs that illustrate each factor degree. Exhibit 5.11 shows NMTA's scaling for the factor of knowledge.

A major problem in determining degrees is to make each degree equidistant from the adjacent degrees (interval scaling). For example, the difference between the first and second degrees in Exhibit 5.11 should approximate the difference between the fourth and fifth degree, since the differences in points will be the same.

---

[13]C. H. Lawshe, "Studies in job evaluation: II. The adequacy of abbreviated point ratings for hourly paid jobs in three industrial plans," *Journal of Applied Psychology* 29 (1945), pp. 177–184; C. H. Lawshe and S. L. Alessi, "Studies in job evaluation: IV. Analysis of another point rating scale for hourly paid jobs and the adequacy of an abbreviated scale," *Journal of Applied Psychology* 40 (1946), pp. 310–319; C. H. Lawshe, E. E. Dudek, and R. F. Wilson, "Studies in job evaluation: VII. A factor analysis of two point rating methods of job evaluation," *Journal of Applied Psychology* 32 (1948), pp. 118–129; C. H. Lawshe and P. C. Farbo, "Studies in job evaluation: VIII. The reliability of an abbreviation and job evaluation system," *Journal of Applied Psychology* 33 (1949), pp. 158–166; C. H. Lawshe and A. A. Maleski, "Studies in job evaluation: III. Analysis of point ratings for salary paid jobs in an industrial plan," *Journal of Applied Psychology* 30 (1946), pp. 117–128; C. H. Lawshe and G. A. Satter, "Studies of job evaluation: I. Factor analysis of point ratings for hourly rated jobs in three industrial plans," *Journal of Applied Psychology* 28 (1944), pp. 189–198; C. H. Lawshe and R. F. Wilson, "Studies in job evaluation: VI. The reliability of two point rating systems," *Journal of Applied Psychology* 31 (1947), pp. 355–366.

EXHIBIT 5.11 Illustration of Factor Scaling from National Metal Trades Association

1. Knowledge

This factor measures the knowledge or equivalent training required to perform the position duties.

1st Degree

Use of reading and writing, adding and subtracting of whole numbers; following of instructions; use of fixed gauges, direct reading instruments and similar devices; where interpretation is not required.

2nd Degree

Use of addition, subtraction, multiplication and division of numbers including decimals and fractions; simple use of formulas, charts, tables, drawings, specifications, schedules, wiring diagrams; use of adjustable measuring instruments; checking of reports, forms, records and comparable data; where interpretation is required.

3rd Degree

Use of mathematics together with the use of complicated drawings, specifications, charts, tables; various types of precision measuring instruments. Equivalent to 1 to 3 years applied trades training in a particular or specialized occupation.

4th Degree

Use of advanced trades mathematics, together with the use of complicated drawings, specifications, charts, tables, handbook formulas; all varieties of precision measuring instruments. Equivalent to complete accredited apprenticeship in a recognized trade, craft or occupation; or equivalent to a 2-year technical college education.

5th Degree

Use of higher mathematics involved in the application of engineering principles and the performance of related practical operations, together with a comprehensive knowledge of the theories and practices of mechanical, electrical, chemical, civil or like engineering field. Equivalent to complete 4 years of technical college or university education.

The following criteria for determining degrees have been suggested: (1) limit to the number necessary to distinguish among jobs, (2) use understandable terminology, (3) anchor degree definition with benchmark job titles, and (4) make it apparent how the degree applies to the job. Using too many degrees makes it difficult for evaluators to accurately choose the appropriate degree. This, in turn, reduces the acceptability of the system.

Weight the Factors According to Importance

Once the degrees have been assigned, the factor weights must be determined. Different weights reflect differences in importance attached to each factor by the employer. For example, the National Electrical Manufacturers Association plan weights education at 17.5 percent; another employer's association weights it at 10.6 percent; a consultant's plan recommends 15.0 percent; and a trade association weights education at 10.1 percent.

EXHIBIT 5.12 Job Evaluation Form

Job *bookstore manager*

Check one: [X] Administrative
[ ] Technical

Compensable Factors	Degree (1 2 3 4 5)	x	Weight	=	Total
Skill:					
Mental	4		45%		180
Experience	3		45%		135
Effort:					
Physical	2		30%		60
Mental	4		30%		120
Responsibility:					
Effect of Error	4		20%		80
Inventiveness/ Innovation	3		20%		60
Working Conditions:					
Environment	1		5%		5
Hazards	1		5%		5
					645

How are the factor weights determined? Obviously, involvement by the organization leaders makes sense. Involvement often occurs through an *advisory committee;* the committee allocates 100 percent of the value among the factors.[14] In the illustration in Exhibit 5.12 a committee allocated 5 percent of the value to working conditions, 45 percent to skill, 30 percent to effort, and 20 percent to responsibility. Each factor has two subfactors, with five degrees each.

In the bookstore manager job in the exhibit, the 4 degrees of the *skill* subfactor *mental,* multiplied by 45, contributes 180 points; *experience* provides another 135 points. The *physical* subfactor of *effort,* rated at 2 degrees for this job, and weighted 30 percent, provides 60 points, and so on. The total—645 for the bookstore manager—determine the job's place in the structure. (Note that choosing zero degrees, say, for *hazardous working conditions*—in a bookstore—is not an option in this plan.)

[14]Charles Fay and Paul Hempel, "Whose Values? A Comparison of Incumbent, Supervisor, Incumbent-Supervisor Consensus and Committee Job Evaluation Ratings" (Working paper, Rutgers University, 1991).

A supplement to committee judgment to determine weights is the use of a *statistical analysis.*[15] In this approach, the committee chooses the *criterion pay structure,* that is, a pay structure they wish to duplicate with the point plan. The criterion structure may be the current rates paid for benchmark jobs, market rates for benchmark jobs, rates for predominantly male jobs (in an attempt to eliminate gender bias), or union-negotiated rates.

Once a criterion structure is agreed on, statistical modeling techniques are used to determine what weight for each factor will reproduce, as closely as possible, the chosen structure. The choice of the criterion is a critical decision since the factor weights and degrees are modeled to reproduce it.

Criterion Pay Structure

Some people object to using market rates since they may not be linked to the firm's business strategy. Still others object because they believe wage rates for jobs held predominantly by women are artificially depressed due to historical gender discrimination.[16] Therefore, duplicating the existing pay structure, whether within the firm or in the market, perpetuates this discrimination.

The statistical approach is often labeled as *policy capturing* to contrast it with the committee judgment approach. Both approaches are policy capturing; only the policy or criterion captured may vary and the method used to capture that policy may vary (statistical versus judgmental).

The criterion structure used clearly makes a difference. Perhaps the clearest illustration can be found in the criterion structures used in municipalities. If market rates were solely used, fire fighters would be paid much less than police. Yet many fire fighters unions have successfully negotiated a link between their pay and police rates. Hence, the negotiated pay structure deviates from a market structure.

Another example is the pay structure for occupational workers at AT&T. These jobs range from operators to clerical workers to highly skilled technicians. All are represented by the Communications Workers of America. Studies show that AT&T's negotiated pay structure pays more than market rates for the lower-skill jobs. The union negotiated this structure in part in response to political pressures within the union. AT&T's job evaluation plan is designed to reflect the negotiated, not the market-based structure. At almost every contract negotiation session, AT&T puts this

---

[15]Paul M. Edwards, "Statistical Methods in Job Evaluation," *Advanced Management* (December 1948), pp. 158–63; J. L. Otis and R. H. Leukart, *Job Evaluation: A Basis for Sound Wage Administration* (Englewood Cliffs, NJ: Prentice Hall, 1954); Kermit Davis, Jr., and William Sauser, Jr., "Effects of Alternative Weighting Methods in a Policy-Capturing Approach to Job Evaluation: A Review and Empirical Investigation," *Personal Psychology* 44 (1991), pp. 85–127.

[16]Donald J. Treiman, "Effect of Choice of Factors and Factor Weights in Job Evaluation," in *Comparable Worth and Wage Discrimination,* ed. H. Remick (Philadelphia: Temple University Press, 1984), pp. 79–89.

issue on the table. But it gets traded off against other issues (layoffs, work rules) which are judged to be more important. Nevertheless, these two examples illustrate that the criterion pay structure on which job evaluation is based really matters.

Apply to Nonbenchmark jobs

Recall that the compensable factors and weights were derived using a sample of benchmark jobs. The final step in the point plan process is to apply the plan to the remaining jobs. To do so, a manual is usually written that describes the method, defines the compensable factors, and provides enough information to permit users to distinguish varying degrees of each factor. The point of the manual is to allow users who were not involved in its development to apply the plan. Obviously, users may also require training as well as background information on the total pay system.

Some organizations have recently discarded point systems for classification plans. IBM recently moved from a point to classification system. They reported that the shift offered simplicity and required less bureaucracy to manage. However, IBM's previous point plan may be so embedded in their culture and so internalized by IBM compensation people that they no longer need a written procedure to apply the plan.

WHO SHOULD BE INVOLVED?

If the internal structure's purpose is to aid managers, and if ensuring high involvement and commitment from employees is important, those managers and employees with a stake in the results need to be involved in the process of designing it.

A common approach is to use committees, task forces, or teams that include representatives from key operating functions, including nonmanagerial employees. In some cases, the group's role is only advisory; in others, it designs the evaluation approach, chooses compensable factors, and approves all major changes.

Management probably will find it advantageous to include union representation as a source of ideas and to help promote acceptance of the results. For example, union–management task forces participated in the design of a new evaluation system for the federal government. Their roles involved mutual problem solving.

But other union leaders believe that philosophical differences prevent their active participation. They take the position that collective bargaining yields more equitable results. In other cases, union and management representatives evaluated jobs jointly and submit disagreements to an arbitrator. So the extent of union participation varies. No single perspective exists on the value of active participation in the process, just as no single management perspective exits.

The Design Process Matters

Procedural equity, discussed in Chapter 2, is highly related to employee involvement and acceptance. Research strongly suggests that attending to the equity of the design process and the approach chosen (job evaluation, skill/competency-based plan, and market pricing) rather than focusing solely on the results (the internal pay structure) is likely to achieve employee and management commitment, trust, and acceptance of the results.[17]

The absence of participation may make it easier for employees and managers to imagine ways the structure might have been rearranged to their personal liking. Two researchers observed ". . . if people do not participate in decisions, there is little to prevent them from assuming that things would have been better, 'if I'd have been in charge.'"[18]

Additional research is needed to ascertain whether the payoffs from increased participation offset potential costs (time involved to reach consensus, potential problems caused by disrupting current perceptions, etc). For example, the involvement of both subunit and corporate managers raises the potential for conflict due to their differing perspectives. Operating managers may wish to gain greater flexibility in order to funnel more pay to key individuals. Corporate types, aware of the difficulties resulting from emphasizing short-term needs rather than the overall corporate strategy, may disagree. Note the difference in focus. The operating manager has operating objectives to achieve, does not want to lose key individuals, and views compensation as a mechanism to help accomplish these goals. Corporate, on the other hand, adopts a wide perspective and focuses on ensuring that the decisions are consistent with overall strategic intent.

Appeals/Review Procedures

No matter the technique, no job evaluation plan anticipates all situations. It is inevitable that some jobs will be incorrectly evaluated, or at least employees and managers may suspect that they were. Consequently, review procedures to handle such cases and to help ensure procedural equity are required. Often the compensation manager handles reviews, but increasingly, peer or team reviews are being used. Very occasionally, these reviews take on the trappings of formal grievance procedures (e.g., documented complaints and responses and levels of approval). Problems may also be

[17]One of the key findings of a National Academy of Science report that examined virtually all research on pay was that the process used to design pay plans is vital to achieving high commitment. George Milkovich and Alexandra Wigdor, eds., *Pay and Performance* (Washington, DC: National Academy Press, 1991). Also, see Edward E. Lawler III and J. Richard Hackman, "Impact of Employee Participation in the Development of Pay Incentive Plans: A Field Experiment," *Journal of Applied Psychology* 53, no. 6 (December 1969), pp. 467–71; Carl F. Frost, John W. Wakely, and Robert A. Ruh, *The Scanlon Plan for Organization Development: Identity, Participation, and Equity* (East Lansing: Michigan State Press, 1974); K. C. Sheflen, E. E. Lawler III, and J. R. Hackman, "Long-Term Impact of Employee Participation in the Development of Pay Incentive Plans: A Field Experiment Revisited," *Journal of Applied Psychology* 55 (1971), pp. 182–86; E. A. Locke and D. M. Schweiger, "Participation in Decision Making: One More Look," *Research in Organization Behavior* (Greenwich, CT: JAI Press, 1979); J. F. Carey, "Participative Job Evaluation," *Compensation Review,* Fourth Quarter 1977, pp. 29–38; G. J. Jenkins, Jr. and E. E. Lawler III, "Impact of Employee Participation in Pay Plan Development," *Organizational Behavior and Human Performance* 28 (1981), pp. 111–28.

[18]R. Crepanzano and R. Folger, "Referent Cognitions and Task Decision Autonomy: Beyond Equity Theory," *Journal of Applied Psychology* (September 1989), pp. 17–23.

handled by managers and the employee relations generalists through informal discussions with employees[19]

When the evaluations are completed, approval by higher levels of management is usually required. The particular approval process differs among organizations. The approval process helps ensure that any changes that result from evaluating work are consistent with the organization's operations and directions.

"I Know I Speak for All of Us When I Say I Speak for All of Us."

A recent study of a university in the western United States found that more powerful departments in the university (as indicated by number of faculty members and size of budget) were more successful in using the appeals process to get jobs paid more or reclassified (higher) than were weaker departments. The authors concluded that in addition to assessing the worth of a job, the entire job evaluation process reflects the political and social context within the organization.[20]

This result is consistent with other research that showed that a powerful member of a job evaluation committee could sway the results.[21] Using students as subjects, a "senior assessor" alternately recommended valuing the shorthand typist over the cost clerk, and then the cost clerk over the shorthand typist with a different group of students. The students generally went along with either suggestion. When a senior assessor talks, other committee members listen.

Consequently, procedures should be judged for their susceptibility to political influences. "It is the decision-making process, rather than the instrument itself that seems to have the greatest influence on pay outcomes," writes one researcher.[22]

THE FINAL RESULT: STRUCTURE

The final result of the job analysis–job description–job evaluation process is a structure; a hierarchy of work.

This hierarchy translates the employer's internal consistency policy into practice. Exhibit 5.13 shows four hypothetical job structures within a single organization. These structures were obtained via different approaches to evaluating work. The jobs are arrayed within four basic functions: managerial, technical, manufacturing, and administrative. The managerial and administrative structures were obtained via a point job

---

[19]B. Carver and A. A. Vondra, "Alternative Dispute Resolution: Why It Doesn't Work and Why It Does," *Harvard Business Review* (May–June 1994), pp. 120–29.

[20]Theresa M. Welbourne and Charlie O. Trevor, "Rational and Coalition Models of Job Evaluation: Do More Powerful University Departments Have an Advantage?" (Working paper, Cornell University, 1998).

[21]A. G. P. Elliott, *Staff Grading* (London: British Institute of Management, 1960); D. Kahneman, "Reference Point, Anchors, Norms, and Mixed Feelings," *Organization Behavior and Human Decision Processes* 51 (1992), pp. 430–54; N. Gupta and G. D. Jenkins, Jr. "The politics of pay," Paper presented at the annual meeting of the Society for Industrial and Organizational Psychology, Montreal, 1992.

[22]Vandra Huber and S. Crandall, "Job Measurement: A Social-Cognitive Decision Perspective" in *Research in Personnel and Human Resources Management,* vol. 12, ed. Gerald R. Ferris (Greenwich, CT: JAI Press, 1994).

EXHIBIT 5.13 Resulting Internal Structures—Job, Skill, and Competency Based

Managerial Group	Technical Group	Manufacturing Group	Administrative Group
		Assembler I Inspector I	
Vice Presidents	Head/Chief Scientist	Packer	Administrative Assistant
Division General Managers	Senior Associate Scientist	Materials Handler Inspector II	Principal Administrative Secretary
Managers	Associate Scientist	Assembler II	Administrative Secretary
Project Leaders	Scientist	Drill Press Operator Rough Grinder	Word Processor
Supervisors	Technician	Machinist I Coremaker	Clerk/Messenger
↑ Job Evaluation	↑ Competency-Based	↑ Skill-Based	↑ Job Evaluation

evaluation plan, and technical and manufacturing work via two different person-based plans (Chapter 6); the manufacturing plan was negotiated with the union. The point of the exhibit is to illustrate the results of evaluating work: structures that support the policy of internal consistency.

Organizations commonly have multiple structures derived through multiple approaches. Consistency in such cases may be interpreted as consistency within each functional group or unit. Although some employees in one structure may wish to compare the procedures used in another structure with their own, the underlying premise in practice is that internal consistency is most influenced by fair and equitable treatment of employees doing similar work in the same skill group.

BALANCING CHAOS AND CONTROL

Looking back at the material we have covered in the past three chapters (determining internal consistency, job analysis, job evaluation), you may be thinking that we have spent a lot of time and a lot of our organization's money to develop some admirable techniques. But we have yet to pay a single employee a single dollar. Why bother with all this? Why not just pay whatever it takes, and get on with it?

Prior to the widespread use of job evaluation, employers in the 1930s and 1940s had irrational pay structures—the legacy of decentralized and uncoordinated wage-setting practices. Pay differences were a major source of unrest among workers. American Steel and Wire, for example, had more than 100,000 pay rates. Employment and wage records were rarely kept before 1900; only the foreman knew with any accuracy how many workers were employed in his department and the rates they received. Foremen were "free to manage," but they used wage information to play favorites by varying the day rate or assigning favored workers to jobs where piece rates were loose.

Job evaluation, with its specified procedures and documentable results, helped to change that. The technique provided work-related and business-related order and logic. But over time, complex procedures and creeping bureaucracy caused many users to lose sight of the objectives. Instead, they focused on "carefully prescribed and described activities." Specialists and researchers became so enamored with their techniques that we were in danger of knowing more and more about less and less.

At the same time, the world of work was changing. Fred Nichols writes on HRNet, the largest internet discussion group related to HR issues, "The work of many if not most people now requires of them that they figure out what to do in a given situation instead of simply invoking a canned routine. They must solve problems, make decisions, plan courses of action, marshal support and, in general, design their own work methods, techniques, and tools." The challenge is to insure that job-evaluation plans afford flexibility to adapt to changing conditions. Sufficient ambiguity usually exists in the compensable factor descriptions to permit interpretation as the situation requires. This inherent flexibility accommodates the introduction of new technology or the restructuring of operations.

Flexibility may be very attractive to managers coping with increased competitive pressures and the need to restructure work. However, the lack of business-and work-related evaluations cut two ways: Generic factors and vague descriptions such as "associates" or "technicians" may not provide sufficient business-and work-related information to justify pay decisions.

This lack of detail clearly avoids bureaucracy, leaving managers "free to manage"—just like the foreman 100 years ago. But it also reduces control and guidelines, which in turn may make it harder to placate disgruntled employees who believe the work they do is undervalued. And it is more difficult to ensure that people are treated fairly.

Some balance between chaos and control is required. History suggests that when flexibility without guidelines exists, chaotic and irrational pay rates too frequently result. Removing inefficient bureaucracy is important, but balanced guidelines are necessary to ensure that employees are treated fairly and that pay decisions support the organization's strategy and help it achieve its objectives.

Summary

The differences in the rates paid for different jobs and skills affect the ability of managers to achieve their business objectives. Differences in pay matter. They matter to employees, because their willingness to take on more responsibility and training, to focus on adding value for customers and improving quality of products, and to be flexible enough to adopt to change all depend at least in part on how pay is structured for different levels of work. Differences in the rates paid for different jobs and skills also influence how fairly employees believe they are being treated. Unfair treatment is ultimately counterproductive.

So far we have examined the most common approach to designing pay differences for different work: job evaluation. In the next chapter, we will examine several alternative approaches. However, any approach needs to be evaluation for how well it will help design an internal pay structure that is based on the work, will help achieve the business objectives, and will be acceptable to the key stakeholders.

Job evaluation has evolved into many different forms and methods. Consequently, wide variations exist in its use and how it is perceived. This chapter discussed some of the many perceptions of the role of job evaluation and reviewed the criticisms leveled at it. No matter how job evaluation is designed, its ultimate use is to help design and manage a work-related, business-focused, and agreed-upon pay structure.

Review Questions

1. How does job evaluation translate internal consistency policies (loosely coupled versus tight fitting) into practice? What does (a) flow of work, (b) fairness, and (c) directing people's behaviors toward organization objectives have to do with job evaluation?
2. Why are there different approaches to job evaluation? Think of several employers in your area (the college, hospital, retailer, 7-11, etc.). What approach would you expect them to use? Why?
3. What are the advantages and disadvantages of using more than one job evaluation plan in any single organization?
4. Why bother with job evaluation? Why not simply market price? How can job evaluation link internal consistency and external market pressures?
5. Consider your college or school. What are the compensable factors required for your college to evaluate jobs? How would you go about identifying these factors? Should the school's educational mission be reflected in your factors? Or are generic factors okay? Discuss.
6. You are the manager of 10 people in a large organization. Everyone becomes very suspicious and upset when they receive a memo from the HR department saying their jobs are going to be evaluated. How do you try to reassure them?

APPENDIX Hay Guide Chart—Profile Method of Position

KNOW-HOW
DEFINITIONS

DEFINITION: Know-How is the sum total to every kind of skill however acquired, required for acceptable job performance. This sum total which comprises the overall savvy has 3 dimensions–the requirements for:

1 Practical procedures, specialized techniques, and scientific disciplines.

2 Know-How of integrating and harmonizing the diversified functions involved in managerial situations occurring i operating, supporting, and administrative fields. This Know-How may be exercised consultatively (about management) as well as executively and involves in some combination the areas of organizing, planning, executing, controlling and evaluating.

3 Active, practicing, face-to-face skills in the area of human relationships (as defined at right).

MEASURING KNOW-HOW: Know-How has both scope (variety) and depth (thoroughness). Thus, a job may require some knowledge about a lot of things, or a lot of knowledge about a few things. The total Know-How is the combination of scope and depth. This concept makes practical the comparison and weighing of the total Know-How content of different jobs in terms of: "How much knowledge about how many things."

2 HUMAN RELATIONS SKILLS

1. **BASIC:** Ordinary courtesy and effectiveness in dealing with others.

2. **IMPORTANT:** Understanding, influencing, and/or serving people are important, but not critical considerations.

3. **CRITICAL:** Alternative or combined skills in understanding, selecting, developing and motivating people are important in the highest degree.

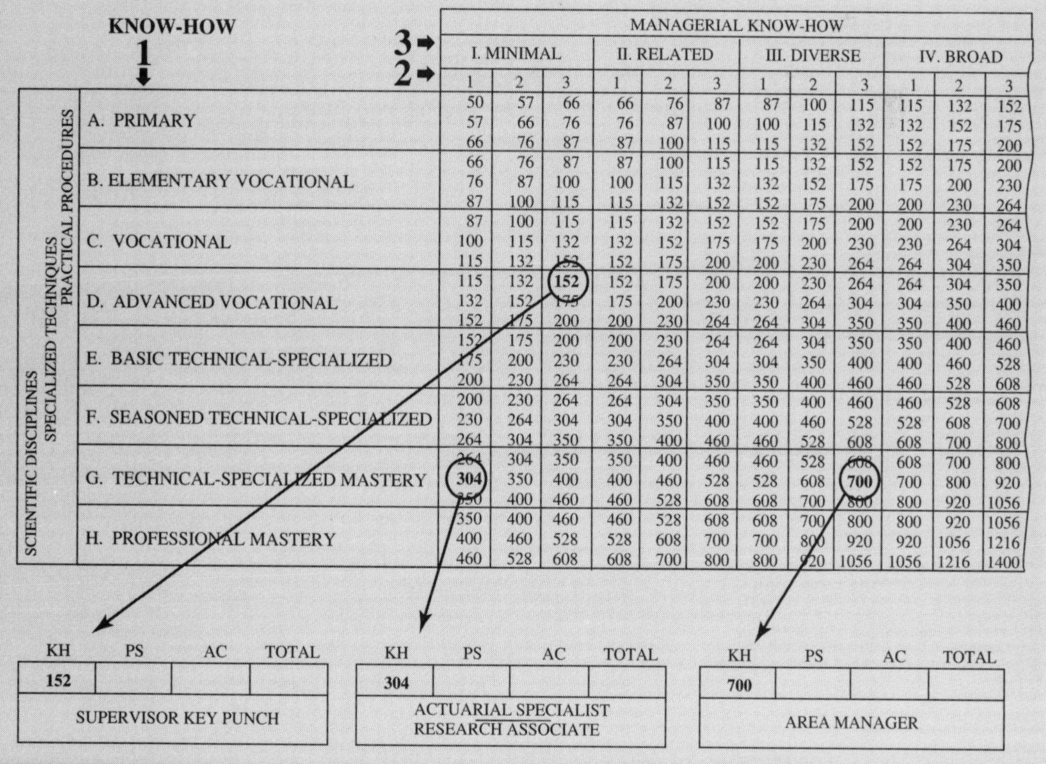

KNOW-HOW

1 ↓ SCIENTIFIC DISCIPLINES / SPECIALIZED TECHNIQUES / PRACTICAL PROCEDURES	3 → 2 → MANAGERIAL KNOW-HOW: I. MINIMAL 1	I. 2	I. 3	II. RELATED 1	II. 2	II. 3	III. DIVERSE 1	III. 2	III. 3	IV. BROAD 1	IV. 2	IV. 3
A. PRIMARY	50	57	66	66	76	87	87	100	115	115	132	152
	57	66	76	76	87	100	100	115	132	132	152	175
	66	76	87	87	100	115	115	132	152	152	175	200
B. ELEMENTARY VOCATIONAL	66	76	87	87	100	115	115	132	152	152	175	200
	76	87	100	100	115	132	132	152	175	175	200	230
	87	100	115	115	132	152	152	175	200	200	230	264
C. VOCATIONAL	87	100	115	115	132	152	152	175	200	200	230	264
	100	115	132	132	152	175	175	200	230	230	264	304
	115	132	152	152	175	200	200	230	264	264	304	350
D. ADVANCED VOCATIONAL	115	132	152	152	175	200	200	230	264	264	304	350
	132	152	175	175	200	230	230	264	304	304	350	400
	152	175	200	200	230	264	264	304	350	350	400	460
E. BASIC TECHNICAL-SPECIALIZED	152	175	200	200	230	264	264	304	350	350	400	460
	175	200	230	230	264	304	304	350	400	400	460	528
	200	230	264	264	304	350	350	400	460	460	528	608
F. SEASONED TECHNICAL-SPECIALIZED	200	230	264	264	304	350	350	400	460	460	528	608
	230	264	304	304	350	400	400	460	528	528	608	700
	264	304	350	350	400	460	460	528	608	608	700	800
G. TECHNICAL-SPECIALIZED MASTERY	264	304	350	350	400	460	460	528	608	608	700	800
	304	350	400	400	460	528	528	608	700	700	800	920
	350	400	460	460	528	608	608	700	800	800	920	1056
H. PROFESSIONAL MASTERY	350	400	460	460	528	608	608	700	800	800	920	1056
	400	460	528	528	608	700	700	800	920	920	1056	1216
	460	528	608	608	700	800	800	920	1056	1056	1216	1400

KH	PS	AC	TOTAL
152			
SUPERVISOR KEY PUNCH			

KH	PS	AC	TOTAL
304			
ACTUARIAL SPECIALIST RESEARCH ASSOCIATE			

KH	PS	AC	TOTAL
700			
AREA MANAGER			

Problem Solving
DEFINITIONS

DEFINITION: Problem Solving is the original, "self-starting" thinking required by the job for analyzing evaluating, creating, reasoning, arriving at and making conclusions. To the extent that thinking is circumscribed by standards, covered by precedents, or referred to others, Problem Solving is diminished, and the emphasis correspondingly is on Know-How.

Problem Solving has two dimensions:

1 The thinking environment in which the problems are solved.

2 The thinking challenge presented by the problem to be solved.

MEASURING PROBLEM SOLVING: Problem Solving measures the intensity of the mental process which employs Know-How to (1) identify, (2) define, and (3) resolves a problem. "You think with what you know." This is true of even the most creative work. The raw material of any thinking is knowledge of facts, principles and means; ideas are put together from something already there. Therefore, Problem Solving is treated as a percentage utilization of Know-How.

PROBLEM SOLVING

1 ↓ / 2 →	THINKING CHALLENGE				
	1. REPETITIVE	2. PATTERNED	3. INTERPOLATIVE	4. ADAPTIVE	5. UNCHARTED
A. STRICT ROUTINE	10% 12%	14% 16%	19% 22%	25% 29%	33% 38%
B. ROUTINE	12% 14%	16% 19%	22% 25%	29% 33%	38% 43%
C. SEMI-ROUTINE	14% 16%	19% 22%	25% 29%	33% 38%	43% 50%
D. STANDARDIZED	16% 19%	22% 25%	29% 33%	38% 43%	50% 57%
E. CLEARLY DEFINED	19% 22%	25% 29%	33% 38%	43% 50%	57% 66%
F. BROADLY DEFINED	22% 25%	29% 33%	38% 43%	50% 57%	66% 76%
G. GENERALLY DEFINED	25% 29%	33% 38%	43% 50%	57% 66%	76% 87%
H. ABSTRACTLY DEFINED	29% 33%	38% 43%	50% 57%	66% 76%	87% 100%

KH	PS	AC	TOTAL
152	**50**		
SUPERVISOR KEY PUNCH			

KH	PS	AC	TOTAL
304	**200**		
ACTUARIAL SPECIALIST RESEARCH ASSOCIATE			

KH	PS	AC	TOTAL
700	**400**		
AREA MANAGER			

ACCOUNTABILITY

DEFINITIONS

DEFINITION: Accountability is the answerability for action and for the consequences thereof. It is the measured effect of the job on end results. It has three dimensions in the following order of importance.

1. **FREEDOM TO ACT**—the degree of personal or procedural control and guidance as defined in the left-hand column of the chart.
2. **JOB IMPACT ON END RESULTS**—as defined at right
3. **MAGNITUDE**—indicated by the general dollar size of the area(s) most clearly or primarily affected by the job.

2 IMPACT OF JOB ON END RESULTS

Indirect

REMOTE: Informational, recording, or incidental services for use by others in relation to some important end result.

CONTRIBUTORY: Interpretive, advisory, or facilitating services for use by others in taking action.

Indirect

SHARED Participating with others (except own subordinates and supervisors), within or outside the organizational unit, in taking action.

PRIMARY: Controlling impact on end results, where shared accountability or others is subordinate.

ACCOUNTABILITY **1** ⬇ / 3 ➡	(1) VERY SMALL OR INDETERMINATE				(2) SMALL				(3) MEDIUM				(4) L	
2 ➡	R	C	S	P	R	C	S	P	R	C	S	P	R	C
	10	14	19	25	14	19	25	33	19	25	33	43	25	33
A. PRESCRIBED	12	16	22	29	16	22	29	38	22	29	38	50	29	38
	14	19	25	33	19	25	33	43	25	33	43	57	33	43
	16	22	29	38	22	29	38	50	29	38	50	66	38	50
B. CONTROLLED	19	25	33	43	25	33	43	57	33	43	57	76	43	57
	22	29	38	50	29	38	50	66	38	50	66	87	50	66
	25	33	43	57	33	43	57	76	43	57	76	100	57	76
C. STANDARDIZED	29	38	50	**66**	38	50	66	87	50	66	87	115	66	87
	33	43	57	76	43	57	76	100	57	76	100	132	76	100
	38	50	66	87	50	66	87	115	66	87	115	152	87	115
D. GENERALLY REGULATED	43	57	76	100	57	76	100	132	76	100	132	1756	100	132
	50	66	87	115	66	87	115	152	87	**115**	152	200	115	152
	57	76	100	132	76	100	132	175	100	132	175	230	132	175
E. DIRECTED	66	87	115	152	87	115	152	200	115	152	200	264	152	200
	76	100	132	175	100	132	175	230	132	175	230	304	175	230
	87	115	152	200	115	152	200	264	152	200	264	350	200	264
F. ORIENTED DIRECTION	100	132	175	230	132	175	230	304	175	230	304	400	230	304
	115	152	200	264	152	200	264	380	200	264	380	460	264	380
	132	175	230	304	175	230	304	400	230	304	400	528	304	400
G. BROAD GUIDANCE	152	200	264	350	200	264	350	460	264	350	460	**608**	350	460
	175	230	304	400	230	304	400	528	304	400	528	700	400	528
	200	264	350	460	264	350	460	608	350	460	608	800	460	608
H. STRATEGIC GUIDANCE	230	304	400	528	304	400	528	700	400	528	700	920	528	700
	264	350	460	608	350	460	608	800	460	608	800	1056	608	800
	304	400	528	700	400	528	700	920	528	700	920	1216	700	920
I. GENERALLY UNGUIDED	350	460	608	800	460	608	800	1056	608	800	1056	1400	800	1056
	400	528	700	920	528	700	920	1216	700	920	1216	1390	920	1216

KH	PS	AC	TOTAL
152	50	**66**	268
SUPERVISOR KEY PUNCH			

KH	PS	AC	TOTAL
304	200	**115**	619
ACTUARIAL SPECIALIST RESEARCH ASSOCIATE			

KH	PS	AC	TOTAL
700	400	**608**	1708
AREA MANAGER			

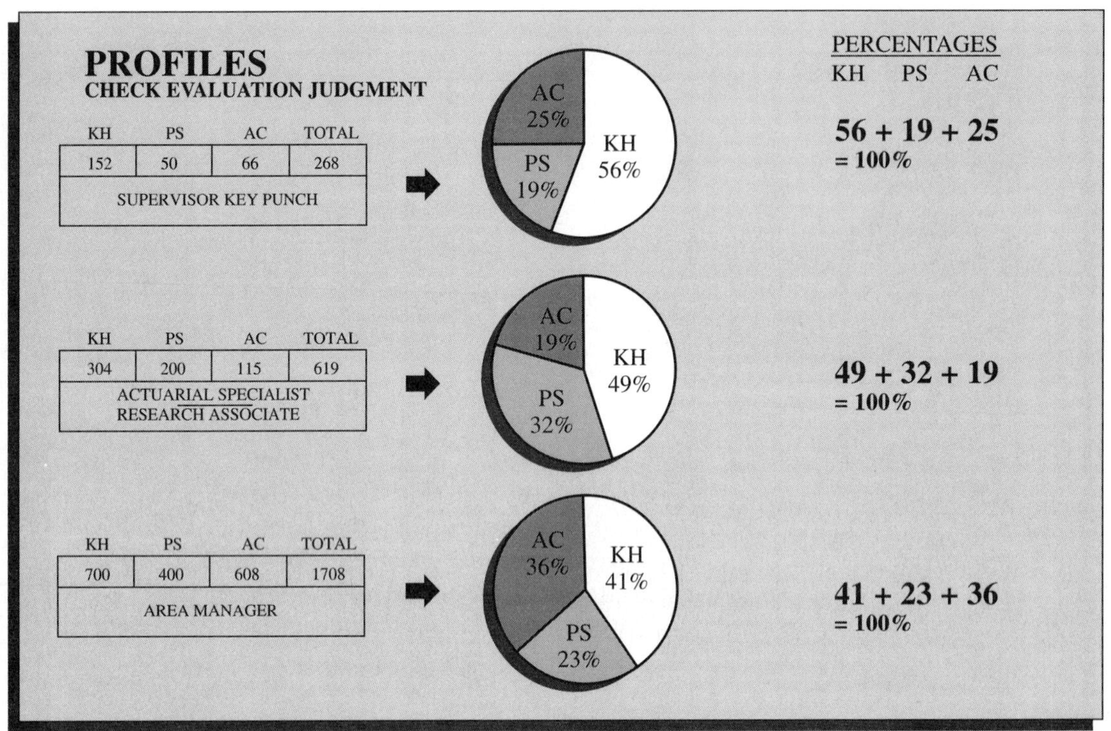
PROFILES
CHECK EVALUATION JUDGMENT
KH PS AC TOTAL
152 50 66 268
SUPERVISOR KEY PUNCH
AC 25%
PS 19%
KH 56%
PERCENTAGES
KH PS AC
56 + 19 + 25
= 100%
KH PS AC TOTAL
304 200 115 619
ACTUARIAL SPECIALIST
RESEARCH ASSOCIATE
AC 19%
KH 49%
PS 32%
49 + 32 + 19
= 100%
KH PS AC TOTAL
700 400 608 1708
AREA MANAGER
AC 36%
KH 41%
PS 23%
41 + 23 + 36
= 100%

Your Turn

Job Evaluation for the State

Your state is enjoying economic growth. Tax revenues are up, but so is the workload for government employees. Recently there have been increasing complaints about pay. Some employees believe that their salary is out of line in comparison to the amount received by other employees. As a first step, the state personnel director hired you to perform job analysis and write job descriptions. The results are shown below. Now a job structure is needed.

1. Divide into teams of four to six students each. Each team should evaluate the eight jobs and prepare a job structure based on its evaluation. Assign titles to each job, and list your structure by title and job letter.
2. Each team should describe the process the group went through to arrive at that job structure. Job evaluation techniques and compensable factors used should be described, and the reasons for selecting them should be stated.
3. Each team should give each job a title and put its job structure on the board. Comparisons can then be made among job structures of the various teams. Does the job evaluation method used appear to affect the results? Do compensable factors chosen affect the results? Does the process affect the results?
4. Evaluate the job descriptions. What parts of them were most useful? How could they be improved?

Job A

Kind of Work. Directs a large and complex fiscal management program in a large state department, agency, or institution. Provides technical and supervisory financial support to carry out policies and programs established by the department head. Serves as the chief liaison to activity managers to ensure coordination of their activities in planning with the accounting division. Maintains a close working relationship with the finance agency controller to ensure compliance with budgetary and financial planning requirements of the Department of Finance. Considerable latitude is granted employee in this class for developing, implementing, and administering financial methods and procedures. Typically reports to a high-level department manager with work reviewed through periodic conferences and reports.

Essential Responsibilities

- Directs all accounting functions of the department, agency, or institution so that adequate financial records and fiscal controls are maintained.
- Provides supervisory and high professional skills for the financial operations of the department consistent with the appropriate state and federal laws and regulations so that state and federal funds are utilized in the most efficient and effective manner.
- Provides coordination with other state and federal agencies relating to financial matters so that the department head and agency controller are informed as to matters pertaining to policies, procedures, and programs that may have an effect on the financial operation of the department.
- Develops authorized department budgets and financial plans, goals,

and objectives for review and approval by the agency controller and the department head so that maximum use will be made of financial resources.

- Consults with and advises the department head, managers, supervisors, and the agency controller on financial policies and procedures, organizational changes, and interpretation of financial data and reports to ensure efficient and effective fiscal management.

Job B

Kind of Work. Keeps financial records where the accounts are relatively complex or assists higher-level accountants and accounting technicians when the accounts are complex and extensive.

Receives direction from higher-level accounting personnel in the form of a review of work for accuracy and completeness. In some cases, may provide lead work direction to account clerks or clerical personnel engaged in the bookkeeping operation. Prepares relatively simple reports, makes preliminary analyses of financial conditions for use by other employees, and implements minor procedural and transactional changes in the fiscal operation. Emphasis is on bookkeeping procedures and the smooth transition of fiscal operations.

Essential Responsibilities

- Maintains the financial records of a moderate-sized department according to established procedures and makes adjustments to the records as directed.
- Prepares special analytical data for use by others in preparing budget requests or other reports.
- Approves and processes travel, account, invoice, and claim documents for payment.
- Codes and records all receipts and disbursement of funds.
- Reviews encumbrance or liquidation documents for accuracy and conformity with procedures and expedites financial transactions.
- Accesses or inputs information to the statewide accounting system.
- Investigates errors or problems in the processing of fiscal transactions and recommends changes in procedures.
- Issues purchase orders.
- Provides lead work direction to other bookkeeping and clerical employees.
- Performs related work as required.

Job C

Kind of Work. Serves as section chief or top assistant to an accounting director or other high-level fiscal management officer in a moderate or large-sized state department. Directs the activities of an accounting or fiscal management section consisting of several subsections or assists the supervisor with the supervision of a very large and complex accounting operation. Works closely with the chief fiscal officer in formulating fiscal policies and independently establishes new accounts in payroll procedures to accomplish the department's program. Considerable independence of action is granted the employee, with work reviewed through reports and conferences.

Essential Responsibilities

- Prepares and administers the department budget, confers with operating officials on projected needs, and devises methods of adjusting budgets so that agency programs may be carried on efficiently and effectively.
- Provides technical accounting assistance and guidance to operational accounting units within a large- or

medium-sized agency so that operating procedures and staff skills will be upgraded on a continuing basis with resultant improvement in quality and reduction in cost.
- Produces special accounting plans, reports, and analyses involving complex accounting methods and principles as a basis for decision making by the chief fiscal officer and the department head.
- Constructs and maintains the department's accounting structure and cost accounting capabilities so the department can conform to legislative intent, meet state and federal regulatory requirements, and provide the department with reporting capabilities.
- Assists in the coordination and ongoing analysis and control of fiscal matters relevant to satellite institutions under departmental supervision.

Job D

Kind of Work. Performs professional accounting work as the fiscal officer of a small department, institution, or major division, or as an assistant to a higher-level accountant in a large fiscal operation. Work involves providing a wide range of accounting services to professional and managerial employees. Assists in the development and maintenance of broad fiscal programs. Regularly performs complex fiscal analysis, prepares fiscal reports for management, and recommends alternative solutions to accounting problems. May supervise account clerks, accounting technicians, or clerical employees engaged in the fiscal operation. Receives supervision from a higher-level accountant, business manager, or other administrative employee.

Essential Responsibilities

- Helps administrative employees develop budgets to ensure that sufficient funds are available for operating needs.
- Monitors cash flow to ensure minimum adequate operating balance.
- Produces reports so that management has proper fiscal information.
- Submits reports to federal and state agencies to ensure that financial reporting requirements are met.
- Analyzes and interprets fiscal reports so that information is available in useful form.
- Instructs technicians and clerks in proper procedures to ensure smooth operation of accounting functions.
- Investigates fiscal accounting problems so that adequate solutions may be developed.
- Recommends and implements new procedures to ensure the efficient operation of the accounting section.
- Interprets state laws and department policies to ensure the legality of fiscal transactions.

Job E

Kind of Work. Performs semiprofessional accounting work within an established accounting system. Responsible for maintaining accounting records on a major set of accounts, preauditing transactions in a major activity, or handling cash receipts in a major facility, and for classifying transactions, substantiating source documents, balancing accounts, and preparing reports as prescribed. Responsible for recognizing errors or problems in the fiscal transactions of an agency and recommending alternative solutions for consideration by other staff.

Must regularly exercise initiative and independent judgment and may provide lead-work direction to account clerks or clerical employees engaged in the fiscal operation. Receives supervision from other accounting personnel.

Essential Responsibilities

- Controls expenditures so they do not exceed budget totals and prepares allotment requests in the agency's budgetary accounts.
- Processes encumbrance changes of expenditures authorization and adjusts budget as necessary and desired.
- Reconciles department accounting records with the statewide accounting system and records documents so that funds may be appropriated, allotted, encumbered, and transferred.
- Authorizes reimbursement for goods and services received by a major department.
- Develops and maintains a system of accounts receivable, including issuance of guidelines for participants and preparation of state and federal reports.
- Provides daily accounting on loans receivable or financial aids for a major college.
- Audits cost vendor statements for conformity within departmental guidelines.
- Supervises cash accounting unit and prepares reports on receipts and deposits.
- Performs related work as required.

Job F

Kind of Work. Keeps financial records when the accounts are relatively simple, or assists others in assigned work of greater difficulty where accounting operations are more complex and extensive. The work involves a combination of clerical and bookkeeping responsibilities requiring specialized training or experience. Receives direction from higher-level accounting personnel in the form of detailed instructions and close review for accuracy and conformance with law, rules, or policy. Once oriented to the work, employee may exercise independent judgment in assigned duties.

Essential Responsibilities

- Maintains complete bookkeeping records independently when scope, volume, or complexity is limited or maintains a difficult part of an extensive bookkeeping operation.
- Codes and records all receipts and disbursement of funds.
- Prepares travel, account, invoice, and claim documents for payment.
- Reviews encumbrance or liquidation documents for accuracy and conformity with procedures and expedites financial transactions.
- Prepares financial information of reports and audits, invoices, and expenditure reports.
- Keeps general, control, or subsidiary books of accounts such as cash book appropriation and disbursement ledgers and encumbrance records.
- Accesses or inputs information to the statewide accounting system as directed.
- Performs related tasks as required.

Job G

Kind of Work. Performs varied and difficult semiprofessional accounting work within an established accounting system. Maintains a complex set of accounts and works with higher management outside the accounting unit in planning and controlling expenditures. Works with higher-level employees in providing technical fiscal advice and service to functional activities. Receives supervision from higher-level management or accounting personnel. May provide lead work to lower-level accounting, bookkeeping, or clerical personnel.

Essential Responsibilities

- Assists the chief accounting officer in the preparation of all budgets to ensure continuity in financial operations.
- Prepares and assembles the biennial budget and coordinates all accounting functions for a small department according to overall plan of department head and needs expressed by activity managers.
- Maintains cost coding and allocation system for a major department to serve as a basis for reimbursement.
- Provides accounting and budgetary controls for federal, state, and private grants including reconciling bank statements and preparing reports on the status of the budget and accounts.
- Evaluates the spending progress of budget activities, ensures that budgetary limits are not exceeded, and recommends or effects changes in spending plans.
- Provides technical services to divisions of an agency in the supervision of deposits, accounts payable, procurement, and other business management areas.
- Performs related work as required.

Job H

Kind of Work. Maintains a large and complex system of accounts. Serves as a section chief in the finance division of a very large department, maintains large state-federal or state-county accounts, and oversees a major statewide accounting function in the Department of Finance. Responsible for coordinating and supervising the various phases of the accounting function. Responsibility extends to the development of procedure and policies for the work involved. Supervises a staff of accounting personnel.

Essential Responsibilities

- Provides regular budget review so that program managers have adequate funds to be effective.
- Conducts financial analysis for economical and equitable distribution or redistribution of agency resource.
- Prepares long- and short-range program recommendations for fiscal action so that agency policies are consistent.
- Plans and directs the computerization of systems applied to fiscal services to ensure efficient operation.
- Develops and defines accounting office procedures to ensure the efficient delivery of fiscal services.
- Reviews and analyzes cost accounting computer output to ensure proper documentation of projected cost as required by federal policy and procedures.
- Prepares and supervises the preparation of federal budgets and grant requests, financial plans, and expenditure reports so that they accurately reflect needs and intent of the agency.

- Develops accounting and documentation procedures for county welfare departments so that state and federal auditing and reporting requirements are met.
- Establishes and maintains a financial reporting system for all federal and other nonstate funding sources so that all fiscal reporting requirements are adhered to on a timely and accurate basis.
- Assists grantee agencies in proper reporting procedures under federal grant programs so that requirements for reimbursement may be made on a timely basis.
- Determines the statewide indirect costs so that all state agencies are allocated their proportionate share of indirect costs.
- Supervises the review and processing of all encumbrance documents submitted to the Department of Finance so that necessary accounting information is recorded accurately and promptly in the accounting system.

Chapter 6 Person-Based Structures

Chapter Outline

History buffs tell us that some form of job evaluation was in use when the pharaohs built the pyramids. Chinese emperors managed the Great Wall construction with the assistance of job evaluation. In the United States, job evaluation in the public sector came into use in the 1880s, when Chicago reformers were trying to put an end to patronage in government hiring and pay practices. Setting pay based not on who you voted for or who you could boast of for family connections but instead on the work you did was a revolutionary old idea.

The logic underlying job-based pay structures flows from scientific management, championed by Taylor in the 1930s. Work was broken into a series of steps and analyzed so that the "one best way," the most efficient way to perform every element of the job (right down to the level of how to shovel coal), could be specified. Strategically, Taylor's approach fit with the mass production technology which was revolutionizing the way work was done and the way companies sought to achieve competitive advantage (cheaper, faster, better).

While academics continue to debate whether Taylorism is out of fashion, its influence pervades our lives. Not only are jobs analyzed and evaluated in terms of the "best way," but cookbooks and software manuals specify the methods for baking a cake or using a program as a series of simple, basic steps. Golf is analyzed as a series of basic tasks that can be combined successfully to lower one's handicap. Work, play, in all daily life, "Taylor's thinking so permeates the soil of modern life we no longer realize it is there."[1]

But in today's "new work," employees are told they must go beyond the tasks specified in their job descriptions. They must know more, think more on the job, take personal responsibility for their results. Continuous learning and improvement, flexibility, participation and partnership are essential for achieving competitive advantage today. Pay systems need to support this new culture. Person-based structures hold out that promise. However, as we discuss person-based systems in this chapter, keep in mind that underlying Tayloristic logic.[2]

The logic supporting person-based approaches is that the resulting structures are believed to be more flexible and reinforce continuous learning. Internal pay structures are based on differences in people's skills or competencies relevant to the work performed.

Person-based approaches are the topic of this chapter. At the end of this chapter, we shall discuss the usefulness of the various approaches—job and person-based—for determining internal structures.

Recall the contrasts in the procedures used in job-based versus people-based structures from Exhibit 4.2. The exhibit points out the similarities in the logic underlying these approaches. No matter the basis for the structure, a way is needed to (1) collect information about the work, (2) organize and summarize that information to permit (3) assessing what is important or of value to the organization, then (4) evaluating similarities and differences in the work. The logic underpins both job- and person-based approaches. The last two chapters discussed the process for job-based structures (job analysis and job evaluation). This chapter will discuss the process for person-based structures. As you will see, similarities abound.

---

[1]Robert Kanigel, *The One Best Way* (New York: Viking, 1997).

[2]C. A.Bartlett and Sumantra Ghoshal, "The Myth of the Generic Manager: New Personal Competencies for New Management Roles,." *California Management Review* 40, no. 1 (1997), pp. 92-105.

PERSON-BASED STRUCTURES: SKILL PLANS

Skill-based plans typically refer to so-called blue collar work; competencies refer to so-called white-collar work. The distinctions are at best ambiguous. But as we begin our discussion of skill-based plans, keep in mind that the majority of applications have been in manufacturing and assembly work.

Structures based on skill pay individuals according to what they have demonstrated rather than on the particular job they are doing. A fundamental distinction is that a person is paid for the skills for which they have been certified regardless of whether the job performed requires those particular skills. Exxon pays operators at its refinery in Baytown, Texas, for the multiple skills in which they are certified, whether Exxon assigns them to operations work or to maintenance tasks. Under job-based plans, employees are paid for the job they perform regardless of the skills they possess.

Skill-based structures link pay to the depth or breadth of the skills, abilities, and knowledge a person acquires that is relevant to the work. Typically applies to operators, technicians, and office work where the work can be specified and defined.

Types of Skill Plans

Skill plans can focus on depth (specialists in corporate law, finance, or welding and hydraulic maintenance) or breadth (generalists with knowledge in all phases of operations including marketing, manufacturing, finance, and human resources).

Specialist: In Depth. Basing pay structures on knowledge possessed by individual employees is not new. The pay structures for your elementary or high school teachers have long been based on their knowledge as measured by education level. A typical teacher's contract specifies a series of steps, with each step corresponding to a level of education. A bachelor's degree in education is step one and is the minimum required for hiring. To advance a step to higher pay requires additional education. For example, an additional nine semester hours of coursework earns an increase of $225 in Ithaca, New York. Of course, an additional advancement in pay is also provided for seniority. The result can be that two teachers may receive different pay rates for doing essentially the same job—teaching English to high school juniors. The pay is based on the knowledge of the individual doing the job (measured by number of college credits and experience) rather than job content. The presumption is that teachers with more knowledge are more effective and more flexible—able to teach seniors, too.

Generalist/Multiskill Based: Breadth. As with teachers, employees in a multiskill system earn pay increases by acquiring new knowledge, but the knowledge is specific to a range of related jobs. An example from Borg-Warner (Exhibit 6.1) illustrates the system. Borg-Warner assembles drive chains for automobile transmissions. Originally, seven different jobs were involved in the assembly process, starting with stackers, and moving up through packers, assemblers, and riveters. When Borg-Warner switched to

Exhibit 6.1 Borg-Warner Automotive Assembly Classifications

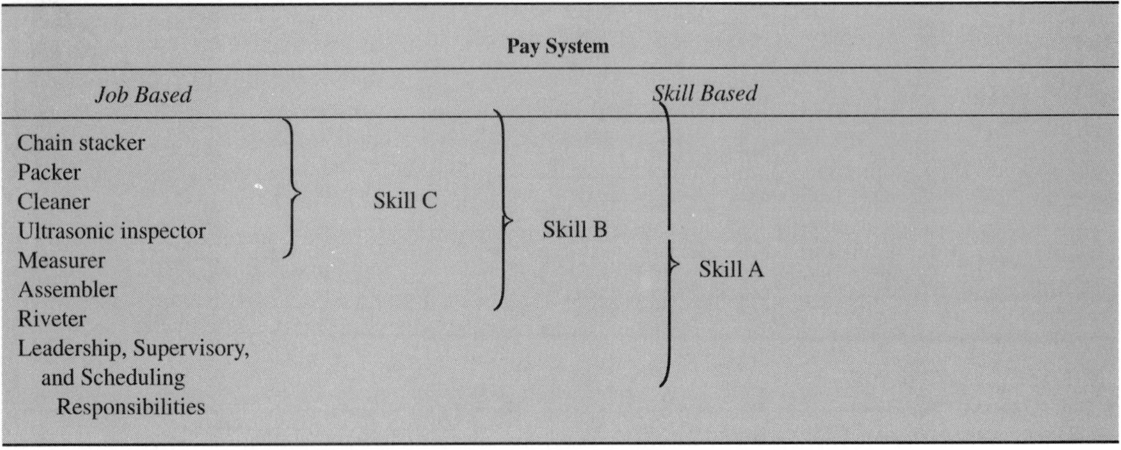

a skill-based pay system, these seven jobs were reorganized into three broad categories: cell operators A, B, and C. Cell operator C is an entry-level position. Once operator Cs can demonstrate mastery of the stacker through measurer jobs, they are eligible to train for operator B jobs. With each mastery comes a pay raise. Operator Bs can be rotated among any of the jobs for which they have demonstrated mastery, including C-level jobs. An operator B can do all the jobs required, including stacking, and still receive operator B pay. Operator As can also do all jobs, plus they assume responsibility for scheduling and supervising teams. The advantage to Borg-Warner is workforce flexibility and, hence, lower staffing levels.

The multiskilled system at Borg-Warner differs from the system for teachers in that the responsibilities assigned to an employee in a multiskill system can change drastically over a short period of time, whereas teachers' job responsibilities do not vary on a day-to-day basis.

Purpose of the Skill-based Structure

Employers who switch from a job-based to a person-based system do so in the hope that the new system will do a better job fulfilling the objectives for an internally consistent structure. Once again we hark back to Chapter 3 to recall that an internally consistent pay structure supports the work flow, is fair to employees, and directs their behavior toward organization objectives.

Support work flow. One of the main advantages of skill based plans is that they can more easily match people to a changing work flow. An example might be a national hotel chain that moves many of its people to the hotel's front desk between 4 P.M. and 7 P.M., when the majority of guests check in. After 7 P.M., many of these same employees move to the food and beverage service area to match the demand for room service and dining room service. By ensuring that guests will not have to wait long to check in or to eat, the hotel provides a high level of service with fewer staff. (Yes, the same thought occurred to us on the quality of the resulting meals.)

Fair to Employees. Employees like the potential of higher pay that comes with skill-based plans. And by encouraging employees to take charge of their own development, skill-based plans may give them more control over their work lives.

However, issues of fairness have not been addressed yet. For example, favoritism and bias may play a role in determining who gets first crack at the training necessary to become certified at higher-paying skill levels. Employees complain that they are forced to pick up the slack for those who are out for training. And the courts have not yet been asked to rule on whether or not it is impermissible discrimination if two people do the same task but for different pay.

Directs Behavior toward Organization Objectives. Person-based plans have the potential to clarify new standards and behavioral expectations. They let employees know that more is expected than just coming to work and doing what they are told.[3] "It's not in my job description" is no longer a relevant response. Skill-based plans try to encourage employees to see their responsibility more broadly than what it does or does not say in a job description. Skill-based plans address the issue of "what difference does it make to what I do."

SKILL ANALYSIS

Skill analysis is a systematic process to identify and collect information about skills required to perform work in an organization.

The parallel to job analysis should be obvious. If structures are to be based on skills, some way is needed to determine the different skills required for the organization to be successful. Data are required to help describe, certify, and value these skills. Exhibit 6.2 identifies the major skill analysis decisions: (1) What information should be collected? (2) What methods should be used? (3) Who should be involved? (4) How useful are the results for pay purposes? These are exactly the same decisions managers face in job analysis.

What Information to Collect?

Exhibit 6.3 defines some of the terms used in skill analysis. Skills, the smallest unit of analysis, are grouped into skill blocks, which is analogous to a job or part of a job. A

[3] G. Douglas Jenkins, Jr., Gerald E. Ledford, Jr., Nina Gupta, and D. Harold Doty, *Skill-Based Pay* (Scottsdale, AZ: American Compensation Association, 1992).

Exhibit 6.2 Determining the Internal Skill-Based Structure

Internal consistency work relationships within the organization → **Skill analysis** → **Skill blocks** → **Skill certification** → **Skill-based structure**

Basic Decisions

- What is the objective of the plan?
- What information should be collected?
- What methods should be used to determine and certify skills?
- Who should be involved?
- How useful are the results for pay purposes?

Exhibit 6.3

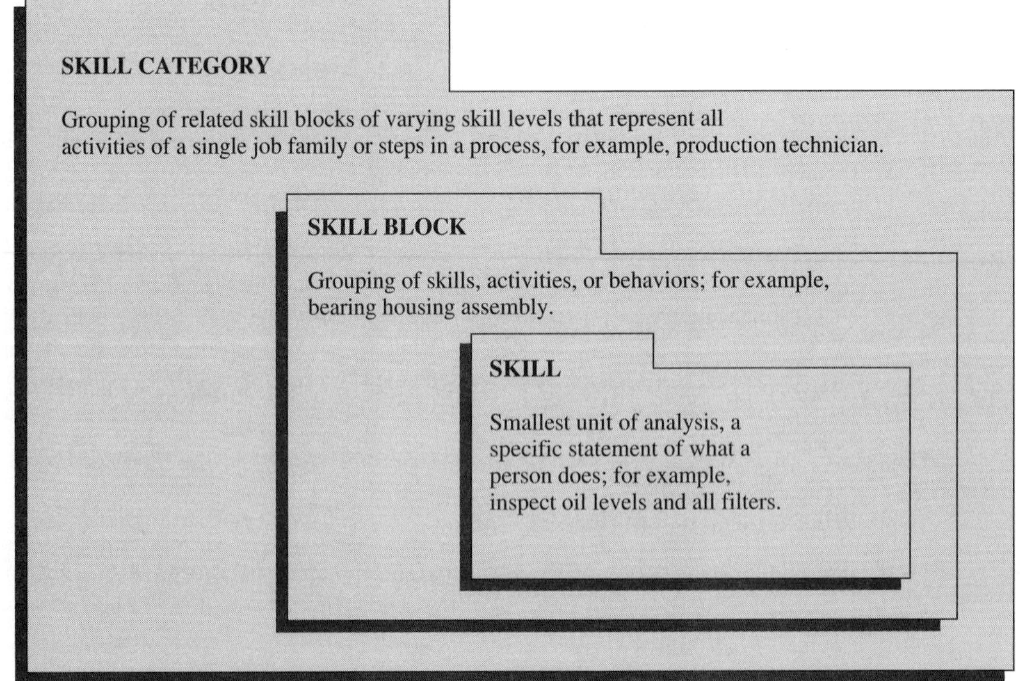

Exhibit 6.4 General Mills Skills-Based Structure

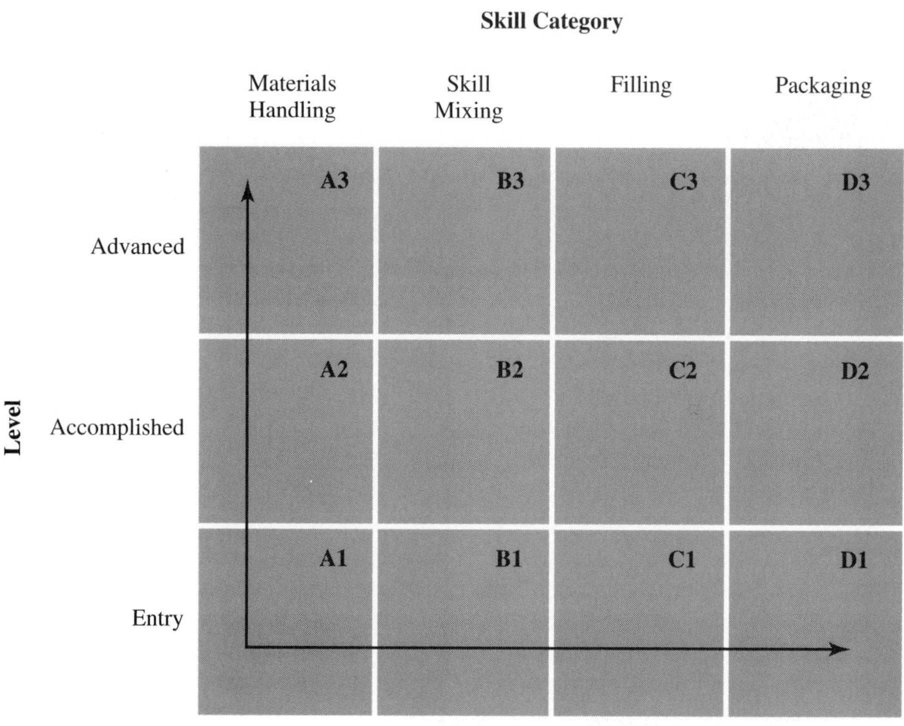

number of related skill blocks of varying levels of difficulty make up a skill category. But a caution—the definitions of terms are still evolving, so they may be used differently in different applications.

Food products manufacturer General Mills uses four skill categories corresponding to the steps in the production process: materials handling, mixing, filling, and packaging.[4] Each skill category has three blocks: (1) entry level, (2) accomplished, and (3) advanced. Exhibit 6.4 is a schematic of their plan. It shows that a new employee can start at entry level in materials handling and, after being certified on all skills included in skill block A1, can begin training for skills in either B1 or A2.

A skill-based plan for technicians at FMC is more fully developed in Exhibit 6.5. The plan has three types of skills: foundation, core electives, and optional electives.

- *Foundation.* This group includes a quality seminar, videos on materials handling and hazardous materials, a three-day safety workshop, and a half-day orientation. All foundation competencies are mandatory and must be certified to reach the Technician I rate ($11).

[4]Gerald E. Ledford, Jr., "Three Case Studies of Skill-Based Pay: An Overview," *Compensation and Benefits Review* (March/April 1991), pp. 11–23. Pages 23–77 of this issue contain case studies of applications at General Mills, Northern Telecom, and Honeywell.

EXHIBIT 6.5 Technician Skill-Based Structure

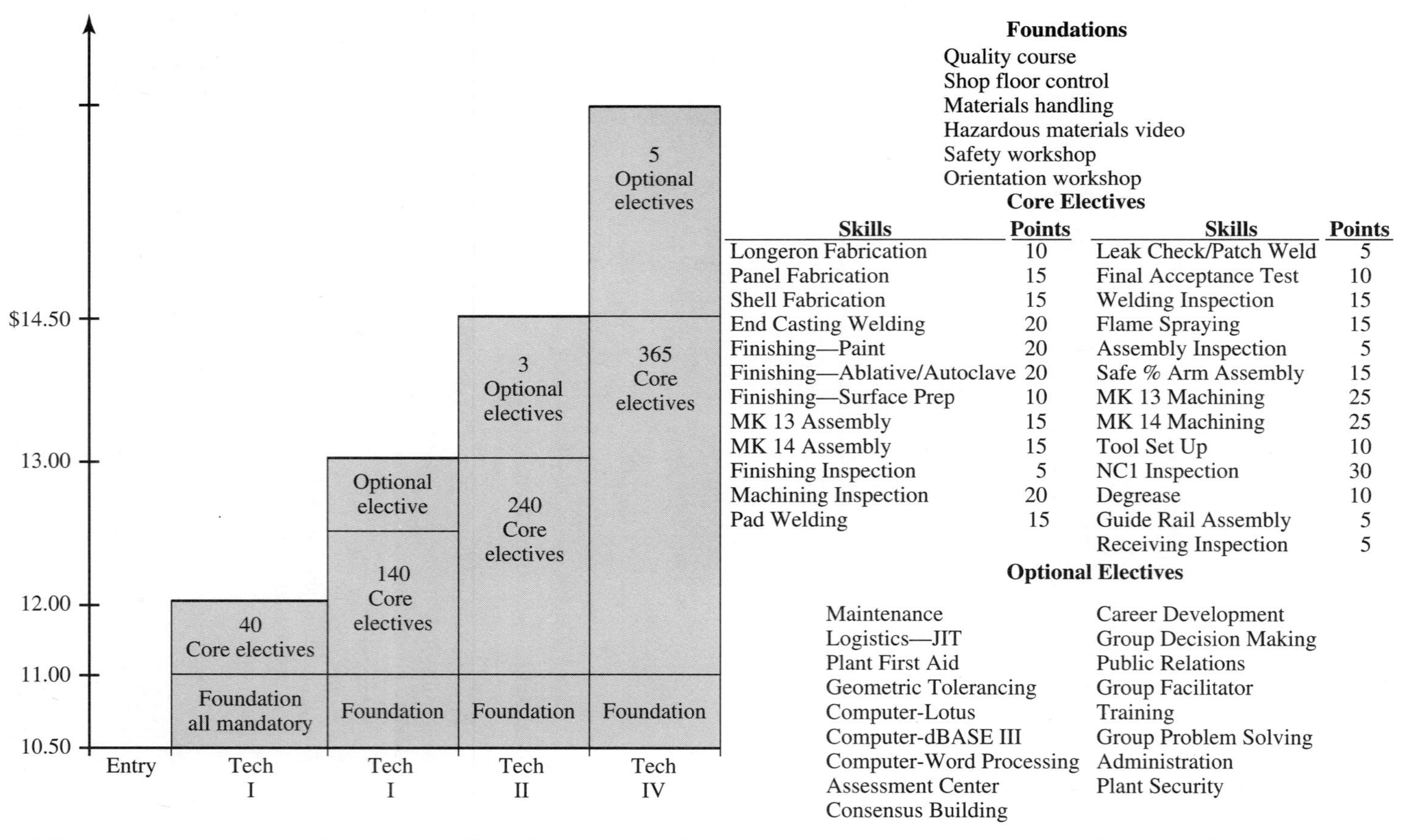

Foundations

Quality course
Shop floor control
Materials handling
Hazardous materials video
Safety workshop
Orientation workshop

Core Electives

Skills	Points	Skills	Points
Longeron Fabrication	10	Leak Check/Patch Weld	5
Panel Fabrication	15	Final Acceptance Test	10
Shell Fabrication	15	Welding Inspection	15
End Casting Welding	20	Flame Spraying	15
Finishing—Paint	20	Assembly Inspection	5
Finishing—Ablative/Autoclave	20	Safe % Arm Assembly	15
Finishing—Surface Prep	10	MK 13 Machining	25
MK 13 Assembly	15	MK 14 Machining	25
MK 14 Assembly	15	Tool Set Up	10
Finishing Inspection	5	NC1 Inspection	30
Machining Inspection	20	Degrease	10
Pad Welding	15	Guide Rail Assembly	5
		Receiving Inspection	5

Optional Electives

Maintenance	Career Development
Logistics—JIT	Group Decision Making
Plant First Aid	Public Relations
Geometric Tolerancing	Group Facilitator
Computer-Lotus	Training
Computer-dBASE III	Group Problem Solving
Computer-Word Processing	Administration
Assessment Center	Plant Security
Consensus Building	

- *Core electives.* These are necessary to the facility's operations (e.g., fabrication, welding, painting, finishing, assembly, inspection). Each skill is assigned a point value.
- *Optional electives.* These are additional specialized competencies ranging from computer applications to team leadership and consensus building.

To reach technician II ($12 per hour), 40 core elective points (of 370) must be certified, in addition to the foundation competencies. To reach Technician III, an additional 100 points of core electives must be certified, plus three optional electives.

A fully qualified Technician IV (e.g., certified as mastering foundations, 365 points of core electives, and five optional electives) is able to perform all work in a cell at the facility. Technician IV earns $14.50 per hour and can be assigned to any task, Technician III earns $13 per hour and can handle more tasks than Technician II, and so on.

Notice that FMC's terminology differs from General Mills' in that the skills are not grouped into blocks, and they are assigned points. Nevertheless, the approach should look familiar to any college student: required courses, required credits chosen among specific categories, electives, and optional electives. There is a minor difference, of course—FMC employees get paid for passing these skills, whereas college students pay to take courses!

Whom to Involve?

Employee involvement is almost built into skill-based plans. Employees are the source of information on defining the skills, arranging them into a hierarchy, and bundling them into skill blocks. Employees and managers are the source of expertise on certifying whether a person actually possesses the skills.

Establish Certification Methods

How should employees be certified that they possess the skill and are able to apply it? Who should be involved in the process? Practice varies widely. Some organizations use peer review, on-the-job demonstrations, and tests for certification. This is similar to the traditional craft approach (i.e., apprentice, journeyman, and master). Still others require successful completion of formal courses, plus time on the job.

In their airbeg facility in Mesa, Arizona, TRW discovered that a problem with this last approach is that sitting in the classroom and doing the time doesn't guarantee that anything was learned.[5] Yet no one was willing to take the responsibility for refusing to certify, since an extra signoff beyond classroom participation was not part of the original system. Northern Telecom uses a preassessment meeting between supervisor and employee to discuss skill accomplishments and goals and training needs. Subsequently, a certification committee made up of employees and supervisors examines employees to determine whether they can be certified in the skills. Honeywell's plan calls for evaluating employees during the six months after they have learned the skills. Again, leaders and peers are used in the certification process.

---

[5]B. Murray and B. Gerhart, "An Empirical Analysis of a Skill-Based Pay Program and Plant Performance Outcomes," *Academy of Management Journal* 41, (1998), pp. 68-78.

Newer skill-based applications appear to be moving away from an on-demand review and toward scheduling fixed review points in the year. The objective is to cut down on administrative time—everything is already on the schedule, so becomes part of the routine—and make it easier to budget and control payroll increases. Other changes include ongoing recertifications, which replace the traditional one-time certification process and help ensure skills are kept fresh, and skill assessments conducted not only by the immediate supervisor but by peers and participants themselves. Again, it may be difficult to add more certification requirements once a system is in place. Plus, all of these changes build bureaucracy.

In light of the detailed bureaucracy that has grown up around job evaluation, we confidently predict a growth of procedures here, too.[6] The whole approach to certification may be fraught with potential legal vulnerabilities if employees who fail to be certified challenge the process. At this point, very little attention has been devoted to assessor training or validating the certification process. On the face of it, just as employment tests used for hiring and promotion decisions are vulnerable to regulatory pressures, so too are certification procedures used to determine pay increases. Clearly, there is a need to ensure that procedures are work related and free of bias.

PERSON-BASED STRUCTURES: COMPETENCIES

There is confusion over what competencies are and what they are supposed to accomplish. As with job evaluation, multiple perspectives abound. Are competencies a skill that can be learned and developed or a trait which is more difficult to learn and includes attitudes and motives? Do competencies focus on the minimum requirements that the organization needs to stay in business or on outstanding performance? Are they characteristics of the organization, or of the employee? Unfortunately, at the present time, the answer to all of these questions, is "yes."[7] A lack of consensus means that competencies can be a number of things; consequently they stand in danger of becoming nothing.

Competency systems have generally been developed for so-called white collar workers. Exhibit 6.6 tries to distinguish among the terms used to discuss competencies. Rather than starting with the most concrete, as we did with skills and tasks in previous exhibits, this time we start at the other extreme with the least concrete. This is the *core competency,* generally defined as a key area of skill and competence required to ensure the success of the organization. These are often taken from mission statements that express an organization's philosophy, mission, values, business strategies, and plans.

Competency sets begin to translate each core competency into action. For "business awareness," for example, competency sets might be related to organizational understanding, cost management, third-party relationships, ability to identify business opportunities.

---

[6]E. E. Lawler III, G. E. Ledford, Jr., and L. Chang, "Who Uses Skill-Based Pay and Why," *Compensation and Benefits Review* 2, no. 5 (1993), pp. 22–26. G. E. Ledford, Jr. "The Effectiveness of Skill-Based Pay," *Perspectives in Total Compensation* 1, no. 1 (1990).

[7]Patricia Zingheim, Gerald E. Ledford, Jr., and Jay R. Schuster, "Competencies and Competency Models: Does One Size Fit All?" *ACA Journal,* Spring 1996, pp. 56–65.

EXHIBIT 6.6

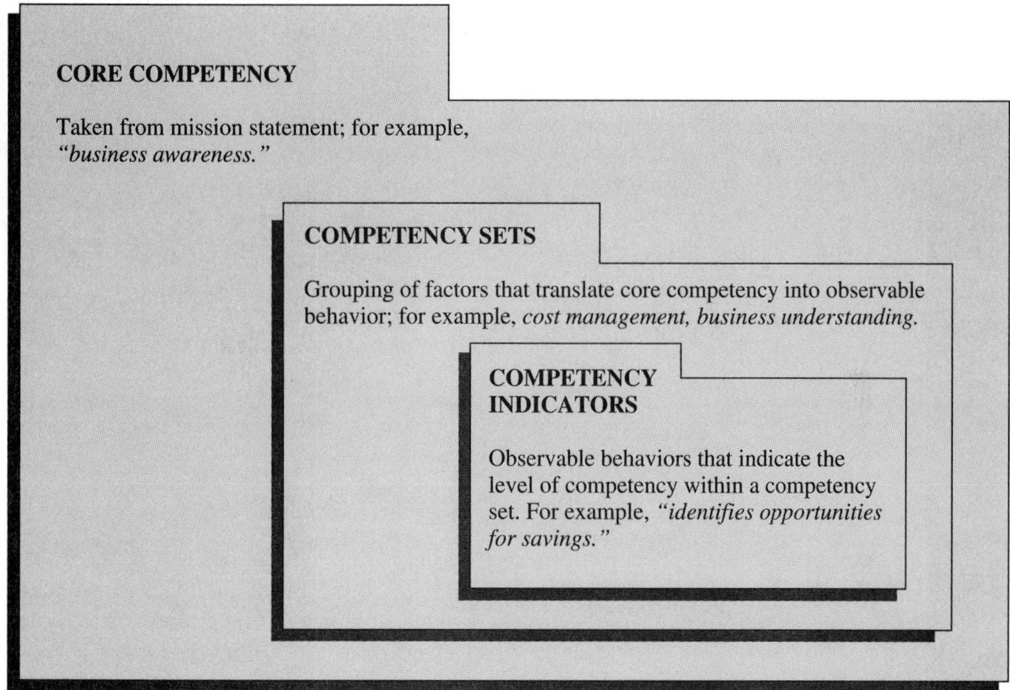

Competency indicators are the observable behaviors which indicate the level of competency within each set. These indicators may be used for staffing and evaluation as well as for pay purposes.

Exhibit 6.7 shows TRW's core competencies and competency sets for its human resource management department. Because the competency sets are assumed to be critical to the success of the business, they should be demonstrated to some degree by all HR employees. However, a single individual would not be expected to reach the highest level in all competencies. Rather, the HR function would want to be sure it possessed all levels of mastery of all the core competencies among its entire HRM group.

The *competency indicators* identify the degree of a competency required at each level of complexity of the work. Exhibit 6.8 shows five levels of competency indicators for the *competency impact and influence.* These behavioral anchors make the competency more concrete. The levels range from "uses direct persuasion" at level one to "uses experts or other third parties to influence" at level five. Dimensions on the behavioral anchored scale might include the intensity of action, the degree of impact of the action, its complexity, and the amount of effort expended. This should all look familiar from the job analysis questionnaires and the process of determining degrees of compensable factors in the previous two chapters.

Exhibit 6.7 TRW's Human Resources Management Core Competencies

Human Resources Success Key Profile Competencies

Integrity — Instilling the trust and respect of others by being reasonably open and candid about opinions and attitudes; keeping sensitive organizational information confidential; behaving in a fair and ethical manner; demonstrating a sense of corporate responsibility.

Efficiency — Performing in an efficient, cost effective manner while maintaining high standards.

Objectivity — Approaching each problem situation with a clear perception of organizational and political reality.

Proactivity — Initiating action to avoid potential problems and anticipating change.

Risk Taking — Expressing opinions and taking action under conditions of uncertainty.

Decisiveness — Making effective and timely decisions.

Professionalism — Maintaining a sensitivity and consciousness about one's professional image and that of the HR function both internal and external to TRW.

Negotiation Skills — Recognizing confrontational situations appropriate to negotiations; persuading others to relinquish demands or accept less than their original position; facilitating a "win-win" situation.

Communication Skills — Communicating information through appropriate organizational channels and effectively using written material, oral presentations, verbal interchange and non-verbal cues.

Team Management Skills — Understanding and utilizing group process skills to accomplish organizationally driven and team-oriented tasks.

Business Skills

Industry Knowledge — Understanding the industry in which the organization competes including the value chain, suppliers, buyers, competitors and potential entrants; understanding the customers and how the organization satisfies customer needs; ability to benchmark key performance measures against centers of excellence from the industry.

Strategic Management — Maintaining an awareness of external and internal forces that will significantly impact the future effectiveness and efficiency of the organization anticipating, understanding and planning for demographic, economic, social and political changes important to the organization.

Organizational Awareness — Understanding the business operations, products/services, how the business competes, what current and future issues confront the organization, near-term and long-range plans, and the cultural/value systems impacting organizational performance; understanding how the organization fits within the TRW corporate structure.

Total Quality Management — Demonstrating the leadership, training, and motivation to improve continuously the organization's management and operations.

General Management Skills — Possessing general knowledge and understanding in business areas such as finance, sales and marketing, law and information technology.

Partnership with Management Team — Ability to serve as a valuable member of the management team and contribute to the accomplishment of the organization's business and financial goals.

HR Functional Leadership

Network Building — Working effectively with others at TRW both within and outside of the HR function, and with people outside TRW ; utilizing these contacts to build and strengthen a support base.

Setting the Vision for HR — Establishing, communicating, and mobilizing the HR Staff with a vision and direction for the function.

Selecting & Developing Staff — Recruiting, selecting, and retaining a high achievement staff; identifying and implementing organizational and individual development plans for increased functional excellence; providing challenging assignments for staff.

Value-Added Perspective of HR — Perceiving and taking advantage of opportunities for the HR function to deliver value-added services and programs in support of the business; communicating to management how HR can contlribute to the organization.

HR Technical Skills

HR Planning — Developing and implementing HR systems, programs and processes which support the business strategies and address the unique challenges facing the organization.

Communications — Developing and implementing an effective two-way employee communications program in the organization that fosters understanding of key business and HR issues.

Work Force Diversity — Understanding the impact demographic changes will have on the characteristics of the work force and determining how current management and HR practices must be modified to address the needs of the new work force; understanding and addressing all EEO/AAP legal requirements.

Selection & Placement — Identifying the organization's human resource needs, understanding recruitment and selection practices to meet those needs; implementing effective external and internal placement processes; designing and implementing an effective performance management system.

Training & Development — Identifying and analyzing employee training and development needs; planning cost effective training activities to meet the needs of the current and future organization; formulating development plans that focus on building the skills of employees.

HR Information Systems — Assessing the type of employee information TRW requires to effectively manage the business; implementing and maintaining the systems to gather, analyze, store and retrieve that information.

Compensation & Benefits — Managing the assessment, design, administration and cost effectiveness of fair, equitable and leading edge compensation, benefits and other reward systems that serve to attract, motivate and retain the diversity of employees required by the organization.

Health, Safety, & Security — Understanding the strategic health, safety, and security issues from both the employee and organizational perspective; understanding the laws and regulations that impact the HR functional area; implementing programs to maintain employee wellness and organizational stability.

Organizational Effectiveness — Effecting organizational change consistent with evolving organizational needs and environmental requirements; designing and putting in place organization structures that reduce bureaucracy and encourage empowerment of employee; managing cultural change within the organization to impact organizational effectiveness.

Employee & Labor Relations — Interpreting the laws and regulations that impact employees from both union and union-free environments; being aware of the issues involved in maintaining union-free status; applying collective bargaining strategies and tactics; instituting discipline and grievance policies for all employees; planning and implementing sound downsizing and outplacement programs when required.

Note on HR Technical Skills: *These skills are considered important for all HR professionals but the weighting of importance and the level of proficiency varies for different positions, organizations and business conditions. HR professionals who are specialists are expected to have expertise in their areas and be familiar with how other HR areas interact with their specialty.*

EXHIBIT 6.8 Sample Behavioral Competency Description

Impact and Influence: The intention to persuade, convince or influence to have a specific impact. It includes the ability to anticipate and respond to the needs and concerns of others.

"Impact and Influence" is one of the competencies considered "most critical".

LEVEL	BEHAVIORS
0: Not shown	• Lets things happen • Quotes policy and issues instruction
1: Direct persuasion	• Uses direct persuasion in a discussion or presentation • Appeals to reason; uses data or concrete examples • Does not adapt presentation to the interest and level of the audience • Reiterates the same points when confronted with opposition
2: Multiple attempts to persuade	• Tries different tactics when attempting to persuade without necessarily making an effort to adapt to the level or interest of an audience (e.g., making two or more different arguments or points in a discussion)
3: Builds trust and fosters win-win mentality (expected performance level)	• Tailors presentations or discussions to appeal to the interest and level of others • Looks for the "win-win" opportunities • Demonstrates sensitivity and understanding of others in detecting underlying concerns, interests or emotions, and uses that understanding to develop effective responses to objections
4: Multiple actions to influence	• Takes more than one action to influence, with each action adapted to the specific audience (e.g., a group meeting to present the situation, followed by individual meetings) • May include taking a well-thought-out unusual action to have a specific impact
5: Influences through others	• Uses experts or other third parties to influence • Develops and maintains a planned network of relationships with customers, internal peers and industry colleagues • When required, assembles "behind the scenes" support for ideas regarding opportunities and/or solving problems

Reprinted from *Raising the Bar:* Using Competencies to Enhance Employee Performance with permission from the American Compensation Association (ACA), 14040 N. Northsight Blvd., Scottsdale, AZ U.S.A. 85260; telephone (602) 483-8352. © ACA.

Defining Competencies

Just as there are competency indicators required in a job (or work role), there are competencies possessed by individuals. Those competencies are most commonly categorized by the so-called "iceberg model," shown in Exhibit 6.9.[8] Individual competence resides in five areas:

Skills (demonstration of expertise)
Knowledge (accumulated information)
Self-concepts (attitudes, values, self image)
Traits (general disposition to behave in a certain way)
Motives (recurrent thoughts that drive behaviors).

As the legions of movie fans who saw the recent megahit "Titanic" can attest, only a small part of an iceberg is visible above water. So, too, with individual competence. Skills and knowledge are relatively observable and measurable. Consequently, the exhibit shows them "above water." These two categories provide the *essential characteristics that everyone needs to be effective in a given job.* In a team environment, for example, these might include effective listening and group problem-solving. These skills can be acquired through training and development.

The other three characteristics—self-concepts, traits and motives—are "under water." That is, they are not visible; they must be inferred from actions. However, according to psychologists, these three are judged to be the *differentiating competencies—critical factors that distinguish superior performance from average performance.*[9] In a team environment, differentiating characteristics might include a strong identification with the team (self-concept), personal flexibility (trait), and the drive to produce results (motive). These competencies are considered a more important basis for long-term success for both the individual and the organization. However, many critics believe that the vagueness and subjectivity (what exactly *are* this person's motives?) make competencies a "risky foundation for a pay system."[10]

One consulting firm says that how you define competencies should be influenced by how the organization plans to apply competencies.[11] If the goal is to integrate an entire HR system, broader definitions are appropriate. If the goal is pay or development decisions only, competencies ought to focus primarily on knowledge- and skill-based behaviors. This firm defines competencies as "those behaviors that excellent performers exhibit much more consistently than average performers; a

---

[8]Lyle M. Spencer, Jr. and Signe M. Spencer, *Competence at Work* (New York: John Wiley and Sons, 1993).

[9]Zingheim, Ledford, and Schuster, "Competencies and Competency Models."

[10]Edward E. Lawler III, "From Job-Based to Competency-Based Organizations," *Journal of Organizational Behavior* 15 (1994), pp. 3–15.

[11]Graham L. O'Neill and David Doig, "Definition and Use of Competencies by Australian Organizations: A Survey of HR Practitioners," *ACA Journal,* Winter 1997, pp. 45–56; Kathleen Guinn, "Performance Management for Evolving Self-Directed Work Teams," *ACA Journal,* Winter 1995, pp. 74–81; Sandra O'Neal, "Competencies and Pay in the Evolving World of Work," *ACA Journal,* Autumn 1995, pp. 72–79.

EXHIBIT 6.9 Iceberg Model of Competency Levels

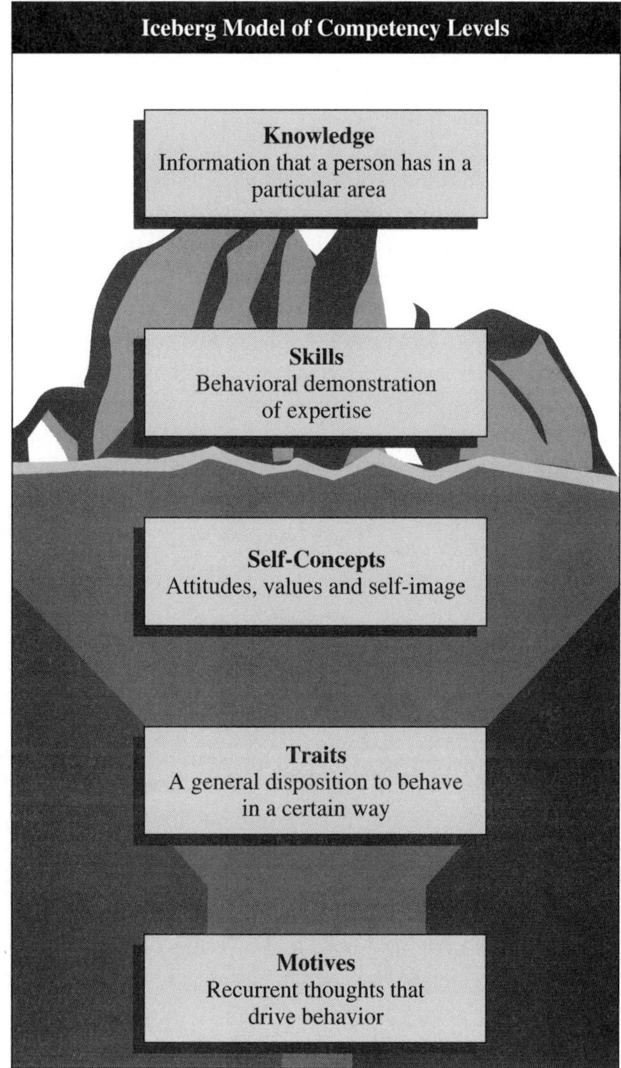

collection of observable behaviors (not a single behavior) that require no inference, assumption or interpretation."[12]

So there is as yet no common agreement on defining competencies. However, that has not stopped a number of compensation consulting companies from moving ahead with them.

[12]*Competencies, Performance and Pay 1995* (New York: William M. Mercer Companies, Inc. 1995).

Purpose of the Competency-Based Structure

Do competencies help provide an internally consistent structure? Using our by-now familiar yardstick, how well do competencies support the work flow, treat employees fairly, and direct their behavior toward organization objectives?

Work Flow. As you can judge from reading the competencies in the previous exhibits, competencies are identified to ensure that all the critical needs of the organization are met. For example, TRW notes on its HR technical skills: "These skills are considered important for all HR professionals but the weighting of importance and the level of proficiency varies for different positions, organizations, and business conditions." So rather than having the skills to smoothly perform today's work, the emphasis is on competence that will serve as conditions change.

Fair to Employees. Advocates of competencies say they can empower employees to take charge of their own development. By focusing on optimum performance rather than average performance, competencies can help employees maintain their marketability.[13] They are consistent with the new employer-employee contract, wherein the organization provides individuals with opportunities to develop in exchange for their labor. Competencies provide the vehicle for this transaction.

On the other hand, critics of competencies worry that the field is going back to the 1950s and 1960s, where basing pay on personal characteristics, including race and sex, was standard practice.[14] Basing pay on personal traits that cannot be documented seems suspect. Trying to justify pay differences based on competencies to employees has risks that need to be managed.

Direct Behavior toward Organization Objectives. The main appeal of competencies is the direct link to the organization's strategy. Rather than involving platoons of employees on committees deciding what tasks they do, the process of identifying competencies starts with the company, or its consultants, deciding what is the heart of the organization: What is it that will spell success for the company? The potential for refocusing and redirecting toward core issues is the biggest selling point for a competency approach.[15]

As with any work analysis, the process may identify the organization's strategy, but its effect on actual behaviors is less apparent. Recall, however, that under a point job evaluation plan, identifying compensable factors also involves identifying the factors that support the organization strategy.

---

[13]Jill Kanin-Lovers, Andrew S. Richter, and Randy Simon, "Competency-Linked Role Evaluation—Management Owned and Operated," *Journal of Compensation and Benefits,* January–February 1995, pp. 53–58.

[14]Lawler, "From Job-Based to Competency-Based Organizations."

[15]C. K. Prahalad and Gary Hamel, "The Core Competence of the Corporation," *Harvard Business Review,* May–June 1990, pp 79–91.

Mercer has posted its *Global Competencies, Performance and Pay* publication on its web site: **http://www.mercer.com** How does Mercer define competencies? Look at another consulting firm's web site (e.g., Towers Perrin at **http://www .towersperrin.com** or Hay at **http://www.haygroup.com**). What information do they offer on competencies? How do other consultants define competencies? If Mercer's competencies can be applied at any company, how can they be strategic (difficult to imitate or unique)?

COMPETENCY ANALYSIS

Because they stem from each organization's mission statement or its strategy to achieve competitive advantage, you might conclude that the core competencies would be unique for each company. They are not. In fact, one analysis showed that most organizations appear to choose from the same list of core competencies.[16] Exhibit 6.10 shows this list of the 20 most popular core competencies. The list takes on the feel of the Boy Scout pledge: trustworthy, kind. . . What may differ among organizations, however, is how they operationalize these core competencies. This parallels an issue we discussed in the strategy chapter: There may be only slight differences in the words, but the actions differ.

Whom to Involve?

Like compensable factors, competencies are derived from the executive leadership's beliefs about the organization and its strategic intent. However, anecdotal evidence indicates that not all employees understand that connection. Employees at one bank insisted that processing student tuition loans was a different competency from processing auto loans. The law department at Polaroid generated a list of over 1,000 competencies they felt were unique to the law department and that created value for the organization.

The issues of employee involvement and employee acceptability are as important with skill-based plans as they are with job-based plans.[17] While initially skill-based plans were heralded for their simplicity, which theoretically made them easier to understand and thus more acceptable, as use of the plans grows, they tend to become more and more bureaucratic. So the initial advantage of simplicity is lost for skill-based systems. Simplicity is a characteristic that never marked competencies. A plan can take up to two years to design.

Exhibit 6.11 shows part of the competencies used by a major toy company. This is one of eight competencies for the marketing department. Other departments have

[16]Zingheim, Ledford, and Schuster, "Competencies and Competency Models," *Raising the Bar: Using Competencies to Enhance Employee Performance* (Scottsdale, AZ: American Compensation Association, 1996).

[17]Graham L. O'Neill and Deirdre Lander, "A Framework for Skill-Based Pay Plans," *ACA Journal,* Winter 1993/94, pp. 14–27.

Exhibit 6.10 The Top Twenty Competencies

Achievement orientation
Concern of quality
Initiative
Interpersonal understanding
Customer-service orientation
Influence and impact
Organization awareness
Networking
Directiveness
Teamwork and cooperation
Developing others
Team leadership
Technical expertise
Information seeking
Analytical thinking
Conceptual thinking
Self-control
Self-confidence
Business orientation
Flexibility

separate competencies. Notice the level of detail. While it may be useful for career development, it is not clear whether all this information is necessary, much less useful, for compensation purposes.

Establish Certification Methods

The heart of the person-based plans is that employees get paid for the relevant skills or competencies they possess, but not necessarily the ones they use. Skill-based plans assume that possessing these skills will make it easier to match work flow with staffing

Exhibit 6.11 Product Development Competency for Marketing Department at a Toy Company

Manages the product development process, by:

- Analyzing and evaluating marketplace to identify niches/opportunities
- Evaluating product/concepts
- Developing marketing strategies
- Coordinating and evaluating research/testing
- Generating product recommendations and obtaining management support
- Driving product schedules/activities

Phase I: Baseline Expectations	*Phase II: Competent/Proficient*	*Phase III: Advanced/Coach*	*Phase IV: Expert/Mentor*
• Analyzes market/competitive data (e.g., TRST, NPD) and provides top-line trend analysis, with supervision • Evaluates products/concepts (see Toy Viability competency) • Contributes to product brainstorming sessions • Oversees market research activities and ensures timely completion • Obtains Account Management input to the product development effort • Develops and implements marketing strategy, with supervision: product, positioning, pricing/financial, promotion, packaging, merchandising, and advertising • Facilitates cost reductions to achieve price/profit goals; ensures execution of cost meeting next steps • Ensures adherence to product schedules • Coordinates licensor approval of product concept/models	• Monitors and analyzes market/competitive data (e.g., TRST, NPD) with minimal supervision, and provides recommendations for product development opportunities • Makes substantial contributions in product brainstorming sessions • Analyzes market research results and makes appropriate product recommendations • Partners with Account Management group to obtain their buy-in to the product development effort • Develops and implements marketing strategy, with minimal supervision • Drives cost reductions to achieve price/profit goals • Drives product schedules and resolves product scheduling issues (late delivery, late debug) • Negotiates with licensors to obtain product approvals.	• Independently monitors and analyzes market/competitive data (e.g., TRST, NPD), provides recommendations for product development opportunities, and coaches others to do so • Leads and facilitates formal product brainstorming sessions • Coaches others in analyzing market research results and making product recommendations • Develops innovative marketing plans (e.g., new channels of distribution, niche markets) • Independently develops and implements marketing strategy, and coaches others to do so • Identifies/evaluates cost reduction opportunities, and coaches others to do so • Identifies and implements product schedule improvement tactics • Coaches others to manage product schedules • Coaches others in managing licensor relationships • Shares product ideas/strategies with other teams/categories	• Reviews/approves recommendations for product development opportunities • Provides short- and long-term vision and goals for developing the corporate product portfolio across categories or brands • Reviews/approves marketing strategy, and proactively adjusts strategy in response to internal/external changes • Approves cost reduction recommendations • Anticipates critical issues that may impact product schedules and develops alternate plans • Ensures on-strategy delivery of product

levels, so whether or not an individual is *using* a particular skill on a particular day is not an issue. Competency-based plans assume—what? That all competencies are used all the time? The assumptions are not clear. What is clear, however, is the requirement that if people are to be paid based on their competencies, then there must be some way to demonstrate or certify to all concerned that a person possesses that level of competency.

Competencies as compensable factors can become obsolete as strategies shift.[18] Under skill-based plans employees often are required to be recertified, since the work they perform may not require them to use all the skills for which they were certified. Airplane pilots, for example, must go through an emergency-landing simulation every 12 months, since the airlines' objective is to ensure that such crucial skills are *not* actually demonstrated on the job with any frequency. Similarly, the introduction of new skill requirements and the obsolescence of previous skills require recertification. At its Ome facility in Tokyo, Toshiba requires all team members to recertify their skills every 24 months. Those who fail have the opportunity to retrain and attempt to recertify before their pay rate is reduced. However, the pressure to keep up-to-date and avoid obsolescence is intense. The same sense of urgency to avoid obsolescence does not pervade competency-based schemes since competencies are more general and less specific to a particular job or project.

Once again, because skills are concrete in the manufacturing settings in which such plans have been successful, they are easier to demonstrate and certify. However, advocates of competencies are relatively silent on the topic of certification. While the literature does discuss competencies as compatible with 360-degree feedback and personal development, it is silent on objectively certifying whether a person possesses a competency, much less how to translate the competency into pay.

ONE MORE TIME: STRUCTURE

Now that we have spent three chapters examining all the trees, let's look again at the forest. The purpose of job- and person-based procedures is to help design and manage an internal pay structure that helps achieve the organization's objectives.

As with job-based evaluation, the final result of the person-based plan is an internal hierarchy of work in the organization. This structure should be consistent with the organization's internal consistency policy, which in turn supports its business operations. Further, managers must insure that the structure *remains* internally consistent by reassessing work/skills/competencies when changes deem it necessary. Failure to do so risks inconsistent structures that lack logic and opens the door to the possibility of favoritism.

ADMINISTERING THE PLAN

Whatever plan is designed, a crucial issue is the fairness of its administration. Details of the plan should be described in a manual that includes all information necessary to apply the plan, such as definitions of compensable factors, degrees, or details of skill blocks, competencies, and certification methods. The manual will help ensure that the plan is administered as its designers intended.

[18]Bartlett and Ghushal, "The Myth of the Generic Manager."

We have mentioned the issue of employee acceptance throughout our discussion of job analysis and job evaluation. Employee acceptance of the process is crucial if the organization is to have any hope that employees will accept the resulting pay as fair. In order to build this acceptance, communication to all employees whose jobs are part of the process used to build the structure is required. This communication may be done through informational meetings, brochures, or other devices.

Most manuals also specify an appeals process for handling problems that occur in the implementation of the plan. for example, employees may believe their jobs were incorrectly evaluated or that the factors chosen ignore valued aspects of certain jobs. Compensation managers, employee teams, or the committee that designed the plan may be charged with handling any reviews.[19]

RESULTS: HOW USEFUL?

The criteria for evaluating the usefulness of pay structures, whether job- or person-based, are much the same: how well they achieve their objectives, as well as their reliability and validity. To date, work on the evaluation of job- versus person-based approaches differs. While there is vast research literature on job evaluation, most of it focuses on the procedures used rather than the effect on employee behaviors. The research treats job-based evaluation as a measurement device and considers its reliability, validity, the costs involved in its design and implementation, and its compliance with laws and regulations. In contrast, research on person-based evaluation tends to focus on its effects and less on procedures or on the approach as a measurement device.

Reliability of Job Evaluation Techniques

A reliable evaluation would be one where different evaluators produce the same results. Reliability can be increased by using evaluators who are familiar with the work. Many organizations use group consensus to increase reliability. Each evaluator makes a preliminary independent evaluation. Then, meeting as a committee, evaluators discuss their results until consensus emerges.[20] However, some studies report that results obtained through group consensus were not significantly different from those obtained by independent evaluators or by averaging individual evaluators' results. Nevertheless, the process may matter in terms of acceptability of results. Others report that a forceful or experienced leader on the committee can sway the results.[21]

---

[19]Folger and M. A. Konovsky, "Effects of Procedural and Distributive Justice on Reactions to Pay Raise Decisions," *Academy of Management Journal,* March 1989, pp. 115–30.

[20]M. K. Mount and R. A. Ellis, "Investigation of Bias in Job Evaluation Ratings of Comparable Worth Study Participants," *Personnel Psychology* 40 (1987), pp. 85–96.

[21]Vandra Huber and S. Crandall, "Job Measurement: A Social-Cognitive Decision Perspective," in *Research in Personnel and Human Resources Management* 12, ed. Gerald R. Ferris (Greenwich, CT: JAI Press, 1994), pp. 223–269.

Validity

Validity refers to the degree to which the evaluation achieves the desired results. Validity of job evaluation has been measured by "hit rates," or agreement of results with a predetermined benchmark structure. The agreed-upon structure may be the structure found in the external market, or a structure negotiated with a union, or a structure defined by a committee, or market rates for jobs held predominantly by men (to try to eliminate any general discrimination reflected in the market), or a combination or variation of these examples. Studies have reported hit rates ranging from 27 to 73 percent of jobs within one, agreed-upon class.[22] The impact of such accuracy depends on the size of the salary discrepancy between classes. If being one class away translates into several hundred dollars in lost pay, then being "close" probably doesn't buy much employee credibility.

Studies of the degree to which different job evaluation plans produce the same results, or convergence of results, start with the assumption that if different approaches produce the same results, then those results must be accurate.

One study looked at three different job evaluation plans applied to the same set of jobs. The study found high consistency among raters using each method, but substantial differences in the plans' impact on pay decisions. For example, when different evaluators used a custom-designed point plan, their pay recommendations for the jobs agreed in only 51 percent of jobs.[23] So it is clear that the definition of reliability needs to be broadened to include impact on pay decisions.

Unfortunately, some studies have found pay discrepancies of up to $427 per month depending on the method used, or consistent results that appeared incorrect. For example, in one study, three plans all gave the same result but all three ranked a police officer higher than a detective.[24] This is contrary to pay practices in the majority of police departments. How did this happen? Either the compensable factors did not pick up something deemed important in the detectives' jobs, or the detectives have more power universally in negotiating higher wages. So while these three plans gave valid results in that their results converged, it is clear that they would have little employee acceptance, at least among detectives.

Acceptability

Several devices are used to assess and improve employee acceptability. An obvious one is the inclusion of a *formal appeals process,* discussed earlier. Employees who believe their jobs are evaluated incorrectly should be able to request reanalysis and/or skills reevaluation. Most firms respond to such requests from managers, but few extend the process to all employees, unless those employees are represented by unions

---

[22]R. M. Madigan and D. J. Hoover, "Effects of Alternative Job Evaluation Methods on Decisions Involving Pay Equity," *Academy of Management Journal,* March 1986, pp. 84–100.

[23]Madigan, "Comparable Worth Judgments"; D. Doverspike and G. Barrett, "An Internal Bias Analysis of a Job Evaluation Instrument," *Journal of Applied Psychology* 69 (1984), pp. 648–62; Kermit Davis, Jr., and William Sauser, Jr., "Effects of Alternative Weighting Methods in a Policy-Capturing Approach to Job Evaluation: A Review and Empirical Investigation," *Personnel Psychology* 44 (1991), pp. 85–127.

[24]Judith Collins, "Job Evaluation" (Working paper, University of Arkansas-Little Rock, 1992).

EXHIBIT 6.12 Illustrations of Audit Indexes

A. Overall indicators.
1. Ratio of number of current descriptions to numbers of employees.
2. Number of job descriptions evaluated last year and previous year.
3. Number of jobs evaluated per unit.
   (a) Newly created jobs.
   (b) Reevaluation of existing jobs.

B. Timeliness of job descriptions and evaluations.
1. Percent of total jobs with current descriptions.
2. Percentage of evaluation requests returned within 7 working days, within 14 working days.
3. Percentage of reevaluation requests returned with changed (unchanged) evaluations.

C. Workability and acceptability of job evaluation.
1. Percentage of employees (managers) surveyed who know the purposes of job evaluation.
2. The number of employees who appeal their job's evaluation rating.
3. The number of employees who receive explanations of the results of their reevaluation requests.

who have negotiated a grievance process. No matter what the outcome from the appeal, the results should be explained in detail to anyone who requests reevaluation.

A second method of assessing acceptability is to include questions about it in *employee attitude surveys.* Questions can assess perceptions of how useful evaluation is as a management tool. Another method is to *audit* how the plan is being used on a series of measures of use. Exhibit 6.12 lists examples of indexes used by various employers. These indexes range from the percentage of employees who understand the reasons for evaluation to the percentage of jobs with current descriptions, to the rate of requests for revaluation. Acceptability is a somewhat vague test of the job evaluation—acceptable to whom is an open issue. Clearly, managers and employees are important constituents because acceptance makes it a useful device. But as we will discuss in the chapter on legislation and pay discrimination (Chapter 17), others outside the firm also have a stake in job evaluation and pay structure.

Bias in Job Evaluation

Much attention has been directed at job evaluation as both a potential source of bias against women and a mechanism to reduce bias.[25] It has been widely speculated that job evaluation is susceptible to gender bias. To date, three ways that job evaluation

[25]D. J. Treiman and H. I. Hartmann, eds., *Women, Work and Wages: Equal Pay for Jobs of Equal Value* (Washington, DC: National Academy of Sciences, 1981); H. Remick, *Comparable Worth and Wage Discrimination* (Philadelphia: Temple University Press, 1984).

can be biased against women have been studied.[26] Unfortunately, no studies of gender effects in skill-based or competency-based plans exist.

Jobholder's Gender. Direct bias occurs if jobs held predominantly by women are undervalued relative to jobs held predominantly by men, simply because of the jobholder's gender. But evidence does not support the proposition that the gender of an individual *jobholder* influences the *evaluation* of the job. One study found no effects when it varied the gender of jobholders using photographs and recorded voices.[27] Another study reported a slight bias *in favor of* female-linked *job titles* (e.g., orderly vs. nurse's aide). The evaluators received extensive training in potential gender bias; hence, they may have "bent over backwards" to avoid it.[28] Simply telling evaluators that varying proportions of men and women performed the jobs made no difference.[29]

However, specific compensable factors may be biased for or against gender-segregated jobs.[30] A study found that those compensable factors related to job content (such as contact with others and judgment) did reflect bias, but others pertaining to employee requirements (such as education and experience) did not.[31] Two job descriptions were evaluated. The female-linked title, executive secretary, was reportedly undervalued on the job content factors. The psychological literature identifies a common tendency to make stereotypical assumptions, usually to the detriment of women and minorities. Perhaps by calling out the job-related criteria for making evaluations, job evaluation is able to avoid this bias.

Wages Criteria Bias. The second potential source of bias affects job evaluation indirectly, through the current wages paid for jobs. In this case, job evaluation results may be biased if the jobs held predominantly by women are incorrectly underpaid. Treiman and Hartmann argue that women's jobs are unfairly underpaid simply because women hold them.[32] If this is the case and if job evaluation is based on the current wages paid, then the job evaluation results simply mirror any bias in the current pay rates. Considering that many job evaluation plans are purposely structured to mirror the existing pay structure, it should not be surprising that the current wages for jobs influence the results of job evaluation. In one study, 400 experienced compensation administrators were sent information on current pay, market, and job evaluation re-

---

[26]This discussion is adapted from D. Schwab and R. Grams, "Sex-Related Errors in Job Evaluation: A 'Real-World' Test," *Journal of Applied Psychology* 70, no. 3 (1985), pp. 533–59; Arvey, "Sex Bias in Job Evaluation Procedures."

[27]Richard D. Arvey, Emily M. Passino, and John W. Lounsbury, "Job Analysis Results As Influenced by Sex of Incumbent and Sex of Analyst," *Journal of Applied Psychology* 62, no. 4 (1977), pp. 411–16.

[28]Michael K. Mount and Rebecca A. Ellis, "Investigation of Bias in Job Evaluation Ratings of Comparable Worth Study Participants," *Personnel Psychology,* Spring 1987, pp. 85–96.

[29]R. Grams and D. Schwab, "An Investigation of Systematic Gender-Related Error in Job Evaluation," *Academy of Management Journal* 28, no. 2 (1985), pp. 279–90.

[30]Gerald V. Barrett and Dennis Doverspike, "Another Defense of Point-Factor Job Evaluation," *Personnel,* March 1989, pp. 33–36.

[31]Arvey, "Sex Bias in Job Evaluation Procedures."

[32]Treiman and Hartmann, *Women, Work and Wages.*

sults. They were asked to use this information to make pay decisions for a set of nine jobs. Half of the administrators received information on jobs traditionally held by men (e.g., security guards) and half received information on jobs traditionally held by women (e.g., secretary II). The results revealed that (1) market data had a substantially larger effect on pay decisions than did job evaluations or current pay data and (2) the jobs' gender had no effect.[33]

This study is a unique look at several factors that may affect pay structures. If market rates and current pay already reflect gender bias, then these biased pay rates could work indirectly through the job evaluation process to deflate the evaluation of jobs held primarily by women.[34] Clearly, the criteria used in the design of evaluation plans are crucial and need to be business and work related.

Evaluator's Gender. The third possible source of gender bias in evaluation is the gender of the individual evaluators. Some argue that male evaluators may be less favorably disposed toward jobs held predominantly by women. However, there is no evidence that the job evaluator's gender affects the results. Several recommendations seek to ensure that job evaluation plans are bias free. The recommendations include the following:

1. Define the compensable factors and scales to include the content of jobs held predominantly by women. For example, working conditions should include the noise and stress of office machines and the repetitive movements associated with the use of word processors.
2. Ensure that factor weights are not consistently biased against jobs held predominantly by women. Are factors usually associated with these jobs always given less weight?
3. Apply the plan in as bias-free a manner as feasible. Ensure that the job descriptions are bias free, exclude incumbent names from the job evaluation process, and train women as evaluators.

Some writers see job evaluation as a friend of those who wish to combat pay discrimination.[35] Without a properly designed and applied system, "employers will face an almost insurmountable task in persuading the government that ill-defined or whimsical methods of determining differences in job content and pay are a business necessity. On the other hand, some lawyers recommend that employers avoid job evaluation on the grounds that the results will lead to lawsuits. Pay discrimination will be discussed again in Chapter 17.

At the risk of pointing out the obvious, all issues concerning job evaluation also apply to skill-based and competency-based plans. For example, the acceptability of

---

[33]S. Rynes, C. Weber, and G. Milkovich, "The Effects of Market Survey Rates, Job Evaluation, and Job Gender on Job Pay," *Journal of Applied Psychology* 74 (1989), pp. 114–23; also see Doverspike and Barrett, "An Internal Bias Analysis."

[34]Grams and Schwab, "Investigation of Systematic Gender-Related Error in Job Evaluation."

[35]Paula England, *Comparable Worth: Theories and Evidence* (New York: Aldine De Gruyter, 1992).

the results of skill-based plans can be studied from the perspective of measurement (reliability and validity) and administration (costs and returns). The various points in skill certification at which errors and biases may enter into judgment (e.g., different views of skill-block definitions, potential favoritism toward team members, defining and assessing skill obsolescence) and whether skill block points and evaluators make a difference all need to be studied. A cynic might observe that one reason skill-based plans seem to be increasing in popularity is that they have yet to take on all the administrative and regulatory baggage to which job evaluation has been subjected.

Research on Skill-based Plans

Two recent empirical studies related use of the skill-based system to productivity. One found positive results, the other did not.[36] However, the plans are well-accepted by employees because it is easy to see the connection between the plan, the work employees do, and the size of their paychecks. Consequently, the plans provide strong motivation for individuals to increase their skills.

However, after several years, many companies are finding that the plans become increasingly expensive, as the majority of employees become certified at the highest pay levels permitted in the plan. As a result, the employer may have an average wage higher than competitors who are using conventional job evaluation. Some employers are combatting this by adding more bureaucracy, requiring that employees stay at a certain rate a certain amount of time before they become eligible to take the training to move to a higher level. Another issue is, what happens when skills that were a basis for pay at one time become obsolete? Should the company cut pay?

Another study looked at the relationship between characteristics of employees and how well they did with a skill-based system.[37] They found that younger, more educated employees with strong growth needs, organizational commitment, and a positive attitude toward workplace innovations were more successful in acquiring new skills. On the other hand, the same researchers suggest that allocating training opportunities by seniority is a key element in transisting from a job-based to a skill-based system, particularly in a unionized setting.[38] They also point out that such a transition incurs substantial up-front costs.

The bottom line is that skill-based approaches may be only short-term initiatives. They may serve to energize and refocus the organization on learning new skills, adapting to a radically different work environment. However, as with any other pay technique, skill-based approaches do not appear suitable for all situations. The acceptability

---

[36]K. Parrent and C. Weber, "Case Study: Does Paying for Knowledge Pay Off?" *Compensation and Benefits Review,* September–October 1994, pp. 44–50; Murray and Gerhart, "Early Organization Outcomes."

[37]Kenneth Mericle and Dong-One Kim, "Determinants of Skill Acquisition and Pay Satisfaction under Pay-for-Knowledge Systems" (Working Paper, Institute of Industrial Relations, University of California Berkeley, 1996).

[38]Kenneth Mericle and Dong-One Kim, "Skill-Based Pay and Work Reorganization in High Performance Firms" (Working Paper, Institute of Industrial Relations, University of California Berkeley, 1996).

may vary, depending on how long the plan has been in place, and whether one is looking at acceptability for the organization or by employees.

Motorola cited the following dilemma as one of their reasons for abandoning a skill-based plan: if at the end of three years, everyone topped out at $10 per hour (by accumulating the necessary skill blocks), what happens next year? Does everybody automatically receive a pay increase? What about the year after that? In a firm with labor intensive products, the increased labor costs under skill-based plans may be a source of competitive disadvantage. In contrast, under a job-based plan, employees are paid according to the value of the job they perform.

Some of the issues to consider before adopting a skill-based plan include the following:[39]

1. Is the facility labor or capital intensive? The financial risks in labor intensive operations may be greater under skill-based approaches.
2. Is the work force individual or team based? Interestingly, Motorola reported that skill-based pay is easier to administer in a setting that adheres to an individual achievement philosophy. Under a team environment, an individual may have to postpone training and the accompanying pay increase in order to meet the needs of the team better.
3. Is the work stable or dynamic? Under rapidly changing technologies, skills may become obsolete rapidly, making constant revision of skill-based plans and recertification an administrative burden.
4. Is a jack-of-all-trades really the master of none? Some research in operations management suggests that the greatest impact on results occurs after just a small amount of increased flexibility. Greater increments in flexibility achieve fewer improvements. More skills may not necessarily improve productivity. So there may be an optimal number of skills for any individual to possess. Beyond that number, productivity returns are less than the pay increases.

TRW's experience is similar to Motorola's. After a few years, people at two manufacturing plants on skill-based systems had all topped out. They were flexible (maxed out on skills) and well trained. So now what? They already had a gainsharing, performance improvement plan. Employees had experienced frequent pay increases under the skill-based plan and had come to think of the increases as an entitlement—not based on new skills at all. So they had come to believe they were entitled to annual across-the-board increases.

Research on Competencies

There is general support, particularly in market-based economies, for the belief that more competent individuals should be paid more than less competent individuals. The challenge is to convert this agreement into defining competencies in a systematic way if pay is to be based on them. While the notion of competencies may have value in identifying what distinguishes typical from truly outstanding performance, there is debate on whether competencies can be translated into a measurable, objective basis for pay.

[39]Jenkins, Ledford, Gupta, and Doty, *Skill-Based Pay.*

A study of 286 competency models found that in higher-level technical, marketing, professional and managerial positions, the distinguishing characteristics of success were motivation, interpersonal influence, and political skills—all of which are competencies.[40] In another study of systems programmers and analysts, where logic, mathematical, and programming skills previously had been thought to be the competencies for success, the competencies that distinguished superior performers were customer-service orientation, leveraging technical information, and influencing others.[41] So the notion of using competencies for developing higher-level "knowledge workers" has some appeal. It fits with the staffing strategy of "hire smart people, give them the tools, then get out of the way."

Competencies also appear to fit nicely with performance evaluation approaches that rely on multirater feedback. However, we have already raised the issue of including "below-the-water" characteristics of a person such as motivation, values, and self-concept in order to predict what a person will do. For example, individuals with high achievement motivation are said to derive personal satisfaction from exceeding established performance standards.[42] The competency "results orientation," which may include developing personal measures of progress even when goals aren't set by management, taking initiative in one's own work methods to improve performance, and setting and striving to reach challenging goals, captures this motivation to achieve. In fact, the "results orientation" has been described as "one of the critical competencies that distinguishes between typical and high performance".

Fair enough. But is it appropriate to pay you for what you have *done* (results) versus what I believe you would *like to do* or are *capable of doing* (results orientation)? As a Nobel-prize-winning physicist noted, "It is difficult to predict, especially the future." Human behavior is celebrated for its variability and unpredictability. So why would an organization try to assess and pay for something that is below the surface? Isn't it "likely to be more effective, for *pay purposes,* to focus on what is easily measurable and directly related to organizational effectiveness" (i.e., knowledge and skills that are task/performance-related)?[43]

THE PERFECT STRUCTURE

Exhibit 6.13 contrasts job-, skill-, and competency-based structures and what they value. Pay increases are gained via promotions to more responsible jobs under job-based structures or by acquiring more valued skills/competencies under the other structures. Logically, employees will focus on how to get promoted (experience, performance) or on how to acquire the required skills or competencies (training).

Managers whose employers use job-based plans focus on placing the right people in the right job. A switch to skill/competency-based plans reverses this procedure.

---

[40]Spencer and Spencer, *Competence at Work.*

[41]Sharon A. Tucker and Kathryn Cofsky, "Competency Based Pay on a Banding Platform," *ACA News* 3, no. 1 (Spring 1994), pp. 30–40.

[42]Spencer and Spencer, *Competence at Work.*

[43]Edward E. Lawler III, "From Job-Based to Competency-Based Organizations."

EXHIBIT 6.13 Contrasting Approaches

	Job-Based	*Skill-Based*	*Competency-Based*
What is valued	• Compensable factors	• Skill blocks	• Competencies
Quantify the value	• Factor degree weights	• Skill levels	• Competency levels
Mechanisms to translate into pay	• Assign points that reflect criterion pay structure	• Certification and price skills in external market	• Certification and price competencies in external market
Pay structure	• Based on job performed/market	• Based on skills certified/market	• Based on competency developed/market
Pay increases	• Promotion	• Skill acquisition	• Competency development
Managers' focus	• Link employees to work • Promotion and placement • Cost control via pay for job and budget increase	• Utilize skills efficiently • Provide training • Control costs via training, certification, and work assignments	• Be sure competencies add value • Provide competency-developing opportunities • Control costs via certification and assignments
Employee focus	• Seek promotions to earn more pay	• Seek skills	• Seek competencies
Procedures	• Job analysis • Job evaluation	• Skill analysis • Skill certification	• Competency analysis • Competency certification
Advantages	• Clear expectations • Sense of progress • Pay based on • value of work performed	• Continuous learning • Flexibility • Reduced work force	• Continuous learning • Flexibility • Lateral movement
Limitations	• Potential bureaucracy • Potential inflexibility	• Potential bureaucracy • Requires cost controls	• Potential bureaucracy • Requires cost controls

Now, managers must assign the right work to the right people, that is, those with the right skills and competencies. As noted earlier, under the skill/competency-based plans, employees are paid for the highest level of skill/competency they have achieved, *regardless of the work they perform.* This is a crucial point about these plans. The top-certified employee at Borg-Warner is certified at A level (which includes B- and C-level skills as well). Even if assigned B- or C-level work, these employees are paid at the higher A rate. This maximizes flexibility in the work force. But it also has risks. If all employees are certified at top rates (which the pay system encourages them to do), an employer may experience higher labor costs than its competitors, which is a price disadvantage in the marketplace. To avoid this, an employer must either control the rate at which employees can certify skill/competency mastery and/or employ fewer people. Absent this offset, the organization's higher labor costs will become a source of competitive disadvantage.

In contrast, a job-based approach controls costs by paying only as much as the work performed is worth, regardless of any greater skills the employee may possess. (Word processors are paid at word-processor rates regardless of whether the person is also qualified to do spreadsheet analysis and fill telephone orders.) So as Exhibit 6.13 suggests, costs are controlled via job rates or via work assignments and budgets.

In addition to potentially higher rates (perhaps offset by fewer employees) and higher training costs, skill/competency plans may have the additional disadvantage of becoming as complex and burdensome as job-based plans. Some recent studies examine the payoffs of skill-based approaches at two facilities. TRW and Ford report that skill-based plans do yield positive productivity improvements while controlling costs. However, no studies have yet been done to assess whether redesigned job-based plans, properly designed and managed, wouldn't be equally effective.[44]

Additionally, questions still remain about a skill/competency system's compliance with the Equal Pay Act. If a member of a protected group has a lower skill-mastery level and lower pay than a white male who is doing the same work, does this violate the equal pay/equal work standard specified in the legislation?[45]

So where does all this come out? What is the best approach to pay structures, and how will we know it when we see it? The answer is, it depends. The best approach may be one which will provide sufficient ambiguity to afford flexibility to adapt to changing conditions. Too generic an approach may not provide sufficient detail to justify pay decisions; too detailed an approach may become rigid. If the work requires tight specifications, as in grilling hamburgers (at McDonalds) or manufacturing computer chips (at Intel), then very detailed job descriptions and evaluation are appropriate.[46]

On the one hand, bases for pay that are too strictly defined may miss changes in work that are inevitable in a changing economy; on the other hand, bases for pay that are too vaguely defined will have no credibility with employees and lead to suspicions of favoritism and bias.

This chapter concludes our section on internal consistency. Before we move on to external considerations, let's once again address the issue of, why bother? Why bother with a pay structure? The answer should be, because it has the potential to improve organization performance. An internally consistent pay structure, whether strategically loosely coupled or tightly fitting, can be designed to (1) help determine pay for the wide variety of work in the organizations, and (2) insure that pay influences peoples' attitudes and work behaviors and directs them toward organization objectives.

---

[44]B. Murray and B. Gerhart, "Early Organization Outcomes from Introduction of Skill-Based Pay" (CAHRS Working paper 94–26, Center for Advanced Human Resource Studies, Ithaca, NY).

[45]K. Davidson, "Motorola Transitions from Skill-Based," *ACA News,* July 1993, p. 3.

[46]T. Jackson, *Inside Intel: Andy Grove and the Rise of the World's Most Powerful Chip Company* (New York: Dutton, 1997); Andy Grove, *Only the Paranoid Survive* (1996).

Summary

This section of the book started by examining pay structures within an organization. The importance placed on internal consistency in the pay structures is a basic strategic issue. The basic premise underlying a policy that emphasizes internal consistency is that internal pay structures need to be consistent with the organization's business strategy and values, the design of the work flow, and a concern for the fair treatment of employees. The work relationships within a single organization are an important part of internal consistency. Structures that are acceptable to the stakeholders involved affect satisfaction with pay, the willingness to seek and accept promotions to more responsible jobs, the effort to undertake additional training, and the propensity to remain with the employer; they also reduce the incidence of pay-related grievances.

The techniques for establishing internally consistent structures include job analysis, job evaluation, and person-based approaches for skill/competency-based plans. Although viewed by some as bureaucratic burdens, these techniques can aid in achieving the objectives of the pay system when they are properly designed and administered. Without them, our pay objectives of improving competitiveness and equity are more difficult to achieve.

We have now finished the first part of the book. We have discussed strategic perspectives on compensation, the key strategic issues in compensation management, and the model that provides a framework for the book. Managing compensation requires adapting the pay system to support the organization strategies, its culture and values, and the needs of individual employees. We examined the internal consistency of the pay structure. We discussed the techniques used to establish consistency as well as its effects on compensation objectives. The next section of the book focuses on the next strategic issue in our pay model: external competitiveness.

Review Questions

1. What are the pros and cons of having employees involved in compensation decisions? What forms can employee involvement take?
2. Why does the process used in the design of the internal pay structure matter? Distinguish between the process used to design and administer the structure and the techniques or mechanics used.
3. If you were managing employee compensation, how would you recommend that your company evaluate the usefulness of its job evaluation or person-based plans?
4. Based on the research on job evaluation, what are the sources of possible gender bias in skill/competency-based plans?
5. How can a manager ensure that job evaluation or skill/competency-based plans support a customer-centered strategy?
6. How would you decide whether to use job-based or person-based structures?

Your Turn

School Board Targets Teachers Pay

A front-page picture in a recent *Ithaca Journal* showed a first-grade teacher getting a hug from one of her six-year-old students at the end of the day at South Hill Elementary School. The teacher holds a bachelor's degree in elementary education, a master's degree in counseling psychology, and a doctoral degree in industrial relations, yet receives only a median salary for first-grade teachers.

The teachers association president says comparing teachers salaries to the average salary earned by others in the district is unfair. "If the average salary of people living in a school district is $24,000, does that mean physicians should get $24,000?"

Should that first-grade teacher with a Ph.D. receive more than the median salary for first-grade teachers?

What would you recommend to the school board? Does person-based logic support your recommendation? Does job-based logic support your recommendation?

EXHIBIT II.1

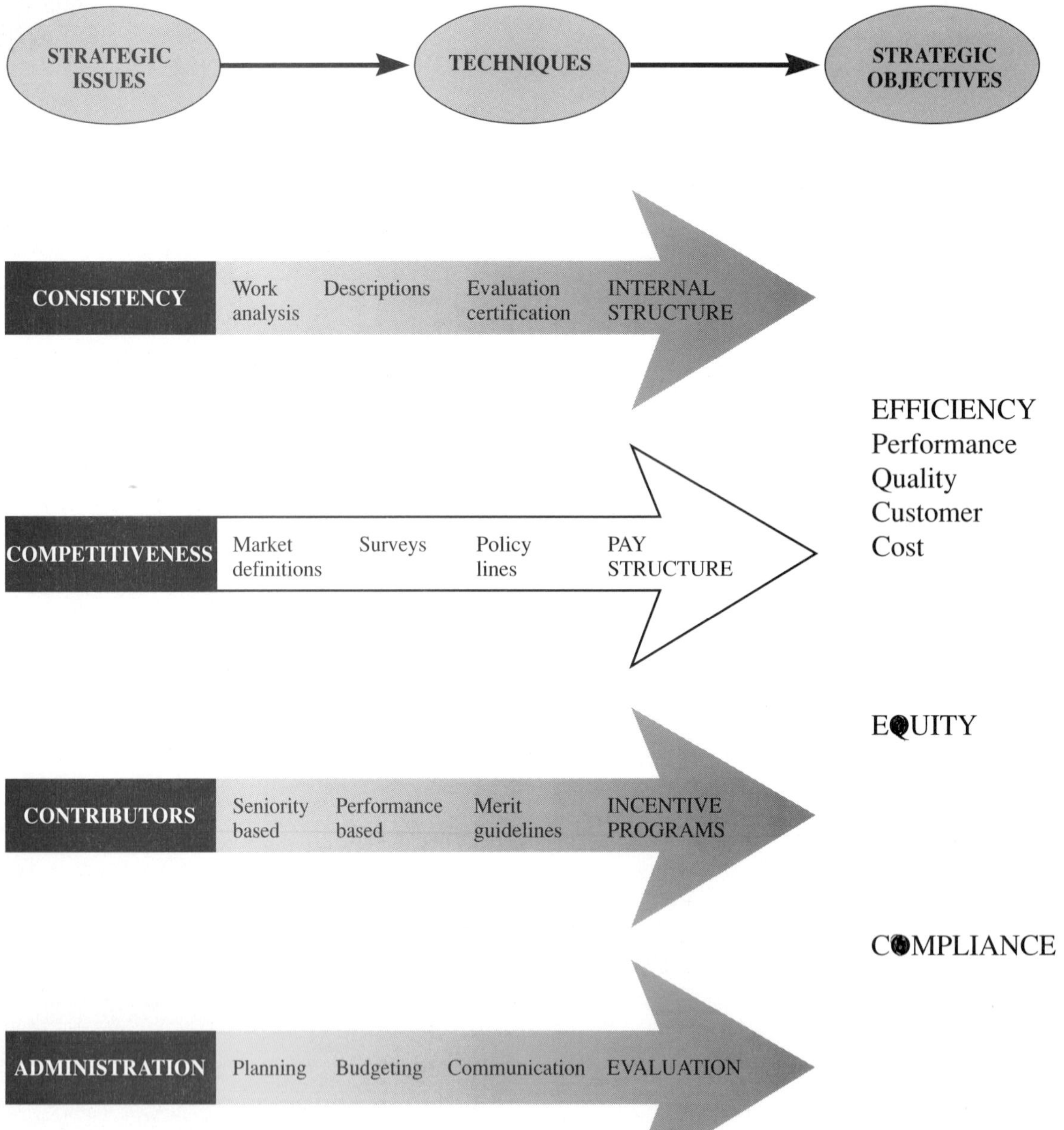

STRATEGIC ISSUES
TECHNIQUES
STRATEGIC OBJECTIVES
CONSISTENCY
Work analysis
Descriptions
Evaluation certification
INTERNAL STRUCTURE
COMPETITIVENESS
Market definitions
Surveys
Policy lines
PAY STRUCTURE
CONTRIBUTORS
Seniority based
Performance based
Merit guidelines
INCENTIVE PROGRAMS
ADMINISTRATION
Planning
Budgeting
Communication
EVALUATION
EFFICIENCY
Performance
Quality
Customer
Cost
EQUITY
COMPLIANCE

External Competitiveness: Determining the Pay Level

Michael Jordan's prowess on the basketball court is legendary. So is his salary. He makes over $300,000 a game. If he averages 30 minutes per game, he gets $10,000 a minute. Totaling his basketball salary plus the $40 million he earns annually in product endorsements, Mr. Jordan has made more than twice as much as all U.S. presidents for all of their terms combined. Salaries earned by Mr. Jordan, the U.S. president, and a host of others are shown in Exhibit II.2. For example, while a Los Angeles lifeguard earns only $800 per week, an actor who plays a lifeguard on television gets $100,000 per episode. Compensation managers don't earn that much, no matter how well their decisions fit the organization's strategy.

How in the world are these salaries determined? For some people, these examples confirm what they have always suspected: that pay is determined without apparent reason or justice. These are figures employers have arrived at when they position their pay relative to other organizations who compete in the same labor and product markets. Michael Jordan is able to command such a high salary because (1) other employers were also interested in his services and (2) they all believe that Mr. Jordan can create a stream of earnings for them that will be greater than his pay.

The objective of this section is to discuss how employers position their pay relative to other employers who compete in the same labor and product/service markets. Exhibit II.1 shows that the external competitiveness policy fits into the total pay model. It represents the next major strategic decision in the model.

External competitiveness varies in its importance among companies and among countries. In the United States and United Kingdom, for example, organizations are continually restructuring and adapting to competitive pressures. Strategic alliances with former competitors, strategic alliances to enter new markets, delayering internal hierarchy and networking teams are but a few examples of the changes.

All these changes have two things in common: (1) de-emphasis of the traditionally stable, internal relationships, and (2) greater reliance on external market-driven relationships.

In contrast, Japanese organizations tend to do very little hiring in the external market for other than entry-level positions. Consequently, pay rates in the external market for many jobs may be less relevant. However, Japanese employers still emphasize comparisons with their competitors on pay level, head count, labor costs, and productivity. Toyota is acutely aware of how much auto assemblers in Germany, Korea, Italy, and South Carolina earn.

External competitiveness translates into practice when the company establishes a pay level. Three pure policy alternatives exist: to lead competitors' pay, to match it, or to lag below it. But as we shall see in Chapter 7, variations exist. Chapter 7 discusses the major factors affecting external competitiveness policies, consequences of these policies, and theories and research related to them. Chapter 8 has two parts. First, it discusses the decisions and techniques that translate an employers' competitiveness policy into pay level. Second, it discusses how to integrate market data with the structures we designed in the previous chapters.

Exhibit II.2 Who Makes How Much?

Gus Bevona	president of the New York City Local of the Service Employees International Union	$412,000
Sandra Bullock	actress, in the hit movie Speed	$500,000
	actress, in the movie flop Speed 2	$12,500,000
Billy Caribou	croupier, Grand Portage, Minnesota	$28,100
William Clinton	president of the United States	$200,000
Michael Cohen	software engineer, Mountain View, California	$45,000
William M. Flynn	first Deputy Attorney General, New York State	$111,000
David Hasselhoff	actor who portrays a Los Angeles lifeguard on Baywatch, per episode	$100,000
Craig Hummer	Los Angeles lifeguard, per week (in season)	$800
Sam Giacobbi	Senate barber, Washington D.C.	$62,000
Michael Jordan	basketball player	$25,000,000
	product endorser	$40,000,000
Lynn Hummel	longshoreman, Port of Los Angeles	$81,000
Ann Lusk	architect, Johnstown, PA	$47,500
Major-General Bryan Dutton	last British head of military troops in Hong Kong; replaced by	$94,700
Major-General Zhou Borong	head of People's Liberation Army in Hong Kong	$1,730
Spiros Mastoras	New York City hot dog and pretzel vendor	$21,000
Sue Mittler	president of Ithaca (New York) Teachers Association	$48,200
Cindy Peck	software engineer, Mountain View, California	$65,000
Addison Piper	Chairman, president, and CEO of Piper brokerage house, (company's profits this year $954,000)	$1,019,360
Wolfgang Puck	chef, mass-market mall cafes and frozen foods	$10,000,000
Margaret Richardson	Commissioner of the Internal Revenue Service	$123,100
Jesus Salvano	front desk clerk, Brownsville, TX	$13,740
Neil Scheuerlein	control room operator at San Onofre, CA nuclear plant	$80,000–100,000
Al Smith	NYPD officer	$58,200
Anders Stoikov	software engineer, Mountain View, California	$95,000
Joanne Tullass	licensed practical nurse, Flagstaff, AZ	$26,480
Eugene Vasser	factory worker, Lincoln Electric	$100,000+
Honey Watrous	money handler, Grand Portage, Minnesota	$14,800
Alice White	nurses aide, Detroit, MI	$12,800

CHAPTER 7 Defining Competitiveness

Chapter Outline

January is always a good month for travel agents in Ithaca, New York. In addition to the permanent population eager to flee Ithaca's leaden skies (our computer has a screen-saver whose color is titled *Ithaca;* it consists of 256 shades of gray), graduating students from Ithaca's two colleges are traveling to job interviews with employers across the country—at company expense, and at full fare. No Saturday night stayovers required. During this recruiting season, students compare notes and find that even for people receiving the same degree in the same field from the same college, the offers vary from company to company.

At first, students attribute these differences to themselves: differences in grades, courses taken, work experience, interviewing skills, and so on. But as students accept offers and reject others, an interesting phenomenon occurs. Many companies whose offers were rejected now extend the identical offer to other students.

If an individual's qualifications do not explain differences in offers, what does? Location has an effect: firms in San Francisco and New York City make higher offers. The work also has an effect: jobs in employment pay a little less than jobs in compensation and employee relations. (Now aren't you glad you didn't drop this course?) And the industry to which the different firms belong has an effect: Pharmaceuticals, brokerage houses, and petroleum firms tend to offer more than consumer products, insurance, banking, and heavy manufacturing firms.[1] What determines these differences in pay levels? What effects do they have? This chapter addresses these questions.

Readers have told us this chapter can be heavy going. The reasons are the sheer volume of relevant theories and research. Another reason is that the reality of the decisions doesn't always match the theories. The key to this chapter is to always ask, So what? How will this information help me?

COMPENSATION STRATEGY: EXTERNAL COMPETITIVENESS

External competitiveness, our second pay policy, addresses pay relationships external to the organization. The key to competitiveness is its relative nature: comparisons with competitors.

External competitiveness is often translated into practical phrases like "being market driven." However, practice is more complex. As you read in Chapter 2, determining external competitiveness for your organization means deciding whether being different regarding compensation really pays off. It also means deciding whether it makes more sense to simply match what competitors are paying and try to do it better (more efficiently).

Although determining your *pay level* versus competitors is a primary decision, competitiveness also includes choosing the *mix of pay forms* (using bonuses, stock options, flexible benefits), career opportunities, challenging assignments, and so on.

Pay competitiveness is expressed in practice by setting pay rates that are above, below, or equal to rates paid by competitors. Within an organization, the average of the array of rates set for various jobs is that organization's pay level.

External competitiveness refers to the pay relationships among organizations—the organization's pay relative to its competitors.
Pay level refers to the average of the array of rates paid by an employer.

Pay level focuses attention on two objectives: (1) control labor costs and (2) attract and retain employees.[2]

Control Labor Costs

Pay level decisions significantly impact most organizations' total expenses. Other things being equal, the higher the pay level, the higher the labor costs (Exhibit 7.1). Furthermore, the higher the pay level relative to what competitors pay, the greater the relative

[1] Richard Thaler, "Interindustry Wage Differentials," *The Winner's Curse* (NY: Free Press, 1992).

[2] S.L. Rynes and A. Barber, "Applicant Attraction Strategies: An Organizational Perspective," *Academy of Management Review* 1990; Margaret L. Williams and George Dreher, "Compensation System Attributes and Applicant Pool Characteristics," *Academy of Management Journal,* August 1992.

costs to provide similar products or services. For example, pilots at major U.S. airlines are nicknamed "flying vice presidents" because of their high salaries and their interest in how the company is managed. Exhibit 7.2 shows that pilot's pay varies by employer. After five years of experience, pilots at US Air ($85,000), Delta ($79,000), and Southwest and United ($78,000) earn the most. But after 10 years Northwest pilots lead the pack ($125,000) and can earn more—over 67 percent more—than Southwest pilots, who max out at about $120,000. The same work is paid differently by different employers. Why would Northwest pay more than America West? What could justify a pay level above whatever minimum amount is required to attract and retain pilots?

Attract and Retain Employees

In fact, all else is rarely equal. Northwest may believe its higher pay for pilots is offset by savings resulting from more productive employees. Northwest pilots may be more experienced, which may reassure white-knuckle passengers. Or maybe they are more flexible and can deal more satisfactorily with the nonroutine (!) events in the air. Or they may be less likely to quit, which can cut down on recruiting and training costs. Or Northwest pilots may just have more negotiating power with Northwest management. These other factors may justify a decision to set a high pay level. In reality, employers set a variety of pay levels. That is why there is no single "going rate" in the labor market for a specific job.

No Single "Going Rate"

Just as graduating students discover each year, the rates paid for similar jobs and skills vary among employers.[3] An array of rates exists. Notice that in Exhibit 7.3, the wages paid to the secretary of the chief executive officer (CEO) vary with the size of the company (top secretaries that report to CEOs in companies with revenues of $5 billion or more can expect to earn approximately 5 to 10 percent more than average); with the region of the country (salaries are highest in the metropolitan New York area, lowest in the South Central region); and with the industry (the top secretaries in financial services average $60,300, but only $46,700 in natural resources and exploration). Although some of this variation may be attributable to such factors as experience and seniority of the secretary (their average tenure in this survey is 18 years with the company and 7 years with the job), much of it also reflects different pay levels among responding companies.

Pay level also varies among job families within a single company. For example, a survey of 21 aerospace firms found that the top-paying firm paid more than 21 percent above the average pay and the bottom one paid more than 13 percent below the overall average pay.[4] Even more interesting are the profiles of different competitive positions for different job families. Company A paid 10.5 percent below the market overall, but

---

[3] *College Placement Council Salary Survey* is published quarterly by the College Placement Council, Bethlehem, PA. It reports starting salary offers to college graduates as collected by college placement offices. Data are reported by curriculum, by functional area, and by degree. It is one of several sources employers may use to establish the offers they extend to new graduates.

[4] Ken Foster, "An Anatomy of Company Pay Practices," *Personnel,* September 1985, pp. 67–71.

Exhibit 7.1 Pay Level Decision Impacts Labor Cost

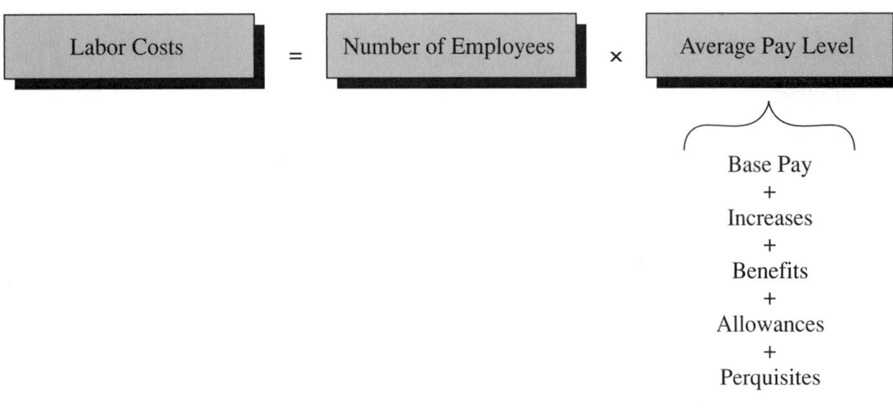

Exhibit 7.2 Structure Differences: Do They Matter?

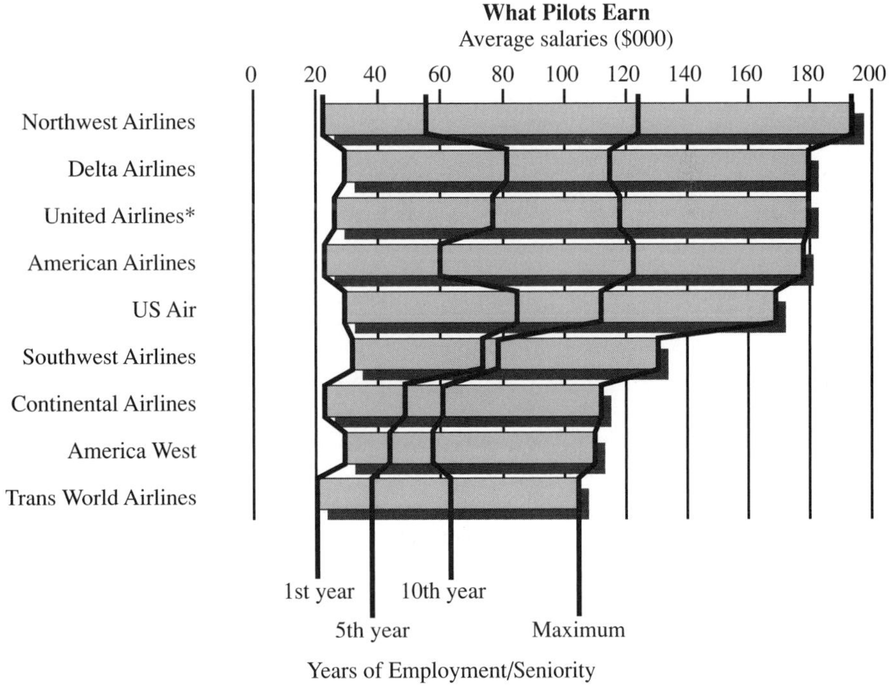

* Adjusted to reflect concessions the pilots made in exchange for an equity stake.

Source: Air Inc., Atlanta.

EXHIBIT 7.3 Secretary to the Chief Executive Officer

	Avg. Base Salary	*Avg. Bonus*	*Avg. Total Cash*
By Revenues (billions)			
$10 and over	$68,800	$5,700	$74,500
$5–10	61,200	6,400	67,600
$2–$5	53,800	2,800	56,600
Less than $2	51,500	4,900	56,400
By Region			
Metro New York	65,900	7,200	73,100
North Central	51,800	3,600	55,400
Northeast*	51,900	2,200	54,100
South Central	50,600	8,500	59,100
Southeast	62,400	4,300	66,700
West Coast	60,300	5,700	66,000

	Avg. Base Salary	*Avg. Bonus*	*Avg. Total Cash*
By Industry			
Chemical and pharmaceuticals	$55,700	—	$55,700
Consumer products	61,100	$7,500	68,600
Technology and equipment	60,800	6,300	67,100
Natural resources and exploration	49,600	—	49,600
Financial services	64,000	4,400	68,400
Utilities	61,200	5,500	66,700
Other service organizations	55,300	5,000	60,300

* Excluding Metro New York

Source: Executive Resource Group

its pay level for sales and market positions was almost 40 percent above the market (Exhibit 7.4). Its CEO was paid 30 percent below the market. Obviously, company A's pay strategy placed great importance on sales and marketing. Company B displayed a completely different pattern. While it was 2.6 percent above the market overall, its CEO's pay was 7 percent above the market and the pay of its sales and marketing people was 3 percent above the market. The internal pay structure at company B closely mirrored the pay relationships found in the external market; company A's pay structure did not. The data suggest that B is a market matcher and A has decided it pays to pay differently.[5]

WHAT SHAPES EXTERNAL COMPETITIVENESS?

The factors that affect the pay level and consequently external competitiveness are grouped in Exhibit 7.5. They include the pressures exerted by (1) competition in labor markets for workers with sought-after skills and abilities; (2) competition in product and service markets, which affects the financial condition of the organization; and (3) characteristics unique to each organization and its work force, such as its business strategies and the productivity and experience of its work force. These factors act in concert to influence pay-level decisions.

---

[5] Barry Gerhart and George Milkovich, "Employee Compensation: Research and Practice," in *Handbook of Industrial and Organizational Psychology,* 2nd ed., ed. M. D. Dunnette and L. M. Hough (Palo Alto, CA: Consulting Psychologists Press, 1992).

EXHIBIT 7.4 The Relationship of Company Pay Scales to Market Average

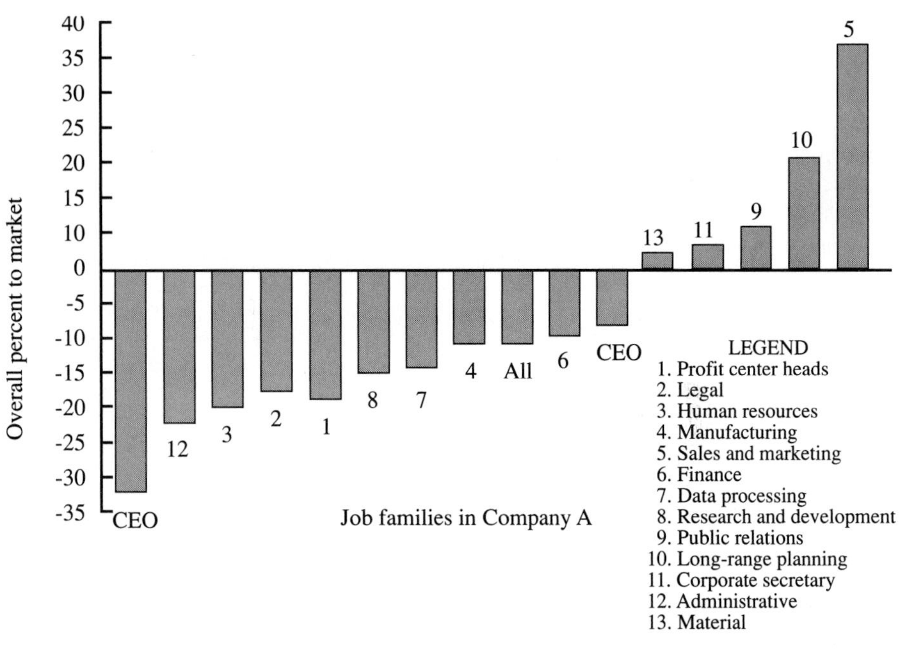

Source: Reprinted by permission of the publisher from Kenneth E. Foster, "An Anatomy of Company Pay Practices," *Personnel,* September 1985, pp. 69-70. © 1985 by the American Management Association.

LABOR MARKET FACTORS

Economists describe two basic types of markets: the quoted price and the bourse. Stores that label each item's price or ads that list a job opening's starting wage are examples of *quoted price markets.* Buying at a flea market or haggling over the terms and conditions in professional athletes' contracts are examples of *bourses.* Graduating students usually find themselves in a quoted labor market, though some haggling over terms may occur.[6] Both types of market involve an exchange between buyers (the employers) and sellers (the workers). If the inducements offered by the employer and the skills offered by the worker are mutually acceptable, a contract is executed. The contract may be formal, such as those made with unions, professional athletes, and executive officers, or informal, with an implied understanding or a brief letter. The result of the workings of the labor market is the allocation of employees to opportunities at specified pay rates.

[6] Barry Gerhart and Sara Rynes, "Determinants and Consequences of Salary Negotiations by Male and Female MBA Graduates," *Journal of Applied Psychology* 76, no. 2 (1991), pp. 256–62.

EXHIBIT 7.5 What Shapes External Competitiveness?

PRODUCT MARKET FACTORS Degree of Competition Level of Product Demand	}	
LABOR MARKET FACTORS Nature of Demand Nature of Supply	}	EXTERNAL COMPETITIVENESS
ORGANIZATION FACTORS Industry, Strategy, Size, Individual Manager	}	

Check this site for its links to the home pages for many companies. **<http://a2z.lycos.com/Business_and_Investing/Corporate_Home_Pages_A2Z/U.S./>** A number of these companies post job openings on their web sites. Select several companies that you believe might be labor market competitors (e.g., Microsoft, Oracle, IBM). Compare their job postings. Do any companies list salaries for their jobs? Do they quote a single salary? Do they allow room for haggling? Do you think any of your companies might be market setters?

How Markets Work

Labor market theory begins with four basic assumptions.

1. Employers always seek to maximize profits.
2. Human resources are homogenous and therefore interchangeable; a business school graduate is a business school graduate is a business school graduate.
3. The pay rates reflect all costs associated with employment (e.g., holidays, benefits, and training).
4. The markets faced by employers are competitive, so there is no advantage for a single employer to pay above or below the market rate.

Although these assumptions oversimplify reality, they provide a framework for understanding labor markets. As we shall see later, as we change our assumptions, our theories change, too.

EXHIBIT 7.6 Supply and Demand for M.B.A.s in the Short Run

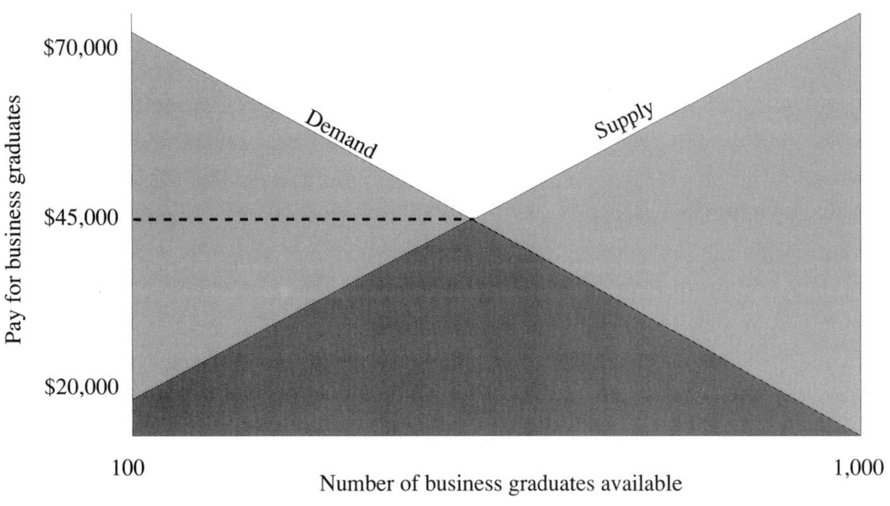

Compensation managers often refer to the "market." "Our pay is market driven," "We pay competitively with the market," or "We are market leaders." Understanding how markets work requires analysis of the demand and supply of labor. The demand side focuses on the *employer:* how many employees they seek and what they are able and willing to pay. The supply side looks at the *workers:* their qualifications and the pay they are willing to accept in exchange for their services.

Exhibit 7.6 shows a simple illustration of demand for and supply of business school graduates. The vertical axis represents pay rates from $20,000 to $70,000 a year. The horizontal axis is the number of business school graduates in the market, ranging from 100 to 1,000. In Exhibit 7.6, the line labeled demand is the sum of all employers' hiring requirements for business graduates at various pay levels. If the pay for business graduates is $70,000, only 100 of them will be hired. (Few firms will be able to afford them.) If the pay is $20,000, then companies can afford to hire 1,000 business graduates. However, as we look at the line labeled supply, we see that there aren't 1,000 business graduates willing to be hired at $20,000. In fact, only 100 are. As pay rates rise, more graduates become interested in working, so the labor supply line slopes upward. The point where the lines for labor demand and labor supply cross determines the market rate. In this illustration, the interaction among all employers and all business graduates determines the $45,000 market rate. Because any single employer can hire all the business graduates it wants at $45,000 and all business graduates are of equal quality (assumption #2), there is no reason for any wage other than $45,000 to be paid.

Labor Demand

So if $45,000 is the market-determined rate for business graduates, how many business graduates will a specific employer hire? The answer requires an analysis of labor demand. In the near term, when an employer cannot change any other factor of production (i.e., technology, capital, or natural resources), its level of production can change only if the level of human resources is changed. Under such conditions, a single employer's demand for labor coincides with the marginal product of labor.

The **marginal product of labor** is the additional output associated with the employment of one additional human resources unit, with other factors held constant.

The **marginal revenue of labor** is the additional revenue generated when the firm employs one additional unit of human resources, with other factors held constant.

Marginal Product

Assume that two business graduates form a consulting firm that provides services to 10 clients. They hire a third person and add five more clients. The marginal product (the change in output associated with the additional unit of labor) of employing the third business graduate is five. But the marginal product of a fourth hire may not be the same as the marginal product of the third. In fact, adding a fourth business graduate generates only four new clients. This diminishing marginal productivity results from the fact that each additional graduate has a progressively smaller share of the other factors of production with which to work. In the short term, other factors of production (e.g., office space, number of computers) are fixed. As more business graduates are brought into the firm without changing other production factors, the marginal productivity must eventually decline.

Marginal Revenue

Now let's look at marginal revenue. Marginal revenue is the money generated by the sale of the marginal product; the additional output associated with the employment of one additional person. In the case of the consulting firm, it's the revenues generated by each additional business graduate. If the graduate's marginal revenue exceeds $45,000, profits are increased by the additional hiring. Conversely, if marginal revenue is less than $45,000, the employer would lose money on the last hire. Recall that our first labor market theory assumption is that employers seek to maximize profits. Therefore, the employer will continue to employ additional graduates until the marginal revenue generated by that last hire is equal to the expenses associated with employing that worker. Because other potential costs will not change in the short run, *the level of demand that maximizes profits is that level at which the marginal revenue of the last hire is equal to the wage rate for that hire.*

EXHIBIT 7.7 Supply and Demand at the Market and Individual Employer Level

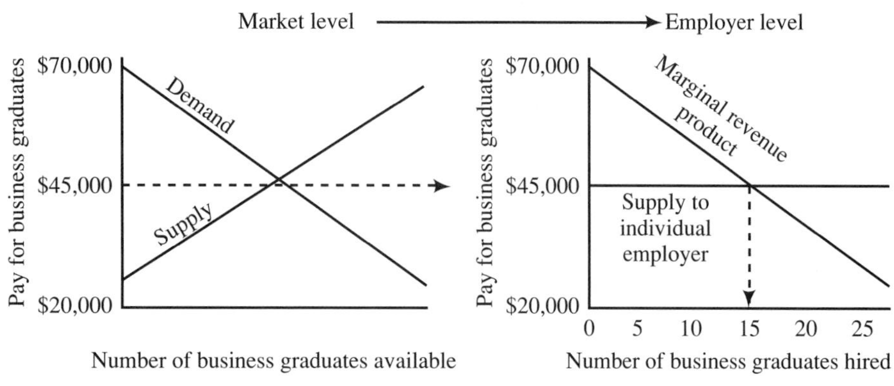

Exhibit 7.7 shows the connection between the labor market model and conditions facing a single employer. On the left is the same supply and demand model from Exhibit 7.6 showing that pay level ($45,000) is determined by the interaction of all employers' demand for business graduates. The right side of the exhibit shows supply and demand at the level of the individual employer. At the market-determined rate ($45,000), the individual employer can hire as many business graduates as desired. Therefore, supply is now a horizontal line representing an unlimited supply of graduates. The demand line still slopes downward, so that the two lines intersect at 15; that is, for this employer, the marginal revenue of the 15th graduate is $45,000. The marginal revenue of the 16th graduate may be $43,000. The point at which the incremental income that hiring the graduate brings to the firm—the marginal revenue product—just equals the wage rate is 15. Until this level of employment is reached, additional graduates contribute more to revenues than they do to costs, so it is worthwhile for the individual employer to continue to hire.[7]

So the manager who uses the marginal product model must do only two things: (1) determine the pay level set by market forces and (2) determine the marginal revenue generated by each potential new employee. These two pieces of information will decide how many people to hire. Simple? Of course not.

Although this model of labor supply and demand provides a valuable analytical framework, it has a number of limitations when applied to managing compensation. The first is that the model's assumptions oversimplify the real world. For example, the assumed degree of competition among buyers and sellers does not exist, nor are factors of production homogeneous, nor are all firms profit maximizers (some maximize market

[7] Paul Milgrom and John Roberts, *Economics, Organization and Management* (Englewood Cliffs, NJ: Prentice Hall, 1992).

share, long-term profits, and so on). The second objection is that managers have no idea what the marginal revenue and marginal products are. Difficulties in trying to operationalize these concepts of marginal revenue and marginal product include the following:

1. Placing a value on the goods or services each individual employee produces.
2. Determining individual values on products and services that are produced through joint efforts of different workers with a variety of talents. Think about this the next time you are in the local supermarket, the symphony hall, or even your college. It will be immediately obvious that labor is heterogeneous, not homogeneous.
3. Factoring out the contributions of other resources (capital and raw materials) in the production process.

Since measuring marginal product and revenue directly is difficult, managers often use other factors that they believe reflect value. In the last two chapters, we discussed compensable factors, skill blocks, and competencies. When the compensable factors define what organizations value in work, job evaluation based on these factors assesses the job's contribution to organization goals. Thus, job evaluation results may be in some sense a proxy for marginal revenue product. However, compensable factors are usually defined as *input* (skills required, problem solving required, responsibilities), rather than as the value of the *output* of a job. The same logic applies to skills and competencies.

Marginal productivity concepts may be relevant to establish the maximum pay rates for jobs or to link pay increases to performance. For example, the highest pay rates or performance payments should not exceed the marginal revenue product, or how much can be received for what the employee produces. Managers may have a "feel" for the link between maximum pay and what the organization can afford, but links to marginal revenue product are theoretical only. As to linking performance to pay, any gains from such a link must be traded off against the cost of measuring, or even estimating, performance.[8] If output from a job is easily measurable, then calculating marginal revenue and linking it to pay may be possible. But for most work, the requirements of having easily measured output and placing a value on it are difficult to meet.

Labor Supply

The labor supply level in Exhibit 7.6 represents different numbers of employees available at different pay rates. Like demand, the exact shape of the line representing the supply of labor depends on the assumptions. In perfectly competitive markets, an individual employer faces a horizontal supply; that is, the market determines the price, and the individual employer can hire all the employees it wants, at that price. (See the right side of Exhibit 7.7.) This model assumes that many workers are seeking jobs, that they possess accurate information about all job openings, and that no barriers to mobility

[8] Charles Brown, "Firms' Choice of Method of Pay," *Industrial and Labor Relations Review* 40 (1990), pp. S165–S182; Edward P. Lazear, *Personnel Economics* (New York: John Wiley & Sons, 1998).

(discrimination, licensing provisions, or union membership requirements) among jobs exist.

As in the analysis of labor demand, these assumptions greatly simplify the real world. As the assumptions of the model change, so does the supply. The upward-sloping line or curve we have looked at so far implies that as pay increases, more people are willing to take a job. But if unemployment rates are low, individual offers of higher pay may not increase supply. If the higher offer is matched quickly by competitors, the employer may face a higher pay level but no increase in supply. For example, when Giant Foods raised its hourly pay 50 cents above the minimum wage in the Chicago area, Wendy's and Burger King quickly followed suit. The result was that the supermarket was paying more for the employees it already had but was still short-handed.

An employer who dominates the local labor market, such as Corning Glass in Corning, New York, may also find that raising wages doesn't necessarily attract more applications simply because the supply has dried up. People who are conveniently located to Corning and interested in work are already there. Any increase in employment requires that additional applicants must be induced to enter the labor supply, perhaps from schools, retirement, or more distant areas. A dominant employer has relatively wide latitude in determining pay levels, since few local labor market competitors exist. However, once the local labor supply is exhausted, small increases in the pay levels may not attract more applicants. The supply curve, although sloping upward, may take on the shape of a "step" function and may require large pay increases to attract additional people. Although many firms find lowering the job requirements and hiring less-skilled workers a better choice than raising wages, any pay savings may be offset by increased training expenses.

MODIFICATIONS TO THE DEMAND SIDE

The story is told of the economics professor and the student who were strolling through campus. "Look," the student cried, "there's a $100 bill on the path!"

"No, you are mistaken," the wiser head replied. "That cannot be. If there were actually a $100 bill, someone would have picked it up."

The point of the story is that economic theories must frequently be revised to account for reality. We started this chapter by observing that different employers offer different pay rates for similar jobs to similar people. This reality differs from what the economic model assumes and predicts. So economists and psychologists modify the model to make it better conform to what actually happens when we change our focus from *all* the employers in an economy to a *particular* employer. A particularly troublesome issue for economists is why an employer would pay more than what theory states is the market-determined rate. Let us look at some modifications to explain this phenomenon. Three modifications to the classic economic model address the pay-level decisions of individual employers: compensating differentials, efficiency wage, and signaling. (See Exhibit 7.8.) Generally, these modifications seek to explain why employers pay rates that may be above or below "market."

EXHIBIT 7.8 Labor Demand Theories and Implications

Theory	*Prediction*	*So What?*
Compensating differentials	Work with negative characteristics requires higher pay to attract workers.	Job evaluation and compensable factors must capture these negative characteristics.
Efficiency wage	Above-market wages will improve efficiency by attracting workers who will perform better and be less willing to leave.	Staffing programs must have the capability of selecting the best employees; work must be structured to take advantage of employees' greater efforts.
Signaling	Pay policies signal the kinds of behavior the employer seeks.	Pay practices must recognize these behaviors by better pay, larger bonuses, and other forms of compensation.

Compensating Differentials

More than 200 years ago, Adam Smith argued that individuals consider the "whole of the advantages and disadvantages of different employments" and make decisions based on the alternative with the greatest "net advantage."[9] If a job has negative characteristics, that is, if the necessary training is very expensive (medical school), job security is tenuous (stockbrokers), working conditions are disagreeable (highway construction), or chances of success are low (professional sports), then employers must offer higher wages to compensate for these negative features.

Such *compensating differentials* explain the presence of various pay rates in the market. Although the notion is appealing, it is hard to document, due to the difficulties in measuring and controlling all the factors that go into a net advantage calculation.

Efficiency Wage Theory

Efficiency wage theory challenges the basic assumption of the employer as a powerless payer of market-determined wages. Instead, this theory posits that sometimes an employer can reduce unit labor costs by paying above-market wages. The high wages may increase efficiency by:

1. Attracting higher-quality applicants.
2. Lowering turnover.
3. Increasing worker effort, out of "gratitude" toward the employer.

[9] Thomas A. Mahoney, *Compensation and Reward Perspective* (Burr Ridge, IL: Richard D. Irwin 1979), p. 123.

4. Reducing worker "shirking" (what economists say when they mean "screwing around") due to the increased cost of being fired.
5. Reducing the need to supervise employees.

Notice that the first four mechanisms assume that the same number of employees will be hired, even at higher rates. The additional costs are offset by increased productivity. Only the last mechanism, reduced supervision, opens the possibility of increasing efficiency by hiring fewer employees. So basically, efficiency increases by hiring better employees or motivating present employees to work harder. The underlying assumption is that pay level determines effort—again, an appealing notion that is difficult to document.

There is some research on efficiency wage theory.[10] One study looked at shirking behavior by examining the relationship between rates of employee discipline and higher wages in several plants of the same firm. Shirking was measured as the number of disciplinary layoffs. (A union contract forbade dismissals without work-related cause.) Higher wages were associated with lower shirking. Shirking was also lower where high unemployment made it more difficult for fired workers to find another job. So while the higher wages cut shirking, the authors were unable to say whether it was cut enough to offset the higher wage bill.[11]

Other research shows that high-wage employers also expend greater efforts on recruiting.[12] This dichotomy is explained by the greater selectivity in hiring that is made possible by the large number of applicants attracted by the high wages. However, although high pay attracts more qualified applicants, it also attracts more unqualified applicants. Few companies evaluate their recruiting programs well enough to show if they do in fact choose superior applicants. So an above-market wage does not always guarantee a more productive work force. Superior recruiting and selection programs are also required.

Does an above-market wage allow an organization to operate with fewer supervisors? Some research evidence says yes. For example, a study of hospitals found that those that paid high wages to staff nurses employed fewer nurse supervisors.[13] However, the researchers did not speculate on whether the higher wages attracted *better* nurses or caused *average* nurses to work harder. Also, we don't know whether the higher wages allowed the hospital to reduce overall nursing costs.

---

[10] Carl M. Campbell III, "Do Firms Pay Efficiency Wages? Evidence with Data at the Firm Level," *Journal of Labor Economics* 11, no. 3 (1993), pp. 442–69.

[11] Peter Cappelli and Keith Chauvin, "An Interplant Test of the Efficiency Wage Hypothesis," *Quarterly Journal of Economics,* August 1991, pp. 769–87.

[12] L. Rynes and J. W. Boudreau, "College Recruiting in Large Organizations: Practice, Evaluation, and Research Implications," *Personnel Psychology* 39 (1986), pp. 729–57.

[13] Erica Groshen, "Why Do Wages Vary Among Employees?" *Economic Review* 24 (1988), pp. 19–38; E. Groshen and A. B. Krueger, "The Structure of Supervision and Pay in Hospitals," *Industrial and Labor Relations Review,* February 1990, pp. 134S–46S.

Signaling

Another variation on the demand model seeks to explain not only the variability in pay levels, but also wages that may be *below* the market.[14] *Signaling theory* says that employers may deliberately design pay policies as part of a strategy that signals to both prospective and current employees what kinds of behaviors are sought. A policy of paying below the market for base pay yet offering generous bonuses or training opportunities sends a different signal, and presumably attracts different applicants, than a policy of paying market wage without bonus tied to performance. An employer who combines low base with high bonuses may be signaling that employees are expected to be risk takers. The proportion of people within the organization who are eligible for bonuses signals the extent to which the reward system is geared to all employees (versus managers only). It may be that in the absence of complete and accurate information about the job, applicants make inferences about nonmonetary job attributes (colleagues, job assignments, etc.) based on what they know about an employer's relative pay level. If this is so, then pay level signals a whole raft of information, both intended and unintended, accurate and inaccurate.

As noted, a number of studies have shown that pay level is a significant factor in attracting applicants. Not surprisingly, employers are reluctant to set low pay for jobs filled from the external market or filled by applicants who are well positioned to exchange information: college students. A study of college students approaching graduation found that a variety of pay characteristics beyond pay level affects their job decisions.[15] Students were more likely to pursue jobs that offer higher pay levels, but they also showed a preference for individual-based (rather than team-based) pay, fixed (rather than variable) pay, job-based (rather than skill-based) pay, and flexible benefits (choices available). This study also rated job seekers on various personal dimensions—materialism, confidence in their abilities, and risk aversion—and then related them to pay preferences. Pay level was extremely important to materialists and less important to those who valued continuous personal improvement and to those who were risk averse. The point is that applicants appear to self-select among job opportunities based on the perceived match between their personal dispositions and the nature of the organization, as signaled by the pay system. Pay level is only one pay characteristic that sends a signal.

Signaling works on the supply side of the model, too, as suppliers of labor signal to potential employers. Individuals who are better trained, have higher grades in relevant courses, and/or have related work experience signal to prospective employers that they are likely to be better performers. Presumably they signal with the same degree of accuracy as employers. So both investments in human capital (degrees, grades, experience) and pay decisions about level (lead, match, lag) and mix (higher bonuses, benefit choices) act as signals and presumably help employees and organizations exchange information.

---

[14] Allison Barber, "Pay as a Signal in Job Choice" (Graduate School of Business Administration, Michigan State University); and J. M. Barron, J. Bishop, and W. C. Dunkelberg, "Employer Search: The Interviewing and Hiring of New Employees," *The Review of Economics and Statistics* 67 (1985), pp. 43–52.

[15] Daniel M. Cable and Timothy A. Judge, "Pay Preferences and Job Search Decisions: A Person-Organization Fit Perspective," *Personnel Psychology,* Summer 1994, pp. 317–48.

EXHIBIT 7.9 Labor Supply Theories and Implications

Theory	*Prediction*	*So What?*
Reservation wage	Job seekers will not accept jobs whose pay is below a certain wage, no matter how attractive other job aspects.	Pay level will affect ability to recruit.
Human capital	The value of an individual's skills and abilities is a function of the time and expense required to acquire them.	Higher pay is required to induce people to train for more difficult jobs.
Job competition	Workers compete through qualifications for jobs with established wages.	As hiring difficulties increase, employers should expect to spend more to train new hires.

MODIFICATIONS TO THE SUPPLY SIDE

Turning to the supply side of the model, which focuses on employees rather than employers, the question becomes: What affects worker behavior? We'll discuss three theories shown in Exhibit 7.9: reservation wage, human capital, and job competition.

Reservation Wage

Economists are renowned for their linguistic creativity and their great sense of humor. So it is not surprising that many of them describe pay as "noncompensatory."[16] What they mean is that job seekers have a *reservation wage* below which they will not accept a job offer, no matter how attractive the other job attributes. If pay does not meet their minimum standard, no other job attributes can make up (i.e., compensate) for this inadequacy. Other theorists go a step further and say that some job seekers—satisfiers—take the first job offer they get where the pay meets their reservation wage. A reservation wage may be above or below the market wage. The theory is seeking to explain differences in workers' responses to offers.

Human Capital

The theory of *human capital,* perhaps the most influential economic theory for explaining pay differences, is based on the premise that higher earnings flow to those who improve their productive capabilities by investing in themselves (e.g., education, training,

[16] C. Brown, "Firms' Choice of Method of Pay," *Industrial and Labor Relations Review,* February 1990, pp. S165–S182.

experience).[17] The theory assumes that people are in fact paid at the value of their marginal product. Improving productive abilities by investing in training or even in one's physical health will increase one's marginal product. The value of an individual's skills and abilities is a function of the time, expense, and resources expended to acquire them. Consequently, jobs that require long and expensive training (engineering, physicians) should receive higher pay levels than jobs that require less investment (clerical work, elementary school teaching). As pay level increases, the number of people willing to overcome these barriers increase, which creates an upward-sloping supply.

Research does support the relationship between years of education or experience and earnings, although some evidence suggests that there is a limit: getting a Ph.D. is not as sound an investment as getting a bachelor's and/or master's degree.

Job Competition

Job competition theory is somewhat similar to human capital theory in that both imply that a decreased labor supply is associated with higher costs for the employer. The human capital theory says these higher costs are the result of higher pay levels. The job competition model says the higher costs take the form of additional training expenses that the employer must bear.

The job competition model asserts that workers do not compete for pay in labor markets. Rather, pay for jobs is "quoted" or established, and workers compete through their qualifications for the job opportunities. A pool of applicants develops for every opportunity. Individuals in the pool are ranked by prospective employers according to the skills, abilities, and experience required for the job. As the employer dips further and further into the applicant pool, individuals require more training and are less productive, even though they receive the same wage. Accordingly, the total costs (pay plus training) associated with each additional unit of labor in the pool increases as the market demand increases.

A number of additional factors affect the supply of labor available to an employer. Geographic barriers to mobility among jobs, union requirements, lack of information about job openings, the degree of risk involved, and the degree of unemployment also influence labor market conditions.

PRODUCT MARKET FACTORS AND ABILITY TO PAY

The supply and demand for labor are major determinants of an employer's pay level. However, any organization must, over time, generate enough revenue to cover expenses, including compensation. It follows that an employer's pay level is constrained by its ability to compete in the product/service market. So product market conditions to a large extent determine what the organization can afford to pay.

---

[17] Gary S. Becker, *Human Capital* (Chicago: University of Chicago Press, 1975); Barry Gerhart, "Gender Differences in Current and Starting Salaries: The Role of Performance, College Major, and Job Title," *Industrial and Labor Relations Review* 43 (1990), pp. 418–33.

The *degree of competition* and *product demand* are the two key product market factors. Both affect the ability of the organization to change the prices it charges for its products and services. If prices cannot be changed without decreasing sales and thereby losing income, then the ability of the employer to set a higher pay level is constrained.

Product Demand

Although the labor market conditions put a floor on the pay level required to attract sufficient employees, the product market puts a lid on the maximum pay level that an employer can set. If the employer pays above the maximum, it must either pass on to consumers the higher pay level through price increases or hold prices fixed and allocate a greater share of total revenues to cover labor costs.

For many years, U.S. automakers solved this affordability dilemma by routinely passing on increased pay in the form of higher car prices. Although competition among the "Big Three" automakers existed, they all passed on the pay increases. But global competitive pressures changed all this. Japanese auto makers like Toyota and Honda produced better quality cars. Faced with lower customer demand for their cars, U.S. automakers responded by restructuring. Some auto workers took pay cuts, accepted smaller wage increases, and agreed to job changes intended to improve productivity. The process is still continuing, with the result that both U.S. and imported autos are of much better quality today than they were ten years ago.

Degree of Competition

Employers in highly competitive markets such as manufacturers of generic drugs are less able to raise prices without loss of revenues. At the other extreme, single sellers of a product, such as Pfizer with its patented drug Viagra, are able to set whatever price they choose. However, setting too high a price encourages other drug companies to fund research and development of competing drugs that can also be patented.

Other factors besides the product market conditions affect pay level. Some of these have already been discussed. The productivity of labor, the technology employed, the level of production relative to plant capacity available, and the extent of nonhuman resource expenses all affect compensation decisions. These factors vary more *across* than *within* industries. The technologies employed and consumer preferences may vary among auto manufacturers, but the differences are relatively small when compared to the technologies and product demand of auto manufacturers versus the technologies and product demand in, say, the oil or banking industry.

A Dose of Reality: What Managers Say

Discussions with compensation managers provide insight into how all of these economic factors translate into actual pay decisions.[18] In one study, a number of scenarios

[18] David I. Levine, "Fairness, Markets, and Ability to Pay: Evidence from Compensation Executives," *American Economic Review,* December 1993, pp. 1241–59.

were presented in which unemployment, profitability, and labor market conditions varied. The managers were asked to make wage adjustment recommendations for several positions. *Level of unemployment* made almost no difference. One manager was incredulous at the suggestion: "You mean take advantage of the fact that there are a lot of people out of work?" (She must not have taken Economics 101.) Differing levels of *profitability* were deemed a factor for higher management to consider in setting the overall pay budget rather than a factor for these compensation managers to consider for individual positions. While numerous indicators of *ability to pay* were mentioned, what it boiled down to was, Whatever the chief financial officer says we can afford! They were sympathetic to a company forced to pay less due to its own financial circumstances, but if a company had the resources, the compensation managers saw it as shortsighted to pay less, even though market conditions would have permitted lower pay. This mind-set probably helps explain *wage's downward stickiness.* Pay goes up more easily than it falls. In direct contradiction to efficiency wage theory, these managers believed that high turnover and difficulty in attracting applicants is a result of poor management rather than a compensation issue. The managers did not recommend increasing wages to solve these problems. Instead, they offered the opinion that, "supervisors try to solve with money their difficulties with managing people."[19]

Another dose of reality comes from companies competing for low-wage, low-skill workers. Nearly 30 percent of all U.S. employees make less than $8 an hour, working at hotels, fast-food restaurants, food processors, or retail outlets. These companies are all facing a scarcity of workers. With unemployment low and turnover high, many of these employers have found it more useful to provide nonwage services to their employees rather than increase wages. McDonald's offers 50 percent food discounts for workers' families. Marriot has a hotline to social workers who assist with child care and transportation crises. English language and citizenship courses are offered for recent immigrants. Seminars on how to manage your finances (and checkbook) and your life (self esteem and family counseling) are offered to low-wage, low-skilled employees.

Why do employers provide such services rather than wage increase? Managers claim that employees value these services more than a wage increase. They would be unable to locate and purchase these services on their own, even if they had more money. Additionally, because of competition for employees, a wage increase would likely be quickly matched by competitors. So everyone would be paying more but getting no advantage from it.[20] A "Your Turn" at the end of this chapter asks you to take a look at what economic theories predict for this segment of the economy.

The point is not that our theories are useless when applied to specific situations. Rather, the point is that reality is complex. Theories are useful when they help us better understand these complexities. More than money matters. Practice is fashioned and tested in the day-to-day world. Compensation theories need to be, too.

---

[19] Ibid., p. 1250.

[20] Family and Work Institute, 1992 Survey; K. Grimsley, "U.S. Corporations Look at Incentives to Entice Low-Wage Workers to Stay," *International Herald Tribune,* March 24, 1997, p. 1.

ORGANIZATION FACTORS

Although product and labor market conditions create a range of possibilities within which managers may set the pay level, other organizational factors such as the type of industry, its business strategy, and even its size may influence pay level decisions.[21]

Industry

The industry in which an organization chooses to compete dictates the particular technologies it employs. Labor intensive industries, such as education and services, tend to be lower paying than are industries whose technologies are less labor intensive, such as petroleum and pharmaceuticals. The importance of qualifications and experience tailored to particular technologies is often overlooked in theoretical analysis of labor markets. But machinists and millwrights who build diesel locomotives for General Electric in Erie, Pennsylvania, have very different qualifications from those machinists and millwrights who build airplanes for Boeing in Seattle, Washington.[22]

Employer Size

There is consistent evidence that large organizations tend to pay more than small ones. For example, earlier you read about CEO secretaries' pay: those in larger organizations received 5 to 10 percent above the average.[23] Another example: a study of manufacturing firms found that firms with 100 to 500 workers paid 6 percent higher wages than did smaller firms; firms of more than 500 workers paid 12 percent more than did the smallest firms.[24]

This relationship between organization size and pay is consistent with economic theory that says the marginal value of having more able people increases with organization size because their talents can influence more people and decisions. The underlying assumption is that the market operates efficiently, that is, the more qualified people are allocated to the more influential positions from where they can have a larger economic impact. Think of the advertising revenue that David Letterman can bring to CBS versus the potential revenue to station WBNS if his late-night show was only seen in Athens, Ohio. WBNS could not generate enough revenue to be able to afford to pay Mr. Letterman $14 million; CBS can.

---

[21] Erica L. Groshen, "Sources of Intra-Industry Wage Dispersion: How Much Do Employers Matter?" *Quarterly Journal of Economics,* August 1991, pp. 869–84.

[22] D. M. Raff, "The Puzzling Profusion of Compensation Systems in the Interwar Automobile Industry," NBER, 1998. Raff attributes the fantastic diversity of compensation programs for blue-collar employees (firm-based, piece rate, company-wide, team-based) to differences in technology employed among competitors.

[23] Executive Secretarial Survey 1993 (Wilton, CT: Executive Resource Group, 1994); Tamar Lewin, "As the Boss Goes, So Goes the Secretary: Is it Bias?" *New York Times,* March 17, 1994, pp. A1, B9.

[24] Wesley Mellow, "Employer Size and Wages," *Review of Economics and Statistics* 64, no. 3 (August 1982), pp. 495–501.

Organization Strategy

As you read in Chapter 2, an organization's strategy also affects its pay-level decision. Some employers adopt a *low-cost/low-wage strategy;* they compete by producing goods and services as cheaply as possible. The Marriotts and McDonald's of the world follow this strategy. Others adopt a *mutual commitment strategy* that combines higher wages with an emphasis on quality, innovation, and customer service.[25] They believe that high wages are essential to reinforce cooperation and participation and will lead the way to a better living standard for all employees. In fact, according to some, the failure to adopt this mutual commitment strategy is what's wrong with the country today.[26] (Who says academics can't be passionate?)

RELEVANT MARKETS

Up to this point, we've examined labor market, product market, and organization factors that influence the pay level. Next, we focus on relevant markets. Economist take the *market* for granted. As in, "the market determines wages." This strikes many compensation managers as bizarrely abstract. Managers pay people. They consider defining the *relevant* market a big part of figuring out how much to pay.

Although the notion of a single homogeneous labor market may be an interesting analytical device, it does not mirror reality. Rather, each organization operates in many labor markets, with unique demand and supply. Managers must define the markets that are relevant for pay purposes and establish the appropriate competitive positions in these markets. The three factors usually used to determine the relevant labor markets are the occupation (qualifications required), geography (willingness to relocate and/or commute), and the other organizations that compete in the same product/service market.

Occupations

The skills and qualifications required in an occupation are important because they tend to limit mobility among occupations. Qualifications include licensing and certification requirements as well as training and education. Accountants, for example, would have difficulty becoming dentists. However, unless they bill themselves as certified public accountants, dentists would break no laws if they started selling accounting services.

---

[25] Thomas Kochan and Paul Osterman, *The Mutual Gains Enterprise: Forging A Winning Partnership Among Labor, Management and Government* (Cambridge: Harvard University Press, 1994); Lee Dyer,"Human Resources as a Source of Competitive Advantage" (Working paper, Cornell University Center for Advanced Human Resource Studies, Ithaca, NY, 1994); Peter Cappelli and Harbir Singh, "Integrating Strategic Human Resources and Strategic Management," in *Research Frontiers in IR and HR,* ed. D. Lewin, O. Mitchell, and P. Sherer (Madison, WI: Industrial Relations Research Association, 1992); Jeffrey Pfeffer, *Competitive Advantage Through People* (Boston: Harvard University Press, 1994).

[26] Thomas Kochan and Lee Dyer, "Managing Transformational Change: The Role of HR Professionals" (Working paper, Cornell University Center for Advanced Human Resource Studies, Ithaca, NY, 1993).

Geography

Qualifications interact with geography to further define the scope of the relevant labor markets. Degreed professionals (accountants, engineers, dentists) are typically recruited nationally. Technicians, craftspeople, and operatives are usually recruited regionally, and office workers, locally. However, the geographic scope of a market is not fixed. It changes in response to workers' willingness to relocate or commute certain distances. This propensity to be mobile in turn may be affected by personal and economic circumstances as well as the employer's pay level. Configurations of local markets are even shaped by the availability of convenient public transportation. Furthermore, the geographic limits may not be the same for all in a broad skill group. Not all accountants operate in a national market; some firms recruit them regionally, others locally. As Exhibit 7.10 shows, pay differentials vary among localities. A job that averages $26,000 nationally can range from $19,225 in Laredo to $29,600 in San Francisco.

Product Market Competitors

In addition to the occupation and geography, the industry in which the employer competes also affects the relevant labor markets by relating the qualifications required to particular technologies. Product market comparisons also focus on comparative labor costs.

Defining the Revelant Market

How do employers choose their relevant market? Surprisingly little research has been done on this issue. But if the markets are incorrectly defined, the estimates of other employer's pay rates may be incorrect and the pay level inappropriately established. One study divided the process of collecting pay rates into two decisions.[27]

1. Which companies to request data from.
2. What data to use and how to weight it.

The first decision is based on known characteristics of the companies: industry, union status, location, size, and hiring practices. But whose data are actually used depends on the quality of the data received. (See Chapter 8 for more specifics.)

What data are weighted most heavily in defining the relevant market, the *product market* competitors' or the *labor market* competitors'? The data from product market competitors are likely to receive greater weight when the following factors apply:

1. Labor costs are a large share of total costs.
2. Product demand is responsive to price changes; that is, people won't pay $4.50 for a bottle of Leinenkugel; they'll have a Bud instead.

[27] Chockalingham Viswesvaran and Murray Barrick, "Decision Making Effects on Compensation Surveys: Implications for Market Wages" *Journal of Applied Psychology* 77, no. 5 (1992), pp. 588–97.

EXHIBIT 7.10 Pay Differences by Location

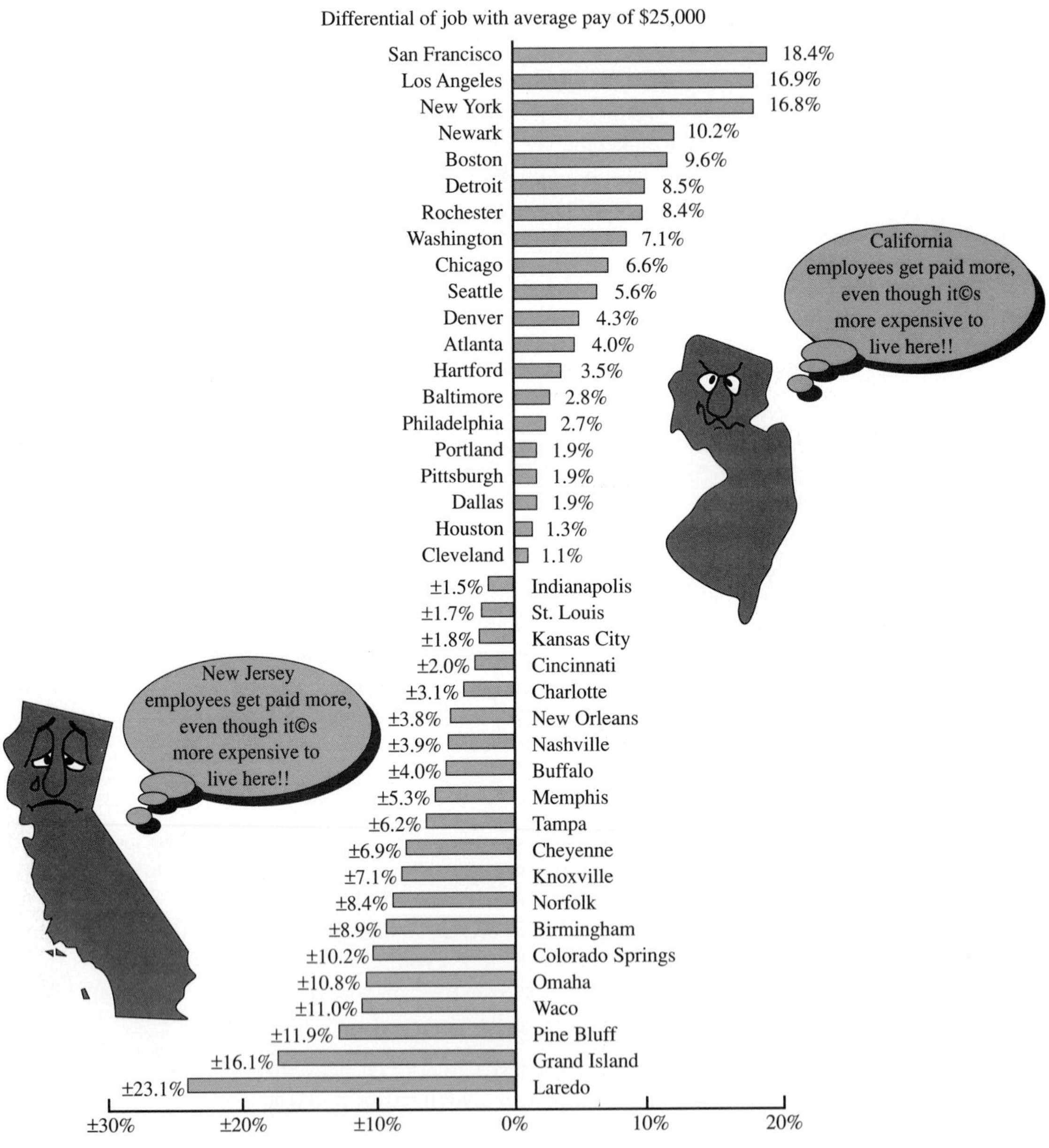

Source: Data from Mercer & Co.

3. Supply of labor is not responsive to changes in pay. Recall the earlier low-wage/low-skill example.
4. Employee skills are specific to the product market and will remain so. (Recall the Boeing millwrights versus the GE Locomotive millwrights.)

On the other hand, labor market comparisons will be more important if the following are true:

1. The organization is having difficulty attracting and retaining employees (the low-wage/low-skill example).
2. Recruiting costs are higher (Microsoft competes with everyone for software engineers).

Economic and behavioral theories offer some help in understanding the variations in pay levels we *observe* among employers. Relevant markets are shaped by pressures from the labor and product market and the organization. But so what? How, in fact, do managers set pay-level policy, and what difference does it make? In the remainder of this chapter, we will discuss those two issues.

COMPETITIVE PAY POLICY OPTIONS

There are three conventional pay-level policies: to lead, to meet, or to follow competition. How do managers choose a policy? Sixty-three firms responding to a survey in 1948 said that the most important factors in setting pay-level policies were rates paid by other employers in the area or industry and union pressures. The least important factors were the firm's financial position and company profits. A Conference Board survey of 280 firms in 1978 and 1983 reports a shift in the importance of factors.[28] As shown in Exhibit 7.11, industry patterns remained the most important factor in 1978, just as they had 30 years earlier. But industry patterns dropped to fourth place in 1983, whereas a firm's specific financial situation and its productivity or labor costs and expected profits (ability to pay) were listed as the most important. Union-related factors, rated extremely important in the 1948 study, were among the least important in the more recent Conference Board studies. Consequently, although the factors considered in setting pay level may be stable, their relative importance may vary over time. It would be interesting to find out what a new study of the factors used as we enter the 21st century would show.

What difference does the competitive pay policy make? The basic premise is that the competitiveness of pay will affect the organization's ability to achieve its compensation objectives, which in turn will affect the organization's performance. The probable effects of alternative policies are shown in Exhibit 7.12.

[28] The Conference Board, *The New Look in Wage Policy and Employee Relations* (New York: The Conference Board, 1983); Levine, "Fairness, Markets, and Ability to Pay."

EXHIBIT 7.11 The Relative Importance of Factors Used to Set Wage Objectives in Corporations in 1978 and 1983

Rank	*1978*	*1983*
1	Industry patterns	Productivity or labor trends in this company
2	Local labor market conditions and wage rates	Expected profits of this company
3	Expected profits of this company	Local labor market conditions and wage rates
4	Productivity or labor cost trends in this company	Industry patterns
5	Consumer price index increases	Consumer price index increases
6	Influence of this settlement on other wage settlements or nonunion wage levels, or both	Internal (company) wage patterns (historical)
7	Potential losses from a strike	Influence of this settlement on other settlements or nonunion wage levels, or both
8	Internal (company) wage patterns (historical)	Internal (company) benefit patterns (historical)
9	Internal (company) benefit patterns (historical)	Potential losses from a strike
10	Major union settlements in other industries	National labor market conditions and wage rates
11	National labor market conditions and wage rates	Major union settlements in other industries

Note: The sample comprised 197 major U.S. corporations, which, in both 1978 and 1983, ranked factors used in setting company wage objectives, with 1 being the most important factor and 11, the least important.

Source: Audrey Freedman, *The New Look in Wage Policy and Employee Relations* (New York: The Conference Board, 1985).

EXHIBIT 7.12 Probable Relationships Between External Pay Policies and Objectives

	Compensation Objectives				
Policy	*Ability to Attract*	*Ability to Retain*	*Contain Labor Costs*	*Reduce Pay Dissatisfaction*	*Increase Productivity*
Pay above market (lead)	+	+	?	+	?
Pay with market (match)	=	=	=	=	?
Pay below market (lag)	–	?	+	–	?
Hybrid policy	?	?	+	?	+
Employer of choice	+	+	+	–	?

Pay with Competition (Match)

Given the choice to match, lead, or lag, the most common policy is to match rates paid by competitors.[29] Managers historically justify the "matching" policy for three reasons:

[29] Brian S. Klaas and John A. McClendon, "To Lead, Lag, or Match: Estimating the Financial Impact of Pay Level Policies," *Personnel Psychology* 49 (1996), pp. 121–40.

(1) failure to match competitors' rates would cause employee dissatisfaction, (2) lower rates would limit the organization's ability to recruit, and (3) management was somehow obligated to pay prevailing rates. Nonunionized companies frequently try to lead or at least match competition to discourage unionism.[30] However, a firm's actual pay policy may differ from its stated policy, depending on which surveys and statistics are used, whether or not all forms of compensation are considered (base pay, incentives, benefits, etc.) and how well jobs are matched across competitors.[31] A pay-with-competition policy tries to ensure that an organization's wage costs are approximately equal to those of its product competitors and that its ability to attract applicants will be approximately equal to its labor market competitors. This policy avoids placing an employer at a disadvantage in pricing products or in maintaining a qualified work force. But it may not provide an employer with a competitive advantage in its labor markets. Most classical economic models, those relying on competitive markets and marginal productivity concepts, would predict that employers would meet competitive wages.

Lead Policy

Does paying differently really pay off? A lead policy maximizes the ability to attract and retain quality employees and minimizes employee dissatisfaction with pay. Or a lead policy may offset less attractive features of the work. Military combat pay is a classic example of this offsetting ability. The relatively high pay offered by brokerage firms that offsets the lack of employment security is another. These illustrate Adam Smith's notion of net advantage.

We have already observed that sometimes an entire industry can pass high pay rates on to consumers if pay is a relatively low proportion of total operating expenses or if the industry is highly regulated. But what about specific firms within a high-pay industry? For example, if Chevron or Exxon adopts a pay leadership position in their industry, do any advantages actually accrue to them? If all firms in the industry have similar technologies and operating expenses, then the lead policy must provide some competitive advantage to Chevron or Exxon that outweighs the higher costs.

Does a lead policy really permit the employer to select the best of the applicant pool? Assuming that the employer is able to select the most qualified from this pool, does this higher quality talent translate into greater productivity, lower unit labor costs, or improved product quality? One study estimated that approximately 50 percent of higher wage costs were offset by benefits in recruiting and training.[32] Although the number of assumptions required for this analysis limits confidence in the precision in the estimate, a number of researchers have linked high wages to ease of attraction, reduced vacancy rates and training time, and better-quality employees. A study of government employees found that as wages increase, both the quality and quantity of

---

[30] P. D. Lineneman, M. L. Wachter, and W. H. Carter, "Evaluating the Evidence on Union Employment and Wages," *Industrial and Labor Relations Review* 44 (1990), pp. 34–53.

[31] "Salary Survey: A Panel of Experts Discusses Key Challenges," *ACA News,* October 1997, pp. 33–37.

[32] J. J. Chrisman, C. W. Hofer, and W. R. Boutton, "Toward a System of Classifying Business Strategies," *Academy of Management Review* 13 (1988), pp. 413–28.

applicants also increased.[33] Research also suggests that increasing pay levels reduces turnover and absenteeism. One study found no evidence that pay level affected an organization's return on assets (ROA).[34] However, this study found that the use of variable forms of pay (bonuses and long-term incentives) was linked to a higher ROA.

The problem with much pay level research is that it focuses on base pay and ignores bonuses, incentives, options, employment security, benefits, or other forms of pay. Yet base pay represents only a portion of compensation. In fact, many managers seem increasingly convinced that they get more bang for the buck by allocating dollars away from base pay and into variable forms that more effectively shape employee behavior.[35] And at the lower wage jobs, it seems that increasing employee services and assistance plans pays off more than wage increases.

A lead policy can have negative effects, too. If an employer does not adjust wages of current employees, these more experienced employees may murmur against the employer just as those vineyard laborers did in Matthew's parable referred to in Chapter 4. Because relatively higher pay makes recruiting easier, it may mask other job attributes that contribute to high turnover later on (e.g., lack of challenging assignments or hostile colleagues). Recall the compensation managers' consensus that high turnover was likely to be a managerial problem rather than a compensation problem.[36]

Lag Policy

Setting a lag pay policy to follow competitive rates may hinder a firm's ability to attract potential employees. However, if pay level is lagged in return for the promise of higher future returns (e.g., stock ownership in a high-tech startup firm), such a promise may increase employee commitment and foster teamwork, which may increase productivity. Andersen Consulting, a software and systems firm, tells college recruits that its starting offers are lower than its competitors but that successful performers will make more than competitors within two to four years. Clearly, Andersen runs a risk of not being able to attract highly qualified talent. But the promise of the bigger carrot seems to attract enough good students, especially in a down economy. Thus, a lag policy's effect on hiring and motivating employees is not clear. Additionally, it is possible to lag competition on pay but to lead on other aspects of rewards (e.g., challenging work, desirable location, outstanding colleagues).

---

[33] A. B. Krueger, "Efficiency Wages,"; M. B. Tannen, "Is the Army College Fund Meeting Its Objectives?" *Industrial and Labor Relations Review* 41 (1987), pp. 50–62; Hyder Lakhani, "Effects of Pay and Retention Bonuses on Quit Rates in the U.S. Army," *Industrial and Labor Relations Review* 41 (1988), pp. 430–38.

[34] B. Gerhart and G. Milkovich, "Organizational Differences in Managerial Compensation and Financial Performance," *Academy of Management Journal* 33 (1990), pp. 663–91. Variable pay is discussed in Chapters 8 through 10. *Variable* indicates that the pay increase (bonus) is not added to base pay; hence, it is not part of fixed costs but is variable, since the amount may vary next year.

[35] The Conference Board, *Variable Pay: New Performance Rewards,* Research Bulletin 246 (New York, 1990).

[36] Levine, "Fairness, Markets, and Ability to Pay."

Match, lead, and lag are the conventional policy options. Some employers adopt nonconventional policies; they may mix policies for different employee groups, or may place their policy in a broader HR context in an effort to become the employer of choice.

Hybrid Policies

In practice, many employers have more than one policy. They may vary the policy for different occupational families, that is, above market for critical skill groups but below or at market for others. Or they may vary the policy for different pay elements. A Denver insurance company describes its policy: "It is our goal to position ourselves competitively above market value in total compensation, slight-to-somewhat-below in base salary, and well-above average in incentive compensation."[37]

Under this multiple competitive policy, higher earnings through profit sharing or incentive pay are offered if the firm's performance is strong. Praxair offers employees the opportunity to earn a bonus of up to 40 days' pay if the division's operating profits exceed certain targets. However, Praxair repositioned its base pay to 5 percent below its usual "match" in the market position. So, in effect, Praxair lags the market by 5 percent but pays a bonus that yields a slight lead position when the company has a good year.

This competitive position has several potential effects. The variable pay policy is intended to focus employee attention on the firm's financial performance and motivate productivity improvements. It also signals to potential job seekers that Praxair wants people willing to perform and able to tolerate some risk. In the meantime, the 5 percent lag reduces labor costs.

Employer of Choice

An *employer of choice* policy is more complex than the other options. It defines compensation more broadly to include all forms of returns from employment. Hence, an organization's position is based on the *total* returns from working for it.

For example, IBM leads its competitors with its extensive training opportunities, employee assistance programs, and the like. But it matches or even follows with its base pay and matches with performance bonuses. A competitor such as Microsoft lags in base, matches on performance bonus, and leads by offering wealth-creating stock options. Plus it offers a supremely challenging work opportunity. Both IBM's and Microsoft's competitiveness policy views pay as part of the total pattern of HR policies.

Which Policy Achieves Competitive Advantage?

Does it pay differently? Adopting a competitive pay policy is akin to establishing a niche in the market. Unfortunately, there is little evidence of the consequences of these different options. It is not known whether the effects of pay level on the financial performance of a firm, its productivity, or its ability to attract and retain employees is suf-

[37] Stephenie Overman, "In Search of Best Practices," *HR Magazine,* December 1993, pp. 48–50.

ficient to offset the effects on payroll costs. Nor is it known how much of a pay level variation makes a difference; will 5 percent, 10 percent, or 15 percent be a noticeable difference? Although lagging competitive pay could have a noticeable reduction in short-term labor costs, it is not known whether this savings is accompanied by a reduction in the quality and performance of the workforce. Similarly, we simply do not know the effects of the variable-pay or employer-of-choice options. It may be that an employer's pay level will not gain any competitive advantage; however, the wrong pay level may put the organization at a serious disadvantage.

Research on the effect of alternative pay-level policies is difficult because companies' stated policies often do not correspond to reality. For example, HR managers at 124 companies were asked to define their firm's target pay level. All 124 of them reported that their companies paid above the median![38] One study proposes a *utility model* to assess the financial impact of alternative pay-level policies.[39] The model looks at the financial trade-offs between wage costs and work force quality. The researchers began with the assumption that the organization's current policy is to match the market. Their model predicted that the payoff is highest when moving from a match position to a lag position, next highest when retaining a match position, and lowest when moving from a match position to a lead position. Their point is not to determine which policy is best; rather, they provide a way to make estimates that, while imprecise, help improve decision making.

So where does this leave the manager? In the absence of convincing evidence, the least-risk approach may be to set the pay level to match competition, though as we noted, some employers set different policies for different skills. They may adopt a lead policy for skills that are critical to the organization's success, a match policy for less critical skills, and a lag policy for jobs that are easily filled in the local labor market. More employers differentiate by using a hybrid policy that includes base pay set at or below competitive market rates plus performance-based bonuses that vary with the unit's profitability. An obvious concern with such decentralization is to achieve some degree of business connectedness if human resources are shared or moved across different business units.

CONSEQUENCES OF PAY LEVEL DECISIONS

Earlier we noted that the degree of competitiveness of the total pay level has two major consequences: (1) its effect on operating expenses and (2) its effect on employee attitudes and work behaviors. These consequences, shown in Exhibit 7.13, have been discussed throughout this chapter. All we will do here is to note again that the competitive policy and the pay level are key decisions that affect the performance of the organization. The pay level directly affects the compensation objectives of efficiency, equity, and compliance.

---

[38] Gerhart and Milkovich, "Employee Compensation."

[39] Brian Klaas and John A. McClendon, "To Lead, Lag, or Match: Estimating the Financial Impact of Pay Level Policies," *Personnel Psychology* 49 (1996), pp. 121–140.

Exhibit 7.13 Some Consequences of Pay Levels

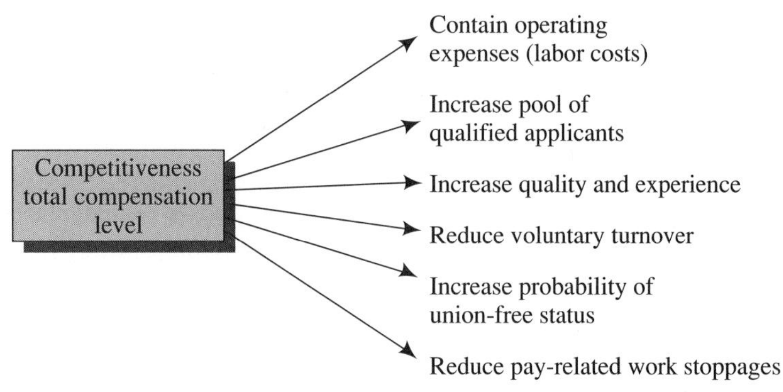

Efficiency

Wages paid represent an expense, so any decision that affects their level is important. A variety of theories make assumptions about the effects of relative pay levels on an organization's effectiveness. Some believe that lead policies diminish shirking, permit hiring better-qualified applicants, and so on. Yet other models (e.g., markets and marginal productivity) support a policy of matching competitors. The utility model just discussed supported a lag policy. Virtually no research evidence guides managers in which policy yields the most efficient results or is the source of competitive advantage under different circumstances.

Pay level indirectly affects revenues through the quality of the work force induced to join and the productivity and experience levels of those who stay. Reduction in turnover of high performers, increased experience levels, increased probability of remaining union free, and reduction of pay-related grievances and work stoppages are examples of the work behaviors presumed to be affected by pay level decisions.

Equity

Employees' sense of fair treatment regarding pay is clearly affected by the level of their pay. Satisfaction with pay is directly related to the pay level: more is better.[40] But as with most things, the relationship between pay and equity is more complex. Employees' sense of pay equity also is related to how others are paid and how they expected to be

[40] H. G. Heneman III, "Pay Satisfaction," *Research in Personnel and Human Resource Management* 3 (1985), pp. 115–39.

paid. A friend of ours at Stanford told us that if all but one of the faculty in the Stanford Business School got $1 million and that one person received $1 million plus $1, the others would all be murmuring against the dean and asking for an explanation of why one person got the extra dollar.

Compliance

It's not enough to say that an employer must pay at or above the legal minimum wage. Provisions of prevailing wage laws and equal rights legislation must also be met. In fact, we will return to the subject of market wages again when we discuss pay discrimination.

No matter the competitive pay policy, it needs to be translated into practice. The starting point is measuring the market through use of a salary survey. For this, we turn to the next chapter.

Summary

One reviewer of this book told us that "there are three important contributions of this chapter. (1) That there is no 'going rate' and so managers make conscious pay level decisions influenced by several factors; (2) that there are both product market and labor market competitors that impact the pay level decisions; and (3) that alternative pay level decisions have different consequences." That is a great summary of the key points.

The pay model used throughout this book emphasizes strategic policy issues: objectives, consistency, competitiveness, contributions, and administration. Policies need to be designed to achieve specific pay objectives. This section is concerned with external competitiveness, or pay comparisons among organizations. Does Apple Computer pay its accountants the same wage that Virginia Electric and Power pays its accountants? Probably not. Different companies pay different rates; the average of the overall array of rates in an organization constitutes the pay level. Each integrated job structure or career path within the organization may have its own pay level and competitive position in the market. To achieve the objectives stipulated for the pay system, the pay level must be properly positioned relative to competitors. The next chapter considers the decisions involved and the variety of techniques available to implement decisions.

Before we proceed, let us reemphasize that the major reason we are interested in the external competitiveness policy and the pay level is that they have profound consequences on the organization's objectives. Theories and practical experience support this belief. As we have also noted, very little research exists to guide us in making pay-level decisions. We have clearly established that differences among organizations' competitive policies and pay levels exist. We have examined the factors that determine these differences. What remains to be better demonstrated are the potential effects that different policies will have.

Review Questions

1. Distinguish policies on external competitiveness from policies on internal consistency. Why is external competitiveness so important?
2. What factors shape an organization's external competitiveness?
3. What does marginal revenue product have to do with pay?
4. What pay level does the efficiency wage theory predict? Does the theory accurately predict organization behavior? Why or why not?
5. What is a relevant market? What difference does it make when determining people's pay?
6. Can you think of any companies that follow a lag and/or lead policy? Why do they believe it pays to pay differently?

Your Turn:

Upstart Airlines

Pilots are critical resources. They directly affect the success of any airline. Suppose you faced a clean slate: A group of investors is about to invest in a new startup, a regional (midwest) airline based at the new Denver airport, but serving the entire midwest, including Laramie, Cody, Jackson Hole, and Rock Springs, Wyoming.

These investors hired you to help them determine pilots' pay. Go back to Exhibit 7.2. Based solely on the information in that exhibit, what would you advise?

1. What policy regarding external competitiveness would you advise? List the options and the pros and cons of each policy option. Offer the rationale for your recommendation.
2. Consider the theories and research presented in this chapter. Which ones did you use to support your recommendation?
3. List three pieces of additional information you would like to have to refine your recommendation. Explain how this information would help you.

Your Turn:

Managing a Low-Wage, Low-Skill Workforce

Take another look at the section about practices of the low-wage, low-skill employers like Marriott and McDonald's. Also take another look at the economic theories highlighted in this chapter.

How, if at all, do these theories help explain the actions Marriott and McDonald's have taken? Would you have predicted these actions *before* the fact?

Chapter 8 Designing Pay Levels and Pay Structures

Chapter Outline

"Average pay of benchmark jobs set to average pay of similar jobs in comparable companies." —3M

"A move to market-based pay to allow a closer alignment with market rates. We will set pay by job family rather than having the same pay policy for all jobs." —IBM

"Pay among the leaders. Base pay will be fully comparable (50th percentile of competitors). Total compensation, including benefits and performance incentives, will bring our compensation to the 75th percentile of competitors." —Colgate

"Our competitive strategy will deliver rewards at the market competitive median for median performance at the 75th percentile for 75th percentile performance, etc." —Medtronic

"Our competitive strategy is based on everyone putting some 'skin in the game' and then sharing our success. Base salaries are below what our competitors pay for similar work, our incentives are equal to our competitors, and our long-term incentives (stock options) are paid to everyone and far exceed our competitors." —Microsoft

"Salaries will be consistent with economic requirements of TRW and compare favorably with those of the markets in areas in which we operate." —TRW Vehicle Safety Systems[1]

All these statements refer to different organizations' external competitiveness policies. Competitive position refers to the comparison of the compensation offered by one employer relative to that paid by its competitors. In the last chapter, we discussed the factors that influenced these policies. The levels and types of compensation that competitors offer—base salary, incentive bonuses, benefits—are critical. Labor market factors that influence policy include the supply of qualified workers and the demand for these workers from other firms. Organizational factors such as the employer's financial condition, technology, size, strategy, productivity, and the influence of unions and employee demographics may also affect a firm's competitive pay policies. In this chapter, we examine how managers use these factors to design pay levels and structures.[2]

[1]Adapted from each company's compensation strategy statements.

[2]Readers have told us that Chapter 8 is one long chapter. We have tried teaching the material in it as two shorter chapters. However, neither the yolk nor the white by itself conveys the idea of an egg. So, too, the material in this chapter loses some important connections if divided. So look over the chapter outline to see where it is we need to go, find a comfortable chair, and let's get going.

EXHIBIT 8.1 Determining Externally Competitive Pay Levels and Structures

External competitiveness: Pay relationships among organizations → **Policy determination** → **Market definition** → **Conduct pay surveys** → **Draw policy lines** → **Competitive pay levels and structures**

Some Major Decisions in Pay Level Determination

- Determine pay level policy.
- Define purpose of survey.
- Design and conduct survey.
- Interpret and apply results.
- Design ranges and bands.

MAJOR DECISIONS

The major decisions involved in setting externally competitive pay and designing the corresponding pay structures are shown in Exhibit 8.1. They include (1) determine the employer's external pay policy; (2) define the purpose of a survey; (3) design and conduct surveys, (4) how to interpret and apply survey results, (5) how to design ranges, flat rates, and/or bands, and (6) balance internal and external considerations.

The first decision, determining the external pay policy, was discussed in the previous chapter. The remaining decisions are discussed in the rest of this chapter. As you read through the chapter, you will become aware that each new decision may cause an employer to revise previous decisions.

For example, the decisions by Microsoft and Medtronic to emphasize incentives in their total pay packages means that these companies will need to ensure that their market surveys collect information on the types of incentives others use. Or a firm may discover that it is losing employees to competitors who offer child care. As information changes, policy decisions may change.

WHY CONDUCT A SURVEY?

Surveys provide the data for setting the pay policy relative to competitors and translating that policy into pay levels and structures.

A **survey** is the systemic process of collecting and making judgments about the compensation paid by other employers.

Most firms conduct or participate in several different pay surveys. Some writers claim that large employers participate in up to 100 surveys in a single year, although they base their compensation decisions on data from only a few surveys.

An employer conducts or participates in a survey for a number of reasons: (1) to adjust the pay level in response to changing competitor pay rates, (2) to establish or price its pay structure, (3) to analyze personnel problems that may be pay related, or (4) to attempt to estimate the labor costs of product market competitors.

Adjust Pay Level

Most organizations make adjustments to employees' pay on a regular basis. Such adjustments can be based on cost of living, performance, ability to pay, seniority, or simply the overall upward movement of pay rates among competitors. Monitoring the changes in rates paid by competitors is necessary to maintain or adjust a firm's pay level in relationship to these competitors.

Adjust Pay Structure

Many employers use market surveys to validate their own job evaluation results. For example, job evaluation may place purchasing assistant jobs at the same level in the job structure as some secretarial jobs. But if the market shows vastly different pay rates for the two types of work, most employers will recheck their evaluation process to see whether the jobs have been properly evaluated. Some may even establish a separate structure for the secretarial work. Thus, the job structure that results from internal job evaluation may not match the pay structures found in the external market. Reconciling these two pay structures is a major issue. Informed judgment based on the organization's specific circumstances and objectives is required.

Recall from our discussion in previous chapters that many fast-changing organizations are keeping the job evaluation but moving to more generic jobs that focus on the person more than the job. Determining pay for such jobs requires even greater reliance on the market, as former relationships between job evaluation points and dollars no longer hold.

Pay-Related Projects

Information from a specialized survey may shed light on a pay-related problem. Many special studies appraise the starting salary offers or current pay practices for targeted groups, for example, patent attorneys, retail sales managers, or software engineers. A recent special survey for software engineers revealed that competitors are using signing bonuses (average 12 percent, about $7,000) to attract these skills. Managers must decide whether to match (or exceed) their competitors or use other forms of total returns.[3]

Estimate Competitors' Labor Costs

Some firms, particularly those in highly competitive businesses, such as retailing, auto, or specialty steel production, use salary survey data in their financial analysis of competitors' product pricing and manufacturing practices. Industrywide labor cost estimates are reported in the Employment Cost Index (ECI), one of four types of salary surveys

[3]Jerrald R. Bratkovich and Joan Ragusa, *The Perils of the Signing Bonus* (New York: Organization Resource Counselors, Inc. 1998).

published regularly by the Department of Labor. The ECI measures quarterly changes in employer costs for employee compensation. It allows a firm to compare its average costs to an all-industry or specific-industry average. However, this comparison has limited value because industry averages may not reflect relevant competitors. Also, the ECI gives a lot of weight to unionized firms.

Survey results serve as crucial input for decisions that ultimately affect a firm's compensation objectives of efficiency, equity, and compliance. An employer's labor costs and the competitiveness of its products can be affected by conclusions drawn from survey data. Because their results are so significant to the organization, businesses should design and manage their surveys carefully. A first step is to identify the key issues the employer seeks to resolve in the survey.

DEFINING THE RELEVANT MARKET

In Chapter 7, we pointed out that employers compete in many labor markets. The relevant market depends on the purpose of the survey. To make decisions about pay levels and structures or to estimate competitors' labor costs, the relevant labor market includes other employers with whom an organization competes for employees. Although a statistician may design a survey to sample a broad population, salary surveys are typically designed to capture a narrower population of employers (i.e., competitor). As we observed in Chapter 7, competitors forming the relevant markets are typically defined by the following:

1. Employers who compete for the same occupations or skills required.
2. Employers who compete for employees within the same geographic area.
3. Employers who compete with the same products and services.

Perhaps a fourth criterion will eventually be added: employers who use the same basis for their structure (e.g., job- versus person-based). As less traditional approaches become more common (skill/competency-based structures, use of contingent and temporary employees, broadbanding, etc.), separate surveys, or at least the flexibility to analyze data from competitors using skill/competencies, will be required. Presently, managers using unique structures face special problems getting comparable market data at the same time that they are relying more on that external market data.[4] So the definition of relevant labor market will vary, depending on the purpose of the survey and the particular jobs and skills being examined.

Exhibit 8.2 shows how qualifications interact with geography to define the scope of relevant labor markets. As the importance of the qualifications and the complexity of qualifications increase, the geographic limits also increase. Competition tends to be national for managerial and professional skills, but local or regional for clerical and production skills.

[4] Consulting firms are in the process of redesigning products to address these needs. For example, Executive Alliance's Semiconductor, Computer, and High Performance Systems Total Compensation Survey (Marlboro, MA) permits customizing reports on a number of options. Towers Perrin and Wyatt are testing methodologies for conducting surveys based on competencies.

EXHIBIT 8.2 Relevant Labor Markets by Geographic and Employee Groups

Geographic Scope	*Production*	*Office and Clerical*	*Technicians*	*Scientists and Engineers*	*Managerial Professional*	*Executive*
Local: Within relatively small areas such as cities or Metropolitan Statistical Areas (e.g., Dallas metropolitan area)	Most likely	Most likely	Most likely			
Regional: Within a particular area of the state or several states (e.g., oil-producing region of southwestern United States)	Only if in short supply or critical	Only if in short supply or critical	Most likely	Likely	Most likely	
National: Across the country				Most likely	Most likely	Most likely
International: Across several countries				Only for critical skills or those in very short supply	Only for critical skills or those in very short supply	Sometimes

EXHIBIT 8.3 Labor Market Competitors

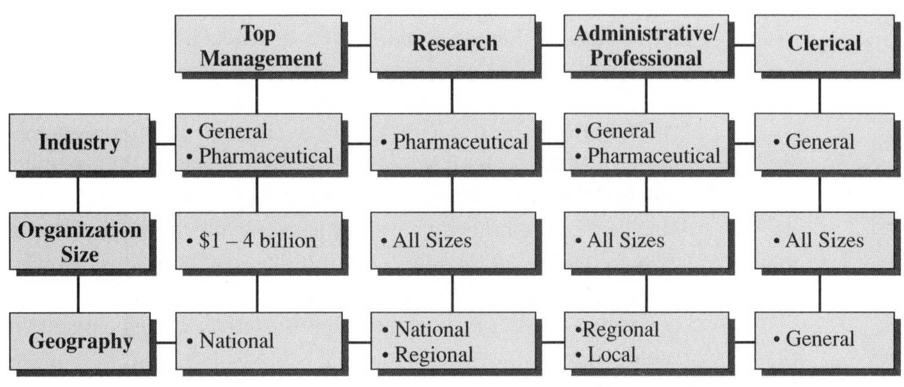

Source: Reprinted from ACA Building Block #2. "Mastering Market Data, An Approach to Analyzing and Applying Salary Survey Information," by Jane A. Bjorndal and Linda K. Ison Employees," with permission from the American Compensation Association (ACA), 14040 N. Northsight Blvd., Scottsdale, AZ U.S.A. 85260: telephone (602) 951-9191, fax: (602) 483-8352 © ACA.

However, these generalizations do not always hold true. In areas with high concentrations of scientists, engineers, and managers (e.g., Boston, Dallas, or Palo Alto), the primary market comparison may be regional, with national data used only secondarily. Exhibit 8.3 translates these generalities into policy for a pharmaceutical manufacturer. For top managerial jobs, national surveys of companies with sales between $1 billion and $4 billion are used. For research jobs, only data from pharmaceutical industry firms are used. For clerical jobs, local data from a wide range of industries and organization sizes are used.

In major metropolitan areas, the relevant market may be further restricted by commuting times and patterns. But the amount of time people are willing to commute varies by locale as well as by personal and economic circumstances. Tokyo's 90-minute bullet train rides and Los Angeles's 90-minute traffic jams are legendary. Further, managers can influence the willingness of people to commute with actions other than setting higher pay levels. For example, a firm may lobby the local transit authority for convenient bus routes and schedules or may sponsor company-owned vans and carpooling programs. One New York City department store buses 160 workers from Brooklyn to its suburban stores during busy holiday seasons so that the stores will have an adequate supply of sales personnel.

From the perspective of cost control and ability to pay, including competitors in the product/service market is crucial.[5] The pay rates of product/service competitors will

[5] Barry Gerhart and George Milkovich, "Employee Compensation," in *Handbook of Industrial and Organizational Psychology,* 2nd ed., ed. M. D. Dunnette and L. M. Hough (Palo Alto, CA: Consulting Psychologists Press, 1992).

affect both costs of operations and financial condition (e.g., ability to pay). However, this becomes a problem when the major competitors are based in countries with far lower pay rates, such as China or Mexico. In fact, the increasingly international character of business has spawned interest in global survey data, particularly for managerial and professional talent.[6]

But even if an employer possesses good international survey data, utilizing that data still requires careful judgment. For example, Sun Microsystems pays its Russian engineers in Moscow between $260 and $320 a month. While these salaries are absurdly low by Western standards, they are 25 to 30 times the salaries paid to other engineers outside the Sun-funded unit at the same institute. Sun probably can afford to pay more, even in light of all the other expenses and bureaucratic headaches associated with such an undertaking. But does it make sense to inflate salaries for some to a U.S. level, when colleagues at other institutes or support staff at the same institute do not receive comparable salaries?

Sun isn't the only U.S. company wrestling with this issue in the former Soviet republics. AT&T's Bell Laboratories supports 120 fiber-optics researchers in Moscow. Corning has a contract with 115 scientists in Saint Petersburg to study optics and silicate chemistry. Borg-Warner has brought Russian scientists to the U.S. to work on projects. Sun's Russian engineers claim they are satisfied with their salaries. "If somebody offers us more, then we'll feel underpaid," their leader comments.[7]

Some writers argue that if the skills are tied to a particular industry, as underwriters, actuaries, and claims representatives are to insurance, it makes sense to define the market on an industry basis.[8] If accounting, sales, or clerical skills are not limited to one particular industry, industry considerations are less important. But this ignores financial objectives of the employer. Pricing labor competitively with others who offer similar products and services is necessary to achieve the organization's financial objectives. Within these product/service market constraints, occupational and geographic factors come into play. Additionally, a firm's size (number of employees, total revenues, and assets) reflects its market dominance. Omitting a dominant firm would not accurately capture the market.

How Many Employers?

There are no firm rules on how many employers to include in a survey.[9] Large firms with a lead policy may exchange data with only a few (6 to 10) top-paying competitors. A small

---

[6] *Expatriate Compensation Survey* (Organization Resource Counselors) and *International Benefit Guidelines and Compensation Benefits Survey* (William M. Mercer) are just some of the surveys conducted annually. Most major consulting firms offer international survey.

[7] Deborah Stead and Robert D. Hof, "Math Genius with Lab. Will Work for Food," *Business Week,* June 14, 1993, pp. 84, 86; Sheila M. Puffer and Stanislav V. Shekshnia, "Compensating Local Employees in Post-Communist Russia: In Search of Talent or Just Looking for a Bargain?" *Compensation and Benefits Review,* September–October 1994, pp. 35–43.

[8] Felicia Nathan, "Analyzing Employers' Costs for Wages, Salaries, and Benefits," *Monthly Labor Review,* October 1987, pp. 3–11.

[9] Chockalingam Viswesvaran and Murray Barrick, "Decision-Making Effects on Compensation Surveys: Implications for Market Wages," *Journal of Applied Psychology* 77, no. 5 (1992), pp. 588–97.

organization in an area dominated by two or three employers may decide to survey only smaller competitors. National surveys conducted by consulting firms may include more than 100 employers. Clients of these consultants often stipulate special analyses that report pay rates by selected industry groups, geographic region, and/or pay levels (e.g., top 10 percent).

Who Should Be Involved?

In most organizations, the responsibility for managing the survey lies with the compensation manager. But since the pricing of HR has a powerful effect on profitability, operating managers and employees need to be involved, too. A recurrent theme in this text has been the need to get user acceptance through involvement in procedure design. Including managers and employees on task forces or surveying employees to discover what firms they use for pay comparisons makes sense.

Outside consulting firms are often used as third-party protection from possible "price-fixing" lawsuits. Suits have been filed alleging that the exchange of survey data violates Section 1 of the Sherman Act, which outlaws conspiracies in restraint of trade. Courts interpret the Sherman Act to find survey participants guilty of price fixing if the overall effect of the information exchange is to *interfere with competitive prices* and *artificially hold down wages.* One case involved the Boston Survey Group, a 34-member association, that exchanged data on wages for a variety of clerical jobs. Each participating firm's information was clearly identified by company name, and the results were reported by industry group. A consent decree agreed to by the Boston Survey Group and the Massachusetts State Attorney General's office stipulates the following:

- The data will no longer be identified by company names.
- Only aggregated information will be reported; salaries of individual employees will not be published.
- No data will be published on a per industry basis.
- Data will not be reported if fewer than 10 people are in a job.
- Members may choose to allow their employees to see the aggregated survey results for their own jobs.

The Utah Society for Healthcare Human Resource Administration, the Utah Hospital Association, and eight hospitals agreed to even stricter requirements.[10] They had been charged with keeping entry-level wages for registered nurses in the Salt Lake City area artificially low by exchanging wage and budget information, including intentions to increase starting pay offers. As a result of the legal agreement, no health care facility in Utah can design, develop, or conduct a wage survey. They can respond in writing (only) to a written request for information for wage survey purposes from a third party, but only after the third party provides written assurance that the survey will be conducted with particular safeguards.

---

[10] Michael B. Shea, "Decrees Offer Survey Guidelines," *ACA News,* June 1994, p. 15; *District of Utah U.S. District Court v. Utah Society For Healthcare Human Resources Administration, et al.,* Federal Register 59, no. 58, March 25, 1994, 14203.

Hiring a third party consultant instead of managing the survey internally buys legal protection at the cost of control over the decisions that determine the quality and usefulness of the data. A consent decree prohibiting exchange of industry data eliminates the ability to make industry or product market comparisons. This might not be important in clerical jobs, but industry groups are important when making comparisons for wages for other skills/competencies and jobs. For example, a Hewlett-Packard marketer's job is probably more similar to that of an AT&T Information Systems marketer than it is to a Union Carbide marketer. If the competencies in question are generalized and thus transferable, then industry data can safely be ignored. However, industry data are crucial from a competitive market labor cost perspective. Further, if the skills are highly specialized (e.g., semiconductors designer), then they may be industry specific and therefore not available across industries.

Make, Buy, Access, or Customize?

The decision to retain outside expertise or to design the survey in-house requires trade-offs. The availability of staff time and expertise and the desire to control the quality of analysis and results are often given as reasons to tailor one's own survey. On the other hand, consulting firms offer a wide choice of ongoing surveys covering almost every job family and industry group imaginable.

Consultant surveys are getting better and better. While we would like to attribute the improvement to the fact that our textbook has improved the sophistication of compensation education in the United States (our book was first published in 1985, and at least some of those early readers ought to be in power positions by now), it is more likely that the improvement is the result of technological advances. Increasingly, consultants offer clients the option of electronically accessing the consultants' survey data base. The client then does the special analysis it desires. General Electric conducts most of its market analysis in this manner. Hay PayNet permits organizations to tie into Hay's vast survey data 24 hours a day seven days a week.

Such ease of access caused one reviewer to ask, "Why go into all this detail about surveys? Consultants do it all now." Carrying that logic forward, we could trash most of the book, since most consultants we know would love to do it all.

The point is that expertise in making compensation decisions is necessary, if only to judge the quality of information provided. Plus, some of our readers may wish to join these consulting firms.

For a demonstration of online surveys, go to **http://www.haypaynet.com.** Also, check out the Radford Survey site **(http://www.radford.com/general.welcome.html).** How do the two sites compare?

Purchasing Criteria. Opinions about the value of consultant surveys are rampant; research is not. Do Hay, Mercer, Towers Perrin, Executive Compensation Services, Executive Alliance, or MCS's 777 surveys of managerial pay yield significantly different results? Many firms select one survey as their primary source and use others to cross-check or "validate" the results.

For staffing decisions, professional consultants who design employment tests report the test's performance against a set of measurements (reliability, validity, etc.). For pay decisions, analogous standards have not yet evolved. Issues of sample design and statistical inference are seldom considered. Some employers routinely combine the results of several surveys and weight each survey in this composite according to the quality of the data reported.[11] Yet little systematic study of differences in market definition, participating firms, types of data collected, analysis performed, and/or results is available.

Publicly Available Data. In the United States, the Bureau of Labor Statistics (BLS) is the major source of publicly available compensation (cash and benefits) data. It publishes extensive information on various occupations (very broadly defined—e.g., secretaries, executives, administrators) in different geographic areas. COMP 2000, a newly revised survey, provides wage and benefit data by occupation in various areas nationwide. They also publish the Employment Cost Index (ECI), which measures changes in employee compensation costs. Their web site (http://stats.bls.gov) offers further information on their surveys.

Exhibit 8.4 illustrates the nature of the BLS data. The data are inexpensive and readily available. Public sector employers seem to use BLS data more often than do private sector employers. Some private firms track the rate of change in BLS data and the ECI as a cross-check on other surveys and to examine geographic differentials for various nonexempt jobs (e.g., secretary I in Washington, D.C., versus secretary I in Durham, North Carolina). However, most private firms find the data are not specific enough to be used alone. The COMP 2000 survey is an attempt to overcome that limitation.

Check out the demonstration of the National Compensation Survey at the Bureau of Labor Statistics' web site: **http://stats.bls.gov.**

WHICH JOBS TO INCLUDE?

A general guideline is to keep things as simple as possible. Select as few employers and jobs as necessary to accomplish the purpose. The more complex the survey, the less likely employers are inclined to participate. There are several approaches to selecting jobs for inclusion.

Benchmark Jobs Approach. Benchmark jobs share the following characteristics:

- The contents are well known, relatively stable, and agreed upon by the employees involved.

[11] L. S. Hartenian and N. B. Johnson, "Establishing the Reliability and Validity of Wage Surveys," *Public Personnel Management* 20, no. 3 (1991), pp. 367–83.

EXHIBIT 8.4 Example of Bureau of Labor Statistics Survey Data

Occupation and level	*Number of workers*	Hourly pay (in dollars) *Mean*	*Median*	*Middle range*
Maintenance and Toolroom Occupations				
General Maintenance Workers	10,041	12.88	12.57	10.00–15.07
Level 1	4,974	10.32	10.00	8.30–12.31
Level 2	4,885	15.56	15.07	13.50–16.75
Maintenance Electricians	4,378	20.07	20.81	17.15–22.41
Maintenance Electronics Technicians	2,303	19.46	20.12	17.64–22.41
Level 2	2,045	19.78	20.12	17.64–22.50
Maintenance Machinists	2,184	18.13	16.97	15.41–19.88
Maintenance Mechanics, Machinery	4,634	18.15	17.85	16.00–20.25
Maintenance Mechanics, Motor Vehicle	2,949	18.28	18.65	16.75–20.22
Maintenance Pipefitters	256	23.90	24.58	20.88–26.60
Skilled Multicraft Maintenance Workers	8,456	19.63	20.61	16.61–22.30
Tool and Die Makers	3,161	19.47	20.22	16.92–21.63
Material Movement and Custodial				
Guards	22,863	7.27	6.75	5.75– 8.00
Level 1	21,000	6.84	6.50	5.75– 7.75
Level 2	1,863	12.08	11.43	9.63–13.96
Janitors	43,148	9.19	8.90	6.87–11.05
Material Movement & Storage Workers	45,433	11.18	11.00	8.32–13.51
Level 1	6,737	9.01	8.32	7.00– 9.50
Level 2	36,481	11.29	11.06	8.55–13.51
Shipping/Receiving Clerks	7,310	10.15	10.00	8.10–11.44
Level 3	2,215	16.01	18.00	13.50–18.20
Truckdrivers	16,707	15.38	15.79	13.45–17.64
Medium Truck	2,709	15.45	17.10	11.80–17.70
Heavy Truck	2,404	18.16	19.30	18.99–19.30
Tractor Trailer	6,631	15.66	15.50	14.95–15.79

Notes:

1. Hourly pay of blue-collar occupations, Chicago-Gary-Kenosha, IL-IN-WI CMSA, June 1996.
2. Standard hours reflect the workweek for which employees receive their regular straight-time salaries (exclusive of pay for overtime at regular and/or premium rates), and the earnings correspond to these weekly hours.
3. Excludes premium pay for overtime and for work on weekends, holidays, and late shifts. Also excluded are performance bonuses and lump-sum payments of the type negotiated in the auto and aerospace industries, as well as profit-sharing payments, attendance bonuses, Christmas or year-end bonuses, and other nonproduction bonuses. Pay increases, but not bonuses, under cost-of-living clauses, and incentive payments, however, are included.

Source: BLS Home Page: http://www.bls.gov

- The supply and demand for these jobs are relatively stable and not subject to recent shifts.
- They represent the entire job structure under study.
- A sizable proportion of the work force is employed in these jobs.

Typically, only benchmark jobs are included in surveys. Descriptions of the benchmark jobs are included in the survey so that participants can match the survey job within the correct job in their organization.

Some employers also use the percentage of incumbents who are women and men as a defining characteristic of a benchmark job to try to ensure that the benchmarks are free of possible employment discrimination.

Generally, the approach is to ensure that benchmark jobs represent all key functions and levels. The employer in Exhibit 8.5 organizes work into four structures. Selecting benchmark jobs from various levels within each structure ensures coverage of the entire work domain.

Global Approach. Rarely do several organizations have identical jobs. This is particularly true in organizations that emphasize semiautonomous teams or continuously adapt jobs to meet changing conditions. The global approach may be better suited to survey pay levels in these situations.

With a global approach, the rates paid to every individual employee in an entire skill group or function (e.g., all chemical engineers or all computer scientists) are used. Exhibit 8.6 shows external market data for engineers with bachelor's degrees. Exhibit 8.7 translates those data into percentiles. A survey user can determine the rates paid to engineers (Exhibit 8.6) as well as the rate's relationship to years since degree (YSD) (Exhibit 8.7). Because of this relationship to YSD, the curves in Exhibit 8.7 are often referred to as maturity curves. A global approach simply substitutes a particular skill (represented by a BS in engineering in the example) and experience or maturity (YSD) for detailed descriptions of work performed.

EXHIBIT 8.5 Benchmarks

Managerial Group	Technical Group	Manufacturing Group	Administrative Group
		Assembler I Inspector I	
Vice Presidents	Head/Chief Scientist	Packer	Administrative Assistant
Division General Managers	Senior Associates Scientist	Material Handler Inspector II	Principal Administrative Secretary
Managers	Associate Scientist	Assembler II	Administrative Secretary
Project Leaders	Scientist	Drill Press Operator Rough Grinder	Word Processor
Supervisors	Technician	Machinist I Coremaker	Clerk/Messenger

EXHIBIT 8.6 Frequency Distribution—All Engineers, All Companies

Years Since BS

Monthly Salary $	0	1	2	3	4	5	6	7	8	9	10	11	12	13	14	15	16	17	18	19	20	21	22	23	24	25	26	27	28	29	30	31	32	33	34	35	36	37	TOTAL
6950+OVER																			1	2	2		3		2	2			2	1	6	1	3	3	1	1		10	40
6825 - 6949																				1			1	1						2	1					1	1	1	9
5700 - 6824																					1	1			2			1	1	1	2			1				2	12
6575 - 6699																	1	1		1	2		2				1	1	1			1				1		2	14
6450 - 6574																1				1	2	2	3	1			2		1	2	1		1		1	2	2	9	31
6325 - 6449														1			1				1	1	1			1		1	1	1		2	2	3		1	2	5	24
6200 - 6324																		1	1	2	1	1	1		1	2	2	2	4	3	1	4	3		2	2	4	5	42
6075 - 6199															1	2	2	1	1		1		6	1		3	2	1	1	2		3	2	2	2	3	1	6	43
5950 - 6074															1	1	1	2	3	1		3	2	1	3	4		3		3	2	2	1	1	2			8	44
5825 - 5949															2	1		2	3	4	4		4	5	2		2	3	2	2	3	1	4	5	2	4	2	6	63
5700 - 5824														1	2	1	1	1	1	3	3	4		5	2	7	4		3	4	3	5	2	2	5	1	2	8	70
5575 - 5699													1	1	1	1		4	6	3	6	2	10	4	3	2	6	4	4	2	4		2	1	5	3	6	14	95
5450 - 5574											1			1		2	1	1	2	2	2	3	5	6	10	4	6	6	5	4	4	2	4	2	3	4	6	11	97
5325 - 5449												1		2	2	5	4	6	5	2	6	2	2	6	8	2	2	4	6	4	3	4	1	6	3	3	3	10	102
5200 - 5324															1	5	3	2	9	4	6	10	5	5	5	4	7	3	5	2	4	5	1	4	5	2	4	15	116
5075 - 5199														2	1	5	8	1	5	7	8	4	5	6	11	9	6	5	11	2	6	8	7	3	3	5	7	16	151
4950 - 5074									1	1	1		1	3	8	7	7	6	7	2	7	7	9	13	8	7	6	7	9	4	3	5	7	7	3	4	2	21	173
4825 - 4949												1	1	1	6	11	8	10	11	13	11	10	12	8	3	8	8	3	7	4	6	2	7	3	1	4	2	17	178
4700 - 4824									1	2		4	2	5	7	10	6	10	9	12	7	9	10	8	9	6	5	8	5	6	3	4	3	3	4	2	2	18	180
4575 - 4699									1	1		8	1	7	8	11	13	6	6	7	11	3	4	7	11	9	9	6	9	8	10	6	11	3	1	5	1	27	210
4450 - 4574									1		2	3	2	4	9	11	9	9	9	13	7	11	13	14	10	9	10	8	6	4	3	4	3	2	1	3	2	10	192
4325 - 4449							1	1	2	1	3	8	6	9	11	11	8	9	6	9	9	7	12	5	16	9	8	7	8	12	7	1	6	7	3	7	4	19	232
4200 - 4324										3	2	8	10	10	8	7	19	12	12	9	6	8	8	3	9	6	7	6	2	8	5	4	2	4	5	7	6	20	216
4075 - 4199								1	4	4	8	5	10	10	19	21	14	11	14	12	9	11	18	13	11	5	7	8	8	12	4	10	3	5	2	3	4	24	290
3950 - 4074							1	4	2	5	10	13	11	17	17	21	15	9	11	8	10	6	5	15	7	9	8	6	3	4	7	7	3	9	4	9	7	18	281
3825 - 3949							3	10	11	7	14	12	13	9	13	21	8	13	15	7	9	8	7	4	5	5	2	7	6	9	7	7	10	3	4	1	3	9	262
3700 - 3824						1	1	10	14	12	8	15	13	15	9	16	14	12	10	11	8	8	6	13	8	4	4	5	3	2	4	6	2		3	3	3	12	255
3575 - 3699							5	10	12	18	9	15	16	14	16	14	13	9	4	6	10	4	9	6	2	4	3	3	2	4	1	6	3	3	1	2	2	8	234
3450 - 3574				2		4	6	8	16	10	12	15	15	10	16	5	8	5	5	6	7	4	5	3	4	7	2	4	6	3	2	1	1	4		1	1	7	205
3325 - 3449					4	5	6	18	13	9	16	12	8	2	9	14	4	9	6	5	3	3	3	6	5	1	3	3	4	3	4	4			4	3	1	3	193
3200 - 3324			2	3	4	8	13	21	19	10	9	8	8	11	7	5	6	5	4	1	6	3	3	1	2	4					1	1		3	1	1	1	5	176
3075 - 3199		1	1	5	9	8	11	13	20	15	13	12	9	5	8	1	1	4	2	4	4	6	1	3	2		2	1	2	2			3		1			5	174
2950 - 3074			4	6	8	4	14	22	7	8	14	10	6		6	2	2	2	2	5	2	3	4	5	3	2	1	2	2		1		4			2	1	1	155
2825 - 2949			14	24	12	11	11	19	18	10	8	5	5	5	2	3	5	2	2		5	1	1	1	2	1			1	1	3		1		1				174
2700 - 2824	4	8	17	19	20	15	18	13	10	8	4	3	4	3	1	3	3	1	1		3		1		1				1	2		3	1			1		1	169
2575 - 2699		11	27	22	25	12	12	7	8	7	3	2	3	5	1	2	1	2				1	1			1	2	1		1								1	158
2450 - 2574	29	42	35	17	14	7	8	4	2		1	3		1	1	1		1	1			1	1	1			1								1				172
2325 - 2449	16	37	28	10	4	10	5	2				1					1					1			1														116
2200 -2324	13	11	8	6	1	1	1	2	3			1								1																			48
UNDER 2200		10	6	3	4	1		2			1	1						1																					29
TOTAL	62	120	142	117	105	87	116	167	165	131	139	166	145	154	193	221	187	170	174	164	179	148	183	170	168	137	128	119	131	124	111	109	103	89	74	91	82	354	5425
MEDIAN	2458	2455	2553	2703	2728	2804	2976	3195	3295	3429	3455	3658	3688	3908	4005	4089	4186	4188	4304	4422	4429	4432	4512	4503	4524	4595	4630	4551	4762	4439	4656	4585	4682	4762	4950	4637	5012	4748	4035
MEAN	2433	2477	2564	2711	2752	2854	3008	3199	3332	3434	3501	3665	3698	3924	4041	4189	4209	4239	4421	4466	4476	4438	4637	4502	4583	4638	4665	4629	4741	4669	4821	4657	4738	4851	4828	4772	4899	4860	4090
STD. DEV.	110	170	243	275	289	344	388	428	479	491	513	583	527	673	678	699	729	798	791	856	932	861	951	807	839	859	819	826	897	979	1097	929	965	1010	1011	943	887	963	1051

Source: Organization Resources Counselors, Inc., New York.

EXHIBIT 8.7 Percentile Curves: Years since First Degree versus Monthly Salary—All Engineers, All Companies

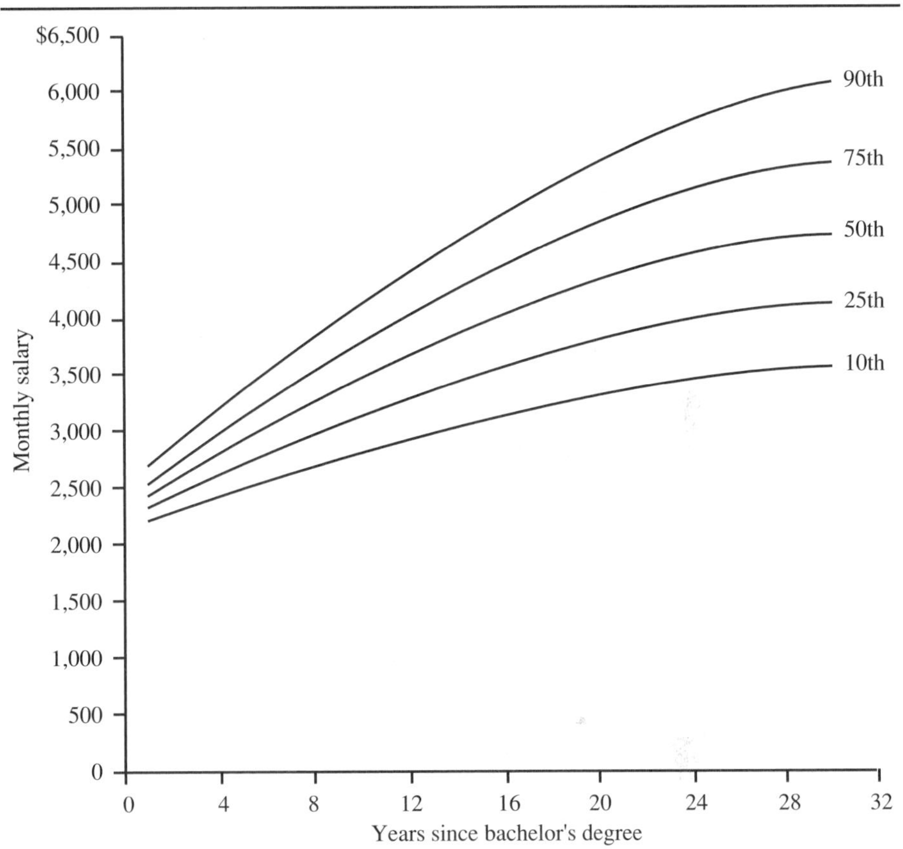

Source: Organization Resources Counselors, Inc., New York.

Low-High Approach. If an organization is using skill/competency-based structures or generic job descriptions, it may not be able to match jobs with competitors who use a traditional job-based approach. Job-based market data must be converted to fit the skill or competency structure. The simplest approach is to identify the lowest- and highest-paid benchmark jobs for the relevant skills in the relevant market and to use the wages for these jobs as anchors for the skill-based structures. Work at various levels within the structure can then be slotted between the anchors. For example, Exhibit 8.8 shows the skill-based system at Borg-Warner. Since the structure begins with unskilled labor, market rates for entry-level unskilled labor would anchor the low end of the structure. Market rates for team leaders should anchor the high end. On a graph with wage rates on the y-axis and the structure on the x-axis, a line can be drawn connecting the rates for the anchors. Wage rates for the rest of the structure can then be slotted on this line. For

EXHIBIT 8.8 Pricing a Skill-Based Structure

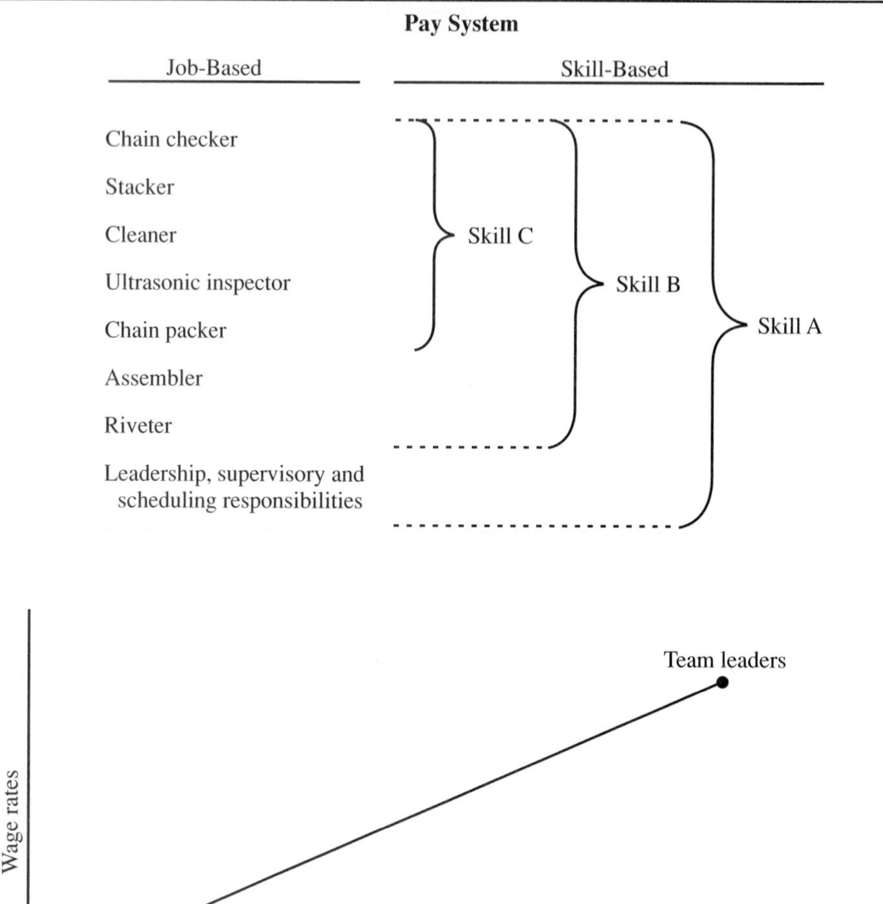

example, if the entry market rate, for operator A, is $8 per hour and the rate for a team leader is $28 per hour, then the rate for operator B can be somewhere between $8 and $28 per hour.

The usefulness of this approach depends on how well the extreme benchmark jobs match the organization's work, and whether they really do tap the entire range of skills.

Hanging a pay system on two pieces of market data raises the stakes on the accuracy of those data.

Using Skills or Competencies

The dilemma facing those using person-based approaches is that the market surveys are typically job based. Thus, matching specific combinations of skills/competencies among competitors in the market requires considerable judgment. Some consultants (e.g., Towers Perrin) are piloting skill/competency-based surveys. Until these products become available, most firms are simply "roughing them in." They are converting competencies to (dare we say it?) jobs, and then going to the market to find matches; for example, the combination of competencies for the financial manager role is matched to financial managers in surveys. If skill/competency-based approaches become more commonly used, then consultants will undoubtedly respond with new survey products to meet those needs.

Benchmark Conversion Approach. This approach to matching survey jobs requires an employer to apply its plan to value the benchmark jobs provided in the survey and to compare those results with internal results. If an organization uses job evaluation, then its job evaluation system is applied to the benchmark jobs, and job evaluation points are assigned to these jobs. If an organization uses skill/competency-based pay, then skill points can be assigned to the survey jobs. The magnitude of difference in skill points or job evaluation points provides a guideline for making similar adjustments in the market data collected for the survey job.

So, the real issue is to ensure that the jobs or skill/competency groups included in the survey provide data that will be useful. Depending on the purpose of the survey, either the benchmark approach, the global approach, the low-high approach, or the benchmark-conversion approach can help.

WHAT INFORMATION TO COLLECT?

Three basic types of data typically are requested: (1) information about the nature of the organization, (2) information about the total compensation system, and (3) specific pay data on each incumbent in the jobs under study. Exhibit 8.9 lists the basic data elements and the logic for including them.

No survey includes all the data that will be discussed. Rather, the data collected depend on the purpose of the survey and the jobs and skills included. Managers must rely on their expertise and experience to decide what data to collect and be sensitive to any guidelines that emerge from consent decrees and legal judgments.

Organization Data. This information assesses the similarities and differences among survey users. Financial information, size, and organization structure are usually included. Surveys of executives and upper-level positions include more detailed financial and reporting relationships data. The logic for including these additional data is that compensation for these jobs is more directly related to the organization's financial performance. More often than not, the financial data are simply used to group firms by size expressed in terms of sales or revenues.

Exhibit 8.9 Data Elements to Consider for Surveys and Their Rationale

Basic Elements	*Examples*	*Rationale*
Nature of Organization		
Identification	Company, name, address, contact person	Further contacts
Financial condition	Assets, sales, profits (after taxes)	Indicates nature of the product/service markets, the ability to pay, size, and financial viability
Size	Profit centers, product lines	Importance of specific job groups to business success
	Total number of employees	Impact on labor market
Structure	Organizational charts	Indicates how business is organized and how important managerial jobs are
Nature of Total Compensation System		
Cash forms used	Base pay, pay increase schedules, long- and short-term incentives, bonuses, cost of living adjustments, overtime and shift differentials	Indicate the mix of compensation offered; used to establish a comparable base
Noncash forms used	Composition of benefits and services, particularly the degree of coverage and contributions to medical and health insurance and pensions	
Incumbent and Job		
Date	Date effective	Need to update rates to current date
Job	Match generic job description	Indicates degree of similarity with survey's key jobs
	Number of employees supervised and reporting levels	Describes scope of responsibilities
Individual	Years since degree, education, date of hire	Indicates training and tenure of incumbents
Pay	Actual rates paid to each individual, total earnings, last increase, bonuses, incentives	

EXHIBIT 8.10 The Total May Be Greater than the Sum of the Parts

Remuneration Comparison for a Specific Job

Company cash compensation	A $100	B $110	C $120	D $130	E $150	F $155	G $170	H $210	I $250	J $255	K $260
Company benefits	J 25	K 30	H 35	A 40	B 45	G 50	D 60	C 65	I 72	E 75	F 77
Company total	**A $140**	**B $155**	**C $185**	**D $190**	**G $220**	**E $225**	**F $232**	**H $245**	**J $275**	**K $290**	**I $322**

Go to two of the compensation consultant web pages listed in the Appendix to Chapter 18. Compare and contrast the information provided. As a manager in a company, which page offers the most useful information—for what purpose? Which of the data elements listed in Exhibit 8.9 does the consultant say is included in their survey information? Would their pages influence which one you might wish to work for? Why?

Total Compensation Data. All the basic forms of pay need to be covered in a survey to assess the similarities and differences in the entire pay packages and to accurately assess competitors' practices.[12] For example, more and more employers offer various forms of team awards and incentives along with the base pay. Some employers roll these awards into the base pay, others do not. Inconsistent reporting (or not reporting) of these awards will distort the data. For example, company I in Exhibit 8.10 may target itself to be at the third quartile among a selected comparison group for cash compensation and benefits. Company I's cash compensation of $250 per week is at the third quartile of comparisons on cash compensation, and Company I's $72 per week for benefits is also at the third quartile of companies for benefits. (See the Appendix for information on quartiles.) But because they surveyed cash compensation and benefits separately, a new profile emerges when the separate surveys are combined. Company I's total pay of $322 is the highest in the group—17 percent higher than its targeted position of third quartile, $275 per week.

[12] Joseph R. Rich and Carol Caretta Phalen, "A Framework for the Design of Total Compensation Surveys," *ACA Journal,* Winter 1992–93, pp. 18–29; Jack Dolmat-Connell, "A New Paradigm for Compensation and Benefits Competitiveness," *Compensation and Benefits Review,* September–October 1994, pp. 51–64; Jill Kanin-Lovers and Sharon Parr, "Developing a Total Compensation Approach," *Compensation Guide,* ed. William A. Caldwell (Boston: Warren Gorham Lamont, December 1996).

EXHIBIT 8.11 Benchmarking Total Compensation

Coverage	Mainstream benefit
Basic term life	1.5 x earnings
Term accidental death & dismemberment	1.5 x earnings
Optional term life	1, 2, 3 x basic earnings
Short-term disability	Average of 100% of pay replaced for 4 weeks; 50% replaced for up to 26 weeks
Long-term disability	60% of pay to age 65 (or recovery or death); integrated with Primary and Family Social Security
Traditional medical	$200 individual/$600 family deductible; 80/20 coinsurance; $1,500 individual/$3,000 family limit on out-of-pocket expenses
Managed medical plan	For POS plan: $10 copay in network; $500 deductible and 70% reimbursement for out of network
Dental	100% coverage of preventive work, 80% of basic services and 50% of major services and orthodontia; $25 individual/$75 family deductible (waived on preventive care)

Source: Alexander & Alexander Consulting Group

It is particularly difficult to include *all* the pay forms in detail. For example, including medical coverage deductibles, flexible benefit options, and vacation policies quickly makes a survey too cumbersome to be useful. Methods to handle this problem range from a brief description of a benchmark benefit package to including only the most expensive and variable benefits or asking for an estimate of total benefit expenses as a percentage of total labor costs.

Exhibit 8.11 shows a benchmark or mainstream benefit package. Each company can describe how, if at all, it differs from the mainstream package.

The greatest limitation on total compensation surveys may be understanding how to use all the information. Perhaps as our experience grows, standards will emerge, and the packaging and interpretation of the data will be simplified. For now, total compensation surveys may be thought of as a database project. A well-designed total compensation database will allow each participating firm to determine the models, financial assumptions, and demographic profiles that best reflect its view of the world. In the best total compensation projects, each firm sees the survey as a custom project.

Incumbent Data. The most important data in the survey are the actual rates paid to each incumbent. Total earnings, hours worked, date and amount of last increase, and bonus and incentive payments are included. However, the usefulness of each element needs to be balanced against the cost of trying to collect it.

Enough data must be available to appraise the match between the benchmark jobs in the survey and jobs within each company. The degree of match between the survey's benchmark jobs and each company's jobs is assessed by various means. The Hay

Group, for example, has installed the same job evaluation plan in many companies that participate in their surveys. Consequently, jobs in different organizations can be compared on their job evaluation points and the distribution of points among the compensable factors. Other surveys simply ask participants to judge the degree of match, using a scale similar to the following one.

> Please check ( ) degree to which your job matches the benchmark job described in the survey:
> My company's job is
> Of moderately less value ( )
> Of slightly less value ( )
> Of equal value ( )
> Of slightly more value ( )
> Of moderately more value ( )

Still other survey designers periodically send teams of employees familiar with the benchmark jobs to visit each participating organization to discuss the matches. Many public agency and trade association surveys simply rely on each participant to match the benchmark jobs as closely as possible. The BLS has perhaps the most rigorous job-matching process. It includes site visits and detailed job analysis.

However, a consultant friend insists that when the compensation manager changes, the job matches often change, too. As we noted earlier, few quality standards exist on market data. This lack of concern for data validity is surprising as more and more employers (i.e., those quoted at the beginning of this chapter) place greater emphasis on "market-based" pay. Clearly, defining "market-based" pay requires judgment.[13]

International Data. International competition requires international pay comparisons. International surveys raise additional issues of comparability because legal regulations and tax policies, as well as customs, vary among countries. For example, because of tax reasons, Korean executives rarely receive incentive pay. However, they do receive company credit cards with significant charge limits that are often used for personal expenses. Some South American countries mandate cost of living adjustments, which makes the timing of the survey data collection crucial. Exhibit 8.12 gives an idea of the type of background information on benefits in more than 60 countries that Mercer provides its clients. Companies with worldwide locations use local surveys for jobs filled locally and international surveys for top executive and managerial jobs.

However, as we will discuss in Chapter 16 on international pay systems, local and regional surveys are of decidedly mixed quality. Some regions (China, Central Europe) still do not have systematic labor markets. Historically, in these countries state agencies set nationwide wage rates. No need for surveys. Japanese companies historically share information among themselves but do not share such information with outsiders.

---

[13] Sara L. Rynes and G. T. Milkovich, "Wage Surveys: Dispelling Some Myths about the 'Market Wage,' " *Personnel Psychology,* Spring 1986, pp. 71–90; Frederic Cook, "Compensation Surveys Are Biased," *Compensation and Benefits Review,* September–October 1994, pp. 19–22; Marlene Kim, "Inside the Black Box: A Subjective Analysis of Salary Surveys," (Working paper, Rutgers University, 1997).

EXHIBIT 8.12 International Benefit Data

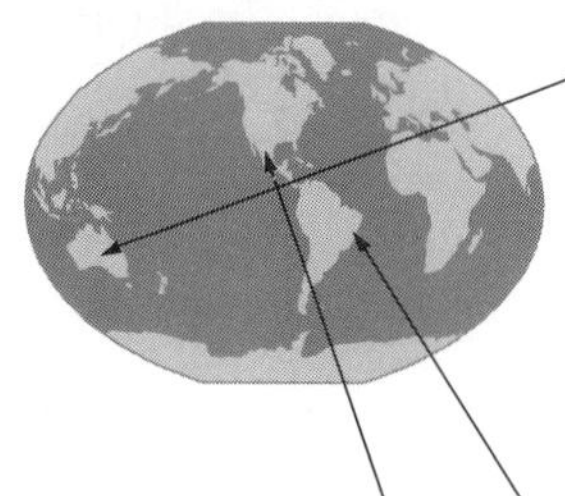

Australia
- An additional 15% tax surcharge on employer superannuation contributions for individuals with incomes of A$85,000 or more. The proposal will significantly add to the complexity of fund administration and also necessitate a review of any 'salary sacrifice' arrangements which may be in place.
- A higher tax free limit and relaxation of the participation rate requirement for qualifying employee share plans.
- A 1% surcharge on the medicare levy for individuals earning more than A$50,000 who do not have private health insurance, with a tax rebate of up to A$450 for lower income earners who do.

Brazil
- Social Security reform is still a top priority, although the Government's proposed reforms are encountering strong opposition.
- Mandatory Profit/Results Sharing legislation has been published by the federal government but not yet voted on by Congress.
- In 1997 the Official Social Security Financing Rules were consolidated and now clearly state that employer contributions to a private retirement programme are not subject to Social Security charges, as long as the plan is extended to all of the employees of the company.

Mexico
- Implementation of the new social security law has been deferred due to administrative problems. The new law introduces a system of privately managed pension fund accounts, in some respects similar to the Chilean model.
- The new social security system will necessitate a review of company retirement plans, many of which have been designed to integrate with the benefits provided under the old system. In the future, there is likely to be a major trend towards defined contribution plans.
- As part of a general review of the Mexican tax laws aimed at reducing tax avoidance, the government is looking at taxation of certain employee benefits, such as savings plans and social welfare allowance plans. In the future, the tax efficiency of these benefits is likely to be reduced.

Source: *1997 International Benefit Guidelines* (William M. Mercer Consultants).

Accuracy of Data. Despite the acceptance of courts of market data as legal justification for salary differentials, the whole area of collection, analysis, and interpretation has not been subject to the same scrutiny as hiring practices and testing. Whether it should have been is another question. Certainly, a sound, business-related rationale for every step in the process is important. But fine distinctions using data that are extremely general may be faulty. Some survey data profile a general guide to assess the adequacy of the whole pay structure, but not necessarily pay of specific jobs. Other surveys are designed to price specific jobs, and still others to assess only the rate of change in the rates paid. The purpose of the survey needs to be kept in mind when judging the accuracy of the data.

Many aspects of surveys have been ignored by researchers. Little can be said about the effects of different formats in the accuracy of the data obtained. Little is known about ensuring comparability of job matches or benefit packages. We don't know how representative surveys are of some markets. The same lack of research plagues the analysis of the data.

How to Collect the Data?

Two basic methods are used to collect pay data: interviews (in person or by phone) and mailed questionnaires. The purpose of the survey and the extensiveness of the data required usually determine the method. Special studies or double-checking results are often performed through phone interviews. Mailed questionnaires are probably most common. The BLS, the most experienced wage surveyor of all, uses extensive field interviews. Some organizations use field visits every second or third year to hold down costs and time requirements.

INTERPRET AND APPLY SURVEY DATA

To discover how survey data are actually analyzed, Belcher interviewed 34 compensation professionals almost 15 years ago. He reports:

> Every organization uses its own methods of distilling information from the survey; uses different surveys for different purposes; and uses different methods for company surveys. I could find no commonality in these methods of analysis by industry, by firm size, or by union presence. For example, some did nothing except read the entire survey, some emphasized industry data, others geographic competitors (commuting distances), some made comparisons with less than five competitors, some emphasized only large firms, others throw out the data from large firms.[14]

His conclusion still holds today. Diversity rules in analyzing survey data. We hope diversity reflects the flexibility of managers who adjust their analysis to deal with a variety of circumstances. We worry that diversity reflects expediency and a lack of business- and work-related logic; such approaches will not be able to withstand close critical scrutiny.

Verify Data

A common first step is to check the accuracy of the job matches. Job descriptions will be included with the survey data. However, even descriptions that match perfectly do not indicate how various companies value the same jobs, or their pay policies in reference to that job.

[14] Letter from D. W. Belcher to G. T. Milkovich, in reference to D. W. Belcher, N. Bruce Ferris, and John O'Neill, "How Wage Surveys Are Being Used," *Compensation and Benefits Review*, September–October 1985, pp. 34–51.

Exhibit 8.13 is a survey report provided by Organization Resources Counselors, Inc., for participants in its Salary Information Retrieval System. This particular survey report was prepared for company P44, a pharmaceutical firm, and reports wages for a business applications programmer/analyst position. We will use this report to illustrate a survey analysis. Examining the number of employees in each company shows that two clusters of wages seem to exist at $44,000 (297 employees) and at $50,000 to $52,000 (231 employees). Such clustering might raise questions with an analyst. Fortunately, the survey report provides assistance. A modifier key with which to assess the goodness of fit of job description is in the upper-left corner of the exhibit. One company, E17, employs by far the largest number of people whose salaries we are analyzing: 297 in MCS 2—Business. But this same company also reports data on 125 people in job MCS 3—Business who earn an average of $50,995. Clearly, company E17 distinguishes between these two jobs and pays them differently. Should both be included here in the same report? Should all the data from company E17 be discarded? Most surveys report only one job match per company, but most surveys also provide little information to assess the strength of that match. The three lines at the bottom of the exhibit disaggregate the salary data according to the goodness of the match.

Leveling. If the job description is similar but not identical, and the survey data are not disaggregated by closeness of match, the data may be weighted according to the match. This technique is called *survey leveling*. Based on a scale such as the one shown on page 237, if the job in the survey has more responsibility, some analysts adjust the survey data (e.g., multiply it by 0.8) to bring its pay closer in comparability to the employer's job. Conversely, the survey data could be adjusted upward. For example, if you believed that your programmers had slightly more responsibility than the survey job description indicated, you might multiply the $43,199 average salary in the survey by 110 percent and use the result, $47,519, instead. Leveling is another example of the use of judgment in the survey analysis process. It clearly leaves the objectivity of the decisions open to challenge.

Typical Analysis

Becoming familiar with the actual data in a survey is a necessary first step to assessing its accuracy and usefulness. In order to do so, we need to review some simple statistics. We will use the data in Exhibit 8.13 to illustrate some possible analyses.

Frequency Distribution. Arranging the data from lowest to highest and then tallying the entries allows construction of a frequency distribution. Frequency distributions include an entry for every single measurement. The frequency table in Exhibit 8.14 displays the salary data in intervals of $2,500. The data are then readily converted to a histogram also shown in the exhibit. The histogram helps visualize the information in the survey and may highlight nonconformities. For example, the one salary above $60,000 may be considered an outlier—an extreme that falls outside the majority of the data points. Whether or not to include outliers is a judgment call.

Exhibit 8.13 Survey Report Prepared by Compensation Consulting Firm

Job: PROGRAMMING/ANALYST-BUSINESS APPLICATIONS

Modifiers: A = Stronger match
B = Exact match
C = Weaker match

Prepared for company P44

Co. #	Modifiers	Job Title	No. of Inc.	Actual Salaries Avg.	Low	High	Range Min.	Mid Pt.	Range Max.
D67	B	Prog/Analyst Sr	2	39,911	39,719	40,040	31,071	38,886	46,702
E08	C	Sr Data Analyst	5	40,231	34,850	43,691	31,519	43,691	55,864
P23	B	Prog Analyst Sr	13	42,987	39,399	48,239	31,519	45,966	60,412
D32	B	Mgmt Syst Analyst	2	42,987	41,705	44,204	38,759	48,688	58,618
E09	B	Prog/Analyst Bus	8	43,597	38,808	47,309	35,925	46,643	57,362
E17	B	MCS 2—Business	297	43,883	35,427	56,184	36,196	48,624	61,052
G02	B	Princ Business Prog	1	44,647	44,647	44,647	39,103	48,491	57,879
P19	B	Prog/Analyst Sr	12	45,421	39,719	54,006	38,759	51,347	63,935
E31	B	Prog Analyst Sr	3	45,904	40,656	48,712	35,599	46,318	55,558
E11	C	Prog Analyst Sr	3	46,244	42,578	51,152	35,599	45,586	55,572
P21	B	Prog/Analyst III	1	46,791	46,791	46,791	38,113	48,787	59,461
E08	B	ADP Analyst	4	47,983	42,922	53,173	33,441	48,496	63,551
E35	B	Sr Sys Analyst Gen	22	48,299	33,264	59,376	41,395	51,744	62,093
P44	**B**	**Sys Dev Spec III**	**3**	**48,358**	**46,067**	**52,114**	**34,180**	**48,831**	**63,482**
A12	B	Info Syst Prog	9	49,328	44,076	53,749	41,193	53,589	65,986
K15	B	Comp Analyst Sr	7	49,521	38,438	54,337	38,310	48,881	59,387
E20	B	Prog/Analyst Sr	1	49,713	49,713	49,713	44,204	56,984	69,765
E15	C	Prog Analyst II	4	49,794	48,048	54,454	38,502	48,112	57,721
C26	B	Sr Syst Analyst	13	50,216	44,736	59,067	38,315	49,773	61,230
E03	B	Prog/Analyst Sr	6	50,280	46,274	54,331	39,325	49,156	58,988
E17	A	MCS 3—Business	125	50,995	40,552	62,783	39,591	52,372	65,153
E11	B	Syst Analyst Sr	3	51,152	50,266	52,483	40,035	51,307	62,580
B10	B	Prog Analyst III	103	51,462	42,578	63,127	42,578	53,222	63,866
F07	A	Sr Prog/Analyst	24	51,729	36,694	64,975	42,400	55,129	67,844
P12	B	Sr Prog/Analyst	1	52,778	52,778	52,778	39,917	51,128	62,339
E09	A	Prog Analyst	10	53,074	49,097	60,510	40,803	53,296	65,789
S37	B	M/S Analyst	2	53,173	52,084	54,198	37,797	50,290	62,783
E34	B	Analyst Bus Syst	1	55,095	55,095	55,095	38,886	52,308	65,729
Q54	A	Prog Analyst Sr	1	55,479	55,479	55,479	44,140	55,607	67,075
E31	A	Prog Analyst Staff	4	58,441	54,922	65,344	45,091	58,648	70,342
Q18	A	Info Syst Analyst	4	58,766	57,465	60,377	40,286	55,181	70,076
E15	B	Prog Analyst I	1	59,514	59,514	59,514	41,320	51,635	61,950
P05	B	Sr MIS Spec	1	62,206	62,206	62,206	42,153	56,184	67,395
	26 companies								
	Total incumbents		696						
	Company P44 average		**3**	**48,358**	**46,067**	**52,114**	**34,180**	**48,831**	**63,482**
	Market weighted average		693	47,519			38,412	50,511	62,588
	Market simple average			47,538	45,640	54,126	38,808	50,502	62,002
	3 companies matching modifier C		12	44,923	41,825	49,765	35,207	45,796	56,386
	23 companies matching modifier B		513	46,239	45,253	52,751	38,431	49,933	61,245
	6 companies matching modifier A		168	51,612	49,035	61,478	42,052	55,040	67,713

Source: Adapted from Organization Resources Counselors, Inc., New York.

Exhibit 8.14 Statistical Analysis of Survey Data

Frequency Table

Wage Interval	*Number of Companies Whose Average Wage Falls in This Interval*
$35,000–$37,500	0
37,501– 40,000	1
40,001– 42,500	1
42,501– 45,000	5
45,001– 47,500	4
47,501– 50,000	6
50,001– 52,500	6
52,501– 55,000	3
55,001– 57,500	2
57,501– 60,000	3
60,001– 62,500	1

Histogram

Quartiles and Percentiles

$39,911 ←	**Minimum**
40,231	
42,987	
$42,987 ←	**10th Percentile**
43,597	
43,883	
44,647	
45,421	
$45,904 ←	**Quartile 1**
46,244	
46,791	
47,983	
48,299	
49,328	
49,521	
49,713	
$49,794 ←	**Quartile 2, 50th Percentile**
50,216	
50,280	
50,995	
51,152	
51,462	
51,729	
52,778	
$53,074 ←	**Quartile 3**
53,173	
55,095	
55,479	
58,441	
$58,766 ←	**90th Percentile**
59,514	
$62,206 ←	**Maximum**

Histograms can vary in their shape. Unusual shapes require further analysis to assess the usefulness of the data. They may reflect problems with job matches, widely dispersed pay rates, or employers with widely divergent pay policies. If the data look reasonable at this point, one wag has suggested that it is probably the result of two large, offsetting errors.

Central Tendency. The vast amount of information contained in a survey must be reduced to a single number that represents the market wage for programming analysts. The arithmetic average, or mean, is the most widely used, calculated by adding all the numbers in the group and then dividing by the number of numbers. The "simple average" for this survey is $49,738 (e.g., $39,911 + $40,231, + $42,987, etc.) and dividing by 32, the number of positions. (*Note:* Data from the company for which the report was prepared are *not* included in any of these calculations.) This calculation of mean, or arithmetic average, gives equal weight to every *company* in the survey. The programmer wage paid by company G02, which has only one individual in that position, counts as much as the wage paid by E17, which has 297 programmers.

An alternative is a *weighted mean,* or weighted average, which gives equal weight to *each individual employee's* wage. Each company's mean wage is weighted by the number of people in that company who occupy that job. A weighted mean gives a more accurate picture of actual labor market conditions, since it better recognizes the size of the supply and demand.

A third measure of central tendency is the *median,* or the middle number of numbers arranged in either increasing or decreasing order.

Although mean is by far the most common measure of central tendency, outliers (extreme values) can distort it. Therefore, some analysts calculate more than one central tendency measure to compare to the scatter plot and/or frequency distribution before deciding which one best represents "market wage."

What difference does all this make? Central tendency measures summarize all the survey responses into a single wage for each job. Although the frequency distribution shows all the wages, central tendency gives just one. Therefore, the analyst must choose the wage measure that gives the most accurate description of the survey data.

Dispersion. The distribution of rates around a measure of central tendency is called *dispersion. Standard deviation* is probably the most common statistical measure of dispersion, although its use in salary surveys is less common. Standard deviation refers to how far from the mean each of the items in a frequency distribution is located. In the frequency distribution based on data in Exhibit 8.13, the standard deviation from the mean is $5,445, which means that 68 percent of the salaries lie between $44,293 and $50,183. Information about dispersion gives the analyst a better idea of the relationship between the central tendency measure and the frequency distribution.

Quartiles and Percentiles. Quartiles and percentiles are the most common measure of dispersion used in salary survey analysis. Recall from the introduction to this chapter that one organization's policy was "to be in the 75th percentile nationally." A 75th percentile means that 75 percent of all companies' pay rates are at or below that point, and 25 percent are above. To calculate quartiles, the measures are ordered from lowest to highest. If the measures are separated into four groups, each group contains 25 percent of the measures, and the numbers that separate the groups are called *quartiles.* There are three quartiles (first, second, and third) for any set of scores. The second quartile always corresponds to the median. To say that a measure is in the fourth quartile means that it falls anywhere above the point of separation between the third and fourth quartile. Exhibit 8.14 shows the survey data with quartiles and percentiles marked.

Exhibit 8.7 shows the 10th, 25th, 50th, 75th, and 90th percentile curves for engineers' salaries. Quartiles correspond to the 25th (Q1), 50th (Q2), and 75th (Q3) percentiles.

The survey report in Exhibit 8.13 also includes range information and indicates whether the programming analysts receive any bonus or incentive compensation. All these issues will be explained in later chapters.

WHERE DO WE GO FROM HERE?

Before we go on to the second half of this chapter, it may be useful to take a break. Spend some time reflecting on what we have been doing, and why. We have looked at the reasons for conducting a survey and the techniques for analyzing survey data. We have summarized data from all the surveyed jobs into a market pay line. But keep in mind what these mechanics are all about. They are about designing a pay line that reflects our competitive position. Why bother? Because external competitiveness is an important part of the compensation strategy.

Next we are going to combine external competitiveness and internal consistency. This is done by merging our external pay line based on external market data with our internal work structure based on job evaluation and skills or competencies.

COMBINE INTERNAL STRUCTURE AND EXTERNAL MARKET RATES

Two components of the pay model are emerging, and their relationship to each other is depicted in Exhibit 8.15.

- An *internally consistent structure* has been developed and is shown on the horizontal axis in Exhibit 8.15. For this illustration, our structure consists of jobs A through P, with P being the most complex job in this structure. Jobs B, D, F, G, H, J, M, and P are benchmark jobs that have been matched in a survey. Job M is the programmer analyst surveyed in Exhibit 8.13.
- External wage rates paid by relevant competitors for those benchmark jobs, as measured by the survey, are shown on the vertical (y) axis. The purpose of the survey is to assist the organization to address external competitiveness, much as job analysis addressed internal consistency.

These two components—internal consistency and external competitiveness—come together in the pay structure. The pay structure has two aspects. One is the actual pay policy line, which reflects market rates adjusted to the job structure and pay level policy decisions of the organization. The second is pay ranges, which build flexibility into the structure.

Calculating the Pay Policy Line

Getting from where we are now—wage rates for a number of benchmark jobs—to an actual pay policy line requires three steps.

1. Construct a market pay line. Recall the frequency distribution for the programmer job M (Exhibit 8.14). If frequency distributions are calculated for all the benchmark jobs B, D, F, H, M, and P, then it is a simple step to transfer all the distributions onto a single graph in Exhibit 8.16, where the employer's job structure (job

Exhibit 8.15 Combining Internal Structure with External Wage Rates

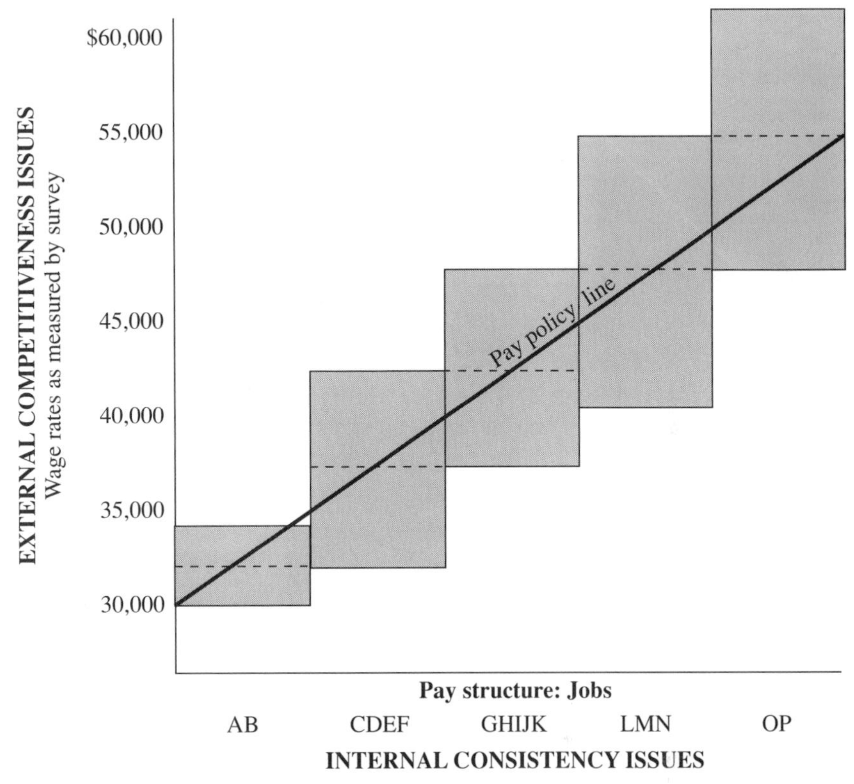

evaluation points) is the x-axis and wage rates are on the y-axis. The frequency distributions are at right angles to the x- and y-axes, similar to a topographic map. (*Note:* For clarity, only four distributions are shown on the exhibit.) Summarizing the data from all these distributions into a market pay line may be as simple as drawing a line that connects the means, percentiles, or other measures of central tendency of the distributions, as in Exhibit 8.16. A straight line or a curve is most useful, even though midpoints for some jobs may not fall on this line. Exactly where this line is drawn will reflect the market pay line. Lines may be drawn to represent various percentiles in the distributions of job rates (e.g., a 60 percent line would indicate that 60 percent of market rates fall below this line). A market line may be drawn freehand on the basis of simple inspection of the data, or statistical techniques, such as regression analysis, may be used. Regression fits a line that minimizes the variance of observations around it. Appendix 8-A provides additional information on regression. The result is a statistically more accurate market pay line that summarizes the distribution of going rates in the market.

Exhibit 8.16 Constructing a Market Pay Line

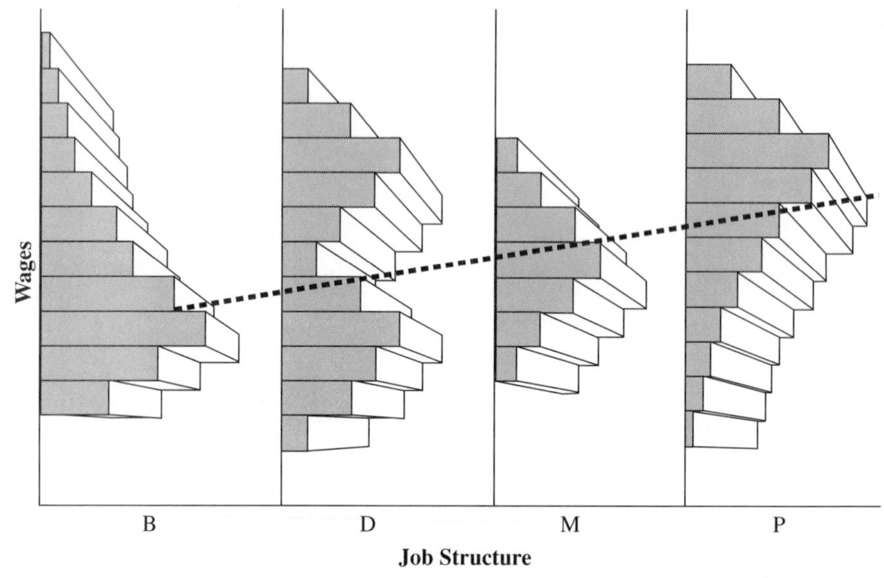

Comparing going rates to the employer's rates will show the competitiveness of the current pay rates. Comparisons may be made across job families or by individual jobs. Exhibit 8.17 shows a comparison based on "market index," or the actual salary divided by the market rate. The market index for personnel representatives is the average salary of the four personnel representatives divided by the market rate for personnel representatives, which yields 86 percent. This low ratio may be the result of deliberate policy choices by the employer (e.g., lag the market for HR positions), the nature of the job, (e.g., personnel reps quickly get promoted into other jobs), or the survey data (e.g., personnel reps in the survey had greater responsibilities). It's up to the analyst to decide whether the variance from the market is explainable and acceptable.

2. Update the survey data. The comparison with the market pay line gives the analyst information on the competitiveness of the current pay. The next step is to update or "age" the market data for comparisons at a future time period.

Because they reflect decisions of employers, employees, unions, and government agencies, wages paid by competitors are constantly changing. And competitors adjust their wages at different times. Universities typically adjust to match the academic year. Unionized employers adjust to correspond to dates negotiated in labor agreements. Many employers adjust each employee's pay on the anniversary of the employee's date of hire. Even though these changes do not occur smoothly and uniformly throughout the year, as a practical matter it is common practice to assume

Exhibit 8.17 Using the Market Index to Determine Competitiveness of Current Pay

Grade	Job Title	Number of Employees	Average Actual Salary	Market Rate Composite	Market Index
1	Personnel representative	4	$19,600	$22,700	86%
3	Senior compensation analyst	2	25,700	28,000	92
4	Security supervisor*	1	33,000	33,500	99
5	Manager, Training*	1	41,000	39,500	104
6	Director, Human Resources*	1	45,000	44,000	102
			Overall market index (Human Resources):		94%
1	Accounting assistant	10	20,000	21,000	95%
2	Accountant	6	24,000	24,500	98
3	Accounting supervisor*	3	31,500	30,000	105
5	Internal auditor	1	38,000	38,000	100
6	Controller*	1	48,000	45,000	107
			Overall market index (Finance):		99%
1	LPN	25	22,000	20,000	110%
2	Registered nurse	100	29,500	27,000	109
3	Nursing instructor	10	34,500	30,500	113
3	Nurse supervisor*	5	38,000	35,000	109
6	Director, Emergency Room*	1	47,500	38,500	123
			Overall market index (Nursing):		110%
1	Programmer	6	21,000	26,500	79%
2	Data entry supervisor*	4	23,500	25,500	92
4	Systems analyst	2	30,000	32,000	94
5	Manager, Computer Operations*	1	38,000	36,500	104
6	Direct, MIS*	1	47,500	46,000	103
			Overall market index (MIS):		90%

* Overall market index for management: 104%.

Overall market index for nonmanagement: 108%.

Source: Reprinted from ACA Building Block #2. "Mastering Market Data, An Approach to Analyzing and Applying Salary Survey Information," by Jane A. Bjorndal and Linda K. Ison Employees," with permission from the American Compensation Association (ACA), 14040 N. Northsight Blvd., Scottsdale, AZ U.S.A. 85260: telephone (602) 951-9191, fax: (602) 483-8352 © ACA.

that they do. Therefore, a survey that requires three to six months to collect, code, and analyze data is probably outdated before it is available. Consequently, the data are usually updated to forecast the competitive rates for the future date when the pay decisions will be implemented.

The amount to update (often called *aging* or *trending*) is based on several factors, including historical trends in the market economic forecasts, prospects for the economy in which the employer operates, and the manager's judgment, among others.

Exhibit 8.18 uses the survey data for the programmer's wage to illustrate updating. In the example, the pay rates collected in the survey were in effect at January 1 of the *current year.* Because this company's stated policy is to "match at the 50th percentile,"

EXHIBIT 8.18 Choices for Updating Survey Data Reflect Pay Policy

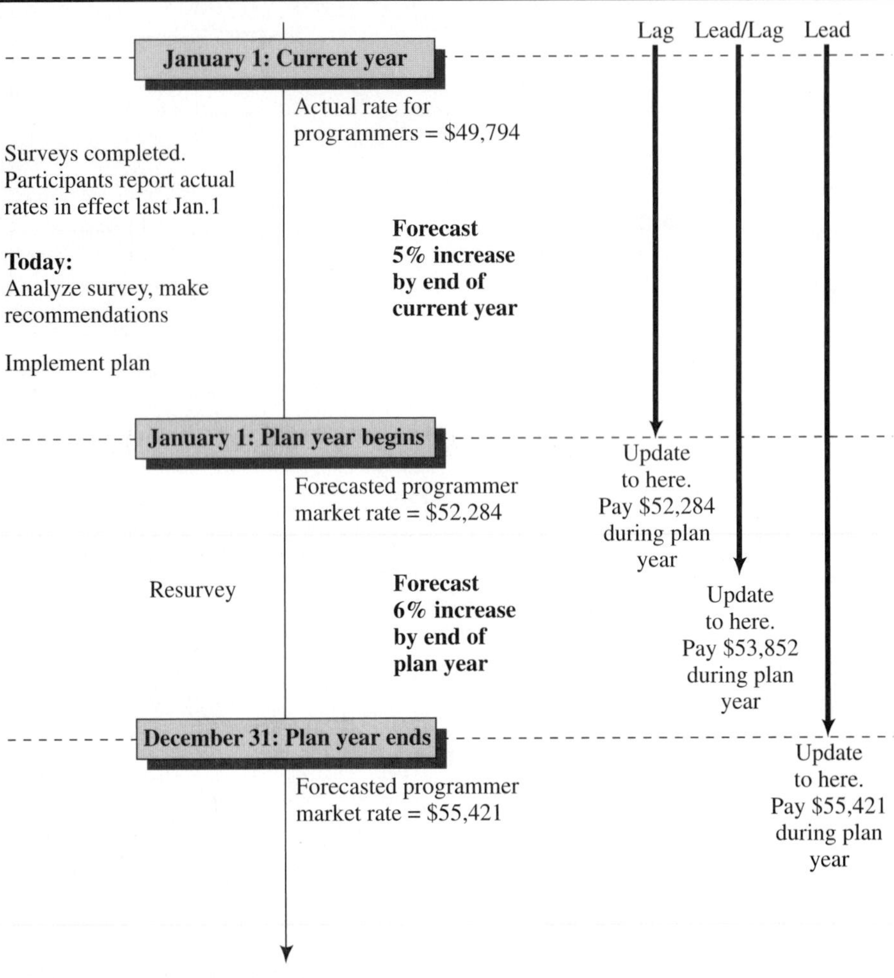

the figure at A ($49,794) is the 50th percentile of the frequency distribution of the market rates for the programmer's job. The compensation manager will use these data for pay decisions that will go into effect on January 1 of the *plan year.* Assume that pay rates have been increasing by approximately 5 percent annually. If we assume that the future will be like the past, then the market data are multiplied by 105 percent, to account for the rise in pay that is expected to occur by the end of the *current year.* The programmer's $49,794 this past January 1 is updated to $50,044 by the end of the *current year.*

To estimate what the market rates will be by the *end* of the *plan* year, a judgment is made about the rate of increase expected during the plan year and survey results are updated again on the basis of this judgment.

3. Translate pay level policy into practice. The arrows on the right-hand side of Exhibit 8.18 show the practical results of updating. Because an individual company typically adjusts its pay level only once per period, its pay will be at the same point at both the beginning and end of the plan year. But whether an organization updates to the end of the current year (programmer rate = $52,284), the end of the plan year (programmer rate = $53,852), or someplace in between depends on its pay-level policy and how it puts that policy into practice. If the company chooses a market rate comparison consistent with its pay-level policy (50th percentile), updates survey data to the end of the current year/start of the plan year (programmer rate = $52,284), and keeps this rate in effect throughout the plan year, the company will actually be lagging the market, since it matches its desired market pay level only at the beginning of the plan year. The market rates continue to rise throughout the year; the company's rates do not.

Aging the market data to a point halfway through the plan year (middle arrow in Exhibit 8.18), is called *lead/lag*. The original survey rates are updated to the end of the current year plus half the projected amount for the plan year ($53,852). To lead competition, an employer can age market data to the *end* of the plan year (programmer = $55,421), then pay at this rate throughout the plan year.

We have oversimplified this discussion by omitting other possible mechanics. For example, some companies lead by matching the competitor's 75th percentile; others match only a few top-paying competitors or lead for some job families and lag for others. The point is that pay-level policy and actual practice may not coincide, depending on how the policy is translated into practice.

DESIGN PAY RANGES AND BANDS

So far we have constructed a line that reflects market pay rates and projected those rates into the future in a way that reflects the organization's pay level policy. All this is part of designing a pay structure that will reflect the organization's policies on internal consistency and external competitiveness. The next step is to design pay ranges *or* pay bands. Once you are familiar with the construction of each, we will examine which approach makes sense under what conditions.

Why Bother with Ranges?

The wide variation of market rates paid for similar jobs and skills reflects two *external* pressures:

1. Quality variations (skills, abilities, experience) among individuals in the external market (e.g., company A has stricter hiring requirements for its buyer position than does company B, even though job descriptions are identical).
2. The recognition of differences in the productivity-related value to employers to these quality variations (e.g., buyers for Nordstrom's are accountable for different results than are buyers for Wal-Mart).

In addition to these external differences in rates, an organization's internal pay policy may call for differences in rates paid to employees on the same job. A pay range exists whenever two or more rates are paid to employees in the same job. Hence, internal pay ranges reflect the following *internal* pressures:

1. The intention to recognize individual performance variations with pay (e.g., buyer A makes better, more timely decisions for Nordstrom's than does buyer B, even though they both hold the same job and have the same responsibilities).
2. Employees' expectations that their pay will increase over time.

From an internal consistency perspective, the range reflects the approximate differences in performance or experience the employer wishes to pay for a given level of work. From an external competitiveness perspective, the range also acts as a control device. A range maximum sets the lid on what the employer is willing to pay for that work; the range minimum sets the floor.

Not all employers use ranges. Skill-based plans establish single *flat rates* for each skill level regardless of performance or seniority. And many collective bargaining contracts establish single flat rates for each job (i.e., all Senior Machinists II receive $14.50 per hour regardless of performance or seniority). This flat rate is often set to correspond to some midpoint on a survey of that job.

Constructing Ranges

Three steps are involved in designing ranges.

1. Develop Grades. A *grade* is a grouping of different jobs that are considered substantially equal for pay purposes. Grades enhance an organization's ability to move people among jobs within a grade with no change in pay. In Exhibit 8.19 the horizontal axis is the job structure with the jobs now slotted into grades.

The question of which jobs are substantially equal and therefore slotted into one grade requires the analyst to reconsider the original job evaluation results. Each grade will have its own pay range, and all the jobs within the grade have that same range. Jobs in different grades (e.g., jobs C, D, E, and F in grade 2) should be dissimilar to those in other grades (grade 1 jobs A and B) and will have a different pay range.

Although grades permit flexibility, they are challenging to design. The objective is for all jobs that are similar for pay purposes to be placed within the same grade. If jobs with relatively close job evaluation point totals fall on either side of grade boundaries (e.g., in Exhibit 8.19, jobs E, F, and G have point totals within 30 points of each other, but E and F are in one grade, and G is in another), the magnitude of difference in salary treatment may be out of proportion to the magnitude of difference in job content. Resolving such dilemmas requires an understanding of the specific jobs, career paths, and the flow of work in the organization. Designing the grade structure that fits each organization involves the use of trial and error until one structure seems to fit the best without too many problems.

2. Establish Ranges (midpoint, minimum, and maximum). The midpoints for each range are usually set to correspond to the competitive pay level established earlier. The point where the pay policy line crosses each grade becomes the midpoint of the pay range for that grade. The midpoint of the range is often called the *control point.* It

EXHIBIT 8.19 Developing Pay Grades

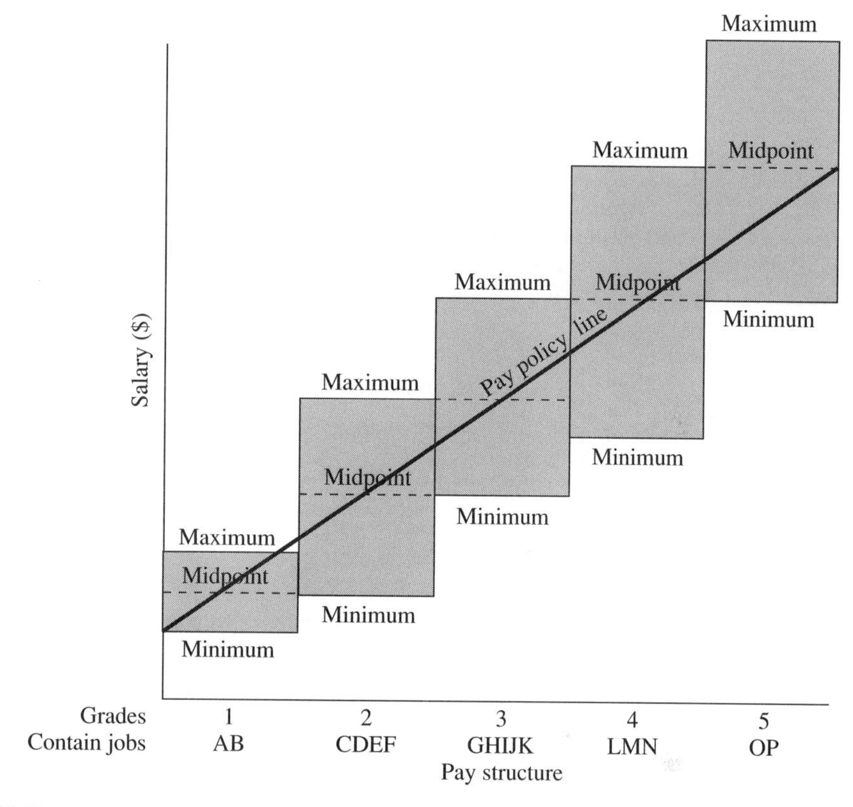

specifies the pay objective for a fully trained employee who is satisfactorily performing a job within that grade. It also reflects the competitive position in the relevant market.

The desired range spread is based on some judgment about how the ranges support career paths, promotions, and other organization systems.[15] Range spreads seem to vary between 10 to 120 percent. Top-level management positions commonly have range spreads of 60 to 120 percent; entry to midlevel professional and managerial positions, between 35 to 60 percent; office and production work, 10 to 25 percent. The underlying logic is that wider range spreads in the managerial jobs are designed to reflect the greater opportunity for individual discretion and performance variations in the work.

Another, perhaps better basis on which to determine the desired range spread is what makes good sense for the particular employer. Surveys usually provide data on

[15] "Alternative Base Salary Approaches," Chapter 22 *Compensation Guide* (New York: Warren Gorham Lamont, 1995).

both the actual maximum and minimum rates paid, as well as the ranges established by policy. Some compensation managers use the actual rates paid, particularly the 75th and 25th percentiles in the survey data, as their maximums and minimums. Others examine alternatives to ensure that the proposed spread includes at least 75 percent of the rates in the survey data. Still others establish the minimum and maximum separately. The amount between the minimum and the midpoint can be a function of the amount of time it takes a new employee to become fully competent. Jobs quickly learned may have minimums much closer to the midpoints. The maximum becomes the amount above the midpoint that the company is willing to pay for sustained performance on the job. In the end, range spread is based on judgment that weighs all these factors.

Once the midpoint (based on the pay policy line) and the range spread (based on judgment) are specified, minimums and maximums are calculated

$$\text{Minimum} = \text{Midpoint} \div [100\% + (1/2 \text{ range spread})]$$
$$\text{Maximum} = \text{Minimum} + (\text{Range spread} \times \text{Minimum})$$

For example, with a range spread of 30 percent, and a midpoint of \$10,000

$$\text{Minimum} = \$10{,}000 \div (1 + 0.15) = \$8{,}695$$
$$\text{Maximum} = \$8{,}695 + (0.30 \times \$8{,}695) = 8695 + 2609 = \$11{,}304$$

Note that these formulas assume symmetrical ranges (i.e., equal distance above and below the midpoint).

An issue related to ranges is the size of pay differentials between supervisors and the employees they supervise. A supervisory job would typically be at least one pay range removed from the jobs it supervises. Although a 15 percent pay differential has been offered as a rule of thumb, large range overlap, combined with possible overtime or incentive pay available in some jobs but not in supervisory jobs, could make it difficult to maintain such a differential. On the other hand, some argue that differentials are counterproductive if they force good technical talent (i.e., engineers) to become managers solely because managers command higher incomes. The issue is one of overlap.

3. Overlap. If A and B are two adjacent pay grades, with B the higher of the two, the degree of overlap is defined as

$$100 \times \frac{\text{Maximum rate grade A} - \text{Minimum rate grade B}}{\text{Maximum rate grade A} - \text{Minimum rate grade A}}$$

What difference does overlap make? Consider the two extremes shown in Exhibit 8.20. The high degree of overlap and low midpoint differentials in Figure A indicate small differences in the value of jobs in the adjoining grades. Such a structure results in promotions (title changes) without much change in pay. On the other hand, in Figure B, few grades and ranges result in wider range midpoint differentials and less overlap between adjacent ranges, and permit the manager to reinforce a promotion (movement into a new range) with a larger pay increase. At some point, the differential must be large enough to induce employees to seek and/or accept the promotion or to undertake the necessary training required. However, there is little research to indicate how much a differential is necessary to influence employees to take on additional responsibilities or invest in training.

EXHIBIT 8.20 Range Overlap

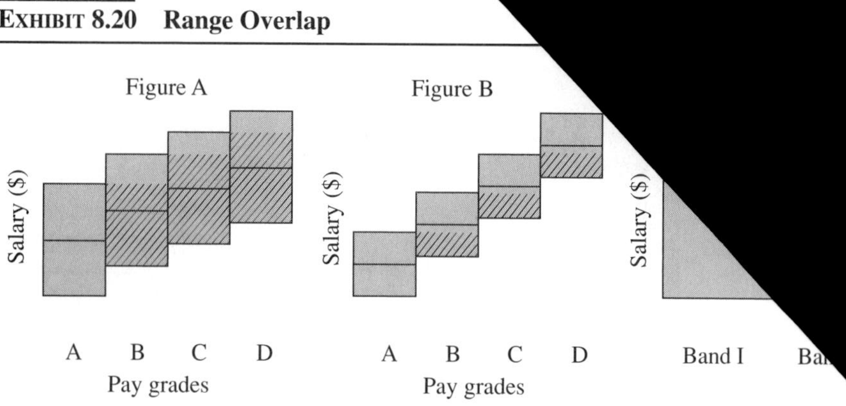

Broadbanding

Figure C collapses the number of salary grades within the structure into only a few broad grades (or bands) with much wider ranges. This technique, known as *broadbanding,* consolidates as many as four or five traditional grades into a single band with one minimum and one maximum. Because the band encompasses so many jobs of differing values, a range midpoint is usually not used.[16]

Contrasts between ranges and broadbands are highlighted in Exhibit 8.21. Supporters of broadbands say they offer several advantages over traditional grade-and-range approaches. First, they provide flexibility to define job responsibilities more broadly. They support redesigned, downsized, or boundaryless organizations that have eliminated layers of managerial jobs. They foster cross-functional growth and development in these new organizations. Employees can move laterally across functions within a band in order to gain depth of experience. The emphasis on lateral movement and deemphasis on pay adjustments tied to such movement helps manage the reality of fewer promotion opportunities in flattened organization structures.

Organizations that use broadbanding as fat grades are likely to follow more traditional salary administration practices by using midpoints, zones, or other control points within bands to keep the system more structurally intact, according to a recent survey.[17] These organizations tend to create bands that are only about twice as wide as the original salary grades. In contrast, organizations that use broadbanding to enhance career mobility and promote significant cultural change tend to reduce the number of pay grades and ranges

[16] Kenan S. Abosch and Beverly L. Hmurovic, "A Traveler's Guide to Global Broadbanding," *ACA Journal,* Summer 1998, pp. 38–47; Kenan S. Abosh and Janice S. Hand, "Characteristics and Practices of Organizations with Broadbanding: A Study of Alternative Approaches," *ACA Journal,* Autumn 1994, pp. 6–17.

[17] Kenan S. Abosch and Janice S. Hand, *Broadbanding Models* (Scottsdale, AZ: American Compensation Association, 1994).

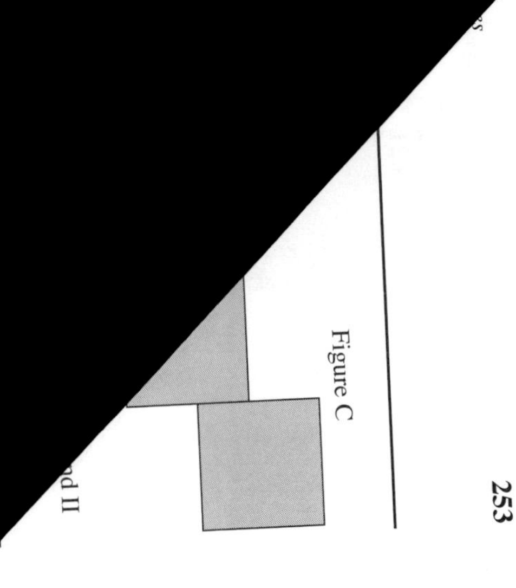

een Ranges and Bands

	Bands support
	Emphasis on flexibility within guidelines
gn	Delayered organizations
rogression	Crossfunctional experience and lateral progression
	Reference market rates, shadow ranges
	Controls in budget, few in system
idelines"	Give managers "freedom to manage" pay
	100–400 percent spreads

more dramatically, and they install bands that are three to eight times wider than the previous salary grades. Further, they are less likely to use control points within bands.

Perhaps the most important differences between grades and broadbanding is where the controls are located. The "grade-and-range" approach has guidelines and controls designed right into the pay system. Range minimums and maximums and midpoint controls are used to guide managers' decisions to help ensure consistency across managers. Under bands, managers are free to manage—with only a total salary budget limiting them. But as experience with bands has advanced, some guidelines are increasingly designed into them (e.g., reference market rates, shadow ranges and zones).

Astra-Merck uses six bands for its entire structure with titles ranging from contributor to executive. General Electric Retailer Financial Services' five bands, shown in Appendix 8-B, replace 24 levels. The appendix lists the objectives, competencies, and training expected at each band.

Bands may be easier to administer, though not all agree. Advocates point to the simplicity of the system. Less time will be spent judging fine distinctions among jobs and building barriers (i.e., that's not in my job description). But others disagree, saying that the time spent judging jobs will now be spent judging individuals, a prospect managers already try to avoid. How will an organization avoid appearance of salary treatment based on personality and politics rather than objective criteria?[18]

Three steps are involved in designing bands.

1. Setting the number of bands. Surveys report companies are using four to eight bands for pay purposes. Usually these are established at the major "breaks," or differences in work or skill/competency requirements. The titles typically used to label each band reflect these major breaks, such as associates (entry level individual contributor),

---

[18] Hill, "Get Off the Broadband Wagon," *Journal of Compensation and Benefits,* January–February 1993, pp. 25–29.

EXHIBIT 8.22 A Four Bands

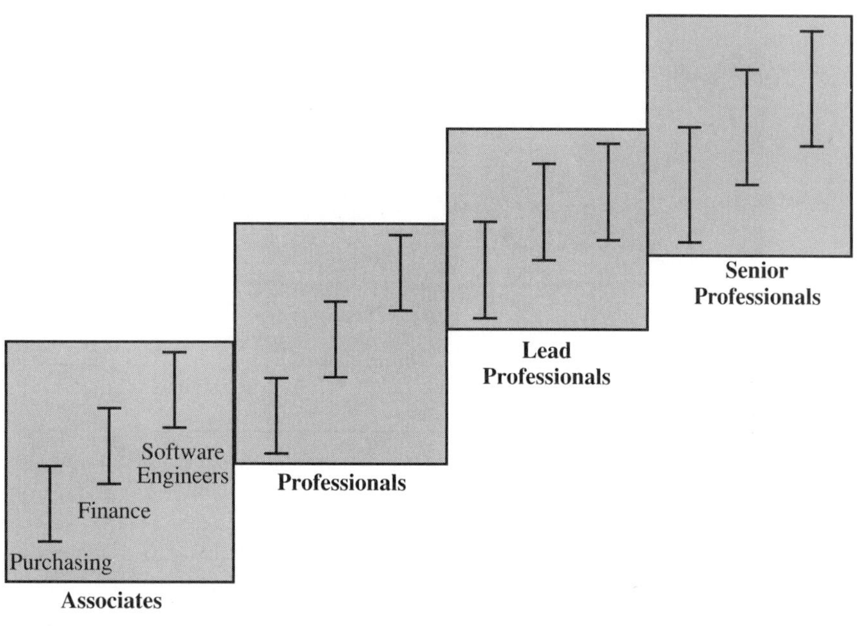

professional (experienced, knowledgeable team member), leader (project or group supervisor), director or "coach" (we don't make this up).

Note that in Exhibit 8.22A, four bands (associates, professionals, lead professionals, senior professionals) include most functions or job families within each band. Each band might include jobs from finance, purchasing, software development and engineering, marketing, and so on. The challenge is how much to actually pay people who are in the same band but in different functions performing different work.

Do associates and professionals at companies like General Electric in purchasing (with degrees in business) receive the same pay as software engineers (with degrees in computer science)? Not likely. Usually external market differences exist, so the different functions or groups within bands must be differently priced.

2. Pricing bands: Reference market rates and zones. As Exhibit 8.22B depicts, within each band each function may have different market rates. In the associate band in the exhibit, the three functions (purchasing, finance, and software engineer) have different *reference rates.* So the next stop is to identify multiple reference rates (much like benchmark market rates) of each function within each band. The reference rates are drawn from market data and reflect rates paid by competitors.

EXHIBIT 8.22 B Reference Rates for Each Discipline within a Band

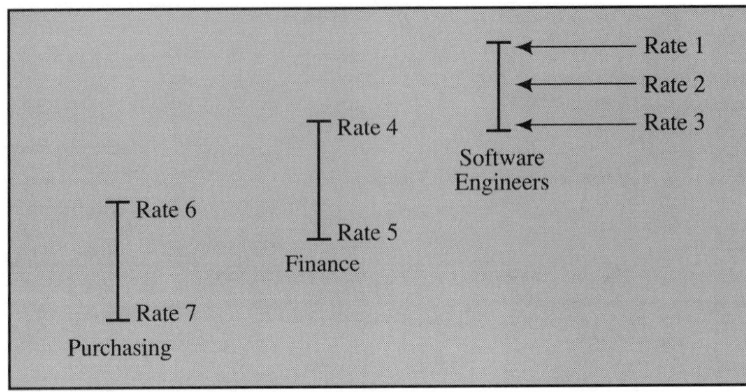

Professionals

Rates 1 through 7 are reference market rates showing the range of rates paid by competitors for jobs within each discipline.

You might say, "this is beginning to look a lot like 'ranges' within each band. You would be correct. Often called *zones,* these shadow ranges reflect the reference rates and serve as guides for managers.

3. Determining within-band (lateral) movement. Within-band pay increases are treated much the same as within-range pay increases. Under banding, employees are encouraged to move cross-functionally (e.g., purchasing to finance, between development and systems design) to increase the organization flexibility and cross-fertilization of ideas. Hence, a career move is more likely to be within-band across zones and less frequently from band A to B.

Flexibility—Control. Recall that according to supporters, the principal payoff of broadbanding is flexibility. Flexibility is one side of the coin; chaos and favoritism is the other. Banding presumes that managers will manage employee pay to accomplish the organization's objectives (and not their own) and treat employees fairly. Historically, this is not the first time greater flexibility has been shifted to managers and leaders. Indeed, the rationale underlying the use of ranges and grades was to reduce the foremen inconsistencies and favoritism that were destructive to employee relations in the 1920s and 1930s.[19] The challenge today is to take advantage of flexibility without increasing labor costs or leaving the organization vulnerable to charges of favoritism or inconsistency.

[19]Robert Kanigel, *The One Best Way* (New York: Viking, 1997).

BALANCING INTERNAL AND EXTERNAL PRESSURES: ADJUSTING THE PAY STRUCTURE

Establishing the pay ranges/bands for work reflects a balance between competitive pressures and pressures for internal consistency and fairness. Up until now, we have tended to make a distinction between the job structure and the pay structure.

A *job structure* orders jobs on the basis of internal organizational factors (reflected in job evaluation or skill certification). The *pay structure,* on the other hand, is anchored by the organization's external competitive position, reflected in its pay policy line.

Reconciling Differences

The problem with using two bases (internal and external) to create a structure is that they are likely to result in two different structures. The order in which jobs are ranked on internal and external factors probably will not completely agree. Differences between market structures and rates and job evaluation rankings warrant a review of the basic decisions in evaluating and pricing that particular job. This may entail a review of the job analysis, the job description, and the evaluation of the job, or the market data for the job in question. Often this reanalysis solves the problem. Sometimes, however, discrepancies persist; sometimes survey data are discarded; sometimes benchmark job matches are changed.

One study of how differences are actually reconciled found that managers weigh external market data more heavily than internal job evaluation data. In light of all the judgments that go into internal evaluation, market data are often considered to be more objective.[20] Yet this chapter has shown that market data are also based on judgments.

Sometimes differences arise because a shortage of a particular skill has driven up the market rate. But reclassifying a market-sensitive job (one in which a supply-and-demand imbalance exists) into a higher salary grade, where it will remain long after the imbalance has been corrected, creates additional problems. Creating a special range that is clearly designated as *market responsive* may be a better approach. However, decisions made on the basis of expediency run the risk of undermining the integrity of the pay system.

MARKET PRICING

Many organizations in the United States are reportedly adopting pay strategies that emphasize external competitiveness (market based) and de-emphasize internal consistency. Called *market pricing,* this approach sets pay structures most exclusively by relying on rates paid in the external market. It requires matching a large percentage of their jobs with market data and collect as much market data as possible. Organizations adopting bands (multiple reference rates—see Exhibit 8.22B) increasingly use market pricing for

[20]S. Rynes, C. Weber, and G. Milkovich, "Effects of Market Survey Rates on Job Evaluation, and Job Gender on Job Pay," *Journal of Applied Psychology* 74 (1989), pp. 114–23.

the specific jobs within each band.[21] Organizations that fill large proportions of their job vacancies with new hires from the outside may also become market pricers.

Market pricers often use the ranking method to determine the pay for jobs unique to their firms. Often called *rank to market,* it involves first determining the competitive rates for positions for which external market data are available and then blending the remaining (nonbenchmark) jobs into the pay hierarchy. At Pfizer, for example, job analysis results in written job descriptions. This is immediately followed by labor market analysis and market pricing for as many jobs as possible Exhibit 8.23 shows Pfizer's pay comparisons with comparable jobs at surveyed companies. After that, the internal job relationships are reviewed to be sure they are *reasonable in light of organization workflow and other uniqueness.* The final step is pricing those jobs not included in the survey. These remaining jobs are compared to the survey positions in terms of their total value to Pfizer. This internal evaluation seeks to ensure consistency with promotion opportunities and with the unique aspects of the organization.

Market Pricing Each Job. Market pricing goes beyond the use of benchmark jobs and then slotting nonbenchmarks. Some employers are basing most if not all of their internal pay structure on external market rates, breaking down the boundaries between the internal organization and external market forces. Increasingly, companies are even specifying the forms of pay for each job according to its competitors in the market. For example, if the average rate paid by competitors for a controller job is $120,000, then the company pays $120,000. If 70 percent of the $120,000 is base pay, 25 percent is annual bonus, and 5 percent is stock options, the company matches not only the amount but also this pattern. Another $120,000 job, say director of market analysis, may have a different pattern among market competitors, which is also matched.

Letting Competitors Determine Pay Structure. Market pricing carried to this extreme de-emphasizes internal consistency completely. Gone is any attempt to align internal pay structures with the business strategy and the work performed. Rather, the internal pay structure is aligned with competitors' decisions that are reflected in the market.

This approach raises several issues. Among them: Just how valid is market data?[22] How specific and finely calibrated is it? Does it really lend itself to such decisions? Why should competitors' pay decisions be the sole or even primary determinant of your company's pay structure? If it is, then *how* your company pays is no longer a source of competitive advantage because it only matches competitors. It is not unique, nor is it difficult to imitate.

---

[21]Frederic W. Cook, "Compensation Surveys Are Biased," *Compensation and Benefits Review,* September–October 1994, pp. 19–22.

[22]S. Rynes and G. Milkovich, "Wage Surveys: Dispelling Some Mythos about the 'Market Wage,'" *Personnel Psychology,* Spring 1986, pp. 71–90; Frederic W. Cook, "Compensation Surveys Are Biased," *Compensation and Benefits Review,* September–October 1994, p. 19–22.

EXHIBIT 8.23 Market Pricing at Pfizer

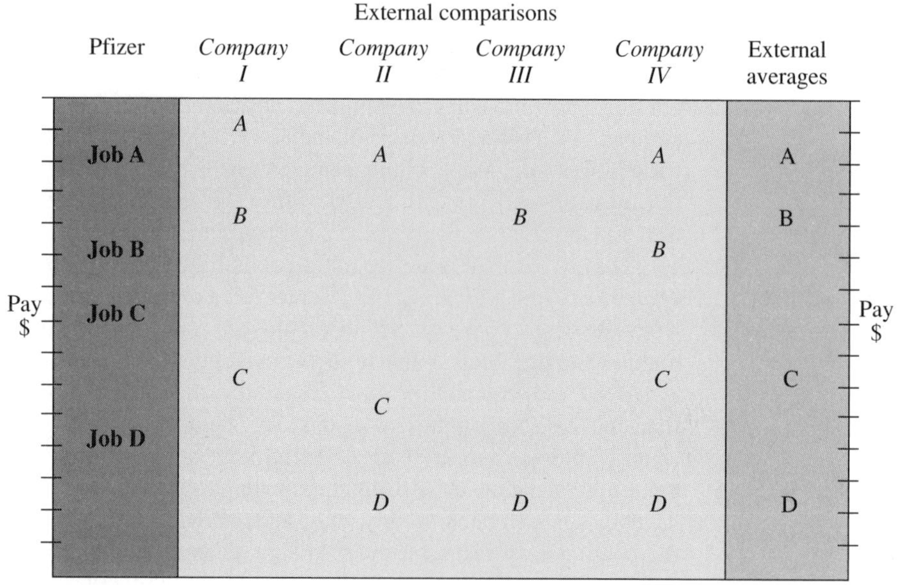

External comparisons

Pfizer | *Company I* | *Company II* | *Company III* | *Company IV* | External averages

Job A

Job B

Job C

Job D

Pay $

A *A* *A* A

B *B* *B* B

C *C* *C* C

D *D* *D* D

Pay $

Any unique or difficult-to-imitate aspects of the organization's pay structure, which may have been based on its flow of work, are de-emphasized by market pricers. Fairness is presumed to be reflected by market base rates; employee behavior is presumed to be reinforced by totally market-priced structures, which are the same as those of competitors.

In sum, the process of balancing internal and external pressures is a matter of judgment, made with an eye to the strategic perspectives and objectives established for the pay system.[23] De-emphasizing internal pay relationships may lead to feelings of inequitable treatment among employees and inconsistency with the fundamental culture of the organization. This in turn may reduce employees' willingness to share new ideas on how to improve the work or the product. Inequitable internal pay relationships may also lead employees to seek other jobs, file grievances, form unions, go out on strike, or refuse to take on increased job responsibilities. Neglecting external pay relationships, however, will affect both the ability to attract job applicants and the ability to hire those applicants who match the organization's needs. External pay relationships also impact labor costs and hence the ability to compete in the product/service market.

[23] Vandra Huber and S. Crandall, "Job Measurement: A Social-Cognitive Decision Perspective" in *Research in Personnel and Human Resources Management,* Vol. 12, pp. 223–269, ed. Gerald R. Ferris (Greenwich, CT: JAI Press, 1994).

Summary

This chapter has detailed the basic decisions and techniques involved in setting pay levels and designing pay ranges. Most organizations survey other employers' pay rates to determine competitive rates paid in the market. An employer using the survey results considers how it wishes to position its pay in the market: to lead, to match, or to follow competition. This policy decision may be different for different business units and even for different job groups within a single organization. Pay policy is translated into practice by setting pay policy lines that reflect the employer's competitive policy and serve as reference points around which pay ranges are established.

The use of ranges is a recognition of both external and internal pressures. No single "going rate" for a job exists in the market; an array of rates exists. This array results from variations in the quality of employees for that job and differences in employer policies and practices. It also reflects the fact that employers differ in the value they attach to the jobs and qualifications. Internally, the use of ranges is consistent with variations in the discretion present in jobs. Some employees will perform better than others; some employees are more experienced than others. Pay ranges permit employers to value and recognize these differences with pay.

Managers are increasingly interested in broadbanding, which offers flexibility to fit the continuously changing work assignments in de-layered organization structures. Broadbanding offers freedom to adapt to changes without requiring approvals, but risks self-serving and potentially inequitable decisions on the part of the manager. Recently, the trend is toward approaches with greater flexibility to adapt to changing conditions.

Let us step back for a moment to review what has been discussed and preview what is coming. We have examined two strategic components of the pay model. A concern for internal consistency meant that analysis and perhaps descriptions and evaluation were important for achieving a competitive advantage. A concern for external competitiveness required competitive positioning, survey design and analysis, setting the pay policy line, and designing pay ranges. The next part of the book is concerned with employee contributions—paying the individuals who perform the work. This is perhaps the most important part of the book. All that has gone before is a prelude, setting up the pay levels and pay structures within which individuals are to be paid.

Review Questions

1. Which competitive pay level policy would you recommend to an employer? Why? Does it depend on circumstances faced by the employer? Which ones?
2. How would you design a survey for setting pay for welders? How would you design a survey for setting pay for financial managers? Do the issues differ? Will the techniques used and the data collected differ? Why or why not?
3. What factors determine the relevant market for a survey? Why is the definition of the relevant market so important?
4. What do surveys have to do with pay discrimination?

5. Contrast pay ranges and grades with bands. Why would you use either? Does their use assist or hinder the achievement of internal consistency? External competitiveness?
6. You are the compensation manager for Lomeli Pharmaceuticals, and you directed the survey reported in Exhibit 8.15. Analyze the results. Specify which measure(s) gives the best representation of the market wage for programming analysts. Make the case that Lomeli's pay for its systems development specialist is too high. Make the case that it's too low.

APPENDIX 8–A

STATISTICS TO CALUCULATE A MARKET LINE USING REGRESSION ANALYSIS

Using the mathematical formula for a straight line,

$$y = a + bx$$

where

y = dollars
x = job evaluation points
a = the y value (in dollars) at which
$x = 0$ (i.e., the straight line crosses the y-axis)
b = the slope of the line

If $b = 0$, the line is parallel to the x-axis and all jobs are paid the same, regardless of job evaluation points. Using the dollars from the market survey data and the job evaluation points from the internal job structure, solving this equation enables the analyst to construct a line based on the relationship between the internal job structure and market rates. An upward sloping line means that more job evaluation points are associated with higher dollars. The market line can be written as

Pay for job A = $a + (b \times$ Job evaluation points for job A)
Pay for job B = $a + (b \times$ Job evaluation points for job B), etc.

The issue is to estimate the values of a and b in an efficient manner, so that errors of prediction are minimized. This is what "least squares" regression analysis does.

For many jobs, particularly high-level managerial and executive jobs, job evaluation is not used. Instead, salaries are related to some measure of company size (sales, volume, operating revenues) as a measure of responsibility through the use of logarithms. In such situations, x and y are converted to logarithms (in base 10), and the equation for a straight line becomes

$$\log y = a + b(\log x)$$

where

x = sales or revenues (in millions of dollars)
y = current compensation (in thousands of dollars)

Example

Given sales and compensation levels for a sample of jobs, assume that

$a = 1.7390$

$b = 0.3000$

Using the equation $\log y = 1.7390 + 0.3000 (\log x)$, one can calculate the current market rate for the chief executive in a company with sales of $500 million.

1. First, set $x = 500$, that is 500,000,000 with six zeros dropped.
2. Log $x = 2.6990$.
3. Multiply log x by 0.3000, which is the coefficient of the variable log x in the given equation. This results in a value of 0.8997.
4. Add to 0.8097 the constant in the equation, 1.7390. The result, 2.5487, is the value of log y.
5. The chief executive's total current compensation is the antilog of log y, which is 354.

Read in thousands of dollars, it is $354,000.

$$\text{Equation: } \log y = 1.7390 + 0.3000 (\log x)$$
$$x = \$500{,}000{,}000 = 500$$
$$\log x = 2.6990$$
$$\log y = 1.7390 + 0.3000 (2.6990)$$
$$\log y = 1.7390 + 0.8097$$
$$\log y = 2.5487$$
$$\text{antilog } y = 354$$
$$y = \$354{,}000$$

APPENDIX 8-B

BROADBANDING AT GENERAL ELECTRIC RETAILER FINANCIAL SERVICES

	Band I
Objectives	• Develop the self-management, interpersonal communication, and technical skills that are needed to effectively manage your work load and successfully perform as a team member. • Develop a working knowledge of other functional areas and their impact as well as an overall understanding of our clients.
Key competencies	• Plan, organize, and follow through on assignments. • Effectively develop co-worker, customer, and client relationships. • Function effectively as a team member. • Add value through innovative ideas.
Recommended training and education	• Service excellence/quality 100. • Customer service/telephone courtesy. • Technical and procedural training and legal requirements. • Number skills/ergonomics. • RFS systems training. • Cultural diversity awareness training. • Interpersonal and communication skills. • Team awareness and skill building.

	Band II
Objectives	• Develop the leadership, communication, and technical skills that are needed to lead teams and manage projects. • Develop a comprehensive knowledge of clients and a full understanding of RFS.
Key competencies	• Provide the interpersonal and technical leadership skills (such as coaching, relationship-building, and training) to facilitate the completion of work assignments. • Manage multiple and complex situations with co-workers, customers, and clients. • Develop strategies and combined resources to meet defined objectives.
Recommended training and education	• Effective written communication. • Time management. • Facilitator training. • Effective meeting skills. • Interviewing skills. • Problem solving/decision making. • Teambuilding/conflict resolution skills.

Band III

Objectives	• Develop the leadership and business skills to effectively lead people or projects with multi-functional perspectives. • Develop the ability to strategize, initiate plans, and implement projects to meet long-term and short-term objectives.
Key competencies	• Coach, motivate, and lead. • Build and guide high-performance work teams. • Influence others to gain a commitment to your plan or strategy. • Integrate a team's work with that of related functions. • Build relationships with internal and external customers and clients.
Recommended training and education	• Corporate entry leadership conference. • Leadership, interview, and presentation skills. • Facilitator/problem-solving training. • New manager development course. • Interpersonal, negotiating, and managing change skills. • Union awareness. • Cultural diversity awareness/management.

Band IV

Objectives	• Develop the ability to provide a strategic direction and perspective that will have a broad business impact. • Develop the ability to effectively manage and lead diverse activities that incorporate multi-functional perspectives in the balanced best interests of the business.
Key competencies	• Establish, communicate, and gain commitment to a vision and to a system of shared values. • Create organizational structures and systems consistent with your vision. • Conceive and implement changes in system, process, structure, staffing, and culture to better serve the customer and client. • Develop talent by identifying and selecting future leaders. • Create and manage internal and external partnerships. • Develop sound business judgment based on an intuitive process and the exploration of diverse information sources. • Manage innovation and risk taking. • Understand the complete business equation.
Recommended training and education	• Manager development course. • Advanced leadership skills. • Creative thinking. • Advanced functional and technical courses. • Cross-functional and cross-business assignments.

Band V

Objectives	• Develop the ability to direct a major segment or a multi-functional area within a major business. • Develop the ability to incorporate a global perspective while proactively establishing a vision.
Key competencies	• Make decisions that reflect global and cross-business considerations. • Translate strategic goals and objectives into specific programs which set the culture for the organization. • Lead a team in the development of a vision and its business-wide communication and acceptance. • Manage community relations.
Recommended training and education	• Business management course. • Executive development course. • Advanced management marketing seminar. • Advanced functional and technical courses. • Cross-functional, cross-business, and cross-cultural developmental assignments.

YOUR TURN:

ARE COMPENSATION SURVEYS UPWARDLY BIASED?

In an article published in the September–October 1994 issue of *Compensation and Benefits Review,* the consultant Frederic W. Cook lambastes current survey practices. He says that the way surveys are constructed, interpreted, and used artificially inflates wages above the "real" market. He lists 12 reasons, 7 of which are included here. Consider each of his charges and discuss whether you agree or disagree. Then suggest ways to respond to Cook's challenges or minimize the problem he identifies in each of his reasons.

1. User Bias. Companies that sponsor surveys often do so with an implicit objective: to show the company as paying either competitively or somewhat below the market, so as to justify positive corrective action.

2. Sample Bias. Companies like to compare themselves against well-regarded, high-paying, and high-performing companies. Those firms that participate in surveys drawing data from a large number of other organizations often have the ability (through computer models) to create a subset of participants with whom they wish to compare. This typically results in a higher competitive pay line than the general survey, thereby showing the user company in a less competitive light in terms of pay rates.

3. Survey Selectivity. Most companies have access to several surveys covering the same population. Compensation managers tend to disregard, challenge, or downplay those surveys that do not show the company in the desired competitive position.

4. Scope Bias. The relative "size" of an organization can be measured in any number of ways: revenues, equity, assets, net income, etc. Sponsoring organizations tend to select size variables that let them compare themselves favorably to the survey companies. It is technically feasible for all companies to show themselves as paying below the market.

5. Compensation Selectivity. A total compensation package is composed of many elements, whereas most surveys tend to focus on a few. If a company surveys only those areas where it is light (cash compensation, for example), it should not interpret or use those findings in isolation.

6. Benchmark Bias. In matching positions against those in the survey, companies tend to match against those that have higher responsibilities and hence higher compensation.

7. Statistical Bias. By manipulating the variables and assumptions in ways favorable to the company, the interpreter may be able to make an above-market practice appear less generous.

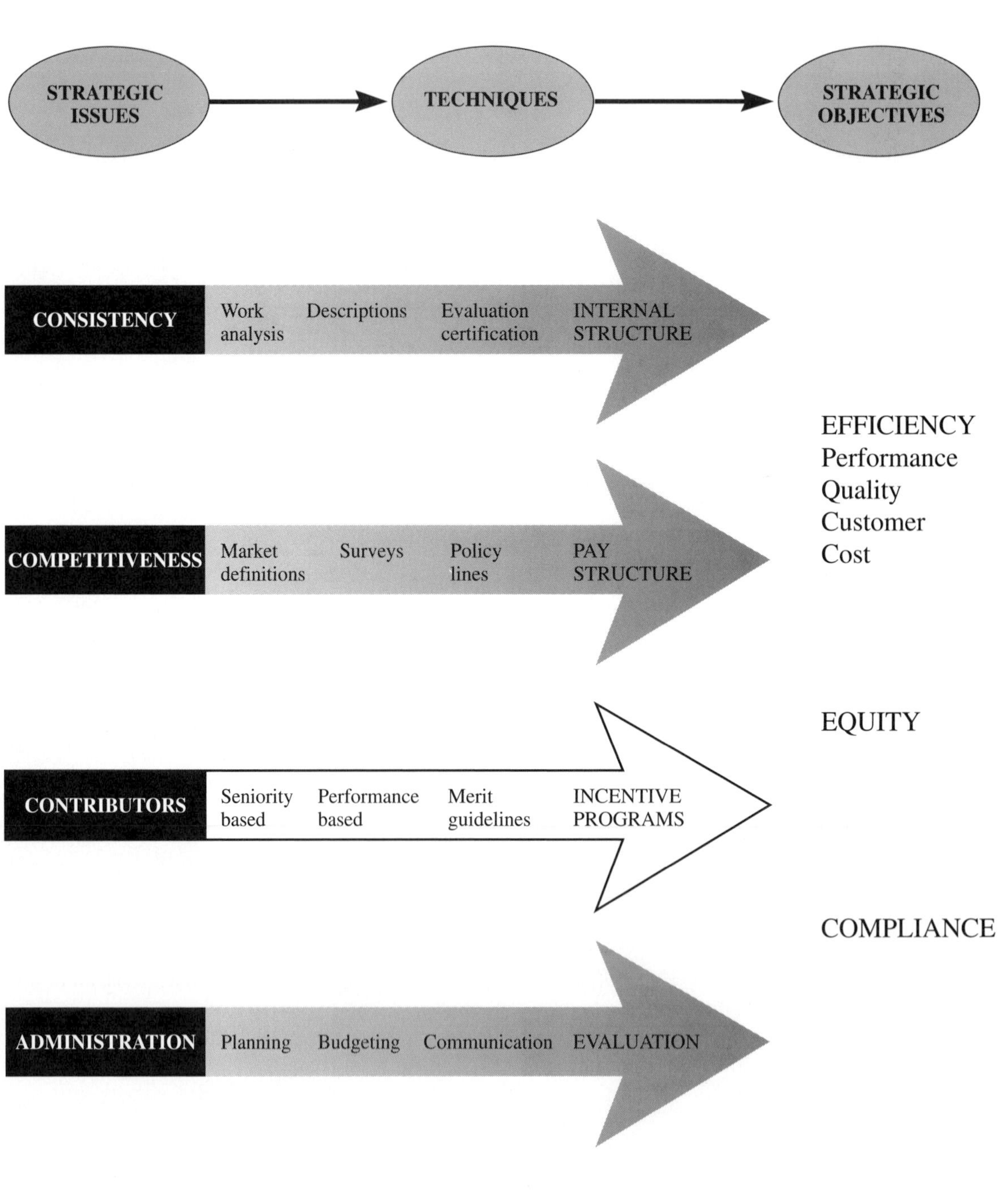

STRATEGIC ISSUES
TECHNIQUES
STRATEGIC OBJECTIVES
CONSISTENCY
Work analysis
Descriptions
Evaluation certification
INTERNAL STRUCTURE
COMPETITIVENESS
Market definitions
Surveys
Policy lines
PAY STRUCTURE
CONTRIBUTORS
Seniority based
Performance based
Merit guidelines
INCENTIVE PROGRAMS
ADMINISTRATION
Planning
Budgeting
Communication
EVALUATION
EFFICIENCY
Performance
Quality
Customer
Cost
EQUITY
COMPLIANCE

Employee Contributions: Determining Individual Pay

Thus far we have concentrated on two components of the pay model (Exhibit III.1). Internal consistency and the practices to ensure it—job analysis and job evaluation—provide guidance relating jobs to each other in terms of the content of the work and the relative contributions of the jobs to the organization's objectives. External competitiveness, or comparisons with the external labor market, raises issues of proper survey definitions, setting policy lines, and arriving at competitive pay levels and equitable pay structures. This part of the book deals with a third critical dimension of the pay system design and administration—paying individual employees performing the job.

How much should one employee be paid relative to another when they both hold the same jobs in the same organization? If this question is not answered satisfactorily, all prior efforts to evaluate and price jobs may have been in vain. For example, the compensation manager determines that all systems analysts should be paid between $38,000 and $46,000. But where in that range is each individual paid? Should a good performer be paid more than a poor performer? If the answer is yes, how should performance be measured and what should be the differential reward? Similarly, should the systems analyst with more years' experience (i.e., higher seniority) be paid more than a coworker with less time on the job? Again, if the answer is yes, what is the trade-off between seniority and performance in assigning pay raises? As Exhibit III.1 suggests, all of these questions involve the concept of employee contribution. For the next three chapters we will be discussing different facets of employee contribution.

Chapter 9 considers how pay affects performance. Is there evidence that companies should invest in pay-for-performance plans? In other words, does paying for performance result in higher performance? The answer may seem obvious, but there are many ways to complicate this elegant notion.

Chapter 10 looks at actual pay-for-performance plans. The compensation arena is full of programs that promise to link pay and performance. We identify these plans and discuss their relative advantages and disadvantages.

Chapter 11 acknowledges that performance can't always be measured objectively. What do we do to ensure that subjective appraisal procedures are as free from error as possible? Much progress has been made here, and we provide a tour of the different strategies to measure performance.

CHAPTER 9

Pay for Performance: The Evidence

Chapter Outline

The primary focus of the last section was to determine the worth of jobs, independent of who performed those jobs. Job analysis, job evaluation, and job pricing all have a common theme. They are techniques to identify the value a firm places on its jobs. Now we introduce people into the equation. Now we declare that different people performing the same job may have different value to the organization. Jim is a better programmer than Sam. Sally knows more programming languages than John.

Entering people into the compensation equation greatly complicates the compensation process. People don't behave like robots. We can't simply tighten a bolt here, oil a joint there, and walk away secure in the knowledge that behaviors will support organizational objectives. Remember, in Chapter 1 we talked about compensation objectives complementing overall human resources objectives, and both of these helping an organization achieve its overall strategic objectives. But this begs the question, "How does an organization achieve its overall strategic objectives?" In this section of the book we argue that organizational success ultimately depends on human behavior. Our compensation decisions and practices should be designed to increase the likelihood that employees will behave in ways that help the organization achieve its strategic objectives. This chapter is organized around employee behaviors. First, we identify the four kinds of behaviors organizations are interested in. Then we note what theories say about our ability to motivate these behaviors. And finally, we talk about our success, and sometimes lack thereof, in designing compensation systems to elicit these behaviors.

WHAT BEHAVIORS DO EMPLOYERS CARE ABOUT? LINKING ORGANIZATION STRATEGY TO COMPENSATION AND PERFORMANCE MANAGEMENT

The simple answer is that employers want employees to perform in ways that lead to better organizational performance. Our focus in this chapter, then, is on employee performance. There is growing evidence that employee performance depends on three general factors:[1]

Employee performance = f (S,K,M) where

S = Skill and ability to perform task

K = Knowledge of facts, rules, principles, and procedures

M = Motivation to perform

Let's use an example from figure skating to illustrate what this equation says. When Michelle Kwan attempts a triple lutz, her performance depends on three things: her physical ability to master the coordination and strength requirements of this jump, her knowledge of the necessary mechanics, and, finally, her motivation. Wanting to succeed isn't enough. Having the ability without the desire to train also isn't enough. The same thing is true in more traditional jobs. For an organization to succeed it needs employees who perform well. And as we noted in Chapter 2, this involves not only good compensation strategy and practice, but also other well-developed H.R. practices.[2] We need to hire people with skill and ability (S). We need to make sure the good employees (High S) stay with the company. If we can succeed at these first two things we can then concentrate on building further knowledge and skills (K & S). And finally, we need to find

[1]Rodney A. McCloy, John P. Campbell & Robert Cuedeck, "A Confirmatory Test of a Model of Performance Determinants," *Journal of Applied Psychology* 79(4) (1994), pp. 493–505.

[2]Brian Becker and Barry Gerhart, "The Impact of Human Resource Management on Organizational Performance: Progress and Prospects," *Academy of Management Journal* 39(4) (1996), pp. 779–801.

EXHIBIT 9.1 Performance Measurement Relates to Compensation Strategy

		Variability in Organizational Performance	
		Low Variability: few swings in overall corporate performance	High Variability: regular and large swings in overall corporate performance
Variability/ease of measurement in individual performance	Unstable, unclear, and changing objectives	Cell A—provide wide range of rewards beyond just money. Include significant incentive component.	Cell B—provide wide range of rewards beyond just money. Emphasize base pay with low incentive portion.
	Stable and easily measured	Cell C—emphasize monetary rewards with large incentive component.	Cell D—emphasize monetary rewards. Large base pay with low incentive portion.

ways to motivate (M) employees to perform well on their jobs—to take their knowledge and abilities and apply them in ways that contribute to organizational performance.

Apparent through all of this is the need to accurately measure performance. We can't tell if we select good employees if we don't know how to measure what constitutes good. We can't tell if employees are building the kinds of knowledge base they need if we can't measure knowledge accumulation. We can't reward performance if we can't measure it! As a simple example, think about where piece-rate systems are used to pay people. Why do many sales jobs use commissions (a form of piece rate) as the primary compensation vehicle? Conventional wisdom has always been that sales jobs are relatively easy to measure performance—dollar sales. There is little ambiguity in the measure of performance, and this makes it easy to create a strong link between units of performance and amount of compensation. One of the biggest recent advances in compensation strategy has been to document and extend this conventional wisdom. Initial evidence suggests that the way we design compensation systems is intimately linked to the stability of our performance measures. Exhibit 9.1 builds on the results of two studies to speculate the following relationship.[3]

Think about what each of the cells suggests in terms of compensation practices under different performance conditions. First, what might cause wide swings in corporate performance—often this occurs when something in the external environment fluctuates widely too (e.g., exchange rate with a major foreign customer, raw material costs). It probably wouldn't be fair, and employees would certainly object, if a large part

[3]This table extrapolates the findings from two studies: Matthew C. Bloom & George T. Milkovich, "The Relationship between Risk, Incentive Pay, and Organizational Performance," *Academy of Management Journal*, forthcoming; Anne Tsui, Jone L. Pearce, Lyman W. Porter, and Angela M. Tripoli, "Alternative Approaches to the Employee-Organization Relationship: Does Investment in Employees Pay Off?" *Academy of Management Journal* 40, no. 5 (1997), pp. 1089–1121.

of pay were incentive based. Things the employees don't control (in the external environment) would be dictating a big part of pay. No employee control translates into unfair treatment. Cells B and D both suggest a low incentive component is appropriate in organizations with highly variable annual performance. Conversely, as cells A and C indicate, larger incentive components are appropriate in companies with stable annual performance.

Employee performance also can vary. Some jobs are fairly stable with expectations fairly consistent across time. In other jobs, though, there might be high fluctuation in the kinds of things expected of employees, and employees willing to be flexible and adjust to changing demand are much in demand here. Evidence suggests that companies are best able to get employees to adjust, be flexible, and show commitment when a broader array of rewards than just money is part of the compensation package.[4] For example, why does Lincoln Electric out-produce other companies in the same industry year after year? Normally we think it's because they have a well-designed incentive system that links to level of production. But when you talk to people at Lincoln Electric, they suggest that part of the success comes from other forms of reward, including the strong commitment to job security—downsizing simply isn't part of the vocabulary here—that reinforce a willingness to try new technologies and new work processes. Cell A describes this kind of reward package that fits the job and organizational performance characteristics.

When we distill all of this, what can we conclude? We think the response depends on how we answer the following four questions.

How do we get good employment prospects to *join* our company?
How do we *retain* these good employees once they join?
How do we get employees to *develop skills* for current and future jobs?
How do we get employees to *perform well* on their current job?

First, how do we get good people to join our company? How did Nike get Tiger Woods to serve as a corporate spokesperson? Part of the answer certainly involves $60 million. Even when the decision doesn't involve millions of dollars, though, the long-run success of any company depends on getting good people to accept employment. And the compensation challenge is to figure out what components of our compensation package are likely to influence this decision to join.

The obvious complement to the decision to join is the decision to stay. How do we retain employees? It doesn't do much good to attract exceptional employees to our company only to lose them a short time later. Once our compensation practices get a good employee in the door, we need to figure ways to ensure it's not a revolving door.

We also need to recognize, though, that what we need employees to do today may change, literally, overnight. A fast-changing world requires employees who can adjust

[4]Anne Tsui, Jone L. Pearce, Lyman W. Porter, and Angela M. Tripoli, "Alternative Approaches to the Employee-Organization Relationship: Does Investment in Employees Pay Off?"

more quickly. How do we get employees, traditionally resistant to change, to willingly develop skills today that may not be vital on the current job but are forecast to be critical as the company's strategic plan adjusts to change? Another compensation challenge!

Finally, we want employees to do well on their current jobs. This means both performing, and performing well, tasks that support our strategic objectives. What motivates employees to succeed? The compensation challenge is to design rewards that enhance job performance.

WHAT DOES IT TAKE TO GET EMPLOYEES TO BEHAVE IN DESIRED WAYS? WHAT MOTIVATION THEORIES SAY

Another way of asking the same question is to ask, "What motivates employees?" If you know the right answer, you're way ahead of the so-called experts. In the simplest sense, motivation involves three elements: (1) what's important to a person, and (2) offering it in exchange for some (3) desired behavior. In Exhibit 9.2 we briefly summarize some of the important motivation theories. Pay particular attention to the last column where we talk about the implications for employee behavior.

Some of the theories in Exhibit 9.2 focus on content—identifying what is important to people. Maslow and Herzberg, for example, both fall in this category. People have certain needs, such as physiological, security, and self-esteem, that influence behavior. Although neither theory is clear on how these needs influence behavior, presumably if we offer rewards that satisfy one or more needs, employees will behave in desired ways. These theories often drive compensation decisions about the breadth and depth of compensation offerings. Flexible pay, with employees choosing from a menu of pay and benefit choices, clearly is driven by the issue of needs. Who best knows what satisfies needs? The employee! So let employees choose, within limits, what they want in their reward package.

A second set of theories, best exemplified by expectancy theory, equity theory, and agency theory, focus less on need states and more on the second element—the nature of the exchange. Many of our compensation practices recognize the importance of a fair exchange. We evaluate jobs using a common set of compensable factors in part to let employees know that an explicit set of rules governs the evaluation process. We collect salary survey data because we want the exchange to be fair compared to external standards. We design incentive systems to align employee behavior with the needs of the organization. All of these pay decisions, and more, owe much to understanding how the employment exchange affects employee motivation.

Expectancy theory argues that people behave as if they cognitively evaluate what behaviors are possible (e.g., the probability that they can complete the task) in relation to the value of rewards offered in exchange. According to this theory, we choose behaviors that yield the most satisfactory exchange. Equity theory also focuses on what goes on inside an employee's head. Not surprisingly, equity theory argues that people are highly concerned about equity, or fairness of the exchange process. Employees look at the exchange as a ratio between what is expected and what is received. Some theorists say we judge transactions as fair when others around us don't have a more (or less)

EXHIBIT 9.2 What Motivation Theories Say

Theory	*Essential Features*	*Predictions About Performance-Based Pay*	*So What?*
Maslow's Need Hierarchy	People are motivated by inner needs. Needs form a hierarchy from most basic (food & shelter) to higher-order (e.g., self-esteem, love, self-actualization). Needs are never fully met; they operate cyclically. Higher-order needs become motivating after lower order needs have been met. When needs are not met, they become frustrating.	1. Base pay must be set high enough to provide individuals with the economic means to meet their basic living needs. 2. An at-risk program will not be motivating since it restricts employees' ability to meet lower-order needs. 3. Success-sharing plans may be motivating to the extent they help employees pursue higher-order needs.	A. Performance-based pay may be de-motivating if it impinges upon employees' capacity to meet daily living needs. B. Incentive pay is motivating to the extent it is attached to achievement, recognition, or approval.
Herzberg's 2-Factor Theory	Employees are motivated by two types of motivators: hygiene factors and satisfiers. Hygiene or maintenance factors, in their absence, prevent behaviors, but in their presence cannot motivate performance. These are related to basic living needs, security, and fair treatment. Satisfiers, such as recognition, promotion, and achievement motivate performance.	1. Base pay must be set high enough to provide individuals with the economic means to meet hygiene needs, but it cannot motivate performance. 2. Performance is obtained through rewards; payments in excess of that required to meet basic needs. 3. Performance-based pay is motivating to the extent it is connected with meeting employees' needs for recognition, pleasure attainment, achievement, and the like. 4. Other factors such as interpersonal atmosphere, responsibility, type of work, and working conditions influence the efficacy of performance-based pay.	A. Pay level is important—must meet minimum requirements before performance-based pay can operate as motivator. B. Security plans will induce minimum, but not extra, performance. Success-sharing plans will be motivating. At-risk plans will be demotivating. C. Other conditions in the working relationship influence the effectiveness of performance-based pay.

Theory	*Essential Features*	*Predictions About Performance-Based Pay*	*So What?*
Expectancy	Motivation is the product of three perceptions: expectancy, instrumentality, and valence. Expectancy is employee's assessment of their ability to perform required job tasks. Instrumentality is employee's beliefs that requisite job performance will be rewarded by the organization. Valence is the value employees attached to the organizational rewards offered for satisfactory job performance.	1. Job tasks and responsibilities should be clearly defined. 2. The pay-performance link is critical. 3. Performance-based pay returns must be large enough to be seen as rewards. 4. People choose the behavior that leads to the greatest reward.	A. Larger incentive payments are better than smaller ones. B. Line-of-sight is critical—employees must believe they can influence performance targets. C. Employee assessments of their own ability are important—organizations should be aware of training and resource needs required to perform at target levels.
Equity	Employees are motivated when perceived outputs (i.e., pay) are equal to perceived inputs (e.g., effort, work behaviors). A disequilibrium in the output-to-input balance causes discomfort. If employees perceive that others are paid more for the same effort, they will react negatively (e.g., shirk) to correct the output-to-input balance.	1. The pay-performance link is critical; increases in performance must be matched by commensurate increases in pay. 2. Performance inputs and expected outputs must be clearly defined and identified. 3. Employees evaluate the adequacy of their pay via comparisons with other employees.	A. Performance measures must be clearly defined and employee must be able to affect them through work behaviors. B. If payouts do not match expectations, employees will react negatively. C. Fairness and consistency of performance-based pay across employees in an organization is important. D. Since employees evaluate their pay-effort balance in comparison to other employees, relative pay matters.
Reinforcement	Rewards reinforce (i.e., motivate and sustain) performance. Rewards must follow directly after behaviors to be reinforcing. Behaviors which are not rewarded will be discontinued.	1. Performance-based payments must follow closely behind performance. 2. Rewards must be tightly coupled to to desired performance objectives. 3. Withholding payouts can be a way to discourage unwanted behaviors.	A. Timing of payouts is very important.

EXHIBIT 9.2 Continued

Theory	*Essential Features*	*Predictions About Performance-Based Pay*	*So What?*
Goal Setting	Challenging performance goals influence greater intensity and duration in employee performance. Goals serve as feedback standards to which employees can compare their performance. Individuals are motivated to the extent that goal achievement is combined with receiving valued rewards.	1. Performance-based pay must be contingent upon achievement of important performance goals. 2. Performance goals should be challenging and specific. 3. The amount of the incentive reward should match the goal difficulty.	A. Line-of-sight is important; employees must believe they can influence performance targets. B. Performance targets should be communicated in terms of specific, difficult goals. C. Feedback about performance is important. D. Performance-based payouts should be contingent upon goal achievement.
Agency	Pay directs and motivates employee performance. Employees prefer static wages (e.g., a salary) to performance-based pay. If performance can be accurately monitored, payments should be based upon satisfactory completion of work duties. If performance cannot be monitored, pay should be aligned with achieving organizational objectives.	1. Performance-based pay must be tightly linked to organizational objectives. 2. Employees dislike risky pay and will demand a wage premium (e.g., higher total pay) in exchange for accepting performance-based pay. 3. Performance-based pay can be used to direct and induce employee performance.	A. Performance-based pay is the optimal compensation choice for more complex jobs where monitoring employees' work is difficult. B. Performance targets should be tied to organizational goals. C. Use of performance-based pay will require higher total pay opportunity.

favorable balance between the give and get of an exchange.[5] Even greater focus on the exchange process occurs in the last of this second set of theories, agency theory.[6] Here employees are depicted as agents who enter an exchange with principals—the owners or their designated managers. It is assumed that both sides to the exchange seek the most favorable exchange possible, and will act opportunistically if given a chance (e.g., try to "get by" with doing as little as possible to satisfy the contract). Compensation is a major element in this theory, because it is used to keep employees in line: employers identify important behaviors and important outcomes and pay specifically for achieving desired levels of each. Such incentive systems penalize employees who try to shirk their duties by giving proportionately lower rewards.

Finally, at least one of the theories summarized in 9.2 focuses on the third element of motivation: desired behavior. A review of this literature indicates that the vast majority of studies on goal setting find a positive impact of goal setting on performance. Workers assigned "hard" goals consistently do better than workers told to "do your best".[7]

WHAT DOES IT TAKE TO GET EMPLOYEES TO BEHAVE IN DESIRED WAYS? WHAT COMPENSATION PEOPLE SAY

In the past, compensation people didn't ask this question very often. Employees learned what behaviors were important as part of the socialization process or as part of the performance management process.[8] If it was part of the culture to work long hours, you quickly learned this. If your performance appraisal at the end of the year stressed certain types of behaviors, or if your boss said certain things were important to her, then the signals were pretty clear: do these things! Compensation might have rewarded people for meeting these expectations, but usually the compensation package wasn't designed to be one of the signals about expected performance. Now compensation people talk about pay in terms of a neon light pointing out expected behaviors. Progressive companies ask the question, "What do we want our compensation package to do?" "How, for example, do we get our product engineers to take more risks?" Compensation is then designed to support this risk-taking behavior. In the next section we begin to talk about the different types of reward components, acknowledging that pay isn't the only reward that influences behavior. The remainder of the chapter looks at pay components and what we know about their effectiveness in motivating desired behaviors.

---

[5] J. S. Adams, "Toward an Understanding of Inequity," *Journal of Abnormal and Social Psychology* 67 (1963), pp. 422–436; J. S. Adams, "Injustice in Social Exchange," in *Advances in Experimental Social Psychology*, vol. 2, ed. L. Berkowitz (New York: Academic Press, 1965); R. Cosier and D. Dalton, "Equity Theory and Time: A Reformulation," *Academy of Management Review* 8 (1983), pp. 311–319.

[6] B. Oviatt, "Agency and Transaction Cost Perspectives on the Manager-Shareholder Relationship: Incentives for Congruent Interests," *Academy of Management Review* 13 (1988), pp. 214–225.

[7] E. A. Locke, K. N. Shaw, L. M. Saari and G. P. Latham, "Goal Setting and Task Performance: 1969–1980," *Psychological Bulletin* 90 (1981), pp. 125–52.

[8] M. R. Louis, B. Z. Posner and G. N. Powell, "The Availability and Helpfulness of Socialization Practices," *Personnel Psychology* 36 (1983), pp. 857–866; E. H. Schein, "Organizational Socialization and the Profession of Management," *Industrial Management Review* 9 (1968), pp. 1–16.

Exhibit 9.3 Components of a Total Reward System

1.	Compensation	Wages, Commissions and Bonuses
2.	Benefits	Vacations, Health Insurance
3.	Social Interaction	Friendly Workplace
4.	Security	Stable, Consistent Position and Rewards
5.	Status/Recognition	Respect, Prominence Due to Work
6.	Work Variety	Opportunity to Experience Different Things
7.	Workload	Right Amount of Work (Not too much, not too little)
8.	Work Importance	Is Work Valued by Society
9.	Authority/Control/Autonomy	Ability to Influence Others; Control Own Destiny
10.	Advancement	Chance to Get Ahead
11.	Feedback	Receive Information Helping to Improve Performance
12.	Work Conditions	Hazard Free
13.	Development Opportunity	Formal and Informal Training to Learn New Knowledge/Skills/Abilities

The International Society for Performance Improvement has web information on performance journals, strategies for improving performance and conferences covering the latest research on performance improvement techniques. **http://www.ispi.org/**

TOTAL REWARD SYSTEM

Compensation is but one of many rewards that influence employee behavior. Sometimes this important point is missed by compensation experts. Going back at least to Henry Ford, we tend to look at money as the great equalizer. Job boring? No room for advancement? Throw money at the problem. Before we commit the same blunder and talk about monetary solutions to problems, please note that at least 13 general categories of rewards exist in organizations (Exhibit 9.3).

Now consider two examples that show how compensation decisions have to be integrated with Total Reward System decisions. If we don't think about the presence or absence of other rewards than money in an organization, we may find the compensation process producing unintended consequences. Example one transports us into a team-based work environment where the culture of the organization strongly supports empowerment of workers. Empowerment is a form of reward. In Exhibit 9.3 we identify the dimensions of empowerment (see #9) as *authority* to make decisions, some *control* over factors that influence outcomes, and the *autonomy* to carry out decisions without over-regulation by upper management. Some people find empowerment a very positive inducement, making coming to work each day a pleasure. Others may view empowerment as just added responsibility—legitimizing demands for more pay. In the first case adding extra compensation may not be necessary. Some have even argued it can lessen motivation.[9] In the second case, extra compensation may be a necessity. Is it any wonder that companies are having trouble finding *one* right answer to the team compensation question.

Our second example illustrates the relationship between the different forms of compensation and another of the general rewards listed in Exhibit 9.3: security. Normally, we think of security in terms of job security. Drastic reductions in middle management layers during the downsizing decade of the 1980s increased employee concerns about job security and probably elevated the importance of this reward to employees today. For example, there is evidence that compensation at risk leaves employees both less satisfied with their pay level and with the process used to determine pay.[10] Security as an issue is creeping into the domain of compensation. It used to be fairly well-established that employees would make more this year than they did last year. And employees counted on such *security* to plan their purchases and other economic decisions. The trend today is towards less stable and secure compensation packages. The decreased security comes in two forms. First, the 80s were some tough cost-cutting years, and wage rollbacks were a part of this trend. Between rollbacks and inflation, average wages declined during the 1980's.[11] Second, the very design of compensation systems today contributes to instability and insecurity. Exhibit 9.4 outlines the different types of wage components.

Notice that Exhibit 9.4 generally orders compensation components from least risky to most risky for employees. We define risky in terms of stability of income, or the ability to accurately predict income level from year to year. Base pay is, at least as far as there are any guarantees, the guaranteed portion of income, as long as employees remain employed. There have been very few years since the Depression when base wages did not rise, or at least stay the same.[12] The next seven components are distinguished by increasing levels of uncertainty for employees. In fact, risk sharing plans actually include a provision for cuts in base pay that are only recaptured in years when the organization meets performance objectives.

All of this discussion of risk is only an exercise in intellectual gymnastics unless we add one further observation. Over the last several decades, companies have been moving more towards compensation programs higher on the risk continuum. New forms of pay are less entitlement oriented and more linked to the uncertainties of individual,

---

[9]E. L. Deci and R. M. Ryan, *Intrinsic Motivation and Self-Determination in Human Behavior* (New York: Plenum Press, 1985). Note, however, the evidence is not very strong.

[10]K. Brown and V. Huber, "Lowering Floors and Raising Ceilings: A Longitudinal Assessment of the Effects of an Earnings-at-Risk Plan on Pay Satisfaction," *Personnel Psychology* 45 (1992), pp. 279–311.

[11]G. Koretz, "Was the Last Decade Really So Cruel? Yes . . . " *Business Week*, January 17, 1994, p. 20.

[12]Please note, though, most of the declines experienced in base pay have occurred since 1980.

Exhibit 9.4 Wage Components

Wage component	*Definition*	*Level of Risk to Employee*
Base Pay	The guaranteed portion of an employee's wage package.	As long as employment continues, this is the secure portion of wages.
Across the Board Increase	Wage increase granted to all employees, regardless of performance. Size related to some subjective assessment of employer about ability to pay. Typically an add-on to base pay in subsequent years.	Some risk to employee since at discretion of employer. But not tied to performance differences, so risk lower in that respect.
Cost of Living Increase	Same as across the board increase, except magnitude based on change in cost of living (e.g., as measured by CPI)	Same as across the board increases.
Merit Pay	Wage increase granted to employee as function of some assessment of employee performance. Adds on to base pay in subsequent years.	Two types of risk faced by employees. Size of total merit pool at discretion of employer (risk element), and individual portion of pool depends on performance, which also is not totally predictable.
Lump Sum Bonus	As with merit pay, granted for individual performance. Does not add into base pay, but is distributed as a one time bonus.	Three types of risks faced here. Both types mentioned under merit pay, plus not added into base—requires annually "re-earning" the added pay.
Individual Incentive Plans	Sometimes this variable pay is an add-on to a fixed base pay. The incentive component ties increments in compensation directly to extra individual production (e.g., commission systems, piece rate). While measures of performance are typically subjective with merit and lump sump components, this form of variable pay differs because measures of performance are objective (e.g., sales volume).	Most risky compensation component if sole element of pay, but often combined with a base pay. No or low fixed base pay means each year employee is dependent upon number of units of performance to determine pay.
Success Sharing Plans	A generic category of pay add-on (variable pay) which is tied to some measure of group performance, not individual performance. Not added into base pay. Distinguished from risk sharing plans below because employees share in any success—performance above standard—but are not penalized for performance below standard.	All success sharing plans have risks noted in above pay components plus the risk associated with group performance measures. Now individual worker is also dependent upon the performance of others included in the group.

Wage component	*Definition*	*Level of Risk to Employee*
• Gain Sharing	Differs from profit sharing in that goal to exceed is not financial performance of organization, but some cost index (e.g., labor cost is most common, might also include scrap costs, utility costs).	Less risk to individual than profit sharing because performance measure is more controllable.
• Profit Sharing	Add-on linked to group performance (team, division, total company) relative to exceeding some financial goal.	Profit measures are influenced by factors beyond employee control (e.g., economic climate, accounting write-offs). Less control means more risk.
Risk Sharing Plans	Generic category of pay add-on (variable pay) that differs from success sharing in that employee shares not only in the successes, but is also penalized during poor performance years. Penalty is in form of lower total compensation in poor corporate performance years. Reward, though, is typically higher than for success sharing programs in high performance years.	Greater risk than success sharing plans. Typically, employees absorb a "temporary" cut in base pay. If performance targets are met, this cut is neutralized by one component of variable pay. Risk to employee is increased, though, because even base pay is no longer totally predictable.

group, and corporate performance.[13] Employees increasingly are expected to bear a share of the risks that businesses have solely borne in the past. It's not entirely clear what impact this shifting of risk will have in the long run, but some authors are already voicing concerns that efforts to build employee loyalty and commitment may be an early casualty of these new pay systems.[14] Some research suggests that employees may need a risk premium (higher pay) to stay and perform in a company with pay-at-risk.[15] To explore what impact these new forms of pay have, the remainder of this chapter summarizes what we know about the ability of different compensation components to motivate the four general behaviors we noted earlier.

---

[13]J. R. Schuster and P. K. Zingheim, *The New Pay: Linking Employee and Organizational Performance* (New York: Lexington Books, 1992).

[14]E. J. Conlon and J. M. Parks, "Effects of Monitoring and Tradition on Compensation Arrangements: An Experiment with Principal-Agent Dyads," *Academy of Management Journal* 33 (1990), pp. 603–622; A. Kohn, *Punished by Rewards: The Trouble With Gold Stars, Incentive Plans, A's, Praise and Other Bribes* (Boston: Houghton-Mifflin, 1993).

[15]Conlon and Parks, "Effects of Monitoring and Tradition."

DOES COMPENSATION MOTIVATE BEHAVIOR: GENERAL COMMENTS

Although there are exceptions, generally, linking pay to behaviors of employees results in better individual and organizational performance.[16] One particularly good study looked at the H.R. practices of over 3,000 companies.[17] One set of questions asked if: (1) the company had a formal appraisal process, (2) was the appraisal tied to the size of pay increases, and (3) did performance influence who would be promoted. Organizations significantly above the mean (by one standard deviation) on these and other "High Performance Work Practices" had annual sales that averaged $27,000 more per employee. So, rewarding employees for performance pays off.

In a more comprehensive review, Heneman reports that 40 of 42 studies looking at merit pay claim performance increases when pay is tied to performance.[18] The strength of this relationship holds even in more scientifically controlled studies. One study of 841 union and non-union companies found gain sharing and profit sharing plans increased individual and team performance 18–20 percent.[19] How, though, does this translate into corporate performance? A review of 26 separate studies gives high marks to profit sharing plans: organizations with such plans had 3.5–5 percent higher annual performance.[20] Gerhart and Milkovich took the performance-based pay question one step further. They found, across 200 companies, there was a 1.5 percent increase in return on assets for every 10 percent increase in the size of a bonus.[21] Further, they found that the variable portion of pay had a stronger impact on individual and corporate performance than did the level of base pay.

IOMA is the Institute of Management and Administration. It specializes in finding studies from a wide variety of places that discuss different aspects of pay for performance. **http://www.ioma.com/newsletters/pfp/index.shtml**

---

[16]W. N. Cooke, "Employee Participation Programs, Group Based Incentives, and Company Performance," *Industrial and Labor Relations Review* 47 (1994), pp. 594–610; G. W. Florkowski, "The Organizational Impact of Profit Sharing," *Academy of Management Review* 12 (1987), pp. 622–636; R. Heneman, *Merit Pay: Linking Pay Increases to Performance Ratings* (Reading, MA: Addison-Wesley, 1992); J. L. McAdams and E. J. Hawk, *Organizational Performance and Rewards* (Phoenix, Ariz.: American Compensation Association, 1994); D. McDonaly and A. Smith "A Proven Connection: Performance Management and Business Results," *Compensation and Benefits Review*, January–February 1995, pp. 59–64; G. T. Milkovich, "Does Performance-Based Pay Really Work? Conclusions Based on the Scientific Research," Unpublished document for 3M, 1994; G. Milkovich and C. Milkovich, "Strengthening the Pay Performance Relationship: The Research," *Compensation and Benefits Review* (1992), pp. 53–62.

[17]Mark A. Huselid, "The Impact of Human Resource Management Practices on Turnover, Productivity, and Corporate Financial Performance," *Academy of Management Journal* 38 (3), pp. 635–672.

[18]Heneman, *Merit Pay*.

[19]Cooke, "Employee Participation Programs."

[20]D. L. Kruse, *Profit Sharing: Does it Make a Difference?* (Kalamazoo, Mich.: Upjohn Institute, 1993).

[21]B. Gerhart and G. Milkovich, "Organizational Differences in Managerial Compensation and Financial Performance," *Academy of Management Journal* 33 (1990), pp. 663–690.

DOES COMPENSATION MOTIVATE BEHAVIOR: SPECIFIC COMMENTS

This section looks at the role of compensation in motivating the four types of behavior outlined earlier.

Do People Join a Firm Because of Pay?

Level of pay and pay system characteristics influence a job candidate's decision to join a firm, but this shouldn't be too surprising.[22] Pay is one of the more visible rewards in the whole recruitment process. Job offers spell out level of compensation, and may even include discussions about kind of pay such as bonuses and profit sharing participation. Less common are statements such as "you'll get plenty of work variety," or "don't worry about empowerment," or "the workload isn't too heavy." These other rewards are subjective, and tend to require actual time on the job before we can decide if they are positive or negative features of the job. Not so for pay. Being perceived as more objective, it's more easily communicated in the employment offer.

Recent research suggests job candidates look for organizations with reward systems that fit their personalities.[23] Below we outline some of the ways that "fit" is important.

Person Characteristics	*Preferred Reward Characteristics*
Materialistic	Relatively more concerned about pay level[24]
Low Self Esteem	Low self esteem individuals want large, decentralized organization with little pay for performance[25]
Risk Takers	Want more pay based on performance[26]
Individualists ("I control my destiny")	Want pay plans based on individual performance, not group performance[27]

None of these relationships is particularly surprising. People are attracted to organizations that that fit their personalities. It's not a big jump, then, to suggest organizations should design their reward systems to attract people with desired personalities and values. For example, if we need risk takers maybe we should design reward systems that have elements of risk built into them.

---

[22]E. E. Lawler, *Pay and Organizational Effectiveness: A Psychological View* (New York: McGraw-Hill, 1971); E. E. Lawler and G. D. Jenkins, "Strategic Reward Systems" in *Handbook of Industrial and Organizational Psychology*, eds. M. D. Dunnette and L. M. Hough (Palo Alto, CA: Consulting Psychologist Press, 1992), pp. 1009–1055; W. Mobley, *Employee Turnover: Causes, Consequences and Control* (Reading, MA.: Addison-Wesley, 1982).

[23]D. M. Cable and T. A. Judge, "Pay Preferences and Job Search Decisions: A Person-Organization Fit Perspective, "*Personnel Psychology* 47 (1994), pp. 317–348.

[24]Cable and Judge, "Pay Preferences."

[25]D. B. Turban and T. L. Keon, "Organizational Attractiveness: An Interactionist Perspective," *Journal of Applied Psychology* 78 (1993), pp. 184–193.

[26]Cable and Judge, "Pay Preferences."; Kohn, *Punished by Rewards*.

[27]Cable and Judge, "Pay Preferences."

Do People Stay in a Firm (or Leave) Because of Pay?

There is clear evidence that poor performers are more likely to leave an organization than good performers.[28] How does pay affect this relationship? Actually, the evidence on pay and retention is mixed. Much of the equity theory research in the 1970s documented that workers who feel unfairly treated in pay react by leaving the firm for greener pastures.[29] This is particularly true under incentive conditions. Turnover is much higher for poor performers when pay is based on individual performance. Conversely, group incentive plans may lead to more turnover of better performers—clearly an undesirable outcome. When AT&T shifted from individual to team-based incentives a number of years ago, star performers either reduced their output or quit. Out of 208 above-average performers, only one continued to report performance increases under the group incentive plan. The rest felt cheated because the incentives for higher individual performance were now spread across all group members.[30]

Clearly, pay can be a factor in decisions to stay or leave. Too little pay triggers feelings of unfair treatment. Result? Turnover. Even the way we pay has an impact on turnover. Evidence suggests that some employees are uncomfortable with pay systems that put any substantial future earnings at risk, or pay systems that link less to personal effort and more to group effort. We need to make sure, as one critic has noted, that we don't let our design of new reward systems rupture our relationships with employees.[31]

Do Employees More Readily Agree to Develop Job Skills Because of Pay?

We don't know the answer to this question. Skill-based pay (Chapter 6) is intended, at least partially, to pay employees for learning new skills—skills that hopefully will help employees perform better on current jobs and adjust more rapidly to demands on future jobs. Whether this promise is fulfilled is unclear. Evidence is starting to accumulate that pay for skill may not increase productivity, but does focus people on believing in the importance of quality and in turning out significantly higher quality products.[32]

Do Employees Perform Better on Their Jobs Because of Pay?

Before answering this question, maybe we should ask if employees think any link at all should be made between pay and performance. Substantial evidence exists that

---

[28]David A. Harrison, Meghna Virick and Sonja William, "Working without a Net: Time, Performance, and Turnover under Maximally Contingent Rewards," *Journal of Applied Psychology* 81(4) (1996), pp. 331–345.

[29]M. R. Carrell and J. E. Dettrich, "Employee Perceptions of Fair Treatment," *Personnel Journal* 55 (1976), pp. 523–524.

[30]A. Weiss, "Incentives and Worker Behavior: Some Evidence" in *Incentives, Cooperation and Risk Sharing*, ed. H. R. Nalbantian (Totowa, NJ: Rowan & Littlefield, 1987), pp. 137–150.

[31]Kohn, *Punished by Rewards.*

[32]IOMA, "Report on Salary Surveys," May 1997, p. 14; Kevin J. Parent and Caroline L. Weber, "Does Paying for Knowledge Pay Off? *Compensation and Benefits Review,* September 1994, pp. 44–50.

management and workers alike believe pay should be tied to performance. Dyer and colleagues asked 180 managers from 72 different companies to rate nine possible factors in terms of the importance they should receive in determining size of salary increases.[33] Workers believed the most important factor for salary increases should be job performance. Following close behind is a factor that presumably would be picked up in job evaluation (nature of job) and a motivational variable (amount of effort expended).

Other research supports these findings.[34] Both college students and a second group of managers ranked job performance as the most important variable in allocating pay raises. Once we move away from the managerial ranks, though, other groups express a different view of the pay-performance link. The role that performance levels should assume in determining pay increases is less clearcut for blue collar workers.[35] As an illustration, consider the frequent opposition to compensation plans that are based on performance (i.e., incentive piece-rate systems). Unionized workers prefer seniority rather than performance as a basis for pay increases.[36] Part of this preference may stem from a distrust of subjective performance measurement systems. Unions ask, "Can management be counted on to be fair?" In contrast, seniority is an objective index for calculating increases. Some evidence also suggests that women might prefer allocation methods not based on performance.[37]

It's probably a good thing that workers believe pay should be tied to performance, because it appears to help the bottom line (profits). Numerous studies indicate that tying pay to individual performance has a positive impact on employee performance.[38] Unfortunately, many of these studies are flawed. In one particularly thorough review of merit pay and performance, Heneman concluded that there are very few good scientific studies to help answer the question, "Can we increase performance of individuals by

---

[33]L. Dyer, D. P. Schwab, and R. D. Theriault, "Managerial Perceptions Regarding Salary Increase Criteria," *Personnel Psychology* 29 (1976), pp. 233–42.

[34]J. Fossum and M. Fitch, "The Effects of Individual and Contextual Attributes on the Sizes of Recommended Salary Increases," *Personnel Psychology* 38 (1985), pp. 587–603.

[35]L. V. Jones and T. E. Jeffrey, "A Quantitative Analysis of Expressed Preferences for Compensation Plans," *Journal of Applied Psychology* 48 (1963), pp. 201–10; Opinion Research Corporation, *Wage Incentives* (Princeton, NJ: Opinion Research Corporation, 1946); Opinion Research Corporation, *Productivity from the Worker's Standpoint* (Princeton, NJ: Opinion Research Corporation, 1949).

[36]D. Koys, T. Keaveny and R. Allen. "Employment Demographics and Attitudes That Predict Preferences for Alternative Pay Increase Policies," *Journal of Business and Psychology* 4 (1989), pp. 27–47.

[37]B. Major, "Gender, Justice and the Psychology of Entitlement," *Review of Personality and Social Psychology* 7 (1988), pp. 124–148.

[38]IOMA, "Incentive Pay Programs and Results: an overview," IOMA, May 1996, p 11; G. Green, "Instrumentality Theory of Work Motivation," *Journal of Applied Psychology* 53 (1965), pp. 1–25; R. D. Pritchard, D. W. Leonard, C. W. Von Bergen, Jr., and R. J. Kirk, "The Effects of Varying Schedules of Reinforcement on Human Task Performance," *Organizational Behavior and Human Performance* 16 (1976), pp. 205–30; D. P. Schwab and L. Dyer, "The Motivational Impact of a Compensation System on Employee Performance," *Organizational Behavior and Human Performance* 9 (1973), pp. 215–25; D. Schwab, "Impact of Alternative Compensation Systems on Pay Valence and Instrumentality Perceptions," *Journal of Applied Psychology* 58 (1973), pp. 308–12.

tying it to pay?"[39] Perhaps in answer to this challenge, one recent study of over 3,000 companies provided convincing evidence that linking pay to performance has a positive impact on the bottom line. Over a five-year period such practices can increase per-employee sales by as much as $100,000.[40]

When we turn to the impact of pay on group performance, the evidence is somewhat clearer. Pay matters! Companies like Corning, Nucor Steel and Pepsico all strongly support variable pay based on group performance (usually the group is all employees in the organization, or some subset). Exhibit 9.5 describes elements of the variable pay plan for these companies.

Most well-controlled studies where companies base part of pay on some measure of corporate or division performance report increases in performance of about 4–6 percent per year.[41] Typical of these studies is a utility company that placed one division on an experimental group incentive plan and left the other division with no pay changes (the control group).[42] The goal in the experimental division was to lower unit cost of electricity. The utility set performance goals for such things as operating expenses, maintenance expenses, and absenteeism. If these goals were exceeded, employees would receive a bonus that grew as the goals were exceeded by a larger amount. After implementing this variable pay plan (or group incentive plan), performance improved significantly over the control division on 11 of 12 objective performance measures. As an example, unit production costs fell 6 percent.

Compensation experts estimate that every dollar spent on any performance-based pay plan yields $2.34 more in organizational earnings.[43] Put differently, there is further documented evidence that every 10 percent increase in bonus paid yields a 1.5 percent increase in R.O.A. (return on assets) to the firm.[44]

Before we rush out and develop a variable pay component to the compensation package, though, we should recognize that such plans can, and do, fail. Sometimes the failure arises, ironically, because the incentive works too well, leading employees to

---

[39]R. Bretz and G. Milkovich, "Performance Appraisal in Large Organizations: Practice and Research Implications," Working paper 87-17, NYSSILLR; E. L. Deci, "The Effects of Contingent and Noncontingent Rewards and Controls on Intrinsic Motivation," *Organizational Behavior and Human Decision Processes* 8 (1972), pp. 217–229; Heneman, *Merit Pay*; F. S. Landy, J. L. Barnes and K. R. Murphy, "Correlates of Perceived Fairness and Accuracy of Performance Evaluations," *Journal of Applied Psychology* 63 (1978), pp. 751–754; J. B. Prince and E. E. Lawler, "Does Salary Discussion Hurt the Developmental Performance Appraisal," *Organizational Behavior and Human Decision Processes* 37 (1986), pp. 357–375; P. M. Wright, "Testing the Mediating Role of Goals in the Incentive-Performance Relationship," *Journal of Applied Psychology* 74 (1989), pp. 699–705.

[40]Mark A. Huselid, "The Impact of Human Resource Management Practices on Turnover, Productivity, and Corporate Financial Performance."

[41]Cooke, "Employee Participation Programs"; Kruse, *Profit Sharing*; G. T. Milkovich, "Does Performance-based Pay"; M. M. Petty, B. Singleton, and D. W. Connell, "An Experimental Evaluation of an Organizational Incentive Plan in the Electric Utility Industry," *Journal of Applied Psychology* 77 (1992), pp. 427–436; J. R. Schuster, "The Scanlon Plan: A Longitudinal Analysis," *Journal of Applied Behavioral Science* 20 (1984), pp. 23–28.

[42]Petty et al., "An Experimental Evaluation."

[43]McAdams and Hawk, *Organizational Performance and Rewards*.

[44]Gerhart and Milkovich, "Organizational Differences."

EXHIBIT 9.5 Examples of Group Incentive Plans

Company	*Pay Component*
Corning	Competitive Base Pay. Group Bonus based on meeting certain quality measures, customer satisfaction measures, and production targets.
Nucor	Plant Manager base pay 25 percent below market. Five percent of excess over target goes to bonus. Bonus often equals base pay in amount
Pepsico	Competitive base pay. All employees get stock options equal to 10 percent of base pay. Employees share in corporate triumphs and failures as stock prices rise or fall.

EXHIBIT 9.6 Sears Makes a Mistake

Strategic Goal	*Supporting Compensation Component As Translated for Tire and Auto Centers*	*Unintended Consequence*
Cut costs by $600 million, provide facelift to stores, cut prices, make every employee focus on profits	Set high quotas for generating dollars from repairs and back up with commissions.	The California Consumer Affairs Division went undercover posing as customers. On 34 of 38 undercover runs Sears charged an average of $235 for unnecessary repairs.

exhibit rewarded behaviors to the exclusion of other desired behaviors. Exhibit 9.6 documents one such embarrassing incident that haunted Sears for much of the early 90s.[45]

Apparently this example is no fluke. Other companies have found poorly implemented incentive pay plans can hurt rather than help. Green Giant, for example, used to pay a bonus based on insect parts screened in its pea packing process. The goal, of course, was to cut the number of insect parts making their way into the final product (anyone planning on vegetables for dinner tonight?). Employees found a way to make this incentive system work for them. By bringing insect parts from home, inserting and inspecting, incentive dollars rose. Clearly, the program didn't work as intended. Experts contend this is evidence the process wasn't managed well. What does this mean?

DESIGNING A PAY-FOR-PERFORMANCE PLAN

According to the Pay Model developed in Chapter 1 we need to be concerned about efficiency, equity, and compliance in designing a pay system.

[45] K. Kelly and E. Schine, "How Did Sears Blow This Gasket?" *Business Week*, June 29, 1992, p.38.

Efficiency

Efficiency involves three general areas of concern.

Strategy: Does the pay-for-performance plan support corporate objectives? For example, is the plan cost effective, or are we making payouts that bear no relation to improved performance on the bottom line? Similarly, does the plan help us improve quality of service? Some pay-for-performance plans are so focused on quantity of performance as a measure that we forget about quality. Defect rates rise. Customers must search for someone to handle a merchandise return. A number of things happen that aren't consistent with the emphasis on quality that top organizations insist upon.

The plan also should link well with H.R. strategy and objectives. If other elements of our total H.R. plan are geared to select, reinforce, and nurture risk-taking behavior, we don't want a compensation component that rewards the status quo.

Finally, we address the most difficult question of all—how much of an increase makes a difference? What does it take to motivate an employee. Is 4 percent, the recent average of pay increases, really enough to motivate higher performance? While there is little hard data on this question, most experts agree that employees don't begin to notice incentive payouts unless they are at least 10 percent, with 15–20 percent more likely to evoke the desired response.[46]

Structure: Is the structure of the organization sufficiently decentralized to allow different operating units to create flexible variations on a general pay-for-performance plan? Different operating units may have different competencies and different competitive advantages. We don't want a rigid pay-for-performance system that detracts from these advantages, all in the name of consistency across divisions.

Standards: Operationally, the key to designing a pay-for-performance system rests in standards. Specifically, we need to be concerned about:

Objectives: Are they specific yet flexible? Can employees see that their behavior influences ability to achieve objectives (called the "line-of-sight" issue in industry)?

Measures: Do employees know what measures (individual appraisals, peer reviews of team performance, corporate financial measures, etc.) will be used to assess whether performance is sufficiently good to merit a payout?

Eligibility: How far down the organization will the plan run? Companies like Pepsico believe all employees should be included. Others think only top management can see how their decisions affect the bottom line.

Funding: Will you fund the program out of extra revenue generated above and beyond some preset standard? If so, what happens in a bad year? Many employees become disillusioned when they feel they have worked harder, but economic conditions or poor management decisions conspire to cut or eliminate bonuses.

---

[46]IOMA, "When Are Bonuses High Enough to Improve Performance?" *IOMA*, November 1996, p. 12.

Equity or Fairness

Our second design objective is to insure the system is fair to employees. Two types of fairness are concerns for employees. The first type is fairness in the amount that is distributed to employees. Not surprisingly, this type of fairness is labeled *distributive justice*.[47] Does an employee view the amount of compensation received as fair? As we discussed earlier in the section on equity theory, perceptions of fairness here depend on the amount of compensation actually received relative to input (e.g., productivity) compared against some relevant standard. Notice several of the components of this equity equation are frustratingly removed from the control of the typical supervisor or manager working with employees. A manager has little influence over the size of an employee's pay check. This is influenced more by external market conditions, pay policy decisions of the organization, and the occupational choice made by the employee. Even decisions about how much of a pay increase to give are typically constrained by budget limitations. Managers do have somewhat more control, though, over the second type of equity. Employees are also concerned about the fairness of *procedures* used to determine the amount of rewards they receive. Employees expect *procedural justice*. Evidence suggests that organizations that use fair procedures and supervisors who are viewed as fair in the means they use to allocate rewards are perceived as more trustworthy and command higher levels of commitment.[48] Some research even suggests that employee satisfaction with pay may depend more on the procedures used to determine pay than on the actual level distributed.[49]

A key element in fairness is communications. Employees want to know in advance what is expected of them. They want the opportunity to provide input into these standards or expectations, too. And, if performance is judged lacking relative to these standards, they want a mechanism for appeals. In a union environment, this is the grievance procedure. Something similar needs to be set up in a non-union environment.[50]

Compliance

Finally, our pay-for-performance system should comply with existing laws. We want a reward system that maintains and enhances the reputation of our firm. Think about the companies that visit a college campus. Some of them students naturally gravitate to—the interview schedule fills very quickly indeed. Why? Because of reputation. We tend to undervalue the reward value of a good reputation. To guard this reputation we need to make sure to comply with compensation laws.

---

[47]John Thibaut and Laurens Walker, *Procedural Justice: A Psychological View*, Hillsdale, NJ: John Wiley & Sons (1975).

[48]Robert Folger and Mary Konovsky, "Effects of Procedural and Distributive Justice on Reactions to Pay Raise Decisions."

[49]S. Alexander and M. Ruderman, "The Role of Procedural and Distributive Justice in Organizational Behavior." *Social Justice Research,* 1 (1987), pp. 177–198.

[50]G. S. Leventhal, J. Karuza and W. R. Fry, "Beyond Fairness: A Theory of Allocation Preferences." In G. Mikula, ed., *Justice and Social* Interaction (New York: Springer Verlag 1980), pp. 167–218.

Summary

Why not admit it? We don't know what makes people tick! Reading this chapter should prove that we have more questions unanswered than we have supposed truths. We know that employee performance depends upon some blend of skill, knowledge and motivation. Absent any of these three ingredients, performance is likely to be suboptimal. This chapter concentrates on the motivation component of this performance triangle. Rewards must help organizations attract and retain employees; they must make high performance an attractive option for employees; they must encourage employees to build new skills and gradually foster commitment to the organization. A tall order, you say! The problem is especially big because we are just starting to realize all the different things that can serve as rewards (or punishments) for employees. This chapter outlines 13 rewards and makes a strong case that fair administration of these rewards can lead a company to higher performance levels.

Review Questions

1. The little girl down the street opens a lemonade stand that is very successful. To keep up with customer demand she decides to hire another little girl who is her best friend. Her dad, author of a stupid book on compensation, counsels his daughter to pay the friend completely on an incentive system—one penny for each glass of lemonade sold. Do you think the pay will motivate faster performance? Is this desirable? How important do you think money is as a motivator in this situation?
2. Roycroft Industries makes C.D. cases that are particularly well-received on the international market. Because of currency fluctuation, the profits Roycroft generates vary widely from year to year. Jim McVeigh, who works for Roycroft, is in charge of a large product development group where the emphasis is on flexible performance, creativity and "doing whatever it takes to get the job done." What kind of reward system would you recommend for this group of employees? In particular, should there be a large incentive component? Should rewards focus mostly on money, or should Roycroft work hard to incorporate the other 12 rewards noted in this chapter?
3. If you wanted workers to perceive their compensation package as secure, what components would you include and which would you avoid?
4. How does procedural justice differ from distributive justice? Defend the position that supervisors have considerable control over procedural justice in their departments but little control over distributive justice? How might you use the principles of procedural justice to avoid having an employee quit because she believes her boss gave her an unfair evaluation?

YOUR TURN:

CLINTON PHARMACEUTICAL

Clinton Pharmaceutical is a medium-sized pharmaceutical company located in Sherwood, New Jersey. Most of Clinton's profits over the past 20 years have been generated by high volume production of drugs that veterinarians use to care for domesticated animals. Since there is only a small markup in this market, Clinton must make its profit from high volume. The somewhat loose quality control laws for drugs distributed to veterinarians has enabled Clinton to achieve unit production levels that are high for the pharmaceutical industry.

Unfortunately, in the past two years productivity has significantly deteriorated at Clinton. (Productivity for the past five years is shown in Exhibit 1.) In addition, turnover and absenteeism are up (Exhibits 2 and 3).

John Lancer, president of Clinton Pharmaceutical, is deeply concerned. The key to Clinton's success has always been its high productivity and resulting low unit production costs. For some reason profits have been down 18 percent during the past two years (1996 = –13 percent; 1997 = –23 percent). Mr. Lancer has an annual stockholders' meeting in two weeks, and he is determined to go in with some answers. Maybe the managers can't correct the decline in time for the meeting, but heads will roll if he doesn't get some answers. All department heads soon receive detailed letters outlining the profit picture and requesting explanations.

Ralph Simpson is the director of Human Resources Management. John Lancer informed him three weeks ago that a marked drop in profits had occurred over the past year. Mr. Simpson offers the data in Exhibit 4 as a possible explanation for the profit decline.

Discussion Questions

1. Do Exhibits 1, 2, and 3 suggest any problems that might explain or be related to the profit declines?
2. Given the discussion of motivation theory in this chapter, do the data in Exhibit 4 suggest that productivity declines may be due to motivation problems? What other human resource management explanations are plausible?

EXHIBIT 1 Clinton Pharmaceutical Productivity Trends

1994	*1995*	*1996*	*1997*	*1998*
127,000	123,000	122,786	104,281	100,222

*Gross revenue generated per employee in constant dollars.

EXHIBIT 2 Turnover Percentages, All Occupations

1994	*1995*	*1996*	*1997*	*1998*
14%	12.5	19.0	26.8	29.3

EXHIBIT 3 Absenteeism, Average Days per Employee

1994	*1995*	*1996*	*1997*	*1998*
*	*	9.6	9.7	10.2

*Records not available.

EXHIBIT 4 Attitude Survey toward Compensation: Level and Administration

N = 1,427 (87 percent response rate)
Questions 1–15

Column A Scaling	*Column B Scaling*	*Column C Scaling*
1 = Very important to me	1 = Very satisfied	1 = Very dependent
2 = Important to me	2 = Satisfied	2 = Dependent
3 = Neither important nor unimportant	3 = Neutral	3 = Unsure
4 = Unimportant to me	4 = Dissatisfied	4 = Rarely dependent
5 = Very unimportant to me	5 = Very dissatisfied	5 = Never dependent

Indicate how important the following rewards available to Clinton employees are to you in column A.
Indicate how satisfied you are with the level Clinton delivers in column B.
How dependent are these rewards on your performance (column C)?

	A	*B*	*C*
1. A good salary	2	2	4
2. An annual raise equal to or greater than the cost of living	1	2	5
3. A profit sharing plan	5	3	1
4. Paid sick days	5	3	5
5. Vacation	3	1	5
6. Life insurance	4	1	5
7. Pension	4	1	5
8. Medical plan	3	1	5
9. Opportunity for advancement	2	5	5
10. Job security	1	2	5
11. Good supervisors	2	2	5
12. Opportunity to develop new skills	2	5	5
13. Good coworkers	3	3	5
14. Steady hours	3	2	2
15. Feedback about performance	1	5	3

Pay for Performance Plans

Chapter Outline

WHAT IS A PAY-FOR-PERFORMANCE PLAN?

What's in a name? The answer is . . . confusion, at least if we are talking about pay-for-performance plans. Listen long enough and you will hear about incentive plans, variable pay plans, compensation at risk, earnings at risk, success sharing, and others. Sometimes these names are used interchangeably. They shouldn't be. The major thing all these names have in common is a shift in thinking about compensation. We used to think of pay as primarily an entitlement—if you went to work and did well enough to avoid being fired, you were entitled to the same size check as everyone else. Pay-for-performance plans signal a movement away from entitlement—sometimes a very *slow* movement—towards pay that varies with some measure of individual or organizational performance. Of the pay components we discussed in Chapter 9, only base pay and across-the-board increases don't fit the pay for performance category. Curiously, though, many of the surveys on pay for performance tend to omit the grandfather of all these plans, merit pay. Maybe the problem is that merit pay is out of favor right now. One survey of 250 companies reports 30 percent are thinking about eliminating merit pay, and another 10 percent already have.[1] Despite this unrest, merit pay is still a pay-for-performance plan used for more than three-quarters of all exempt, clerical, and administrative employees.[2] While more innovative pay-for-performance plans may get more and better press, as Exhibit 10.1 suggests, there is still no widespread evidence of their adoption.

Exhibit 10.1 illustrates the wide variety of variable pay plans in use today. What used to be primarily a compensation tool for top management is gradually becoming more prevalent for lower level employees too. Exhibit 10.2 indicates that variable pay is commanding a larger share of total compensation for all employee groups.

The greater interest in variable pay probably can be traced to two trends. First, the increasing competition from foreign producers forces American producers to cut costs and/or increase productivity. Well-designed variable pay plans have a proven track record in motivating better performance and helping cut costs. Second, today's fast-paced business environment means that workers must be willing to adjust what they do and how they do it. There are new technologies, new work processes, new work relationships. All these require workers to adapt in ways and with a speed that is unparalleled. Failure to move quickly means market share goes to competitors. If this happens, workers face possible layoffs and terminations. To avoid this scenario, compensation experts are focusing on ways to design reward systems so that workers will be able and willing to move quickly into new jobs and new ways of performing old jobs. The ability and incentive to do this come partially from reward systems that more closely link worker interests with the objectives of the company.

---

[1]American Management Association, "Survey of Merit Pay," *Compflash* (January 1994), p. 8.

[2]American Management Association, "Merit Raises Remain Popular among Fortune 1000," *Compflash* (December 1994), p. 1.

Exhibit 10.1 Frequency of Adoption for Different Variable Pay Plans

Type of Plan	*Percentage Use*
Pay for Competencies**	31%
Pay for Skill/Knowledge	7
Gain Sharing	12
Profit Sharing (excluding retirement programs)	14
Lump Sum Payments	25
Spot Awards (after the fact)	27
Long Term Incentives** (Below executive level)	15
Individual Incentives	9

Source: 1995 Wyatt data services; those designated by ** come from 1996 Hay Fall Conference Survey

Exhibit 10.2 Base vs. Variable Pay

	Percentage of Total Compensation			
	Today		**Expected in 3 Years**	
Employee Group	*Base*	*Variable*	*Base*	*Variable*
Nonexempt	98%	2	96%	4
Exempt	92	8	87	13
Executive	76	24	71	29

DOES VARIABLE PAY IMPROVE PERFORMANCE RESULTS: THE GENERAL EVIDENCE

As the evidence pointed out in Chapter 9, pay-for-performance plans—those that introduce variability into the level of pay you receive—seem to have a positive impact on performance. An extensive survey of 473 companies by the Hay Group supports this belief: well-designed variable pay plans can be effective.

	Impact on Performance of Organization		
Plan Type	*Improved*	*Not Improved*	*Can't Tell*
Gain Sharing	39	9	52
Profit Sharing (excluding retirement programs)	30	25	45
Key Contributor	45	11	45
Suggestion Awards	37	23	40
Team-based Awards	32	9	59

Source: Hay Compensation Reports, 1995

Notice, we qualified our statement that variable pay plans can be effective—*if they are designed well*. In the next sections we talk about issues in design and the impacts they can have.

SPECIFIC PAY-FOR-PERFORMANCE PLANS: SHORT TERM

Merit Pay

A merit pay system links increases in base pay (called merit increases) to how highly employees are rated on a subjective performance evaluation. Chapter 11 covers performance evaluation, but as a simple illustration consider the following typical merit pay setup.

	Well Above Average	*Above Average*	*Average*	*Below Average*	*Well Below Average*
Performance Rating →	1	2	3	4	5
Merit Pay Increase →	6%	5%	4%	3%	0%

At the end of a performance year, the employee is evaluated, usually by the direct supervisor. The performance rating, 1 to 5 in the above example, determines the size of the increase added into base pay. This last point is important. In effect, what you do this year in terms of performance, is rewarded *every year* you remain with your employer. By building into base pay, the dollar amount, just like the Energizer bunny, keeps on going! With compounding, this can amount to tens of thousands of dollars over an employee's work career.[3]

Increasingly, merit pay is under attack. Not only is it expensive, but many argue it doesn't achieve the desired goal: improving employee and corporate performance.[4] In a thorough review of merit pay literature, Heneman concludes that merit pay does have a small, but significant, impact on performance.[5]

If we want merit pay to live up to its potential, it needs to be managed better.[6] This requires a complete overhaul of the way we allocate raises: improving the accuracy of performance ratings, allocating enough merit money to truly reward performance, and making sure the size of the merit increase differentiates across performance levels. To illustrate this latter point, consider the employee who works hard all year, earns a 6 percent increase as our guidelines above indicate, and compares himself with the average performer who coasts to a 4 percent increase. First we take out taxes on that extra two percent. Then we spread it out over 52 pay checks. It's only a slight exaggeration to

---

[3]Jerry M. Newman and Daniel J. Fisher, "Strategic Impact Merit Pay," *Compensation and Benefits Review*, July/August 1992, pp. 38–45.

[4]Glenn Bassett, "Merit Pay Increases are a Mistake," *Compensation and Benefits Review*, March/April 1994, pp. 20–25.

[5]Robert Heneman, *Merit Pay: Linking Pay Increases to Performance Ratings* (Reading, MA: Addison-Wesley, 1992).

[6]Ibid.

EXHIBIT 10.3 Relative Cost Comparisons

	Merit Pay		*Lump-sum Bonus*
Base Pay	$50,000		$50,000
Year 1 payout 5%	(2,500)	5%	(2,500)
New Base Pay	52,500		50,000
Extra Cost Total	2,500		2,500
Year 2 Payout 5%	($2,625 = .05 × 52,500)	5%	(2,500 =.05 × 50,000)
New Base Pay	55,125 (52,500 + 2,625)		50,000
Extra Cost Total	5,125		5,000
After 5 years			
Year 5 Payout	3,039		2,500
New Base Pay	63,814		50,000

suggest that the extra money won't pay for a good cup of coffee. Unless we make the reward difference larger for every increment in performance, many employees are going to say "Why bother?"

Lump-sum Bonuses

Lump-sum bonuses are an increasingly used substitute for merit pay. Based on employee or company performance, employees receive an end-of-year bonus that does not build into base pay. Because employees must earn this increase every year, it is viewed as less of an entitlement than merit pay. As Exhibit 10.3 indicates, lump-sum bonuses also can be considerably less expensive than merit pay over the long run.

Notice how quickly base pay rises under a merit pay plan. After just five years, base pay is almost $14,000 higher than under a lump-sum bonus plan. It should be no surprise that cost-conscious firms report switching to lump-sum pay. Forty percent of all companies reported using lump-sum bonuses in 1997, up from 30 percent in 1996.[7] It also should be no surprise that employees aren't particularly fond of lump-sum bonuses. After all, the intent of lump-sum bonuses is to cause shock waves in an entitlement culture. By giving lump-sum bonuses for several years, a company is essentially freezing base pay. Gradually this results in a repositioning relative to competitors. The message becomes loud and clear: "Don't expect to receive increases in base pay year after year—new rewards must be earned each year."

Individual Spot Awards

Technically, spot awards should fall under pay-for-performance plans. About 30 percent of all companies use spot awards.[8] Usually these payouts are awarded for exceptional

[7]IOMA, "Lump Sum Merit Pay," *Ioma Report on Salary Surveys*, July 1997, pp. 10–11.

[8]American Management Association, "A Growing Trend: Variable Pay for Lower Level Employees," *Compflash* (1992), p. 1.

performance, often on special projects or for performance that so exceeds expectations as to be deserving of an add-on bonus. The mechanics are simple. After the fact, someone in the organization alerts top management to the exceptional performance. If the company is large, there may be a formal mechanism for this recognition, and perhaps some guidelines on the size of the spot award (so named because it is supposed to be awarded on the spot). Smaller companies may be more casual about recognition and more subjective about deciding the size of the award. One creative user of spot awards is Mary Kay Cosmetics. Top sales women get pink Cadillacs, mink coats, and diamond rings.[9]

INDIVIDUAL INCENTIVE PLANS: TYPES

These plans differ from the above because they offer a promise of pay for some objective, pre-established level of performance. For example, Cellular One pays its car phone installers on a very simple incentive system. Every customer complaint costs $10. Damage a car during installation—expect to lose $20. When this reverse incentive plan (penalty for poor performance rather than reward for good) was first implemented, vehicle damage dropped 70 percent.

All incentive plans have one common feature: an established standard against which worker performance is compared to determine the magnitude of the incentive pay. For individual incentive systems, this standard is compared against individual worker performance. From this basic foundation, a number of seemingly complex and divergent plans have evolved. Before discussing the more prevalent of these plans, however, it is important to note that each varies along two dimensions and can be classified into one of four cells illustrated in Exhibit 10.4.

EXHIBIT 10.4 Individual Incentive Plans

		Method of Rate Determination	
		Units of production per time period	*Time period per unit of production*
Relationship between production level and pay	*Pay constant function of production level*	(1) Straight piecework plan.	(2) Standard hour plan.
	Pay varies as function of production level	(3) Taylor differential piece rate system. Merrick multiple piece rate system.	(4) Halsey 50–50 method. Rowan plan. Gantt plan.

[9]Bob Nelson, *1001 Ways to Reward Employees* (New York: Workman Publishing, 1994).

The first dimension on which incentive systems vary is in the *method of rate determination*. Plans either set up a rate based on units of production per time period or in time period per unit of production. On the surface, this distinction may appear trivial but, in fact, the deviations arise because tasks have different cycles of operation.[10] Short-cycle tasks, those that are completed in a relatively short period of time, typically have as a standard a designated number of units to be produced in a given time period. For long-cycle tasks, this would not be appropriate. It is entirely possible that only one task or some portion of it may be completed in a day. Consequently, for longer cycle tasks, the standard is typically set in terms of time required to complete one unit of production. Individual incentives are based on whether or not workers complete the task in the designated time period.

The second dimension on which individual incentive systems vary is the specified relationship between production level and wages. The first alternative is to tie wages to output on a one-to-one basis, so that wages are some constant function of production. In contrast, some plans vary wages as a function of production level. For example, one common alternative is to provide higher dollar rates for production above the standard than for production below the standard.

Each of the plans discussed in this section has as a foundation a standard level of performance determined by some form of time study or job analysis completed by an industrial engineer or trained personnel administrator. (Exhibit 10.5 provides an illustration of a time study.) The variations in these plans occur in either the way the standard is set or the way wages are tied to output. As in Exhibit 10.4, there are four general categories of plans.

1. *Cell 1.* The most frequently implemented incentive system is a straight piecework system (Exhibit 10.6). Rate determination is based on units of production per time period, and wages vary directly as a function of production level. A standard is developed reflecting the units of output a worker is expected to complete in, say, an hour. Workers are paid for each unit of output. Consequently, workers who consistently exceed the established standard receive higher than average wages.

The major advantages of this type of system is that it is easily understood by workers and, perhaps consequently, more readily accepted than some of the other incentive systems. The major disadvantages center on the difficulty in setting a standard. For example, the industrial engineer charged with establishing a standard for the drilling operation in Exhibit 10.5 may be expected to observe numerous drillers performing the task. The time study expert would then derive a standard indicating the number of holes it should be possible to drill in a given time period by workers performing at a normal rate. The accuracy of the industrial engineer's measurements, the workers chosen to observe, and the definition of a normal rate of speed all influence the final standard.[11] An inappropriate standard can result in labor dissension (too high a standard) or excessive

---

[10]Thomas Patten, *Pay: Employee Compensation and Incentive Plans* (New York: Macmillan, 1977).

[11]Stephen Carroll and Craig Schneider, *Performance Appraisal and Review Systems* (Glenview, IL: Scott, Foresman, 1982).

EXHIBIT 10.5 Example of a Time Study

Task: Drilling operation.
Elements:
1. Move part from box to jig.
2. Position part in jig.
3. Drill hole in part.
4. Remove jig and drop part in chute.

		Elements			
Notes and Remarks	*Observation Number*	*(1)*	*(2)*	*(3)*	*(4)*
	1	.17	.22	.26	.29
	2	.17	.22	.27	.34
	3	.16	.21	.28	.39
	4	.18	.21	.29	.29
	5	.19	.20	.30	.36
	6	.25	.21	.31	.31
	7	.17	.23	.29	.33
Observed time		.17 (mode)	.21 (mode)	.29 (median)	.33 (mean)
Effort rating	(130%)	1.30	1.30	1.30	1.30
Corrected time		.2210	.2730	.3370	.4290
Total corrected time					1.2600
Allowances:					
Fatigue	5%				
Personal needs	5%				
Contingencies	10%				
Total	20% (of total corrected time of 1.2600)				.2520
Total allotted time for task					1.5120

Source: From Stephen J. Carroll and Craig E. Schneider, *Performance Appraisal and Review Systems* (Glenview, IL: Scott, Foresman, 1982). Copyright © 1982 by Scott, Foresman and Company. Reprinted by permission.

EXHIBIT 10.6 Illustration of a Straight Piece Rate Plan

Piece rate standard (e.g., determined from time study): 10 units/hour
Guaranteed minimum wage (if standard is not met): $5/hour
Incentive rate (for each unit over 10 units): $.50/unit

Examples of Worker Output	*Wage*
10 units or less	$5.00/hour (as guaranteed)
20 units	20 × $.50 = $10/hour
30 units	30 × $.50 = $15/hour

labor costs (too low a standard). Either outcome is likely to result in deteriorating labor-management relations. Consequently, great care must be taken to ensure that both management and workers have a role in establishing standards. In unionized firms this is often formally ensured through inclusion of standards as a negotiable issue in the contract language.

2. *Cell 2.* Two relatively common plans set standards based on time per unit and tie incentives directly to level of output: (1) standard hour plans and (2) Bedeaux plans. A *standard hour plan* is a generic term for plans setting incentive rate based on completion of a task in some expected time period. A common example can be found in any neighborhood gasoline station or automobile repair shop. Let us assume that you need a new transmission. The estimate you receive for labor costs is based on the mechanic's hourly rate of pay, multiplied by a time estimate for job completion derived from a book listing average time estimates for a wide variety of jobs. If the mechanic receives $30 per hour and a transmission is listed as requiring four hours to remove and replace, the labor costs would be $120. All this is determined in advance of any actual work. Of course, if the mechanic is highly experienced and fast, the job may be completed in considerably less time than indicated in the book. However, the job is still charged as if it took the quoted time to complete. This is the basic mechanism of a standard hour incentive plan. If a task can be completed in less than the designated time, a worker is still paid at a rate based on the standard time allotted for that job times an hourly rate. Standard hour plans are more practical than a straight piecework plan for long-cycle operations and jobs that are nonrepetitive and require numerous skills for completion.[12]

A *Bedeaux plan* provides a variation on straight piecework and standard hour plans. Instead of timing an entire task, a Bedeaux plan requires division of a task into simple actions and determination of the time required by an average skilled worker to complete each action. After the more fine time analysis of tasks, the Bedeaux system functions similarly to a standard hour plan. Workers receive a wage incentive for completing a task in less than standard time. This incentive is a direct function of the time saved in completing the task.

3. *Cell 3.* The two plans included in cell 3 provide for variable incentives as a function of units of production per time period. Both the Taylor plan and the Merrick plan provide different piece rates, depending on the level of production relative to the standard. To illustrate this, consider the contrasts of these plans with a straight piece rate plan. A straight piece rate plan varies wages directly with output. If workers reach standard production, they receive the standard wage. Eighty percent of standard production results in 80 percent of standard wage. Plotting a graph with percentage of standard production on one axis and percentage gain in base hourly rate on the other, the slope for a straight piece rate system would be 1.00. Both the Taylor and Merrick plans would have variable slopes, depending on production levels of workers. For example, the Taylor plan establishes two piecework rates. One rate goes into effect when a worker exceeds the published standard for a given time period. This rate is set higher than the regular wage incentive level. A second rate is established for production below standard, and this rate is lower than the regular wage.

[12]Thomas Wilson, "Is It Time to Eliminate the Piece Rate Incentive System?" *Compensation and Benefits Review*, March–April, pp. 43–49.

EXHIBIT 10.7 Illustrations of the Taylor and Merrick Plans

Piece rate standard: 10 units per hour
Standard wage: $5.00/hour
Piecework rate:

Output	*Taylor Rate per Unit*	*Taylor Wage*	*Merrick Rate per Unit*	*Merrick Wage*
7 units/hour	$.50/unit	$3.50	$.50/unit	$3.50
8 units/hour	$.50/unit	$4.00	$.50/unit	$4.00
9 units/hour	$.50/unit	$4.50	$.60/unit	$5.40
10 units/hour	$.50/unit	$5.00	$.60/unit	$6.00
11 units/hour	$.70/unit	$7.70	$.70/unit	$7.70
12 + units	Calculations at same rate as for 11 units.			

The Merrick system operates in the same way, except that three piecework rates are set: (1) high—for production exceeding 100 percent of standard; (2) medium—for production between 83 and 100 percent of standard; and (3) low—for production less than 83 percent of standard. Exhibit 10.7 compares these two plans.

Both systems are designed to reward highly the efficient worker and penalize the inefficient worker. Quite obviously, there are infinite variations on the number and type of piecework rates that could be established. Although these two plans are designed to encourage the highly efficient, they are not as penalty-laden for less efficient workers as their now defunct predecessors.

4. *Cell 4.* The three plans included in cell 4 provide for variable incentives linked to a standard expressed as time period per unit of production. The three plans include the Halsey 50–50 method, the Rowan plan, and the Gantt plan.

The *Halsey 50–50 method* derives its name from the shared split between worker and employer of any savings in direct cost. An allowed time for a task is determined via time study. The savings resulting from completion of a task in less than the standard time are allocated 50–50 (most frequent division) between the worker and the company.

The *Rowan plan* is similar to the Halsey plan in that an employer and employee both share in savings resulting from work completed in less than standard time. The major distinction in this plan, however, is that a worker's bonus increases as time required to complete the task decreases. For example, if the standard time to complete a task is 10 hours and it is completed in 7 hours, the worker receives a 30 percent bonus. Completion of the same task in 6 hours would result in a 40 percent bonus above the hourly wage for each of the 6 hours.

The *Gantt plan* differs from both the Halsey and Rowan plans in that standard time for a task is purposely set at a level requiring high effort to complete. Any worker who fails to complete the task in standard time is guaranteed a preestablished wage. However, for any task completed in standard time or less, earnings are pegged at 120 percent of the time saved. Consequently, workers' earnings increase faster than production whenever standard time is met or exceeded.

Exhibit 10.8 Advantages and Disadvantages of Individualized Incentive Plans

Advantages

1. Substantial contribution to raise productivity, to lower production costs, and to increase earnings of workers.
2. Less direct supervision is required to maintain reasonable levels of output than under payment by time.
3. In most cases, systems of payment by results, if accompanied by improved organizational and work measurement, enable labor costs to be estimated more accurately than under payment by time. This helps costing and budgetary control.

Disadvantages

1. Greater conflict may emerge between employees seeking to maximize output and managers concerned about deteriorating quality levels.
2. Attempts to introduce new technology may be resisted by employees concerned about the impact on production standards.
3. Reduced willingness of employees to suggest new production methods for fear of subsequent increases in production standards.
4. Increased complaints that equipment is poorly maintained, hindering employee efforts to earn larger incentives.
5. Increased turnover among new employees discouraged by the unwillingness of experienced workers to cooperate in on-the-job training.
6. Elevated levels of mistrust between workers and management.

Source: T. Wilson, "Is It Time to Eliminate the Piece Rate Incentive System?" *Compensation and Benefits Review* 24, no. 2 (1992), pp. 43–49; Pinhas Schwinger, *Wage Incentive Systems* (New York: Halsted, 1975).

Individual Incentive Plans: Advantages and Disadvantages

We already mentioned that incentive plans can lead to unexpected, and undesired, behaviors. Certainly Sears, our example from Chapter 9, did not want mechanics to sell unnecessary repairs. But the incentive program encouraged that type of behavior. This is a common problem with incentive plans: employees and managers end up in conflict because the incentive system often focuses only on one small part of what it takes for the company to be successful.[13] Employees, being rational, do more of what the incentive system pays for. Exhibit 10.8 outlines some of the other problems, as well as advantages, with individual incentive plans.

Individual Incentive Plans: Examples

Even though incentive systems are less popular than they used to be, there are still notable successes. Of course, most sales positions have some part of pay based on commissions, a form of individual incentives. Perhaps the longest running success with individual incentives, going back to before World War I, belongs to a company called

[13]Kenneth Chilton, "Lincoln Electric's Incentive System: A Reservoir of Trust," *Compensation and Benefits Review*, Nov.–Dec. 1994, pp. 29–34.

EXHIBIT 10.9 Lincoln Electric's Compensation System

Description of Culture:	Reservoir of Trust. Long history of employment stability even under severe economic downturns. Employees with 3+ years seniority are guaranteed (on one-year renewable basis) at least 75 percent full-time work for that year. In exchange, employees agree to flexible assignment across jobs.
Base Wages:	Market rate determined. Time study department sets piece rate so average worker can earn market rate.
Bonus (short term):	Board of Directors sets year-end bonus pool as function of company performance. Employee's share in pool is function of semi-annual performance review (see below).
Incentive (long term):	Employees share in long term company successes/failures in form of employee stock ownership plan (ESOP). Employees now own 28 percent of outstanding stock shares.
Performance Review:	Employees rated on four factors: 1) dependability, 2) quality, 3) output, 4) ideas and cooperation in comparison to others in department. To insure against rating inflation, the average score in department cannot exceed 100.

Lincoln Electric. As we describe in Exhibit 10.9 the compensation package for factory jobs at Lincoln Electric, notice how the different pieces fit together. This isn't a case of an incentive plan operating in a vacuum. All the pieces fit together. Lincoln Electric's success is so striking that it's the subject of many case analyses.[14]

TEAM INCENTIVE PLANS: TYPES

Corporate America is thinking teams.[15] When we move away from individual incentive systems and start focusing on people working together, we shift to group incentive plans. The group might be a work team. It might be a department. Or we might focus on a division or the whole company. The basic concept is still the same, though. A standard is established against which worker performance is compared to determine magnitude of the incentive pay. With the focus on groups, now we are concerned about group performance in comparison against some standard, or level of expected performance. The standard might be an expected level of operating income for a division; for a smaller group with no traceable income accountability, the standard might be a 93 percent customer satisfaction rating on questionnaires mailed to new purchasers. Indeed, as Exhibit 10.10 suggests, the range of performance measures for different types of corporate objectives is indeed impressive.

Historically, financial measures have been the most widely used performance indicator for group incentive plans. Increasingly, though, top executives express concern that these measures do a better job of communicating performance to stock analysts than

[14]Jon Katzenbach and Douglas Smith, *The Wisdom of Teams* (New York: Harper Collins 1993).

[15]Brian McWilliams, "The Measure," *The Conference Board Magazine* (February 1996), pp. 16–20.

EXHIBIT 10.10 A Sampling of Performance Measures

Customer-Focused Measures

Time to Market Measures
- On time delivery
- Cycle time
- New product introductions

Customer Satisfaction Measures
- Market share
- Customer satisfaction
- Customer growth and retention
- Account penetration

Financially Focused Measures

Value Creation
- Revenue growth
- Resource yields
- Profit margins
- Economic value added

Shareholder Return
- Return on invested capital
- Return on sales/earnings
- Earnings per share
- Growth in profitability

Capability-Focused Measures

Human Resources Capabilities
- Employee satisfaction
- Turnover rates
- Total recruitment costs
- Rate of progress on developmental plans
- Promotability index
- Staffing mix/head-count ratio

Other Asset Capabilities
- Patents/copyrights/regulations
- Distribution systems
- Technological capabilities

Internal Process-Focused Measures

Resource Utilization
- Budget-to-actual expenses
- Cost-allocation ratios
- Reliability/rework
- Accuracy/error rates
- Safety rates

Change Effectiveness
- Program implementation
- Teamwork effectiveness
- Service/quality index

to managers trying to figure out how to improve operating effectiveness.[16] The outgrowth has been what is called **The Balanced Scorecard.** Mobil Oil, for example, uses a constellation of measures that better indicate exactly where a company is succeeding, and what needs to be improved. The process begins, just as we suggested ought to be the case in Chapter 2, with a careful analysis of strategic objectives for both the corporation and all of its divisions. Then, leaders of all the strategic business units are challenged to identify measures that best reflect the directions being taken by the business. This leads to a constellation of measures such as customer satisfaction, quality, innovation, employee development and the ever familiar financial measures. The balanced scorecard forces discussions about priorities among these different measures. But dissent is viewed positively. A picture begins to emerge about what is most important, and what the necessary tradeoffs are to achieve the different objectives. What evolves is a series

[16]Ibid.

EXHIBIT 10.11 The Choice between Individual and Group Plans

Characteristic	*Choose an Individual Plan when . . .*	*Choose a Group Plan when . . .*
Performance measurement	Good measures of individual performance exist. Task accomplishment not dependent on performance of others.	Output is group collaborative effort. Individual contributions to output cannot be assessed.
Organizational adaptability	Individual performance standards are stable. Production methods and labor mix relatively constant.	Performance standards for individuals change to meet environmental pressures on relatively constant organizational objectives. Production methods and labor mix must adapt to meet changing pressures.
Organizational commitment	Commitment strongest to individual's profession or superior. Supervisor viewed as unbiased and performance standards readily apparent.	High commitment to organization built upon sound communication of organizational objectives and performance standards.
Union status	Nonunion. Unions promote equal treatment. Competition between individuals inhibits "fraternal" spirit.	Union or nonunion. Unions less opposed to plans that foster cohesiveness of bargaining unit and which distribute rewards evenly across group.

of objectives with different weights in terms of importance. These objectives send clear signals to managers, and then to their employees, about what is important. At places like Whirlpool, results on these scorecards become the subject of healthy discussion: what can we do to improve results on key dimensions, and how will this influence our progress on other objectives?[17]

Whatever our thinking is about appropriate performance measures, the central point is still that we are now concerned about group performance. This presents both problems and opportunities. As Exhibit 10.11 illustrates, we need to decide if a group incentive plan is a better choice than an individual plan.

Comparing Group and Individual Incentive Plans

In this era of heightened concern about productivity, we frequently are asked if setting up incentive plans really boosts performance. As we noted in Chapter 9, the answer is yes. We also are asked which is better, group or individual incentive plans. Often this is a misleading question. As we noted in Exhibit 10.7, things like the type of task, the organizational commitment to teams, and the type of work environment may preclude one or the other. When forced to answer the question anyway, experts agree that individual

[17]Miriam Erez and Anit Somech, "Is Group Productivity Loss the Rule or the Exception? Effects of Culture and Group-based Motivation," *Academy of Management Journal* 39, no. 6 (1996), pp. 1513–1537; Daniel G. Hansen, "Worker Performance and Group Incentives: A Case Study," *Industrial and Labor Relations Review* 51, no. 1 (1997), pp. 37–49.

incentive plans have better potential, and probably better track records, in delivering higher productivity. Group plans suffer from what is called the "free-rider" problem. See if this sounds familiar: you are a team member on a school project and at least one person doesn't carry his share of the load. Yet, when it comes time to divide the rewards, they are typically shared equally. Problems like this caused AT&T to phase out many of their team reward packages. Top performing employees readily grew disenchanted with having to carry free riders. End result—turnover of the very group that is most costly to lose.

Recent research on free riders suggests that the problem can be lessened through use of good performance measurement techniques. Specifically, free riders have a harder time loafing when there are clear performance standards. Rather than being given instructions to "do your best," when asked to deliver specific levels of performance at a specific time, the poorer performers actually showed the most performance improvement.[18]

Team Compensation

Despite an explosion of interest in teams and team compensation, many of the reports from the front lines are not encouraging. Companies report they generally are not satisfied with the way their team compensation systems work.[19] Failures can be attributed to at least five causes. First, one of the problems with team compensation is that teams come in many varieties. There are full-time teams (work group organized as a team). There are part-time teams that cut across functional departments (experts from different departments pulled together to improve customer relations). There are even full-time teams that are temporary (cross-functional teams pulled together to help ease the transition into a partnership or joint venture).

With so many varieties, it's hard to argue for one consistent type of compensation plan. We are still at the stage of trying to find the *one best way*. Maybe the answer is to look at different compensation approaches for different types of teams. Perhaps the best illustration of this differential approach for different teams comes from Xerox.

Xerox has a gain-sharing plan that pays off for teams defined at a very broad level—usually at the level of a strategic business unit. For smaller teams, primarily intact work teams (e.g., all people in a department or function), there are group rewards based on supervisory judgments of performance. Units that opt to have their performance judged as teams (it is also possible to declare that a unit wouldn't be fairly judged if team measures were used) have managers who judge the amount to be allocated to each team based on its specific performance results. In new teams, the manager might also decide how much of the total will go to each individual in the team. More mature teams do individual allocations on their own. In Xerox's experience, these teams start out allocating equal shares, but as they evolve the teams allocate based on performance. Out of about 2,000 work teams worldwide at Xerox, perhaps 100 have evolved to this

[18]American Management Association, "Team-Based Pay: Approaches Vary, but Produce no Magic Formulas," *Compflash* (April 1994), p.4.

[19]Conversersation with Thomas Ruddy, Manager of Research, Xerox Corporation, 1997.

level of sophistication.[20] For problem-solving teams and other temporary teams, Xerox also has a reward component called the Xerox achievement awards. Teams must be nominated for exceptional performance. A committee decides which teams meet a set of predetermined absolute standards. Awards vary up to $10,000 per team and $1,000 per team member. Even contributors outside the core team can share in the award. If nominated by team members, extended members who provide crucial added value are given cash bonuses equal to those of team members.

A second problem with rewarding teams is called "the level problem." If we define teams at the very broad level—the whole organization being an extreme example—much of the motivational impact of incentives can be lost. As a member of a 1,000-person team, I'm unlikely to be at all convinced that my extra effort will significantly affect our team's overall performance. Why, then, should I try hard? Conversely, if we let teams get too small, other problems arise. TRW found that small work teams competing for a fixed piece of incentive awards tend to gravitate to behaviors that are clearly unhealthy for overall corporate success. Teams hoard star performers, refusing to allow transfers even for the greater good of the company. Teams are reluctant to take on new employees for fear that time lost to training will hurt the team—even when the added employees are essential to long run success. Finally, bickering arises when awards are given. Because teams have different performance objectives, it is difficult to equalize for difficulty when assigning rewards. Inevitably complaints arise.[21]

The last three major problems with team compensation involve the three Cs: complexity, control and communications. Some plans are simply too complex. Xerox's Houston facility has a gain-sharing plan for teams that requires understanding a three-dimensional performance matrix. Employees (and these authors!) threw their hands up in dismay when they tried to understand the "easy to follow directions." On the other hand, Xerox's San Diego unit has had great success with a simple program called "bet the boss." Employees come to the boss with a performance saving idea and bet their hard effort against the bosses incentive that they can deliver. Such plans have a simplicity that encourages employee buy-in.

The second C is control. Praxair, a worldwide provider of gases (including oxygen) extracted from the atmosphere, works hard to make sure all its team pay comes from performance measures under the control of the team. If mother nature ravages a construction site, causing delays and skyrocketing costs, workers aren't penalized with reduced team payouts. Such uncontrollable elements are factored into the process of setting performance standards. Indeed, experts assert that this ability to foretell sources of problems and adjust for them is a key element in building a team pay plan.[22] Key to the control issue is the whole question of fairness. Are the rewards fair given our ability

---

[20]Conversation with Ann Killian, V.P. of H.R., Harvey Minkoff, Director of Compensation, and Roberta Bixhorn, Manager of Compensation—all at TRW, 1997.

[21]John G. Belcher, *Results Oriented Variable Pay System* (New York: AMACOM, 1996); Steven E. Gross, *Compensation for Teams* (New York: AMACOM, 1995).

[22]Theresa M. Welbourne, David B. Balkin, and Luis R. Gomez-Mejia, "Gainsharing and Mutual Monitoring: A Combined Agency-Organizational Justice Interpretation," *Academy of Management Journal* 38, no. 3 (1995), pp. 881–899.

to produce results? Recent research suggests this perception of fairness is crucial. With it, employees feel it is appropriate to monitor all members of the group—slackers beware! Without fairness, employees seem to have less sense of responsibility for the team's outcomes.[23]

The final C is a familiar factor in compensation successes and failures: communication. Team-based pay plans simply are not well communicated. Employees asked to explain their plans often flounder because more effort is devoted to the mechanics by the design team than to deciding how to explain the plan.

Although there is much pessimism about team-based compensation, many companies still seek ways to reward groups of employees for their interdependent work efforts. Companies that do use team incentives typically set team performance standards based on productivity improvements (38 percent of plans), customer satisfaction measures (37 percent), financial performance (34 percent), or quality of goods and services (28 percent).[24] For example, Kraft Foods uses a combination of financial measures (e.g., income from operations and cash flow) combined with measures designed to gauge success in developing managers, building diversity, and adding to market share.[25]

Gain-sharing Plans

Our discussion of team-based compensation often mentioned gain-sharing plans as a common component. As the name suggests, employees share in the gains in these types of group incentive plans. With profit sharing plans—surprise—the sharing involves some form of profits. Realistically, though, most employees feel as if little they can do will affect profits—that's something top management decisions influence more. So gain sharing looks at cost components of the income ledger, and identifies savings over which employees have more impact (e.g., reduced scrap, lower labor costs, reduced utility costs).

The following issues are key elements in designing a gain-sharing plan:

1. Strength of reinforcement. What role should base pay assume relative to incentive pay? Incentive pay tends to encourage only those behaviors that are rewarded. For example, try returning an unwanted birthday present to a store that pays its sales force solely for new sales. Tasks carrying no rewards are only reluctantly performed (if at all).
2. Productivity Standards. What standard will be used to calculate whether employees will receive an incentive payout? Almost all group incentive plans use a historical standard. A historical standard involves choice of a prior year's performance to use for comparison with current performance. But which baseline year should be used? If too good (or too bad) a comparison year is used, the standard will be too hard (or easy)

[23]American Management Association, "Team-Based Pay: Approaches Vary, but Produce no Magic Formulas," *Compflash* (April 1994), p. 4.

[24]Conversation with Sharon Knight, Director of Compensation, and Martha Kimber, Manager of Compensation, both at Kraft Foods, 1997.

[25]John G. Belcher, *Results Oriented Variable Pay System* (New York: AMACOM, 1996).

to achieve, with obvious motivational and cost effects. One possible compromise is to use a moving average of several years (for example, the average for the past five years, with the five-year block changing by one year on an annual basis).

One of the major problems with historical standards is the problems that changing environmental conditions can cause. For example, consider the company that sets a target of 6 percent return on investment based on historical standards. When this level is reached, it triggers an incentive for eligible employees. Yet, in a product market where the average for that year is 15 percent return on investment, it is apparent that no incentive is appropriate for our underachiever.[26] Such problems are particularly insidious during economic swings and for organizations facing volatile economic climates. Care must be taken to ensure that the link between performance and rewards is sustained. This means that environmental influences on performance, not controllable by plan participants, should be factored out when identifying incentive levels.

3. Sharing the gains: split between management and workers. Part of the plan must address the relative cuts between management and workers of any profit or savings generated. This also includes discussion of whether an emergency reserve (gains withheld from distribution in case of future emergencies) will be established in advance of any sharing of profits.

4. Scope of the formula. Formulas can vary in the scope of inclusions for both the labor inputs in the numerator and productivity outcomes in the denominator.[27] Recent innovations in gain-sharing plans largely address broadening the types of productivity standards considered appropriate. Arguing that organizations are complex and require more complex measures, performance measures have expanded beyond traditional financial measures. For example, with the push for greater quality management, we could measure retention of customers or some other measure of customer satisfaction. Similarly, other measures include delivery performance, safety, absenteeism, turnaround time, and number of suggestions submitted. Four specific examples are:[28]

What is rewarded	*Goal*	*Bonus/Mo*
Productivity	38,500 lbs./month	$ 20
Cost	.009 lbs. below standard	$ 40
Product Damage	15 per 10,000 cases	$ 10
Customer Complaints	14 per million lbs.	$ 15

[26]Robert Masternak, "How to Make Gainsharing Successful: The Collective Experience of 17 Facilities," *Compensation and Benefits Review,* September/October 1997, pp. 43–52.

[27]John G. Belcher, "Gainsharing and Variable Pay: The State of the Art," *Compensation and Benefits Review*, May/June 1994, pp. 50–60.

[28]John Belcher, "Design Options for Gain Sharing," American Productivity Center, unpublished paper, 1987.

Great care must be exercised with these alternative measures, though, to ensure that the behaviors reinforced actually affect the desired bottom-line goal. Getting workers to expend more effort, for example, might not always be the desired behavior. Increased effort may bring unacceptable levels of accidents. Or it may be preferable to encourage cooperative planning behaviors that result in more efficient work.

5. Perceived fairness of the formula. Most incentive systems do not cover all employees in a firm. In fact it is common to limit eligibility to individuals in key positions whose income exceeds certain minimum standards. When multiple plans with different goals covering different employee groups are implemented, coordination to ensure equity becomes increasingly important.

6. Ease of administration. Sophisticated plans with involved calculations of profits or costs can become too complex for existing company information systems. Increased complexities also require more effective communications and higher levels of trust among participants.

7. Production variability. One of the major sources of problems in group incentive plans is failure to set targets properly. At times the problem can be traced to volatility in sales. Large swings in sales and profits, not due to any actions by workers, can cause both elation (in good times) and anger (in bad times). A good plan insures that environmental influences on performance, not controllable by plan participants, should be factored out when identifying incentive levels. One alternative would be to set standards that are relative to industry performance. To the extent data are available, a company could trigger gain sharing when performance exceeds some industry norm. The obvious advantage of this strategy is that economic and other external factors hit all firms in the industry equally hard. If our company performs better, relatively, it means we are doing something as employees to help achieve success.

Exhibit 10.12 illustrates three different formulas that can be used as the basis for gain-sharing plans. The numerator, or input factor, is always some labor cost variable, expressed in either dollars or actual hours worked. Similarly, the denominator is some output measure such as net sales or value added. Each of the plans determines employees' incentives based on the difference between the current value of the ratio and the ratio in some agreed-upon base year. The more favorable the current ratio relative to historical standard, the larger the incentive award.[29] The three primary types of gain-sharing plans, differentiated by their focus on either cost savings (the numerator of the equation) or some measure of revenue (the denominator of the equation), are noted below.

Scanlon Plan. Scanlon plans are designed to lower labor costs without lowering the level of a firm's activity. Incentives are derived as a function of the ratio between labor

[29]A. J. Geare, "Productivity from Scanlon Type Plans," *Academy of Management Review* 1, no. 3 (1976), pp. 99–108.

EXHIBIT 10.12 Three Gain Sharing Formulas

	Scanlon Plan (single ratio volume)	*Rucker Plan*	*Improshare*
Numerator of ratio (input factor)	Payroll costs	Labor cost	Actual hours worked
Denominator of ratio (outcome factor)	Net sales (plus or minus inventories)	Value added	Total standard value hours

Source: Adapted from M. Bazerman and B. Graham-Moore, "PG. Formulas: Developing a Reward Structure to Achieve Organizational Goals," in *Productivity Gainsharing*, ed. B. Graham-Moore and T. Ross (Englewood Cliffs, NJ: Prentice Hall, 1983).

EXHIBIT 10.13 Examples of a Scanlon Plan

1997 Data (base year) for Alton, Ltd.		
SVOP	=	$10,000,000
Total wage bill	=	4,000,000
Total wage bill / SVOP	=	4,000,000 ÷ 10,000,000 = .40 = 40%
Operating Month, March 1998		
SVOP	=	$950,000
Allowable wage bill	=	.40 ($950,000) = $380,000
Actual wage bill (August)	=	330,000
Savings	=	50,000
$50,000 available for distribution as a bonus.		

costs and sales value of production (SVOP).[30] The SVOP includes sales revenue and the value of goods in inventory. To illustrate how these two figures are used to derive incentives under a Scanlon plan, consider Exhibit 10.13.

In practice, the $50,000 bonus in Exhibit 10.13 is not all distributed to the workforce. Rather, 25 percent is distributed to the company, 75 percent of the remainder is distributed as bonus, and 25 percent of the remainder is withheld and placed in an emergency fund to reimburse the company for any future months when a "negative bonus" is earned (i.e., when the actual wage bill is greater than the allowable wage bill). The excess remaining in the emergency pool is distributed to workers at the end of the year. Appendix 10-A illustrates a variant of the Scanlon plan adopted at Dresser Rand's Painted Post facility.

IOMA is the Institute of Management and Administration. It specializes in finding studies from a wide variety of places that discuss different aspects of pay for performance. Its website is **http://www.ioma.com/newsletters/pfp/index.shtml.**

[30]Ibid.

Rucker Plan. The Rucker plan involves a somewhat more complex formula than a Scanlon plan for determining worker incentive bonuses. Essentially, a ratio is calculated that expresses the value of production required for each dollar of total wage bill. Consider the following illustration.[31]

1. Assume accounting records show the company expended $.60 worth of electricity, materials, supplies, and so on, to produce $1.00 worth of product. The value added is $.40 for each $1.00 of sales value. Assume also that 45 percent of the value added was attributable to labor; a productivity ratio (PR) can be allocated from the formula:
2. PR × .45 = 1.00. Solving yields PR = 2.22.
3. If the wage bill equals $100,000, the *expected* production value is the wage bill ($100,000) × PR (2.22) = $222,222.22.
4. If *actual* production value equals $280,000, then the savings (actual production value minus expected production value) is $57,777.78.
5. Since the labor contribution to value added is 45 percent, the bonus to the workforce should be .45 × $57,777.78 = $26,000 (rounded).
6. The savings are distributed as an incentive bonus according to a formula similar to the Scanlon formula—75 percent of the bonus is distributed to workers immediately and 25 percent is kept as an emergency fund to cover poor months. Any excess in the emergency fund at the end of the year is then distributed to workers.

Implementation of the Scanlon/Rucker Plans. There are two major components vital to the implementation and success of a Rucker or Scanlon plan: (1) a productivity norm and (2) development of effective worker committees. Development of a productivity norm requires both effective measurement of base year data and acceptance by workers and management of this standard for calculating bonus incentives. Effective measurement requires that an organization keep extensive records of historical cost relationships and make them available to workers or union representatives to verify cost accounting figures. Acceptance of these figures, assuming they are accurate, requires that the organization choose a base year that is neither a "boom" nor a "bust" year. The logic is apparent. A boom year would reduce opportunities for workers to collect bonus incentives. A bust year would lead to excessive bonus costs for the firm. The base year chosen also should be fairly recent, allaying worker fears that changes in technology or other factors would make the base year unrepresentative of a given operational year.

The second ingredient of Scanlon/Rucker plans is a series of worker committees (also known as productivity committees or bonus committees). The primary function of these committees is to evaluate employee and management suggestions for ways to improve productivity and/or cut costs. Operating on a plantwide basis in smaller firms, or a departmental basis in larger firms, these committees have been highly successful in

[31]Ibid.

eliciting suggestions from employees. It is not uncommon for the suggestion rate to be above that found in companies with standard suggestion incentive plans.[32]

It is this climate the Scanlon/Rucker plans foster that is perhaps the most vital element of success. Numerous authorities have pointed out that these plans have the best chance for success in companies with competent supervision, cooperative union-management attitudes, strong top management interest and participation in the development of the program, and management open to criticism and willing to discuss different operating strategies. It is beyond the scope of this discussion to outline specific strategies adopted by companies to achieve this climate, but the key element is a belief that workers should play a vital role in the decision-making process.

Similarities and Contrasts between Scanlon and Rucker Plans. Scanlon and Rucker plans differ from individual incentive plans in their primary focus. Individual incentive plans focus primarily on using wage incentives to motivate higher performance through increased effort. While this is certainly a goal of the Scanlon/Rucker plans, it is not the major focus of attention. Rather, given that increased output is a function of group effort, more attention is focused on organizational behavior variables. The key is to promote faster, more intelligent, and more acceptable decisions through participation. This participation is won by developing a group unity in achieving cost savings, a goal that is not stressed, and is often stymied, in individual incentive plans.

Even though Scanlon and Rucker plans share this common attention to groups and committees through participation as a linking pin, there are two important differences between the two plans. First, Rucker plans tie incentives to a wide variety of savings, not just the labor savings focused on in Scanlon plans.[33] Second, this greater flexibility may help explain why Rucker plans are more amenable to linkages with individual incentive plans.

Improshare. Improshare (IMproved PROductivity through SHARing) is a relatively new gain-sharing plan that has proven easy to administer and to communicate.[34] First, a standard is developed which identifies the expected hours required to produce an acceptable level of output. This standard comes either from time and motion studies conducted by industrial engineers or from a base period measurement of the performance factor. Any savings arising from production of the agreed-upon output in fewer than the expected hours is shared by the firm and by the worker.[35] So, for example, if 100 workers can produce 50,000 units over 50 weeks, this translates into 200,000 hours (40 hours × 50 weeks) for 50,000 units, or 4 hours per unit. If we implement an Improshare plan, any gains resulting in less than 4 hours per unit are shared 50/50 between employees and management (wages times number of hours saved).[36]

---

[32] Patten, "Pay: Employee Compensation and Incentive Plans"; Schwinger, *Wage Incentive Plans.*

[33] B. Graham-Moore and T. Ross, *Productivity Gainsharing* (Englewood Cliffs, NJ: Prentice Hall, 1983).

[34] Newman, "Selecting Incentive Plans to Complement Organizational Strategy."

[35] Marshall Fein, "Improshare: A Technique for Sharing Productivity Gains with Employees. In *The Compensation Handbook*, ed. Rock, M. L. and Berger, L.A. (New York: McGraw-Hill 1993), pp. 158–175.

[36] R. Kaufman. "The Effects of Improshare on Productivity," *Industrial and Labor Relations Review*, 45 no. 2 (1992), pp. 311–322.

One survey of 104 companies with an Improshare plan found a mean increase in productivity during the first year of 12.5 percent.[37] By the third year the productivity gain rose to 22 percent. A significant portion of this productivity gain was traced to reduced defect rates and down time (e.g., repair time).

Profit Sharing Plans

If you were to read most books or articles on variable pay today, you would see less discussion of profit sharing plans and much energy devoted to gain-sharing plans or related variants. An erroneous conclusion to draw from this is that profit sharing is dead. In reality, many variable pay plans still require some profit target to be met before any payouts occur. Our experience with chief executive officers is that they have a hard time giving employees extra compensation if the company isn't also profiting. So, many variable pay plans have some form of profit "trigger" linked to revenue growth or profit margins or some measure of shareholder return such as earnings per share or return on capital. Profit sharing continues to be popular because the focus is on the measure that matters most to the most people: some index of profitability. When payoffs are linked to these measures, employees spend more time learning about financial measures and the business factors that influence them.

On the downside, most employees don't feel their jobs have a direct impact on profits. A small cog in a big wheel doesn't serve to motivate very well. Further, even if workers are able to improve operating efficiency there is no guarantee that profits will automatically increase. Strength of the market, global competition, even the way we enter accounting information into the balance sheet all can affect profits and serve to disenchant workers.

The trend in recent variable pay design is to combine the best of gain-sharing and profit sharing plans.[38] The company will specify a funding formula for any variable payout that is linked to some profit measure. As experts say, the plan must be self-funding. Dollars going to workers are generated by additional profits gained from operational efficiency. Along with the financial incentive, employees feel they have a measure of control. For example, an airline might give an incentive for reductions in lost baggage, with the size of the payout dependent on hitting profit targets. Such a program combines the need for fiscal responsibility with the chance for workers to affect something they can control.

Earnings-at-Risk Plans

We probably shouldn't separate earnings-at-risk plans as a distinct category. In fact, any incentive plan could be an at-risk plan. Think of incentive plans as falling into one of two categories: success sharing or risk sharing. In success sharing plans, employee base

---

[37]Darlene O'Neill, "Blending the Best of Profit Sharing and Gainsharing," *HR Magazine*, March 1994, pp. 66–69.

[38]K. Brown and V. Huber, "Lowering Floors and Raising Ceilings: A Longitudinal Assessment of the Effects of an Earnings-at-Risk Plan on Pay Satisfaction," *Personnel Psychology* 45 (1992), pp. 279–311.

wages are constant and variable pay adds on during *successful years*. If the company does well, you receive some amount of variable pay. If the company does poorly, you simply forgo any variable pay—there is no reduction in your base pay, though. In a risk-sharing plan, base pay is reduced by some amount relative to the level that would be offered in a success sharing plan. Let's say base pay is set at 80 percent of its previous level. The risk you assume occurs in bad years for the company. Your total compensation remains at 80 percent. In good years, though, you are rewarded for having assumed some of the risk. If, for example, the company meets all its goals, you might receive your 80 percent base pay, a 20 percent bonus to make you "whole," another 20 percent that you might rightfully have received under any success sharing plan, plus (and this is the difference) a 20 percent premium for having assumed some of the business risk. To summarize, in bad years you get 80 percent, and in good years you get (at least under this example) 140 percent. Under a success sharing plan the range would have been 100 percent to 120 percent. Risk sharing means just that. You gamble along with the company. For taking on part of the gamble things are worse in bad years and better in good years.

Clearly, at-risk plans shift some of the risk of doing business from the company to the employee. The company hedges against the devastating effects of a bad year by mortgaging some of the profits that would have accrued during a good year. Companies like Dupont and Saturn report that these programs, admittedly fairly new, are meeting with some success. Reports on the employee front are not so positive, though. At-risk plans appear to be met with decreases in satisfaction with both pay in general and with the process used to set pay.[39]

Group Incentive Plans: Advantages and Disadvantages

Clearly, group pay-for-performance plans are gaining popularity while individual plans are stable or declining in interest. Why? A big part of the reason is the changing nature of work processes. Teams as the basic work unit are growing in popularity. The interdependence of jobs and the need for cooperation means compensation must reinforce working together. Efforts to reinforce these group efforts with compensation generally have been successful (Chapter 9). Exhibit 10.14 outlines some of the general positive and negative features of group pay-for-performance plans.[40]

[39]These observations are drawn from a variety of sources, including: K. Brown and V. Huber, "Lowering Floors and Raising Ceilings: A Longitudinal Assessment of the Effects of an Earnings-at-Risk Plan on Pay Satisfaction," *Personnel Psychology* 45 (1992), pp. 279–311; D. Collins, L. Hatcher and T. Ross (1993), "The Decision to Implement Gainsharing: The Role of Work Climate, Expected Outcomes and Union Status," *Personnel Psychology* 46 (1993), pp. 77–103; Compflash, Team-based Pay: Approaches Vary, but Produce no Magic Formulas," April 1994, p. 4; W.N. Cooke, "Employee Participation Programs, Group Based Incentives and Company Performance," *Industrial and Labor Relations Review* 47 (1994), pp. 594–610.; G.W. Florowski, "The Organizational Impact of Profit Sharing," *Academy of Management Review* 12 no. 4 (1987), pp. 622–636.

[40]T.H. Hammer and R.N. Stern, "Employee Ownership: Implications for the Organizational Distribution of Power," *Academy of Management Journal* 23 (1980), pp. 78–100.

EXHIBIT 10.14 Advantages and Disadvantages of Group Incentive Plans

Advantages
1. Positive impact on organization and individual performance of about 5-10 percent per year. 2. Easier to develop performance measures than for individual plans. 3. Signals that cooperation, both within and across groups, is a desired behavior. 4. Teamwork meets with enthusiastic support from most employees. 5. May increase participation of employees in decision making process.
Disadvantages
1. Line of sight may be lessened, i.e., employees may find it more difficult to see how their individual performance affects their incentive payouts. 2. May lead to increased turnover among top individual performers who are discouraged because they must share with lesser contributors. 3. Increases compensation risk to employees because of lower income stability. May influence some applicants to apply for jobs in firms where base pay is larger compensation component.

Group Incentive Plans: Examples

Incentive plans, as we noted earlier, all can be described by common features: 1) how large a group participates in the plan, 2) what is the standard against which performance is compared, and 3) what is the payout schedule. Exhibit 10.15 illustrates some of the more interesting components of plans for leading companies.

EXPLOSIVE INTEREST IN LONG-TERM INCENTIVE PLANS

Long-term incentives (LTIs) focus on performance beyond the one-year time line used as the cutoff for short-term incentive plans. Recent growth in long-term plans appears to be spurred in part by a desire to motivate longer term value creation. The most common LTIs are employee stock ownership plans (ESOPs) and performance plans. The hottest new trend in long-term incentives, though, is broad-based option plans. We will discuss these in greater detail at the end of this section.

Employee Stock Ownership Plans (ESOPs)

Some companies believe that employees can be linked to the success or failure of a company in yet another way—through employee stock ownership plans.[41] At places like PepsiCo, Lincoln Electric, and others the goal is to increase employee involvement in the organization, and hopefully this will influence performance. Toward this end,

[41]Chilton, "Lincoln Electric's Incentive System . . ."; Howard Rudnitsky, "You Have to Trust the Workforce," *Forbes*, July 19, 1993, pp. 78–81.

EXHIBIT 10.15 Corporate Examples of Group Incentive Plans

GE Information systems	A team-based incentive that also links to individual payouts. Team and individual performance goals are set. If the team hits its goals, the team members earn their incentive only if they also hit their individual goals. The team incentive is 12–15 percent of monthly base pay.
Corning Glass	A gain-sharing program (goal sharing) where 75 percent of the payout is based on unit objectives such as quality measures, customer satisfaction measures and production targets. The remainder is based on Corning's return on equity.
3M	Operates with an earnings-at-risk plan. Base pay is fixed at 80 percent of market. Employees have a set of objectives to meet for pay to move to 100 percent of market. Additionally there is a modest profit sharing component.
Saturn	Earnings-at-risk plan where base pay is 93 percent of market. Employees meet individual objectives to capture at-risk component. All team members must meet objectives for any to get at-risk money. A profit sharing component is based on corporate profits.
Dupont Fibers	Earnings-at-risk plan where employees receive reduced pay increases over 5 years—resulting in 6 percent lower base pay. If department meets annual profit goal, employees collect all 6 percent. Variable payout ranges from 0 (reach less than 80 percent of goal) to 12 percent (150 percent of goal).

employees own 28 percent of stock at Lincoln Electric. At Worthington Industries, an oft-praised performer in the steel industry, the typical employee owns $45,000 in stock.[42]

Despite these high-profile adoptions, ESOPs don't make sense as an incentive. First, the effects are generally long term. How I perform today doesn't have much of an impact on the stock price at the time I exercise my option. Nor does my working harder mean more for me. Indeed, we can't predict very well what makes stock prices rise—and this is the central ingredient in the reward component of ESOPs. So the performance measure is too complex to figure out how we can control our own destiny. Sounds like ESOPs do poorly on two of the three Cs we mentioned earlier as causing incentive plans to fail. Why then do about 9,500 companies have ESOPs covering more than 10 million employees with holdings of over $150 billion in the stock of their companies?[43] The answer may well be that ESOPs foster employee willingness to participate in the decision-making process.[44] And companies that take advantage of that willingness can harness a considerable resource—the creative energy of its workforce.

[42]IOMA, *IOMA's Pay for Performance Report*, May 1996, p. 3.

[43]Ibid.

[44]Ibid.

Performance Plans (Performance Share and Performance Unit)

Performance plans typically feature corporate performance objectives for a time frame three years in the future. They are driven by financial earnings or return measures, and pay out for meeting or exceeding specific goals.

Broad-Based Option Plans (BBOP)

The latest trend in long-term incentives, and probably the component of compensation generating the most discussion in the late 1990s, is in the area of broad-based option plans. BBOPs are stock grants: the company gives employees shares of stock over some time frame. The strength of BBOPs is in their versatility. Depending on the way they are distributed to employees, they can either reinforce a strong emphasis on performance (performance culture) or inspire greater commitment and retention (ownership culture) of employees.

Some of the best known companies in the country offer stock grants to employees at all levels. For example, Starbucks has a stock grant program called Beanstock, and all employees who work at least 500 hours per year up to the level of vice president are eligible (broadbased participation). If company performance goals are reached, all employees receive equal stock grants worth somewhere between 10–14 percent of their earnings. The grants vest 20 percent each year, and the option expires 10 years after the grant date. This program exists to send the CEOs a clear signal that all employees, especially the two-thirds who are part-timers, are business partners. This effort to create a culture of ownership is viewed as the primary reason Starbucks has turnover that is only a fraction of the usually high turnover in the retail industry.

Microsoft's program shares one common feature with Starbucks. The stock grant program, again, is broadbased. By rewarding all employees, Microsoft hopes to send a strong signal to all employees that reinforces its culture: take reasoned risks that have long-run potential for contributing to the company. Microsoft's BBOP is targeted at all permanent employees. Unlike Starbuck's plan, though, the size of the stock grant is linked to individual performance and estimated long-run contribution to the company. Starting 12 months after the stock grant date, 12.5 percent is vested every 6 months.

Kodak provides a third example. Only nonmanagement employees are eligible, and grants are only given to that small percentage of employees who are recognized for extraordinary accomplishments. Based on recommendations by an individual or team's manager, Kodak prides itself on giving immediate grant options for outstanding contributions.

Other LTI Plans

Exhibit 10.17 illustrates some of the remaining LTI alternatives and examples of companies using them.

EXHIBIT 10.17 Other LTI Alternatives

Long-Term Incentive Plan	*Adopting Company*
Premium Priced Stock options: stock options granted with exercise prices in excess of fair market value on the date of grant. Goal is to create a stronger incentive to perform than exists with a standard stock option.	Transamerica Monsanto
Long-term Vest stock options: extend stock option terms beyond 10 years and lengthen vesting period to period longer than traditional 3–4 years. Goal is to tie top executives to the company longer. Useful when company has difficulty keeping top talent.	Chiquita Disney
Indexed Stock Options: exercise price moves up or down with a stock index. Creates incentive to outperform the stock market.	Becton Dickinson
External Standards LTI: Base payouts on external standards, not internal budgets/goals. Forces a comparison with other strong companies, typically in the same industry and yields payouts only when performance exceeds these comparisons.	Procter & Gamble Motorola
Career Grants: stock grants that do not fully vest until retirement. Used for key employees that company cannot afford to lose. Improves retention of this group.	Coca-Cola Procter & Gamble AMR

Source: Michael Davis, "Long Term Incentives—Going beyond the Typical Use". Conference Board Compensation Conference, New York City, 1997.

Summary

Pay-for-performance plans can work. But as this chapter demonstrates, the design and effective administration of these plans is key to their success. Having a good idea is not enough. The good idea must be followed up by sound practices that recognize rewards can, if used properly, shape employee behavior.

Review Questions

1. Your boss had lunch yesterday with a CEO in the same town who just implemented a gain-sharing plan. You guessed it . . . he wants you to see if it would work in your company. What conditions would you like to see exist before you would be comfortable making a positive recommendation?
2. You are the V.P. of H.R. for a *Fortune* 500 company that has trouble with turnover at the top levels. The chairman of the board has issued an ultimatum: fix the problem. While your primary emphasis might be on having a competitive base pay, is there anything you can do in the incentive department? Justify your answer.

3. How is an earnings-at-risk plan different from an ordinary gain-sharing or profit sharing plan? How might earnings-at-risk plans affect attraction and retention of employees?
4. If you wanted to create a work environment where employees offered more new product suggestions, what type of plan might you recommend? What are some of the problems you need to be aware of?

Appendix 10–A

Gain-Sharing at Dresser Rand

History

Let's start with some background on the history of gain-sharing and the Painted Post Gain-Sharing Plan.

Gain-sharing plans have been on the American industrial scene for almost 50 years. One of the first gain-sharing plans was developed by the late Joseph Scanlon. Scanlon was a one-time prize fighter; cost accountant; later, he went to work in a steel mill where he became a local union president. Scanlon eventually joined the United Steelworkers of America staff as its research director.

In 1938 the steel mill where Scanlon worked was on the verge of bankruptcy. The men were desperately anxious to protect their jobs. Scanlon, who had worked on the management side as an accountant and on the union side as union president, realized that the productivity of the plant was exceedingly low.

Scanlon convinced the president of the company to join him in a visit to the office of Mr. Clinton S. Golden, vice president of the Steelworkers, to talk things over. Mr. Golden encouraged them to go back and devise a plan whereby the union and management could work together to save the company. As a result, the first plan of its type was worked out between the management and the union. A new principle was introduced—the principle of employee participation. Later on, Scanlon became a professor at the Massachusetts Institute of Technology, but he died an untimely death in 1956.

Scanlon's work is being carried on by a small group of mostly university professors who are committed to cooperation and team work in American industry. One of those professors, Dr. Michael Schuster of Syracuse University, was commissioned by Ingersoll-Rand management to conduct a feasibility study to see if gain-sharing was an idea that might help Painted Post.

The results of the feasibility study were positive. A recommendation was made to implement a productivity gain-sharing program at Painted Post. The plan is modeled after plans used in many other companies, but has several unique features which are unique to Painted Post. Painted Post was the first Ingersoll-Rand location to attempt a gain-sharing plan. It was started July 1, 1985. If you would like more details about gain-sharing, stop into the Plant Personnel Office.

Now let's get down to the plan itself. Its basic purpose is to tap the huge reservoir of know-how, skill, and experience that is present in every workforce. The plan permits and encourages all employees to participate in the solution to productivity, quality, and cost problems.

In addition, each employee shares in the success of the plan through the bonus program. In short, the plan gives each employee a financial stake in the business.

Key Features of the Painted Post Gain-Sharing Plan

1. A productivity, quality, and cost reduction formula to recognize employees for their efforts. Employees can earn a bonus by:
   - Increasing productivity
   - Improving quality
   - Saving on shop supplies

   This element of the plan gives employees a triple opportunity to be productive and, at the same time, conscious of quality, material, and shop supplies.
2. An expansion of the Employee Involvement Teams (EITs) to provide employees with an opportunity to solve problems that can increase productivity and quality, while reducing the costs of material and shop supplies.
3. A Bonus Committee composed of four union and four management representatives responsible for the overall administration of the program.
4. The program recognizes Painted Post employees for performance efforts that exceed the plant's 1984 levels.
5. Teamwork and employee participation are the key ingredients of the plan. Both require your support and commitment in order for the program to be successful.

The Employee Involvement Teams

The success of the Painted Post Gain-Sharing Plan will largely be determined by the extent to which all employees, hourly and salary, get involved in making Painted Post a successful business once again. The vehicle for doing this is through an expanded and modified process of employee involvement. ALL EMPLOYEES MUST GET INVOLVED IF WE ARE TO MAKE THIS GAIN-SHARING PLAN A SUCCESS.

You know more about your work operations than anyone else. You know best how they can be improved, what shortcuts can be taken, how materials can be saved and scrap minimized, and how work can be performed more efficiently.

The best suggestions are those which recognize the problem and propose a solution.

There will be Employee Involvement Teams (EITs) in each department of the plant, and where possible on the second shift as well. The primary purpose of the EITs should be in the areas of cost reduction, quality, and productivity. The teams will have the option of seeking their own projects. The Steering Committee will also form task forces, task teams, and project teams to work on specific projects, which, in the view of the Steering Committee, might contribute to reducing costs, increasing quality, or reducing production inefficiencies and bottlenecks. Other companies have found that expansion of the EITs will allow us to:

- Use our creative powers in our daily tasks to make suggestions which will improve productivity and quality that will result in better earnings and bonuses.
- Communicate clearly with each other—management to employees and employees to management.
- Join fully and cooperatively in the common effort to increase productivity, quality, and earnings.
- Keep an open-minded attitude to change.

When an EIT team has developed a solution to a problem and the supervisor agrees with the solution, it may be implemented immediately if the cost of the solution is less than $200 and it does not impact on another department. The reason for this is that we want all employees to take greater responsibility for the success of the business.

If, after discussion and analysis, the employees feel the idea is still a good one, and the supervisor or area manager does not, the employees may ask for a review by the EIT Steering Committee. The reason for this is that no one employee, hourly or salaried, can be permitted to stand in the way of a good idea being heard.

The only bad idea is one that is not suggested. You may think your suggestion is not important enough to bring up. **WRONG.** It may prove to be catalyst needed by your fellow employee to trigger another idea.

There will be an Employee Involvement Steering Committee which will coordinate all employee involvement activities. The EIT Steering Committee will have the following functions:

- Oversee the operation of the EIT teams.
- Encourage the teams to take on significant projects.
- Review ideas that have been rejected by supervisors or managers.
- Coordinate review of ideas that cut across more than one department.
- Provide regular communications on the activities of the EITs.
- Act as a mechanism that will create greater trust, confidence, and teamwork.

The Bonus Committee

The Bonus Committee is made up of four union and four company representatives. It is one of the most effective means of communication between employees and management. The committee meets once each quarter to review the bonus computation for the previous quarter and analyze why it was, or was not, favorable. Accurate minutes will be kept by the Bonus Committee.

The Gain-Sharing Bonus

The productivity bonus is paid to recognize employees for their efforts. **The bonus is not a gift.** It will be paid when it has been earned by exceeding 1984 performance levels for labor costs, quality, and shop supplies.

The program utilizes three measurement points when calculating the bonus payout:

Productivity (as measured in labor costs)

Quality (as measured by spoilage, scrap, and reclamations)

Shop supplies

The Painted Post Gain-Sharing Plan permits gains in productivity to be enhanced by savings in scrap and reclamation expenses and shop supplies. Thus, a bonus is determined by the following formula:

Gain-sharing bonus = Productivity (Labor costs) ± Quality (Spoilage, scrap, & reclamation) ± Shop supplies

However, if quality falls below the stated target, it will reduce the bonus earned from a productivity gain. Conversely, if productivity falls below the stated target, it will reduce a bonus that could have been earned from a quality improvement.

Thus, employees are required to focus on three very important indicators of plant performance. This measurement system ensures that productivity gains are not achieved at the expense of quality and prudent shop supply usage. At Painted Post, the dual importance of productivity and quality must be recognized by all employees.

The Role of Quality

Maintaining and increasing the quality of Painted Post products is achieved with this measurement formula in two ways.

First, only "good product" is to be recognized in accounting for sales.

Second, "bad product" will be scrapped and will adversely affect spoilage, scrap, and reclamation, as well as labor costs.

Thus, there is a double benefit for employees to produce good quality products and a severe penalty for failure to do so.

Calculation of the Gain-Sharing Bonus

Employees will receive a bonus when they exceed their own levels of performance in 1984. Bonuses from the Painted Post Gain-Sharing Plan are not based upon management or employee opinion of how much work should be done and of what quality. Instead, the bonus is based upon improvements in how the work force actually performed in 1984. Following is an example of how the gain-sharing bonus will be calculated.

PAINTED POST
Gain-Sharing Calculation Example

Net sales	$ 9,000,000
Inventory change sales value	+ 1,000,000
Sales value of production	10,000,000
Labor Bonus Pool	
Target labor and fringe (16.23%)	1,623,000
Actual labor and fringe	1,573,000
Labor/fringe savings bonus	50,000
Actual percent of sales value	15.73%

Waste Savings Bonus Pool	
Target spoiled and reclamation (3.34)	$ 334,000
Actual spoiled and reclamation	294,000
Waste savings bonus	40,000
Actual percent of sales value	2.94%
Operating Supplies Bonus Pool	
Target operating supplies (4.00%)	$ 400,000
Actual operating supplies	370,000
Operating supplies savings bonus	30,000
Actual percent of sales value	3.70%
Distribution	
Total all savings bonus pools	$ 120,000
Less: Current quarter reserve provision	40,000
Apply to prior quarter loss	–0–
Available for distribution	80,000
Employee share (65%)	52,000
Participating payroll	1,000,000
Employee share—percentage of participating payroll	5.20%
Reserve balance	$ 40,000

The reserve is established in order to safeguard the Company against any quarters with lower than normal output. At the end of each plan year, whatever is left in the reserve will be paid out with 65 percent going to the employees and 35 percent to the Company.

On the next several pages we examine the bonus formula in detail. Please read this information carefully. It is very important for every employee to understand how we arrive at a bonus.

Questions and Answers

Q: What should an employee do if he or she has a question about the plan or an idea that might increase the bonus?
A: Questions or ideas should be referred to the employee's supervisor, the EIT Steering Committee, the Plant Personnel office, or the Gain-Sharing Committee.
Q: Will being absent or tardy affect my bonus?
A: Employees will only receive a bonus for actual hours worked. The employee who has lost time will not be paid a bonus for that period of absences.
Q: What about other pay-for-time-not-worked benefits?
A: Bonuses will be excluded from all pay-for-time-not-worked benefits, such as vacations, holidays, death in family, jury duty, etc.
Q: What if there is ever a question as to the accuracy of the calculation of the bonus formula?
A: If there is ever a question as to the accuracy of the information, the company has agreed to permit Price Waterhouse to conduct an audit.
Q: How long will the program last?
A: The Gain-Sharing Plan will exist for the life of the present collective bargaining agreement. Since the plan is an annual plan, each year the nature of the plan will be reviewed. The Union and the Company will have the right to meet to review the plan if either becomes dissatisfied with it.

Painted Post Gain-Sharing Plan
XXXX Quarter 19XX
(Example 1)

Net Sales are the combination of the following:	$ 9,000,000
Gas compressor sales	
Air compressor transfers	
V & R transfers	
Transfers to repair centers	
Transfers to DRCS	
In short, **Net Sales** is what Painted Post receives for what it does.	
± Inventory Change Sales Value	±1,000,000
Inventory is work in progress and finished goods that have not been shipped.	
SALES VALUE OF PRODUCTION	$10,000,000
The actual quarterly sales plus or minus the inventory increases or decreases.	
Incidentally, if we can get some price increases, that should increase the sales value of production and help us to earn a bonus.	

Painted Post Gain-Sharing Plan
XXXX Quarter 19XX
(Example 2)

SALES VALUE OF PRODUCTION	$10,000,000
Target Labor and Fringe (16.23%)	1,623,000
The historical relationship between payroll cost (less pension) and sales for the year 1984. Payroll costs were adjusted to reflect the 1985 contract changes.	
This is the amount of labor we would expect if we had $10,000,000 in sales. It is the target we must beat if we are to earn a bonus.	
Actual Labor and Fringes	1,573,000
The actual monies paid during the quarter for wages and fringes.	
LABOR COSTS SAVINGS	$ 50,000
The difference between what we would have expected in labor costs from what actually occurred.	
Can we do better than the past and earn a bonus?	
Answer: There is nothing the Painted Post work force can't do when it tries.	

Painted Post Gain-Sharing Plan
XXXX Quarter 19XX
(Example 3)

Target Spoilage and Reclamation (3.34%)	$334,000
The historical relationship between spoilage, scrap, and reclamations and sales for the year 1984.	
This is the cost of spoilage, scrap, and reclamation we would expect if we had $10,000,000 in sales.	
Actual Spoilage and Reclamation	294,000
The actual costs of spoilage, scrap, and reclamations for the quarter.	
QUALITY SAVINGS	$ 40,000
The difference between what we would have expected in quality costs and what actually occurred.	
Can we reduce the costs of quality?	
Answer: Painted Post has one of the most highly skilled work forces anywhere.	
We can improve our quality and probably increase our sales as a result.	

Painted Post Gain-Sharing Plan
XXXX Quarter 19XX
(Example 4)

Target Operating Supplies (4.00%)	$400,000
The historical relationship between operating supplies and sales for the year 1984.	
This is the cost of shop supplies we would expect if we had $10,000,000 in sales.	
Actual Operating Supplies	370,000
The actual costs of operating supplies for the quarter.	
OPERATING SUPPLIES SAVINGS	$ 30,000
The difference between what we would have expected in operating supply costs and what actually occurred.	
Does anyone know where savings might be found in operating supplies?	
Answer: Everyone knows.	

Painted Post Gain-Sharing Plan
XXXX Quarter 19XX
(Example 5)

TOTAL ALL SAVINGS BONUS POOLS		$120,000
Labor	+ $ 50,000	
Quality	+ 40,000	
Supplies	+ 30,000	
	$120,000	
Less 1/3 as current Qtr. Reserve Provision		40,000
Apply to prior quarter loss		-0-
Available for Distribution		80,000
Employee share of savings 65%		52,000
Participating Payroll		1,000,000
Employee Share—% of Participating Payroll		5.20%
(Participating payroll is total wages for all hours worked.)		
RESERVE BALANCE		40,000

The Reserve is established to provide some safeguard for the Plan against quarters with lower than normal efficiency where we fail to meet our stated labor costs, spoilage, scrap and reclamation, and shop supplies goals. At the end of the gain-sharing year, the money remaining in the Reserve Account will be distributed.

APPENDIX 10–B

PROFIT-SHARING AT 3M

Prologue

". . . In years of unusual company prosperity, incomes under a properly designed plan may go up, allowing the employee to participate in the company's prosperity; and during lean years, incomes automatically decrease. It seems to me that those in important positions should recognize that it is proper to expect their incomes to vary somewhat in relation to the prosperity of their division, subsidiary, and/or the prosperity of the company as a whole."

William L. McKnight
Chairman 1949–1966

3M's management compensation system is designed to reinforce the manager's responsibility to improve profitability. The formula is based on a simple philosophy; the individual manager's income should vary with the business unit's profitability. This booklet explains how "profit-sharing" converts this philosophy into practice.

Salary Surveys

Our management compensation system starts with a review of competitive pay rates in the marketplace. For 3M, the "marketplace" is not the average U.S. corporation, but rather, respected companies that are similar to us in management philosophies and human resource principles. In other words, the "peer" companies with which we compete for talent.

The survey process involves asking our peers for information about base salaries, discretionary bonuses, and any special incentive programs. These components are added together to provide the basis for 3M's salary range structure.

As you'll see, as a manager part of your total cash compensation is paid to you as base salary, and the remainder as profit-sharing. The relationship of your total pay to the market rate determined by survey is illustrated by this diagram.

MARKET	**3M RANGE MIDPOINT**
BONUS/ SPECIALS	PROFIT-SHARING (VARIABLE)
BASE SALARY	BASE SALARY
PEERS	3M

The diagram helps to illustrate a very important concept. Your profit-sharing is not an "over and above" payment, nor is it a bonus. Rather, it is a variable portion of your total cash compensation that will fluctuate with the success of your business unit.

Definitions

Before explaining how a profit-sharing plan is developed, we must discuss two important terms.

As noted earlier, profit-sharing is a variable part of your cash compensation. In order to calculate the variable payment, it is first necessary to assign a fixed number of profit-sharing "shares." These shares are not owned, nor do they have a market value; they are a device to calculate profit-sharing. Then, after the end of each quarter, the number of shares is multiplied by the profit-sharing "rate." The rates vary with profitability; hence, your profit-sharing payment will increase or decrease, depending upon profitability.

The Rate Calculations section of this booklet describes how profit-sharing rates are determined.

Your Initial Plan

When you are first appointed to management, 5 percent to 10 percent of your new total compensation is normally allocated to profit-sharing. Let's go through an example to show how the initial plan is developed. The example assumes you work for an operating division; if you are a staff manager, you will normally receive company shares instead of the division shares referred to in the example.

Let's assume that when you are appointed, your total cash compensation is $45,600 per year, and you receive a promotional increase of approximately 15 percent. The computation works like this.

$45,600	Total compensation
×1.15	15% promotional increase
$52,520	New total compensation
×0.05	5% allocated to profit-sharing
$ 2,600	Amount allocated to profit-sharing

The next step is to determine your number of shares. To do this, your profit-sharing dollar allocation is divided by your division's four-quarter profit-sharing rate (the sum of the most recent four quarter's rates). In our example, the four-quarter rate is $0.17391. Accordingly,

$$\frac{\$2{,}600 \text{ Dollar Allocation}}{\$0.17391 \text{ Division Rate}} = 14{,}950 \text{ Division Shares}$$

Your annualized profit-sharing compensation plan would then be:

Base Salary	$49,920 Paid Monthly
Division Profit-Sharing	
14,950 Shares at $0.17391	2,600 Paid Quarterly
	$52,520 Total Compensation

Generally, your initial share assignment is division shares only, since, as a new manager, your most significant contributions will be at the division level. However, as your responsibilities increase, you may be assigned group and company shares. As a staff manager, you will receive company shares which will be increased as responsibilities increase.

Rate Calculations

The 3M profit-sharing system provides for profit-sharing at the division, group, and company level. All three types of profit-sharing rates are described in this section.

All profit-sharing rates are calculated quarterly. Quarterly profit is determined as follows:

Year-to-date profit, current quarter
– Year-to-date profit, previous quarter
= Current quarter profit

Division Rates. A division's quarterly profit-sharing rate is determined by dividing the division's current quarter profit by the number of 3M common shares outstanding at the end of the previous quarter. As an example, let's assume your division had a $5,000,000 profit and there were 115 million shares of 3M common stock outstanding.

$$\frac{\$\ 5{,}000{,}000 \text{ Quarterly Profit}}{115{,}000{,}000 \text{ 3M Common Stock}} = \$0.04348 \text{ (Division Profit-Sharing rate per share)}$$

Since the number of outstanding shares of 3M common stock remains relatively constant, the quarterly rate will increase if division profit increases. This creates the opportunity for you to earn more than your planned income; remember, your share allocation was based on the four-quarter rate at the time your shares were assigned. Conversely, if profit declines, the quarterly rate declines and you will be paid less than your planned income.

Group Rates. Group quarterly profit-sharing rates are calculated using the same formula as division rates. That is, group quarterly profit is divided by the number of 3M common shares outstanding. For example, if your group's quarterly income was $18,750,000 your group rate would be:

$$\frac{\$18{,}750{,}000 \text{ Group Profit}}{115{,}000{,}000 \text{ 3M Common Stock}} = \$0.16304 \text{ (Group Profit-Sharing rate per share)}$$

The assignment of group shares is determined using the most recent four-quarter group rate in the manner described for division share assignments.

Company Rates. The formula used to calculate company quarterly profit-sharing rates differs from the division/group formula.

The formula is: Current quarter 3M consolidated net income, minus 2.5% of the previous quarter's Stockholders' Equity (Assets minus Liabilities), divided by the previous quarter's number of 3M common shares outstanding. Using representative numbers, the quarterly calculation looks like this:

Reserve for Return on Stockholders' Equity	
Total Assets	$6,593,000,000
Less Total Liabilities	2,585,000,000
Stockholders' Equity	$4,008,000,000
	× 2 ½%
Minimum Reserve	$ 100,200,000
Income Available for Profit-Sharing	
Consolidated Net Income	$ 186,450,000
Less Minimum Reserve	100,200,000
Adjusted Net Income	$ 86,250,000
Company Share Rate	

$$\frac{\$86{,}250{,}000 \text{ Profit-Sharing Income}}{115{,}000{,}000 \text{ 3M Common Stock}} = \$0.750 \text{ (Company Profit-Sharing rate per share)}$$

By establishing the minimum reserve, this formula recognizes the fact that the shareholders own the company and are entitled to a reasonable return before profits are shared with management. And, the inclusion of assets and liabilities in the calculation provides an incentive for managers to use assets wisely in their efforts to increase profits.

The assignment of company shares uses the same four-quarter rate method described for division share assignments.

Another Example

Now that you understand rate calculations, let's go through another example that will build on the first.

Your initial plan was designed to pay you a total of $52,520, of which $2,600 was to be profit-sharing. However, since that plan became effective, your division's four-quarter rate increased from $0.17391 to $0.20000. As a result, your plan is now paying at an annual rate of $52,910, as follows:

Base Salary	$49,920 Paid Monthly
Division Profit-Sharing	2,990 Paid Quarterly
14,950 shares @ $0.20000	$52,910 Total

Your manager has decided that:

- You have earned a 6 percent merit increase.
- You should have 10 percent of your total pay in profit-sharing (up from 5 percent).
- You should receive some group and company shares.
- The value of the group/company profit-sharing should be 10 percent of your profit-sharing.

Assuming that the four-quarter group and company rates are $0.65216 and $3.000 respectively, your new plan would look like this.

Base Salary	$50,460 Paid Monthly
Division Profit-Sharing:	
25,200 shares @ $0.2000	5,040 Paid Quarterly
Group Profit-Sharing:	
425 shares @ $0.65216	277 Paid Quarterly
Company Profit-Sharing:	
100 shares @ $3.000	300 Paid Quarterly
	$56,077 Total Planned Pay

It's important to note that your 6 percent increase was calculated at a value determined by the current four-quarter rate, and not from the rate used when your shares were originally assigned. In other words, $56,077 is 106 percent of $52,910.

The addition of group/company shares and a change in the percent allocated to profit-sharing is most often timed to correspond with a merit or promotional increase. Other changes to your plan, called "conversions," are explained in the last section of this booklet.

You've noted that your profit-sharing allocation was not divided equally between division, group, and company profit-sharing. The reasons are explained in the next section.

Profit-Sharing Mix

Our example illustrated an important feature of the 3M profit-sharing system. Because your most important contributions will always be at the division level (as long as you have a division job), division profit-sharing will always be the most important. However, as your responsibility level increases, the value of the group/company portion may increase, to about 40 percent of the total profit-sharing allocation. When group shares are used, the value of group and company profit-sharing will normally be kept approximately equal (up to 20 percent for each). The desired mix is achieved by adjusting the number of shares (without subtracting division shares), generally at the time of an increase.

Profit-Sharing/Base Salary Balance

It is also important to maintain a proper relationship between profit-sharing and base salary. As you advance in management, more dollars are assigned to profit-sharing, increasing your potential for an increase or decrease in earnings as a result of business unit profitability. For example, as a new or first-level manager, no more than 15 percent of your total planned compensation will be assigned to profit-sharing, whereas senior managers may have up to 40 percent of their total planned compensation in profit-sharing. At the time of compensation plan changes, increases are planned so as to retain the desired balance between base salary and profit-sharing in your plan (without reducing base salary).

Participation Limits

Profit-sharing is intended to provide significant increases in total cash compensation during periods of improving profitability; however, profit growth rates vary by division, and sometimes dramatically. As a consequence, managers in divisions experiencing rapid or even explosive growth can significantly outearn their counterparts in divisions with lower profit growth or even declining profits. When profit growth is more related to the business/product cycle of the division than to relative managerial effectiveness, excessive earnings are not justified. To maintain internal equity while still permitting increased earnings through profit-sharing, participation limits have been established.

Participation limits are calculated as a percent of your base salary, and they vary by salary grade. Participation limits are calculated on a year-to-date basis. It is important to emphasize that participation limits do not stop profit-sharing; they only restrain the rate at which you participate in profit growth.

Suppose, using our last example, your division is extremely successful. The division, group, and company four-quarter profit-sharing rates have jumped to $0.75000, $1.00000, and $3.500, respectively. At those rates, the annualized value of your profit-sharing has increased by approximately 350 percent.

Type	*Planned*	*Now Paying*
25,200 Division Shares	$5,020	$18,900
425 Group Shares	277	425
100 Company Shares	300	350
	$5,597	$19,675

However, at your salary grade, the participation limit is 35 percent. Here's how it works.

Base Salary	$50,420
	× 35%
100% participation up to	$17,647
50% participation in the next	$17,647
25% participation in the remainder	

So, in our example you would receive:

100% participation	$17,647
50% participation in excess ($2,028)	1,014
Total	$18,661

Normally, after participation limits are reached, the plan will be revised to provide the desired balance between base salary and profit-sharing without a loss in planned total compensation. The resulting new plan effectively captures the level of compensation attained and allows for full participation in future profit growth.

Conversions

Occasionally, events such as the sale or transfer of commodities, the acquisition or divestiture of a subsidiary or business, or the reorganization of a division will affect division profits, resulting in an increase or decrease in the profit-sharing rate that does not reflect operating results. If the event results in a net change of 3 percent in a division's rate or a 6 percent change in a group rate, the Compensation Department will automatically "convert" your plan.

Conversion is simply restating the number of shares you have in your plan, based on the four-quarter profit-sharing rates. For example, the number of division shares you are assigned will decrease if your division rate increased because of added profit, and they will increase if your division lost profit. The intent, of course, is to cancel the influence of the event and allow the profit-sharing rate to reflect normal changes in business operations.

Summary

The 3M Management Profit-Sharing Compensation system has and continues to:

- Focus management attention on profits and the effective use of assets,
- Provide a measure of variable compensation,
- Allow managers to participate in the growth and decline of the profits of their division, group, and the company.

If there are any questions still unanswered, you should contact your manager, your Human Resource Manager, or the Compensation Department.

YOUR TURN:

J. MARTIN GAMES: COSTING OUT AN INDIVIDUAL INCENTIVE SYSTEM

A competitor to GTM Toys has decided to implement an individual incentive plan to improve productivity. As a first step in this process, the company hired an industrial engineer to do time studies for the three assembler positions involved in assembling the Dunk-it Basketball Game. General descriptions of the three positions follow:

Position 1: Remove basketball hoop and miniature backboard from feeder lines and attach hoop to backboard with available screws.

Position 2: Remove net from number 2 feeder line and attach to hoop.

Position 3: Assemble Dunk-it Basketball Game box and enclose foam rubber basketball and assembled hoop.

Time studies indicate that each of the jobs should take an allotted time (with allowance for fatigue and other contingencies) (see Exhibit 1). Current pay and productivity for the three position incumbents is also available (see Exhibit 2).

What is the likely response of the three position incumbents if they are put on a straight piecework schedule as noted in Exhibit 1 and they continue to perform at the level noted in Exhibit 2?

EXHIBIT 1 Time Study

Position	*Allotted Time (minutes, seconds)*		*Established Standard (units/hour)*
1	-0-	45	80
2	-0-	36	100
3	-0-	54	66

EXHIBIT 2 Productivity and Wage Data

Position	*Incumbent*	*Wages/Hour*	*Units/Hour*
1	Arnold	$7.50	71
2	Ramirez	$7.50	88
3	Friedman	$7.50	59

CHAPTER

Performance Appraisals

Chapter Outline

Chapters 9 and 10 covered the merits of pay-for-performance plans. A key element of these plans is some measure of performance. Sometimes this measure is objective and quantifiable. Certainly, when we are measuring performance for a group incentive plan, objective financial measures may be readily available. As we move down to the level of the individual and the team, these "hard" measures are not as readily available. This chapter discusses in more detail the difficulties of measuring performance, particularly when we use subjective procedures.

THE ROLE OF PERFORMANCE APPRAISALS IN COMPENSATION DECISIONS

By the year 2000 employees may have between 10–15 percent of their pay determined by their level of performance. This would be up from 5 percent in 1980 and 6.8 percent in 1991.[1] If we also add in other forms of compensation tied to performance (group performance and company performance), another 10–15 percent of total compensation depends on some accurate measure of performance.[2] This emphasis on performance and effective use of human resources is further evident in the continuing emphasis on total quality management. One of the major requirements for winning the Baldrige Award, the superbowl of quality recognition, is effective measurement of performance.[3]

At times, measurement of performance can be quantifiable. Indeed, some good estimates suggest between 13 percent of the time (hourly workers) and 70 percent of the time (managerial employees) employee performance is tied to these quantifiable measures.[4] Just because something is quantifiable, though, doesn't mean it is an objective measure of performance. As any accounting student knows, financial measures are arrived at through a process that involves some subjective decision making. Which year we choose to take writeoffs for plant closings, for example, affects the bottom line reported to the public. Such potential for subjectivity has led some experts to warn that so-called objective data can be deficient and may not tell the whole story.[5] Despite these concerns, most HR professionals probably would prefer to work with objective data. Sometimes, though, objective performance standards are not feasible. Either job output is not readily quantifiable or the components that are quantifiable do not reflect important job dimensions. A secretarial job could be reduced to words per minute and errors per page of typing. But many secretaries, and their supervisors, would argue this captures only a small portion of the job. Courtesy in greeting clients and in answering phones, initiative in solving problems without running to the boss, dependability under deadlines—all of these intangible qualities can make the difference between a good and a poor secretary. Such subjective goals are less easily measured. The end result, all too often, is a performance appraisal process that is plagued by errors.

Perhaps the biggest attack against appraisals in general, and subjective appraisals in particular, comes from top names in the total quality management area. Edward Deming, the grandfather of the quality movement here and in Japan, launched an attack of appraisals because, he contended, the work situation (not the individual) is the major determinant of performance.[6] Variation in performance arises many times because employees don't have necessary information, technology or control to adequately perform

---

[1]Amanda Bennett, "Paying workers to meet goals spreads, but gauging performance proves tough," *The Wall Street Journal,* June 7, 1990, pp. B1, B8.

[2]Ibid.

[3]Towers Perrin, *1991 Survey of Top HR Goals* (New York: Towers Perrin, 1992).

[4]Susan E. Jackson, Randall S. Schuler and J. Carlos Rivero, "Organizational Characteristics as Predictors of Personnel Practices," *Personnel Psychology* 42 (1989), pp. 727–786.

[5]Robert L. Cardy and Gregory H. Dobbins, *Performance Appraisal: Alternative Perspectives* (Cincinnati: Southwestern Publishing, 1994).

[6]W.E. Deming, *Out of the Crisis* (Cambridge, Mass.: MIT Press, 1986).

their jobs.[7] Further, Deming argued, individual work standards and performance ratings rob employees of pride and self-esteem.

Some experts argue that rather than throwing out the entire performance appraisal process, we should apply total quality management principles to improving the process.[8] A first step, of course, is recognition that part of performance is influenced more by the work environment and system than by employee behaviors. For example, sometimes when students say the dog ate my paper (1990s version, the computer ate my disk) . . . it really happened. When we tell teachers, or other raters, that the system sometimes does control performance, raters are more sympathetic and rate higher.[9]

A second step in this direction, one that involves most of the remainder of this chapter, concerns identifying strategies to understand and measure job performance better. This may help us reduce the number and types of rating errors illustrated in Exhibit 11.1.

EXHIBIT 11.1 Common Errors in the Appraisal Process

Halo error	An appraiser giving favorable ratings to all job duties based on impressive performance in just one job function. For example, a rater who hates tardiness rates a prompt subordinate high across all performance dimensions *exclusively because of this one characteristic.*
Horn error	The opposite of a halo error. Downgrading an employee across all performance dimensions *exclusively because of poor performance on one dimension.*
First impression error	Developing a negative or positive opinion of an employee early in the review period and allowing that to negatively or positively influence all later perceptions of performance.
Recency error	The opposite of first impression error. Allowing performance, either good or bad, at the end of the review period to play too large a role in determining an employee's rating for the entire period.
Leniency error	Consistently rating someone higher than is deserved.
Severity error	The opposite of leniency error. Rating someone consistently lower than is deserved.
Central tendency error	Avoiding extremes in ratings across employees.
Clone error	Giving better ratings to individuals who are like the rater in behavior and/or personality.
Spillover error	Continuing to downgrade an employee for performance errors in prior rating periods.

[7]David Waldman, "The Contributions of Total Quality Management to a Theory of Work Performance" *Academy of Management Review* 19 (1994), pp. 510–536.

[8]David Antonioni, "Improve the Performance Management Process before Discontinuing Performance Appraisals," *Compensation and Benefits Review,* May–June 1994, pp. 29–37.

[9]R.L. Cardy, C.L. Sutton, K.P. Carson and G.H. Dobbins, "Degree of Responsibility: An Empirical Examination of Person and System Effects on Performance Ratings," (Paper presented at the national meeting of the Academy of Management, San Francisco, CA 1990).

COMMON ERRORS IN APPRAISING PERFORMANCE

Suppose you supervised 1,000 employees. How many would you expect to rate at the highest level? How many would be average or below? If you're tempted to argue the distribution should look something like a normal curve, you might get an A in statistics, but fail Reality 101. One survey of 1,816 organizations reported the following distribution of performance ratings (Exhibit 11.2) for its managers.

EXHIBIT 11.2 Ratings of Managers

Rating Received	*Percent of Managers Receiving Rating*
Above average employee	46.4
Average employee	49.0
Below Average	4.6

Now, we might argue that managers got to that organization level because they are better than average performers.[10] So, of course they rate mostly average or better in their jobs. But the truth is, as raters we tend to make mistakes. Our ratings differ from what would occur if we could somehow, in a moment of clarity, divine the truth. We make errors in ratings. Recognizing and understanding the errors, such as those noted in Exhibit 11.1, are the first steps to communicating and building a more effective appraisal process.

Not surprisingly, the potential for errors causes employees to lose faith in the performance appraisal process. One poll, in fact, found that 30 percent of employees believed their performance appraisals were ineffective. Employees, quite naturally, will be reluctant to have pay systems tied to such error-ridden performance ratings. At the very least, charges that the evaluation process is political will abound.[11] There are several factors that lead raters to give inaccurate appraisals: (1) guilt, (2) embarrassment about giving praise, (3) taking things for granted, (4) not noticing, (5) halo effect, (6) dislike of confrontation, (7) spending too little time on preparation of the appraisal.[12] To counter such problems, companies and researchers alike have expended considerable time and money to identify ways performance ratings can be improved.

STRATEGIES TO BETTER UNDERSTAND AND MEASURE JOB PERFORMANCE

Early research designed to understand and measure job performance centered on identifying the best appraisal format. If only the ideal format could be found, so the argument goes, raters would use it to measure job performance better; that is, make more accurate

[10]American Management Association, "Top performers? Most Managers Rated Average or Better," *Compflash*, September 1992, p. 3.

[11]Clinton Longnecker, Henry Sims, and Dennis Gioia, "Behind the Mark: The Politics of Employee Appraisal," *Academy of Management Executive* 1, no. 3 (1987), pp. 183–93.

[12]Timothy D. Schellhardt, "Annual Agony," *The Wall Street Journal*, November 19, 1996, p. A1.

ratings. More recent attention has focused less on the rating format and more on the raters themselves. One branch of this work identifies possible categories of raters (supervisor, peers, subordinates, customers, self) and examines whether a given category leads to more or less accurate ratings. The second branch of this research about raters attempts to identify how raters process information about job performance and translate it into performance ratings. Such information, including an understanding of the role irrelevant information plays in the evaluation of employees, may yield strategies to reduce the flaws in the total process. Finally, data also suggest that raters can be trained to increase the accuracy of their ratings. The following sections discuss each of these different approaches to better understand and measure performance.

Strategy One: Improve Appraisal Formats

Types of Formats. Evaluation formats can be divided into two general categories: ranking and rating.[13] *Ranking formats* require the rater to compare employees against each other to determine the relative ordering of the group on some performance measure (usually some measure of overall performance). Exhibit 11.3 illustrates three different methods of ranking employees.

The *straight ranking procedure* is just that: employees are ranked relative to each other. *Alternation ranking* recognizes that raters are better at ranking people at extreme ends of the distribution. Raters are asked to indicate the best employee and then the worst employee. Working at the two extremes permits a rater to get more practice prior to making the harder distinctions in the vast middle ground of employees. Finally, the *paired comparisons ranking* method simplifies the ranking process by forcing raters to make ranking judgments about discrete pairs of people. Each individual is compared separately with all others in the work group. The person who "wins" the most paired comparisons is ranked top in the group, and so on. Unfortunately, as the size of the work group goes above 10 to 15 employees, the number of paired comparisons becomes unmanageable.

The second category of appraisal formats, ratings, is generally more popular than ranking systems.

The various *rating formats* have two elements in common. First, in contrast to ranking formats, rating formats require raters to evaluate employees on some absolute standard rather than relative to other employees. Second, each performance standard is measured on a scale where appraisers can check the point that best represents the employee's performance. In this way, performance variation is described along a continuum from good to bad. It is the types of descriptors used in anchoring this continuum that provide the major difference in rating scales.

These descriptors may be adjectives, behaviors, or outcomes. When adjectives are used as anchors, the format is called a *standard rating scale*. Exhibit 11.4 shows a typical rating scale with adjectives as anchors ("well above average" to "well below average").

---

[13]Daniel Ilgen and Jack Feldman, "Performance Appraisal: A Process Focus," *Research in Organizational Behavior*, vol. 5 (1983), pp. 141–97.

Exhibit 11.3 Three Ranking Formats

Straight Ranking Method

Rank	*Employee's Name*
Best	1. ________
Next Best	2. ________
Next Best	3. ________
etc.	

Alternation Ranking

Rank	*Employee's Name*
Best performer	1. ________
Next best	2. ________
Next best	3. ________
etc.	4. ________
Next worst	3. ________
Next worst	2. ________
Worst performer	1. ________

(alternate identifying best then worst, next best then next worst, etc.)

Paired Comparison Ranking Method

	John	*Pete*	*Sam*	*Tom*	*# times ranked higher*
Bill	x	x	x	x	4
John		x	x	x	3
Pete			x	x	2
Sam				x	1

x indicates person in row ranked higher than person in column. Highest ranking goes to person with most "ranking wins."

Exhibit 11.4 Rating Scales Using Absolute Standards

Standard Rating Scale with Adjective Anchors

Communications skills: Written and oral ability to clearly and convincingly express thoughts, ideas, or facts in individual or group situations.

Circle the number that best describes the level of employee performance	1	2	3	4	5
	well above average	above average	average	below average	well below average

Behaviorally anchored rating scales (BARS) seem to be the most common behavioral format, although there are variants on this scale and small differences in construction and explanation. BARS help to more completely rate an employee's performance. Manager A and manager B could both have met their individual objectives, but we don't know what means they used to attain them, nor do we know how difficult these objectives were in comparison to each other. Without this knowledge, ratings can't be used to compare the achievements of these two managers.[14] By anchoring scales with concrete behaviors, firms adopting a BARS format hope to make evaluations less subjective. When raters try to decide on a rating, they have a common definition (in the form of a behavioral example) for each of the performance levels. Consider, as an example, the following behaviors as recorded on fictitious officer fitness reports for the British Royal Navy. They are easily identifiable and, hopefully, humorous:

> "This Officer reminds me very much of a gyroscope—always spinning around at a frantic pace, but not really going anywhere."
>
> "He would be out of his depth in a car park puddle."
>
> "Works well when under constant supervision and cornered like a rat in a trap."
>
> "This man is depriving a village somewhere of an idiot."
>
> "Only occasionally wets himself under pressure."[15]

This rating format directly addresses a major criticism of standard rating scales: Different raters carry with them into the rating situation different definitions of the scale levels (e.g., different raters have different ideas about what "average work" is). Exhibit 11.5 illustrates a behaviorally anchored rating scale.

In both the standard rating scale and BARS, overall performance is calculated as some weighted average (weighted by the importance the organization attaches to each dimension) of the ratings on all dimensions. The appendices to this chapter give examples of rating scales and the total appraisal form for some well-known organizations. As a brief illustration, though, consider Exhibit 11.6.

The employee evaluated in Exhibit 11.6 is rated slightly above average. An alternative method for obtaining the overall rating would be to allow the rater discretion not only in rating performance on the individual dimensions, but in assigning an overall evaluation. Then, the weights (shown in the far right column of Exhibit 11.6) would not be used and an overall evaluation would be based on a subjective and internal assessment by the rater.

In addition to adjectives and behaviors, *outcomes* also are used as a standard. The most common form is management by objectives (MBO). Management by objectives is both a planning and appraisal tool that has many different variations across firms.[16] As a first step, organization objectives are identified from the strategic plan of the company.

---

[14]Lloyd S. Baird, Richard W. Beatty, Craig Eric Schneider, and Douglas G. Shaw, *The Performance, Measurement, Management, and Appraisal Sourcebook* (Amherst, MA: Human Resources Development Press, 1995).

[15]Royal Navy and Marines fitness reports form S206.

[16]Mark L. McConkie, "A Clarification of the Goal Setting and Appraisal Processes in MBO," *Academy of Management Review* 4, no. 1 (1979), pp. 29–40.

Exhibit 11.5 Standard Rating Scale with Behavioral Scale Anchors

Teamwork:		Ability to contribute to group performance, to draw out the best from others, to foster activities building group morale, even under high pressure situations.
Exceeds Standards	1	Seeks out or is regularly requested for group assignments. Groups this person works with inevitably have high performance and high morale. Employee makes strong personal contribution and is able to identify strengths of many different types of group members and foster their participation. Wards off personality conflicts by positive attitude and ability to mediate unhealthy conflicts, sometimes even before they arise. Will make special effort to insure credit for group performance is shared by all.
	2	Seen as a positive contributor in group assignments. Works well with all types of people and personalities, occasionally elevating group performance of others. Good ability to resolve unhealthy group conflicts that flare up. Will make special effort to insure strong performers receive credit due them.
Meets Standards	3	Seen as a positive personal contributor in group assignments. Works well with most types of people and personalities. Is never a source of unhealthy group conflict and will encourage the same behavior in others.
	4	When group mission requires skill this person is strong in, employee seen as strong contributor. On other occasions will not hinder performance of others. Works well with most types of people and personalities and will not be the initiator of unhealthy group conflict. Will not participate in such conflict unless provoked on multiple occasions.
	5	Depending on the match of personal skill and group mission, this person will be seen as a positive contributor. Will not be a hindrance to performance of others and avoids unhealthy conflict unless provoked.
Does Not Meet Standards	6	Unlikely to be chosen for assignments requiring teamwork except on occasions where personal expertise is vital to group mission. Not responsive to group goals, but can be enticed to help when personal appeals are made. May not get along with other members and either withdraw or generate unhealthy conflict. Seeks personal recognition for team performance and/or may downplay efforts of others.
	7	Has reputation for noncontribution and for creating conflicts in groups. Cares little about group goals and is very hard to motivate towards goal completion unless personal rewards are guaranteed. May undermine group performance to further personal aims. Known to seek personal recognition and/or downplay efforts of others.
Rating:		Documentation of Rating (optional except for 6 and 7):

Each successively lower level in the organizational hierarchy is charged with identifying work objectives that will support attainment of organizational goals. Exhibit 11.7 illustrates a common MBO objective. Notice that the emphasis is on outcomes achieved by employees. At the beginning of a performance review period, the employee and supervisor discuss performance objectives (column 1).[17] Months later, at the end of the review period, the two again meet to record results formally (of course, multiple informal discussions should have occurred before this time). Results are then compared against

[17]Mark L. McConkie, "A Clarification of the Goal Setting and Appraisal Processes in MBO," *Academy of Management Review* 4, no. 1 (1979), pp. 29–40.

EXHIBIT 11.6 An Example of Employee Appraisal

Employee: Kelsey T. Mahoney
Job Title: Supervisor, Shipping and Receiving

Performance Dimension	Dimension Rating					Dimension Weight
	Well Below Average 1	*Below Average 2*	*Average 3*	*Above Average 4*	*Well Above Average 5*	
Leadership ability				×		0.2 (× 4) = 0.8
Job Knowledge					×	0.1 (× 5) = 0.5
Work Output				×		0.3 (× 4) = 1.2
Attendance			×			0.2 (× 3) = 0.6
Initiative			×			0.2 (× 3) = 0.6

Sum of Rating × weight = 3.7
Overall Rating = 3.7

EXHIBIT 11.7 Example of MBO Objective for Communications Skill

1. Performance objective	2. Results
By July 1 of this year Bill will complete a report summarizing employee reactions to the new performance appraisal system. An oral presentation will be prepared and delivered to all non-exempt employees in groups of 15–20. All oral presentations will be completed by August 31, and reactions of employees to this presentation will average at least 3.0 on a 5-point scale.	Written report completed by July 1. All but one oral presentation completed by August 31. Last report not completed until September 15 because of unavoidable conflicts in vacation schedules. Average rating of employees (reaction to oral presentation) was 3.4, exceeding minimum expectations.

objectives, and a performance rating is then determined based on how well objectives were met.

A review of firms using MBO indicates generally positive improvements in performance both for individuals and the organization. This performance increase is accompanied by managerial attitudes toward MBO that become more positive over time, particularly when the system is revised periodically to reflect feedback of participants. Managers are especially pleased with the way that MBO provides direction to work units, improves the planning process, and increases superior/subordinate communication. On the negative side, MBO appears to require more paperwork and increase both performance pressure and stress.[18]

[18]J. S. Hodgson, "Management by Objectives: The Experiences of a Federal Government Department," *Canadian Public Administration* 16, no. 4 (1973), pp. 422–31.

Exhibit 11.8 shows some of the common components of an MBO format and the percentage of experts who judge this component vital to a successful evaluation effort.

A final type of appraisal format does not easily fall into any of the categories yet discussed. In an *essay format*, supervisors answer open-ended questions in essay form describing employee performance. Since the descriptors used could range from comparisons with other employees to the use of adjectives describing performance, types of behaviors, and goal accomplishments, the essay format can take on characteristics of all the formats discussed previously.

Exhibit 11.9 illustrates the relative popularity for these formats in industry.

EXHIBIT 11.8 Components of a Successful MBO Program

	*Total Number of Responses**	*Percentage of Authorities in Agreement*
1. Goals and objectives should be specific.	37	97%
2. Goals and objectives should be defined in terms of measurable results.	37	97
3. Individual goals should be linked to overall organization goals.	37	97
4. Objectives should be reviewed "periodically."	31	82
5. The time period for goal accomplishment should be specified.	27	71
6. Wherever possible, the indicator of the results should be quantifiable; otherwise, it should be at least verifiable.	26	68
7. Objectives should be flexible; changed as conditions warrant.	26	68
8. Objectives should include a plan of action for accomplishing the results.	21	55
9. Objectives should be assigned priorities of weights.	19	50

*In this table the total number of responses actually represents the total number of authorities responding; thus, percentages also represent the percentage of authorities in agreement with the statements made.

Source: Mark L. McConkie, "A Clarification of the Goal Setting and Appraisal Process in MBO," Academy of Management Review 4, no. 1 (1979), pp. 29–40. © 1979, Academy of Management Review.

EXHIBIT 11.9 Usage of Performance Evaluation Formats

Type of System	**Usage (%) by Type of Employee**	
	Nonexempt	*Exempt*
1. Standard Rating Scale	52	32
2. Essay	30	3
3. Management by objectives or other objective-based system	19	73
4. Behaviorally Anchored Scale	28	24
5. Other	33	32

Percentages total more than 100 percent because of multiple systems in different companies.

Source: Based on a survey of 256 firms from a population of 1,300 large organizations completed by Drake, Beam and Morin, New York, 1983.

Evaluating Performance Appraisal Formats. Appraisal formats are generally evaluated against five criteria: (1) employee development potential (amount of feedback about performance that the format offers), (2) administrative ease, (3) personnel research potential, (4) cost, and (5) validity. Admittedly, different organizations will attach different weights to these dimensions. For example, a small organization in its formative years is likely to be very cost conscious. A large organization with pressing affirmative action commitments might place relatively high weight on validity and nondiscrimination and show less concern about cost issues. A progressive firm concerned with employee development might demand a format allowing substantial employee feedback. Other organizations may be concerned solely with costs. These criteria are explained below.[19]

Employee Development Criterion. Does the method communicate the goals and objectives of the organization? Is feedback to employees a natural outgrowth of the evaluation format, so that employee developmental needs are identified and can be attended to readily?

Administrative Criterion. How easily can evaluation results be used for administrative decisions concerning wage increases, promotions, demotions, terminations, and transfers? Comparisons among individuals for personnel action require some common denominator for comparison. Typically this is a numerical rating of performance. Evaluation forms that do not produce numerical ratings cause administrative headaches.

Personnel Research Criterion. Does the instrument lend itself well to validating employment tests? Can applicants predicted to perform well be monitored through performance evaluation? Similarly, can the success of various employees and organizational development programs be traced to impacts on employee performance? As with the administrative criterion, though, evaluations typically need to be quantitative to permit the statistical tests so common in personnel research.

Cost Criterion. Does the evaluation form require a long time to develop initially? Is it time-consuming for supervisors to use in rating their employees? Is it expensive to use? All of these factors increase the format cost.

Validity Criterion. By far the most research on formats in recent years has focused on reducing error and improving accuracy. Success in this pursuit would mean that decisions based on performance ratings (e.g., promotions, merit increases) could be made with increased confidence. In general, the search for the perfect format to eliminate rating errors and improve accuracy has been unsuccessful. The high acclaim, for example, accompanying the introduction of BARS has not been supported by research.[20]

---

[19]Bruce McAfee and Blake Green, "Selecting a Performance Appraisal Method," *Personnel Administrator* 22, no. 5 (1977), pp. 61–65.

[20]H. John Bernardin, "Behavioral Expectation Scales v. Summated Ratings: A Fairer Comparison," *Journal of Applied Psychology* 62 (1977), pp. 422–27; H. John Bernardin, Kim Alvares, and C. J. Cranny, "A Re-comparison of Behavioral Expectation Scales to Summated Scales," *Journal of Applied Psychology* 61 (1976), pp. 284–91; C. A. Schriesheim and U. E. Gattiker, "A Study of the Abstract Desirability of Behavior-Based v. Trait-Oriented Performance Rating," *Proceedings of the Academy of Management* 43 (1982), pp. 307–11; and F. S. Landy and J. L. Farr, "Performance Rating," *Psychological Bulletin* 87 (1980), pp. 72–107.

Exhibit 11.10 provides a report card on the five most common rating formats relative to the criteria just discussed.

Which of these appraisal formats is the best? Unfortunately, the answer is a murky "it depends." Keeley suggests that the choice of an appraisal format is dependent on the type of tasks being performed.[21] He argues that tasks can be ordered along a continuum from those that are very routine to those for which the appropriate behavior for goal accomplishment is very uncertain. In Keeley's view, different appraisal formats require assumptions about the extent to which correct behavior for task accomplishment can be specified. The choice of an appraisal format requires a matching of formats with tasks that meet the assumptions for that format. At one extreme of the continuum are behavior-based evaluation procedures that define specific performance expectations against which employee performance is evaluated. Keeley argues behaviorally anchored rating scales fall into this category. The behavioral anchors specify performance expectations representing different levels of performance possible by an employee. Only for highly routine, mechanistic tasks is it appropriate to specify behavioral expectations. For these routine tasks it is possible to identify the single sequence of appropriate behaviors to accomplish a goal. Consequently, it is possible to identify behavioral anchors for a performance scale that illustrate varying levels of attainment of the proper sequence of activities.

However, when tasks become less routine, it becomes more difficult to specify a single sequence of procedures that must be followed to accomplish a goal. Rather, multiple strategies are both feasible and appropriate to reach a final goal. Under these circumstances, Keeley argues the appraisal format should focus on evaluating the extent to which the final goal can be specified.[22] Thus, for less certain tasks an MBO strategy would be appropriate. As long as the final goal can be specified, performance can be evaluated in relation to that goal without specifying or evaluating the behavior used to reach that goal. The focus is exclusively on the degree of goal accomplishment.

At the other extreme of the continuum are tasks that are highly uncertain in nature. A relatively low consensus exists about the characteristics of successful performance. Moreover, the nature of the task is so uncertain it may be difficult to specify expected goals. For this type of task, Keeley argues that judgment-based evaluation procedures—as exemplified by standard rating scales—may be most appropriate. Raters make subjective estimates about the levels of employee performance on tasks for which neither the appropriate behavior nor the final goal are well specified. The extent of this uncertainty makes this type of appraisal very subjective and may well explain why trait-rating scales are openly criticized for the number of errors that result in performance evaluation.

Strategy Two: Select the Right Raters

A second way that firms have tried to improve the accuracy of performance ratings is to focus on who might conduct the ratings and which of these sources is more likely to be

[21]Michael Keeley, "A Contingency Framework for Performance Evaluation," *Academy of Management Review* 3 (July 1978), pp. 428–38.

[22]Ibid.

EXHIBIT 11.10 An Evaluation of Performance Appraisal Formats

	Employee Development Criterion	*Administration Criterion*	*Personnel Research Criterion*	*Economic Criterion*	*Validity Criterion*
Ranking	Poor—ranks typically based on overall performance, with little thought given to feedback on specific performance dimensions.	Poor—comparisons of ranks across work units to determine merit raises are meaningless. Other administrative actions similarly hindered.	Average—validation studies can be completed with rankings of performance.	Good—inexpensive source of performance data. Easy to develop and use in small organizations and in small units.	Average—good reliability but poor on rating errors, especially halo.
Standard rating scales	Average—general problem areas identified. Some information on extent of developmental need is available, but no feedback on necessary behaviors/outcomes.	Average—ratings valuable for merit increase decisions and others. Not easily defended if contested.	Average—validation studies can be completed, but level of measurement contamination unknown.	Good—inexpensive to develop and easy to use.	Average—content validity is suspect. Rating errors and reliability are average.
Behaviorally anchored rating scales	Good—extent of problem and behavioral needs are identified.	Good—BARS good for making administrative decisions. Useful for legal defense because job relevant.	Good—validation studies can be completed and measurement problems on BARS less than many other criterion measures.	Average—expensive to develop but easy to use.	Good—high content validity. Some evidence of inter-rater reliability and reduced rating errors.
Management by objectives	Excellent—extent of problem and outcome deficiencies are identified.	Poor—MBO not suited to merit income decisions. Level of completion and difficulty of objectives hard to compare across employees.	Poor—nonstandard objectives across employees and no overall measures of performance make validity studies difficult.	Poor—expensive to develop and time-consuming to use.	Excellent—high content validity. Low rating errors.
Essay	Unknown—depends on guidelines or inclusions in essay as developed by organization or supervisors.	Poor—essays not comparable across different employees considered for merit or other administrative actions.	Poor—no quantitative indices to compare performance against employee test scores in validation studies.	Average—easy to develop but time-consuming to use.	Unknown—unstructured format makes studies of essay method difficult.

accurate. A method known as 360-degree feedback has grown more popular in recent years. Generally, this system is used in conjunction with supervisory reviews.[23] This method assesses employee performance from five points of view: supervisor, peer, self, customer, and subordinate. The flexibility of this process makes it appealing to employees at all levels within an organization; most companies using this system report that their employees are satisfied with its results.[24] They felt that the 360-degree system out-performed their old systems in improving employee understanding and self-awareness, promoting communication between supervisors and staff, and promoting better performance and results.[25] Regardless of the positive responses from those who have implemented the 360-degree feedback system, today most companies still only use it for evaluation of their top level personnel[26] and for employee development rather than for appraisal or pay decisions.[27] Let's take a closer look at the role and benefit of each of these raters.

Supervisors as Raters. Who rates employees? Some estimates indicate more than 80 percent of the input for performance ratings comes from supervisors.[28] There is good reason supervisors play such a dominant role. Supervisors assign (or jointly determine) what work employees are to perform. This makes a supervisor knowledgeable about the job and the dimensions to be rated. Also, supervisors frequently have considerable prior experience in rating employees, thus giving them some pretty firm ideas about what level of performance is required for any given level of performance rating.[29] Supervisor ratings also tend to be more reliable than those from other sources.[30] On the negative side, though, supervisors are particularly prone to halo and leniency errors.[31]

Peers as Raters. One of the major strengths of using peers as raters is that they work more closely with the ratee and probably have an undistorted perspective of typical performance, particularly in group assignments (as opposed to what a supervisor might observe in a casual stroll around the work area). Balanced against this positive are at least two powerful negatives. First, peers may have little or no experience in conducting appraisals, leading to rather mixed evidence about the reliability of this rating source.

---

[23]Mark R. Edwards and Ann J. Ewen, *360 Degree Feedback: The Powerful New Model for Employee Assessment and Performance Improvement* (Toronto: American Management Association, 1996).

[24]Ibid.

[25]Ibid.

[26]IOMA, *Ioma Pay For Performance Report,* March 1997, p. 8.

[27]Mark R. Edwards and Ann J. Ewen, *360 Degree Feedback: The Powerful New Model for Employee Assessment and Performance Improvement* (Toronto: American Management Association, 1996).

[28]Susan E. Jackson, Randall S. Schuller and J. Carlos Rivero. "Organizational Characteristics as Predictors of Personnel Practices," *Personnel Psychology* 42, (1989) pp. 727–86.

[29]E. Pulakos and W. Borman, *Developing the Basic Criterion Scores for Army-wide and MOS-specific Ratings*. (Alexandria, VA: U.S. Army Research Institute).

[30]Deniz S. Ones, Frank L. Schmidt, and Chockalingam Viswesvaran, "Comparative Analysis of the Reliability of Job Performance Ratings," *Journal of Applied Psychology* 81, no. 5 (1996), pp. 557–574.

[31]F.S. Landy and J.L. Farr, "Performance Rating," *Psychological Bulletin 87* (1980), pp. 72–107;

Second, in a situation where teamwork is promoted, placing the burden of rating peers on coworkers can either create group tensions (in the case of low evaluations) or yield ratings second only to self-ratings in level of leniency.[32] However, Motorola, one of the leaders in the use of teams and in peer ratings, reports that peer ratings help team members exert pressure on fellow workers to perform better.[33]

Self as Rater. Some organizations have experimented with self-ratings. Obviously self-ratings are done by someone who has the most complete knowledge about the ratee's performance. Unfortunately, though, self-ratings are generally more lenient and possibly more unreliable than ratings from other sources.[34] One compromise in the use of self-ratings is to use them for developmental rather than administrative purposes. Increasingly firms are asking employees to rate themselves as the first step in the appraisal process. Forcing employees to think about their performance in advance may lead to more realistic assessments, ones that are also more in tune with a supervisor's own perceptions.

Customer as Rater. This is the decade of the customer. The drive for quality means more companies are recognizing the importance of customers. One logical outcome of this increased interest is ratings from customers. For example, Burger King surveys its customers, sets up 800 numbers to get feedback, and hires mystery customers to order food and report back on the service and treatment they receive. Increasingly we can expect the boundaries between organizations and the outside world to fade. While much of the customer-rating movement is directed at performance of business units, we can expect some of this to distill down to individual workers.

Subordinate as Rater. Historically, upward feedback has been viewed as countercultural, but the culture within organizations has undergone a revolution in the past 10 years and views are everchanging.[35] The notion of subordinates as raters is appealing since most employees want to be successful with the people who report to them. Hearing how they are viewed by their subordinates gives them the chance to see both their strengths and weaknesses as a leader and to modify their behavior.[36] The difficulty with this type of rating is in attaining candid reviews and also with counseling the ratee on how to deal with the feedback. Changes in behavior will not necessarily occur, but proper training can help to elicit change based on subordinates' feedback.

---

[32]M.M. Harris and J. Schaubroeck, "A Meta Analysis of Self-supervisor, Self-peer and Peer-supervisor ratings," *Personnel Psychology* 4 (1988), pp. 43–62.

[33]Personal communication from Jack Barry, Director of Compensation, Motorola, May 20, 1997.

[34]Harris and Schaubroeck, "A Meta Analysis of Self-supervisor, Self-peer and Peer-supervisor Ratings."

[35]Mark R. Edwards and Ann J. Ewen, *360 Degree Feedback: The Powerful New Model for Employee Assessment and Performance Improvement* (Toronto: American Management Association, 1996).

[36]William L. Bearly, and John E. Jones, *360 Degree Feedback: Strategies, Tactics, and Techniques for Developing Leaders* (Amherst, MA: HRD Press, 1996).

The American Compensation Association has an extensive web site, including the address noted below. Go to this address if you want information about other books on performance measurement, including books that talk about the advantages and disadvantages of using multiple raters. **http://www.acaonline.org/bookstore/generic/html/ acabookfra004000.html**

Strategy Three: Understand Why Raters Make Mistakes

A third way to improve job performance ratings is to understand how raters think. When we observe and evaluate performance, what else influences ratings besides an employee's performance? We know, for example, that feelings, attitudes, and moods influence raters. If your supervisor likes you, independent of how well you perform, you are likely to get better ratings.[37] Your boss's general mood also influences performance ratings. Hope for a rater who is generally cheerful rather than grumpy; it could influence how you are evaluated.[38] Interestingly, when researchers examined ratings, they found that administrative ratings tended to be more lenient, while research ratings were significantly more accurate. Essentially, administrative ratings seem to be more directly related to the human involved, so the rater is more prone to error, whereas research ratings seem to be removed from the person who will be affected by the appraisal, and thus are more commonly related to predictors.[39]

Researchers continue to explore how raters process information about the performance of the people they rate. In general, we think the following kinds of processes occur. First, the rater observes behavior of a ratee. Second, the rater encodes this behavior as part of a total picture of the ratee (i.e., one way of saying that the rater forms stereotypes). Third, the rater stores this information in memory, which is subject to both short- and long-term decay. Simply put, they forget things. Fourth, when it comes time to evaluate a ratee, the rater reviews the performance dimensions and retrieves stored observations/impressions to determine their relevance to the performance dimensions. Finally, the information is reconsidered and integrated with other available information as the rater decides on the final ratings.[40] Quite unintentionally, this process can produce information errors and they can occur at any stage.

---

[37]R.L. Cardy and G.H. Dobbins, "Affect and Appraisal Accuracy: Liking as an Integral Dimension in Evaluating Performance," *Journal of Applied Psychology* 71 (1986), pp. 672–678; Robert C. Liden and Sandy J. Wayne, "Effect of Impression Management on Performance Ratings: A Longitudinal Study," *Academy of Management Journal* 38, no. 1 (1995), pp. 232–260; Angelo S. Denisi, Lawrence H. Peters, and Arup Varma, "Interpersonal Affect and Performance Appraisal: A Field Study," *Personnel Psychology* 49 (1996), pp. 341–360.

[38]G. Alliger and K.J. Williams, "Affective Congruence and the Employment Interview." In *Advances in Information Processing in Organizations,* vol. 4, ed. J.R. Meindl, R.L. Cardy and S.M. Puffer (Greenwich, CT: JAI Press).

[39]Denise Champagne, Michael M. Harris, and David E. Smith, "A Field Study of Performance Appraisal Purpose: Research- Versus Administrative-Based Ratings," *Personnel Psychology* 48 (1995), pp. 151–160.

[40]Landy and Farr, "Performance Rating"; A.S. Denisi, T. P. Cafferty, and B.M. Meglino, "A Cognitive View of the Performance Appraisal Process: A Model and Research Propositions," *Organizational Behavior and Human Performance* 33 (1984), pp. 360–96; Jack M. Feldman, "Beyond Attribution Theory: Cognitive Processes in Performance Appraisal," *Journal of Applied Psychology* 66, no. 2 (1981), pp. 127–48; and W. H. Cooper, "Ubiquitous Halo," *Psychological Bulletin* 90 (1981), pp. 218–44.

Errors in the Rating Process. Ideally raters should notice only performance-related factors when they observe employee behavior. In fact all of the processing stages should be guided by *performance relevancy*. Unless a behavior (or personality trait) affects performance it should not influence performance ratings. Fortunately, studies show that performance actually does play an important role, perhaps the major role, in determining how a supervisor rates a subordinate.[41] Employees who are technically proficient and who do not create problems on the job tend to receive higher ratings than others who score lower on these dimensions.[42] On the negative side, though, performance-irrelevant factors appear to influence ratings, and they can cause errors in the evaluation process.[43]

Errors in Observation (Attention). Generally, researchers have varied three types of input information to see what raters pay attention to when they are collecting information for performance appraisals. First, it appears that raters are influenced by general appearance characteristics of the ratees. Males are rated higher than females (other things being equal). A female ratee is observed, not as a ratee, but as a female ratee. A rater may form impressions based on stereotypic beliefs about women rather than the reality of the work situation and quite apart from any performance information. Females are rated less accurately when the rater has a traditional view of women's "proper" role; raters without traditional stereotypes of women are not prone to such errors.[44] Race also matters in performance ratings; ratings are higher when the rater is of the same race.[45] In general, it seems that if supervisors see ratees as similar to themselves, there is a positive influence on performance ratings, independent of actual performance.[46]

---

[41]Angelo Denisi and George Stevens, "Profiles of Performance, Performance Evaluations, and Personnel Decisions," *Academy of Management* 24, no. 3 (1981), pp. 592–602; Wayne Cascio and Enzo Valenzi, "Relations among Criteria of Police Performance," *Journal of Applied Psychology* 63, no. 1 (1978), pp. 22–28; William Bigoness, "Effects of Applicant's Sex, Race, and Performance on Employer Performance Ratings: Some Additional Findings," *Journal of Applied Psychology* 61, no. 1 (1976), pp. 80–84; Dorothy P. Moore, "Evaluating In-Role and Out-of-Role Performers," *Academy of Management Journal* 27, no. 3 (1984), pp. 603–18;W. Borman, L. White, E. Pulakos & S. Oppler, "Models of Supervisory Job Performance Ratings". *Journal of Applied Psychology* 76, no. 6 (1991), pp. 863–872.

[42]W. Borman, L. White, E. Pulakos & S. Oppler, "Models of Supervisory Job Performance Ratings," *Journal of Applied Psychology* 76, no. 6 (1991), pp. 863–872.

[43]H. J. Bernardin and Richard Beatty, *Performance Appraisal: Assessing Human Behavior at Work* (Boston: Kent Publishing, 1984).

[44]G. Dobbins, R. Cardy and D. Truxillo, "The Effects of Purpose of Appraisal and Individual Differences in Stereotypes of Women on Sex Differences in Performance Ratings: A Laboratory and Field Study," *Journal of Applied Psychology* 73, no. 3 (1988), pp. 551–558.

[45]Edward Shaw, "Differential Impact of Negative Stereotyping in Employee Selection," *Personnel Psychology* 25 (1972), pp. 333–38; Benson Rosen and Thomas Jurdee, "Effects of Applicant's Sex and Difficulty of Job on Evaluations of Candidates for Managerial Positions," *Journal of Applied Psychology* 59 (1975), pp. 511–12; Gail Pheterson, Sara Kiesler, and Philip Goldberg, "Evaluation of the Performance of Women as a Function of Their Sex, Achievement, and Personal History," *Journal of Personality and Social Psychology* 19 (1971), pp. 114–18; W. Clay Hamner, Jay Kim, Lloyd Baird, and William Bigoness, "Race and Sex as Determinants of Ratings by Potential Employers in a Simulated Work Sampling Task," *Journal of Applied Psychology* 59, no. 6 (1974), pp. 705–11; and Neal Schmitt and Martha Lappin, "Race and Sex as Determinants of the Mean and Variance of Performance Ratings," *Journal of Applied Psychology* 65, no. 4 (1980), pp. 428–35.

[46]D. Turban and A. Jones, "Supervisor-subordinate Similarity: Types, Effects and Mechanisms." *Journal of Applied Psychology*. 73, no. 2 (1988), pp. 228–234.

Researchers also look at change in performance over time to see if this influences performance ratings. Both the pattern of performance (performance gets better vs. worse over time) and the variability of performance (consistent vs. erratic) influence performance ratings, even when the overall level of performance is controlled.[47] Workers who start out high in performance and then get worse are rated lower than workers who remain consistently low.[48] Not surprisingly, workers whose performance improves over time are seen as more motivated, while those who are more variable in their performance are tagged as lower in motivation. All of us have seen examples of workers and students who intuitively recognize this type of error and use it to their advantage. The big surge of work at the end of an appraisal period is often designed to "color" a rater's perceptions.

Errors in Storage and Recall. Research suggests that raters store information in the form of traits.[49] More importantly, people also tend to recall information in the form of trait categories. For example, a rater observes a specific behavior such as an employee resting during work hours. The rater stores this information not as the specific behavior, but rather in the form of a trait, such as, that worker is lazy. Specific instructions to recall information about the ratee, as for a performance review, elicit the trait—lazy. Further, in the process of recalling information, a rater may remember events that didn't actually occur, simply because they are consistent with the trait category.[50] The entire rating process then, may be heavily influenced by these trait categories that the rater adopts, regardless of their accuracy.

Errors in storage and recall also appear to arise from memory decay. At least one study indicates that rating accuracy is a function of the delay between performance and subsequent rating. The longer the delay, the less accurate the ratings.[51] Some research suggests that memory decay can be avoided if raters keep a diary and record information about employee performance as it occurs.[52]

---

[47]Denisi and Stevens, "Profiles of Performance, Performance Evaluations, and Personnel Decisions"; William Scott and Clay Hamner, "The Influence of Variations in Performance Profiles on the Performance Evaluation Process: An Examination of the Validity of the Criterion," *Organizational Behavior and Human Performance* 14 (1975), pp. 360–70; and Edward Jones, Leslie Rock, Kelly Shaver, George Goethals, and Laurence Ward, "Pattern of Performance and Ability Attributions: An Unexpected Primacy Effect," *Journal of Personality and Social Psychology* 10, no. 4 (1968), pp. 317–40.

[48]B. Gaugler, & A. Rudolph, "The Influence of Assessee Performance Variation on Assessor's Judgments," *Personnel Psychology* 45 (1992), pp. 77–98.

[49]Landy and Farr, "Performance Rating"; Bernardin and Beatty, *Performance Appraisal: Assessing Human Behavior at Work.*

[50]N. Cantor and W. Mischel, "Traits v. Prototypes: The Effects on Recognition and Memory," *Journal of Personality and Social Psychology* 35 (1977), pp. 38–48; R. J. Spiro, "Remembering Information from Text: The `State of Schema' Approach," in *Schooling and the Acquisition of Knowledge*, eds. R.C. Anderson, R. J. Spiro, and W. E. Montague (Hillsdale, CA: Erlbaum Assoc., 1977); and T.K. Srull and R.S. Wyer, "Category Accessibility and Social Perception: Some Implications for the Study of Person Memory and Interpersonal Judgments," *Journal of Personality and Social Psychology* 38 (1980), pp. 841–56.

[51]Robert Heneman and Kenneth Wexley, "The Effects of Time Delay in Rating and Amount of Information Observed on Performance Rating Accuracy," *Academy of Management Journal* 26, no. 4 (1983), pp. 677–86.

[52]B.P. Maroney and R.M. Buckely, "Does Research in Performance Appraisal Influence the Practice of Performance Appraisal? Regretfully Not." *Public Personnel Management* 21 (1992), pp. 185–196.

Errors in the Actual Evaluation. The context of the actual evaluation process also can influence evaluations.[53] Several researchers indicate that the purpose of an evaluation affects the rating process.[54] For example, performance appraisals sometimes serve a political end. Supervisors have been known to deflate performance to send a signal to an employee—You're not wanted here.[55] Supervisors also tend to weigh negative attributes more heavily than positive attributes; you are likely to receive a much lower score if you perform poorly, than you are to receive a proportionally higher score if you perform well.[56]

If the purpose of evaluation is to divide up a fixed pot of merit increases, ratings also tend to be less accurate. Supervisors who know ratings will be used to determine merit increases are less likely to differentiate among subordinates than when the ratings will be used for other purposes.[57] Being required to provide feedback to subordinates about their ratings also yields less accuracy than a secrecy policy.[58] Presumably anticipation of an unpleasant confrontation with the angry ratee persuades the rater to avoid confrontation by giving ratings higher than are justified. However, when raters must justify their scoring of subordinates in writing, the rating is more accurate.[59]

TRAINING RATERS TO RATE MORE ACCURATELY

Although there is some evidence that training is not effective,[60] or is less important in reducing errors than other factors,[61] most research indicates rater training is an effective method to reduce appraisal errors.[62] Rater-training programs can be divided into three

[53]Robert Liden and Terence Mitchell, "The Effects of Group Interdependence on Supervisor Performance Evaluations," *Personnel Psychology* 36, no. 2 (1983), pp. 289–99.

[54]See, for example, Dobbins, Cardy and Truxillo, "The Effects of Purpose of Appraisal and Individual Differences in Stereotypes of Women on Sex Differences in Performance Ratings: A Laboratory and Field Study."

[55]G.R. Ferris and T.A. Judge, "Personnel/Human Resource Management: A Political Influence Perspective," *Journal of Management* 17 (1991), pp. 1–42.

[56]Yoav Ganzach, "Negativity (and Positivity) in Performance Evaluation: Three Field Studies," *Journal of Applied Psychology* 80, no. 4 (1995), pp. 491–499.

[57]Winstanley, "How Accurate are Performance Appraisals?"; Landy and Farr, "Performance Rating"; and Heneman and Wexley, "The Effects of Time Delay in Rating and Amount of Information Observed on Performance Rating Accuracy."

[58]Cummings and Schwab, *Performance in Organizations.*

[59]Neal P. Mero, and Stephan J. Motowidlo, "Effects of Rater Accountability on the Accuracy and the Favorability of Performance Ratings," *Journal of Applied Psychology* 80, no. 4 (1995), pp. 517–524,

[60]H.J. Bernardin and E.C. Pence, "Effects of Rater Training: Creating New Response Sets and Decreasing Accuracy," *Journal of Applied Psychology* 6 (1980), pp. 60–66.

[61]Sheldon Zedeck and Wayne Cascio, "Performance Appraisal Decision as a Function of Rater Training and Purpose of the Appraisal," *Journal of Applied Psychology* 67, no. 6 (1982), pp. 752–58.

[62]H.J. Bernardin and M.R. Buckley, "Strategies in Rater Training," *Academy of Management Review* 6, no. 2 (1981), pp. 205–12; D. Smith, "Training Programs for Performance Appraisal: A review," *Academy of Management Review* 11, no. 1 (1986), pp. 22–40; B. Davis and M. Mount, "Effectiveness of Performance Appraisal Training Using Computer Assisted Instruction and Behavioral Modeling," *Personnel Psychology* 3 (1984), pp. 439–52; H.J. Bernardin, "Effects of Rater Training on Leniency and Halo Errors in Student Ratings of Instructors," *Journal of Applied Psychology* 63, no. 3 (1978), pp. 301–8; and J.M. Ivancevich, "Longitudinal Study of the Effects of Rater Training on Psychometric Error in Ratings," *Journal of Applied Psychology* 64, no. 5 (1979), pp. 502–08.

distinct categories:[63] (1) *Rater-error training*, in which the goal is to reduce psychometric errors (e.g., leniency, severity, central tendency, halo) by familiarizing raters with their existence; (2) *performance dimension training*, which exposes supervisors to the performance dimensions to be used in rating; and (3) *performance-standard training*, which provides raters with a standard of comparison or frame of reference for making appraisals. Several generalizations about ways to improve rater training can be summarized from this research.

First, straightforward lecturing to ratees (the kind we professors are notorious for) about ways to improve the quality of their ratings generally is ineffective. Second, individualized or small group discussion sections are more effective in conveying proper rating procedures. Third, when these sessions are combined with extensive practice and feedback sessions, rating accuracy significantly improves. Fourth, longer training programs (more than 2 hours) generally are more successful than shorter programs. Fifth, performance-dimension training and performance-standard training generally work better than rater-error training, particularly when they are combined. Finally, the greatest success has come from efforts to reduce halo errors and improve accuracy. Leniency errors are the most difficult form of error to eliminate. This shouldn't be surprising. Think about the consequences to a supervisor of giving inflated ratings versus accurate or even deflated ratings. The latter two courses are certain to result in more complaints and possibly reduced employee morale. The easy way out is to artificially inflate ratings.[64] Unfortunately, this positive outcome for supervisors may come back to haunt them—with everyone receiving relatively high ratings there is less distinction between truly good and poor performers. Obviously, it is also harder to pay for real performance differences.

PUTTING IT ALL TOGETHER: THE PERFORMANCE EVALUATION PROCESS

A good performance evaluation doesn't begin on the day of the performance interview. We outline here some of the key elements in the total process, from day one, that make for a good outcome in the appraisal process.[65] First, we need a sound basis for establishing the performance appraisal dimensions and scales associated with each dimension. Performance dimensions should be relevant to the strategic plan of the company. If innovation of new products is key to success, we'd better have something in our performance dimensions that assesses individual performance. And these performance dimensions also should reflect what employees are expected to do in their jobs, that is, their job descriptions. If the job descriptions include nothing on quality (admittedly an unlikely event), the appraisal should not measure quality. Unclear job expectations are one of the most significant barriers to good performance. If an employee doesn't know what you expect of him, how can he possibly please you?[66]

[63]Bernardin and Buckley, "Strategies in Rater Training."

[64]Longnecker, Sims, and Gioia, "Behind the Mask: The Politics of Employee Appraisal."

[65]Robert Heneman, *Merit Pay: Linking Pay Increases to Performance Ratings* (Reading, MA: Addison-Wesley 1992).

[66]Ann Podolske, "Creating a Review System That Works," *IOMA's Pay For Performance Report*, March 1996, pp. 2–4.

Second, we need to involve employees in every stage of developing performance dimensions and building scales to measure how well they perform on these dimensions. In given cases, employees who were involved in all stages of these processes often received lower ratings, but had more positive reactions. They were happier with the system's fairness and the appraisal accuracy. They gave better evaluations of managers and indicated intentions to stay with their organization. Managers also responded well to this type of "due process" system. They felt they had a greater ability to resolve work problems. They had higher job satisfaction and less distortion of appraisal results to further their own interests.[67] Third, we need to make sure raters are trained in use of the appraisal system and that all employees understand how the system operates and what it will be used for. Fourth, we need to make sure raters are motivated to rate accurately. One way to achieve this is to ensure that managers are rated on how well they utilize and develop human resources. A big part of this would be evaluation and feedback to employees. Less than one-half of managers report that they provide feedback, and of those who do give feedback, most admit they are unsure if their feedback is worthwhile.[68] Regardless of the quality of feedback one receives, performance is not uniformly improved.[69]

Fifth, raters should maintain a diary of employee performance, both as documentation and to jog the memory.[70] This will help ensure that supervisors are knowledgeable about subordinate performance.[71] Sixth, raters should attempt a performance diagnosis to determine in advance if performance problems arise because of motivation, skill deficiency, or external environmental constraints;[72] this process in turn tells the supervisor whether the problem requires motivation building, training, or efforts to remove external constraints. Lastly, the actual appraisal process should follow the guidelines outlined in Exhibit 11.11.[73] At a minimum this performance measurement system should provide:

1. A clear sense of direction
2. An opportunity for employees to participate in setting the goals and standards for performance

---

[67]Stephen J. Carroll, J. Kline Harrison, Monika K. Renard, Kay B. Tracy, and M. Susan Taylor, "Due Process in Performance Appraisal: A Quasi-experiment in Procedural Justice," *Administrative Science Quarterly* 40 (1995), pp. 495–523.

[68]Ann Podolske, "Creating a Review System That Works," *IOMA's Pay For Performance Report,* March 1996, pp. 2–4.

[69]Avraham N. Kluger, and Angelo DeNisi, "The Effects of Feedback Interventions on Performance: A Historical Review, a Meta-Analysis, and a Preliminary Feedback Intervention Theory," *Psychological Bulletin* 119, no. 2 (1996), pp. 254–284.

[70]A. DeNisi, T. Robbins, and T. Cafferty. "Organization of information used for performance appraisals: Role of diary-keeping." *Journal of Applied Psychology* 74, no. 1 (1989), pp. 124–129.

[71]Angelo S. Denisi, Lawrence H. Peters, and Arup Varma, "Interpersonal Affect and Performance Appraisal: A Field Study," *Personnel Psychology* 49 (1996), pp. 341–360; F.J. Landy, J.L.Barnes and K.R. Murphy, "Correlates of Perceived Fairness and Accuracy of Performance Evaluations," *Journal of Applied Psychology* 63 (1978), pp. 751–754.

[72]S. Snell and K. Wexley, "Performance Diagnosis: Identifying the Causes of Poor Performance," *Personnel Administrator,* April 1985, pp. 117–27.

[73]Ann Podolske, "Creating a Review System That Works," *IOMA's Pay For Performance Report,* March 1996, pp. 2–4.

Exhibit 11.11 Tips on Appraising Employee Performance

Preparation for the Performance Interview

1. Keep a weekly log of individual's performance. Why?
   A. It makes the task of writing up the evaluation simpler. The rater does not have to strain to remember six months or a year ago.
   B. It reduces the chances of some rating errors (e.g., recency, halo).
   C. It gives support/backup to the rating.
2. Preparation for the interview should *not* begin a week or two before it takes place. There should be continual feedback to the employee on his/her performance so that (*a*) problems can be corrected before they get out of hand, (*b*) improvements can be made sooner, and (*c*) encouragement and support are ongoing.
3. Allow sufficient time to write up the evaluation. A well-thought-out evaluation will be more objective and equitable. Sufficient time includes (*a*) the actual time necessary to think out and write up the evaluation, (*b*) time away from the evaluation, and (*c*) time to review and possibly revise.
4. Have employees fill out an appraisal form prior to the interview. This prepares employees for what will take place in the interview and allows them to come prepared with future goal suggestions, areas they wish to pursue, and suggestions concerning their jobs or the company.
5. Set up an agreed-upon, convenient time to hold the interview (at least one week in advance). Be sure to pick a nonthreatening day.
6. Be prepared!
   A. Know what you are going to say. Prepare an outline (which includes the evaluation and future goal suggestions).
   B. Decide on developmental opportunities *before* the interview. Be sure you know of possible resources and contacts.
   C. Review performance interview steps.
7. Arrange the room in such a way as to encourage discussion.
   A. Do not have barriers between yourself and the employee (such as a large desk).
   B. Arrange with secretary that there be no phone calls or interruptions.

Performance Appraisal Interview (Steps)

1. Set the subordinate at ease. Begin by stating the purpose of the discussion. Let the individual know that it will be a two-way process. Neither the superior nor subordinate should dominate the discussion.
2. Give a general, overall impression of the evaluation.
3. Discuss each dimension separately. Ask the employee to give his/her impression on own performance first. Then explain your position. If there is a problem on some, try *together* to determine the cause. When exploring causes, urge the subordinate to identify three or four causes. Then, jointly determine the most important ones. Identifying causes is important because it points out action plans which might be taken.
4. Together, develop action plans to correct problem areas. These plans will flow naturally from the consideration of the causes. Be specific about the who, what, and when. Be sure to provide for some kind of follow-up or report back.
5. Close the interview on an optimistic note.

Communication Technique Suggestions

1. Do not control the interview—make it two-way. Do this by asking open-ended questions rather than submitting your own solutions. For example, rather than saying, "Jim, I'd like you to do these reports over again," it would be better to say, "Jim, what sort of things might we do here?" Avoid questions that lead to one-word answers.
2. Stress behaviors and results rather than personal traits. Say, "I've noticed that your weekly report has been one to two days late in the last six weeks," rather than, "You tend to be a tardy, lazy person."

EXHIBIT 11.11 ***(concluded)***

Communication Technique Suggestions

3. Show interest and concern. Instead of saying, "Too bad, but we all go through that," say, "I think I know what you're feeling. I remember a similar experience."
4. Allow the subordinate to finish a sentence or thought. This includes being receptive to the subordinate's own ideas and suggestions. For example, rather than saying, "You may have something there, but let's go back to the real problem," say, "I'm not certain I understand how that relates to this problem. Why don't you fill me in on it a bit more?"

These last four suggestions emphasize problem analysis rather than appraisal. Of course, appraisal of past performance is a part of the problem analysis, but these suggestions should lead to a more participative and less defensive subordinate role. These suggestions will also help improve creativity in problem solving. The subordinate will have a clearer understanding of why and how he/she needs to change work behavior. There should be a growth of climate of cooperation, which increases motivation to achieve performance goals.

3. Prompt, honest, and meaningful feedback
4. Immediate and sincere reinforcement
5. Coaching and suggestions for improving future performance
6. Fair and respectful treatment
7. An opportunity for employees to understand and influence decisions which affect them(6)

EQUAL EMPLOYMENT OPPORTUNITY AND PERFORMANCE EVALUATION

Equal employment opportunity (EEO) and affirmative action have influenced H.R. decision making for almost 30 years now. While there are certainly critics of these programs, at least one important trend can be traced to the civil rights vigil in the workplace. Specifically, EEO has forced organizations to document decisions and to ensure they are firmly tied to performance or expected performance. Nowhere is this more apparent than in the performance appraisal area. Performance appraisals are subject to the same scrutiny as employment tests. Consider the use of performance ratings in making decisions about promotions. In this context, a performance appraisal takes on all the characteristics of a test used to make an initial employment decision. If employees pass the test—are rated highly in the performance evaluation process—they are predicted to do well at higher level jobs. This interpretation of performance evaluation as a test, subject to validation requirements, was made in *Brito v. Zia Company*.[74] In this case, Zia Company used performance evaluations based on a rating format to lay off employees. The layoffs resulted in a disproportionate number of minorities being discharged. The court held that:

[74]*Brito v. Zia Company*, 478 F.2d. 1200 (1973).

> Zia, a government contractor, had failed to comply with the testing guidelines issued by the Secretary of Labor, and that Zia had not developed job-related criteria for evaluating employees' work performance to be used in determining employment promotion and discharges which is required to protect minority group applicants and employees from the discriminatory effects of such failure.[75]

Since the *Brito* case there has been growing evidence that the courts have very specific standards and requirements for performance appraisal.[76] The courts stress six issues in setting up a performance appraisal system.[77]

1. Courts are favorably disposed to appraisal systems that give specific written instructions on how to complete the appraisal. Presumably, more extensive training in other facets of evaluation would also be viewed favorably by the courts.
2. Organizations tend to be able to support their cases better when the appraisal system incorporates clear criteria for evaluating performance. Performance dimensions and scale levels that are written, objective, and clear tend to be viewed positively by courts in discrimination suits.[78] In part, this probably arises because behaviorally oriented appraisals have more potential to provide workers feedback about developmental needs.
3. As pointed out by every basic personnel book ever printed, and reinforced by this text, the presence of adequately developed job descriptions provides a rational foundation for personnel decision. The courts reinforce this by ruling more consistently for defendants (company) when their appraisal systems are based on sound job descriptions.
4. Courts also approve of appraisal systems that require supervisors to provide feedback about appraisal results to the employees affected. Absence of secrecy permits employees to identify weaknesses and to challenge undeserved appraisals.
5. The courts seem to like evaluation systems that incorporate a review of any performance rating by a higher level supervisor.
6. Perhaps most importantly, the courts consistently suggest that the key to fair appraisals depends on consistent treatment across raters, regardless of race, color, religion, sex, and national origin.

The focal question then becomes, Are similarly situated individuals treated similarly? This standard is particularly evident in a recent court case involving performance

---

[75]Ibid.

[76]G.L. Lubben, D.E. Thompson, and C.R. Klasson, "Performance Appraisal: The Legal Implications of Title VII," *Personnel* 57, no. 3 (1980), pp. 11–21; H. Feild and W. Halley, "The Relationship of Performance Appraisal System Characteristics to Verdicts in Selected Employment Discrimination Cases," *Academy of Management Journal* 25, no. 2 (1982), pp. 392–406; *Albermarle Paper Company v. Moody,* U.S. Supreme Court, no. 74-389 and 74-428, 10 FEP Cases 1181 (1975); also *Moody v. Albermarle Paper Company*, 474 F.3d. 134.

[77]Feild and Hally, "The Relationship of Performance Appraisal System Characteristics to Verdicts in Selected Employment Discrimination Cases"; and Gerald Barrett and Mary Kernan, "Performance Appraisal and Terminations: A Review of Court Decisions Since Brito v. Zia with Implications for Personnel Practices," *Personnel Psychology* 40 (1987), pp. 489–503.

[78]D. Martin and K. Bartol, "The Legal Ramifications of Performance Appraisal: An Update." *Employee Relations* 17, no. 2 (1991), pp. 286–93.

appraisal and merit pay.[79] A Black male filed suit against General Motors, claiming race discrimination in both the timing and amount of a merit increase. The court found this case without merit. General Motors was able to show that the same set of rules was applied equally to all individuals.

TYING PAY TO SUBJECTIVELY APPRAISED PERFORMANCE

Think, for a moment, about what it really means to give employees merit increases. Bill Peterson makes $40,000 per year. He gets a merit increase of 3 percent, the approximate average increase over the past few years. Bill's take-home increase (adjusted for taxes) is a measly $16 per week more than he used to make. Before we console Bill, though, consider Jane Krefting, who is a better performer than Bill, and receives a 6 percent merit increase. Should she be thrilled by this pay-for-performance differential and motivated to continue as a high achiever? Probably not. After taxes, her paycheck (assuming a base salary similar to Bill's) is only $15 dollars per week more than Bill's check.

The central issue involving merit pay is: How do we get employees to view raises as a reward for performance? Chapter 9 illustrated this difficulty in theoretical terms. Now it is addressed from a pragmatic perspective. Very simply, organizations frequently grant increases that are not designed or communicated to be related to performance. Perhaps the central reason for this is the way merit pay is managed. Many companies view raises not as motivational tools to shape behavior, but as budgetary line items to control costs.[80] Frequently this results in pay increase guidelines with little motivational impact. The three pay increase guidelines that particularly fit the low motivation will be discussed briefly before outlining a standard that attempts to link pay to performance.[81]

Two types of pay increase guidelines with low motivation potential are those that provide equal increases to all employees regardless of performance. The first, a general increase, typically is found in unionized firms. A contract is negotiated that specifies an across-the-board, equal increase for each year of the contract. Similar increases would occur because of cost-of-living adjustments but these would be triggered by changes in the consumer price index (Discussed in more detail in Chapter 17).

The third form of guideline comes somewhat closer to tying pay to performance. Seniority increases tie pay increases to a preset progression pattern based on seniority. For example, a pay grade might be divided into 10 equal steps, with employees moving to higher steps based on seniority. To the extent that performance improves with time on the job, this method has the rudiments of paying for performance.

By far the most prevalent form of pay guideline for exempt employees is one intended to link pay and performance.[82] Of course, the first problem we run into is, What is our measure of performance? If the measure is objective, our ability to link pay to

---

[79]*Payne v. General Motors*, 53 FEP Cases 471 (D. C. Kan. 1990).

[80]Milkovich and Milkovich, "Strengthening the Pay-for-performance Relationship . . ."

[81]*Compensating Salaried Employees During Inflation: General vs. Merit Increases* (New York: Conference Board, Report no. 796, 1981).

[82]Jackson, Schuller and Rivero, "Organizational Characteristics as Predictors of Personnel Practices."

performance is a bit easier. But here we talk about subjective measures. One set of subjective measures, as we discussed in Chapter 6, involves the competencies that people possess or acquire. Increasingly companies assert that corporate performance depends on having employees who possess key competencies. Xerox identifies 17 core competencies. As a company with strong strategic objectives linked to customer satisfaction and quality, it's not surprising to find that Xerox values such competencies as quality orientation, customer care, dependability, and teamwork. Recent trends in compensation center on finding ways to build competencies in employees. Merit increases may be linked to employee ability and willingness to demonstrate key competencies. For example, showing more of the following behaviors might be tied to higher merit increases:

Competency: Customer Care

1. Follows through on commitments to customers in a timely manner
2. Defines and communicates customer requirements
3. Resolves customer issues in a timely manner
4. Demonstrates empathy for customer feelings
5. Presents a positive image to the customer
6. Displays a professional image at all times
7. Communicates a positive image of the company and individuals to customers

In practice, tying pay to performance requires three things. First, we need some definition of performance. Whether we measure it by behaviors, competencies, or traits, there must be agreement that higher levels of performance will have positive impacts on corporate strategic objectives. Second, we need some continuum that describes different levels from low to high on the performance measure. And third, we need to decide how much of a merit increase will be given for different levels of performance. Decisions about these three questions lead to some form of merit pay guide. In its simplest form a guideline specifies pay increases permissible for different levels of performance (see Exhibit 11.12).

Increases expressed in the form of ranges may be warranted if the goal is to give supervisors some discretion in the amount of increases. A twist on this guideline would vary the time between increases. Better performers might receive increases every 8 months; the poorest performers might have to wait 15 months to two years for their next increase.

A more complex guideline ties pay not only to performance but also to position in the pay range. Exhibit 11.13 illustrates such a system for a food market firm. The

EXHIBIT 11.12 Performance-based Guideline

	1	2	*3*	*4*	5
Performance Level	Outstanding	Very Satisfactory	Satisfactory	Marginally Unsatisfactory	Unsatisfactory
Merit Increase	6–8 %	5–7 %	4–6%	2–4%	0 %

percentages in the cells of Exhibit 11.13 are changed yearly to reflect changing economic conditions. Despite these changes, though, two characteristics remain constant. First, as would be expected in a pay-for-performance system, lower performance is tied to lower pay increases. In fact, in many organizations the poorest performers receive no merit increases. The second relationship is that pay increases at a decreasing rate as employees move through a pay range. For the same level of performance, employees low in the range receive higher percentage increases than employees who have progressed farther through the range. In part this is designed to forestall the time when employees reach the salary maximum and have salaries frozen. In part, though, it is also a cost-control mechanism tied to budgeting procedures, as discussed in Chapter 18.

Performance- and Position-Based Guidelines

Given a salary increase matrix, merit increases are relatively easy to determine. As Exhibit 11.13 indicates, an employee at the top of his pay grade who receives a "competent" rating would receive a 4 percent increase in base salary. A new trainee starting out below the minimum of a pay grade would receive a 10 percent increase for a "superior" performance rating.

Designing Merit Guidelines

Designing merit guidelines involves answering four questions. First, what should the poorest performer be paid as an increase? Notice that this figure is seldom negative. Wage increases are, unfortunately, considered an entitlement. Wage cuts tied to poor performance are very rare. Most organizations, though, are willing to give no increases to very poor performers.

The second question involves average performers. How much should they be paid as an increase? Most organizations try to ensure that average performers are kept whole (wages will still have the same purchasing power) relative to cost of living. This dictates that the midpoint of the merit guidelines equals the percentage change in the local or national consumer price index (CPI). Following this guideline, the six percent increase for an average performer in the second quartile of Exhibit 11.13 would reflect the change in

EXHIBIT 11.13 Performance Rating Salary Increase Matrix

Performance Rating / *Position in Range*	*Unsatisfactory*	*Needs Improvement*	*Competent*	*Commendable*	*Superior*
Fourth quartile	0%	0%	4%	5%	6%
Third quartile	0	0	5	6	7
Second quartile	0	0	6	7	8
First quartile	0	2	7	8	9
Below minimum of range	0	3	8	9	10

EXHIBIT 11.14 Merit Grids

Merit grids combine 3 variables: level of performance, distribution of employees within their job's pay range, and merit increase percentages.

Example:

1. Assume a performance rating scale of A through D: 30 percent of employees get A, 35 percent get B, 20 percent get C, and 15 percent get D. Change to decimals.

A	B	C	D
.30	.35	.20	.15

2. Assume a range distribution as follows: 10 percent of all employees are in the top (fourth) quartile of the pay range for their job, 35 percent are in the third quartile, 30 percent in second quartile, and 25 percent in lowest quartile. Change to decimals.

1	.10
2	.35
3	.30
4	.25

3. Multiply the performance distribution by the range distribution to obtain the percent of employees in each cell. Cell entries = Performance × Range.

	A	*B*	*C*	*D*
1	.30 × .10 = .03	.35 × .20 = .035	.30 × .10 = .02	.15 × .10 = .015
2	.30 × .35 = .105	.35 × .35 = .1225	.20 × .35 = .07	.15 × .35 = .0525
3	.30 × .30 = .09	.35 × .30 = .105	.20 × .30 = .06	.15 × .30 = .045
4	.30 × .25 = .075	.35 × .25 = .1225	.20 × .25 = .05	.15 × .25 = .0375

Cell entries tell us that 3 percent of employees are in top quartile of pay range AND received an A performance rating, 10.5 percent of employees are in second quartile of pay range AND received an A performance rating, etc.

4. Distribute increase percentage among cells, varying the percentages according to performance and range distribution, for example, 6 percent to those employees in cell A1, 5 percent to those employees in B1.

5. Multiply increase percentages by the employee distribution for each cell. Sum of all cells should equal the total merit increase percentage.

   Example: 6% × cell A1 = .06 × .03 = .0018

   5% × cell B1 = .05 × .035 = .00175

   etc. ______

   Targeted merit increse percentage = Sum

6. Adjust increase percentage among cells if needed in order to stay within budgeted increase.

CPI for that area. In a year with lower inflation, all the percentages in the matrix probably would be lower.

Third, how much should the top performers be paid? In part, budgetary considerations (Chapter 18) answer this question. But there is also growing evidence that employees do not agree on the size of increases that they consider meaningful (Chapter 8). Continuation of this research may help determine the approximate size of increases needed to make a difference in employee performance.

Finally, matrices can differ in the size of the differential between different levels of performance. Exhibit 11.13 basically rewards successive levels of performance with 1 percent increases (at least in the portion of the matrix in which any increase is granted). A larger jump between levels would signal a stronger commitment to recognizing performance with higher pay increases. Most companies balance this, though, against cost considerations. Larger differentials cost more. When money is tight this option is less attractive. Exhibit 11.14 shows how a merit grid is constructed when cost constraints (merit budget) are known.

PROMOTIONAL INCREASES AS A PAY-FOR-PERFORMANCE TOOL

Let's not forget that firms have methods of rewarding good performance other than raises. One of the most effective is a promotion accompanied by a salary increase, generally reported as being in the 8 to 12 percent range. This method of linking pay to performance has at least two characteristics that distinguish it from traditional annual merit pay increases. First, the very size of the increment is approximately double a normal merit increase. A clearer message is sent to employees, both in the form of money and promotion, that good performance is valued and *tangibly rewarded***.** Second, promotion increases represent, in a sense, a reward to employees for commitment and exemplary performance over a sustained period of time. Promotions are not generally annual events. They complement annual merit rewards by showing employees that there are benefits to both single-year productivity and to continuation of such desirable behavior.

Summary

The process of appraising employee performance can be both time-consuming and stressful. These difficulties are compounded if the appraisal system is poorly developed or if a supervisor lacks the appropriate training to collect and evaluate performance data. Development of sound appraisal systems requires an understanding of organizational objectives balanced against the relative merits of each type of appraisal system. For example, despite its inherent weaknesses, an appraisal system based on ranking of employee performance may be appropriate in small organizations which, for a variety of reasons, choose not to tie pay to performance; a sophisticated MBO appraisal system may not be appropriate for such a company.

Training supervisors effectively to appraise performance requires an understanding of organizational objectives. We know relatively little about the ways raters process information and evaluate employee performance. However, a thorough understanding of organizational objectives combined with a knowledge of common errors in evaluation can make a significant difference in the quality of appraisals.

Review Questions

1. LeBoy corporation manufactures specialty equipment for the auto industry (e.g., seat frames). One job involves operation of machines that form heat-treated metal into various seat shapes. The job is fairly low-level and routine. Without any further information, which of the five types of appraisal formats do you think would be most appropriate for this job? Justify your answer.
2. Employees in your department have formed semiautonomous work teams (they determine their own production schedule and individual work assignments). Individual performance is assessed using four performance dimensions: quantity of work, quality of work, interpersonal skills, and teamwork. Should the supervisor have a role in the rating process? What role, if any, should other members of the work team have in the assessment process?
3. What do you think should be included in the design of a performance appraisal process to lessen the probability that your company would be accused of discrimination in performance appraisal?
4. If you wanted to ensure that employees had good feedback about performance problems and strengths, which appraisal format would you recommend using? Why?
5. Assume that you had one employee fall into each of the cells in Exhibit 11.13 (25 employees in the company). How much would base salary increase in dollars if the current average salary in the company is $15,000? (Assume that ratings are randomly distributed by salary level: you can use $15,000 as your base salary for calculation in each of the cells.)

Appendix 11–A

Sample Appraisal Form: Outokumpu American Brass

outokumpu american brass

Salaried Personnel Performance Appraisal

Name (Last) (First) (MI)	OAB Employee #	OAB Service Date Appraisal Date
Location	Function	Department
Classification Title	Pay Grade	Time in present position _____ Years _____ Months

Performance Rating (check one)		
A copy of this form is to be provided to the employee upon completion of the appraisal process. Submit the original to the Human Resources Department	Exceeds Standards 1 ☐ 2 ☐ Meets Standards 3 ☐ 4 ☐ 5 ☐ Does Not Meet Standards 6 ☐ 7 ☐	Comment (if any)

Completed by: ______________________ Employee Signature: ______________________
(your signature does not imply agreement)

Reviewed by: ______________________

Job Knowledge:	The ability to effectively understand, utilize and demonstrate technical concepts and operating procedures applicable to all aspects of the job. People differ in the breadth of knowledge across jobs, the depth of knowledge within jobs, and the ability to innovatively use this knowledge to complete tasks.

Exceeds Standards	1	Displays broad knowledge and innovative ability on technical concepts and operating procedures for even the most complex tasks. Most people in the department consider this person the expert on a wide variety of department jobs.
	2	Broad knowledge of technical and operating procedures for all aspects of own and closely related jobs. If you needed to know both standard and alternative procedures for performing any aspect of this job you would think of this person as the source.
Meets Standards	3	Broad knowledge of standard technical and operating procedures for all aspects of own job. If you needed to know existing or alternative procedures for any aspect of this job, this person could be expected to provide correct information.
	4	Generally knowledgeable about all standard technical and operating aspects of own job. Might be expected to occasionally double check procedures with others on the most complex of tasks.
	5	Generally understands standard job components but may not be versed in all the more complex aspects. Wouldn't normally expect others to go to this person for technical and/or operating information because of these knowledge gaps. Would expect this person to go to others for information rather than perform inadequately because of knowledge gaps.
Does Not Meet Standards	6	Technical and/or operating information about some standard aspects of job may be faulty, leading to occasional improper performance of job. May show desire to improve but progress has been minimal thus far.
	7	Regularly makes mistakes because of faulty knowledge on many standard and more complex aspects of job. Shows little sign of improvement despite prior counseling.

Rating:	Documentation of Rating (optional except for 6 and 7):

Interpersonal Skills:		The ability to show understanding, support, courtesy, tact and cooperation in interactions with coworkers, subordinates, customers, and visitors. People differ in the extent they are recognized and sought out to show this skill, the frequency and nature of lapses in this skill, and the ability to recognize and correct lapses as they occur.
Exceeds Standards	1	The understanding, support and tact shown by these employees make them the choice for: difficult negotiations with others; reaction to sensitive business ideas; ability to resolve conflict between individuals. Is recognized company-wide for consistency in interpersonal skills.
	2	This person is seen by others as genuinely interested in their welfare. Able to make others feel comfortable when asked to conduct discussions of even the most sensitive and stressful subjects. Is recognized department wide for consistency in interpersonal skills.
Meets Standards	3	This person could be expected to show courtesy, tact and understanding in interactions with coworkers, subordinates, customers and visitors even under sensitive circumstances.
	4	This person occasionally might have lapses in courtesy, tact and understanding in sensitive and stressful situations, but lapses would be confined to internal employees and not customers/visitors. Person could be expected to recognize and seek to repair damage to relationship immediately.
	5	This person occasionally might have lapses in courtesy, tact and understanding, but lapses would be confined to internal employees. Would be expected to seek to repair damage to relationship immediately if recognized.
Does Not Meet Standards	6	Lapses in courtesy, tact and understanding are not uncommon and not confined to just internal employees. Could be expected to attempt to repair damage to relationship, when it is recognized or pointed out. Seems genuinely interested in improving.
	7	Lapses in courtesy, tact and understanding are not uncommon and not confined to just internal employees. Could be expected to show little remorse and not feel damage repair is personal responsibility.
Rating:		Documentation of Rating (optional except for 6 and 7):

Organization and Planning: Ability to systematically make plans and set objectives, structure tasks to achieve objectives, establish priorities and make schedules.		
Exceeds Standards	1	Can be relied upon to have a plan for accomplishing tasks, even when working from unclear directions or vague strategic goals. Plan shows clear recognition of problems and constraints. Tasks have reasonable timeframes and accurately reflect company or supervisory priorities.
	2	Once understands overall responsibilities as explained by supervisor, could be expected to develop a clear plan for tasks to be completed without being prompted. Plan usually shows clear recognition of problems and constraints. Tasks have reasonable timeframes and accurately reflect supervisor's priorities.
Meets Standards	3	Supervisor explains overall responsibilities. Without prompting, this employee could be expected to develop an effective plan of attack with only occasional assistance from supervisor in one or more of the following: defining tasks to be performed, establishing priorities and timeframes, identifying constraints.
	4	Supervisor explains overall responsibilities. Occasionally requires prompting to develop plan for completing tasks. Supervisor provides occasional assistance in: defining tasks to be performed, establishing priorities and timeframes, identifying constraints.
	5	Supervisor explains overall responsibilities. Occasionally requires prompting to develop plan for completing tasks. Supervisor occasionally (on complex tasks) must monitor planning and organizing to ensure no gaps in: defining tasks to be performed, establishing priorities and timeframes, identifying constraints.
Does Not Meet Standards	6	Supervisor explains overall responsibilities and must assist employee in outlining tasks to be performed. Planning and organization still show gaps and possible errors. Employee misses deadlines because of poor plan of attack or prioritization of tasks.
	7	Without direct intervention by supervisor this employee could be expected to work without any clear plan for completing tasks; has only vague ideas about priorities, time tables and constraints.
Rating:		Documentation of Rating (optional except for 6 and 7):

Communication Skills:		Written and oral ability to clearly and convincingly express thoughts, ideas or facts in individual or group situations.
Exceeds Standards	1	Through clarity and logic of communications is able to persuade others to adopt policies and practices, even those which may have been unpopular initially. Makes complex ideas understandable for all levels and types of audiences. Would be a top choice for presenting an unpopular subject to a hostile audience.
	2	Clearly and logically presents ideas in a way that makes even complex subjects easy to grasp for a wide variety of audiences. Frequently is able to persuade others to adopt policies and practices, even those which may have been unpopular initially. Not normally among the first people considered to present an unpopular subject to a hostile audience.
Meets Standards	3	Typically presents ideas clearly and logically without assistance from others. Recognizes when content of message is not understood and is able to reexplain ideas in a different manner to clarify. Communications ability may not have the power to convert unsympathetic listeners.
	4	Ideas are clear and logical, but success may come only after pretesting arguments with others and clarifying content of message. Recognizes when content of message is not understood and usually is able to rephrase in a way that clarifies.
	5	With help of others can develop clear and logical communications. Occasionally, may not be clear when ideas are first presented in casual conversations or in written drafts, but on own or with help, recognizes where message is not understood. Struggles to find ways to clarify message and is usually successful.
Does Not Meet Standards	6	Occasionally unclear in formal presentations and in final papers, either because of failure to seek input from others or because of inability to act upon that input. May not be able to recognize when listeners or readers do not understand message. May not be able to clarify message even when gap in understanding is recognized. Gives appearance of trying to improve these skills.
	7	Frequently unclear in communications of both casual and great importance. Shows little ability or interest in understanding where misunderstanding is or in correcting same.
Rating:		Documentation of Rating (optional except for 6 and 7):

Judgment: Ability to obtain and evaluate information from all relevant sources. Uses information effectively to arrive at conclusions which are appropriate to the situation.

Exceeds Standards	1	Readily perceives existent or potential problems, collects information relevant to solution from affected sources. Makes effective decisions which reflect sensitivity to Financial, Operating and Human Resource constraints of both short- and long-term nature.
	2	Readily perceives existing problems. Usually able to identify potential problems before they occur. With occasional direction from others is able to identify and obtain information from parties who will be affected by decision. Decisions effective for short-term perspective and usually reflect consideration of long-term concerns.
Meets Standards	3	Good at perceiving existing problems. May need help to identify many of these sources on own. Usually needs help, though, to identify input sources. Decisions are typically quite good from a short-term perspective and at least reflect consideration of long-term issues.
	4	Responsive to claims by others that potential or current problems exist. Frequently is aware of these concerns on own. Seeks and obtains help in identifying appropriate sources for input information. First pass at problem solution may be incomplete, but is diligent in seeking input from others before errors result. Final decisions are typically good from a short-term perspective and at least reflect consideration of long-term issues.
	5	Responsive to claims by others that potential or current problems exist. Not always perceptive on own, though, that problems exist or are developing. First pass at problem solution may be incomplete, but is diligent in seeking input from others before errors result. Final decisions are acceptable but sometimes not optimal, either in short- or long-term perspective.
Does Not Meet Standards	6	Occasionally fails to recognize existing or potential problems and may let them magnify before acting on advice of others. Once acts, though, can be spurred by others to seek information from some, but not always all, relevant sources. Not always diligent in getting input to final decision. Decisions regularly are unacceptable from short- and/or long-term perspective.
	7	Shows little effort to recognize or deal with problems unless forced by others. Decisions lack input of relevant sources and are usually unacceptable.

Rating:	Documentation of Rating (optional except for 6 and 7):

Initiative-Dependability:		Ability to fulfill responsibilities on time and according to expectations of supervisor. Includes recognition and quality completion of necessary tasks beyond the scope of initial instructions.
Exceeds Standards	1	Recognizes tasks which need to be performed to complete overall mission. Undertakes such tasks, even if beyond initial instructions of supervisor, checking for approval where appropriate. Completes these and other assigned tasks on time, even if efforts beyond the norm are required.
	2	Receives task assignments from supervisor and regularly finds ways to exceed requirements. Completes tasks on time and according to directions of supervisor, even if efforts beyond the norm are required.
Meets Standards	3	Receives task assignments from supervisor and occasionally finds ways to exceed requirements. Completes tasks on time and according to directions of supervisor, even if efforts beyond the norm are required.
	4	Receives task assignments from supervisor and occasionally finds ways to exceed requirements. Completes top priority tasks on time, and few modifications are needed. Usually completes less important tasks on time and without reminders. This work may have minor flaws which employee might catch and correct immediately, causing deadline to be narrowly missed. Occasionally exerts efforts beyond those normally required.
	5	Rarely would expect this person to complete tasks beyond those assigned by supervisor. Completes top priority tasks accurately and on time, but occasionally may need to be reminded to do so. Less important tasks are completed, but sometimes reminders are needed when deadlines are drawing close. May leave these tasks to the last minute such that, to meet deadline, minor flaws are not corrected. Corrects flaws immediately when noted. Wouldn't be expected to regularly and willingly exert efforts beyond those normally required.
Does Not Meet Standards	6	Does work assigned but occasionally misses important deadlines, and more often misses lesser deadlines, unless closely supervised. Work regularly does not meet supervisor expectations, but employee can be expected to try to make corrections. Only reluctantly exerts efforts beyond those normally required.
	7	Can not be counted on to meet deadlines except under very close supervision. Employee begrudgingly corrects work if demanded, but errors may still exist. Only works beyond normal hours when directly instructed.
Rating:		Documentation of Rating (optional except for 6 and 7):

Teamwork: Ability to contribute to group performance, to draw out the best from others, to foster activities building group morale, even under high pressure situations.

Exceeds Standards	1	Seeks out or is regularly requested for group assignments. Groups this person works with inevitably have high performance and high morale. Employee makes strong personal contribution and is able to identify strengths of many different types of group members and foster their participation. Wards off personality conflicts by positive attitude and ability to mediate unhealthy conflicts, sometimes even before they arise. Will make special effort to insure credit for group performance is shared by all.
	2	Seen as a positive contributor in group assignments. Works well with all types of people and personalities, occasionally elevating group performance of others. Good ability to resolve unhealthy group conflicts that flare up. Will make special effort to insure strong performers receive credit due them.
Meets Standards	3	Seen as a positive personal contributor in group assignments. Works well with most types of people and personalities. Is never a source of unhealthy group conflict and will encourage the same behavior in others.
	4	When group mission requires skill this person is strong in, employee seen as strong contributor. On other occasions will not hinder performance of others. Works well with most types of people and personalities and will not be the initiator of unhealthy group conflict. Will not participate in such conflict unless provoked on multiple occasions.
	5	Depending on the match of personal skill and group mission, this person will be seen as a positive contributor. Will not be a hindrance to performance of others and avoids unhealthy conflict unless provoked.
Does Not Meet Standards	6	Unlikely to be chosen for assignments requiring teamwork except on occasions where personal expertise is vital to group mission. Not responsive to group goals, but can be enticed to help when personal appeals are made. May not get along with other members and either withdraw or generate unhealthy conflict. Seeks personal recognition for team performance and/or may downplay efforts of others..
	7	Has reputation for noncontribution and for creating conflicts in groups. Cares little about group goals and is very hard to motivate towards goal completion unless personal rewards are guaranteed. May undermine group performance to further personal aims. Known to seek personal recognition and/or downplay efforts of others.

Rating:	Documentation of Rating (optional except for 6 and 7):

Quantity/Quality: Amount of high quality work completed in a variety of situations relative to expectations.		
Exceeds Standards	1	Consistently exceeds expectations in both quality and quantity of work for tasks requiring widely different skills.
	2	Output often exceeds standards and is of the highest quality, even across tasks requiring widely different skills.
Meets Standards	3	Consistently exceeds expectations in both quality and quantity of work for tasks in area of known competence. For tasks requiring developed skill, meets expectations for both quantity and quality.
	4	Consistently meets, and occasionally exceeds, expectations in both quality and quantity of work for tasks in area of known competence. For tasks requiring less developed skills, may initially not meet expectations, but will quickly develop to a satisfactory level.
	5	Meets expectations in quality and quantity of work for tasks in area of known competence. On rare occasions when expectations aren't met initially, employee makes effort to correct problem immediately. For tasks requiring less developed skills, may initially not meet expectations but will quickly develop to a satisfactory level.
Does Not Meet Standards	6	Does not consistently meet expectations in quality and quantity of work for tasks in areas of known competence. May attempt to correct problem, but still fall below expectations. Shows little interest and capability to achieve acceptable quantity/quality standards in areas of less developed skills.
	7	Frequently marginally misses quality/quantity expectations on a wide variety of tasks or misses by a wide margin on a few tasks, even after prior counseling.
Rating:		Documentation of Rating (optional except for 6 and 7):

Management of Human Resources:	The ability to effectively select, utilize and develop subordinates. Also requires recognition and compliance with accepted and required personnel policies and procedures. (RATING IN THIS AREA REQUIRED ONLY FOR SUPERVISORY POSITIONS).

Exceeds Standards	1 Widely recognized in the company as very good at selecting good people, placing them in jobs which utilize their skills effectively, and providing developmental experiences which increase their value to the organization. Is conscientious in keeping current and following accepted and required personnel policies and procedures. Insists on same from subordinates.
	2 Employees within the department would characterize this person as one of the top people in selecting, utilizing and developing subordinates. Complaints by subordinates about treatment rarely occur, and are never traceable to improper behavior by this person. Is conscientious in keeping current and following accepted and required personnel policies and procedures. Insists on same from subordinates.
Meets Standards	3 Good at utilizing and developing better employees. Occasionally has employees who don't meet expectations. Likely to consult HR staff and others for strategies to assist these employees. Such strategies are typically successful. Complaints by subordinates about treatment rarely occur, handled appropriately when they do. Conscientious in keeping current and following accepted and required personnel policies and procedures. Subordinates don't always follow these guides as closely.
	4 Has a mixed group of employees in terms of effectiveness. Is concerned about placement and development and will respond to suggestions if offered, but not particularly proactive except for top subordinates. Complaints by subordinates about treatment are handled quickly and effectively. Few lapses of the same type arise later. Will attempt to comply with accepted and required personnel policies and procedures, but both self and subordinates have occasional lapses which are quickly corrected when pointed out.
	5 Mixed group of employees in terms of effectiveness. Concerned about placement and development and will respond to suggestions offered, but not particularly proactive except for top subordinates. Complaints by subordinates about treatment sometimes follow patterns previously observed, but are handled quickly and usually effectively, at least in short run. Attempts to comply with accepted and required personnel policies and procedures, but both self and subordinates have occasional lapses which are quickly corrected when pointed out.
Does Not Meet Standards	6 Seems concerned about selecting and developing good employees, but is a continuing source of complaints. Shows the same pattern of mistakes over time. Corrects problems with help from HR department, but does not seem to have sense of ways to avoid problem in the future. Lapses in compliance with accepted and required personnel policies and procedures are not uncommon for self and subordinates. Responds, at least in short run, to notification about infractions.
	7 Regularly has complaints from employees about treatment. Will respond only when complaint is voiced and pursued outside department. Not unusual to trace violations of accepted personnel policies and procedures back to this department. Shows little talent and/or motivation for changing treatment of employees.

Rating:	Documentation of Rating (optional except for 6 and 7):

Performance Against Standards: The ability to achieve objectives as agreed upon by supervisor and employee.
(RATING IN THIS AREA OPTIONAL FOR NONEXEMPT EMPLOYEES)

Exceeds Standards	1	Exceeds expectations on all objectives.
	2	Exceeds expectations on all priority objectives and most remaining objectives. Any problems are generally traceable to external constraints not under control of employee.
Meets Standards	3	Meets or exceeds expectations on all objectives. Exceeds expectations on one, but not all, priority objectives.
	4	Meets expectations on all priority objectives. May occasionally fall below standards on one or a few remaining objectives, but this is balanced against performance exceeding expectations on an equal number of other objectives.
	5	On average, performance meets expectations, but there is variability across objectives. Performance which does not meet standards on one objective is balanced against high performance on another objective of approximately equal importance.
Does Not Meet Standards	6	On average, performance does not meet expectations. Either the employee generally meets standards on most objectives with a few (more than one) sub marginal ratings, or, on average, good performance (exceeds standards) does not balance out occasions of poor performance. Does not meet standards on at least one priority objective.
	7	On average, does not meet standards for a majority of objectives. More than one objective not met.

Rating:	Documentation of Rating (optional except for 6 and 7):

1st Priority Objective and Desired Results (One of top three of four priorities in this business unit)	**Actual Results and Comments**	**Rating** (Exceeded, met, not met or deferred)

2nd Priority Objective and Desired Results	**Actual Results and Comments**	**Rating** (Exceeded, met, not met or deferred)

3rd Priority Objective and Desired Results	Actual Results and Comments	**Rating** (Exceeded, met, not met or deferred)

4th Priority Objective and Desired Results	Actual Results and Comments	**Rating** (Exceeded, met, not met or deferred)

3. *PERFORMANCE FACTORS:* Explain specific strengths and weaknesses.
You may check "*IMPROVEMENT REQUIRED*" in conjunction with "*MEETS OR EXCEEDS AN ACCEPTABLE LEVEL OF PERFORMANCE*" when the trend of the employee's performance is declining or is approaching unacceptable for the performance factor.

TECHNICAL COMPETENCE/JOB KNOWLEDGE Demonstrates the skills needed to perform the job. Understands the work environment, the job requirements, and the customer needs. Completed assignments with minimum direction.	[ ] Meets or exceeds an acceptable level of performance. Improvement Required [ ] [ ] Unacceptable
EXPLAIN:	

QUALITY Demonstrates a commitment to quality and the quality process. Completes assignments in an accurate and thorough manner. Produces work that meets standards.	[ ] Meets or exceeds an acceptable level of performance. Improvement Required [ ] [ ] Unacceptable
EXPLAIN:	

PRODUCTIVITY Organizes work activities to improve results. Uses resources efficiently and effectively.	[ ] Meets or exceeds an acceptable level of performance. Improvement Required [ ] [ ] Unacceptable
EXPLAIN:	

Appendix 11–B

Sample Appraisal Form: Stanley Tools

STANLEY EMPLOYEE GOAL SHEET

Individual: ______________________ Manager: ______________________

COMPANY GOALS:
- To grow the Company revenues by 10% per year to reach $4bn revenues
- To reduce the Company's asset base by $250m
- To reduce the Company's costs by $150m

DIVISION or FUNCTION GOALS:
DEPARTMENT or TEAM GOALS:

(List in priority the key goals you are accountable for achieving to support business goals. You are responsible for reviewing your goals quarterly. Use the above quarterly box to (√) review dates.)

S.M.A.R.T. Goal Statement	*Target Outcome*	*Review Dates*	*Comments*
1.			
2.			
3.			
4.			
5.			

Determine the percentage of your work time needed to attain your goal (e.g., 25%, 50%, etc.). List in the % column. If the % of time required exceeds 100%, renegotiate time frames. Assess the degree of difficulty of the goal, and your own experience relative to the goal. Negotiate with your manager for the support requirements that you will need in order to accomplish each goal.

Support Plan	*% of Time*	*Degree of Difficulty (high/med/low)*	*Degree of Experience (high/med/low)*	*Support required in order to accomplish the goals (e.g. Financial resources, management support, training, technology, etc.)*
Goal #1				
Goal #2				
Goal #3				
Goal #4				
Goal #5				

______________________ ______________________

Individual: Date Manager: Date

STANLEY WORKS PROFESSIONAL DEVELOPMENT PLAN

Name:	Current Role:	Division:
Development Period:	Date:	

The Stanley Works Professional Development Plan is to be completed jointly by the supervisor and individual. List 3–4 key development needs (e.g., skills and/or competencies required for success and mastery for the individual's current role, etc.). Clearly outline the actions (e.g., training, participation on teams, etc.), resources needed and target completion dates to fulfill development plan commitments.

Development Needs: Current Role *List 3–4 development needs within your current job.*	**Action Plans** *Identify specific, measurable actions that will allow you to fill your development need(s).*	**Involvement of Others** *List individuals who can provide resources and support to assist you in achieving your development needs.*	**Target Dates**
Needs:	1. 2. 3.		
Needs:	1. 2. 3.		
Needs:	1. 2. 3.		
Needs:	1. 2. 3.		

Career Development Planning

Career Aspirations:

Discuss and record career aspirations, roles of expressed interest, and what development is needed for competency and success in that role.

Potential Career Paths & Timing:

Indicate specific roles the individual could assume in the near and long-term.

Development Needs: Long-Term *List the key skills, competencies and goals needed to assume future role(s).*	**Action Plans** *Identify specific actions to fill development need(s).*	**Involvement of Others** *List individuals who need to contribute to the development plan by providing opportunities, resources, etc.*	**Target Dates**
Needs:	1. 2. 3.		

Individual's Signature   Date   Manager's Signature   Date

THE STANLEY WORKS PERFORMANCE REVIEW FOR SALARIED PERSONNEL

Name ______________________ Position ______________________ As Of ______
(Date)

Department ______________________ Division ______________________

RESULTS Summarize your evaluation of performance in relation to established goals. (Attach goal sheet). Give specific examples of the individual's contribution to the Company's Goals and Strategies—4 X 4 Plans—Profitable Growth—Operational Excellence—Customer Intimacy—Resource Sharing—Diversity—Product/Process Innovation

Core Success Skills Assessment	*Give specific examples of the presence or absence of the Core Success Skills.*
• Is Proactive/Gets the Job Done	
• Acts as an Involved Business Partner	
• Uses Good Judgment	
• Communicates Effectively	
• Demonstrates Effective Teamwork	
• Provides Technical Leadership	
• Operates in Accordance with Stanley Values	

(Complete only if you lead people or projects)

Global Leadership Competencies	*Give specific examples of the presence or absence of these competencies (if applicable).*
• Takes a Global Perspective	
• Develops Competitive Strategies	
• Leads Change	
• Drives Innovation	
• Builds Capability in People and Organizations	
• Manages Performance of People	

STRENGTHS & NEEDS From your analysis of your performance in relation to goals and to the demonstration of Core Success Skills, describe your strongest abilities and those that could be developed.

Strongest Abilities Demonstrated in This Year's Performance	*Abilities that Could Be Developed*

PERFORMANCE DEVELOPMENT PLAN

What can my boss do to develop my performance? What can I do to further my performance both personally and professionally?

CAREER GOALS

What job would I like to be doing next?

Five to ten years from now?

What do I need to do to qualify?

SIGNATURE OF INDIVIDUAL

Signed ______________________________ Date ______________

YOUR TURN:

POLICY IMPLICATIONS OF MERIT PAY GUIDES

GEMCAR is a manufacturer of decals and hood ornaments for all varieties of American cars. During the past four years, profits have plummeted 43 percent. This decline is attributed to rising costs of production and is widely believed to have triggered the resignation of GEMCAR's longtime president, C. Milton Carol. The newly hired CEO is Winston McBeade, a former vice president of finance and of human resources management at Longtemp Enterprises, a producer of novelty watches. As his first policy statement in office, Mr. McBeade declared a war on high production costs. As his first official act, Mr. McBeade proposed implementing a new merit pay guide (see Exhibits 1 and 2 for former and revised pay guides). What can you deduce about Mr. McBeade's "philosophy" of cost control from both the prior and newly revised merit guides? What implications does this new philosophy have for improving the link between pay and performance and, hence, productivity?

EXHIBIT 1 Merit Pay Guide for Last Year

		Performance				
		Well Below Average	*Below Average*	*Average*	*Above Average*	*Well Above Average*
Above Grade Maximum (red circle)		0 0	2 0	3 10	4 5	6 15
Position in Salary Range	Q4	0 0	3 0	4 5	5 10	7 15
	Q3	0 0	4 0	5 10	6 25	8 10
	Q2	2 	5 2	6 9	7 9	9 10
	Q1	2 0	6 3	7 6	8 5	10 9

Notes: 1. Cost of living rose 3 percent last year.

2. The number at the lower right corner of each cell represents the number of employees falling into that cell during the previous year.

EXHIBIT 2 Revised Pay Guide

		Performance				
		Well Below Average	*Below Average*	*Average*	*Above Average*	*Well Above Average*
Position in Salary Range	Above grade maximum (red circle)	0	0	0	0	0
	Q4	0	0	2	3	4
	Q3	0	0	3	4	5
	Q2	0	0	4	5	6
	Q1	0	0	5	6	7

Note: Cost of living is expected to rise 3 percent this year.

EXHIBIT IV.1 The Pay Model

STRATEGIC ISSUES → TECHNIQUES → STRATEGIC OBJECTIVES

STRATEGIC ISSUES	TECHNIQUES				STRATEGIC OBJECTIVES
CONSISTENCY	Work analysis	Descriptions	Evaluation certification	INTERNAL STRUCTURE	EFFICIENCY Performance Quality Customer Cost
COMPETITIVENESS	Market definitions	Surveys	Policy lines	PAY STRUCTURE	EQUITY
CONTRIBUTORS	Seniority based	Performance based	Merit guidelines	INCENTIVE PROGRAMS	COMPLIANCE
ADMINISTRATION	Planning	Budgeting	Communication	EVALUATION	

Employee Benefits

Take $14,000 and bury it in the backyard. Leave it there as very expensive fertilizer for your geraniums. Why $14,000 you ask? Why bury it in the backyard, you ask? Well, $14,000 is the average amount we spend on a full-time employee's benefits in one year. Burying the $14,000 in the backyard is our way of saying it's not clear the money is any worse off in the ground than invested in employee benefits. A bit harsh? An exaggeration, you say! Think about what we know that is fact—not faith—in the benefits area. Which of the issues covered in the pay model (Exhibit IV.1), for example, can we answer with respect to benefits? Does effective employee benefits administration facilitate organization performance? The answer is unclear. We do know that benefit costs can be cut, and this affects the bottom line (admittedly an important measure of organization performance). But what about other design and administrative efforts? Do they complement organization strategy and performance? We don't know. Or do employee benefits impact upon an organization's ability to attract, retain, and motivate employees? Conventional wisdom says employee benefits can affect retention, but there is little research to support this conclusion. A similar lack of research surrounds each of the other potential payoffs to a sound benefits program.

Employee benefits cost over one trillion dollars today. Is it any wonder, then, that firms are increasingly paying attention to this reward component? It represents a labor cost with no apparent returns.

Compounding this concern is the ever present entitlement problem. Employees perceive benefits as a right, independent of how well they or the company perform. Efforts to reduce benefit levels or eliminate parts of the package altogether would meet with employee resistance and dissatisfaction.

Assuming that organizations must find ways to control costs of benefits wherever possible, this chapter focuses on identifying ways to maximize the returns from benefit expenditures. As a first step in this direction, Chapter 12 identifies issues organizations should face in developing and maintaining a benefits program. A model of the benefits determination process also is presented to provide a structure for thinking about employee benefits.

Chapter 13 provides a summary of the state of employee benefits today. Hopefully this will provide the groundwork for the innovative and effective benefit packages of tomorrow.

CHAPTER 12

The Benefits Determination Process

Chapter Outline

What can you do with a trillion dollars? Help balance the budget? Buy two used copies of this book? Cover the cost of employee benefits in the United States today? It's hard to believe that employee benefits cost this much—it works out to $14,659 per full-time worker in 1995, more than double the 1983 cost of $7,000 per worker.[1]

[1]U.S. Chamber of Commerce, *Employee Benefits* (U.S. Chamber of Commerce: Washington, D.C., 1996).

These figures are particularly revealing when we consider what passed as benefits in the not-too-distant past:

- A carriage shop published a set of rules for employees in 1880 that stated, in part: "Working hours shall be from 7 A.M. to 9 P.M. every day except the Sabbath. . . . After an employee has been with this firm for five years he shall receive an added payment of five cents per day, provided the firm has prospered in a manner to make it possible. . . . It is the bounden duty of each employee to put away at least 10 percent of his monthly wages for his declining years so he will not become a burden upon his betters."
- In 1915, employees in the iron and steel industry worked a standard 60 to 64 hours per week. By 1930 that schedule had been reduced to 54 hours.
- It was not until 1929 that the Blue Cross concept of prepaid medical costs was introduced.
- Prior to 1935 only one state (Wisconsin) had a program of unemployment compensation benefits for workers who lost their jobs through no fault of their own.
- Before World War II very few companies paid hourly employees for holidays. In most companies employees were told not to report for work on holidays and to enjoy the time off, but their paychecks were smaller the following week.

In comparison to these "benefits" from the past, today's reality seems staggering. Consider the following examples, only somewhat outrageous in their generosity.

- At Andersen Consulting's office in Boston, on-site concierge service is only one of the perks. A shoeshine service sets up shop on Fridays. Dry cleaning is dropped off every morning at the front desk.
- At MBNA America Bank, America's second-largest credit card company, employees at some sites can have their clothes hemmed by an on-site tailor. Just down the hall is an espresso bar with Belgian chocolates and French pastries, a barber shop, shoe repair, film processing and free travel service.
- Need door-to-desk dry cleaning, or chef-prepared take-home dinners such as blackened chicken or handmade ravioli? Consider working at Autodesk.[2]

Clearly these firms would argue that these extra services are important benefits of employment, perhaps making attraction, retention, and motivation of employees just that much easier. But the truth is, we don't know if even ordinary benefits have positive payoffs. Until we can clearly identify the advantages of employee benefits, we need to find ways to control their costs, or at least slow their growth. Exhibit 12.1 illustrates the rapid rise in employee benefit costs, moving from about 25 percent of payroll costs in 1959 to just over 42 percent today.[3]

---

[2]Stephanie Armour, "Fringe Benefits on the Rise," *USA Today*, October 8, 1997, p. 1B.

[3]U.S. Chamber of Commerce, *Employee Benefits*.

EXHIBIT 12.1 Changes in Benefit Costs: 1959, 1969, 1990, 1995

	1959	*1969*	*1990*	*1995*
Percentage of payroll (total)	24.7	31.1	38.4	42

Source: U.S. Chamber of Commerce Annual Benefits Surveys, 1996.

Employee Benefits that part of the total compensation package, other than pay for time worked, provided to employees in whole or in part by employer payments (e.g., life insurance, pension, workers' compensation, vacation).

Employee benefits can no longer realistically be called "fringe benefits." As an example, visualize a $20,000 car rolling down the assembly line at General Motors. A cost accountant would tell you that $1,200 of this cost is due to worker health insurance alone. Compare this to the cost of all the steel for the same car—$500—and the impact is evident. Now compare this to amounts as low as $100 for foreign automakers in their U.S. factories (with their younger, healthier workers and hardly any retirees), and the global implications of benefit costs are all too frightening.[4]

Over one 20-year period (1955–1975), employee benefit costs rose at a rate almost four times greater than employee wages or the consumer price index.[5] A similar comparison for the period 1963–1987 shows the rate of growth has slowed (benefit costs rose twice as fast as wage costs). Indeed, between 1993 and 1995 the cost of benefits have actually stabilized at about $14,500 per full-time employee. Nevertheless, organizations still express concern for controlling the cost of benefits, particularly with the aging, and increasingly costly, baby boomer generation.[6]

WHY THE GROWTH IN EMPLOYEE BENEFITS?

Wage and Price Controls

During both World War II and the Korean War the federal government instituted strict wage and price controls. The compliance agency charged with enforcing these controls was relatively lenient in permitting reasonable increases in benefits. With strict limita-

---

[4]Rebecca Blumenstein, "Seeking a Cure: Auto Makers Attack High Health-care Bills with a New Approach," *The Wall Street Journal*, December 9, 1996, p. A1.

[5]John Hanna, "Can the Challenge of Escalating Benefits Costs Be Met?" *Personnel Administration* 27, no. 9 (1977), pp. 50–57.

[6]U.S. Chamber of Commerce, *Employee Benefits* (Washington, D.C.: U.S. Chamber of Commerce, 1988).

tions on the size of wage increases, both unions and employers sought new and improved benefits to satisfy worker demands.

Unions

The climate fostered by wage and price controls created a perfect opportunity for unions to flex the muscles they had acquired under the Wagner Act of 1935. Several National Labor Relations Board rulings during the 1940s freed unions to negotiate over employee benefits. With little freedom to raise wages during the war, unions fought for the introduction of new benefits and the improvement of existing benefits. Success on this front during the war years led to further postwar demands. Largely through the efforts of unions, most notably the auto and steelworkers, several benefits common today were given their initial impetus: pattern pension plans, supplementary unemployment compensation, extended vacation plans, and guaranteed annual wage plans.[7]

Employer Impetus

Many of the benefits in existence today were provided at employer initiative. Much of this initiative can be traced to pragmatic concerns about employee satisfaction and productivity. Rest breaks often were implemented in the belief that fatigue increased accidents and lowered productivity. Savings and profit-sharing plans (e.g., Procter & Gamble's profit-sharing plan was initiated in 1885) were implemented to improve performance and provide increased security for worker retirement years. Indeed, many employer-initiated benefits were designed to create a climate in which employees perceived that management was genuinely concerned for their welfare. Notice, though, these supposed benefits were taken on faith. But their costs were quite real. And absent hard data about payoffs, employee benefits slowly became a costly entitlement of the American workforce.

Cost Effectiveness of Benefits

Another important and sound impetus for the growth of employee benefits is their cost effectiveness in two situations. The first cost advantage is that most employee benefits are not taxable. Provision of a benefit rather than an equivalent increase in wages avoids payment of federal and state personal income tax. Remember, though, recurrent tax reform proposals continue to threaten the favorable tax status granted to many benefits.

A second cost effectiveness component of benefits arises because many group-based benefits (e.g., life, health, and legal insurance) can be obtained at a lower rate than could be obtained by employees acting on their own. Group insurance also has relatively easy qualification standards, giving security to a set of employees who might not otherwise qualify.

---

[7] McCaffery, *Managing the Employee Benefits Program* (New York: American Management Association, 1983).

Government Impetus

Obviously the government has played an important role in the growth of employee benefits. Three employee benefits are mandated by either the state or federal government: workers' compensation (state), unemployment insurance (federal), and social security (federal). In addition, most other employee benefits are affected by such laws as the Employee Retirement Income Security Act (ERISA affects pension administration) and various sections of the Internal Revenue Code.

THE VALUE OF EMPLOYEE BENEFITS

Exhibit 12.2 shows the relative importance employees attached to different types of benefits across three different studies.[8]

In general the three studies reported in Exhibit 12.2 show fairly consistent results. For example, medical payments regularly are listed as one of the most important benefits employees receive. These rankings have added significance when we note over the past decade that health care costs are the most rapidly growing and the most difficult to control of all the benefit options offered by employers.[9] In 1996 health care costs alone

EXHIBIT 12.2 Ranking of Different Employee Benefits

	STUDY		
	1	*2*	*3*
MEDICAL	1	1	3
PENSION	2	3	8
PAID VACATION AND HOLIDAYS	3	2	X
SICKNESS	4	X	5
DENTAL	5	X	6
PROFIT SHARING	6	X	2
LONG TERM DISABILITY	7	X	7
LIFE INSURANCE	8	X	4

x = not rated in this study

[8]This table was compiled from three different sources. Some of the reward components rated in some of the studies were not traditional employee benefits and have been deleted from the rankings here. The three studies were: "The Future Look of Employee Benefits," *The Wall Street Journal*, September 8, 1988, p. 23 (Source: Hewitt Associates); Kermit Davis, William Giles, and Hubert Feild, *How Young Professionals Rank Employee Benefits: Two Studies* (International Foundation of Employee Benefit Plans: Brookfield, WI, 1988); Kenneth Shapiro and Jesse Sherman, Employee Attitude Benefit Plan Designs," *Personnel Journal*, July 1987, pp. 49–58.

[9]Mary Fruen and Henry DiPrete, *Health Care in the Future* (Boston, MA: John Hancock, 1986); HRM Update, "Health Plan Increases" (New York: The Conference Board, May 1988); Kintner and Smith, "General Motors Provides Health Care Benefits to Millions"; Health Research Institute, "1985 Health Care Cost Containment Survey," Walnut Creek, CA: Health Research Institute; North West National Life Insurance Co., "Ten Ways to Cut Employee Benefit Costs," 1988.

were estimated at $3,915 per employee, up 54 percent from 1988 and a whopping 78 percent from 1987.[10]

These costs would not seem nearly so outrageous if we had evidence that employees place high value on the benefits they receive. Unfortunately, there is evidence that employees frequently are not even aware of, or undervalue, the benefits provided by their organization. For example, in one study employees were asked to recall the benefits they received. The typical employee could recall less than 15 percent of them. In another study MBA students were asked to rank the importance attached to various factors influencing job selection.[11] Presumably the large percentage of labor costs allocated to payment of employee benefits would be justified if benefits turned out to be an important factor in attracting good MBA candidates. Of the six factors ranked, employee benefits received the lowest ranking. Opportunity for advancement (1), salary (2), and geographic location (3) all ranked considerably higher than benefits as factors influencing job selection. Compounding this problem, these students also were asked to estimate the percentage of payroll spent on employee benefits. Slightly less than one half (46 percent) of the students thought that benefits comprised 15 percent or less of payroll. Nine out of 10 students (89 percent) thought benefits accounted for less than 30 percent of payroll. Only 1 in 10 students had a reasonably accurate (42 percent of payroll) or inflated perception of the magnitude of employee benefits.[12]

The ignorance about the value of employee benefits inferred from these studies can be traced to both attitudinal and design problems. Looming largest is the attitude problem. Benefits are taken for granted. Employees view them as a right with little comprehension of, or concern for, employer costs.[13]

One possible salvation from this money pit comes from recent reports that employees are not necessarily looking for more benefits, but rather greater choice in the benefits they receive.[14] In fact, up to 70 percent of employees in one study indicated they would be willing to pay more out of pocket for benefits if they were granted greater choice in designing their own benefits package. Maybe better benefits planning, design, and administration offer an opportunity to improve benefits effectiveness. Indeed, preliminary evidence indicates employers are making serious efforts to educate employees about benefits, with an outcome of increased employee awareness.[15]

---

[10]"Large Employers Report Moderate Healthcare Cost Increases," *Compensation and Benefits Review*, July/August 1997, p 13; U.S. Chamber of Commerce, *Employee Benefits*, (Washington, D.C.: U.S. Chamber of Commerce 1991).

[11]M.L. Williams and E. Newman, "Employees' Definitions of and Knowledge of Employer-provided Benefits" (Paper presented at 1993 Academy of Management Meetings, Atlanta, 1993); Richard Huseman, John Hatfield, and Richard Robinson, "The MBA and Fringe Benefits," *Personnel Administration* 23, no. 7 (1978), pp. 57–60.

[12]Ibid.

[13]Foegen, "Are Escalating Employee Benefits Self-Defeating?"

[14]Employee Benefit Research Institute, *America in Transition: Benefits for the Future* (Washington, D.C.: EBRI 1987).

[15]Carol Danehower and John Lust, "How aware are employees of their benefits?" *Benefits Quarterly* 12, no. 4, pp. 57–61.

KEY ISSUES IN BENEFITS PLANNING, DESIGN, AND ADMINISTRATION

Benefits Planning and Design Issues

First and foremost, the benefits planning process must address the vital question: "What is the relative role of benefits in a total compensation package?"[16] For example, if a major compensation objective is to attract good employees, we need to ask, "What is the best way to achieve this?" The answer is not always, nor even frequently, "Let's add another benefit."

Consider a company that needs to fill some entry-level jobs that pay minimum wage. One temptation might be to set up a day care center to attract more mothers with preschool children. Certainly this is a popular response today, judging from all the press day care centers are receiving. A more prudent compensation policy would ask the question: "Is day care the most effective way to achieve my compensation objective?" Sure, day care may be popular to working mothers. But can the necessary workers be attracted to the company using some other compensation tool that better meets company needs? For example, we know that day care is relatively popular in the insurance industry. If we went to compensation experts in that industry they might say (and we would be impressed if they did): "We target recruitment of young females for our entry-level jobs. Surveys of this group indicate day care is an extremely important factor in the decision to accept a job." If we heard this kind of logic it would certainly illustrate the kind of care firms should use before adopting expensive benefit options.

As a second example, How do we deal with undesirable turnover? We might be tempted to design a benefits package that improves progressively with seniority, thus providing a reward for continuing service. This would only be the preferred option, though, if other compensation tools (e.g., increasing wages, introducing incentive compensation) are less effective.

In addition to integrating benefits with other compensation components, the planning process also should include strategies to ensure external competitiveness and adequacy of benefits. Competitiveness requires an understanding of what other firms in your product and labor markets offer as benefits. Firms conduct benefits surveys much as they conduct salary surveys. Either our firm must have a package comparable to survey participants, or there should be a sound justification of why deviation makes sense for the firm.

In contrast, ensuring that benefits are adequate is a somewhat more difficult task. Most organizations evaluating adequacy consider the financial liability of employees with and without a particular benefit (e.g., employee medical expenses with and without medical expenses benefits). There is no magic formula for defining benefits adequacy.[17] In part, the answer may lie in the relationship between benefits adequacy and the third plan objective: cost of effectiveness. More organizations need to consider

---

[16]Burton Beam, Jr. and John J McFadden, *Employee Benefits* (Chicago: Dearborn Financial Publishing 1996).

[17]Burton Beam, Jr. and John J McFadden, *Employee Benefits*.

whether employee benefits are cost justified. All sorts of ethical questions arise when we start asking this question. How far should we go with elder care? Can we justify a $250,000 operation that will likely buy only a few months more of life? Companies face these impossible questions when designing a benefits system.

The compensation link site listed below will give you general information about compensation and benefits. The second address, to Benefitslink, will provide a wealth of information about types of benefits, a message board to interact in discussions with others interested in benefits, and a question and answer column to "ask the expert." **http://www.compensationlink.com/** and **http://www.benefitslink.com/index.shtml**

Benefits Administration Issues

Three major administration issues arise in setting up a benefits package: (1) Who should be protected or benefited? (2) How much choice should employees have among an array of benefits? (3) How should benefits be financed?[18]

The first issue—who should be covered—ought to be an easy question. Employees, of course. But every organization has a variety of employees with different employment statuses. Should these individuals be treated equally with respect to benefits coverage? Exhibit 12.3 illustrates that companies do indeed differentiate treatment based on

EXHIBIT 12.3 Comparison of Full- and Part-Timer Benefits

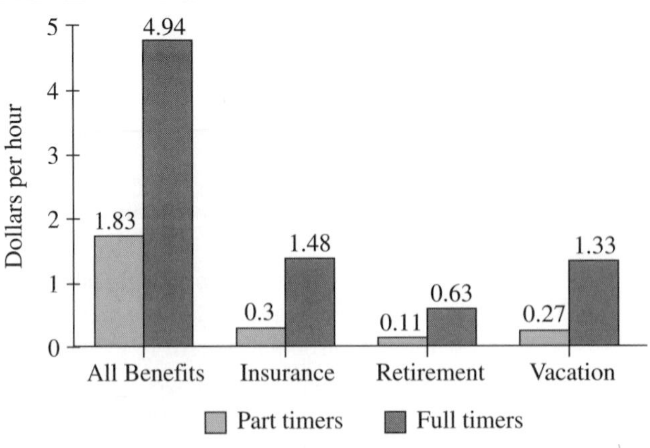

Source: U.S. Department of Labor, Bureau of Labor Statistics. *Employer Costs for Employee Compensation*. March 1994 (Washington D.C.: U.S. Government Printing Office, 1994).

[18]Ibid.

employment status. The dollar value of benefits is much lower, even when we factor in the difference in hours worked, for part-timers than full-time employees.

As a second example, should retired automobile executives be permitted to continue purchasing cars at a discount price, a benefit that could be reserved solely for current employees? In fact, a whole series of questions need to be answered:

1. What probationary periods (for eligibility of benefits) should be used for various types of benefits? Does the employer want to cover employees and their dependents immediately upon employment or provide such coverage for employees who have established more or less permanent employment with the employer? Is there a rationale for different probationary periods with different benefits?
2. Which dependents of active employees should be covered?
3. Should retirees (as well as their spouses and perhaps other dependents) be covered, and for which benefits?
4. Should survivors of deceased active employees (and/or retirees) be covered? And if so, for which benefits? Are benefits for surviving spouses appropriate?
5. What coverage, if any, should be extended to employees who are suffering from disabilities?
6. What coverage, if any, should be extended to employees during layoff, leaves of absence, strikes, and so forth?
7. Should coverage be limited to full-time employees?[19]

The answers to these questions depend on the policy decisions regarding adequacy, competition, and cost effectiveness discussed in the last section.

The second administrative issue concerns choice (flexibility) in plan coverage. In the standard benefits package, employees typically have not been offered a choice among employee benefits. Rather, a package is designed with the average employee in mind and any deviations in needs simply go unsatisfied. The other extreme (discussed in greater detail later) is represented by "cafeteria-style," or flexible benefit plans. Under this concept employees are permitted great flexibility in choosing the benefits options of greatest value to them. Picture an individual allotted *x* dollars walking down a cafeteria line and choosing menu items (benefits) according to their attractiveness and cost. The flexibility in this type of plan is apparent. Exhibit 12.4 illustrates a typical choice among packages offered to employees under a flexible benefits system. Imagine an employee whose spouse works and already has family coverage for health, dental, and vision. The temptation might be to select package A. A second employee with retirement in mind might select option B with its contributions to a 401K pension plan.

Even companies that are not considering a flexible benefits program are offering greater flexibility and choice. Such plans might provide, for example, (1) optional levels of group term life insurance; (2) the availability of death or disability benefits under pension or profit-sharing plans; (3) choices of covering dependents under group medical expense coverage; (4) a variety of participation, cash distribution, and investment options under profit-sharing, thrift, and capital accumulation plans.[20]

---

[19]Ibid.

[20]Kenneth Shapiro, "Flexibility in Benefit Plans," *1983 Hay Compensation Conference Proceedings* (Philadelphia: Hay Management Consultants, 1983).

Exhibit 12.4 Example of Possible Options in a Flexible Benefits Package

	Package			
	A	*B*	*C*	*D*
Health	No	No	Yes	Yes
Dental	No	No	No	Yes
Vision	No	Yes	Yes	Yes
Life Insurance	1 X AE*	2 X AE	2 X AE	3 X AE
Dependent Care	Yes	No	No	No
401K Savings	No	Yes	No	No
Cash Back	Yes	No	No	No

* AE = Average Earnings

Exhibit 12.5 Advantages and Disadvantages of Flexible Benefit Programs

Advantages

1. Employees choose packages that best satisfy their unique needs.
2. Flexible benefits help firms meet the *changing* needs of a *changing* workforce.
3. Increased involvement of employees and families improves understanding of benefits.
4. Flexible plans make introduction of new benefits less costly. The new option is added merely as one among a wide variety of elements from which to choose.
5. Cost containment: Organization sets dollar maximum. Employee chooses within that constraint.

Disadvantages

1. Employees make bad choices and find themselves not covered for predictable emergencies.
2. Administrative burdens and expenses increase.
3. Adverse selection. Employees pick only benefits they will use. The subsequent high benefit utilization increases its cost.
4. Subject to nondiscrimination requirements in Section 125 of the Internal Revenue Code.

Exhibit 12.5 summarizes some of the major advantages and disadvantages of flexible benefits. Judging from increased adoption of flexible benefits over the past decade, it seems that employers consider the advantages noted in Exhibit 12.5 to far outweigh the disadvantages. Current estimates put the rate of flexible benefit adoption at 25 percent for large employers.[21]

[21]Burton Beam, Jr. and John J McFadden, *Employee Benefits*.

The level at which an organization finally chooses to operate on this choice/flexibility dimension really depends on its evaluation of the relative advantages and disadvantages of flexible plans noted in Exhibit 12.5.[22] Many companies cite the cost savings from flexible benefits (46 percent of those that adopt) as a primary motivation.[23]

A key consideration in the continued popularity of flexible benefit plans may well be the increased scrutiny by the Internal Revenue Service. Section 125 of the Internal Revenue Code outlines a series of requirements a company must meet in setting up a flexible benefits package.[24] The most important of these restrictions is a nondiscrimination clause; that is, a plan may not give significantly higher benefits to highly compensated executives relative to average employees. In fact, the average benefits for non-highly compensated employees must equal or exceed 75 percent of the average benefits for highly compensated executives.

The final administrative issue involves the question of financing benefits plans. Alternatives include:

1. Noncontributory (employer pays total costs).
2. Contributory (costs shared between employer and employee).
3. Employee financed (employee pays total costs for some benefits—by law the organization must bear the cost for some benefits).

In general, organizations prefer to make benefits options contributory, reasoning that a "free good," no matter how valuable, is less valuable to an employee. Furthermore, employees have no personal interest in controlling the cost of a free good.

COMPONENTS OF A BENEFITS PLAN

Exhibit 12.6 outlines a model of the factors influencing benefits choice, from both the employer and employee perspective. The remainder of this chapter briefly examines each of these factors.

Employer Preferences

As Exhibit 12.6 indicates, a number of factors affect employer preference in determining desirable components of a benefits package.

Relationship to Total Compensation Costs. A good compensation manager considers employee benefit costs as part of a total package of compensation costs. Frequently employees think that just because an employee benefit is attractive, the company should

---

[22]Commerce Clearing House, *Flexible Benefits* (Chicago: Commerce Clearing House, 1983); American Can Company, *Do It Your Way* (Greenwich, Conn.: American Can Co., 1978); L.M. Baytos, "The Employee Benefit Smorgasbord: Its Potential and Limitations," *Compensation Review*, First Quarter 1970, pp. 86–90; "Flexible Benefit Plans Become More Popular," *Wall Street Journal*, December 16, 1986, p. 1; Richard Johnson, *Flexible Benefits: A How To Guide*, (Brookfield, WI: International Foundation of Employee Benefit Plans 1986).

[23]Christopher Conte, "Flexible Benefit Plans Grow More Popular as Companies Seek to Cut Costs," *The Wall Street Journal*, March 19, 1991, p A1.

[24]Johnson, *Flexible Benefits: A How To Guide*.

EXHIBIT 12.6 Factors Influencing Choice of Benefits Package

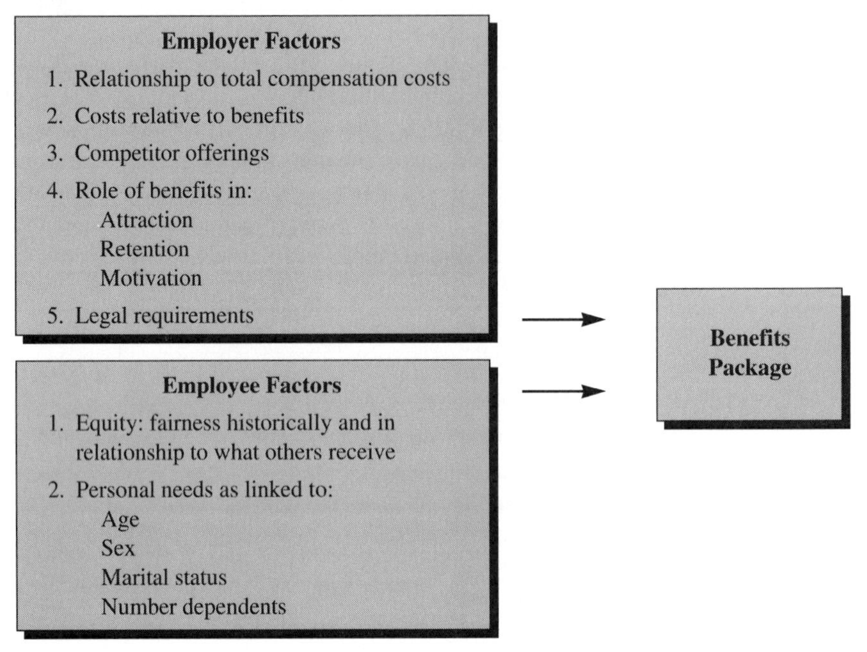

provide it. A good compensation manager thinks somewhat differently: "Is there a better use for this money? Could we put the money into some other compensation component and achieve better results?" Benefit costs are only one part of a total compensation package. Decisions about outlays have to be considered from this perspective.

Costs Relative to Benefits. A major reason for the proliferating cost of benefits programs is the narrow focus of benefits administrators. Too frequently the costs/advantages of a particular benefit inclusion are viewed in isolation, without reference to total package costs or forecasts of rising costs in future years. To control spiraling benefit costs, administrators should adopt a broader, cost-centered approach. As a first step, this approach would require policy decisions on the level of benefit expenditures acceptable both in the short and long run. Historically, benefits managers negotiated or provided benefits on a package basis rather than a cost basis. The current cost of a benefit would be identified and, if the cost seemed reasonable, the benefit would be provided for or negotiated with employees. This failed to recognize that rising costs of this benefit were expected to be borne by the employer. The classic example of this phenomenon is health care coverage. An employer considering a community-based medical plan like Blue Cross during the early 1960s no doubt agreed to pay all or most of the costs of one of the Blue Cross options. As costs of this plan skyrocketed during the 60s and 70s, the employer was expected to continue coverage at the historical level. In effect, the employer became locked into a level of coverage rather than negotiating a level of cost. In subsequent years, then, the spiraling costs were essentially out of the control of the benefits manager.

A cost-centered approach would require benefits administrators, in cooperation with insurance carriers and armed with published forecasts of anticipated costs for particular benefits, to determine the cost commitments for the existing benefits package. Budget dollars not already earmarked may then be allocated to new benefits that best satisfy organizational goals. Factors affecting this decision include an evaluation of benefits offered by other firms and the competitiveness of the existing package. Also important is compliance with various legal requirements as they change over time (Chapter 13). Finally, the actual benefit of a new option must be explored in relation to employee preferences. Those benefits that top the list of employee preferences should be evaluated in relation to current and future costs. Because future cost estimates may be difficult to project, it is imperative that benefits administrators reduce uncertainty.

If a benefit forecast suggests future cost containment may be difficult, the benefit should be offered to employees only on a cost-sharing basis. Management determines what percentage of cost it can afford to bear within budget projections, and the option is offered to employees on a cost-sharing basis, with projected increases in both employer and employee costs communicated openly. In the negotiation process, then, employees or union representatives can evaluate their preference for the option against the forecasted cost burden. In effect, this approach defines the contribution an employer is willing to make, in advance. And it avoids the constraints of a defined benefit strategy that burdens the employer with continued provision of that defined benefit level despite rapidly spiraling costs.

Competitor Offerings. Benefits must be externally equitable, too. This begs the question, what is the absolute level of benefits payments relative to important product and labor market competitors? A policy decision must be made about the position (market lead, market lag, or competitive) the organization wants to maintain in its absolute level of benefits relative to the competition. One of the best strategies to determine *external equity* is to conduct a benefits survey. Alternatively, many consulting organizations, professional associations, and interest groups collect benefits data that can be purchased. Perhaps the most widely used of these surveys is the annual benefits survey conducted by the U.S. Chamber of Commerce.[25]

Role of Benefits in Attraction, Retention and Motivation. Given the rapid growth in benefits and the staggering cost implications, it seems only logical that employers would expect to derive a fair return on this investment. In fact, there is at best only anecdotal evidence that employee benefits are cost justified. This evidence falls into three categories.[26] First, employee benefits are widely claimed to help in the retention of

---

[25]U.S. Chamber of Commerce, *Employee Benefits.*

[26]Donald P. Crane, *The Management of Human Resources*, 2nd ed. (Belmont, CA: Wadsworth, 1979); Foegen, "Are Escalating Employee Benefits Self-Defeating?" *Pension World* 14, no. 9 (September 1978), pp. 83–84, 86.

workers. Benefit schedules are specifically designed to favor longer term employees. For example, retirement benefits increase with years of service, and most plans do not provide for full employee eligibility until a specified number of years of service has been reached. Equally, amount of vacation time increases with years of service; and finally, employees' savings plans, profit-sharing plans, and stock purchase plans frequently provide for increased participation or benefits as company seniority increases. By tying these benefits to seniority, it is assumed that workers are more reluctant to change jobs.

There is also some research to support this common assumption that benefits increase retention. Two studies found that higher benefits reduced mobility.[27] More detailed follow-up studies, though, found only two specific benefits curtailed employee turnover: pensions and medical coverage.[28] Virtually no other employee benefit had a significant impact on turnover.

We've been assuming here that turnover is bad and stability is good. In fact, there are times when turnover may be good—something we may not want to discourage. For example, at one time or another three Americans in ten have stayed in a job they wanted to leave simply because they could not give up their health care coverage.[29] This job lock probably is not a desirable outcome for employers.

Employee benefits also might be valued if we could prove they increase employee satisfaction. Unfortunately, though, today only 50 percent of workers consider their benefits adequate. This is down from 83 percent in the early 80s.[30] The lowest satisfaction marks go to disability, life, and health insurance.[31] Why have satisfaction ratings fallen? One view holds that benefits satisfaction falls as cost-cutting companies attempt to reduce coverage and also shift more of the costs to employees.[32] A second view is more pessimistic, arguing that benefits plans fail to meet either employer or employee needs. In this view simply pumping more money into benefits is inappropriate. Rather, employers must make fundamental changes in the way they approach the benefits planning process. Companies must realize that declining satisfaction with benefits is a result of long-term changes in the workforce. Ever increasing numbers of women in the labor force, coupled with increasing numbers of dual career families and higher educational

---

[27]Olivia Mitchell, "Fringe Benefits and Labor Mobility," *Journal of Human Resources* 17, no. 2 (1982), pp. 286–98; Bradley Schiller and Randal Weiss, "The Impact of Private Pensions on Firm Attachment," *Review of Economics and Statistics* 61, no. 3 (1979), pp. 369–80.

[28]Olivia Mitchell, "Fringe Benefits and the Cost of Changing Jobs," *Industrial and Labor Relations Review* 37, no. 1 (1983), pp. 70–78. William E. Even, David A. MacPherson, "Employer Size and Labor Turnover: The Role of Pensions," *Industrial and Labor Relations Review*, 49, No. 4 (July 1996), p. 707.

[29]New York Times and CBS poll as reported in the *Human Resource Management News* (Chicago: Remy Publishing, 1991).

[30]Christopher Conte, "Flexible Benefit Plans Grow More Popular as Companies Seek to Cut Costs," *The Wall Street Journal*, March 19, 1991, p A1.

[31]*The Wall Street Journal*, April 30, 1985, p. 1.

[32]George Dreher, Ronald Ash, Robert Bretz, "Benefit Coverage and Employee Cost: Critical Factors in Explaining Compensation Satisfaction," *Personnel Psychology* 41 (1988), 237–254.

attainments, suggest changing values of employees.[33] Changing values, in turn, necessitate a reevaluation of benefits packages.

Finally, employee benefits also are valued because they may have an impact on the bottom line. Although supporting evidence is slim, there are some glimmers of potential. For example, employee stock ownership plans (Chapter 12) reportedly improve company productivity.[34] Presumably, owning stock motivates employees to be more productive. After all, part of the reward returns to them in the form of dividends and increased stock value. Similar productivity improvements are reported for employee assistance programs (e.g., alcohol and drug treatment programs for employees), with reports of up to 25 percent jumps in productivity after their implementation.[35]

Legal Requirements. Employers obviously want a benefits package that complies with all aspects of the law. Exhibit 12.7 shows part of the increasingly complex web of legislation in the benefits area. Greater details on the three legally mandated benefits (workers' compensation, social security, and unemployment insurance) are provided in Chapter 13.

Absolute and Relative Compensation Costs. Any evaluation of employee benefits must be placed in the context of total compensation costs. Cost competitiveness means the total package must be competitive—not just specific segments. Consequently, decisions on whether to adopt certain options must be considered in light of the impact on total costs and in relationship to expenditures of competitors (as determined in benefits surveys such as the Chamber of Commerce survey discussed earlier in this chapter).

Employee Preferences

Employee preferences for various benefit options are determined by individual needs. Those benefits perceived to best satisfy individual needs are most highly desired. In part these needs arise out of feelings of perceived equity or inequity.

Equity. To illustrate the impact of equity, consider the example of government employees working in the same neighborhood as auto workers. Imagine the dissatisfaction with government holidays that arises when government employees leave for work every morning, knowing that the auto workers are home in bed for the whole week between Christmas and New Year's Day. The perceived unfairness of this difference need not be rational. But it is, nevertheless, a factor that must be considered in determining employee needs. Occasionally this comparison process leads to a "bandwagon" effect where new benefits offered by a competitor are adopted without careful consideration, simply because the employer wants to avoid hard feelings. This phenomenon is particularly apparent for employers with strong commitments to maintaining a totally or

---

[33]Ibid.

[34]"ESOPs Key to Performance," *Employee Benefit News*, no. 5, 1987, p. 16.

[35]Lynn Densford, "Bringing Employees Back to health," *Employee Benefit News* 2 (February 1988), p.19.

EXHIBIT 12.7 Impact of Legislation on Selected Benefits

Legislation	*Impact on Employee Benefits*
Fair Labor Standards Act 1938	Created time-and-a-half overtime pay. Benefits linked to pay (e.g., social security) increase correspondingly during those overtime hours.
Employee Retirement Income Security Act 1974	If an employer decides to provide a pension (it is not mandated), specific rules must be followed. Plan must vest (employee has right to both personal and company contributions into pension) after five years employment. Pension Benefit Guaranty Corporation, as set up by this law, provides worker some financial coverage when a company and its pension plan goes bankrupt.
Tax reform–1982, 1986	Permit Individual Retirement Accounts (IRAs) for eligible employees. Established 401K programs, a matched contributions saving plan (employer matches part or all of employee contribution) that frequently serves as part of a retirement package.
Health Maintenance Act 1973	Required employers to offer alternative health coverage (e.g., Health Maintenance Organizations) options to employees
Discrimination Legislation (Age Discrimination in Employment Act, Civil Rights Act, Pregnancy Disability Act, various state laws)	Benefits must be administered in a manner that does not discriminate against protected groups (on basis of race, color, religion, sex, national origin, age, pregnancy)
Consolidated Omnibus Budget Reconciliation Act (COBRA) 1984	Employees who resign or are laid off through no fault of their own are eligible to continue receiving health coverage under employer's plan at a cost borne by the employee.

partially nonunion work force. Benefits obtained by a unionized competitor or a unionized segment of the firm's workforce are frequently passed along to nonunion employees. While the effectiveness of this strategy in thwarting unionization efforts has not been demonstrated, many nonunion firms would prefer to provide the benefit as a safety measure.

Personal Needs of Employees. A major assumption in empirical efforts to determine employee preferences is that preferences are somehow systematically related to what are termed demographic differences. The demographic approach assumes that demographic groups (e.g., young versus old, married versus unmarried) can be identified for which benefits preferences are fairly consistent across members of the group. Furthermore, it assumes that meaningful differences exist between groups in terms of benefit preferences.

There is some evidence that these assumptions are only partially correct. In an extensive review of employee preference literature, Glueck traced patterns of group preferences for particular benefits.[36] As one might expect, older workers showed stronger preferences than younger workers for pension plans.[37] Also, families with dependents had stronger preferences for health/medical coverage than families with no dependents.[38] The big surprise in all these studies, though, is that many of the other demographic group breakdowns fail to result in differential benefit preferences. Traditionally, it has been assumed that benefit preferences ought to differ among males versus females, blue collar versus white collar and married versus single. Few of these expectations have been borne out by these studies. Rather, the studies have tended to be more valuable in showing preference trends that are characteristic of all employees. Among the benefits available, health/medical and stock plans are highly preferred benefits, while such options as early retirement, profit sharing, shorter hours, and counseling services rank among the least-preferred options. Beyond these conclusions, most preference studies have shown wide variation in individuals with respect to benefit preferences.

The weakness of this demographic approach has led some organizations to undertake a second and more expensive empirical method of determining employee preference: surveying individuals about needs. One way of accomplishing this requires development of a questionnaire on which employees evaluate various benefits. For example, Exhibit 12.8 illustrates a questionnaire format.

While other strategies for scaling are available (e.g., paired comparison), the most important factor to remember is that a consistent method must be used in assessing preferences on a questionnaire. Switching between a ranking method and a Likert-type scale may, by itself, affect the results.[39]

A third empirical method of identifying individual employee preferences is commonly known as a flexible benefit plan (also called, at various times, a cafeteria-style plan or a supermarket plan). As previously noted, employees are allotted a fixed amount of money and permitted to spend that amount in the purchase of benefit options. From a theoretical perspective, this approach to benefits packaging is ideal. Employees directly identify the benefits of greatest value to them, and by constraining the dollars employees have to spend, benefits managers are able to control benefits costs.

ADMINISTERING THE BENEFITS PROGRAM

The job description for an employee-benefits executive found in Exhibit 12.9 indicates that administrative time is spent on three functions requiring further discussion: (1) communicating about the benefits program, (2) claims processing, and (3) cost containment.[40]

---

[36]William F. Glueck, *Personnel: A Diagnostic Approach* (Plano, Tex.: Business Publications, 1978).

[37]Ludwig Wagner and Theodore Bakerman, "Wage Earners' Opinions of Insurance Fringe Benefits," *Journal of Insurance*, June 1960, pp. 17–28; Brad Chapman and Robert Otterman, "Employee Preference for Various Compensation and Benefits Options," *Personnel Administrator* 25 (November 1975), pp. 31–36.

[38]Stanley Nealy, "Pay and Benefit Preferences," *Industrial Relations* (October 1963), pp. 17–28.

[39]George T. Milkovich and Michael J. Delaney, "A Note on Cafeteria Pay Plans," *Industrial Relations* (February 1975), pp. 112–16.

[40]McCaffery, *Managing the Employee Benefits Program.*

Exhibit 12.8 Questionnaire Formats for Benefits Surveys

Employee Benefit Questionnaire

1. In the space provided in front of the benefits listed below indicate how important each benefit is to you and your family. Indicate this by placing a "1" for the most important, and "2" for the next most important, etc. Therefore, if life insurance is the most important benefit to you and your family, place a "1" in front of it.

Importance		*Improvement*
________	Dental insurance	________
________	Disability (pay while sick)	________
________	Educational assistance	________
________	Holidays	________
________	Life insurance	________
________	Medical insurance	________
________	Retirement annuity plan	________
________	Savings plan	________
________	Vacations	________
________	____________________	________
________	____________________	________

Now, go back and in the space provided after each benefit, indicate the priority for improvement. For example, if the savings plan is the benefit you would most like to see improved, give it a "1," the next a priority "2," etc. Use the blank lines to add any benefits not listed.

2. Would you be willing to contribute a portion of your earnings for new or improved benefits beyond the level already provided by the Company?

☐ Yes ☐ No

If yes, please indicate below in which area(s):

☐ Dental insurance ☐ Medical insurance

☐ Disability benefits ☐ Retirement annuity plan

☐ Life insurance ☐ Savings plan

Source: Pfizer Corporation

Employee Benefits Communication

Much of the effort to achieve benefit goals focuses on identifying methods of communication. The most frequent method for communicating employee benefits today is probably still the employee benefits handbook.[41] A typical handbook contains a description of all benefits, including levels of coverage and eligibility requirements. To be most effective, this benefits manual should be accompanied by group meetings and videotapes.[42] While some organizations may supplement this initial benefits discussion

[41]Towers, Perrin, Forster, and Crosby, "Corporate Benefit Communication . . . Today and Tomorrow," 1988.

[42]Ibid.

EXHIBIT 12.9 Job Description for Employee-Benefits Executive

Position

The primary responsibility of this position is the administration of established company benefits programs. Develops and recommends new and improved policies and plans with regard to employee benefits. Assures compliance with ERISA requirements and regulations.

Specific Functions

1. Administers group life insurance, health and accident insurance, retirement programs, and savings plans.
2. Processes documents necessary for the implementation of various benefits programs and maintains such records as are necessary.
3. Recommends and approves procedures for maintenance of benefits programs and issues operating instructions.
4. Participates in the establishment of long-range objectives of company benefits programs.
5. Conducts surveys and analyzes and maintains an organized body of information on benefits programs of other companies.
6. Informs management of trends and developments in the field of company benefits.
7. Gives advice and counsel regarding current developments in benefits programs.
8. Acts as liaison between company and banks, insurance companies, and other agencies.
9. Conducts special studies as requested by management.

In addition, the employee-benefits executive may be responsible for various employee services, such as recreation programs, advisory services, credit unions, and savings bond purchase programs.

Source: Robert McCaffery, *Managing the Employee Benefits Program* (New York: American Management Association, 1983), p. 25.

with periodic refreshers (e.g., once per year), a more typical approach involves one-on-one discussions between the benefits administrator and an employee seeking information on a particular benefit. In recent years the dominance of the benefits handbook is being challenged by personalized benefits statements generated by computer software programs specially designed for that purpose. These tailor-made reports provide a breakdown of package components and list selected cost information about the options.[43]

Despite this and other innovative plans to communicate employee benefit packages, failure to understand benefits components and their value is still one of the root causes of employee dissatisfaction with a benefits package.[44] We believe an effective communications package must have three elements. First, an organization must spell out its

[43]Ibid.

[44]"Yoder-Heneman Creativity Award Supplement," *Personnel Administration* 26, no. 11 (1981), pp. 49–67.

Exhibit 12.10 Typical Benefits Objectives

Objective	*Respondents Indicating This Is a Primary Objective (in Percents)**
1. Increase Employee Understanding of Plan Objectives	82
2. Increase Employee Appreciation of the Benefits Program	81
3. Increase Employee Knowledge of the Cost of Providing Benefits	41
4. Obtain Employee Cooperation in Controlling Benefit Costs	36
5. Encourage Employee Responsibility for Own Financial Security	16
6. Maintain the Company's Commitment to Open Employee Communications	16

*Multiple responses permitted

Source: Towers, Perrin, Forster and Crosby (1988), "Corporate Benefit Communication . . . Today and Tomorrow."

benefit objectives and ensure that any communications achieve these objectives. Exhibit 12.10 outlines typical benefits objectives.

The second element of an effective communications package is to match the message with the appropriate medium. Exhibit 12.11 indicates the effectiveness ratings for a variety of communications tools.

And finally, the content of the communications package must be complete, clear, and free of the complex jargon which so readily invades benefits discussions. The amount of time/space devoted to each issue should vary closely with both perceived importance of the benefit to employees and with expected difficulty in communicating option alternatives.[45]

Claims Processing

As noted by one expert, claims processing arises when an employee asserts that a specific event (e.g., disability, hospitalization, unemployment) has occurred and demands that the employer fulfill a promise of payment.[46] As such, a claims processor must first determine whether the act has, in fact, occurred. If the answer is yes, the second step involves determining if the employee is eligible for the benefit. If payment is not denied at this stage, the claims processor calculates payment level. It is particularly important

[45]Benefits, "How Do You Communicate? It May Not Be Nearly As Well As You Think," *Benefits*, December 1988, pp. 13–15; Kevin Greene, "Effective Employee Benefits Communication," in David Balkin and Luis Gomez-Mejia, *New Perspectives on Compensation* (Englewood Cliffs, NJ: Prentice-Hall 1987).

[46]Bennet Shaver, "The Claims Process," in *Employee Benefit Management*, ed. H. Wayne Snider, pp. 141–52.

EXHIBIT 12.11 Effectiveness of Different Communications Tools

Communications Tool	*Rating*
	5 = highly effective 1 = highly ineffective
MEMOS	3.4
SPECIAL BROCHURES	3.8
EMPLOYEE HANDBOOKS	3.3
SMALL GROUP MEETINGS	4.2
PERSONALIZED BENEFIT STATEMENTS	4.3
LETTERS TO EMPLOYEE'S HOME	3.5
COMPANYWIDE PUBLICATIONS	3.3
"LIVE" SLIDE SHOWS	3.8
LARGE GROUP MEETINGS	3.6
BULLETIN BOARDS	3.1
VIDEOTAPES	4.0
EMPLOYEE ANNUAL REPORTS	2.4
SLIDES/AUDIOTAPES	3.7
INDIVIDUAL DISCUSSIONS WITH SUPERVISORS	3.4
BENEFIT NEWSLETTERS	3.6
TELEPHONE HOTLINES	3.6
ELECTRONIC COMMUNICATIONS	3.3
FILMS	3.5

Source: Towers, Perrin, Forster and Crosby (1988), "Corporate Benefit Communication . . . Today and Tomorrow."

at this stage to ensure coordination of benefits. If multiple insurance companies are liable for payment (e.g., working spouses covered by different insurers), a good claims processor can save from 10 to 15 percent of claims cost by ensuring that the liability is jointly paid.[47]

While these steps are time consuming, most of the work is quite routine in nature. The major job challenges come in those approximately 10 percent of all claims where payment is denied. A benefits administrator must then become an adroit counselor, explaining the situation to the employee in a manner that conveys the equitable and consistent procedures used.

Cost Containment

Cost containment is easily the biggest issue in benefits planning and administration today. Escalating costs of the 1960s, 1970s and 1980s, combined with disappointing evidence that benefits have little impact on shaping positive employee behaviors, have

[47]Thomas Fannin and Theresa Fannin, "Coordination of Benefits: Uncovering Buried Treasure," *Personnel Journal*, May 1983, pp. 386–91.

molded the cost-cutting drives of the 1990s. Increasingly, employers are auditing their benefits options for cost containment opportunities. The most prevalent practices include:

1. Probationary periods—excluding new employees from benefits coverage until some term of employment (for instance, 3 months) is completed.
2. Benefits limitations—it is not uncommon to limit disability income payments to some maximum percentage of income, and to limit medical/dental coverage for specific procedures to a certain fixed amount.
3. Co-pay—requires employees to pay a fixed or percentage amount for coverage
4. Administrative cost containment—includes such things as seeking competitive bids for program delivery.

So prevalent is the cost issue today that the terminology of cost containment is becoming a part of every employee's vocabulary. Exhibit 12.12 provides definitions of some common cost containment terms.

Probably the biggest cost containment strategy in recent years is the movement to outsourcing. By hiring vendors to administer their benefits programs, many companies, such as GTE and Tenneco, claim greater centralization, consistency, and control of costs and benefits.[48] Other companies like Digital Equipment Corporation outsource so they may focus on their core businesses, "leaving benefits to the benefits experts."[49]

EXHIBIT 12.12 A Basic Primer of Cost Containment Terminology

Deductibles—an employee claim for insurance coverage is preceded by the requirement that the first $*x* dollars be paid by the claimant.
Coinsurance—a proportion of insurance premiums are paid by the employee.
Benefit Cutbacks—corresponding to wage concessions some employers are negotiating with employees to eliminate or reduce employer contributions to selected options.
Defined Contribution Plans—employers establish the limits of their responsibility for employee benefits in terms of dollar contribution maximum.
Defined Benefits Plans—employers establish the limits of their responsibility for employee benefits in terms of a specific benefit and the options included. As the cost of these options rises in future years the employer is obligated to provide the benefit as negotiated, despite its increased cost.
Dual Coverage—in families where both spouses work there is frequently coverage of specific claims from each employer's benefit package. Employers cut costs by specifying payment limitations under such conditions.
Benefit Ceiling—establishing a maximum payout for specific claims (e.g., limiting liability for extended hospital stays to $150,000.)

[48]E. Scott Peterson, "From Those Who've Been There . . . Outsourcing Leaders Talk about Their Experiences," *Benefits Quarterly*, 6, no. 1 (First Quarter 1997), pp. 6–13
[49]Ibid.

Summary

Given the rapid escalation in the cost of employee benefits over the past 15 years, organizations would do well to evaluate the effectiveness of their benefits adoption, retention, and termination procedures. Specifically, how does an organization go about selecting appropriate employee benefits? Are the decisions based on sound evaluation of employee preferences balanced against organizational goals of legal compliance and competitiveness? Do the benefits chosen serve to attract, retain and/or motivate employees? Or are organizations paying billions of dollars of indirect compensation without any tangible benefit? This chapter has outlined a benefits determination process that identifies major issues in selecting and evaluating particular benefit choices. The next chapter catalogs the various benefits available and discusses some of the decisions confronting a benefits administrator.

Review Questions

1. You have just been hired as the first H.R. person ever at Krefting Electric. The CEO made it clear that your first priority is to "handle this benefits thing." His concern is that employees don't seem very happy, but he is spending over $4,000 per employee. He wants you to fix things, and he leaves it to you to figure out what and how. What should you do, and why?
2. Your CEO is living proof that a little bit of knowledge is dangerous. He just read in the *Wall Street Journal* that employee benefits cost, on average, 38 percent of payroll. To save money, he suggests the company fire its two benefits administrators, do away with all benefits, and give employees a 38 percent pay hike. What arguments could you provide to persuade the CEO this is not a good idea?
3. You live in Buffalo, New York, where population declines are the most evident sign of decay in this self-styled "gateway to the East." The average age of your 600-person workforce is 43. Turnover is low, and the want ad page is just that—one page. Not much is happening on the job front. How do these facts influence your decisions about designing an employee benefits program?
4. How is the concept of external equity similar or different in discussing pay versus benefits?
5. Describe how a flexible benefits program might increase worker satisfaction with benefits at the same time that costs are being reduced.

Your Turn:

Mondaille Hydraulics

Mondaille Hydraulics manufactures pumps for construction equipment and residential homes. In six months contract negotiations are scheduled with the bargaining representative for all blue-collar workers, Local 1099 of the United Auto Workers. The president of your company, Forrest Sutton, is convinced that he must get concessions from the workers if Mondaille is to compete effectively with increasing foreign competition. In particular, Mr. Sutton is displeased with the cost of employee benefits. He doesn't mind conceding a small wage increase (maximum 3 percent), but he wants the total compensation package to cost 3 percent less for union employees during the first year of the new contract. Your current costs are shown in Exhibit 1.

Your labor relations assistant has surveyed other companies obtaining concessions from UAW locals. You also have data from a consulting firm that indicates employee preferences for different forms of benefits (Exhibit 2). Based on all this information, you have two possible concession packages that the union just might accept, labeled Option 1 and Option 2 (Exhibit 3).

1. Cost out these packages given the data in Exhibits 1 and 2 and the information contained from various insurance carriers and other information sources (Exhibit 4).
2. Which package should you recommend to the president? Why?
3. Which of the strategies do you think need not be negotiated with the union before implementation?

Exhibit 1 Current Compensation Costs

Average yearly wage	$26,769
Average hourly wage	13.12
Dollar value of yearly benefits, per employee	8,923
Total compensation (wages plus benefits)	35,692
Daily average number of hours paid	8.0

Benefits (by category)	*Dollar Cost/ Employee/Year*
1. Legally required payments (employer's share only)	$2,141.00
a. Old-age, survivors, disability, and health insurance (FICA) taxes	1,509.00
b. Unemployment compensation	292.00
c. Workers' compensation (including estimated cost of self-insured)	311.00
d. Railroad retirement tax, railroad unemployment and cash sickness insurance, state sickness benefits insurance, etc.	29.00
2. Pension, insurance, and other agreed-upon payments (employer's share only)	$3,124.00
a. Pension plan premiums and pension payments not covered by insurance-type plan (net)	1,460.00
b. Life insurance premiums; death benefits; hospital, surgical, medical, and major medical insurance premiums, etc. (net)	1,427.00

EXHIBIT 1 (concluded)

Benefits (by category)	*Dollar Cost/ Employee/Year*
c. Short-term disability	83.00
d. Salary continuation or long-term disability	57.00
e. Dental insurance premiums	51.00
f. Discounts on goods and services purchased from company by employees	27.00
g. Employee meals furnished by company	-0-
h. Miscellaneous payments (compensation payments in excess of legal requirements, separation or termination pay allowances, moving expenses, etc.)	24.00
3. Paid rest periods, lunch periods, wash-up time, travel time, clothes-change time, get-ready time, etc. (60 minutes)	$ 727.00
4. Payments for time not worked	$2,769.00
a. Paid vacations and payments in lieu of vacation (16 days average)	1,558.00
b. Payments for holidays not worked (9 days)	973.00
c. Paid sick leave (10 days maximum)	172.00
d. Payments for state or national guard duty; jury, witness, and voting pay allowances; payments for time lost due to death in family or other personal reasons, etc.	66.00
5. Other items	$ 157.00
a. Profit-sharing payments	-0-
b. Contributions to employee thrift plans	71.00
c. Christmas or other special bonuses, service awards, suggestion awards, etc.	-0-
d. Employee education expenditures (tuition refunds, etc.)	40.00
e. Special wage payments ordered by courts, payments to union stewards, etc.	46.00
Total	$8,923.00

EXHIBIT 2 Benefit Preferences

Benefit Type or Method of Administering	*Importance to Workers*
Pensions	87
Hospitalization	86
Life insurance	79
Paid vacation	82
Holidays	82
Long-term disability	72
Short-term disability	69

(continued)

EXHIBIT 2 *(concluded)*

Benefit Type or Method of Administering	*Importance to Workers*
Paid sick leave	70
Paid rest periods, lunch periods, etc.	55
Dental insurance	51
Christmas bonus	31
Profit sharing	21
Education expenditures	15
Contributions to thrift plans	15
Discount on goods	5
Fair treatment in administration	100

Note: 0 = Unimportant; 100 = Extremely important.

EXHIBIT 3 Two Possible Concession Packages

Option 1

Implement COPAY for Benefit	*Amount of COPAY*
Pension	$300.00
Hospital, surgical, medical, and major medical premiums	350.00
Dental insurance premiums	75.00

Reduction of Benefit

Eliminate 10-minute paid break (workers leave work 10 minutes earlier)
Eliminate one paid holiday per year
Coordination with legally required benefit; Social Security coordinated with
  Mondaille pension plan

Option 2

Improved claims processing
  Unemployment compensation
  Workers' compensation
  Long-term disability
Require probationary period (one year) before eligible for
  Discounts on goods
  Employee meal paid by company
  Contributions to employee thrift plans
Deductible ($100 per incident)
  Life insurance; death benefits; hospital, etc.
  Dental insurance

COPAY	*Amount of COPAY*
Hospital, surgical, medical and major medical premiums	$350.00

EXHIBIT 4 Analysis of Cost Implications for Different Cost-Cutting Strategies: Mondaille Hydraulics

Cost-Saving Strategy	*Savings as Percent of Benefit-Type Cost*
COPAY	Dollar-for-dollar savings equal to amount of COPAY
Deductible ($100 per incident)	
Life insurance premiums, death benefits, hospital, etc.	10%
Dental insurance	15
Require probationary period before eligible (one year)	
Discount on goods and services	10
Employee meals furnished by company	15
Contributions to employee thrift plans	10
Improved claims processing	
Unemployment compensation	8
Workers' compensation	3
Long-term disability	1
Coordination with legally required benefits	
Coordinate Social Security with Mondaille pension plan	15

Chapter 13 Benefits Options

Chapter Outline

At times the number of benefits options and choices can be quite overwhelming. Even trained human resource professionals can err in their evaluation of a benefits package. For example, one study asked both college graduates and human resource professionals to rank 11 different benefits, equated for costs, to a company.[1] The HR professionals' role was to estimate the graduates' responses. Surprisingly, at least to the recruiters, the college graduates placed high value on medical and life insurance, company stocks, and pensions. Lesser importance was placed on holidays and scheduling conveniences (e.g., flextime, four-day work week). The recruiters systematically underestimated the value of most of the top benefits and overestimated the value of the leisure and work-schedule benefits. Our goal in this chapter is to give you a clearer appreciation of employee benefits. We begin with a widely accepted categorization of employee benefits in Exhibit 13.1. The U.S. Chamber of Commerce issues an annual report based on a nationwide survey of employee benefits.[2] This report identifies seven categories of benefits in a breakdown that is highly familiar to benefits plan administrators. These seven categories will be used to organize this chapter and illustrate important principles affecting strategic and administrative concerns for each benefit type.

Exhibit 13.2 provides data from both the private sector (both small and large firms) and the public sector on employee participation in selected benefits programs.[3] Notice the high rate of participation for such common benefits as life and health insurance and pension plans in all except small firms. Only for legally required benefits (social security, workers' compensation and unemployment insurance) is the participation rate higher.

Exhibit 13.2 shows that a greater percentage of employees is covered in the private sector. The one major exception is with pension coverage. Typically, state and local government employees are more likely to have some form of retirement coverage than their private sector counterparts.

LEGALLY REQUIRED BENEFITS

Virtually every employee benefit is *somehow affected* by statutory or common law (many of the limitations are imposed by tax laws). In this section the primary focus will be on benefits that are *required* by statutory law: workers' compensation, social security, and unemployment compensation.

Workers' Compensation

What costs employers 83 billion dollars a year and is a major cost of doing business? Answer: workers' compensation.[4] The cost of workplace injuries and illnesses, includ-

---

[1]Kermit Davis, William Giles, and Hubert Feild, "Compensation and Fringe Benefits: How Recruiters View New College Graduates' Preferences," *Personnel Administrator*, January 1985, pp. 43–50.

[2]U.S. Chamber of Commerce, *Employee Benefits*, 1996 edition (Washington, D.C.: Chamber of Commerce, 1996).

[3]U.S. Department of Labor, *Employee Benefits in Medium and Large Firms*, 1986, Bulletin 2281, 1987.

[4]Fay Hansen, "Who Gets Hurt, and How Much Does It Cost?" *Compensation and Benefits Review*, May–June, 1997, pp. 6–11.

EXHIBIT 13.1 Categorization of Employee Benefits

Type of Benefit

1. Legally required payments (employers' share only)
   a. old-age, survivors, disability, and health insurance (employer FICA taxes) and railroad retirement tax
   b. Unemployment compensation
   c. Workers' compensation (including estimated cost of self-insured)
   d. State sickness benefits insurance
2. Retirement and savings plan payments (employers' share only)
   a. Defined benefit pension plan contributions (401K type)
   b. Defined contribution plan payments
   c. Profit sharing
   d. Stock bonus and employee stock ownership plans (ESOP)
   e. Pension plan premiums (net) under insurance and annuity contracts (insured and trusted)
   f. Administrative and other costs
3. Life insurance and death benefits (employers' share only)
4. Medical and medical-related benefit payments (employers' share only)
   a. Hospital, surgical, medical, and major medical insurance premiums (net)
   b. Retiree hospital, surgical, medical, and major medical insurance premiums (net)
   c. Short-term disability, sickness or accident insurance (company plan or insured plan)
   d. Long-term disability or wage continuation (insured, self-administered, or trust)
   e. Dental insurance premiums
   f. Other (vision care, physical and mental fitness benefits for former employees)
5. Paid rest periods, coffee breaks, lunch periods, wash-up time, travel time, clothes-change time, get-ready time, etc.
6. Payments for time not worked
   a. Payments for or in lieu of vacations
   b. Payments for or in lieu of holidays
   c. Sick leave pay
   d. Parental leave (maternity and paternity leave payments)
   e. Other
7. Miscellaneous benefit payments
   a. Discounts on goods and services purchased from company by employees
   b. Employee meals furnished by company
   c. Employee education expenditures
   d. Child care
   e. Other

ing medical treatment, wage replacement benefits, and lost productivity more than doubled between 1985 and 1993.[5] Workers' compensation is a form of no-fault insurance (employees are eligible even if their actions caused the accident) that covers injuries and diseases that arise out of, and while in the course of employment. Benefits are given for:[6]

[5]National Council on Compensation Insurance, Inc., 1996 Annual Statistical Bulletin.

[6]Ronald G. Ehrenberg, "Workers' Compensation, Wages, and the Risk of Injury." in *New Perspectives in Workers' Compensation,* ed. John Burton (Ithaca, NY: ILR Press, 1988).

EXHIBIT 13.2 Percentage Participation in Selected Benefits

	Small Firms			Medium and Large Firms		State and Local Governments	
Benefit Type	*1990*	*1992*	*1994*	*1991*	*1993*	*1992*	*1994*
Paid holiday	81%	79%	80%	92%	91%	75%	73%
Paid vacation	86	85	86	96	97	67	66
Sickness and accident insurance	23	24	24	45	44	22	21
Long-term disability	14	13	14	40	41	28	30
Health insurance	67	64	62	83	82	90	87
Life insurance	57	54	54	94	91	89	87
Retirement	35	34	35	78	78	93	96
Defined benefit plan	12	12	9	59	56	87	91
Defined contribution plan	28	27	29	48	49	9	9

Source: U.S. Department of Labor, Bureau of Labor Statistics, *Employee Benefits in Small Private Establishments, 1990, 1992, and 1994* (U.S. Government Printing Office, Washington, DC: 1992, 1994, and 1996); *Employee Benefits in Medium and Large Private Establishments, 1991 and 1993* (Washington, DC: U.S. Government Printing Office, 1993 and 1995); *Employee Benefits in State and Local Governments, 1992 and 1994* (Washington DC: U.S. Government Printing Office, 1994 and 1996).

1. Permanent total disability and temporary total disability
2. Permanent partial disability—loss of use of a body member
3. Survivor benefits for fatal injuries
4. Medical expenses
5. Rehabilitation

Of these five categories, temporary total disability is both the most frequent type of claim and one of the two most costly (along with permanent partial disability).[7] The amount of compensation is based on fixed schedules of minimum and maximum payments. Disability payments are often tied to the employee's earnings, modified by such economic factors as the number of dependents. Exhibit 13.3 shows the average benefit payment for different injury categories.

Some states provide "second injury funds." These funds relieve an employer's liability when a pre-employment injury combines with a work-related injury to produce a disability greater than that caused by the latter alone. For example, if a person with a known heart condition is hired, and then breaks an arm in a fall triggered by a heart attack, medical treatments for the heart condition would not be paid from workers' compensation insurance; treatment for the broken arm would be compensated.

Workers' compensation is covered by state, not federal laws. As Exhibit 13.4 shows, the types of coverage are fairly uniform. The primary difference across states is in benefits levels and costs. In fact, some employers argue these high costs are forcing them to uproot established businesses in states with high costs to relocate in lower cost states.[8]

---

[7]Ibid.

[8]Ibid.

Exhibit 13.3 Benefits by Type of Accident

Type of Accident	*Average Benefit Payment*
Fatality	$162,847
Permanent Total Disability	$173,660
Permanent Partial Disability	$ 21,093
All Cases	$ 4,832
Temporary Total Disability	$ 2,419
Medical Only	$ 419

Source: National Council on Compensation Insurance, Inc. 1996 Annual Statistical Bulletin.

Exhibit 13.4 Commonalities in State Workers' Compensation Laws

Issue	*Most Common State Provision*
Type of law	Compulsory (in 47 states) Elective (in 3 states)
Self insurance	Self-insurance permitted (in 48 states)
Coverage	All industrial employment Farm labor, domestic servants and casual employees usually exempted. Compulsory for all or most public sector employees (in 47 states)
Occupational diseases	Coverage for all diseases arising out of and in the course of employment. No compensation for "ordinary diseases of life."

Source: U.S. Chamber of Commerce, *Analysis of Workers' Compensation Laws*, 1985 (Washington, D.C.: Chamber of Commerce, 1985), Publication no. 6803.

This website from the Department of Labor provides extensive information about legally required benefits and specific requirements for compliance: **http://www.dol.gov/dol/public/regs/main.htm**

Why these rapid cost increases? At least three factors seem to play a role.[9] First, medical costs continue to skyrocket. Over 30 percent of workers' compensation costs can be traced to medical expenses. Second, some employees use workers' compensation as a surrogate for more stringent unemployment insurance programs. Rising numbers of employees, fearing recession and possible layoffs, fake new illnesses or stall reporting back after existing illnesses.

[9]Ibid.

Recent evidence suggests companies are beginning to control workers' compensation costs. For example, Bob Evans Farms Inc. has cut claims by 30 percent through safety committees and a safety program that charges managers for workplace injuries. If Pete the short-order cook is hit in the eye by a flying tomato seed, his manager's budget is reduced $1,000.[10] Besides better safety training, greater use of managed care techniques such as HMO's, self-insurance, reengineering the workplace, and better monitoring techniques to uncover fraud have all helped to regulate workers' compensation costs.[11]

Social Security

When social security was introduced in 1937, only about 60 percent of all workers were eligible.[12] By 1993, 97.6 percent of the labor force was covered.[13] Whether a worker retires, becomes disabled, or dies, social security benefits are paid to replace part of the lost family earnings. Indeed, ever since its passage, the Social Security Act has been designed and amended to provide a foundation of basic security for American workers and their families. Exhibit 13.5 identifies initial coverage of the law and subsequent broadening of this coverage over the years.[14]

The money to pay these benefits comes from the social security contributions made by employees, their employers, and self-employed people during working years. As contributions are paid in each year, they are immediately used to pay for the benefits to current beneficiaries. Herein lies a major problem with social security. While the number of retired workers continues to rise (because of earlier retirement and longer life spans), no corresponding increase in the number of contributors to social security has offset these costs. Combine these increases with other cost stimulants (e.g., liberal cost-of-living adjustments) and the outcome is not surprising. To maintain solvency, there has been a dramatic increase in both the maximum earnings base and the rate at which that base is taxed. Exhibit 13.6 illustrates the trends in tax rate, maximum earnings base, and maximum tax for social security.

Several points immediately jump out from this exhibit. First, with the rapid rise in taxable earnings, most of us will pay some amount of social security tax on every dollar we earn. This wasn't always true. Notice, in 1980 the maximum taxable earnings were $25,900. Every dollar earned over that amount was free of social security tax. Now the maximum is over $60,000, and for one part of social security (medicare) there is no earnings maximum. If Tiger Woods makes 30 million next year, he will pay 7.65 % social security tax on the first 60,000+ and 1.45% (the health/medicare portion) on all the

[10]Fay Hansen, "Who Gets Hurt, and How Much Does It Cost?" p. 11.

[11]Charles Lorenz, "Nine Practical Suggestions for Streamlining Worker's Compensation Costs," *Compensation and Benefits Review*, May–June 1995, pp. 40–44.

[12]Employee Benefit Research Institute, *Fundamentals of Employee Benefit Programs* (Washington, D.C.: EBRI, 1990).

[13]Jefferey A. Miron, David N. Weil, "The Genesis and Evolution of Social Security," National Bureau of Economic Research, Inc., Working Paper Series, (Working Paper 5949, p. 19).

[14]William J. Cohen, "The Evolution and Growth of Social Security," in *Federal Policies and Worker Status Since the Thirties*, ed. J.P. Goldberg, E. Ahern, W. Haber, and R.A. Oswald (Madison, WI: Industrial Relations Research Association, 1976), p. 62.

EXHIBIT 13.5 Social Security through the Years

	Original Provisions of the 1935 Law
	Federal old-age benefits program
	Public assistance for the aged, blind, and dependent children who would not otherwise qualify for social security
	Unemployment compensation
	Federally funded state program for maternity care, crippled children's services, child-welfare services
	Public health services
	Vocational rehabilitation services
	Changes in the Law since 1935
1939	Survivor's insurance added to provide monthly life insurance payments to the widow and dependent children of deceased workers.
1950-1954	Old-age and survivor's insurance was broadened.
1956	Disability insurance benefits provided to workers and dependents of such employees.
1965	Medical insurance protection to the aged, and later (1973) the disabled under age 65 (Medicare).
1972	Cost-of-living escalator tied to the consumer price index—guaranteed higher future benefits for all beneficiaries.
1974	Existing state programs of financial assistance to the aged, blind, and disabled were replaced by SSI (supplemental security income) administered by the Social Security Administration.
1983	Effective 1984, all new civilian federal employees are covered. All federal employees covered for purpose of Medicare.

remaining. For the super rich (even with royalties, textbook authors need not apply), this elimination of the cap is costly.

Second, remember that for every dollar deducted as an employees' share of social security, there is a matching amount paid by employers. For employees making in the $70,000 or more range, this means an employer contribution of about $6,000 . Because social security is retirement income to employees, employers should decrease private pension payouts by a corresponding amount.

It is generally agreed that current funding levels will produce a massive surplus throughout the 1990s. In 1996 the social security surplus was $66 billion.[15] Current baby boomers are just now reaching their peak earnings potential. And their social security payments now subsidize a much smaller generation born during the 1930s. There are now almost 3.5 workers paying into the system for every one collecting benefits. Within the next 40 years this ratio will drop to about two to one.[16] Many experts believe this statistic foreshadows the collapse of social security as we know it. In anticipation of this

[15]"Social Securities?," *The Economist* 341, Dec. 14, 1996.

[16]Thomas H. Paine, "Alternative Ways to Fix Social Security," *Benefits Quarterly*, Third Quarter 1997, pp. 14–18

EXHIBIT 13.6 What Social Security Does to Your Pay Check

	Employers and Employees each pay amounts shown						
Year	**OASDI**			**Health**		**Total Contribution**	
	max. taxable earning	*% OASI (old age, survivors)*	*% DI (Disability)*	*max. taxable earnings*	*% health*	*%*	*$*
1980	25,900	4.52	.56	25,900	1.05	6.13	1,587.67
1990	51,300	5.6	.6	51,300	1.45	7.65	3,924.45
1995	61,200	5.26	.94	No Max	1.45	7.65	No Max because of uncapped health care
1997–1999	increases with market wage movement	5.35	.85	No Max	1.45	7.65	No Max, uncapped health
2000+	increases with market wage movement	5.3	.9	No Max	1.45	7.65	No Max, uncapped health

Source: Social Security Bulletin, Annual Statistical Supplement (1996).

possibility, Congress currently is debating different reform plans, including several that call for social security payments going straight to your own individual account and to be earmarked for your own personal retirement (rather than going into a general fund used for subsidizing all retirees in general).[17]

Benefits Under Social Security. The majority of benefits under social security fall into one of four categories: (1) old age or disability benefits, (2) benefits for dependents of retired or disabled workers, (3) benefits for surviving family members of a deceased worker, and (4) lump-sum death payments. To qualify for these benefits, a worker must work in a covered employment and earn a specified amount of money (about $650 today) for each quarter-year of coverage.

Forty quarters of coverage will insure any worker for life. The amount received under the four benefits categories noted above varies, but in general is tied to the amount contributed during eligibility quarters. The average monthly retirement benefit rose from $571 in 1990 to $720 in early 1996.[18]

Unemployment Insurance

The earliest union efforts to cushion the effects of unemployment for their members (c. 1830s) were part of benevolent programs of self-help. Working members made

[17]Kelly Olsen, "A Point by Point Comparison of Social Security Reform Plans," *Benefits Quarterly*, Third Quarter 1997, p. 88.

[18]*Social Security Bulletin*, Annual Statistical Supplement 1996, p. 31.

contributions to their unemployed brethren.[19] With passage of the unemployment insurance law (as part of the Social Security Act of 1935), this floor of security for unemployed workers became less dependent upon the philanthropy of fellow workers. Since unemployment insurance laws vary state by state, this review will cover some of the major characteristics of different state programs.

Financing. Unemployment compensation paid out to eligible workers is financed exclusively by employers who pay federal and state unemployment insurance tax. The tax amounts to 6.2 percent of the first $7,000 earned by each worker.[20] All states allow for experience rating, charging lower percentages to employers who have terminated fewer employees. The tax rate may fall to almost 0 percent in some states for employers who have had no recent experience (hence the term experience rating) with downsizing, and rise to 10 percent for organizations with large numbers of layoffs.

Coverage. All workers except a few agricultural and domestic workers are currently covered by unemployment insurance (U.I.) laws. These covered workers (97 percent of the workforce), though, must still meet eligibility requirements to receive benefits.

Eligibility. To be eligible for benefits, an unemployed worker must: (1) be able, available, and actively seeking work; (2) not have refused suitable employment; (3) not be unemployed because of a labor dispute (except Rhode Island and New York); (4) not have left a job voluntarily; (5) not have been terminated for gross misconduct; and (6) have been previously employed in a covered industry or occupation, earning a designated minimum amount for a designated period of time.

Duration. Until 1958 the maximum number of weeks any claimant could collect U.I. was 26 weeks. However, the 1958 and 1960–61 recessions yielded large numbers of claimants who exhausted their benefits, leading many states temporarily to revise upward the maximum benefits duration. The most recent modification of this benefits duration (1982) involves a complex formula that ensures extended benefits in times of high unemployment. Extended benefits will be paid when either of two conditions prevails: (1) when the number of insured unemployed in a state reaches 6 percent, or (2) when the unemployment rate is greater than 5 percent and at least 20 percent higher than in the same period of the two preceding calendar years, and remains that way for 13 weeks.[21]

Weekly benefits amount. Those unemployed workers who do meet eligibility requirements are entitled to a weekly benefit amount designed to equal 50 percent of the

[19]Raymond Munts, "Policy Development in Unemployment Insurance," in *Federal Policies and Worker Status Since the Thirties*, ed. Goldberg, Ahern, Haber, and Oswald (Madison, WI: Industrial Relations Research Association, 1976).

[20]Burton T. Beam & John J. McFadden, *Employee Benefits* (Chicago: Dearborn Financial Publishing, 1996), p. 64.

[21]C. Arthur Williams, John S. Turnbull, and Earl F. Cheit, *Economic and Social Security*, 5th ed. (New York: John Wiley & Sons, 1982).

claimants' lost wages. Most states don't reach this target level, though, with the average payout being 36 percent of lost wages.[22] Nor do benefits appear to cover even the minimum outlay necessary for food and housing faced by the average recipient.[23] Recognizing this problem, some states recently raised their benefits levels.

Controlling unemployment taxes. Every unemployed worker's unemployment benefits are "charged" against the firm or firms most recently employing a currently unemployed worker. The more money paid out on behalf of a firm, the higher is the unemployment insurance rate for that firm. Efforts to control these costs quite logically should begin with a well-designed human resources planning system. Realistic estimates of human resource needs will reduce the pattern of hasty hiring followed by morale-breaking terminations. Additionally, though, a benefits administrator should attempt to audit prelayoff behavior (e.g., lateness, gross misconduct, absenteeism, illness, leaves of absence) and compliance with U.I. requirements after termination (e.g., job refusals can disqualify an unemployed worker).

Family and Medical Leave Act

The 1993 Family and Medical Leave Act (F.M.L.A.) entitles all eligible employees to receive unpaid leave up to 12 weeks per year for specified family or medical reasons. Under F.M.L.A. employees may be required to provide 30 days' notice for intended leave, proof of illness when appropriate, and periodic status reports. Common reasons for leave under F.M.L.A. include caring for an ill family member or adopting a child.

Consolidated Omnibus Budget Reconciliation Act (COBRA)

In 1985 Congress enacted this law to provide current and former employees and their spouses and dependents with a temporary extension of group health insurance when coverage is lost due to qualifying events (e.g., layoffs). All employers with 20 or more employees must comply with COBRA. An employer may charge individuals up to 102 percent of the premium for coverage that can extend up to 36 months, depending on the category of the qualifying event.

RETIREMENT AND SAVINGS PLAN PAYMENTS

The last chapter noted that a high relationship exists between employee age and preference for a pension plan. While this need for old-age security may become more pronounced as workers age, it is evident among younger workers also.

This security motive and certain tax advantages have fostered the rise of pension programs. As Exhibit 13.2 indicated, the vast majority of employers choose to provide this benefit as part of their overall package. Perhaps because of their prevalence,

[22] *Social Security Bulletin*, Annual Statistical Supplement 1996, p. 350.

[23] Ibid.

pension plans are also one of the targets for cost control. Owens-Corning, for example, is decreasing the cost of its retirement package by 20 percent. To make up for the decrease, Owens-Corning is adding a variable sum linked to profitability of the company. In good years the company pays out. In bad years the 20 percent savings makes the company that much more competitive.[24]

Pension programs provide income to an employee at some future time as compensation for work performed now. Two types of pension plans will be discussed to varying degrees here: (1) defined benefit and (2) defined contribution plans. As you read these descriptions keep in mind that defined benefit plans may be a dying breed. Today 9 of 10 new plans are defined contribution plans.[25] To understand why this rapid change is occurring, we have to explain the cost-saving distinctions between the two types of plans.

Defined Benefit Plans

In a defined benefit plan an employer agrees to provide a specific level of retirement pension, which is expressed as either a fixed dollar or percentage-of-earnings amount that may vary (increase) with years of seniority in the company. The firm finances this obligation by following an actuarially determined benefits formula and making current payments that will yield the future pension benefit for a retiring employee.[26]

Defined benefit plans generally follow one of three different formulas. The most common approach (54 percent) is to calculate average earnings over the last 3–5 years of service for a prospective retiree and offer a pension about one-half this amount (varying from 30–80 percent) adjusted for years of seniority. The second formula (14 percent of companies) for a defined benefits plan uses average career earnings rather than earnings from the last few years: other things being equal, this would reduce the level of benefit for pensioners. The final formula (28 percent of companies) commits an employer to a fixed dollar amount that is not dependent on any earnings data. This figure generally rises with seniority level.

The level of pension a company chooses to offer depends on the answer to several questions. First, what level of retirement compensation would a company like to set as a target, expressed in relation to preretirement earnings? Second, should Social Security payments be factored in when considering the level of income an employee should have during retirement? About one-half of the private sector plans monitored by the Department of Labor have a provision for integration with social security benefits.[27] One integration approach reduces normal benefits by a percentage (usually 50 percent) of social security benefits.[28] Another feature employs a more liberal benefits formula on earnings that exceed the maximum income taxed by social security. Regardless of the formula

[24]"Benefits are Being Picked to Death," *Business Week*, December 4, 1995, p. 42.

[25]Kevin Dent, David Sloss, "The Global Outlook for Defined Contribution Versus Defined Benefit Pension Plans," *Benefits Quarterly*, First Quarter 1996, pp. 23–28.

[26]*Fundamentals of Employee Benefit Programs,* Employee Benefit Research Institute, 1997, pp. 69–73.

[27]*EBRI Databook on Employee Benefits,* Employee Benefit Research Institute, 1995, p. 172.

[28]Burton T. Beam & John J. McFadden, *Employee Benefits*.

used, about one-half of U.S. companies do not employ the cost-cutting strategy. Once a company has targeted the level of income it wants to provide employees in retirement, it makes sense to design a system that integrates private pension and social security to achieve that goal. Any other strategy is not cost effective.

Third, should other post retirement income sources (e.g., savings plans that are partially funded by employer contributions) be integrated with the pension payment? Fourth, a company must decide how to factor seniority into the payout formula. The larger the role played by seniority, the more important pensions will be in retaining employees. Most companies believe that the maximum pension payout for a particular level of earnings should only be achieved by employees who have spent an entire career with the company (e.g., 30–35 years). As Exhibit 13.7 vividly illustrates, job hoppers are hurt financially by this type of strategy. In our example, a very plausible scenario, job hopping cuts final pension amounts in half.

Defined Contribution Plans

Defined contribution plans require specific contributions by an employer, but the final benefit received by employees is unknown, depending on the investment success of those charged with administering the pension fund.

There are two popular forms of defined contribution plans. A 401K plan, so named for the section of the Internal Revenue Code describing the requirements, is a savings

EXHIBIT 13.7 The High Cost of Job Hopping

		Years in Company	*Percentage of Salary for Pension*	*X*	*Salary at Company (final)*	*Annual Pension*
Sam's Career History	Job 1	10	10 %	X	$ 35,817	= $ 3,582
	Job 2	10	10 %	X	$ 64,143	= $ 6,414
	Job 3	10	10 %	X	$114,870	= $11,487
	Job 4	10	10 %	X	$205,714	= $20,571
					Sam's Total Pension	= $42,054
Ann's Career History	Job 1	40		X	$205,714	= $82,286
					Ann's Total Pension	= $82,286

Assumptions: 1. Starting Salary of $20,000 with 6 percent annual inflation rate. 2. Both employees receive annual increases equal to inflation rate. 3. Pensions based on one percentage point (of salary) for each year of service multiplied by final salary at time of exit from company.

Source: Federal Reserve Bank of Boston

plan in which employees are allowed to defer income up to a $9,500 maximum (moves upward with changes in the Consumer Price Index). Employers typically match employee savings at a rate of 50 cents on the dollar.[29]

The second type of plan is an Employee Stock Ownership Plan (ESOP). In a basic ESOP a company makes a tax-deductible contribution of stock shares or cash to a trust. The trust then allocates company stock (or stock bought with cash contributions) to participating employee accounts. The amount allocated is based on employee earnings. When an ESOP is used as a pension vehicle (as opposed to an incentive program), the employees receive cash at retirement based upon the stock value at that time. ESOPs have one major disadvantage which limits their utility for pension accumulations. Many employees are reluctant to "bet" most of their future retirement income on just one investment source. If the company's stock takes a downturn, the result can be catastrophic for employees approaching retirement age. Despite this disadvantage, ESOPs continue to be popular. One public opinion poll found that about half of employees would trade their next pay increase for a share in ownership of the company.[30] Further evidence of ESOP popularity comes from the growth of participation by employees. In 1975 about 250,000 employees were enrolled in ESOPs. That number exceeded 11.5 million by 1992.[31]

Finally, profit sharing can also be considered a defined contribution pension plan if the distribution of profits is delayed until retirement. Chapter 10 explains the basics of profit sharing.

The advantages and disadvantages of these two generic categories of pensions (defined benefit and defined contribution) are outlined in Exhibit 13.8.

EXHIBIT 13.8 Relative Advantages of Different Pension Alternatives

Defined Benefit Plan	*Defined Contribution Plan*
1. Provides an explicit benefit which is easily communicated	Unknown benefit level is difficult to communicate
2. Company absorbs risk associated with changes in inflation and interest rates which affect cost	Employees assume these risks
3. More favorable to long service employees	More favorable to short-term employees
4. Employer costs unknown	Employer costs known up front

[29]Poterba, Venti, and Wise, "401(K) Plans and Tax-Deferred Saving," in *Studies in the Economics of Aging*, ed. D. Wise (Chicago: University of Chicago Press, 1994), pp. 105–138.

[30]Employee Benefit Research Institute, *Fundamentals of Employee Benefit Programs* (Washington, D.C.: EBRI, 1990).

[31]National Center for Employee Ownership, "Employee Ownership Continues to Grow in 1992," News release, March 15, 1993.

Possibly the most important of the factors noted in Exhibit 13.8 is the differential risk borne by employers on the cost dimension. Defined contribution plans have known costs from year one. The employer agrees to a specific level of payment that only changes through negotiation or through some voluntary action. This allows for quite realistic cost projections. In contrast, defined contribution plans commit the employer to a specific level of benefit. Errors in actuarial projections can add considerably to costs over the years and make the budgeting process much more prone to error. Perhaps for this reason, defined contribution plans have been more popular for new adoptions over the past 15 years.[32]

Not surprisingly, both of these deferred compensation plans are subject to stringent tax laws. For deferred compensation to be exempt from current taxation, specific requirements must be met. To qualify (hence it is labeled a "qualified" deferred compensation plan), an employer cannot freely choose who will participate in the plan. This requirement eliminated the common practice of building tax-friendly, extravagant pension packages for executives and other highly compensated employees. The major advantage of a qualified plan is that the employer receives an income tax deduction for contributions made to the plan even though employees may not yet have received any benefits. The disadvantage arises in recruitment of high-talent executives. A plan will not qualify for tax exemptions if an employer pays high levels of deferred compensation to entice executives to the firm, unless proportionate contributions also are made to lower level employees.

The Employee Retirement Income Security Act (ERISA)

The early 1970s were a public relations and economic disaster for private pension plans. Many people who thought they were covered were the victims of complicated rules, insufficient funding, irresponsible financial management, and employer bankruptcies. Some pension funds, including both employer-managed and union-managed funds, were mismanaged; other pension plans required long vesting periods. The result was a pension system that left far too many life-long workers poverty stricken. Enter the Employee Retirement Income Security Act in 1974 as a response to these problems.

ERISA *does not require* that employers offer a pension plan. But if a company decides to have one, it is rigidly controlled by ERISA provisions. These provisions were designed to achieve two goals: (1) to protect the interest of 35 million workers who are covered today by private retirement plans, and (2) to stimulate the growth of such plans.

The actual success of ERISA in achieving these goals has been mixed at best. In the first two full years of operation (1975–76) more than 13,000 pension plans were terminated. A major factor in these terminations, along with the recession, was ERISA. Employers complained about the excessive costs and paperwork of living under ERISA.

---

[32]Kevin Dent, David Sloss, "The Global Outlook for Defined Contribution Versus Defined Benefit Pension Plans," *Benefits Quarterly*, First Quarter 1996, pp. 23–28.

Some disgruntled employers even claimed ERISA was an acronym for "Every Ridiculous Idea Since Adam." To examine the merits of these claims, let us take a closer look at the major requirements of ERISA.

General Requirements. ERISA requires that employees be eligible for pension plans beginning at age 21. Employers may require one year of service as a precondition for participation. The service requirement may be extended to three years if the pension plan offers full and immediate vesting.

Vesting and Portability. These two concepts are sometimes confused but have very different meanings in practice. Vesting refers to the length of time an employee must work for an employer before he or she is entitled to employer payments made into the pension plan. The vesting concept has two components. First, any contributions made by the employee to a pension fund are immediately and irrevocably vested. The vesting right becomes questionable only with respect to the employer's contributions. As mandated by ERISA, and amended by the tax reform act of 1986, the employer's contribution must vest at least as quickly as one of the following two formulas: (1) full vesting after five years, or (2) 20 percent after three years and 20 percent each year thereafter (full in seven years).

The vesting schedule an employer uses is often a function of the demographic makeup of the work force. An employer who experiences high turnover may wish to use the five-year service schedule. By so doing, any employee with fewer than 5 years' service at time of termination receives no vested benefits. Or the employer may use the second schedule in the hopes that earlier benefits accrual will reduce undesired turnover. The strategy adopted is, therefore, dependent on organizational goals and workforce characteristics.

Portability of pension benefits becomes an issue for employees moving to new organizations. Should pension assets accompany the transferring employee in some fashion?[33] ERISA does not require mandatory portability of private pensions. On a voluntary basis, though, the employer may agree to let an employee's pension benefits transfer to the new employer. For an employer to permit portability, of course, the pension rights must be vested.

Pension Benefit Guaranty Corporation. Despite the wealth of constraints imposed by ERISA, the potential still exists for an organization to go bankrupt, or in some way fail to meet its vested pension obligations. To protect individuals confronted by this problem, employers are required to pay insurance premiums to the Pension Benefit Guaranty Corporation (PBGC) established by ERISA. In turn, the PBGC guarantees payment of vested benefits to employees formerly covered by terminated pension plans.

---

[33]Susan M. Philips and Linda P. Fletcher, "The Future of the Portable Pension Concept," *Industrial and Labor Relations Review* 30 (1977), p. 197.

LIFE INSURANCE

One of the most common employee benefits offered by organizations (about 91 percent of medium to large private-sector firms) is some form of life insurance.[34] Typical coverage would be a group term insurance policy with a face value of one to two times the employee's annual salary.[35] Most plan premiums are paid completely by the employer (79 percent of employers).[36] Slightly over 40 percent include retiree coverage. About two-thirds of all policies include accidental death and dismemberment clauses.[37] To discourage turnover, almost all companies make this benefit forfeitable at the time of departure from the company.

Life insurance is one of the benefits heavily affected by movement to a flexible benefits program. Flexibility is introduced by providing a core of basic life coverage (e.g., $ 25,000). The option then exists to choose greater coverage (usually in increments of $10,000–25,000) as part of the optional package.

MEDICAL AND MEDICALLY RELATED PAYMENTS

General Health Care

The American health system today costs in excess of $800 billion annually.[38] Health care costs represented 5.9 percent of gross national product in 1965, 10.5 percent in 1983, and are expected to exceed 14 percent this year. One out of every seven dollars spent by Americans in 1992 were spent on health care.[39] More costly technology, increased numbers of elderly, and a system that does not encourage cost savings have all contributed to the rapidly rising costs of medical insurance. In the past 10 years, though, employers have begun to take steps designed to curb these costs. After a discussion of the types of health care systems, these cost-cutting strategies will be discussed. Exhibit 13.9 provides a brief overview of the three most common health care options.

An employer's share of health care costs is contributed into one of five health care systems: (1) a community-based system, such as Blue Cross; (2) a commercial insurance plan; (3) self-insurance; (4) a health maintenance organization (HMO); or (5) a preferred provider organization (PPO).

Of these five, plans 1 through 3 (labeled as traditional coverage in Exhibit 13.9) operate in a similar fashion. Two major distinctions exist, however. The first distinction is

---

[34]U.S. Department of Labor, Bureau of Labor Statistics, *Employee Benefits in Medium and Large Private Establishments*, 1993 (Washington, DC: U.S. Government Printing Office, 1995); Employee Benefit Research Institute, *Fundamentals of Employee Benefit Programs*.

[35]U.S. Department of Labor, Bureau of Labor Statistics, *Employee Benefits in Medium and Large Private Establishments*, 1993 (Washington, DC: U.S. Government Printing Office, 1995).

[36]Ibid.

[37]Ibid.

[38]Katharine R. Levit, et al., "National Health Expenditures, 1993," *Health Care Financing Review* (Fall 1994), pp. 247–294.

[39]Ibid.

EXHIBIT 13.9 How Health Insurance Options Differ on Key Dimensions

Issue	*Traditional Coverage*		*Health Maintenance Organization (HMO)*		*Preferred Provider Organization (PPO)*	
Who is eligible?	May live anywhere		May be required to live in HMO designated service area		May live anywhere	
Who provides health care?	Doctor and health care facility of patient's choice		Must use doctors and facilities designated by HMO		May use doctors and facilities associated with PPO; if not, may pay additional copayment/deductible	
How much coverage on routine, preventive level?	Does not cover regular checkups and other preventive services; diagnostic tests may be covered in part or full		Covers regular checkups, diagnostic tests, other preventive services with low or no fee per visit		Same as with HMO if doctor and facility are on approved list; copayments and deductibles are assessed at much higher rate for others not on list	
Hospital care	Covers doctors and hospital bills		Covers doctors and hospital bills if HMO-approved hospital		Covers doctors and hospitals if PPO-approved.	
Percent of all employees enrolled in these programs yearly	1993	1997	1993	1997	1993	1997
	48 %	15 %	19 %	30%	27 %	35 %

Source: Wall Street Journal, January 20, 1998. Enrollment data from William M. Mercer, Inc.

in the manner payments are made. With Blue Cross the employer-paid premiums guarantee employees a direct service, including room, board, and necessary health services covered by the plan. Coverage under a commercial insurance plan guarantees fixed payment for hospital service to the insured, who in turn reimburses the hospital. And finally, a self-insurance plan implies that the company provides coverage out of its own assets, assuming the risks itself within state legal guidelines. To protect against catastrophic loss, the most common strategy for self-insurers is to have stop-loss coverage, with an insurance policy covering costs in excess of some predetermined level (e.g., \$50,000).

The second distinction is in the way costs of medical benefits are determined. Blue Cross operates via the concept of community rating. In effect, insurance rates are based on the medical experience of the entire community. Higher use of medical facilities and services results in higher premiums. In contrast, insurance companies operate off a narrower experience rating base, preferring to charge each company separately according to its medical facility usage. Finally, of course, the cost of medical coverage under a self-insurance program is directly related to usage level, with employer payments going directly to medical care providers rather than to secondary sources in the form of premiums.

As a fourth delivery system, health maintenance organizations offer comprehensive benefits for a fixed fee. Health maintenance organizations offer routine medical services at a specific site. Employees make prepayments in exchange for guaranteed health care services on demand. By law employers of more than 25 employees are required to provide employees the option of joining a federally qualified HMO. If the employee opts for HMO coverage the employer is required to pay the HMO premium or an amount equal to the premium for previous health coverage, whichever is less.

Finally, preferred provider organizations represent a variation on health care delivery in which there is a direct contractual relationship between and among employers, health care providers, and third-party payers.[40] An employer is able to select certain providers who agree to provide price discounts and submit to strict utilization controls (for example, strict standards on number of diagnostic tests that can be ordered). In turn, the employer influences employees to use the preferred providers through financial incentives. Doctors benefit by increasing patient flow. Employers benefit through increased cost savings. And employees benefit through wider choice of doctors than might be available under an HMO.

Health Care: Cost Control Strategies

There are three general strategies available to benefit managers for controlling the rapidly escalating costs of health care.[41] First, organizations can motivate employees to change their demand for health care, through changes in either the design or the administration of health insurance policies.[42] Included in this category of control strategies are: (1) deductibles (the first *x* dollars of health care cost are paid by the employee); (2) coinsurance rates (premium payments are shared by company and employee); (3) maximum benefits (defining a maximum payout schedule for specific health problems); (4) coordination of benefits (ensure no double payment when coverage exists under the employee's plan and a spouse's plan); (5) auditing of hospital charges for accuracy; (6) requiring preauthorization for selected visits to health care facilities; (7) mandatory second opinion whenever surgery is recommended.[43]

The second general cost control strategy involves changing the structure of health care delivery systems and participating in business coalitions (for data collection and dissemination). Under this category falls the trend toward HMOs and PPOs. Even under more traditional delivery systems, though, there is more negotiation of rates with hospitals and other health care providers. Indeed, one recent trend involves direct contracting, which allows self-insured companies or employer associations to buy health care

[40]Thomas Billet, "An Employer's Guide to Preferred Provider Organizations," *Compensation Review* 16, No. 4 (1984), pp. 58–62.

[41]Regina Herzlinger and Jeffrey Schwartz, "How Companies Tackle Health Care Costs: Part I," *Harvard Business Review* 63 (July–August 1985), pp. 69–81.

[42]David Rosenbloom, "Oh Brother, Our Medical Costs Went Up Again," Paper presented for the Health Data Institute, March 16, 1988.

[43]Herzlinger and Schwartz, "How Companies Tackle Health Care Costs: Part I"; Regina Herzlinger, "How Companies Tackle Health Care Costs: Part II," *Harvard Business Review* 63 (July–August 1985).

Exhibit 13.10 Use of Selected Cost Control Strategies

Strategy	*Percent of Companies Using*
Preadmission certification	79%
Required second surgical opinion	35
Limited patient choice of physicians	53
Exclusionary clauses	65

Source: 1996 Employee Benefits Report, U.S. Chamber of Commerce, p. 44.

services directly from physicians or provider-sponsored networks. Some experts contend that direct contracting can save 30 to 60 percent over fee-for-service systems.[44]

The final cost strategy involves promotion of preventive health programs. No-smoking policies and incentives for quitting smoking are popular inclusions here. But there is also increased interest in healthier food in cafeterias and vending machines, on-site physical fitness facilities, and early screening to identify possible health problems before they become more serious. One review of physical fitness programs found fitness led to better mental health and improved resistance to stress; there also was some evidence of increased productivity, increased commitment, decreased absenteeism, and decreased turnover.[45]

The Health Insurance Association of America provides research about a wide variety of specific health related issues at its website: **http://www.hiaa.org/hiaapubs/index.html#Research**

Short- and Long-Term Disability

A number of benefit options provide some form of protection for disability. For example, workers' compensation covers disabilities that are work related. Even social security has provisions for disability income to those who qualify. Beyond these two legally required sources, though, there are two private sources of disability income: employee salary continuation plans and long-term disability plans.

Many companies have some form of salary continuation plan that pays out varying levels of income depending on duration of illness. At one extreme is short-term illness covered by sick leave policy and typically reimbursed at a level equal to 100 percent of salary.[46] After such benefits run out, disability benefits become operative. The benefit level is typically 50 to 67 percent of salary, and may be multitiered.[47] For example, a

[44]Business & Health, March 1997, in Compensation & Benefits Review, July/August 1997, p. 12

[45]Loren Falkenberg, "Employee Fitness Programs: Their Impact on the Employee and the Organization," *Academy of Management Review* 12, no. 3, 1987, pp. 511–522.

[46]Employee Benefit Research Institute, *Fundamentals of Employee Benefit Programs.*

[47]Ibid.

long-term disability plan might kick in when the short term plan expires, typically after 26 weeks.[48] Long-term disability is usually underwritten by insurance firms and provides 60 to 70 percent of predisability pay for a period varying between two years and life.[49] Only about 35 percent of all U.S. businesses are estimated to provide long-term disability insurance.[50]

Dental Insurance

A rarity 20 years ago, dental insurance is now quite prevalent. Dental insurance is a standard inclusion for 82 percent of employers.[51]

In many respects dental care coverage follows the model originated in health care plans. The dental equivalent of HMOs and PPOs are standard delivery systems. For example, a dental HMO enlists a group of dentists who agree to treat company employees in return for a fixed monthly fee per employee.[52]

Fortunately for all of us, dental insurance costs have not spiraled like other health care costs. In 1996 the typical cost for employee dental coverage was $186.[53] In part these relatively modest costs are due to stringent cost control strategies (e.g. plan maximum payouts are typically $1,000 or less per year), but the excess supply of dentists in the United States also has helped keep costs competitive.[54]

Vision Care

Vision care dates back only to the 1976 contract between the United States Auto Workers and the Big 3 auto makers. Since then, this benefit has spread to other auto-related industries and parts of the public sector. Most plans are noncontributory and usually cover partial costs of eye examination, lenses and frames. About 48 percent of employees have some form of vision care program.[55]

MISCELLANEOUS BENEFITS

Paid Time off during Working Hours

Paid rest periods, lunch periods, wash-up time, travel time, clothes-change time, and get-ready time benefits are self-explanatory.

---

[48]Ibid.

[49]Employee Benefit Research Institute, *Fundamentals of Employee Benefit Programs*, Fifth Edition (Washington, DC: EBRI, 1997), p. 297.

[50]Employee Benefit Research Institute, *Fundamentals of Employee Benefit Programs.*

[51]1997 Employee Benefits Report, U.S. Chamber of Commerce, p. 50.

[52]"Dental Insurance Program Gains Favor Among Firms," *The Wall Street Journal*, September 21, 1984, p. 31.

[53]1996 Employee Benefits Report, U.S. Chamber of Commerce, p. 45–46.

[54]Harry Sutton, "Prescription Drug and Dental Programs," *Compensation and Benefits Review* 18, no. 4, 1986, pp. 67–71.

[55]1997 Employee Benefits Report, U.S. Chamber of Commerce, p. 50.

Payment for Time Not Worked

Included within this category are several self-explanatory benefits:

1. Paid vacations and payments in lieu of vacation
2. Payments for holidays not worked
3. Paid sick leave
4. Other (payments for National Guard or Army or other reserve duty; jury duty and voting pay allowances; payments for time lost due to death in family or other personal reasons).

Judging from employee preferences discussed in the last chapter and from analysis of negotiated union contracts, pay for time not worked continues to be a high-demand benefit. Twenty years ago it was relatively rare, for example, to grant time for anything but vacations, holidays, and sick leave. Now many organizations have a policy of ensuring payments for civic responsibilities and obligations. Any outside pay for such civic duties are usually nominal, so companies often supplement this pay, frequently to the level of 100 percent of wages lost. There is also increasing coverage for parental leaves. Maternity and, to a lesser extent, paternity leaves are much more common than 25 years ago. Indeed, passage of the Family and Medical Leave Act in 1993 provides up to 12 weeks of unpaid leave (with guaranteed job protection) for birth, adoption, or care of a family member with a serious illness.

Exhibit 13.11 outlines the average paid leave time for covered employees.

Interestingly, paid time off is one of the areas where firms are trying to cut employee benefits. In 1980 every medium and large private employer offered at least one paid holiday per year. Now that number is 10 percent lower. Part of the change can be explained by the good job market in recent years. Paid time off is linked to seniority. But in good years more people change jobs, and loss of seniority means fewer paid days off.[56]

EXHIBIT 13.11 Payment for Time Not Worked

	Medium and Large private firms	*State and local Government*	*Small private firms*
Paid Holidays (days)	10.2	14.2	9.2
Paid Vacation at 1 year (days)	9.4	12.4	7.6
Lunch break (minutes)	29	34	not available
Rest time (minutes)	26	29	26
Personal leave (days)	3.1	2.9	2.6
Funeral leave (days)	3	3.7	2.9
Military leave (days/year)	14	17	12.2
Maternity leave (months)	4.3	10.5	3.5

Source: EBRI Databook on Employee Benefits, 1995.

[56] "Benefits are Being Picked to Death," *Business Week*, December 4, 1995, p. 42.

Child Care

Few companies provide day care as a paid employee benefit. There appears to be greater concentrations of this benefit in certain industries. In the insurance industry child care is viewed as a tool to attract and retain employees. Indeed, Traveler's Insurance reports reduced turnover (at a cost of $1,200 per child per year) and Mutual Insurance believes child care is an excellent recruitment tool.[57] Notice that John Hancock, discussed in the appendix, also has child care coverage.

Legal Insurance

Prior to the 1970s, prepaid legal insurance was practically nonexistent. Coverage is still limited to about 7 percent of all employees, and generally only in medium to large firms.[58] Tremendous variety exists in the structure, options, delivery systems, and attorney compensation mechanisms. Across these plans, though, there are still some commonalities. A majority of plans provide routine legal services (e.g., divorce, real estate matters, wills, traffic violations) but exclude provisions covering felony crimes, largely because of the expense and potential for bad publicity. Employees with legal problems either select legal counsel from a panel of lawyers selected by the firm or freely choose their own lawyers with claims reimbursed by an insurance carrier.

BENEFITS FOR CONTINGENT WORKERS

Approximately 1 out of every 10 workers is employed in an alternative work arrangement.[59] These contingent work relationships include working through a temporary help agency, working for a contract company, working on-call, and working as an independent contractor. Both to reduce costs and to permit easier expansion and contraction of production/services, contracting offers a viable way to meet rapidly changing environmental conditions.

Contingent workers cost less primarily because the benefits offered are lower than for regular employees. As Exhibit 13.12 shows, the fewer hours employees work in a week, the more severe is the benefits' penalty.

Summary

Since the 1940s employee benefits have been the most volatile area in the compensation field. From 1940 to 1980 these dramatic changes came in the form of more and better forms of employee benefits. The result should not have been unexpected. Employee

[57]Sue Shellenbargen, "Employers Report Gains from Babysitting Aid." *The Wall Street Journal*, July 22, 1991, p. B1.

[58]U.S. Department of Labor, Bureau of Labor Statistics, *Employee Benefits in Medium and Large Private Establishments, 1993* (Washington, DC: U.S. Government Printing Office, 1994).

[59]Steven Hipple and Jay Stewart, "Earnings and benefits of workers in alternative work arrangements," *Monthly Labor Review*, October 1996, pp. 46–54.

Exhibit 13.12 Comparison of Benefit Coverage (Full Time versus Contingent)

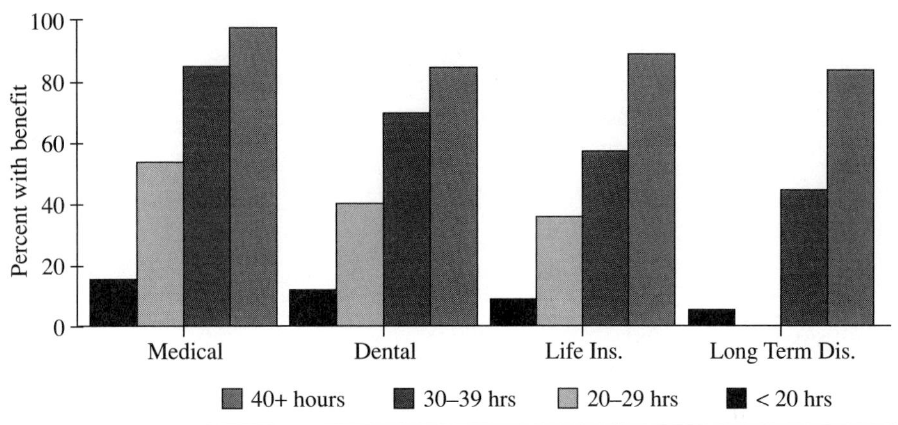

benefits are now a major, and many believe prohibitive, component of doing business. Look for the remainder of this decade on into the millennium to be dominated by cost-saving efforts to improve the competitive position of American industry. A part of these cost savings will come from tighter administrative controls on existing benefit packages. But another part, as already seen in the auto industry, may come from a reduction in existing benefits packages. If this does evolve as a trend, benefits administrators will need to develop a mechanism for identifying employee preferences (in this case "least preferences") and use those as a guideline to meet agreed upon savings targets.

Review Questions

1. Your company has a serious turnover problem among employees with fewer than five years' seniority. The CEO wants to use employee benefits to lessen this problem. What might you do, specifically, in the areas of pension vesting, vacation and holiday allocation, and life insurance coverage in efforts to reduce turnover?
2. Assume you are politically foolhardy and decide to challenge your CEO's decision in question 1 to use benefits as a major tool for reducing turnover. Before she fires you, what arguments might you try to use to persuade her? (Hint: Are there other compensation tools that might be more effective in reducing turnover? Might the changes in benefits have unintended consequences on more senior employees? Could you make a cost argument against such a strategy? Is turnover of these employees necessarily bad, and how would you demonstrate that this turnover isn't a problem?
3. Why are defined contribution pension plans gaining in popularity in the United States and defined benefit plans losing popularity?

4. Some people claim that workers' compensation and unemployment compensation create a disincentive to work. What does this mean? In your opinion is there any validity to this argument?
5. One of the authors of this book counsels companies he deals with that spending more money on employee benefits is like throwing dollars down a black hole. Assuming he isn't crazy (a huge leap of faith), what might be the basis of this argument?

APPENDIX:

THE TOP TEN COMPANIES IN EMPLOYEE BENEFITS[1]

The top ten companies in terms of employee benefit programs are also companies with reputations for treating their employees well. These companies are:

1. Xerox
2. Quaker Oats
3. John Hancock Insurance
4. Chrysler
5. Merck
6. Bell Atlantic
7. AT&T
8. Citibank
9. Johnson & Johnson
10. Hewlett Packard

Just to give you an idea of what it takes to be one of the top ten, consider the following highlights taken from the first three on the list.

Xerox

Health Care and Other Insurance. Xerox employees receive an annual allowance of $2,296 ($5,438 for families) to buy health, dental, and other insurance coverage. The amount not spent from this total is reimbursed to employees (average rebate: $270 per year). Seventy-three percent of all employees are enrolled in HMOs with no annual premiums and modest co-pays of $5–10 per doctor visit.

---

[1]*The Buffalo News*, Monday, March 25, 1996, p. A–8.

Retirement Plans. Outstanding pension flexibility, including a choice between annuity, lump-sum payout or transfer of an equal dollar amount to an income mutual fund or IRA. Retirees also receive an allowance for health insurance coverage.

Time Off and Special Features. As a "family friendly" organization, Xerox gives a $10,000 lifetime stipend (up to $2,000 a year) for expenses such as child care, extended health care, or down payments of first homes.

Also available is a reimbursement for as much as $3,000 for adoption-related expenses.

Quaker Oats

Health Care and Other Insurance. Quaker Oats scores phenomenally well among employees on its health care package, with 92 percent of employees rating the plans satisfactory or higher. No wonder, health care and other insurance is nearly free for employees, no matter what the coverage.

Retirement Plans. From the first day of employment, Quaker Oats employees are enrolled in an Employee Stock Ownership Plan that is immediately vested. The contribution averages 12 percent of annual earnings in recent years.

Time Off and Special Features
Quaker Oats gives employees flex credits that can be used to buy up to five vacation days. They also can sell up to 10 days.

John Hancock

Health Care and Other Insurance. In an interesting customer service approach, John Hancock polls its employees to check satisfaction with HMO, PPO and fee-for-service plans. Satisfaction levels are routinely above 80 percent.

Retirement Plans. Employees can contribute up to 15 percent of regular and overtime pay to a 401K. This money is matched by the company dollar for dollar up to 2 percent of compensation. John Hancock also contributes to a 401K for employees at a rate of 4–5 percent of annual compensation.

Time Off and Special Features. John Hancock is one of those rare firms with an on-site child care facility, and it serves about 30 percent of employees at an average charge of $220 per week. In another family-friendly policy the company offer new parents up to one year's unpaid leave with full benefits.

YOUR TURN:

KRAMER TOOL COATING COMPANY

Background

Kramer Tool Coating company (KTC) is a high technology firm that coats cutting tools by bombarding them with ions of a patented substance. Because of the high cost of the ion chambers needed for this process, KTC has yet to make a profit in its 10 years of existence. Forecasts project, however, that KTC will make money next year, and by 10 years from now (barring drastic changes in cutting tool technology) will boast a return after taxes of $30 million.

KTC is unionized by an independent union comprising workers who used to be employed at a nearby company unionized by the United Auto Workers. When that company went bankrupt, KTC hired 20 of its most skilled individuals. These people are now key members in the independent union. Remembering the bankruptcy, these employees have been reluctant to press for too much, too fast, lest history repeat itself. But it is evident now that the company is past its danger point. The new contract will be the first to include any but the bare minimum of benefits. The old package included the legally required benefits (e.g., workers' compensation, unemployment insurance, Social Security) and a relatively low-cost health care package.

The Situation

The union insists that the next package include a substantial growth in employee benefits. Hard negotiation has determined that the union is willing to forgo substantial wage increase demands in exchange for some gains in the following areas: (1) life insurance, (2) dental insurance, (3) package of short-term (sick days) and long-term disability coverage, and (4) a contributory 401K pension plan. Life insurance and dental insurance coverage as proposed by the union cost approximately the same amount. Similarly, the disability package and the pension package are about equally expensive. You believe the union will settle for one of the two insurance packages and either the pension or disability coverage. Basically, you are indifferent in terms of costs.

Your Task

The president wants a recommendation about which way to have the labor lawyer negotiate. Consider how current and long-term corporate goals might influence your decision making. Also, do you want any other cost data or projections before making a decision? Are there any benefits that, if adopted, might make another of the requested benefits less necesary? What other information should you collect?

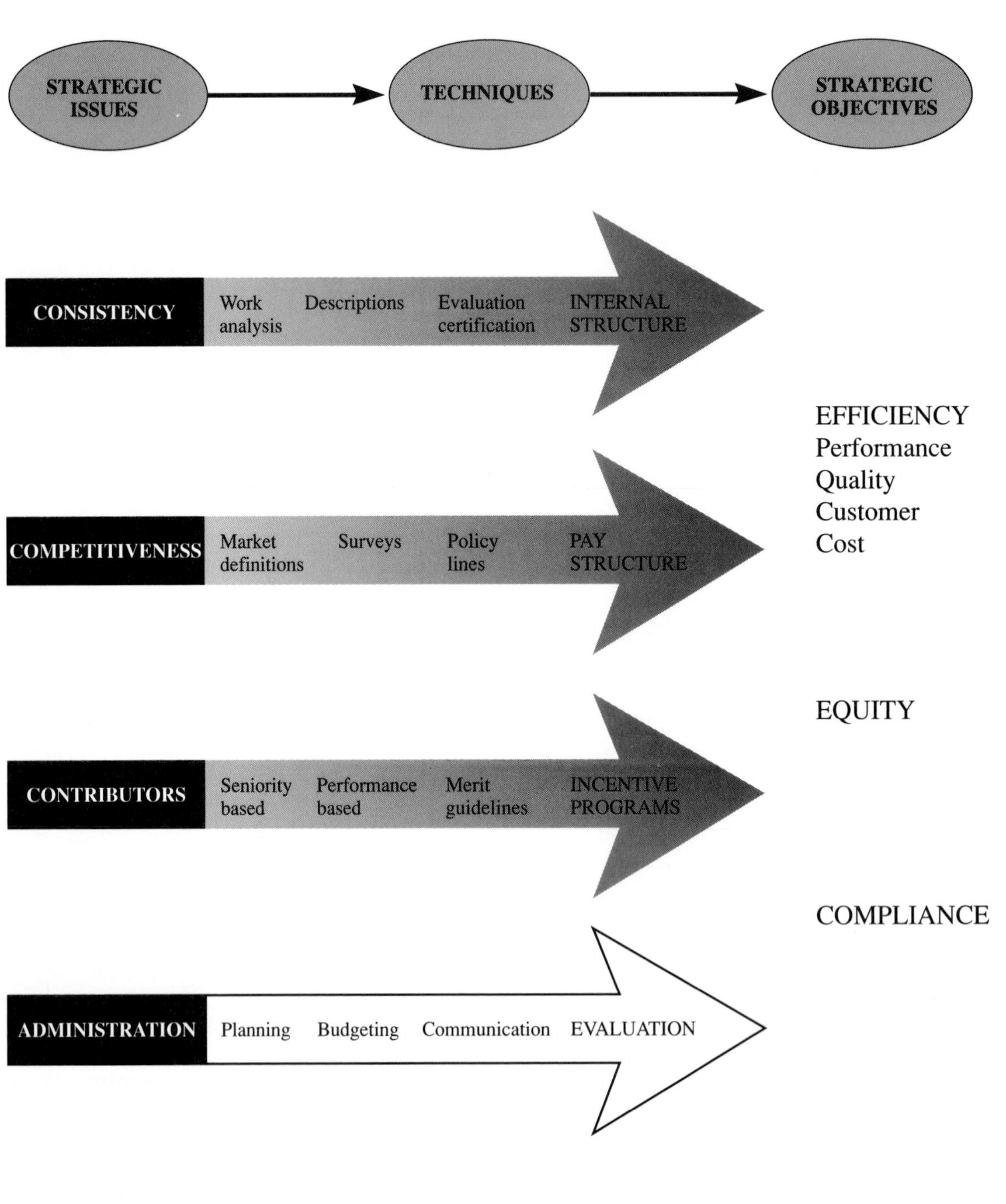
STRATEGIC ISSUES
TECHNIQUES
STRATEGIC OBJECTIVES
CONSISTENCY
Work analysis
Descriptions
Evaluation certification
INTERNAL STRUCTURE
COMPETITIVENESS
Market definitions
Surveys
Policy lines
PAY STRUCTURE
CONTRIBUTORS
Seniority based
Performance based
Merit guidelines
INCENTIVE PROGRAMS
ADMINISTRATION
Planning
Budgeting
Communication
EVALUATION
EFFICIENCY
Performance
Quality
Customer
Cost
EQUITY
COMPLIANCE

Extending the System

We have now completed the discussion of three strategic policies in the pay model used in this book. The first, which focused on determining the structure of pay, dealt with internal consistency. The second was determining the pay level based on external competitiveness, and the third dealt with determining the pay for employees according to their contributions. Strategic decisions regarding consistency, competitiveness, and contributions are directed at achieving the objectives of the pay system. Specific objectives vary among organizations; helping achieve competitive advantage and treating employees fairly are basic ones.

We now extend the basic pay model to the strategic issue of administration. A number of employee groups require, because of their importance to strategic success, special consideration in the way we design the administration of their compensation packages. In fact, Chapter 14 is titled just that: Compensation of Special Groups. Here we talk about employee groups that don't quite fit our basic model. Their special employment status, for reasons we will discuss in a moment, dictates the design of compensation administration programs that sometimes differ from the more traditional designs covered in parts I–IV.

In chapter 15 we look at compensation in unionized firms. Although less than 15% of the workforce in the U.S.A. is unionized, the role of unions in wage determination extends far beyond this small group. Firms looking to remain non union often pay considerable attention to the way rewards are distributed to union employees. And as we shall see, the role of a compensation person in a unionized organization is, indeed, different.

Our final extension of the system focuses on international employees. Different cultures, different laws, and different economies all can lead to different strategic and administrative decisions for international employees. And if we are truly to embrace the globalization of business, the globalization of compensation must be a key ingredient.

CHAPTER 14 Compensation of Special Groups

Chapter Outline

> The country's in a bind, but I'm cheerful and I'm chipper,
> As I slash employee wages like a fiscal Jack the Ripper.
> And I take away their health care and never mind their hollers.
> And pay myself a bonus of a couple of million dollars.
>
> Mark Russell
> Comedian

Mark Russell's satirical song is a reflection of our worst fears about pay: injustice hits the common worker first. This chapter takes a look at groups that, for reasons we will discuss, receive compensation that is anything but common. Our goal is to show the logic of compensation practices for these special groups.

So far we have described compensation programs as if they were fairly uniform across all jobs in an organization: jobs are analyzed; then job evaluation determines a job's internal worth; salary surveys give an indication of what other competitors pay for the job; discrepancies are reconciled and provisions are made to recognize that variation in performance across individuals in the same job should be recognized with compensation differences. Not all jobs follow all these stages, though. Indeed, all we have to do is open a newspaper to see that some jobs and some people are singled out for special compensation treatment in an organization. Why do 300-pound linemen regularly make more than $2–3 million per year? Why does Michael Eisner (Chief Executive Officer, Walt Disney Company) regularly make over $10 million per year? Is the value of these jobs determined in the same way as compensation is determined for other jobs in a company? The answer is probably no. But why? To answer this question it is useful to work backwards. What jobs get special compensation treatment in a company? Are they basically the same kinds of jobs across companies? If they are the same kinds of jobs, is there any common characteristic(s) the jobs share that would cause companies to devise special compensation packages?

WHO ARE SPECIAL GROUPS?

When we begin to look at company practices with these questions in mind, a pattern begins to emerge. Special treatment, either in the form of add-on packages not received by other employees, or in the form of compensation components entirely unique in the organization, tends to focus on a few specific groups. This chapter argues that special groups share two characteristics. First, special groups tend to be placed in positions that have built-in conflict, conflict that arises because different factions place incompatible demands on members of the group. And second, simply facing conflict is not sufficient; the way that this conflict is resolved has important consequences for the success of the company.

When both of these characteristics are present, we tend to find distinctive compensation practices adopted to meet the needs of these special groups. Exhibit 14.1 describes the nature of the conflicts faced by such special groups as supervisors, top management, boards of directors, scientists and engineers, sales personnel and contingent workers.

As the second characteristic explains, the conflict these special groups face has important consequences for the success of the firm. As an example, consider the contrast in compensation treatment for engineers in two different organizations. One is a high-technology firm with a strong research and development component. The other organization employs a few engineers, but their role is not central to the mission of the organization. A survey of this type of difference in employee composition and organizational strategy found that research and development organizations with heavy concentrations of engineers had evolved unique compensation systems that were responsive to the special needs of the engineering contingent. Organizations with a different focus and with fewer engineers merged this group's compensation with the standard package offered other employees.

EXHIBIT 14.1 Conflicts Faced by Special Groups

Special Group	*Type of Conflict Faced*
Supervisors	Caught between upper management and employees. Must balance need to achieve organization's objectives with importance of helping employees satisfy personal needs. If unsuccessful, either corporate profit or employee morale suffers.
Top Management	Stockholders want healthy return on investment. Government wants compliance with laws. Executive must decide between strategies that maximize short-run gains at expense of long run versus directions that focus on long run.
Board of Directors	Face possibility that disgruntled stockholders may sue over corporate strategies that don't "pan out."
Professional Employees	May be torn between goals, objectives, and ethical standards of their profession (e.g. should an engineer leak information about a product flaw, even though that information may hurt corporate profits) and demands of an employer concerned more with the profit motive.
Sales Staff	Often go for extended periods in the field with little supervision. Challenge is to stay motivated and continue making sales calls even in the face of limited contact or scrutiny from manager.
Contingent Workers	Play an important "safety valve" role for companies. When demand is high, more are hired. When demand drops, these are the first workers downsized. Employment status is highly insecure and challenge is to find low cost ways to motivate.

COMPENSATION STRATEGY FOR SPECIAL GROUPS

Supervisors

Remember, supervisors are caught between the demands of upper management in terms of production and the needs of employees in terms of rewards and reinforcements. The major challenge in compensating supervisors centers on equity. Some incentive must be provided to entice nonexempt employees to accept the challenges of being a supervisor. For many years, the strategy was to treat supervisors like lower-level managers. But in so doing, the existing job evaluation system sometimes left these supervisors making less money than *the top paid employees they supervised*. As you might imagine, this created little incentive to take on the extra work involved. More recently organizations have devised several strategies to attract workers into supervisory jobs. The most popular method is to key base salary of supervisors to some amount exceeding the top paid subordinate in the unit (5 percent to 30 percent represents the typical size of the differential).

Another method to maintain equitable differentials is simply to pay supervisors for scheduled overtime. Companies that do pay overtime are about evenly split between paying straight-time versus time-and-one-half for overtime hours.

The biggest trend in supervisory compensation centers on increased use of variable pay. Slightly more than half of all companies now have a variable pay component for supervisors, up 16 percent from last year.[1]

Corporate Directors

A typical board of directors comprises 10 outside and 3 inside directors, each having a term averaging three years. Historically, directors frequently were given the role of "rubber stamping" decisions made by top management. Such boards were stacked with people affiliated in some way with the organization (e.g., retired corporate officers, suppliers, attorneys). Modern corporate boards have changed considerably. Approximately two-thirds of boards now include more outside directors than inside directors (e.g., CEO, corporate officers). Outside members now include unaffiliated business executives, representatives from important segments of society, and major shareholders. Outside directors are usually paid higher compensation, probably because it takes a greater incentive to get them to participate. The pay differential between the two groups is about $10,000. Exhibit 14.2 shows the cash components of this compensation package.

EXHIBIT 14.2 Board of Directors' Direct Compensation (mean)

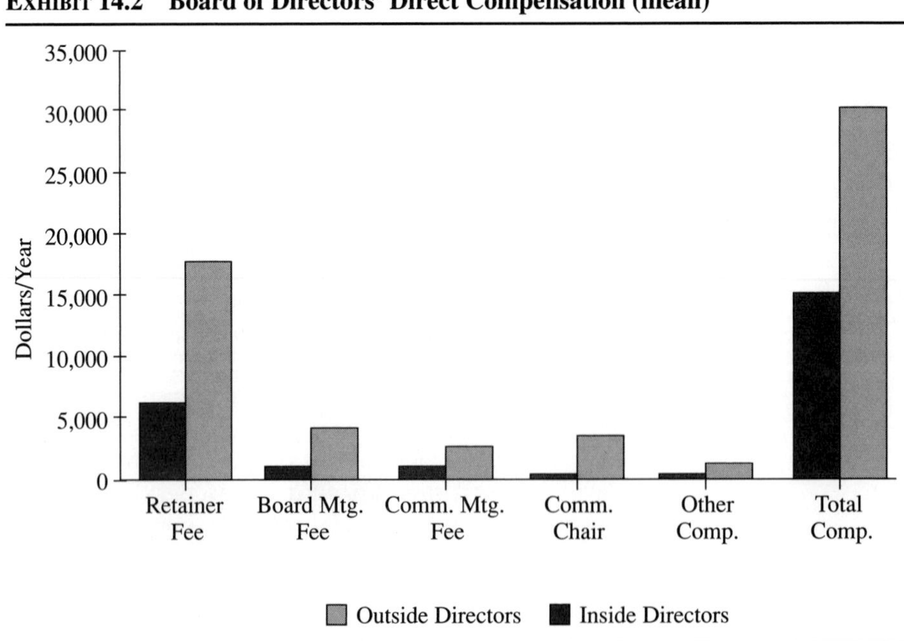

Source: IOMA, "Non Cash Compensation Prevails for Directors," March 1996, p. 2.

[1]ECS Supervisory Management Compensation Survey, Wyatt Data Services 1996.

In addition to cash compensation, there is an increasing emphasis on director rewards that link to corporate performance. Shareholders are holding directors accountable for firm performance. Reflecting this trend of linking pay to performance, more pay is stock based, with 62 percent of companies giving directors some form of outright stock grant or more restricted stock options.[2]

Executive Compensation

How would you like to make $2.3 million per year? That is the 1996 average (salary plus bonus) for Chief Executive Officers (CEOs).[3] Add retirement benefits, incentive plans, and stock option gains and the dollar value of total compensation for executives rises to a mind-boggling $5,781,300.[4] Exhibit 14.3 gives a brief history of how executive compensation climbed to such lofty heights. Pay attention to the way the granting of stock options gradually plays a bigger role in executive compensation.

Exhibit 14.4 shows the total compensation for the top five executives in the United States. Notice how most of the top five, as is true for many highly paid executives, reap the greatest rewards from long-term incentives, usually by exercising stock options. Many critics argue that this level of compensation for executives is excessive.[5] Are the

EXHIBIT 14.3 A Brief History of Executive Compensation

The Year	*The Key Event*
1974	Michael Bergerac cracks the $1 million mark when recruited to Revlon.
1979	Chrysler's Lee Iaocca takes $1 million plus 400,000 option shares.
1983	William Bendix of Bendix becomes the first executive to collect a huge golden parachute (contract clause for payment in a takeover leading to termination) of $3.9 million over five years.
1984	Congress tries to limit excessive golden parachutes with unintended consequences—the rules actually lead to larger amounts.
1986	New law gives favorable tax treatment to stock option awards. Sizes increase.
1987	Lee Iacocca receives first megagrant of stock options: 820,000 option shares worth 15.3 times his salary and bonus that year.
1987	Junk bond expert Michael Milkin explodes through $500,000,000 mark in salary and bonus.
1987	Leon Hirsch of US Surgical gets even larger megastock option award worth 126 times his salary and bonus.
1992	Securities and Exchange Commission rules CEO salaries must be disclosed more often in proxy statements. Easier availability of peer compensation data serves to drive up the standard.
1992	Michael Eisner of Walt Disney exercises low-cost stock options for pretax profit of 126 million.
1993	New tax law sets upper limit on tax-deductible executive compensation at $1 million. Has unintended effect of raising bar to that level.

Source: *The Wall Street Journal,* Thursday April 11, 1996. p. R4.

---

[2]American Management Association, "More Companies Pay Board Members with Stock," *Compflash*, September 1995, p. 4.

[3]"Executive Pay," *Business Week*, April 21, 1997, p. 59.

[4]Ibid.

[5]Graef S. Crystal, *In Search of Excess* (New York: W.W. Norton, 1991)

EXHIBIT 14.4 The Top Five Executives in Total Compensation

Person	Company	1996 Salary + Bonus	Long Term Compensation	Total
Lawrence Cos	Green Tree Financial	$102,449,000	$None	$102,449,000
Andrew Grove	Intel	3,003,000	94,587,000	97,590,000
Sanford Well	Travelers Group	6,330,000	87,828,000	94,157,000
Theodore Waitt	Gateway 2000	965,000	80,361,000	81,326,000
Anthony O'Reilly	H.J. Heinz	2,736,000	61,500,000	64,236,000

Source: *Business Week*, April 21, 1997, p.58–59.

critics right? One way to answer the question is to look at the different ways people say executive compensation is determined and ask, "Does this seem reasonable?"

This site is maintained by the AFL-CIO and is designed to monitor executive compensation. Their view is that CEOs are overpaid, and monitoring is the first step to curbing excess: **http://aflcio.paywatch.org/ceopay/**

Possible Explanations for CEO Compensation. One approach to explain why executives receive such large sums of money involves social comparisons.[6] In this view executive salaries bear a consistent relative relationship to compensation of lower level employees. When salaries of lower-level employees rise in response to market forces, top executive salaries also rise to maintain the same relative relationship. In general, managers who are in the second level of a company earn about two-thirds of a CEO's salary, while the next level down earns slightly more than half of a CEO's salary.[7] Much of the criticism of this theory, and an important source of criticism about executive compensation in general, is the gradual increase in the spread between executives' compensation and the average salaries of the people they employ. In 1980 CEOs received about 42 times the average of workers. By 1996 top executives were paid 209 times the average factory worker.[8] As a point of reference, the corresponding differential in Japan is under 20.[9] Both these pieces of information suggest that a social comparison explanation is not sufficient to explain why executive wages are as high as they are.

A second approach to understanding executive compensation focuses less on the *difference* in wages between executive and other jobs, and more on explaining the *level* of executive wages. The premise in this economic approach is that the worth of a CEO should correspond closely to some measure of company success, such as profitability or

[6]Herbert A. Simon, *Administrative Behavior*, 2nd ed. (New York: Macmillan, 1957).

[7]The Conference Board, *Top Executive Compensation: 1995.*

[8]"Executive Pay," *Business Week*, April 21, 1997, p. 59.

[9]This comparison needs to be interpreted with some caution. One counterargument (the Hay Group, *Compflash*, April 1992, p. 3) notes that American companies are generally much larger than their foreign counterparts. When compared to like-sized companies in other countries the U.S. multiple is comparable to the international average.

sales. Intuitively, this explanation makes sense. There is also empirical support. Numerous studies over the past 30 years demonstrate executive pay bears some relationship to company success.[10]

One recent study combined both social comparison and economic explanations to try to better understand CEO salaries. Both of these explanations turned out to be significant. Size and profitability affected level of compensation. But social comparisons also did. In this study the social comparison was between CEOs and the wages of the board of directors. It seems that CEO salaries rose, on average, 51 percent for every $100,000 more that was earned by directors on the board.[11] Recognizing this, CEOs sometimes lobby to get a board loaded with directors who are highly paid in their primary jobs.

A third view of CEO salaries, called agency theory, incorporates the political motivations that are an inevitable part of the corporate world. Sometimes, this argument runs, CEOs make decisions that aren't in the economic best interest of the firm and its shareholders. One variant on this view suggests that the normal behavior of a CEO is self-protective—CEOs will make decisions to solidify their position and to maximize the rewards they personally receive.[12] As evidence of this self-motivated behavior, consider the following description of how executives ensure themselves high compensation.[13] The description comes from the experience of a well-known executive compensation consultant, now turned critic, who specialized for years in the design of executive compensation packages.

1. If the CEO is truly underpaid: A compensation consultant is hired to survey true competitors of the company. The consultant reports to the board of directors that the CEO is truly underpaid. Salary is increased to a competitive or higher level.
2. If the CEO is not underpaid and the company is doing well: A compensation consultant is hired. A list of companies is recommended to the consultant as appropriate for surveying. Companies tend to be selected because they are on the top end in terms of executive compensation. The consultant reports back to the board that its CEO appears to be underpaid. Salary is increased.
3. If the CEO is not underpaid and the company is doing poorly: A compensation consultant is hired. The CEO laments with the consultant that wages are so low for top management that there is a fear that good people will start leaving the company and going to competitors. Of course, no one ever asks why the company is underperforming if it has such a good management team. Anyway, the result is that the consultant recommends a wage increase to avoid future turnover.

In each of these scenarios CEO wages rise. And at times the blatant manipulation is depressing.

---

[10]Marc J. Wallace, "Type of Control, Industrial Concentration, and Executive Pay," *Academy of Management Proceedings* (1977), pp. 284–288; W. Lewellan and B. Huntsman, "Managerial Pay and Corporate Performance," *American Economic Review* 60 (1977), pp. 710–720.

[11]Charles O'Reilly, Brian Main, and Graef Crystal, "CEO Compensation as Tournament and Social Comparison: a Tale of Two Theories," *Administrative Science Quarterly* 33 (1988), pp. 257–274.

[12]Kathyrn M. Eisenhardt, "Agency Theory: An Assessment and Review," *Academy of Management Review* 14 (1989), pp. 57–74.

[13]Graef Crystal, *In Search of Excess.*

Agency theory argues that executive compensation should be designed to ensure executives have the best interests of stockholders in mind when they make decisions. The outcome has been to use some form of long-term incentive plan, most commonly stock options. A survey of 500 firms found the use of long-term incentives rising for CEOs from 33 percent of the package in 1990 to 39 percent in 1995.[14] In the simplest form, an executive is given the option to purchase shares of the company stock at some future date for an amount equal to the fair market price at the time the option is granted. There is a built-in incentive for an executive to increase the value of the firm. Stock prices rise. The executive exercises the option to buy the stock at the agreed-upon price. Because the stock price has risen in the interim, the executive profits from the stock sale.

Although this sounds like an effective tool to motivate executives, there are still many critics.[15] The major complaint is that stock options don't have a downside risk. If stock prices rise, the stock options are exercised. If stocks don't improve, the executive suffers no out-of-pocket losses. Some argue that executive compensation should move more towards requiring executives to own stock, and not just to the option to buy.[16] With the threat of possible financial loss and the hopes of possible substantial gains, motivation may be higher. Some early evidence supports this position. In three industries where executives had large stock holdings, firms outperformed other industries where executives had little or no current stock investment.

The second trend in response to complaints about excessive executive compensation is increasing government regulation. In 1992 the Securities and Exchange Commission entered the controversy.[17] Stockholders are now permitted to propose and vote on limits to executive compensation. The 1993 Revenue Reconciliation Act limited employer deductions for executive compensation to $1 million and capped the amount of executive compensation used in computing contributions to and benefits from qualified retirement plans. Ironically, this very law may be contributing to the growth of executive compensation. The $1 million mark now serves as a new standard, with many executives making less than this quickly finding their pay rise to this level.

Components of an Executive Compensation Package. There are five basic elements of most executive compensation packages: (1) base salary, (2) short-term (annual) incentives or bonuses, (3) long-term incentives and capital appreciation plans, (4) employee benefits, and (5) perquisites. Because of the changing nature of tax legislation, each of these at one time or another has received considerable attention in designing executive compensation packages. Exhibit 14.5 traces the trend in these components over time.

One obvious trend is apparent from these data. Companies are placing more and more emphasis on incentives at the expense of base salary. Such a change in emphasis

[14]"Executives Pay: On the Rise but Increasingly at Risk," *Compflash*, November, 1995, p. 5.

[15]Nancy C. Pratt, "CEOs Reap Unprecedented Riches while Employees' Pay Stagnates," *Compensation and Benefits Review,* September/October 1996, p. 20.

[16]Ira T. Kay, "Beyond Stock Options: Emerging Practices in Executive Incentive Programs," *Compensation and Benefits Review* 23, no. 6 (1991), pp. 18–29.

[17]Michelle Osborn, "SEC: Executive Pay Is an Issue for Shareholders," *USA Today*, 1994, p. B1.

EXHIBIT 14.5 Percentage Breakdown of Executive Compensation Components

Compensation Component	*Percent During 1970s*	*Percent During 1980s*	*Percent During 1990s*
Base Salary	60	40	27
Benefits	*	15	7
Perks	*	5	unknown
Short-term Incentive	25	20	43
Long-term Incentive	15	20	23

*—Unreported

Source: various issues of *The Wall Street Journal*, data from Towers Perrin, Wyatt Co; Michael Bishko, "Compensating Your Overseas Executives, Pt. 1: Strategies for the 1990s," *Compensation and Benefits Review* 22, May–June 1990, American Management Association.

EXHIBIT 14.6 The Top Base Salaries Across Industries

Industry	*Person*	*Base Salary*
Basic Materials	Alston Correll: Georgia-Pacific	$1,050,000
Energy	Ray Irani: Occidental	1,900,000
Industrial	Lawrence Bossidy: Allied Signal	2,000,000
Technology	John Welch: General Electric	2,300,000
Financial	John Reed: Citicorp	1,466,000
Utilities	William Esrey: Sprint	987,000

Source: "Executive Pay Survey," *The Wall Street Journal*, April 10, 1997, pp. R16–17.

signals the growing importance attached to making decisions that ensure profitability and survival of a company.

Base Salary. As noted earlier, being competitive is a very important factor in the determination of executive base pay. But competitive levels of compensation vary widely across industries. Exhibit 14.6 shows the top base salaries of CEOs in different industries.

Although formalized job evaluation still plays an occasional role in determining executive base pay, other sources are much more important. Particularly important is the opinion of a compensation committee, composed usually of the company's board of directors or a subset of the board. Frequently this compensation committee will take over some of the data analysis tasks previously performed by the chief personnel officer, even going so far as to analyze salary survey data and performance records for executives of comparably sized firms.[18] One empirical study suggests the most common

[18]Ernest C. Miller, "How Companies Set the Base Salary and Incentive Bonus Opportunity for Chief Executive and Chief Operating Officers . . . A Compensation Review Symposium," *Compensation Review* 9 (Fourth Quarter 1976), pp. 30–44; Monci Jo Williams, "Why Chief Executives' Pay Keeps Rising," *Fortune*, April 1, 1985, pp. 66–72, 76.

behavior (60 percent of the cases) of executive compensation committees is to identify major competitors and set the CEO's compensation at a level between the best and worst of these comparison groups.[19]

Bonuses. Annual bonuses often play a major role in executive compensation and are primarily designed to motivate better performance. Most striking is the rapid rise in popularity of this type of compensation. Only 15 years ago just 36 percent of companies gave annual bonuses. Today bonuses are given to 90 percent of executives.[20] And these incentives on average are 72 percent of total compensation.

Incentives vary markedly across industries. In the financial industry they are 2.5 times higher than base pay. In contrast utility companies only pay incentives averaging 38 percent of base pay.[21] The variation often can be traced to legal or company policy prohibitions. The types of organizations relying almost exclusively on base salary for total direct compensation typically have one or more of the following characteristics:[22] (1) tight control of stock ownership, (2) not-for-profit institutions, or (3) firms operating in regulated industries.

Long-term Incentive and Capital Appreciation Plans. Long-term incentives now account for 35 percent of total executive compensation, up from 28 percent a decade ago.[23] By far the most common long-term incentive remains the executive stock option. Because many of the highest reported executive pay packages can be traced to stock options, critics have focused on their use and abuse. One clear complaint is that stock options don't pay for performance of the executive. In a stock market that is rising on all fronts, executives can exercise options at much higher prices than the initial grant price—and the payouts are more likely attributed to general market increases than any specific action by the executive. Efforts to counter this undeserved reward are linked to the rise of other types of long term incentives, some of which require the executive to "beat the market" or hit certain performance targets specifically linked to firm performance. Exhibit 14.7 identifies other types of long-term incentives and generally describes their main features.[24]

Executive Benefits. Since many benefits are tied to income level (e.g., life insurance, disability insurance, pension plans), executives typically receive higher benefits than most other exempt employees. Beyond the typical benefits outlined in Chapter 13, however, many executives also receive additional life insurance, exclusions from de-

---

[19]Daniel J. Miller, "CEO Salary Increases May Be Rational after All: Referents and Contracts in CEO Pay," *Academy of Management Journal* 38, no. 5, pp. 1361–1385.

[20]Arreglado, *Top Executive Compensation: 1990 Edition*, The Conference Board.

[21]The Conference Board, "Top Executive Compensation: 1995 Edition," in IOMA, *Pay for Performance Report*, June 1996, p. 10.

[22]William H. Cash, "Executive Compensation," *Personnel Administrator* 22, no. 7 (1977), pp. 11–19.

[23]The Conference Board, *Executive Annual Incentive Plans: 1996,* p10.

[24]Other tax reform issues are discussed in Gregory Wiber, "After Tax Reform, Part I: Planning Employee Benefit Programs," *Compensation and Benefits Review* 19, no. 2 (1987), pp. 16–25; and Irwin Rubin, "After Tax Reform, Part 2," *Compensation and Benefits Review* 20, no. 1 (1988), pp. 26–32.

Exhibit 14.7 Long-term Incentives for Executives

Type	*Description*	*Comments*
Incentive Stock Options	Purchase of stock at a stipulated price, conforming with Internal Revenue Code (Section 422A).	No taxes at grant. Company may not deduct as expense.
Nonqualified Stock Options	Purchase of stock at a stipulated price, not conforming with Internal Revenue Code.	Excess over fair market value taxed as ordinary income. Company may deduct.
Phantom Stock Plans	Cash or stock award determined by increase in stock price at a fixed future date.	Taxed as ordinary income. Does not require executive financing.
Stock Appreciation Rights	Cash or stock award determined by increase in stock price during any time chosen (by the executive) in the option period.	Taxed as ordinary income. Does not require executive financing.
Restricted Stock Plans	Grant of stock at a reduced price with the condition they may not be sold before a specified date.	Excess over fair market value taxed as ordinary income.
Performance Share/ Unit Plans	Cash or stock award earned through achieving specific goals.	Taxed as ordinary income. Does not require executive financing.

Source: Sibson & Co. 1990 Executive Compensation Report.

ductibles for health-related costs, and supplementary pension income exceeding the maximum limits permissible under ERISA guidelines for qualified (eligible for tax deductions) pension plans.

Of course, various sections of ERISA and the tax code restrict employer ability to provide benefits for executives that are too far above those of other workers. The assorted clauses require that a particular benefits plan: (1) cover a broad cross-section of employees (generally 80 percent), (2) provide definitely determinable benefits, and (3) meet specific vesting (see Chapter 13) and nondiscrimination requirements. The nondiscrimination requirement specifies that the average value of benefits for low-paid employees must be at least 75 percent of the average value for highly paid employees.[25]

Executive Perquisites. Perquisites, or "perks," probably have the same genesis as the expression "rank has its privileges." Indeed, life at the top has its rewards, designed to satisfy several types of executive needs. One type of perk could be classified as internal, providing a little something extra while the executive is inside the company: luxury offices, executive dining rooms, special parking. A second category also is designed to be

[25]Dennis Blair and Mark Kimble, "Walking Through the Discrimination Testing Wage for Welfare Plans," *Benefits Quarterly* 3, no. 2 (1987), pp. 18–26. Author's note: At press time Section 89 of the Tax Code was under serious attack. If repealed, the nondiscrimination laws would change again.

company-related, but for business conducted externally: company-paid membership in clubs/associations, payment of hotel, resort, airplane, and auto expenses.

The final category of perquisites should be totally isolated from the first two because of the differential tax status. This category, called personal perks, includes such things as low-cost loans, personal and legal counseling, free home repairs and improvements, personal use of company property, and expenses for vacation homes.[26] Since 1978, various tax and regulatory agency rulings have slowly been requiring companies to place a value on perks.[27] If this trend continues, the taxable income of executives with creative perk packages may increase considerably.

Exhibit 14.8 illustrates different types of perks and the percentage of companies that offer them.

Compensation of Scientists and Engineers in High-technology Industries

Scientists and engineers are classified as professionals. According to the Fair Labor Standards Act, this category includes any person who has received special training of a

EXHIBIT 14.8 Popular Perks Offered to Executives

Type Of Perk	*Percent of Companies Offering Perk*
Physical Exam	91
Company Car	68
Financial Counseling	64
Company Plane	63
Income Tax Preparation	63
First-Class Air Travel	62
Country Club Membership	55
Luncheon Club Membership	55
Estate Planning	52
Personal Liability Insurance	50
Spouse Travel	47
Chauffeur Service	40
Reserved Parking	32
Executive Dining Room	30
Home Security System	25
Car Phone	22
Financial Seminars	11
Loans at low or no interest	9
Legal Counseling	6

Source: Hewitt Associates, 1990.

[26]Michael F. Klein, "Executive Perquisites," *Compensation Review* 12 (Fourth Quarter 1979), pp. 46–50.

[27]R.L. VanKirk and L.S. Schenger, "Executive Compensation: The Trend is Back to Cash," *Financial Executive*, May 1978, pp. 83–91.

scientific or intellectual nature and whose job does not entail more than a 20 percent time allocation for supervisory responsibilities.

The compensation of scientists and engineers focuses on rewarding them for their special scientific or intellectual training. Here lies one of the special compensation problems that scientists and engineers face. Consider the freshly minted electrical engineer who graduates with all the latest knowledge in the field. For the first few years after graduation this knowledge is a valuable resource on engineering projects where new applications of the latest theories are a primary objective. Gradually, though, this engineer's knowledge starts to become obsolete. Team leaders begin to look to the newer graduates for fresh new ideas. If you track salaries of these employees, there is a close resemblance between pay increases and knowledge obsolescence. Early years bring larger than average (relative to employees in other occupations) increases. After ten years, increases drop below average, and become down right puny in the 15–20-year timeframe. Partly because salary plateaus arise, many scientists and engineers make career changes such as moving into management or temporarily leave business to update their technical knowledge. In recent years some firms have tried to deal with the plateau effect and also accommodate the different career motivations of mature scientists and engineers.

The result has been the creation of dual career tracks. Exhibit 14.9 shows a typical dual career ladder.

Notice that dual ladders provide exactly that: two different ways of progressing in an organization, each reflecting different types of contributions to the organization's mission. The first, or managerial ladder, ascends through increasing responsibility for supervision or direction of people. The professional track ascends through increasing contributions of a professional nature which do not mainly entail the supervision of employees. Scientists and engineers have the opportunity at some stage in their careers to consider a management track or continue along the scientific track. Not only do dual tracks offer greater advancement opportunities for scientists and engineers, but maximum base pay in the technical track can approximate that of upper management positions.

A second problem in designing the compensation package of scientists and engineers centers on the question of equity. The very nature of technical knowledge and its dissemination requires their relatively close association across organizations. In fact, scientists and engineers tend to compare themselves for equity purposes with the graduates who entered the labor market at the same time period. Partially because of this and partially because of the volatile nature of both jobs and salaries in these occupations, organizations rely very heavily on external market data in pricing their base pay.[28] This has resulted in the use of maturity curves.

Maturity curves reflect the relationship between scientist/engineer compensation and years of experience in the labor market. Generally, surveying organizations ask for information about salaries as a function of years since the incumbent(s) last received a degree. This is intended to measure the half-life of technical obsolescence. In fact, a plot

[28]Jo C. Kail, "Compensating Scientists and Engineers," in *New Perspectives on Compensation*, ed. David B. Balkin & Luis R. Gomez-Mejia (Englewood Cliffs, N.J.: Prentice-Hall, 1987), pp. 247–281.

EXHIBIT 14.9 IBM Dual Ladders

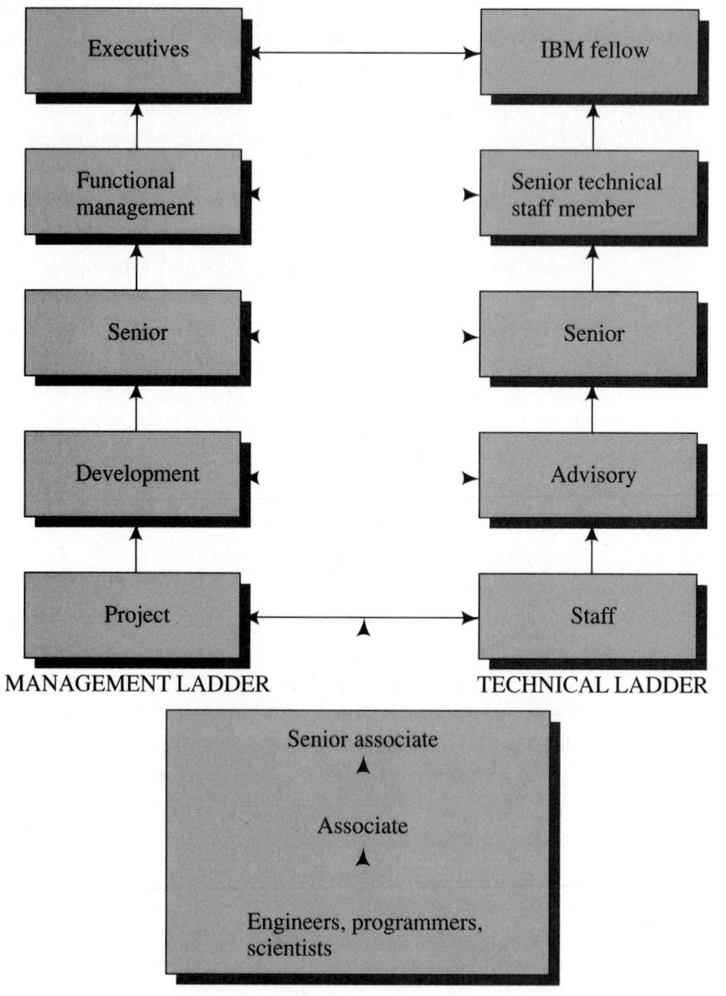

of this data, with appropriate smoothing to eliminate aberrations, typically shows curves that are steep for the first 5–7 years and then rise more gradually as technical obsolescence erodes the value of jobs. Exhibit 14.10 illustrates such a graph with somewhat greater sophistication built into it, in that different graphs are constructed for different levels of performance. To construct such graphs, the surveying organization must also ask for data broken down by broad performance levels. Notice in the illustration that the high performers begin with somewhat higher salaries, and the differential continues to broaden over the first few years.

EXHIBIT 14.10 Maturity Curve Showing Years Since Last Degree Relative to Salary

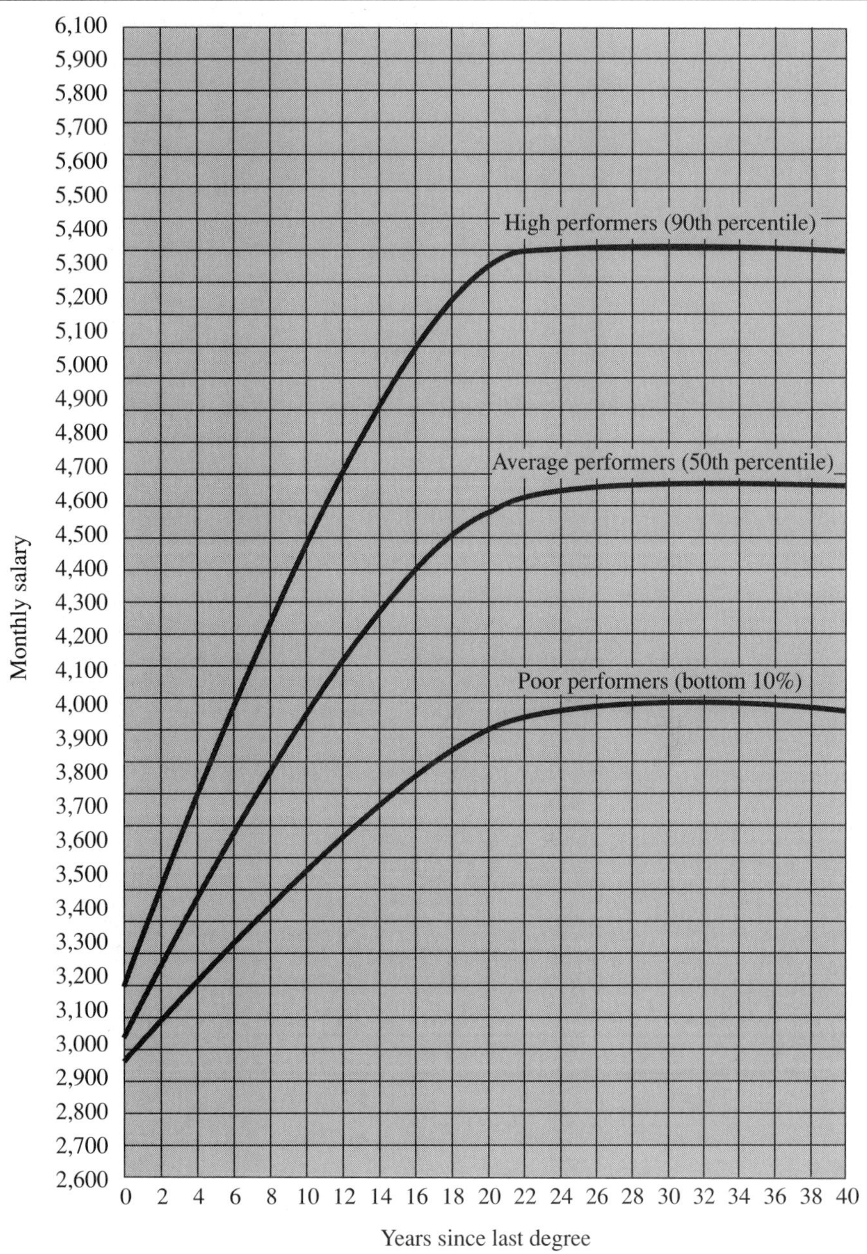

Scientists and engineers also receive compensation beyond base pay. In general, high-technology firms place a great emphasis on the use of performance-based incentives.[29] Common forms of incentives include profit sharing and stock ownership incentives. Other incentives link payment of specific cash amounts to completion of specific projects on or before agreed-upon deadlines. Post-hiring bonuses are also paid for such achievements as patents, publications, elections to professional societies, and attainment of professional licenses.

Finally, organizations have devoted considerable creative energy to development of perks that satisfy the unique needs of scientists and engineers. These perks include flexible work schedules, large offices, campus-like environments and lavish athletic facilities. The strategic importance of these groups dictates that both mind and body be kept active.

Sales Force Compensation

The sales staff spans the all-important boundary between the organization and consumers of the organization's goods or services. Besides the sales function, or even as part of selling, the sales staff must be sensitive to changing consumer tastes and provide rapid feedback to appropriate departments. Indeed, there is a growing trend toward linking sales compensation to customer satisfaction measures, with about one-third of all companies reporting use of such quality-based measures.[30] The role of interacting in the field with customers requires individuals with high initiative who can work under low supervision for extended periods of time. The standard compensation system is not designed for this type of job. As you might expect, there is much more reliance on incentive payments tied to individual performance. Thus, even when salespeople are in the field—and relatively unsupervised—there is always a motivation to perform. Exhibit 14.11 shows that most sales employees at every organization level have some component of pay, usually a large one, that is an incentive tied to performance.

EXHIBIT 14.11 Sales Compensation Components

	Percent receiving this form of Compensation				
Sales Position	*Straight Salary*	*Straight Commission*	*Salary + Commission*	*Salary + Bonus*	*Salary + Bonus + Commission*
Top Sales Executive*	8	3	27	28	26
Senior Sales Representative	6	13	42	6	34
Entry Sales Representative	6	8	54	3	31

* does not add up to 100 % because of other compensation components not listed.

Source: Dartnell, *The 28th Sales Force Compensation Survey*, 1994–1995.

---

[29]George T. Milkovich, "Compensation Systems in High Technology Companies," in *New Perspectives on Compensation*, ed. Balkin & Gomez-Mejia, pp. 269–277.

[30]"Sales Compensation Is Increasingly Tied to Quality," *Compflash,* (Englewood Cliffs, N.J.: Prentice-Hall, 1987), July 1995, p. 1.

Exhibit 14.12 Average Annual Compensation Change: Mid-level Salesperson

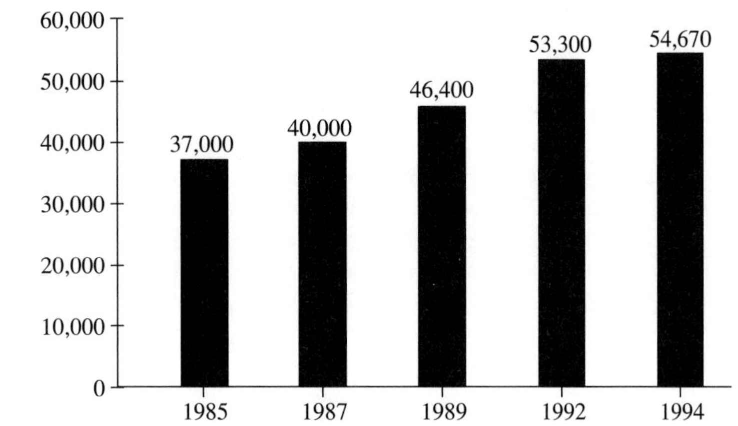

Source: Dartnell Corporation, *28th Sales Force Compensation Survey* 1994–1995.

Designing a Sales Compensation Plan. Four major factors influence the design of sales compensation packages: (1) the nature of people who enter the sales profession, (2) organizational strategy, (3) competitor practices, and (4) product to be sold.

People Who Enter the Sales Profession. Popular stereotypes of salespeople characterize them as heavily motivated by financial compensation. One study supports this perception, with salespeople ranking pay significantly higher than five other forms of reward.[31] As a source of satisfaction, pay rated a mean of 83.7 on a 100-point scale. Promotional opportunities, sense of accomplishment, personal growth, recognition, and job security were all less highly regarded. These values almost dictate that the primary focus of sales compensation should be on direct financial rewards (base pay + incentives). Exhibit 14.12 shows the level of, and change in, average annual compensation for a senior salesperson over a 10-year period. In general, compensation growth has slowed down, perhaps reflecting the slower inflation rate in recent years.

Organizational Strategy. A sales compensation plan should link desired behaviors of salespeople to organizational strategy.[32] Salespeople must know when to stress customer service and when to stress volume sales. And when volume sales are the goal, which products should be pushed hardest? Strategic plans signal which behaviors are important. For example, emphasis on customer service to build market share, or movement into geographic areas with low potential, may limit sales volume. Ordinarily, sales rep-

[31]N. Ford, O. Walker & G. Churchill, "Differences in the Attractiveness of Alternative Rewards among Industrial Salespeople: Additional Evidence," *Journal of Business Research* 13, no. 2 (1985), pp. 123–138.

[32]Bill O'Connell, "Dead Solid Perfect: Achieving Sales Compensation Alignment," *Compensation and Benefits Review*, March/April 1996, pp. 41–48.

resentatives under an incentive system will view customer service as an imposition, taking away from money-making sales opportunities. And woe be to the sales supervisor who assigns a commission-based sales person to a market with low sales potential. Salespeople asked to forgo incentive income for these low sales tasks should be covered under a compensation system with a high base pay and small incentive component.

Alternatively, an organization may want to motivate aggressive sales behavior. A straight commission-based incentive plan will focus sales efforts in this direction, to the possible exclusion of supportive tasks such as processing customer returns. These incentive plans include both a statement about the size of the incentive and a discussion of the performance objective necessary to achieve the incentive. Typical performance measures include: overall territory volume, market share, number of product placements in retail stores, number of new accounts, gross profit, percentage of list price attainment (relative to other salespeople in the organization), consistency of sales results, expense control productivity per square foot (especially popular in retail stores), and bad debt generated by sales.[33] Each measure, of course, corresponds to a different business goal. For example, an organization might use some volume measure such as number of units, orders, invoices, or cash received if the business goal is to increase sales growth. Alternatively, if the goal is profit improvement, the appropriate measurement would be gross margin on sales or price per unit. Percentage account erosion would be stressed if improved account retention became a major focus of attention, while customer satisfaction indices are increasingly popular because of greater emphasis on quality.

Competitor Practices. In selecting an appropriate pay level, organizations should recognize that external competitiveness is essential. The very nature of sales positions means that competitors will cross paths, at least in their quest for potential customers. This provides the opportunity to chat about relative compensation packages, an opportunity which salespeople will frequently take. To ensure that the comparison is favorable, the organization should identify a compensation level strategy that explicitly indicates target salaries for different sales groups and performance levels.

Product to Be Sold. The very nature of the product or service to be sold may influence the design of a compensation system. Consider a product which, by its very technical nature, takes time to understand and thus to fully develop an effective sales presentation. Such products are said to have high barriers to entry, meaning considerable training is needed to become effective in the field. Compensation in this situation usually includes a large base pay component, minimizing the risk a sales representative will face and encouraging entry into the necessary training program. At the opposite extreme are products with lower barriers to entry, where the knowledge needed to make an effective sales presentation is relatively easy to acquire. These product lines are sold more often using a higher incentive component, thus paying more for actual sales than for taking the time to learn the necessary skills.

Products or services that sell themselves, where sales ability isn't as crucial, inspire different compensation packages than opportunities where the salesperson is more

---

[33]John K. Moynahan, *The Sales Compensation Handbook,* (New York: AMACOM, 1991).

prominent. Base compensation tends to be more important with easily sold products. Not surprisingly, incentives become more important when willingness to work hard may make the difference between success and failure.

Most jobs do not fit the ideal specifications for either of the two extremes, represented by straight salary or straight commission plans. A combination plan is intended to capture the best of both these plans. A guaranteed straight salary can be linked to performance of nonsales functions such as customer service, while a commission for sales volume yields the incentive to sell. A plan combining these two features signals the intent of the organization to ensure that both types of activities occur in the organization.

Compensation for Contingent Workers

About 1 of every 10 workers is employed in a nontraditional work relationship.[34] For our purposes let's call contingent workers anyone who works through a temporary help agency, on an on-call basis, a contract company, or as an independent contractor. The first two of these groups typically earn less than workers in traditional arrangements; the latter two earn more. For example, working through a temporary help agency usually means low pay in administrative or day labor positions. In contrast, the wages for an independent contractor might be higher than for the more permanently employed counterpart. Indeed, independent contractors often are people who have been downsized and then reemployed by the company. DuPont cut its workforce by 47,000 between 1990–1997. About 14,000 of these workers were subsequently hired as vendors or contractors.[35] Because the employment status of contingent workers is temporary and employee benefits are less or nonexistent, wages at times tend to compensate by being somewhat higher. Exhibit 14.13 illustrates these wage and benefit characteristics.

Why the move to contingent workers? Part of the answer may be cost savings. Employee benefit costs are about half for contingent workers.[36] But sometimes wages are higher. The real reason for contingent workers may be the added flexibility such em-

EXHIBIT 14.13 Wage and Benefits of Contingent Workers

		Percentage of Workers Eligible for Employer Benefit	
Type of Worker	*Median Weekly Earnings*	*Health Insurance*	*Pensions*
Temp from agency	$290	45%	3%
Contract worker	512	70	29
On-call worker	386	66	19
Independent contractor	518	73	35
Worker in traditional arrangement	480	83	49

Source: Steven Hipple and Jay Stewart, "Earnings and Benefits of Workers in Alternative Work Arrangements," *Monthly Labor Review*, October 1996, pp. 46–54.

[34]Steven Hipple and Jay Stewart, "Earnings and Benefits of Workers in Alternative Work Arrangements," *Monthly Labor Review*, October 1996, pp. 46–54.

[35]Kim Clark, "Manufacturing's Hidden Asset: Temp Workers," *Fortune*, November 10, 1997, pp. 28–29.

[36]Ibid.

ployment offers the employer. In today's fast-paced marketplace, lean and flexible are desirable characteristics. And contingent workers offer this option.

A major compensation challenge for contingent workers, as with all our special group employees, is identifying ways to deal with equity problems. Contingent workers may work alongside permanent workers, yet often receive lower wages and benefits for the same work. Employers deal with this potential source of inequity on two fronts, one traditional and one that challenges the very way we think about employment and careers. One company response is to view contingent workers as a pool of candidates for more permanent hiring status. High performers may be moved off contingent status and afforded more employment stability. Cummins Engine, for example, is famous for its hiring of top-performing contingent workers. The traditional reward of a possible "promotion," then, becomes a motivation to perform.

A second way to look at contingent workers is to champion the idea of boundaryless careers.[37] At least for high-skilled contingent workers, it is increasingly popular to view careers as a series of opportunities to acquire valuable increments in knowledge and skills. Sometimes these opportunities arise in one organization through transfers across different jobs. But knowledge acquisition may even be faster for employees willing to forgo traditional job security and accept temporary assignments that quickly enhance their skill repertoire. In this framework, contingent status isn't a penalty or cause of dissatisfaction. Rather, employees who accept the idea of boundaryless careers may view contingent status as part of a fast-track developmental sequence. Lower wages are offset by opportunities for rapid development of skills—opportunities that might not be so readily available in more traditional employment arrangements. Companies like General Electric that promote this reward—enhanced employability status through acquisition of highly demanded skills—may actually have tapped an underutilized reward dimension.

Summary

Special groups are portrayed here as sharing two common characteristics: they all have jobs with high potential for conflict, and resolution of this conflict is central to the goals of the organization. Probably because of these characteristics, special groups receive compensation treatment that differs from other employees. Unfortunately, most of this compensation differentiation is prescriptive in nature, and little is known about the specific roles assumed by special groups and the functions compensation should assume in motivating appropriate performance. Future practice and research should focus on answering these questions.

[37]Janet H. Marler, George T. Milkovich, & Melissa Barringer, "Boundaryless Organizations and Boundaryless Careers: A New Market for High Skilled Temporary Work" (Unpublished Paper submitted to 1998 Academy of Management Annual Conference, Human Resource Division).

Review Questions

1. When we first wrote this book, back when pterodactyls circled the earth, we didn't even mention contingent workers as a special group. What has changed about the way corporations function to make this group of workers increasingly important?
2. Why are firms moving to different types of long-term incentives for executives in a shift away from stock options?
3. Is it possible for occupational groups other than those discussed in this chapter to assume the status of a special group for the purposes of compensation? If your answer is no, explain why not. If your answer is yes, explain why. Use as your example the job of a lawyer in an industry going through deregulation (elimination or revision of some of the rules governing the way firms in the industry do business). Given what you see in wage treatment for special groups in this chapter, what changes might you expect in lawyer compensation?
4. For each of the special groups discussed in this chapter, explain how the issue of equity is especially important. Who are the comparison groups against which special group members might compare themselves to determine if compensation is fair?

YOUR TURN:

COMPENSATION OF SPECIAL GROUPS

Madeira Research, Inc., is a government contractor providing design and testing for all-terrain combat vehicles and functional weaponry. Fifty-five percent of all MRI costs are traceable to wages and benefits. Of the 312 employees, 118 are scientists/engineers. Salary surveys for competitors in the region (basically a 200-mile radius) show the following information (randomly chosen from a larger survey printout).

Employee #	*Company*	*Highest Relevant Degree Received*	*Number Years since Degree Received*	*Salary ($ per Year)*
1	A	B.S.	3	39,000
2	B	M.S.	6	58,800
3	B	M.S.	3	50,400
4	A	Ph.D.	7	95,900
5	C	B.S.	6	48,000
6	A	Ph.D.	9	105,300
7	A	M.S.	4	53,200
8	C	Ph.D.	3	77,100
9	C	B.S.	7	51,000
10	D	Ph.D.	6	91,200
11	D	M.S.	9	67,200
12	D	M.S.	7	61,600
13	C	Ph.D.	4	81,800
14	B	B.S.	9	57,000
15	A	B.S.	4	42,000

Discussion Questions

1. From the information provided can you identify any pattern to the market rates for scientists/engineers? What is the pattern and how strong is it?
2. Assuming you want to lead the market by 10 percent, how much should you pay the following two scientists from your company?

	Degree	*Yrs. since Degree Received*	*Last Performance Rating*	*Salary*
#1	M.S.	5	Very Good	____
#2	Ph.D.	8	Excellent (top rating)	____

CHAPTER 15

Union Role in Wage and Salary Administration

Chapter Outline

Many experts believe that unions are facing their most critical challenge of the last 50 years.[1] Between 1954 and 1987 union membership fell 50 percent.[2] During roughly that same period, the union success rate in certification elections (winning rights to represent previously nonunion workers) fell from 60 percent to approximately 45 percent.[3] Today 14.5 percent of wage and salary employees are unionized, down from 36 percent in the heyday of unions.[4]

---

[1]Thomas A. Kochan, Harry C. Katz, and Robert B. McKersie, *The Transformation of American Industrial Relations* (New York: Basic Books, 1986), pp. 221–23.

[2]Kirkland Ropp, "State of the Unions," *Personnel Administrator* 32, no. 7 (1987), pp. 36–41.

[3]Richard B. Freeman, *On the Divergence of Unionism Among Developed Countries.* (Working paper no. 2817. Cambridge, Mass.: National Bureau of Economic Research.)

[4]Bureau of Labor Statistics, "Union Member Summary," January 1998, http://stats.bls.gov:80/newsrels.htm

One popular explanation for this decline is that management is taking an increasingly hard stance against unions in general, and union demands in particular.[5] A large portion of this management opposition to unions is spurred by increasing pressure from both domestic and international competitors. Management increasingly resists wage increases that would give nonunion competitors, both domestic and foreign, a competitive price advantage. The end result of these competitive pressures is a declining union–nonunion wage differential. In fact, one study shows that a 10 percent rise in import share (a popular measure of international competition) has the effect of lowering the union wage differential by approximately 2 percent.[6]

Such competitive pressures during the 1980s and early 1990s have triggered lower than normal wage increases in unionized firms and even some wage concessions. Accompanying these wage trends is an increasing pessimism about the continued viability of yesterday's unions in today's marketplace. Although the statistics indicate a decline in unionism, some of the issues that are important cornerstones of unionization continue to be important for workers. Fully 63 percent of employees say they want to have more influence in their workday decisions. If need be, 40 percent of workers would vote union to achieve their needs. Admittedly, this is less than a majority, but it is far more than the 15 percent unionization today.[7] This percentage supporting unionization is comparable to a figure reported 15 years ago in a similar survey, and suggests antiunion support may have bottomed out.[8]

THE IMPACT OF UNIONS IN WAGE DETERMINATION

Despite the strong management efforts to lessen the impact of unions, they still assume an important role in wage determination. Even in a nonunion firm, the protective actions taken by wage and salary administrators are influenced by external union activity. This chapter outlines the general factors affecting wages in unionized firms and then illustrates the specific impact of unions in wage determination. Four specific areas of impact are discussed: (1) impact on general wage and benefit levels, (2) impact on the structure of wages, (3) impact on nonunion firms (also known as spillover), and (4) impact on wage and salary policies and practices in unionized firms. The final discussion focuses on union response to the changing economic environment of the 1980s and the alternative compensation systems which have evolved in response to these changes.

This site gives detailed information about dozens of unions, including specifics of union contracts: **http://www.geocities.com/WallStreet/3088/labor.htm**

[5]Gail McCallion, "Union Membership Decline: Competing Theories and Economic Implications," CRS Report for Congress, August 23, 1993, p. 13.

[6]David A. Macpherson and James B. Steward, "The Effect of International Competition on Union and Non Union Wages," *Industrial and Labor Relations Review* 43, no. 4 (1990), pp. 434–446.

[7]Richard B. Freeman and Joel Rogers, "Worker Representation and Participation Survey," *CQ Researcher*, June 28,1996, p. 574.

[8]R. Wayne Mondy and Shane Preameaux, "The Labor Management Power Relationship Revisited," *Personnel Administrator,* May 1985, pp. 51–54.

Union Impact on General Wage Levels

Do unions raise wages? Are unionized employees better off than they would be if they were nonunion? Unfortunately, comparing what is versus what might have been is no easy chore. Several measurement problems are difficult to overcome. The ideal situation would compare numerous organizations that were identical except for the presence or absence of a union.[9] Any wage differences among these organizations could then be attributed to unionization. Unfortunately, few such situations exist. One alternative strategy adopted has been to identify organizations within the same industry that differ in level of unionization. For example, consider company A which is unionized, and company B which is not. It is difficult to argue with assurance that wage differences between the two firms are attributable to the presence or absence of a union. First, the fact that the union has not organized the entire industry weakens its power base (strike efforts to shut down the entire industry could be thwarted by nonunion firms). Consequently, any union impact in this example might underestimate the role of unions in an industry where percentage of unionization is greater. A second problem in measuring union impact is apparent from this example. What if company B grants concessions to employees as a strategy to avoid unionization? These concessions, indirectly attributable to the presence of a union, would lead to underestimation of union impact on wages.

Another strategy in estimating union impact on wages is to compare two different industries that vary dramatically in the level of unionization.[10] This strategy suffers because nonunionized industries (e.g., agriculture, service) are markedly different from unionized industries in the types of labor employed and their general availability. Such differences have a major impact on wages independent of the level of unionization and make any statements about union impact difficult to substantiate.

One source of continuing data on unionized and nonunionized firms is the Bureau of Labor Statistics. Between 1969 and 1985 the union wage premium more than doubled from 17.6 to 35.6 percent.[11] In 1996 workers represented by unions had median weekly earnings of $610 compared to nonunion wages of $462, a 32 percent difference.[12] Historically, union wages have experienced multiple-year upswings followed by multiple-year downswings. The 1950s were characterized by a widening of the union wage premium, followed by a constriction in the 1960s, an enlargement from 1969 to 1983, and another constriction from 1983 to the present.[13] Since 1983, the nonunion sector has been securing larger wage increases than the unionized sector, partially due to unions' acceptance of lump-sum payments in lieu of increases in base wage.[14]

---

[9]Allan M. Carter and F. Ray Marshall, *Labor Economics* (Homewood, Ill.: Richard D. Irwin, 1982).

[10]Ibid.

[11]Michael L. Wachter and William H. Carter, "Norm Shifts in Union Wages: Will 1989 Be a Replay of 1969?" in *Brookings Papers on Economic Activity*, eds. William C. Brainard and George L. Perry (Washington, D.C.: The Brookings Institution, 1989), pp. 233–276.

[12]http://stats.bls.gov/news.release/union2.t02.htm, January 28, 1998.

[13]Wachter and Carter, "Norm Shifts in Union Wages: Will 1989 Be a Replay of 1969?"

[14]Fehmida Sleemi, "Collective Bargaining Outlook for 1995," *Compensation and Working Conditions* 47, no. 1 (January 1995), pp. 19–39.

Perhaps the best conclusion about union versus nonunion wage differences comes from a summary analysis of 114 different studies.[15] Two important points emerged:

1. Unions do make a difference in wages. Union workers earn somewhere between 8.9 percent and 12.4 percent more than their nonunion counterparts.
2. The size of the gap varies from year to year. During periods of higher unemployment, the impact of unions is larger. During strong economies the union–nonunion gap is smaller. Part of the explanation for this time-based phenomenon is related to union resistance to wage cuts during recessions and the relatively slow response of unions to wage increases during inflationary periods (because of rigidities or lags introduced by the presence of multiyear labor contracts).

This site provides union employment and wage information: **http://stats.bls.gov/news.release/union2.nws.htm**

Unions also have an impact on the difference between wages for selected groups. Wage differentials among workers who are different in terms of race, age, service, skill level, and education appear to be lower under collective bargaining.[16]

Similar studies of union–nonunion wage differentials exist for employees in the public sector.[17] Union employees in the public sector earn, on average, about 7–12 percent more than their nonunion counterparts.[18] However, this range masks some large variations in wage increases for different occupational groups in the public sector. The largest gains for public-sector employees are reported for firefighters, with some studies reporting as much as an 18 percent wage differential attributable to the presence of a union. At the other extreme, however, teachers' unions (primarily affiliates of the National Education Association and the American Federation of Teachers) have not fared as well, with reported impacts generally in the range of 1 to 4 percent.[19]

In recent years, with low unemployment and reports of record profits, little mention is made of one old union nemesis: wage concessions, or wage cuts. Some experts claim that wage concessions are more prevalent in unionized firms, and this reduces the advantage union workers hold in wages, particularly during downturns in the economy. For example, in 1908 the glass bottle blowers accepted a 20 percent wage cut in the hopes of fighting automation. During the 1930s concessions were a regular feature in

---

[15]Stephen B. Jarrell and T.D. Stanley, "A Meta Analysis of the Union–Non Union Wage Gap," *Industrial and Labor Relations Review* 44, no. 1 (1990), pp. 54–67.

[16]Freeman, "The Impact of Collective Bargaining: Illusion or Reality?"

[17]David Lewin, "Public Sector Labor Relations: A Review Essay," in *Public Sector Labor Relations: Analysis and Readings*, ed. David Lewin, Peter Feuille, and Thomas Kochan (Glen Ridge, N.J.: Thomas Horton and Daughters, 1977), pp. 116–144.

[18]Dale Belman, John S. Heywood, & John Lund, "Public Sector Earnings and the Extent of Unionization," *Industrial and Labor Relations Review* 50, no. 4 (July 1997), pp. 610–628; H. Gregg Lewis, "Union/Nonunion Wage Gaps in the Public Sector," *When Public Sector Workers Unionize,* ed. Richard B. Freeman and Casey Ichniowski (Chicago: University of Chicago Press, 1988), pp. 169–193.

[19]For a discussion of the reasons for this smaller public sector–union impact see Lewin et al., *Public Sector Labor Relations: An Analysis and Readings.*

the construction, printing, and shoe industries. Concessions were also made in the apparel and textile industries during the 1950s. Continuing into the 1980s, major contract concessions occurred in 8 industries: air transport, food stores, shoe manufacturing, primary metals, metal cans, transportation equipment, textiles, and trucking.[20] Recent research suggests that concessions aren't solely, or even primarily, a tool used in unionized firms. Concessions are most likely in small firms, in high-wage paying firms, and in firms where only a small portion of the workforce is unionized.[21]

The Structure of Wage Packages

The second compensation issue involves the structuring of wage packages. One dimension of this issue concerns the division between direct wages and employee benefits. Research indicates that the presence of a union adds about 20–30 percent to employee benefits.[22] Whether because of reduced management control, strong union–worker preference for benefits, or other reasons, unionized employees also have a greater percentage of their total wage bill allocated to employee benefits. In 1997 benefits accounted for 36 percent of the total compensation package for union workers, and 26 percent for nonunion employees.[23] Typically the higher costs show up in the form of higher pension expenditures or higher insurance benefits.[24] One particularly well-controlled study found unionization associated with a 24 percent higher level of pension expenditures and 46 percent higher insurance expenditures.[25]

A second dimension of the wage structure issue is the evolution of two-tier pay plans. Basically a phenomenon of the union sector, two-tier wage structures differentiate pay based upon hiring date. A contract is negotiated which specifies that employees hired after a given target date will receive lower wages than their higher seniority peers working on the same or similar jobs. From management's perspective, wage tiers represent a viable alternative compensation strategy. Tiers can be used as a cost control strategy to allow expansion or investment, or as a cost-cutting device to allow economic survival.[26] Two-tier pay plans initially spread because unions viewed them as less painful than wage freezes and staff cuts among existing employees. The tradeoff was to bargain away equivalent wage treatment for future employees. Remember, this is a

---

[20]Robert Gay, "Union Contract Concessions and Their Implications for Union Wage Determination" (Working paper no. 38, Division of Research and Statistics, Board of Governors of the Federal Reserve System, 1984).

[21]Linda A. Bell, "Union Wage Concessions in the 1980s: The Importance of Firm-specific Factors," *Industrial and Labor Relations Review* 48, no. 2 (January 1995), pp. 258–275.

[22]Richard Freeman and James Medoff, *What Do Unions Do?* (New York: Basic Books, 1981).

[23]http://stats.bls.gov/news.release/ecec.nws.htm; January 28, 1998.

[24]http://stats.bls.gov/news.releases/ecec.t07.htm., January 28, 1998 Table 7; Robert Rice, "Skill, Earnings and the Growth of Wage Supplements," *American Economic Review* 56 (1966), pp. 583–93; George Kalamotousakis, "Statistical Analysis of the Determinants of Employee Benefits by Type," *American Economist*, Fall 1972, pp. 139–47; William Bailey and Albert Schwenk, "Employer Expenditures for Private Retirement and Insurance Plans," *Monthly Labor Review* 95 (1972), pp. 15–19.

[25]Loren Solnick, "Unionism and Fringe Benefits Expenditures," *Industrial Relations* 17, no. 1 (1978), pp. 102–07.

[26]James E. Martin and Thomas D. Heetderks, *Two-Tier Compensation Structures: Their Impact on Unions, Employer, and Employees* (Kalamazoo, Mich.: W.E. Upjohn Institute for Employment Research, 1990).

radical departure from the most basic precepts of unionization. Unions evolved and continue to endure, in part based on the belief that all members are equal. Two-tier plans are obviously at odds with this principle. Lower-tier employees, those hired after the contract is ratified, receive wages 50–80 percent lower than employees in the higher tier.[27] The contract may specify that the wage differential may be permanent, or the lower tier may be scheduled ultimately to catch up with the upper tier. Eventually the inequity from receiving different pay for the same level may cause employee dissatisfaction.[28] Consider the Roman Emperor who implemented a two-tier system for his army in A.D. 217.[29] He was assassinated by his disgruntled troops shortly thereafter. Although such expressions of dissatisfaction are unlikely today, unions are much more reluctant to accept a two-tier structure, and may view it as a strategy of last resort.[30]

Union Impact: The Spillover Effect

Although union wage settlements have declined in recent years, the impact of unions in general would be understated if we did not account for what is termed the "spillover effect." Specifically, employers seek to avoid unionization by offering workers the wages, benefits, and working conditions won in rival unionized firms. The nonunion management continues to enjoy the freedom from union "interference" in decision making, and the workers receive the spillover of rewards already obtained by their unionized counterparts. Several studies document the existence and importance of this phenomenon, providing further evidence of the continuing role played by unions in wage determination.[31]

Role of Unions in Wage and Salary Policies and Practices

Perhaps of greatest interest to current and future compensation administrators is the role unions play in administering wages. The role of unions in administering compensation is outlined primarily in the contract. The following illustrations of this role are taken from major collective bargaining agreements in effect today.

Basis of Pay. The vast majority of contracts specify that one or more jobs are to be compensated on an hourly basis and that overtime pay will be paid beyond a certain number of hours. Notice the specificity of the language in the following contract clause:

---

[27]Mollie Bowers and Roger Roderick, "Two-Tier Pay Systems: The Good, The Bad and the Debatable," *Personnel Administrator* 32, no. 6 (1987), pp. 101–112.

[28]James Martin and Melanie Peterson, "Two-Tier Wage Structures: Implications for Equity Theory," *Academy of Management Journal* 30, no. 2 (1987), pp. 297–315.

[29]"Two-Tier Wage Systems Falter as Companies Sense Worker's Resentment," *The Wall Street Journal*, June 16, 1987, p. 1.

[30]Fehmida Sleemi, "Collective Bargaining Outlook for 1995," *Compensation and Working Conditions* 47, no. 1 (January 1995), pp. 19–39.

[31]David Neumark & Michael L. Wachter, "Union Effects on Nonunion Wages: Evidence from Panel Data on Industries and Cities," *Industrial and Labor Relations Review* 49, no. 1 (1995), pp. 20–38; Lawrence Kahn, "The Effect of Unions on the Earnings of Nonunion Workers," *Industrial and Labor Relations Review* 31, no. 1 (1978), pp. 205–16.

A. Overtime pay is to be paid at the rate of one and one-half (1 $^{1}/_{2}$) times the base hourly straight-time rate.
B. Overtime shall be paid to employees for work performed only after eight (8) hours on duty in any one service day or forty (40) hours in any one service week. Nothing in this Section shall be construed by the parties or any reviewing authority to deny the payment of overtime to employees for time worked outside of their regularly scheduled work week at the request of the Employer.
C. Penalty overtime pay is to be paid at the rate of two (2) times the base hourly straight-time rate. Penalty overtime pay will not be paid for any hours worked in the month of December.
E. Excluding December, part-time flexible employees will receive penalty overtime pay for all work in excess of ten (10) hours in a service day or fifty-six (56) hours in a service week.
(United States Postal Workers Union and United States Postal Service, expires 11/98)

Further, many contracts specify a premium be paid above the worker's base wage for working nonstandard shifts:

> The shift bonus for second (2nd) shift employees shall be thirty-eight cents ($.38) per hour, and the shift bonus for third (3rd) shift employees shall be forty-five cents ($.45) per hour. (TRW Inc. *and* Auto Workers 10/98)

Alternatively, agreements may specify a fixed daily, weekly, biweekly or monthly rate. In addition, agreements often indicate a specific day of the week as payday, and sometimes require payment on or before a certain hour. The following contract clause illustrates this requirement.

> Payday shall be on Wednesday of each week between the hours of 6:30 A.M.–7:30 A.M., and between the hours of 2:30 P.M.–4:00 P.M. covering wages earned during the payroll week occurring two weeks prior.
> (U.S. Agri-Chemicals and Chemical Workers, expires 12/98)

Much less frequently, contracts specify some form of incentive system as the basis for pay. The vast majority of clauses specifying incentive pay occur in manufacturing (as opposed to nonmanufacturing) industries.

> Section 7. Establishment of Labor Standards. The Company and the Union, being firmly committed to the principle that high wages can result only from high productivity, agree that the Company will establish Labor Standards that:
> (a) Are fair and equitable to both the Company and the workers; and
> (b) Are based on the working capacity of a normally qualified worker properly motivated and working at an incentive pace; and
> (c) Give due consideration to the quality of workmanship and product required; and
> (d) Provide proper allowances for fatigue, personal time, and normal delays, and
> (e) Provide for payment of incentive workers based on the earned hours produced on-standard (except when such Employees are working on a Preliminary Estimate, etc.), and for each one per cent (1%) increase in acceptable production over standard, such workers shall receive a one per cent (1%) increase in pay over the applicable incentive rate.

The Company will, at its discretion as to the time and as to jobs to be placed on or removed from incentive, continue the earned-hour incentive system now in effect, and extend it to jobs in such other job classifications which, in the opinion of the Company, can properly be placed on incentive, with the objective of increasing productivity and providing an opportunity for workers to enjoy higher earnings thus made possible. The plan shall be maintained in accordance with the following principles: . . .
(Maytag, Maytag and Admiral Products and Auto Workers, expires June 1, 2001)

Occupation-wage Differentials. Most contracts recognize that different occupations should receive different wage rates. Within occupations, though, a single wage rate prevails.

Occupation	*Hourly Wage*
Production Line Operator	$ 7.85
QC Inspector	$ 8.11
Set Up I	$ 7.75
Set Up II	$ 8.39
Set Up III	$12.02

IUE Local 386 and Gowanda Electronics Corporation, 1997.

Although rare, there are some contracts that do not recognize occupational/skill differentials. These contracts specify a single standard rate for all jobs covered by the agreements. Usually such contracts cover a narrow range of skilled groups.

Experience/Merit Differentials. Single rates are usually specified for workers within a particular job classification. Single-rate agreements do not differentiate wages on the basis of either seniority or merit. Workers with varying years of experience and output receive the same single rate. Alternatively, agreements may specify wage ranges. The following example is fairly typical:

Job Title	*Start*	*2 mo*	*6 mo*	*9 mo*	*1 yr*	*2 yr*	*5 yr*	*7 yr*	*10 yr*	*15 yr*
Shop Clerk	$4.76	$5.15	$5.54	$5.94	$6.67	$6.96	$7.12	$7.40	$7.55	$7.85
QC Inspector	4.76	5.21	5.60	5.99	6.79	7.09	7.25	7.56	7.83	8.11

IUE Local 386 and Gowanda Electronics Corporation, 1997

The vast majority of contracts, as in the example above, specify seniority as the basis for movement through the range. Automatic progression is an appropriate name for this type of movement through the wage range, with the contract frequently specifying the time interval between movements. This type of progression is most appropriate when the necessary job skills are within the grasp of most employees. Denial of a raise is rare, and frequently is accompanied by the right of the union to submit any wage denial to the grievance procedure.

A second strategy for moving employees through wage ranges is based exclusively on merit. Employees who are evaluated more highly receive larger or more rapid increments than average or poor performers. Within these contracts, it is common to specify that disputed merit appraisals may be submitted to grievance. If the right to grieve is not explicitly *excluded*, the union also has the implicit right to grieve.

The third method for movement through a range combines automatic and merit progression in some manner. A frequent strategy is to grant automatic increases up to the midpoint of the range and permit subsequent increases only when merited on the basis of performance appraisal.

Other differentials. There are a number of remaining contractual provisions that deal with differentials for reasons not yet covered. A first example deals with differentials for new and probationary employees. About one-half of major agreements refer to differentials for these employees. The most common rate designation is below or at the minimum of the rate range. For example:

> New hires shall start at 85% of the maximum rate, progress to 90% after completion of 1040 hours worked, 95% after 2080 hours worked and to the maximum after completion of 3120 hours worked. This will apply only to employees hired on or after the effective date of the Agreement.
>
> (Chrysler Corp. and Auto Workers; expired 9/97)

A second example of contract differentials deals with different pay to unionized employees who are employed by a firm in different geographic areas. Very few contracts provide for different wages under these circumstances, despite the problems that can arise in paying uniform wages across regions with markedly different costs of living.

A final category where differentials are mentioned in contracts deals with part-time and temporary employees. Few contracts specify special rates for these employees. Those that do, however, are about equally split between giving part-time and temporary employees wages above full-time workers (because they have been excluded from the employee benefits program) or below full-time workers.

Vacations and Holidays. Vacation and holiday entitlements are among clauses frequently found in labor contracts. They, too, use very specific language, as the following example illustrates:

> The following holidays shall be observed by all employees in this bargaining unit as paid holidays:
>
> 1. New Year's Day
> 2. Martin Luther King, Jr. Day
> 3. Patriot's Day
> 4. Good Friday
> 5. Memorial Day
> 6. Independence Day
> 7. Labor Day
> 8. Columbus Day
> 9. Election Day
> 10. Veterans Day
> 11. Thanksgiving
> 12. Christmas

Section 14.2
If any of the aforementioned holidays falls on a Saturday the County will observe the holiday on the prior Friday. If a holiday falls on a Sunday, the following Monday will be observed as the holiday.

Section 14.3
An employee who is required to work on a day celebrated as a holiday as provided in this Agreement, will be paid his regular straight time pay plus one & one-half times his straight time hourly rate for every hour actually worked on such holiday, except when an employee elects compensatory time off as provided under Section 16.10 of Article 16 of this contract. Any employee who works in excess of eight (8) hours on a holiday or a day celebrated as a holiday shall receive double time (2x) their regular hourly rate for all hours worked over eight hours on such holiday.
(The County of Erie *and* Civil Service Employees Association, Inc., expires 99)

Wage Adjustment Provisions. Frequently in multiyear contracts some provision is made for wage adjustment during the term of the contract. There are three major ways these adjustments might be specified: (1) deferred wage increases, (2) reopener clauses, and (3) cost-of-living adjustments (COLA) or escalator clauses. A deferred wage increase is negotiated at the time of initial contract negotiations with the timing and amount specified in the contract. A reopener clause specifies that wages, and sometimes such nonwage items as pension and benefits, will be renegotiated at a specified time or under certain conditions. Finally, a COLA clause, as noted earlier, involves periodic adjustments based typically on changes in the consumer price index:

A cost of living allowance, if applicable, shall be placed in effect and adjusted semiannually effective with the first pay period beginning on or after January 1 and July 1. The calculation of the cost of living adjustment will be based on the 1967 Index (CPI-W). Under the Index, a one cent ($.01) per hour wage increase will be made effective for each .3 point increase in the index.
(Swift-Eckrich Inc. and Teamsters, expired 1/97)

UNIONS AND ALTERNATIVE REWARD SYSTEMS

International competition causes a fundamental problem for unions. If a unionized company settles a contract and raises prices to cover increased wage costs, there is always the threat that an overseas competitor with lower labor costs will capture market share. Eventually, enough market share means the unionized company is out of business. To keep this from happening unions have become much more receptive in recent years to alternative reward systems that link pay to performance. After all, if worker productivity rises, product prices can remain relatively stable even with wage increases.

About 20 percent of all U.S. collective bargaining agreements permit some alternative reward system (e.g., lump sum, piece rate, gain sharing, profit sharing, skill-based pay).[32] Willingness to try such plans is higher when the firm faces extreme competitive

[32]J.L. McAdams and E.J. Hawk, *Organizational Performance and Reward: 663 Experiences in Making the Link* (Scottsdale, AZ: American Compensation Association, 1994).

pressure.[33] In the unionized firms that do experiment with these alternative reward systems, though, the union usually insists on safeguards that protect both the union and its workers. The union insists on group-based performance measures with equal payouts to members. This equality principle cuts down strife and internal quarrels among the members and reinforces the principles of equity that are at the very foundation of union beliefs. To minimize bias by the company, performance measures tend more often in unionized companies to be objective. Most frequently the measures rely on past performance as a gauge of realistic targets rather than some time study or other engineering standard that might appear more susceptible to tampering.[34] Below we offer specific feedback about union attitudes towards alternative reward concepts.

Lump-Sum Awards

As discussed in Chapter 10, lump sum awards are one-time cash payments to employees that are not added to an employee's base wages. These awards are typically given in lieu of merit increases which are more costly to the employer. This higher cost results both because merit increases are added on to base wages and because several employee benefits (e.g., life insurance and vacation pay) are figured as a percentage of base wages. Lump-sum payments are a reality of union contracts. For the past 10 years a stable one-third of all major collective bargaining agreements in the private sector have contained a provision for lump-sum payouts.[35]

Employee Stock Ownership Plans (ESOP)

An alternative strategy for organizations hurt by intense competition is to obtain wage concessions in exchange for giving employees part ownership in the company. For example, the Teamsters have experimented with contract provisions permitting local trucking companies and Teamster employees to set up ESOP plans.[36] One National Master Freight Agreement specified that employees would receive 49 percent ownership in a trucking company in exchange for wage concessions of no more than 15 percent over 5 years. So far, these plans have not been very effective in keeping marginal firms from eventually declaring bankruptcy.[37]

Pay-for-Knowledge Plans

Pay-for-knowledge plans do just that: pay employees more for learning a variety of different jobs or skills. For example, the U.A.W. negotiates provisions giving hourly wage

---

[33]L.B. Cardinal and I.B. Helburn, "Union versus Nonunion Attitudes toward Share Agreements," *Proceedings of the 39th Annual Meeting of the Industrial Relations Research Association* (Madison, WI. 1987), pp. 167–173.

[34]R.L. Heneman, C. von Hippel, D.E. Eskew and D.B. Greenberger, "Alternative Rewards in Unionized Environments," *ACA Journal,* Summer 1997, pp. 42–55.

[35]Fehmida Sleemi, "Collective Bargaining Outlook for 1995," *Compensation and Working Conditions* 47, no. 1 (January 1995), pp. 19–39, Table 4.

[36]*Changing Pay Practices: New Developments in Employee Compensation,* Washington, D.C.: Bureau of National Affairs, 1988.

[37]Ibid.

increases for learning new skills on different parts of the assembly process. By coupling this new wage system with drastic cuts in the number of job classifications, organizations have greater flexibility in moving employees quickly into high-demand areas. Unions also may favor pay-for-knowledge plans because they make each individual worker more valuable, and less expendable, to the firm. In turn, this also lessens the probability that work can be subcontracted out to nonunion organizations.

Gain-Sharing Plans

Gain-sharing plans are designed to align workers and management in efforts to streamline operations and cut costs. Any cost savings resulting from employees working more efficiently were split according to some formula between the organization and the workers. Some reports indicate gain sharing is more common in unionized than nonunionized firms.[38] In our experience success is dependent on a willingness to include union members in designing the plan. Openness in sharing financial and production data, key elements of putting a gain-sharing plan in place, are important in building trust between the two parties.

While unions aren't always enthusiastic about gain sharing, they rarely directly oppose it, at least initially. Rather, the most common union strategy is to delay taking a stand until real costs and benefits are more apparent.[39] Politically, this may be the wisest choice for a union leader. As Exhibit 15.1 illustrates, there are numerous possible costs and benefits to union membership for agreeing to a gain-sharing plan. Until the plan is actually implemented, though, it is unclear what the impact will be in any particular firm.

Profit-Sharing Plans

Unions have debated the advantages of profit-sharing plans for at least 80 years.[40] Walter Reuther, then President of the C.I.O. in 1948 (which became the A.F.L.–C.I.O. in 1955) championed the cause of profit sharing in the auto industry. The goal of unions is to secure sound, stable income levels for the membership. When this is achieved, subsequent introduction of a profit-sharing plan allows union members to share the wealth with more profitable firms while still maintaining employment levels in marginal organizations. We should note, though, that not all unions favor profit-sharing plans. As indicated by recent grumblings of employees at General Motors, inequality in profits among firms in the same industry can lead to wage differentials for workers performing the same work. Ford regularly distributes profit-sharing checks several times larger than the employees at G.M. receive. Most General Motors employees would argue the dif-

---

[38]R.L. Heneman, C. von Hippel, D.E. Eskew and D.B. Greenberger, "Alternative Rewards in Unionized Environments."

[39]T. Ross and R. Ross, "Gainsharing and Unions: Current Trends," in *Gainsharing: Plans for Improving Performance*, ed. B. Graham-Moore and T. Ross (Washington, D.C.: Bureau of National Affairs), pp. 200–213.

[40]J. Zalusky, "Labor's Collective Bargaining Experience with Gainsharing and Profit-Sharing"; William Shaw, "Can Labor be Capitalized?" *American Federationist* 17 (June 1910), p. 517.

EXHIBIT 15.1 Union Perceptions of Advantages/Disadvantages of Gain Sharing

Advantages of Gain sharing (% agreement)	*Disadvantages of gain sharing (% agreement)*
1. Increased recognition (95)	1. Management may try to substitute for wage increases (94)
2. Better job security (94)	2. Management can't be trusted (88)
3. More involvement in job activities (94)	3. Peer pressure to perform may increase (77)
4. More money (94)	4. Don't trust/understand bonus calculations (76)
5. More feeling of contributing to firm (86)	5. Union influence is undermined (66)
6. Increased influence of union (70)	6. Increased productivity may reduce need for jobs (64)

Source: T. Ross and R. Ross, "Gainsharing and Unions: Current Trends," in *Gainsharing: Plans for Improving Performance,* ed. B. Graham-Moore and T. Ross (Washington, D.C.: Bureau of National Affairs, 1990).

ference in payout cannot be traced to the fact that Ford employees work harder or smarter. In fact, the difference in profitability, the U.A.W. argues, is due to management decision making. Therefore, the argument runs, workers should not be penalized for factors beyond their control.

Summary

Other countries continue to make inroads in product areas traditionally the sole domain of American companies. The impact of this increased competition has been most pronounced in the compensation area. Labor costs must be cut to improve our competitive stance. Alternative compensation systems to achieve this end are regularly being devised. Unions face a difficult situation. How should they respond to these attacks on traditional compensation systems? Many unions believe that the crisis demands changing attitudes from both management and unions. Labor and management identify compensation packages that both parties can abide. Sometimes these packages include cuts in traditional forms of wages in exchange for compensation tied more closely to the success of the firm. We expect the remainder of the 1990s will be dominated by more innovation in compensation design and increased exploration between unions and management for ways to improve the competitive stance of American business.

Review Questions

1. Most union contracts do not include provisions for merit pay. Given what you have learned here and in Chapter 11, explain why unions oppose merit pay.
2. The late 90s have enjoyed a rare combination of low unemployment and low inflation. Explain why this combination would make COLA clauses less likely to appear in union contracts than was true in the 1980s.

3. It is probably true that, if given a choice, unions would prefer to implement a skill-based pay system than some form of gain-sharing plan. Why?
4. Assume, as local union president, you have just received valid information that the company employing your workers is close to bankruptcy. What types of wage concessions might your union be able to make? Which of these are likely to have the least negative impact on your union workers' wages in the short run (one year)? Which represent the greatest cost-saving potential for the union in the short run? Which is most likely to create internal dissension between different factions of the union?

YOUR TURN:

GENERAL TECHNOLOGY

The Company

General Technology (GT) is an international producer of burglar alarm systems. To crack the international market, GT must comply with quality standards as set by the International Organization for Standardization (ISO). Compliance requires that all products and processes pass a series of 17 strict criteria, the so-called ISO 9000 audit.

The Union

The Technology Workers of America (TWA) organized GT's Buffalo division in 1979. In the last control, both parties agreed to have a three-person panel listen to all disputes between union and management concerning the proper classification of jobs.

Your Role

You are the neutral third party hired to hear the dispute described below. The union representative has voted in the union's favor, and management has sided with management's position. You will break the tie. How do you vote and why? Some experts would argue that enough evidence is presented here for you to make a decision. See if you can figure out what the logic was that led to this conclusion. Further, list what other information you would like to have and how that might influence your decision.

The Grievance

A job titled Technical Review Analyst I with responsibility for ISO 9000 audits is slotted as a tier 3 job.[1] Union believes that this job should be evaluated as a tier 4 job. Management contends that both this job and its counterpart in tier 4 (Senior Technical Review Analyst) should be graded in tier 3.

Summary of Important Points in the Union Case

The union asserts, and management agrees, that the only difference historically between auditors classified as Technical Review Analysts I (tier 3) and those classified as Senior Technical Review Analysts (tier 4) was the presence or absence of one task. That task was the performance of systems tests.

[1] Tier 1 is the low end and tier 5 is the highest for all skilled craft jobs. Different evaluation systems are used for management and for clerical employees.

Only tier 4 personnel performed this work, and this yielded the higher tier classification. With the introduction of ISO 9000 audits, the systems test component of the tier 4 job was eventually phased out and both tier 3 and tier 4 auditors were asked to perform the ISO 9000 audit. The union and management agree that the systems test work previously performed by tier 4 employees was easier (and less valuable to the company) than the new ISO 9000 work now being performed. However, the union maintains that this added responsibility from the ISO 9000 audit, which involves about 150 hours of training, is sufficiently complex to warrant tier 4 classification. As partial support, the union provided a list of attendees to one ISO 9000 training session and noted that many of the attendees from other companies are managers and engineers, asserting this as evidence of the complexity involved in the audit material and the importance attached to this job by other firms.

The union also presented evidence to support the assertion that tier 3 personnel performing ISO 9000 audits are doing work of substantially the same value as the old grade 310 work.[2] This grade, as agreed by both the union and the company, is equivalent to the new tier 4.

Summary of Important Points in Management Case

Management's case includes four major points. First, management argues that a Technical Review Analyst performing ISO 9000 audits has a job that is similar in complexity, responsibility, and types of duties to jobs previously classified as grade 308 and 309. Jobs in these old grades are now slotted into tier 3, per the contract.

Second, management presented evidence that many of the duties performed in the ISO 9000 audits were performed in a series of prior audits, variously labeled Eastcore MPA, QSA 1981, and QPS 1982. This long and varied history of similar duties, management contends, is evidence that ISO 9000 does not involve higher level or substantially different (and hence no more valuable) duties than have been performed historically.

Third, management presented both notes and a memorandum from W. P. Salkrist (the company job evaluation expert) in support of his argument that the audit job with ISO 9000 responsibilities should be classified as a tier 4 job. Prior to introduction of the ISO 9000 audit, neither the union nor management had found any reason to complain about the existing prior job evaluations of the tier 3 and tier 4 review analysts.

Fourth, management provided evidence that these jobs at other facilities, *with other local contract provisions and conditions*, were all classified into tier 3.[3]

[2] The former job evaluation system broke jobs down into many more grades. As of the last contract, jobs are now classified into one of five tiers or grades.

[3] Union strongly contests the introduction of this information. In the past, management has vehemently argued that conditions at other facilities should not be introduced because local contracts were negotiated, with different trade-offs being made by the different parties. Union believes that this same logic should now apply if a consistent set of rules is to evolve.

CHAPTER 16 International Pay Systems

Chapter Outline

Change is part of modern market-based economies and consequently part of the employment relationships embedded in them. It is yesterday's news that the terms and conditions under which people work are changing. Over 70 percent of the *Fortune* 500 multinationals report that they have restructured over the past five years. Forty percent responded that they were either in the midst of restructuring or that it was ongoing and continuous. This means downsizing, layoffs, redefined work roles, more variable pay, greater risk, and general uncertainty.

Change in the employment relationship is not isolated in the United States. It is happening globally. Major Japanese employers are restructuring. Nissan and Toyota have modified their lifetime employment promises to long-term security within a group of companies, not necessarily the parent company.[1] Japanese employers report they are increasingly using ability and performance-based pay with less emphasis on seniority.[2] European companies are searching for ways to control the rate of labor cost increases and beginning to experiment with variable pay and performance-based appraisal. Deutsche Bank in Germany is controlling costs by cutting up to 9,000 jobs.[3]

And talk about jolting change—consider China, Russia and Central Europe, where employees in these communist and postcommunist economies face the challenge of revising pay systems that had been dictated by central government authorities without business or market-related logic. The Chinese government is shrinking its welfare state and requiring people to pay for their pensions and health care. Even the government organ *The People's Daily* hectors workers to care for themselves: "City dwellers are used to eating from one big rice bowl . . . They could learn from the rural people how to fend for themselves."[4] And in Russia, a friend recently suggested that "the most effective pay delivery system is a brown bag under the table."

So employment relationships are changing, and pay systems around the world are changing, too. A framework can help understand and manage this change. Without such a framework, the changes appear chaotic. With the framework, they may appear only ambiguous, ill-conceived, or inappropriate. However, they may also become more understandable and manageable.

---

[1] M. Morishima, "The evolution of HRM Policies and Practices in Japan," (Working paper, Keio University, Kyoto, Japan, 1996).

[2] Hayashi and Ohta, "Performance Evaluation and Remuneration for Gaishi Presidents," *Gaishi,* January–February 1997, pp. 50–53; Ida, "Overview: The Dichotomy between Japanese and Western HRM No Longer So Clear," *Gaishi,* March–April 1996, pp. 53–63; Survey of Japanese Personnel Management Practices," *Gaishi,* March–April 1996, pp. 64–68.

[3] Lowell Turner, ed. *Negotiating the New Germany: Can Social Partnership Survive?* (Ithaca, New York: Cornell University Press, 1998); D. Murphy, "Paying People in Europe," *International HR Journal,* Winter 1997, pp. 23–28; Puffer & Shekshnia, "Compensating Local Employees in Post-Communist Russia," *Compensation and Benefits Journal,* September–October 1994, pp. 35–42; J. Giacobbe-Miller, D. Miller, and V. Victorov, "Comparisons of Russian and U.S. Pay Allocation Decisions, Distributive Justice, and Productivity" (Working Paper, Amherst, University of Massachusetts, 1997); D. Soskice, "Wage Determination: The Changing Role of Institutions in Advanced Industrialized Countries," *Oxford Review of Economic Policy* 6, no. 4, pp. 36–61.

[4] "China Tries to Shrink Welfare State," *The Wall Street Journal,* January 20, 1997, p. C12.

EXHIBIT 16.1 Social Contract: Government, Organizations, and Employees

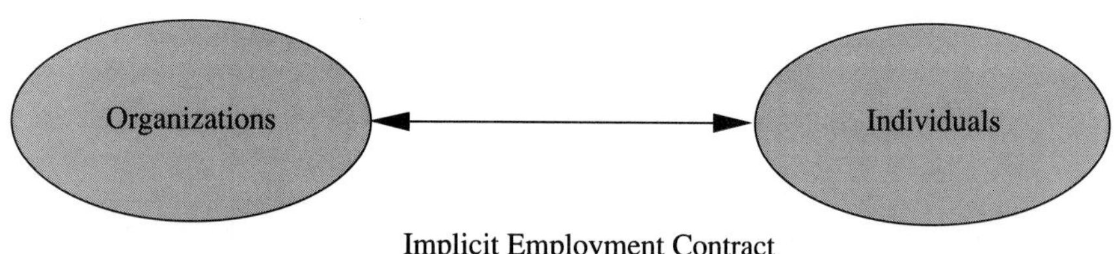

Implicit Employment Contract

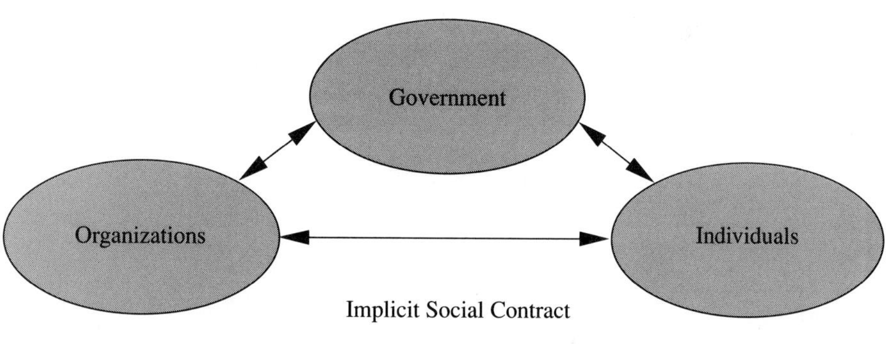

Implicit Social Contract

Check out the consultant web pages listed in the Appendix to Chapter 18 to see which ones provide information on wages, benefits, and legal requirements *outside* North America. For example, Watson Wyatt Worldwide offers information in your choice of five languages at **http://www.watsonwyatt.com.** Mercer, at **http:// www.mercer.com,** discusses new issues in major countries.

SOCIAL CONTRACTS

As we noted in Chapter 1, looking at compensation as part of the social contract offers a useful framework for understanding and managing employee pay. Exhibit 16.1 depicts the employment relationship with the actions employees believe are expected of them and the responses (e.g., pay, benefits, opportunities) they expect in return. This concept can expand to include the role of government. The implicit employment and social contracts are the keystones of modern societies' economic and social well-being. As you read this chapter, it should be clear that people in different countries and cultures hold differing beliefs about the roles and responsibilities of governments, employers, unions, and employees.

A recent study contrasting U.S. and German pay systems illustrates the point. It concluded that "in the U.S. you work hard to advance to keep a good job, to keep from falling into a shallow social safety net . . . . whereas the German pay system and social benefits system is close to a guaranteed annual income."[5] A typical German employee's marginal tax rate (percent tax on each additional dollar or mark earned) is 30 percent higher than in the United States. As a result, the return for working extra hours or working harder to receive a gain-sharing bonus is smaller in Germany. But in exchange for their higher taxes, German employees receive more generous social benefits, such as welfare and unemployment payments, national health care, plus subsidized college and apprenticeship programs.

So understanding how to manage employee compensation in Germany requires an understanding of the social contract; that is, understanding the roles played by government, employees, and employers. Efforts to change employee compensation systems—for example, to make them more responsive to customers, encourage innovative and quality service, or control costs—must be managed within the context of the relevant social contract.

A note of caution as you read this chapter. National and regional generalizations are often as misleading as personal stereotypes.[6] To claim that all organizations in Germany or Japan or the United States operate in some similar way ignores variations and differences. Considerable variety among company practices within any country exists. The basic premise of this section is that social, cultural, and economic conditions within each nation or region, taken as a whole, form distinct social and employment relationships. Understanding these relationships is useful for managing employee compensation. But do not assume uniformity within a country.

GLOBAL WORKPLACE COMPARISONS

Three related factors define the differences in various employment relationships: (1) managerial autonomy based on culture and laws, (2) patterns of ownership within financial markets, and (3) structures to accommodate trade union and employee involvement.[7]

---

[5] Linda Bell and Richard Freeman, "Why Do Americans and Germans Work Different Hours?" (Working Paper 4808, National Bureau of Economic Research, 1994).

[6] G. Milkovich and M. Bloom, "Rethinking International Compensation: From Exaptriate and National Cultures to Strategic Flexibility," *Compensation and Benefits Review,* April 1998; L. Markoczy, "Us and Them," *Across the Board,* February 1998, pp. 44–48.

[7] A. Hegewisch, C. Brewster, and J. Koubek, "Different Roads: Changes in Industrial Relations in the Czech Republic and East Germany since 1989," *Industrial Relations Journal,* 27 (1996), pp. 50–63; C. Brewster, "Different Paradigms in Strategic HRM: Questions Raised by Comparative Reasearch" (paper presented at Cornell Conference on Strategic HRM, Ithaca, NY, October 1997); Miriam Rothman, Dennis R. Briscoe, and Raoul C.D. Nacamulli, eds. *Industrial Relations Around the World* (Berlin: Walter deGruyter, 1993); Klaus Schwab and Claude Smadja, "Power and Policy: The New Economic World Order," *Harvard Business Review,* November–December 1994, pp. 40–45.

Managerial Autonomy

Managerial autonomy refers to the degree of freedom or discretion to make choices. Most U.S.-based organizations have relatively greater freedom (i.e., it is less costly) to change employee pay practices than in Europe. 3M, a global company based in St. Paul, Minnesota, is currently encouraging all its units to pursue performance-based pay in order to sustain growth. 3M units in the United States are trying out a variety of gain-sharing and bonus plans. At 3M Singapore, the notion of performance-based bonuses is old hat. Bonuses equivalent to two months' salary are paid every six months. On the other hand, 3M Europe, headquartered in Brussels, was told by the Belgian government that its proposed performance-based pay plan may be illegal. In an effort to control inflation and promote egalitarian values, Belgium passed a law that made all forms of new pay beyond that set by the nationally negotiated labor agreements illegal. Generally, European Union (E.U.) countries constrict actions at the national level via wage agreements negotiated by industrywide or nationwide employer and union associations.[8]

Japanese employment relationships have also been changing. Traditionally, Japan's employment relationship has been supported by "three pillars":

1. Lifetime security within the company.
2. Seniority-based pay and promotion systems.
3. Enterprise unions (decentralized unions that represent blue-collar workers within a single company). This structure contrasts with industrywide unions such as United Auto Workers in the United States or I.G. Metall, the largest trade union in Germany.[9]

Increasingly, Japanese companies are using performance-based approaches for pay and promotion (though seniority still is important, as you will read later in this chapter), MBO-style performance appraisal is commonly used to assess managerial performance, and employment security is defined as *long time* rather than *lifetime*.[10] The Japanese government regulates layoffs.[11]

On the whole, businesses have greatest freedom of action in the United States, less in Japan, and are the most constrained in Europe, particularly in Germany. In both Europe and Japan, government has a greater involvement in social policy and welfare

---

[8] *Social Europe: The Social Dimension of the Internal Market* (Brussels: Directorate-General for Employment, Social Affairs, and Education, 1988); Sandford M. Jacoby, ed., *The Workers of Nations* (New York: Oxford University Press, 1995); Soskice, "German Wage Bargaining System."

[9] Yoko Sano, "Changes and Continued Stability in Japanese HRM Systems: Choice in the Share Economy," *International Journal of Human Resource Management*, February 1993, pp. 11–27; Motohiro Morishima, "The Japanese Human Resource Management System: A Learning Bureaucracy," in *Human Resource Management in the Pacific Rim: Institutions, Practices and Values*, ed. J. Devereaux Jennings and Larry Moore (New York: Walter deGruyter, 1997).

[10] "The Appreciation of 'Lifetime Employment System and Job Mobility' in Toyota" (Toyota White Paper, Tokyo, 1993); "Business Restructuring and Effective Use of Human Resources," *Productivity in Japan* 7, no. 3 (Alexandria, VA: Japan Productivity Center for Socio-Economic Development).

[11] Johannes Schregle, "Dismissal Protection in Japan," *International Labour Review* 132, no. 4 (1993), pp. 507–20.

EXHIBIT 16.2 Pay and Social Costs Adjusted to Reflect Purchasing Power (Comparative Compensation Costs in U.S. Dollars*)

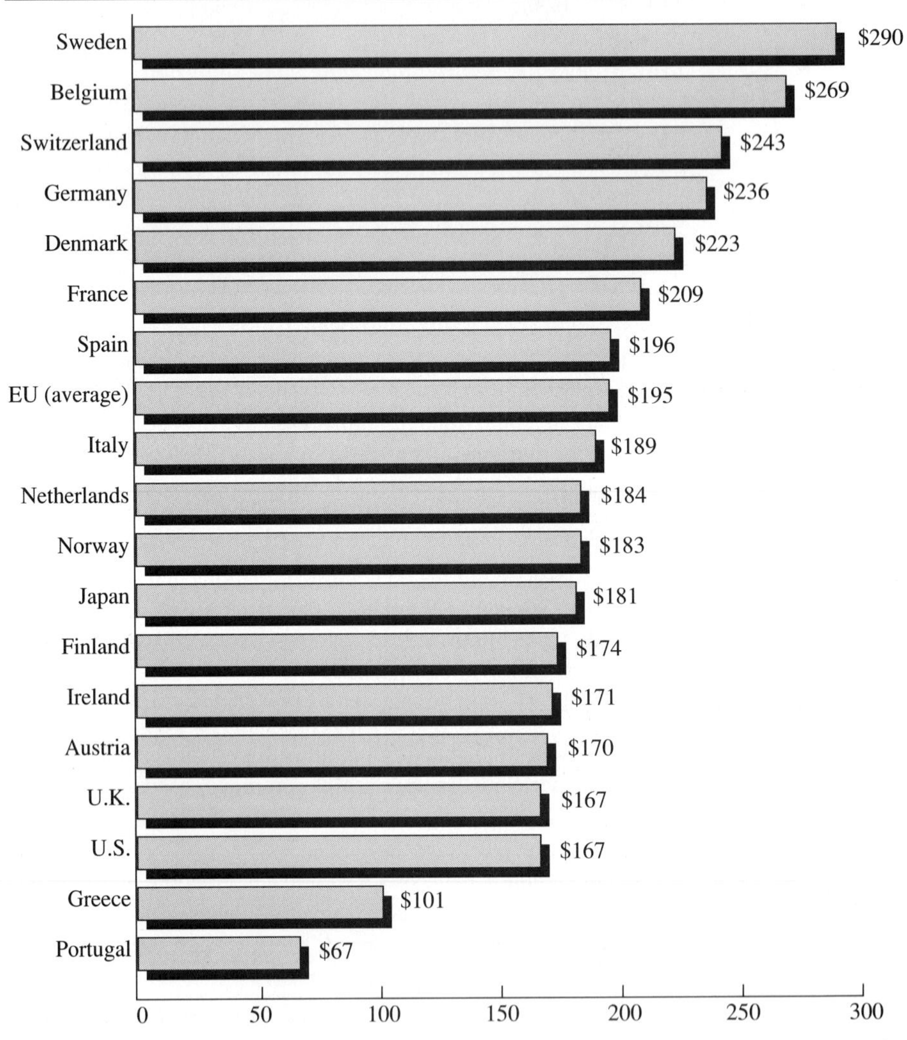

* Using OECD average 1997 exchange rates adjusted for GDP purchasing parities relative to those in the United States.
Source: Information adapted from Sedgwick Noble Lowndes (1997).

programs. And the costs of these social welfare programs are considerable. As Exhibit 16.2 shows, U.S. employers' *total employment costs,* including pay and social programs, are lower than in Japan and most of Europe. Employer costs for pay and social programs are 8 percent higher in Japan, 25 percent higher in France, 41 percent higher in Germany, and 61 percent higher in Belgium.

EXHIBIT 16.3 Trade union density

	1995	*%chg since 1985*
Sweden	91.1	+8.7
Italy	44.1	−7.4
South Africa	40.9	+130.8
Australia	35.2	−29.6
U.K.	32.9	−27.7
Germany	28.9	−17.6
New Zealand	24.3	−55.1
Japan	24.0	−16.7
U.S.	14.2	−21.1
South Korea	12.7	+2.4
France	9.1	−37.2

Source: Data from *ILO Labour Report,* 1997.

Ownership and Financial Markets

Patterns of ownership also affect the employment relationship and social contract. In the United States, corporate ownership and access to capital is far less concentrated than in most other countries. In Korea, for example, six conglomerates control a significant portion of the Korean economy, and the six are closely linked with specific families (e.g., Hyundai and Samsung). In Germany, most major companies are closely allied and owned largely by a small number of influential banks and the Bundesbank, its national bank. These patterns of ownership make certain types of pay systems almost nonsensical. For example, linking performance bonuses to increased shareholder value or offering stock options to employees makes little sense for German, Korean, or Japanese firms.[12] Japanese, Korean, and European governments take a greater interventionist role in their economies.

Trade Unions and Employee Involvement

As Exhibit 16.3 shows, Europe is highly unionized: in Sweden, 91 percent of the workforce belongs to unions; in the U.K., 33 percent, and in Italy, 44 percent. In Asia, Japan's unionization rate is 24 percent, and South Korea's almost 13 percent. Although the exhibit might cause you to conclude that union power is declining in Europe, caution is in order. In many countries, workers are covered by collective agreements, even though they may not be union members. In France, for example, 90 percent of workers

[12] Michael Byungnam Lee, Vida Scarpello, and B. Wayne Rockmore, "Strategic Compensation in South Korea's Publicity Traded Firms," Presentation at 10th World Congress of the International Industrial Relations Association, June 1995, Washington DC; Michael Byungnam Lee, "Business Strategy, Participative Human Resource Management and Organizational Performance: The Case of South Korea" (Working Paper, Georgia State University, 1994).

are covered by collective agreements, even though only 9 percent are members of unions.

In addition to higher rates of unionization, Belgium, Germany, and the European Union (E.U.) require the establishment of worker councils. While the exact rules may vary among nations, worker councils and unions significantly affect any proposed changes in pay. The E.U. is committed to maintaining the role of the *social partners,* as it calls employers and trade unions. The E.U. is trying to provide common labor standards in all its member countries. The purpose of standards is to avoid "social dumping," or the relocation of a business in a country with lower standards and labor costs. At present, hourly labor costs vary substantially among the countries, although sometimes the low labor costs are accompanied by low productivity.[13]

Exhibit 16.4 summarizes some of the different approaches to pay and benefits regulations. The United Kingdom specifies the fewest requirements with no minimum wage, no maximum hours, and no formal methods for employee participation. France, Belgium, and the Netherlands have the most generous minimum annual vacations.

Perhaps most striking for managing pay is that many European countries have nationally negotiated wage agreements that set the floor for wages of all unionized employees in the country. Such national-level decision making reduces the ability of organization-level managers to attempt to tailor or craft their pay system to fit their organization's unique business strategy. Hence the basic business strategy-based model

Business Strategy → HR Strategy → Compensation Strategy → Employee Behaviors → Competitive Advantage

needs to be modified to include the direct impact of various laws and regulations.

In summary, employee compensation is part of the overall employment relationship that in turn operates within the social context or environment. A region's history, culture, economic conditions, laws, regulations, and political factors all influence pay decisions. These contextual factors are in turn reflected by the autonomy managers have to make pay decisions, the patterns of corporate and capital ownership, the power of the trade unions, and the social contracts.

These interrelationships bring to mind the old children's game of rock crushes scissors, scissors cuts paper, and paper covers rock. Rock, scissors, and paper interact with each other in the same way that culture, employment relationships, and economic forces interact. Culture and laws shape the employment relationships, which in turn shape how organizations and employees economically compete. Economic competitiveness recalibrates and forces changes in the culture and laws. Thus, the forces are inevitably intertwined.

---

[13] Barbara A. Lee, "The Effect of the European Community's Social Dimension on Human Resource Management in U.S. Multinationals: Perspectives from the United Kingdom and France," *Human Resource Management Review* 4, no. 4 (1994), pp. 333–61; Neil Millward, Mark Steens, David Smart, and W. R. Hawes, *Workplace Industrial Relations in Transition* (Brookfield, VT: Dartmouth Publishing Company, 1992); John T. Addison and W. Stanley Siebert, "Recent Developments in Social Policy in the New European Union," *Industrial and Labor Relations Review*, October 1994, pp. 5–27; Christopher L. Erickson and Sarosh Kuruvilla, "Labor Costs and the Social Dumping Debate in the European Union," *Industrial and Labor Relations Review*, October 1994, pp. 28–47.

EXHIBIT 16.4 Employment Practices and Policies among EC Countries

Country	*Minimum Pay*	*Maximum Hours (including overtime)*	*Minimum Annual Vacation*	*Employee Participation*
Belgium	Yes	8 per day; 40 per week	4 weeks	Works councils
Denmark	No, but must conform to one of two compulsory wage systems	Depends on collective agreement	2.5 days per month	Employee representation on board of directors where there are more than 30 employees
France	Yes	10 per day 39 per week (includes 5 Saturdays)	2.5 days per month	Employee and union representatives
Germany	No, but if a collective agreement exists, this provision must be included	8 per day 48 per week	18 days	Works councils
Greece	Yes	48 per week	4 weeks (after 1 year's employment)	Works councils
Ireland	No	No, Generally applicable statutory maximum	3 weeks	No formal requirements
Italy	Collective agreement	48 per week 8 per day	Collective agreement	National collective bargaining agreements; requires consultation
Luxembourg	Yes	40 per week 8 per day	25 works days (5 days' holiday equals 1 week)	Employee representatives; joint works councils; employee directors
The Netherlands	Yes	48 per week 8.5 per day 5.5 days per week	4 weeks	Works council if 35 or more employees
Portugal	Yes	Office workers: 42 hours per week Others: 48 per week; 8 per day.	Not less than 21 days nor more than 30 days	Workers' commissions and registered trade unions
Spain	Yes	40 per week 9 per day	2.5 days per month	Employee delegates and committees; employee directors
United Kingdom	No	No	No requirements	No formal requirements

EXHIBIT 16.5 Comparing Labor Costs

Caterpillar compared its hourly U.S. labor costs with those of its own joint venture in Japan, under the theory that the Japanese venture has costs similar to those of Komatsu:

Caterpillar	*Shin Caterpillar Mitsubishi*
$22.26/hour cash compensation plus $10/hour in benefits	About $20.25/hour plus $5/hour in benefits

The UAW examined cash compensation at Cat and Komatsu, but didn't include the added cost of benefits:

Caterpillar	*Komatsu*
$20.91/hour	$19.66/hour

Add in recent wage increases and changes in exchange rates, and there's little difference in annual cash compensation:

Caterpillar	*Komatsu*
$39,350	$39,700

Source: Adapted from Robert L. Rose and Masayoshi Kanabayashi, "Comparing U.S.–Japan Labor-Cost Data Can be Murky," *The Wall Street Journal*, June 4, 1992, p. B4.

GLOBAL WAGE COMPARISONS

In Chapter 8 we discussed the numerous difficulties in measuring a market wage rate. Many large companies face difficulties of even greater magnitude when they try to compare their labor costs with those of foreign competitors. Comparisons among nations as different as the United States and Japan, for example, can be very misleading. Even if wages appear the same, expenses for health care, living costs, and typical company-provided perquisites such as dormitories and commuting allowances all complicate the picture. Comparisons between a specific U.S. firm and a specific Japanese firm may be even more misleading. Accurate data are difficult to obtain. Statistics may not be publicly available or may not completely specify what is or is not included. A number of different comparisons may all be valid, but all may paint different pictures. Exhibit 16.5, for example, shows three different wage comparisons between Caterpillar, Inc., in the United States and Komatsu, Ltd., a Japanese competitor. These comparisons were offered by various parties during a strike by the UAW against Caterpillar in Peoria, Illinois.

Mexico provides a closer-to-home example. A Bureau of Labor Statistics comparison of hourly compensation costs in 29 countries (Exhibit 16.6) shows wages in Mexico at only 8 percent of those in the United States. However, another source, Hewitt Associates, puts the "effective labor cost" in Mexico at about $6.00 per hour compared to $18.17 in

EXHIBIT 16.6 Indexes of Hourly Compensation Costs for Production Workers in Manufacturing
[Index, United States = 100]

Country or Area	*1975*	*1980*	*1985*	*1990*	*1992*	*1993*	*1994*	*1995*	*1996*
United States	100	100	100	100	100	100	100	100	100
Canada	94	88	84	107	106	97	94	93	94
Mexico	23	22	12	11	14	16	15	9	8
Australia	88	86	63	88	81	73	83	88	93
Hong Kong	12	15	13	21	24	26	27	28	29
Israel	35	38	31	57	56	—	54	61	62
Japan	47	56	49	86	101	114	125	138	119
Korea	5	10	9	25	30	32	38	43	46
New Zealand	50	54	34	56	49	48	53	59	62
Singapore	13	15	19	25	31	32	37	43	47
Sri Lanka	4	2	2	2	—	—	3	3	—
Taiwan	6	10	12	26	32	31	33	34	33
Austria	71	90	58	119	126	120	128	148	141
Belgium	101	133	69	129	137	127	138	156	147
Denmark	99	110	62	120	124	114	121	141	137
Finland	72	83	63	141	123	99	113	144	138
France	71	91	58	102	104	97	101	113	109
Germany*	100	125	74	149	157	152	159	185	180
Greece	27	38	28	45	46	—	45	52	—
Ireland	48	60	46	79	83	—	75	80	80
Italy	73	83	59	119	121	95	95	96	102
Luxembourg	100	121	59	110	—	—	119	134	—
Netherlands	103	122	67	123	127	120	124	141	132
Norway	106	117	80	144	142	120	124	142	141
Portugal	25	21	12	25	32	27	27	31	—
Spain	40	60	36	76	83	69	68	74	75
Sweden	113	127	74	140	152	107	112	126	138
Switzerland	96	112	74	140	144	135	148	170	160
United Kingdom	53	77	48	85	89	76	76	80	80

Notes: *Former West Germany; dash indicates data are not available.
Source: U.S. Department of Labor, Bureau of Labor Statistics, June 1997.

the United States, for a ratio of 33 percent.[14] The difference between the two estimates stems largely from supplemental pay required by either Mexican law or custom. Hewitt reports that it is standard practice in Mexico to pay one month's pay as a Christmas bonus plus 80 percent of base for vacation bonuses plus punctuality bonuses. In addition, Mexican law dictates workers be paid 365 days per year.[15] Arthur Andersen, another consulting firm, reports that due to shortages of trained Mexican managers, they often earn 20 to 30

[14] "Mexican Labor's Hidden Costs," *Fortune,* October 17, 1994, p. 32.
[15] *International Benefit Guidelines* (New York: William M. Mercer, 1994).

percent more than their U.S. counterparts. The point of including all this information is to show that some data are useful only for gross comparisons and understanding trends over time. But anyone designing a pay system in one of these countries must obtain current local data and understand local culture and customs.

Standard of Living: Basket of Goods versus Big Mac

If comparing labor costs is difficult, comparing living costs and standards is even more complex. The Bank of Switzerland uses a uniform basket of goods based on European consumer habits, which includes the prices for 137 items from clothing to transportation to personal care.[16] A woman shopping for a summer dress, jacket, skirt, shoes, and stockings will find Tokyo the most expensive place to shop ($2,300), whereas Nairobi ($50) and Bombay ($120) are best buys. Tokyo is equally expensive for a man. If he wants a blazer, shirt, jeans, socks, and shoes, he will need to come up with $1,800 to pay for a medium-priced outfit.

If your tastes don't run to blazers and jackets, the *Economist* takes a Big Mac approach. Rather than pricing a complex basket of goods and services, the magazine uses the price of a Big Mac in different locations.[17] According to Exhibit 16.7, the average price of a Big Mac in the United States is $2.36 (average of 4 cities), in China 9.60 yuan ($1.15 U.S.), in Canada $2.86 ($2.10 U.S.), and in Russia 9,500 rubles, which is only about $1.93 in U.S. dollars, but up from only 2,900 rubles 3 years earlier.

Why is this standard of living data important for managing compensation? These comparisons permit adjustments for international employees who transfer among countries to maintain *purchasing power parity.*[18] Purchasing power parity comes up again in this chapter when we discuss expatriate pay.

Purchasing Power

There are several ways to calculate purchasing power. A common approach is to divide hourly wages by the cost of a standard basket of goods and services. Another approach is to calculate the working time required to buy an item such as a one-kilogram loaf of bread: 7 minutes in London, 15 minutes in Tokyo, 27 minutes in Montreal, and 12 minutes in Chicago. Or to buy a Big Mac: 14 minutes in Chicago, 36 minutes in London, and 90 minutes in Mexico City. The Big Mac (plus fries) attains luxury status in Nairobi, Caracas, and Lagos; an employed person must toil three hours (Nairobi), four hours (Caracas) or almost two days (Lagos) to afford it. (Hold the fries.)

---

[16] Daniel Kalt and Manfred Gutmann, eds., *Prices and Earnings Around the Globe* (Zurich: Union Bank of Switzerland, 1998).

[17] "Big Mac Currencies," *Economist*, April 9, 1997, p. 82.

[18] J. Abowd and M. Bognanno, "International Differences in Executive & Managerial Compensation," (Working Paper, Cornell Univeristy, 1997).

EXHIBIT 16.7 The Hamburger Standard

	Big Mac Prices	
	In local currency	*In dollars*
United States*	**$2.36**	**2.36**
Argentina	Peso3.00	3.00
Australia	A$2.50	1.97
Austria	Sch36.00	3.40
Belgium	BFr109	3.50
Brazil	Real2.95	2.98
Britain	£1.79	2.70
Canada	C$2.86	2.10
Chile	Peso950	2.33
China	Yuan9.60	1.15
Czech Republic	CKr51.0	1.85
Denmark	DKr25.75	4.40
France	FFr17.5	3.41
Germany	DM4.90	3.22
Hong Kong	HK$9.90	1.28
Hungary	Forint214	1.43
Israel	Shekel9.50	3.00
Italy	Lire4,500	2.90
Japan	¥288	2.70
Malaysia	M$3.76	1.51
Mexico	Peso14.9	2.02
Netherlands	Fl5.45	3.21
New Zealand	NZ$2.95	2.01
Poland	Zloty3.80	1.44
Russia	Ruble9,500	1.93
Singapore	S$3.05	2.16
South Africa	Rand7.00	1.64
South Korea	Won2,300	2.95
Spain	Pta365	2.89
Sweden	SKr26.0	3.87
Switzerland	SFr5.90	4.80
Taiwan	NT$65.0	2.39
Thailand	Baht48.0	1.90

*Average of New York, Chicago, San Francisco and Atlanta
Source: McDonald's

COMPARING SYSTEMS

We have made the point that pay systems differ around the globe, and those differences relate to the nature of the social contracts in various cultures. In this section we compare several compensation systems. Examples from Japanese and European companies are contrasted with the U.S. examples that have been discussed throughout the book. The caution about stereotyping raised earlier applies here as well. Even in nations described by some as homogeneous, pay systems differ from business to business. For example, two well-known Japanese companies, Toyota and Toshiba, have designed different pay systems. Toyota places greater emphasis on external market rates, uses far fewer levels in its structure, and places greater emphasis on individual-based merit and performance pay than does Toshiba. So as we discuss "typical" systems, remember that differences and experimentation exist everywhere.

The Pay Model: Strategic Choices

The pay model used throughout the book guides our discussion of pay systems in different countries. Our experience suggests that all organizations face similar strategic issues, but that the relative importance among them differs greatly. You will recognize the basic choices, which seem universal:

- Objectives of pay systems
- External competitiveness
- Internal consistency
- Employee contributions
- Administration

But if the choices are universal, the decisions are not.

Comparing Apples and Oranges: Strategic Relevance Differs

We have noted that each nation has its own laws regulating pay determination. Some of these support national-level pay setting, others industrywide decision making, and still others operate at the organization level. In Sweden, national wage bargaining results from centralized negotiation involving national union leaders, government officials, and representatives from leading Swedish employers. The nationwide compensation agreement guarantees equal pay for equal work across all employers, regardless of differences in each company's productivity.[19]

In the Slovak Republic, vestiges of the recent communist past remain. We interviewed government officials in the Slovak Labor Ministry who were responsible for ensuring that a nationwide salary structure was adhered to across all industries and companies. By comparison, in Germany, industrywide wage agreements result from negotiation between industry employers' associations and national trade unions. These apply to all firms within an industry. Each industry negotiates separate agreements.[20]

---

[19] R. Locke and K. Thelen, "Apples and Oranges Revisited: Contextualized Comparisons and Comparative Labor Policies," *Politics and Society* 23, no. 2 (1996), pp. 337–67.

[20] M. Wallerstein, M. Golden, P. Lange, "Unions, Employers' Associations, and Wage Setting Institutions in Northern and Central Europe, 1950–1992," *Industrial and Labor Relations Review* 50, no. 3 (1997), pp. 379–400.

In the central European country of Slovenia, where nationwide agreements also exist, the building fabrication company Trimo adds three steps to each base rate set by the agreements. Trimo hopes to establish a lead position in its market and attract and hold on to more highly educated and skilled workers. However, Trimo's structure is the exception. More often, when national-level negotiations establish the "going rate," pay is no longer used to help achieve competitive advantage. In contrast to U.S.-based companies, organizations in the E.U. place relatively less importance on market surveys and competitive positions.

In addition to national and industrywide negotiated agreements, regulation in some countries is so strict that it is difficult to manage any part of employee compensation to help achieve competitive advantage. In effect, decisions about pay are taken out of the hands of the organization and placed in the hands of regulators and nationwide associations. For example, Sweden is so constrained by laws and national agreements that all Swedish organizations have very similar pay systems. However, global competitive forces are pressuring organizations in all countries to seek to control labor costs and attempt to use performance-based pay plans. This in turn is putting pressure on regulators and negotiators to modify their social contracts.

So while the choices in the pay model are universal, their strategic importance differs around the globe. We need to be cautious about comparing apples and oranges, since laws, history, culture, and ideologies differ.

JAPANESE PAY SYSTEMS

Traditional Japanese pay systems tend to emphasize the person rather than the job; seniority and skills possessed rather than job or work performed; promotions based upon supervisory evaluation of trainability, skill/ability levels, and performance rather than on performance alone; internal consistency and equity over competitors' market rates; and lifetime job security rather than security based on the performance of the organization and the individual.

Components of Pay in Japan

It is convenient to describe Japanese pay systems in terms of three basic components: base pay, bonuses, and allowances/benefits.[21]

Base Pay. Base pay accounts for 60 to 80 percent of an employees' monthly pay, depending on the rank in the organization. Base pay is not based on job evaluation or market pricing (as predominates in North America), nor is it attached to specific job titles. Rather, it is based on a combination of employee characteristics: career category, years of service, and skill/performance level.

---

[21] C. Hitoshi, S. Osamu, and I. Ryuko, "Salaryman Today and into Tomorrow," *Compensation and Benefits Review*, September–October 1997, pp. 67–75; M. Yashiro, *Human Resource Management in Japanese Companies in the Future* (New York: Organization Resource Counselors, 1996).

EXHIBIT 16.8 Salary and Age Chart for General Administration Work in a Japanese Company

*Age	†Salary	Age	Salary	Age	Salary	Age	Salary
		31	$1,900	41	$2,900	51	$3,800
22	$1,000	32	2,000	42	3,000	52	3,700
23	1,100	33	2,100	43	3,100	53	3,600
24	1,200	34	2,200	44	3,200	54	3,500
25	1,300	35	2,300	45	3,300	55	3,400
26	1,400	36	2,400	46	3,400	56	3,300
27	1,500	37	2,500	47	3,500	57	3,200
28	1,600	38	2,600	48	3,600	58	3,100
29	1,700	39	2,700	49	3,700	59	3,000
30	1,800	40	2,800	50	3,800	60	2,900

Notes: *Age 22 is typical entry age with college degree. † Monthly salary.

Career. Five career categories prevail in Japan: (1) general administration, (2) engineer/scientific, (3) secretary/office, (4) technician/blue collar job, and (5) contingent. Workers in the first two categories are called white-collar workers.

Years of Service. Seniority is a major factor in determining base pay. Management creates a matrix of pay and years of service for each career category. Exhibit 16.8 shows a matrix for general administration work. Age is often used rather than years of service because they are equivalent in the Japanese system of lifetime employment. Companies meet periodically to compare their matrices, which accounts for the similarity among companies. In general, salary increases with age until 50 years old and then is reduced. Employees can expect annual increases no matter what their performance level until age 50, though the amount of increase varies according to individual skills and performance.

Skills and Performance. Each skill is defined by its class (usually 7–13) and rank (1–9) within the class. Exhibit 16.9 illustrates a skill salary chart for the General Administration career category. Classes 1 and 2 typically include associate (entry) and senior associate work; 2, 3, and 4 supervisor and managerial; 5, 6, and 7 managerial, general director, and so on. Employees advance in rank as a result of their supervisor's evaluation of their

- Effort (e.g., enthusiasm, participation, responsiveness)
- Skills required for the work (e.g., analytical, decision making, leadership, planning, process improvement, teamwork)
- Performance (increasingly, MBO-style ratings)

Mitsui's appraisal form in Exhibit 16.10 is typical of most appraisals.

To illustrate how the system works, let us consider a graduate fresh from college who enters at class 1, rank 1. After one year, this new *salaryman* and all those hired at

EXHIBIT 16.9 Skill Chart for General Administration Work

	Associate	Senior Associate	Supervisor		Manager	General Director	
	Class 1	*Class 2*	*Class 3*	*Class 4*	*Class 5*	*Class 6*	*Class 7*
Rank 1	$ 600	$1,600	$2,600	$3,100	$3,600	$4,500	$5,500
Rank 2	700	1,700	2,650	3,150	3,750	4,700	6,000
Rank 3	800	1,800	2,700	3,200	3,800	4,900	
Rank 4	900	1,900	2,750	3,250	3,900	5,100	
Rank 5	1,000	2,000	2,800	3,300	4,000		
Rank 6	1,100	2,100	2,850	3,350	4,100		
Rank 7	1,200	2,200	2,900	3,400			
Rank 8	1,300	2,300	2,950	3,450			
Rank 9	1,400	2,400	3,000	3,500			

the same time are evaluated by their supervisors on their effort, abilities, and performance. Early in the career (the first three years), effort is more important; in later years abilities and performance receive more emphasis. The number of ranks an employee moves each year (and therefore the increase in base pay) depends on this supervisory rating (e.g., A = 3 ranks; B = 2 ranks; C = 1 rank; D = 0 ranks).

Theoretically, a person with an A rating could move up three ranks in class each year and shift to the next class in three years. However, most companies require both minimum and maximum years of service within each class. So even if you receive four straight A ratings, you would still remain in class 1 for the minimum of six years. Class 2 may also have a six year minimum time, and so on. Conversely, if you received four straight D grades, you would still get promoted to the next skill class after spending the maximum of 10 years in class 1. These minimum and maximum times in class effectively change this skill system into one based on both seniority and skill.

The logic underlying this approach is revealing. On the one hand, setting a minimum time in each class helps ensure that the employee knows the work and returns value to the company. On the other hand, the system also slows the progress of high-potential performers. And even the weakest performers eventually advance. Indeed, some report that weak performers eventually can get to the top of the pay structure though they do not get the accompanying job titles or responsibility.

The system reflects the traditional Japanese saying, "A nail that is standing too high will be pounded down." An individual employee will not want to stand out. Employees work to advance the performance of the group or team rather than themselves.

We can use Exhibits 16.8 and 16.9 to calculate base salary using a Japanese system. Sato-san joined a Japanese company after his graduation from Keio University. After 11 years in general administration work, he is at skill class 2, rank 7. His recent A appraisal means he could move three ranks, which would promote him to class 3, rank 1. However, classes 1 and 2 require six years minimum in each, so he must wait another year

Exhibit 16.10 Mitsui Annual Appraisal of Performance (Summary)

Name: Job grade:

Age: Years in the grade:

School:

Appraisal	Rating				
	A	B	C	D	E
Last year's appraisal:					
First-half appraisal	___	___	___	___	___
Second-half appraisal	___	___	___	___	___
Attendance					
Performance:					
Quantity	___	___	___	___	___
Quality	___	___	___	___	___
Ability:					
Planning/judgment	___	___	___	___	___
Improvement	___	___	___	___	___
Negotiation	___	___	___	___	___
Leadership	___	___	___	___	___
Work attitude:					
Positiveness	___	___	___	___	___
Cooperation	___	___	___	___	___
Responsibility	___	___	___	___	___
General Appraisal					
First appraisal	___	___	___	___	___
Second appraisal	___	___	___	___	___
Adjustment	___	___	___	___	___
General appraisal	___	___	___	___	___
All-company adjustment	___	___	___	___	___
Final decision	___	___	___	___	___

Key: Outstanding (A); Superior (B); Standard (C); Inferior (D); Very inferior (E).

before receiving the promotion to skill class 3 (six years in class one and six years in class 2). So his base pay is calculated as

Salary for years of seniority (10) or age 33 (Exhibit 16.8, $2,100) +
Salary for class 2 and skill rank 9 (Exhibit 16.9, $2,400)
= $2,100 + $2,400
= $4,500 per month or $54,000/year

The increase this year was $100 per month for the additional age (or year of service) plus $200 per month for the increase from rank 7 to rank 9 in class 2. The $300 per month total increase equals 7 percent.

Under the traditional Japanese system, increases in annual base pay are relatively small (7 percent for Sato-san's superior performance, compared to 10 to 12 percent for star performers in many U.S. merit systems), though they compound over time just as conventional merit and across-the-board increases in the United States. However, since the Japanese system is so seniority based, labor costs increase as the average age of the work force increases. In fact, one of the major problems facing Japanese employers is the increasing labor costs caused by the cumulative effects of annual increases combined with lifetime employment security.[22]

Bonus. Bonuses account for between 20 and 40 percent of annual salary, depending on the level in the organization. Generally, the higher up you are, the larger the percent of annual salary received as bonus. Many writers assume that the Japanese bonus is similar to the U.S. profit-sharing bonus in that it is based on some measure of performance.[23] But some caution in interpretation is required. For blue-collar and unionized employees, management calls the bonus a *gratuity.*[24] Unions avoid this term, however; they describe bonuses as an *expectable* additional payment to be made regularly, twice a year (July and December), even in bad financial times. Each bonus for workers is the equivalent of about two months' salary. While there is some fluctuation based on the firm's performance, the differences over time are small. According to the Japan Institute of Labour, for most employees (managers excepted), bonuses are in reality variable pay that helps control the employers' cash flow and labor costs, but are not intended to act as a motivator or to support improved corporate performance.

Japanese labor laws encourage the use of bonuses to achieve cost savings by omitting bonuses from calculations of many other benefits costs. For example:

- Calculations for pension plan contributions (2.25 percent of each employees' salary) exclude bonuses.
- Health insurance premiums are 4.1 percent of salary, but only .5 percent of bonus.
- Overtime pay calculations (at least 25 percent of base pay) exclude bonuses.
- Calculations for severance pay and earlier retirement allowances exclude bonuses.

So the cost savings offered by emphasizing bonuses rather than base pay can add up. Sano has observed, "In the rest of the world a bonus is defined as a reward or dividend of profits to employees. In Japan, however, the bonus is assumed to be a part of regular

---

[22] Brenton R. Schlender, "Japan's White Collar Blues," *Fortune*, March 21, 1994, pp. 67–69; Yoko Sano, "Changes and Continued Stability in Japanese HRM Systems: Choice in the Share Economy"; Morishima, "The Japanese Human Resource Management System: A Learning Bureaucracy."

[23] Martin Weitzman, *The Share Economy* (Cambridge, MA: Harvard University Press, 1984).

[24] Ryohei Magota, "The Bonus System in Japan," *Labor Issues Quarterly*, Summer 1994, pp. 6–8; Sano, "Changes and Continued Stability in Japanese HRM Systems: Choice in the Share Economy."

earnings, except for top management. In the recent past, the actual amount of bonus never decreases, even in hard times."[25]

She further emphasizes the traditional importance of the timing of the bonuses. In Japan both the summer festival and new year are traditional gift-giving times; in addition, consumers tend to make major purchases during these periods. Employees use their bonuses to cover these expenses. Thus, the bonus system is deeply rooted in Japanese life and is considered an indispensable source of income.

Even though bonuses for blue-collar employees are not strongly linked to performance, bonuses for white-collar employees are increasingly performance based. While they continue to retain elements of the traditional guaranteed payment, Japanese banks, automobile companies, and other large companies are beginning to base bonuses on corporate, unit, and individual performance, much like many U.S. companies. At the highest executive level, it is even becoming common for bonuses to be cut if the firm's performance slips. Indeed, poor corporate earnings is such a loss of face that some executives resign.

Allowances. The third characteristic of Japanese pay systems, the allowance, comes in a variety of forms: family allowances, commuting allowances, housing and geographic differential allowances, and so on. Company housing, which often includes rent or mortgage subsidies as well as dormitories for single employees, is a substantial cost. Life-passage payments are made when an employee marries or experiences a death in the immediate family. Commuting allowance is also important. A recent survey reported that employees who took public transportation received about 9,000 yen (approximately $90 per month) for commuting. Family allowances include extra pay that varies with number of dependents. Toyota provides about 17,500 to 18,000 yen ($175 to $180) a month for the first dependent and about 4,500 to 5,500 yen ($45 to $55) for additional dependents.[26] Some employers even provide matchmaking allowances for interested employees.

Experience suggests that many of these allowances would be considered discriminatory in the United States. For example, housing allowances for unmarried women have traditionally been lower than men's because the women were expected to live with their parents. Many Japanese employers still expect women to retire upon marriage or motherhood. These practices and expectations appear to be changing, albeit slowly.

The history of some of these allowances reveals very pragmatic roots. But like many practices in the United States, the allowances remain long after the need. An example is the contemporary family allowance that originated as a "rice allowance" during the late 1940s and early 1950s. At that time, Japanese workers needed extra money to feed their families because of the country's hyperinflation.

---

[25] Sano, "Changes and Continued Stability in Japanese HRM Systems: Choice in the Share Economy."

[26] Sangyo Rodo Chosasho, "Prevalence of Preferences," *Industry and Labor Research Center*, Chingin-Jijo, March 5, 1993.

Legally Mandated Benefits. Legally mandated benefits in Japan include Social Security, unemployment, and workers' compensation. Although these three are similar to the United States, Japanese employers also pay premiums for mandated health insurance, preschool child support, and employment of the handicapped. The references include more detail on Japanese benefits.[27]

Changing and Building on Traditional Approaches

Japan's traditional seniority-based approach, based not on specific jobs or performance but rather on the length of service with a company, is changing. The traditional approach resulted in very similar treatment of all employees of the same age with similar education. However, contemporary pay systems are more complex. Aging workforces mean increased labor costs. Controlling labor costs under a seniority-based system requires rapid expansion so that younger, lower-wage employees can also be hired in order to keep average labor costs down. The slowed expansion that Japan has been experiencing in the last few years, coupled with seniority-based pay, means that Japanese labor costs have climbed faster than their international competitors'. Faced with these pressures, many Japanese companies are trying to maintain *long-time* (rather than lifetime) employment while they also look for other ways to reward younger and more flexible employees. As a result, considerable variation in pay systems is beginning to emerge among Japanese companies.[28]

Strategic Comparisons

Japanese and U.S. organizations appear to have different strategic approaches to pay. Exhibit 16.11 uses the basic strategic choices outlined in the pay model—objectives, internal consistency, competitiveness, contribution, and administration—as a basis for comparisons. Japanese organizations set pay objectives that focus on the long term (age and security), support high commitment (seniority-ability-based), are more egalitarian (smaller pay differences), signal the importance of company and individual performance (company bonuses, individual promotions), and encourage flexible workers (person-based pay). U.S. companies, in contrast, focus on the short term (less job security); emphasize cost control (variable pay based on performance); reward performance improvement (individual, unit, and corporate), meritocracy, and innovation (individual rewards); and encourage flexibility (broadbanding and skill-based).

These objectives are achieved by emphasizing different policies. U.S. firms generally set base pay according to market pricing (competitive position), the work (job and person), and employee contributions (performance-based pay). In Japan, person-based factors (seniority–ability and performance) are generally used to set base pay. Market comparisons are monitored in Japan, but internal consistency remains far more important.

---

[27] William M. Mercer, *International Benefit Guidelines*.

[28] Sano, "Changes and Continued Stability in Japanese HRM Systems: Choice in the Share Economy"; Morishima, "The Evolution of HRM Policies and Practices in Japan."

Exhibit 16.11 Strategic Similarities and Differences: An Illustrated Comparison

	Japan	*U.S.*
Objectives	Long-term focus High commitment Egalitarian—internal fairness Flexible work force Control cash flow with bonuses	Short/intermediate focus High commitment Performance—market—meritocratic Flexible work force Cost control; varies with performance
Internal consistency	Person based: age, ability, performance determines base pay Many levels Small pay differences	Work based; jobs, skills, accountabilities Fewer levels Larger pay differences
External competitiveness	Monitor age-pay charts Consistent with competitors	Market determines base pay Compete on variable and performance-based pay
Employee contribution	Bonuses vary with performance only at higher levels in organization Performance appraisal influences promotions and small portion of pay increases	Increases based on individual, unit, and corporate performance Increased percentage of total pay
Advantages	Supports low to normal/high commitment Greater predictability Flexibility—person based Performance over long term	Supports performance–competitor focus Costs vary with performance Encourages "wild ducks" (innovators) Focus on short-term payoffs (speed to market)
Disadvantages	High cost of aging work force Discourages unique contributors Discourages women and younger employees	Skeptical workers, less security Fosters "What's in it for me?" No reward for investing in long-term projects

Each approach has advantages and disadvantages. Clearly, the Japanese approach is consistent with low turnover/high commitment, greater acceptance of change, and the need to be flexible. U.S. firms face higher turnover (which is not always a disadvantage) and greater skepticism about change (i.e., what's in it for me?). U.S. firms clearly encourage innovation and wild ducks; they also recognize the enormous talent and contributions to be tapped from work force diversity. Japanese pay systems face challenges from the high costs associated with an aging white-collar workforce, its limited use of women's capabilities, and emerging efforts to reward innovative individuals. The U.S. challenges include the impact of increased uncertainty and risk among employees, its short-term focus, and employees' skepticism about change.

GLOBAL SNAPSHOTS

Discussing how companies approach pay plans in other countries in the same detail as we did the Japanese system requires another textbook. (Groan!) So an appendix to this chapter offers some highlighted comparisons (sigh of relief . . .) based on the major strategic decisions in the pay model.

Internal Consistency. Person-based systems are used to determine base pay in Japan and Korea and in high-technology firms in Egypt and Mexico.[29] Most companies in the E.U. and the United States use some form of job basis for setting base pay, though some careers (engineering and computer related) are based on person factors (type of degree, years since degree, maturity-curve performance). And knowledge and competency approaches are receiving increased attention.

External Competitiveness. North America and the United Kingdom still remain relatively unique in the autonomy and discretion employers have to adapt to labor and product market competitors.[30] Japanese and Korean companies emphasize internal more than external factors. However, global competition is forcing strategic changes in both cultures.

As already noted, employers and union associations negotiate national rates of pay in many countries in Europe and Asia. These rates act as the going rates for entire industries. By establishing national rates for different types of work, pay is no longer a variable to be managed.

Employee Contributions. An increased interest in performance-based pay seems to be a global trend. The United Kingdom and United States seem to place greatest emphasis on performance-based approaches. The percentage of total pay that is based on performance varies greatly due to tax rates, culture, and ideology. For example, the communist party objected to wage differences by saying they do no good and lead to social inequality. In the past, China rationalized communism with a Confucian quote: "Do not worry about scarcity, only about unevenness." Now they have a new rationalization that condemns "averagism."

---

[29] Gordon Betcherman, Kathryn McMullen, Norm Leckie, and Christina Caron, eds., *The Canadian Workplace in Transition* (Kingston, Ontario: IRC Press, 1994); "Focus on International Benefits," *Employee Benefit Plan Review*, November 1994, pp. 32–37; Gilian Flynn, "HR in Mexico: What You Should Know," *Personnel Journal*, August 1994, pp. 34–44; Richard D. Kantor and Michael Richerson, "The Egyptian Compensation Environment: Where Change is the Only Constant," *Benefits and Compensation International*, March 1993, pp. 188–22; Bronstein, "Labour Law Reform in Latin America: Between State Protection and Flexibility," *International Labour Law Review*, Spring 1997; Gustavo Amparan, "Comparative Compensation Systems Between Two Mexican Companies," (Working Paper, 1996).

[30] W. Vanhonacker "Entering China: An Unconventional Approach," *Harvard Business Review*, March–April 1997, pp. 130–140; Korea Labor Institute, *Korea's Labor Unions* (Seoul, Korea: Korea Labor Institute, 1997), Korea Labor Institute, *Quarterly Labor Review* (Seoul, Korea: Korea Labor Institute, 1991); Michael Byungnam Lee, "Bonuses, Unions, and Labor Productivity in South Korea," *Journal of Labor Research, 1997*; *Benefit Policies for Third Country Nationals, U.S. Expatriates, and Key Local Nationals* (New York: Kwasha Lipton, 1997); Tony Buxton, Paul Chapman, and Paul Temple, *Britain's Economic Performance* (London: Routledge, 1994), G. R. Ungson, R. M. Steers, and S. H. Park, *Korean Enterprises: The Quest for Globalization* (Boston: Harvard Business School Press, 1997).

Benefits. Taxes and government regulation are major influences on the management of pay around the globe. In Mexico, an *acquired rights* law requires that if a benefit, service, or bonus is paid two years in a row, it becomes an employee's right. So consultants caution employers new to Mexico to go slow with benefits and other services. Both India and Mexico mandate profit sharing; 10 percent of pretax profits must be distributed to employees. In addition, most developed and emerging economies have some form of national health care supplied by employer- and employee-paid premiums.

In centralized command-control economies that are experimenting with market-based approaches such as China, managing employee compensation presents unique challenges.[31] Government agencies still control base-pay determination, but noncash payments are highly valued by employees. A survey reported that after higher pay, Chinese employees say they want scarce goods and services such as housing; medical care; access to hard-currency goods like fresh fruit, meat, and fish; transportation; and allowances for meals, clothing, and laundry. Similar conditions existed in the United States in earlier periods. Ford Motor Company provided cafeterias, dentists, social workers, home economists, and English tutors to its work force in the 1920s and 1930s, since so many of the workers were immigrants who were unfamiliar with American customs.

This brief review of the national differences in pay determination should convince you that ***international compensation involves more than exporting U.S.-style systems.***

EXPATRIATE PAY

When multinational organizations decide to open facilities in an international location, one of the many decisions they face is the type of personnel to hire. International subsidiaries choose among a mix of expatriates (expats, someone whose citizenship is that of the employer's base country; for example, a Japanese citizen working for Sony in Toronto), third country nationals (TCNs, someone whose citizenship is neither the employer's base country nor the location of the subsidiary; for example, a German citizen working for Sony in Toronto), and local country nationals (LCNs, citizens of the country in which the subsidiary is located; for example, Canadian citizens working for Sony in Toronto). One obvious choice is to staff the subsidary with individuals whose citizenship corresponds to the country of origin for the subsidiary: LCNs. Hiring LCNs has advantages. The company saves relocation expenses and avoids concerns about employees adapting to the local culture. Employment of LCNs satisfies nationalistic demands for hiring locals. Only rarely do organizations decide that hiring LCNs is inappropriate.

---

[31] Li Hua Wang, "Research in Pay Policies and Determination in China. What We Know and What We Don't Know" (Working Paper, Cornell University, 1998); L. Farh, C. Early, Lin, "Impetus for Action: Cultural Analysis or Justice and Organization Citizenship in Chinese Society," *Administrative Science Quarterly* 42 (1997), pp. 421–444; Meng, "An Examination of Wage Determination in China's Rural Sector," *Applied Economics* 28 (1996), pp. 715–724; Chen, "New Trends in Reward Allocation Preferences, A Sino–U.S. Comparison," *Academy of Management Journal* 38, no. 2 (1995), pp. 418–428; A. Verma & Zhiming, "The Changing Face of HRM in China," Chapter 9 in *Employment Relations in the Growing Asian Economies*, ed. Verma (London: Routledge, 1996); Boisot and Child, "From Fiefs to Clans to Network Capitalism: Explaining China's Emerging Economic Order," *Administrative Science Quarterly* 41 (1996), pp. 600–628.

Expats or TCNs may be brought in for a number of reasons.[32] The foreign assignment may represent an opportunity for selected employees to develop an international perspective; the position may be sufficiently confidential that information is entrusted only to a proven domestic veteran; the particular talent demanded for a position may not be readily available in the local labor pool. Exhibit 16.12 catalogues a number of reasons for asking employees to take work assignments in another country. Designing expatriate pay systems that help achieve such varied objectives is a challenge.

Only about 1 percent of the international workforce composed of U.S. and European multinational companies is expatriates. About 4.2 percent of the international workforce for Japanese manufacturing companies are expatriates (i.e., Japanese nationals working in other countries). Sony manufacturing facilities in Italy employ mostly Italians, although a regional operations manager is a Japanese expatriate; Sony manufacturing facilities in Mexico employ mostly Mexicans. However, the plant manager and controller are Japanese expatriates. The greater use of expatriates by Japanese companies maintains greater control of the subsidiaries. However, there is some evidence that managerial job satisfaction and even profitability of the subsidiaries suffer as a result.[33]

Varying Objectives

Expatriates are a relatively small, yet critical and costly group of international employees; and the number of expatriates per large U.S. multinational company has declined over the past decade. There are two explanations for this decline. One is that the objectives for overseas assignments are shifting. Earlier, transferring technologies and the need for specific skills in scarce supply in local economies were the primary reasons for hiring expatriates. More recently, developing a global perspective among key employees has become more important. This shift is consistent with the increasing educational levels globally and the growing importance of international sales for U.S. firms. Indeed, our experience is that two very different groups of employees are receiving global assignments. One group is higher-level managers and executives who must make strategic decisions about global opportunities and competition. The other group is recent college graduates who receive relatively short overseas assignments as part of their career development.

Costs. It is a challenge to design a pay system for employees who are being assigned overseas to meet a variety of corporate objectives. In addition, expatriate assignments are expensive. For example, a company that sends a U.S. employee (base salary of $80,000) with a spouse and two children to London for three years can expect to spend

---

[32] Frank McGoldrick, "Expatriate Compensation and Benefit Practice of U.S. and Canadian Firms: Survey Results," *International Human Resource Journal*, Summer 1997, pp. 13–17; C. Reynolds, *Compensating Globally Mobile Employees* (Scottsdale, AZ: American Compensation Association, 1995); C. Reynolds, "Expatriate Compensation in Historical Perspective," *International Human Resource Journal*, Summer 1997, pp. 118–131; G. Wederspahn and L. Solow, "Multicultural Teams: From Chaos to Synergy," *International Human Resource Journal*, Winter 1998, pp. 20–24.

[33] Vlado Pucik, "The Challenges of Globalization: The Strategic Role of Local Managers in Japanese-Owned U.S. Subsidiaries," (Paper presented at Cornell Conference on Strategic HRM, Ithaca, NY, October 1997).

EXHIBIT 16.12 Why Expatriates Are Selected

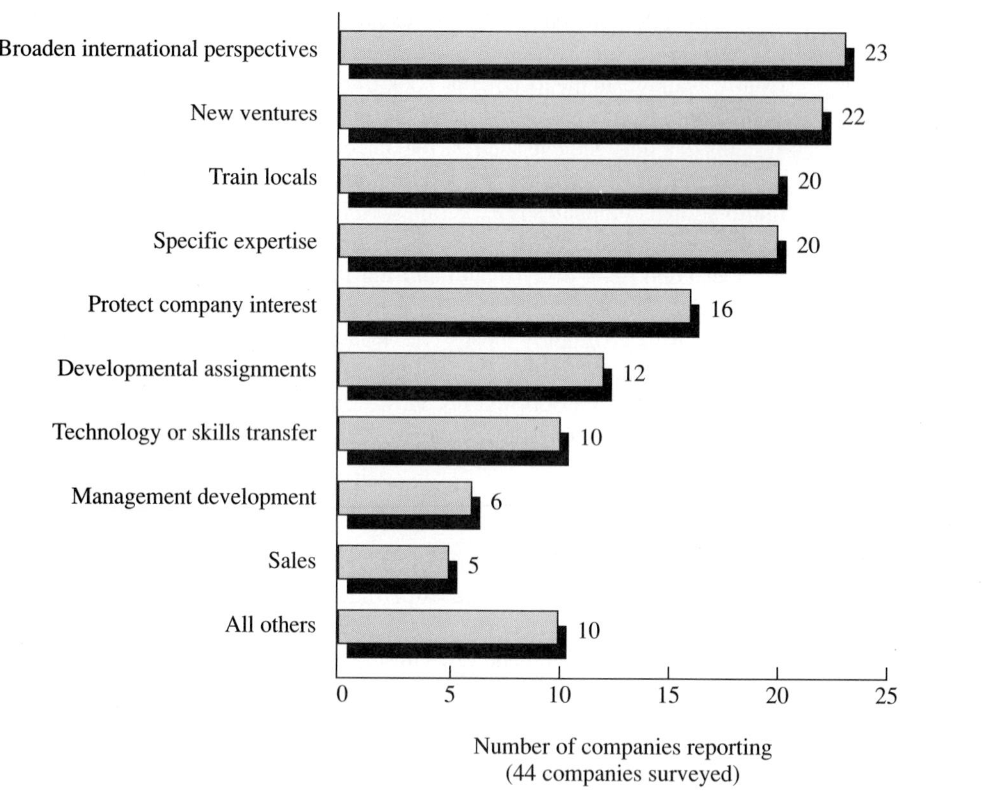

Source: Organization Resources Counselors Inc.

$800,000 to $1,000,000. Obviously, the high cost of expatriate assignments needs to be offset by the value of the contributions the employee makes.[34]

Fairness. Fairness is in the eye of the beholder. In expatriate compensation, fairness is measured against the compensation expatriates would have received had they stayed in their home country and by comparisons to the pay received by local nationals. The expatriate pay must be sufficient to encourage the employee to take the assignment yet not so attractive that local nationals will feel unfairly treated or that the expatriate will refuse any future reassignments. Expatriate compensation systems are forever trying to be like Goldilocks' porridge: not too high, not too low, but just right. However, the relevant standard for judging fairness may not be home-country treatment. It may be the pay of other

[34] "What It Costs to House Expatriates Worldwide" (New York: Runzheimer International, 1998).

expats, that is, the expat community, or it may be local nationals. And how do local nationals feel about the allowances and pay levels of their expat coworkers? Very little research tells us how expats and those around them judge the fairness of expat pay.[35]

Employee Preferences. Beyond work objectives, costs, and fairness, an additional consideration is employees' preferences for international assignments. For many European and Asian companies, their home markets are a relatively small part of the total product market. So working in another country at some point in a career is part of understanding your market. Yet for many U.S. employees, leaving the United States means leaving the action. They may worry that expatriate experience sidetracks rather than enhances a career. Employees undoubtedly differ in their preferences for overseas jobs, and preferences can vary over time. Having children in high school, elderly parents to care for, divorce, and other life factors exert a strong influence on whether an offer to work overseas is a positive or negative opportunity. Research does inform us of the following:

- 68 percent of expatriates do not know what their jobs will be when they return home.
- 54 percent return to lower-level jobs. Only 11 percent are promoted.
- Only 5 percent believe their company values overseas experience.
- 77 percent have less disposable income when they return home.
- More than half of returning expatriates leave their company within one year.

Unfortunately, while research does highlight the problem, it does not offer much guidance for designers of expat pay systems.[36] Consequently, we are at the mercy of conjecture and beliefs.

Elements of Expatriate Compensation

A shopping list of items, such as those in Exhibit 16.13, that can make up expatriate compensation includes everything from household furnishing allowances to language and culture training, spousal employment assistance, and rest and relaxation leaves for

[35] Angelo DeNisi and T. P. Sommers, "In Search of Adam's Other: Re-Examination of Referents Used in the Evaluation of Pay," *Human Relations* 43 (1990), pp. 497–511; Farh, et al, "Impetus for Action."

[36] *Expatriate Dual Career Survey Report* (New York: Windham International and National Foreign Trade Council, 1997); Garry M. Wederspahn, "Costing Failures in Expatriate Human Resources Management," *Human Resource Planning* 15, no. 3, pp. 27–35; Michael S. Schell and Ilene L. Dolins, "Dual-Career Couples and International Assignments," *International Compensation and Benefits*, November–December 1992, pp. 25–29; Carolyn Gould, "Can Companies Cut Costs by Using the Balance-Sheet Approach?" *International Compensation and Benefits*, July–August 1993, pp. 36–41; David E. Molnar, "Repatriating Executives and Keeping Their Careers on Track," *International Compensation and Benefits*, November–December 1994, pp. 31–35; Ken I. Kim, Hun-Joon Park, and Nori Suzuki, "Reward Allocations in the United States, Japan, and Korea: A Comparison of Individualistic and Collectivistic Cultures," *Academy of Management Journal* 33, no. 1 (1990), pp. 188–98; Anne S. Tsui, Jone L. Pearce, Lyman W. Porter, and Angela M. Tripoli, "Alternative Approaches to the Employee-Organization Relationship: Does Investment in Employees Pay Off?" *Academy of Management Journal* 40, no. 5 (1997), pp. 1089–1121.

Exhibit 16.13 Common Allowances in Expatriate Pay Packages

Financial Allowances
- Reimbursement for tax return preparation
- Tax equalization
- Housing differential
- Children's education allowance
- Temporary living allowance
- Goods and services differential
- Transportation differential
- Foreign service premium
- Household furnishing allowance
- Currency protection
- Mobility premium
- Home-leave allowance
- Stopover allowance
- Subsidized health and fitness facilities
- Hardship premium
- Completion bonus
- Assignment extension bonus
- Extended work week payment

Social Adjustment Assistance
- Emergency leave
- Home leave
- Language training (manager)
- Company car/driver
- Assistance with locating new home
- Access to western health care
- Club membership
- General personal services (e.g., translation)
- Personal security (manager and family)
- General culture-transition training (manager)
- Social events
- Career development and repatriation planning
- Training for local culture customs (manager)
- Orientation to community (manager and family)
- Counseling services
- Rest and relaxation leave
- Domestic staff (excluding child care)
- Use of company-owned vacation facilities

Family Support
- Language training (family)
- Assistance locating schools for children
- General culture-transition training (family)
- Training for local culture's customs (family)
- Child care providers
- Spousal employment in firm
- Assistance locating spousal employment outside firm

longer-term assignments. Usually such lists are organized into four major components: salary, taxes, housing, and general-services allowances and premiums.

Salary. The base salary plus incentives (merit, eligibility for profit sharing, bonus plans, etc.) for expatriate jobs is usually determined via job evaluation or competency-based plans. 3M, for example, applies a recently designed international job evaluation plan for its international assignments. Common factors describe different 3M jobs around the world. With this system, the work of a regional human resource manager in Brussels can be compared to the work of a human resource manager in Austin, Texas, or Singapore. Most companies attempt to apply the procedures they use to value domestic operations to expatriate jobs.

Beyond salaries and incentives, the intent of the other components is to help keep expatriate employees financially whole and minimize the disruptions of the move. This basically means maintaining a standard of living about equal to their peers in their home or base country. This is a broad standard, one that has often resulted in very costly packages from the company's perspective, but provide good deals for the expatriate.

Taxes. Income earned in foreign countries has two potential sources of income tax liability.[37] With few exceptions (Saudi Arabia is one), foreign tax liabilities are incurred on income earned in foreign countries. For example, money earned in Japan is subject to Japanese income tax, whether earned by a Japanese or a Korean citizen. The other potential liability is the tax owed in the employees' home country. The United States has the dubious distinction of being the only developed country that taxes its citizens for income earned in another country, even though that income is taxed by the country in which it was earned. So money beyond $70,000 earned in Japan by an American citizen is subject to both Japanese income tax and U.S. income tax. Employers handle this through *tax equalization.*[38] The employer takes the responsibility of paying whatever income taxes are due to either the host country and/or the home country. Taxes are deducted from employees' earnings up to the same amount of taxes they would pay had they remained in their home country.

This allowance can be a substantial amount. For example, the marginal tax rates in Belgium, the Netherlands, and Sweden can run between 70 to 90 percent. So if the expatriate is sent to a lower-tax country (lower than the United States), the company keeps the difference. If the expatriate's assignment is in a higher-tax country, the company makes up the difference. The logic here is that if the employee kept the windfall from being assigned to a low-tax country, then getting this person to accept assignments elsewhere would become difficult. Additionally, the unearned windfall has the potential to create a sense of unfairness among other employees (local nationals and other expatriates). Tax equalization takes income tax considerations out of the equation when an employee is deciding whether to accept an expatriate position.

---

[37] Monica M. Sabo, "Tax-Effective Compensation Planning for International Assignments," *International Compensation and Benefits,* January–February 1995, pp. 24–28; Charles J. Boyland, "A Short Guide to U.S. Expatriate Taxes," *Journal of International Compensation and Benefits,* July–August 1992, pp. 45–50.

[38] Reynolds, "Expatriate Compensation."

Housing. Most international companies pay allowances for housing or provide company-owned housing for expatriates. "Expatriate colonies" often grow up in sections of major cities where international companies tend to locate their expatriates. The difficulty comes in determining what is appropriate housing, and in some cases, finding affordable versions of it. Depending on the type of package used, an employee may be given some or all of the choice in the matter. Our experience is that this allowance is a very important part of the expatriate's compensation package, especially for American employees. Americans often face challenges adapting to relatively less spacious conditions compared to expatriates from other countries. Japanese citizens working for Toshiba in the U.S. are often delighted with the available housing when coming to the United States, since it tends to be more spacious than what is available in Tokyo. Perhaps Americans take their wide open spaces for granted. Providing expatriates with appropriate housing seems to have a major impact on the success of the assignment.

Service Allowances and Premiums. A friend in Moscow cautions that when we take the famed Moscow subway, we must be sure to pay the fare at the beginning of the ride. The reason is that inflation is so high that if we wait to pay until the end of the ride, the fare will be more than we can afford! Cost of living allowances, club memberships, transportation assistance, child care and education, spousal employment, local culture training, and personal security are some of the many service allowances and premiums expatriates receive.

The logic supporting these allowances is that foreign assignments require the expatriate to (1) work with less direct supervision than a domestic counterpart, (2) often live and work in strange and sometimes uncongenial surroundings, and (3) represent the employer in the host country. The size of the premium is a function of both the expected hardship and hazards in the host country and the type of job. So an assignment in London will probably yield less service and premium allowances than one in Tehran, where Death to Americans Day is still a national holiday.[39] Balance against this the objectives for the expatriate assignment and the type of job. A more senior career expatriate assigned for three to five years to manage a joint venture in Tehran will receive very different service and premium allowances than a newly graduated software engineer on an 18-month product design and support assignment in London.

Some research tells us that the components of expatriate compensation packages do affect expenses, commitment to the employer, job satisfaction, and willingness to accept other assignments.[40] A recent study reported that expatriates' beliefs about how sufficient the allowances were plus their perceptions of the employers' support for their situation influences their commitment and intentions. Thus, managing the implicit psychological contract via good communications is an important part of expatriate compensation.

---

[39] *Guide to Major Holidays Around the Globe* (Zurich: Union Bank of Switzerland, 1998).

[40] Fred K. Piker, "Attracting, Retaining, Motivating Senior-Level Expatriates: What's Fair to Both Company and Employee," *Innovations in International HR*, Summer 1997, pp. 1–5; Hal B. Gregersen and Linda K. Stroh, "Coming Home to the Arctic Cold: Antecedents to Finnish Expatriate and Spouse Repatriation Adjustment," *Personnel Psychology* 50 (1997), pp. 635–654; Richard A. Guzzo, Katherine A. Noonan, and Efrat Elron, "Expatriate Managers and the Psychological Contract," *Journal of Applied Psychology* 7, no. 4 (1994), pp. 617–26.

The Balance Sheet Approach

Most North American, European, and Japanese global firms use the balance sheet approach to pay expatriates.[41] As you can tell from the name, this approach borrows from accounting, where credits and debits must balance. It is based on the premise that employees on overseas assignments should have the same spending power as employees in the home country. Therefore, the home country is the standard for all payments. The approach has three objectives:

1. Ensure mobility of expatriate talent to global assignments as cost effectively as feasible.
2. Ensure that expatriates neither gain nor lose financially.
3. Minimize adjustments required of expatriates and their dependents.

Of these, the last two, minimizing financial effects and adjustments, seem to receive the major emphasis. Until recently, efforts to link expatriate pay to improving performance and cost effectiveness received less attention.

Exhibit 16.14 depicts the balance sheet approach. Home country salary is the first column. The salary (based on job evaluation, market surveys, merit and incentives) is divided into the components discussed earlier (taxes, housing, service allowances and premiums) plus a "reserve" to cover savings or other financial obligations (e.g., alimony) or discretionary payments. These components are used because each varies as salary and number of dependents change. As salary increases, taxes and reserves may increase, but the percentage of salary going for housing and goods and services may decline. As number of dependents increase, percent salary going for reserve may decrease, and housing and goods and services increase.

Note that the proportion set for each of the components are *norms* (i.e., assumed to be "normal" for the typical expatriate) set to reflect consumption patterns in the home country. They are not actual expenditures. These norms are based on surveys conducted by consulting firms. Using these norms is supposed to avoid negotiating with each individual. But any experienced expatriate will tell you no one is "typical"; this approach permits a lot of flexibility.

So now two basic building blocks for expatriate salaries are in place: the home country's salary for the job the expatriate will be doing plus the norms of home-country expenditures (four categories) for someone earning that salary. If any building block is wrong, the rest of the system is also wrong.

The next building block is the equivalent costs experienced by the typical expatriate in the host country where the assignment is located. For example, if a profile for a manager earning $80,000 shows typical housing costs of $2,000 a month in the United States, the expatriate will be expected to pay $2,000 a month for housing in the host country. If similar housing costs $3,000, the company pays the difference. In the illustration, taxes, housing, and goods and services components are all greater in the host country than in the

---

[41] *International Total Remuneration*, certification course T9 (Scottsdate, AZ: American Compensation Association, 1998); Cal Reynolds, "International Compensation," in *Compensation Guide*, ed. WIlliam A. Caldwell (Boston: Warren, Gorham and Lamont, 1998).

EXHIBIT 16.14 Balance Sheet Approach

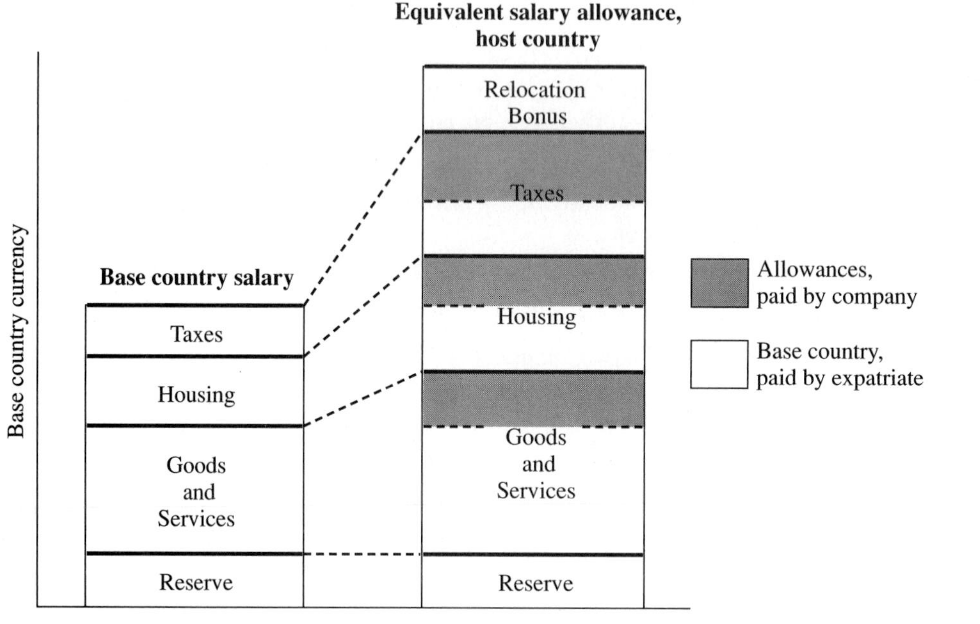

home country. The expatriate bears the same level of costs (white area of column two) as at home. The employer is responsible for the additional costs (shaded area). (Changing exchange rates among currencies are considered in these allowance calculations.)

Despite the inherent difficulties in comparing apples and oranges (and other goods and services), most major companies use some index of cost of living abroad provided by consulting firms, the State Department, or the United Nations. For example, Runzheimer International supplies comparative cost of living data for different cities around the globe.[42] A $75,000 cost for a typical family of four in Chicago translates into about $41,000 in Warsaw, $73,000 in Rome, $151,000 in Seoul, and $210,000 in Tokyo. Exhibit 16.15 shows recent Runzheimer comparisons for housing costs.

Relocation Incentive. The balance sheet approach is really designed to equalize the purchasing power of expatriates in similar jobs across the globe with what they would have in their home country. However, equalizing pay may not motivate an employee to move to another country, particularly if the new location has less personal appeal. Therefore, many employers also offer some form of financial incentive or bonus to encourage the move. Column 2 of Exhibit 16.14 shows relocation bonuses or lump sum payments that some companies use at each transfer or move. These bonuses typically

[42] Runzheimer International, "What It Costs to House Expatriates Worldwide."

EXHIBIT 16.15 What It Costs to House Expatriates Worldwide

This chart shows typical annual housing costs of relocated employee families based on a U.S. expatriate family of four, having a moderate base salary. The housing costs listed coincide with typical housing costs for both homes or apartments rented by the expatriate families. Homes that expatriates rent vary in size from three to four bedrooms, depending on location. In addition to rental costs, the annual expenses include utilities, insurance, maintenance, and taxes.

Location	*Total Annual Housing Cost*
Tokyo	$118,200
Hong Kong	84,645
Paris	71,359
London	51,634
Caracas	46,258
Frankfurt	46,083
Mexico City	44,806
Rio de Janeiro	38,195
Chicago	28,894

Source: Runzheimer International.

equal around three months of base pay. Four out of five U.S. multinational corporations pay relocation bonuses to induce people to take expatriate assignments.

If gaining international experience is really one of the future competencies required by organizations, then the need for such premiums ought to be reduced, since the overseas experience should increase the likelihood of future promotions. However, research reveals that U.S. expatriates feel their U.S. organizations still do not appreciate or value their international expertise.[43] So the rhetoric of the value of global competencies has yet to match the reality; hence the need for relocation incentives.

Alternatives to Balance Sheet Approach. The balance sheet approach was refined in the 1960s and 1970s when most expatriates were technical employees of U.S. oil companies. But the business environment and the reasons for expatriate assignments have changed since then. Consequently, many employers are exploring changes. A few of these alternatives are described below.[44]

Negotiation simply means the employer and employee find a mutually agreeable package. This approach is most common in smaller firms with very few expatriates. The arrangements tend to be relatively costly (or generous, depending on your point of

[43] Gregersen and Stroh, "Coming Home to the Arctic Cold."

[44] Milkovich and Bloom, "Rethinking International Compensation;" Mary E. Myhr, "Linking Expatriate Pay to Assignment Objectives," *International Compensation and Benefits,* March–April 1994, pp. 37–43; S. E. Wimbush, "Expatriate Compensation and the High Price of Old Assumptions," *International Compensation and Benefits,* March–April 1994, pp. 51–56.

view), create comparability problems when other people are asked to locate overseas ("but Mike and Sarah got . . ."), and need to be renegotiated with each transfer ("You are going to take away my chauffeur and three domestic servants here in the Philippines just to send me to London? Guess again!").

Another alternative, *localization,* ties salary to the host (local) country salary scales and provides some cost of living allowances for taxes, housing, and dependents. The allowances tend to be similar to those under the balance sheet, but the salary can vary. The down side is that individual salaries vary with the location (average rate for an engineer in Geneva is $55,000 compared to $41,300 in Rome and $32,000 in Bristol) rather than with the job or performance.

While the balance sheet approach ties salary to the home country, the *modified balance sheet* ties salary to a region (Asia-Pacific, Europe, North America, Central America, and South America). The logic is that if an employee of a global business who relocates from San Diego, California, to Portland, Maine, receives only a moving allowance, why should all the extras be paid for international moves of far less distance (i.e., from Germany to Spain)? In Europe, many companies no longer view those European managers who work outside their home country as expats. Instead, they are Europeans running their European businesses.

Another common modification is to decrease allowances over time. The logic is that the longer the employee is in the host country, the standard of living should become closer to that of a local employee. For example, if Americans eat a $10 pizza twice a week in the United States, should they eat a $30 pizza twice a week in Tokyo, at the employer's expense? More typically, after a couple of months, the expatriate will probably learn where the nationals find cheaper pizza or will develop a taste for the local cuisine; in any event, the yearnings for Chicago-style deep dish with pepperoni ought to diminish. So while these modified plans minimize the impact of changes in standards of living at the first stage (one to three years) of the assignment, after three to five years some of the allowance becomes equal to allowances paid to local national employees. The major exception seems to be taxes and housing. The main purpose of the modified balance sheet seems to be to reduce costs; it pays little attention to performance, ensuring fairness, or satisfying preferences of expats.

The *lump-sum/cafeteria approach* offers expats more choices. This approach sets salaries according to the home-country system and simply offers employees lumps of money to offset differences in standards of living. So, for example, a company will still calculate differences in cost of living. But instead of breaking them into housing, transportation, goods and services, and so on, the employee simply receives a total allowance. Perhaps one employee will trade less spacious housing for private schooling and tutors for the children; another employee will make different choices. The logic is to avoid paying for items the employee does not value. These approaches may offer employees flexibility to minimize their taxes. We know of one expatriate, for example, who purchased a villa and a winery in Italy with his allowance. He has been reassigned to Chicago, but still owns and operates his winery. This arrangement was probably not an objective of the expatriate pay system; however, the expatriate made tradeoffs in his living arrangements to retain most of his lump sum.

Expatriate Systems → Objectives? *Quel Dommage!*

Talk to experts in international compensation, and you soon get into complexities of taxes, exchange rates, housing differences, and the like. What you do not hear is how the pay system affects competitive advantage, customer satisfaction, quality, or other performance concerns. It does emphasize maintaining employee purchasing power and minimizing disruptions and inequities. But the lack of attention to improving performance or ensuring that the expatriate assignment is consistent with organization objectives remains.

BORDERLESS WORLD → BORDERLESS PAY?

Many multinational corporations are attempting to create a cadre of global managers, managers who operate anywhere in the world in a borderless manner.[45] According to Jack Welch, CEO of General Electric, "The aim in a global business is to get the best ideas from everyone, everywhere."[46] To support this global flow of ideas and people, some are also designing borderless or at least regionalized pay systems. One testing ground for this approach is the E.U. One of the difficulties with borderless pay is that base pay levels and the other components depend so much on national laws and customs about executive pay.

Nevertheless, perhaps the strongest pressure to harmonize managerial pay systems is that managers in global companies are no longer expatriates from their home countries but true global managers running global businesses.

Focusing on expatriate compensation may blind companies to the issue of adequate rewards for employees who are seeking global career opportunities. Ignoring such employees causes them to focus only on the local operations and pay less attention to the broader goals of the global firm. It is naive to expect commitment to a long-term global strategy in which local executives have little input and receive limited benefits. Paradoxically, attempts to localize top management in subsidiaries may reinforce the gap in focus between local and global management.

Creating Global Mindsets

Globalizing an organization goes beyond developing and paying a cadre of people who move around the world to different assignments. It involves a *mindset*—adapting alternative courses to create a common mental programming that views the company's operations on a worldwide scale. This view requires balancing priorities of corporate, business unit, and different regions. Pay systems can support such a mindset.

A successful global organization must learn from its experiences in each locality in order to become truly global rather than "multilocal." At least a partial disassociation of

---

[45] Valdo Pucik, Noel Tichy, and Carole K. Barnett, eds., *Globalizing Management* (New York: Wiley, 1992).

[46] "The Global Company: Series on Global Corporations," *Financial Times,* November 7, 1995.

pay from national customs and linking them to the organization's values and strategy may help foster behavior consistent with the notion of a borderless organization.

While human resource systems in Japanese, U.S., and European multinationals may be strikingly dissimilar, they share a challenge of rewarding potentially promising employees with adequate opportunities that lead to more responsibility and opportunities for career growth. The successful mix of talent from locals, third country nationals, and home-office employees is a goal that has so far eluded most of the multinationals. The belief is that those who do manage to mobilize global human resources will gain a substantial competitive edge. However, global utilization of intellectual capital will probably not be achieved without a restructuring of global reward systems.[47]

Summary

Studying employee compensation only in your neighborhood, city, or country is like a horse with blinders. Removing the blinders by adopting a global perspective will deepen your understanding of local or national issues. Anyone interested in compensation needs to adopt a global perspective. The internationalization of businesses, financial markets, trade agreements, and even labor markets is affecting every workplace and every employment relationship. And employee compensation, so central to the workplace, is embedded in the political–socioeconomic arrangements found in each nation—the social contract. Examining employee compensation in the framework of the implicit social contracts offers insights into various approaches to pay.

Any attempt to manage employee compensation to help achieve organization success and competitive advantage while sustaining fair treatment for employees needs to take place within the changing social contracts that are occurring globally.

The basic premise of this book has been that compensation systems have a profound impact on individual behavior, organization success, and social well-being. We believe this holds true within all national boundaries and among nations as well.

Review Questions

1. Why is the social contract so important in managing compensation? How do the expectations and beliefs about compensation differ among your peers? Between your parents and you? Between international peers? How do expectations about the government's role affect these views?
2. Distinguish between nationwide and industrywide pay determination. How do they compare to a business strategy-based approach?
3. Development arguments for and against "typical" Japanese-style and "typical" U.S.-style approaches to pay. What factors are causing each approach to change?

[47] Milkovich and Bloom, "Rethinking International Compensation."

4. Distinguish between global, expatriates, local nationals, and third-country nationals.
5. Under the balance sheet approach to paying expats, most of total compensation is linked to costs of living. Some argue that expatriate pay resembles traditional Japanese pay. Evaluate this argument.
6. Select any country included in the appendix to this chapter (or another country, if you are familiar with compensation systems there). Discuss which of the strategic policies are most important in that country (internal consistency, external competitiveness, employee contributions, administration). Explain your answer and discuss the implications for the pay objectives and a strategic perspective toward pay.

Appendix

Global Comparisons

China (PRC)	Egypt	Germany	India	Japan
Internal Consistency				
• Hierarchical levels • Small differentials • Job based and negotiated with government agencies	• Relatively hierarchical • Skill/knowledge based, especially technical • Small differentials	• Relatively hierarchical • Primarily job based • Modest differentials between levels	• Job based and *caste based;* jobs at the bottom levels determined by the caste system • Higher level jobs are job based	• Person based; seniority–ability factors • Hierarchical with small differentials • Differences compound with tenure
External Competitiveness				
• Lack of data and markets • Emphasis on preferential access to scarce goods and services • Government agencies control wages; shift to noncash and off-the-books forms	• Lack salary surveys • Government guarantees jobs with low pay to college graduates	• National rates negotiated by employer and union association • Government and Bundesbank major players in negotiations • Increasing interest in surveys and market data	• Oversupply of highly qualified labor, forcing wages down; many highly educated workers leave the country	• Comparisons within industry • Relative labor costs and work force productivity important factors • Private comparisons among Japanese firms • Consultant surveys among multinationals

Employee Contribution				
• Growing interest in incentives based on individual and facility performance	• High interest in performance based; up to 40% of pay based on company results • High inflation and high taxes decrease impact of performance increases	• Increases based on seniority, inflation, and across-the-board guarantees • Increasing interest in performance bonuses, up to 20% in some cases • Performance small percentage of total pay	• Low-caste workers have little incentive to do better; excellence by the individual threatens the caste system and is not rewarded • Payment Bonus Act of 1965 requires profit sharing with a minimum of 8.33%	• Increased interest in individual merit and group-based pay • Traditional bonuses (twice yearly) used as variable cost • Performance based pay small percentage of total pay • Emerging use of performance appraisal
Benefits				
• Major strategic tool; company provides services such as housing, showers, medical, scarce commodities, transportation, and day care	• Moderate mandatory benefits of vacation pay, medical, and retirement	• National health care and national pensions • High mandated; costly layoff severance allowance • Discretionary; cars	• Mandatory retirement and pension benefits • Typical package includes housing, traveling, and geographic allowances	• Mandated: national health care, and retirement; layoff allowances • Discretionary; commuting, housing, family, sports facilities, vacation retreats
Nature of Administration				
• Centralized • Emphasize government connections • Focus on benefits/ services	• Government taxes and regulations limit the use of pay as a strategic tool • Centralized with low participation • Search for nontaxable "payments"	• Government policies and regulations major factor • Centralized • Less use of pay as strategic source of competitive advantage	• Government laws major factor; regardless of profit level or performance level, employee's pay cannot go down • Layoffs are illegal	• Increasingly using pay as strategic device • Tax regulations major influence: retaining allowances; only base pay included in pension medical, retirement calculations

(continued)

	Korea	Mexico	Russia	Slovenia	United Kingdom
Internal Consistency	• Person based, seniority, ability, and competencies • Hierarchical with small differentials	• Relatively hierarchical levels • Primarily job based with skill based in high tech • Modest differentials	• Hierarchical • Appearance of job based • Small differentials	• Modest to low hierarchies • Small differentials • Job and skill based	• Relatively hierarchical levels • Primarily job based • Modest differences among levels
External Competitiveness	• Mobility among companies relatively common • Surveys of wages and labor costs • Competitive position important for attracting and retaining workers	• Competitive forces influencing pay of higher-skilled workers • Surveys based upon work conduct • Overall labor cost relatively low; yet, 10 to 25 % premium for scarce talent	• Lacks markets and data; setting pay is guessing game • Personal negotiations based on expertise	• National negotiated rates with unions, employers, and the government • Rates paid above negotiated rate to attract needed talent	• Reduced reliance on national rates negotiated by employers and union associations; more on industry specific data • White-collar based on "London rates" • Increasing use of surveys and competitive market data
Employee Contribution	• Increasing use of performance-based pay • Companywide bonuses at least once a year	• Increases based on seniority, inflation, and across-the-board guarantees • Growing interest in performance based • Performance about 5% of total pay	• Transition from old, out-of-date piece rates and across-the-board government mandated increases • Facility level incentives	• Increasing use of profit sharing, gain-sharing, and performance appraisals	• Increase based on seniority, inflation, and across-the-board guarantees • Growing use of performance based (75% use individual based and 50% use unit or firm based) • Performance still small percentage of total pay

Benefits				
• Mandatory national health care and retirement • Generally sparse benefits; few companies pay overtime or holidays	• Moderate mandatory medical, retirement, low cash allowances • Christmas bonus (15 days' pay) and vacation bonus (25 percent of pay) • Mandated profit sharing; 10% of pretax profits	• Major strategic tool; offer scarce goods and services, medical care, improved housing, access to quality products	• High mandated coverage: medical care, pensions, and vacations/holidays	• Slight trend away from company cars, though it is still a major symbol of status • National health care and pensions • Paid leaves (25 days) plus national holidays • Lunch and parking allowance
Nature of Administration				
• Government policies and regulations not enforced stringently	• Government regulations major factor • Acquired rights; if a benefit or bonus is paid for two years, employee has a right to it • Centralized • Low costs and increased use of incentives as strategic aspects	• High inflation and uncertainty • Preferential access to scarce goods and service (nontaxed) • Individual negotiations	• Government policies major factor • Increased use of performance based as a strategic tool	• Government policies and regulations a major influence • Centralized and open • Early efforts at using pay strategically have not had impact on administration • Increasing effort to use employee reviews

Your Turn:

International Compensation

Your Assignment

1. Recommend a new compensation policy that will attract and retain U.S.engineers to the Madrid office.
2. Analyze and assess the present policy on expatriates, specifically the mix of U.S. expatriates and local country nationals (L.C.N.s).

The following information is provided for use in this case:

1. A memo outlining Medico's present expatriate pay policy.
2. Some definitions of pay elements in the expatriate policy.
3. Letter from a consultant describing approaches to expatriate pay.
4. A memo from a former Medico expatriate outlining reasons for quitting.

Use this information to answer the questions at the end of the case.

Background

Medico Instruments is a manufacturer of specialty medical instruments. The C.E.O. has asked you to look at their expatriate pay system. The company is headquartered in Provo, Utah, with branch offices all over the world. Many of these offices are staffed by some United States citizens, called expatriates, who work in these foreign locations, usually on a temporary basis. The rest of the office is staffed by local country nationals (L.C.N.s), who are citizens of the country in which the office is located.

By an examination of internal Medico memos and discussions with their H.R. department, you learned that last week, one of the U.S. expatriates, an instruments engineer, quit in Madrid. This made three voluntary quits in six months for the Madrid office. All three expatriates cited low pay among the reasons for their departure.

Medico InterOffice Memorandum

Here is the summary you requested of the features we presently offer to employees working in our overseas offices. Most of the policy was updated two years ago. We follow a "balance sheet" approach with the following additional elements:

- A pre-move visit to the foreign location for the employee and his/her spouse.
- Pre-move cultural and language training for employees and their families.
- Provision of a company-paid car in the foreign location for the duration of the employee's stay.
- Shipping and/or storage costs for the employee's belongings.

- Emergency travel arrangements in case of death or illness of a family member back in the United States.

The following is compensation information you requested about our expatriate engineers in Madrid. Please note that when this plan was implemented, the dollar was worth 140 pesetas.

	Pesetas	*U.S. Dollars*
Base salary	10,920,000	$ 78,000
Profit sharing	280,000	2,000
Foreign service premium	700,000	5,000
Tax equalization	574,000	4,100
Housing allowance	980,000	7,000
Subtotal	*13,454,000*	*96,100*
Benefits	3,640,000	26,000
Total	17,094,000	$122,100

From: The Gray Group
To: Medico Instruments

Here is the information you requested on the different types of expatriate plans.

Balance Sheet Approach

This is by far the most common method used to pay expatriates. It attempts to enable the expatriate to maintain a standard of living roughly equivalent to the standard of living prior to taking the assignment. Expenses are broken down into four major categories: Income taxes, housing, goods and services, and reserve (or as discretionary accounts, such as savings, investments, etc.). Each component is measured in home country currency and varies with income level and family size. Costs of comparable income taxes, housing, and goods and services are then measured in the host country, and the expatriate is "equalized" to the base country for each component.

Here is an example based upon the information you sent me regarding the Madrid location.

	U.S. Expenditures	*Madrid Equivalent*	*Allowance in U.S. Dollars*
Taxes	$17,000	$ 20,000	$ 3,000
Housing	13,000	21,000	8,000
Goods and services	34,000	40,000	6,000
Discretionary account	24,000	24,000	—
Total	$88,000	$105,000	$17,000

Notice that total U.S. expenditures were $88,000, about equivalent to the employee's salary (excluding benefits). The company pays the expatriate the amounts in Allowance (the third column) plus usual salary (column 1). Therefore, the expatriate will be paid $105,000. However, the purchasing power of the expatriate will be about the same as it was back in the United States at a salary of $88,000. The intent is that financially the expat will neither gain nor lose.

The balance sheet has been criticized as too complex and too expensive: the expat ends up spending the extra allowance. An alternative is simply lump the allowance into base and incentives.

Lump-Sum Approach

In this method, the company provides the expatriate with an amount of money (a lump sum), in addition to base pay and any incentive pay, that the expatriate can spend in any way. This method is similar to the balance sheet approach in that many of the calculations to determine the lump are the same. However, the major difference is that all of the money can be spent on one thing without drastically affecting the compensation. For example, under a lump-sum approach, choosing to live in a small apartment would free up funds for other items. But under the balance sheet approach, the smaller apartment would mean a smaller allowance. So there is little incentive to not spend the entire allowance.

The major drawback to lump sum is that variations in currency exchange rates may severely cut buying power; it depends upon which goods the lump-sum calculation is based.

Cafeteria Style

This method is very similar to the lump-sum approach, except that the employer offers a number of options the employee can choose from. Usually a list is created, and expatriates are given a limit on the number of options they can choose. This method only works if it does not force expatriates to choose between two highly desirable options such as a life insurance policy and home leave.

Please note that all methods are designed to keep the expats purchasing power the same on assignment as in their home country. The expat allowances are not based on performance or what competitors do, but rather on the estimates of a particular location's living costs. However, competitors' practices can be surveyed to gauge your practices.

Medico InterOffice Memorandum

To: C. Me
From: Seedy Rom, Project Engineer
Re: Expatriate Pay

I was an expatriate on assignment in Madrid only four months ago. However, I could not stand to live there any longer, so I requested a transfer back to stateside. I have a wife and two small children, and I could no longer expect them to face the poor living standards and working conditions in Madrid.

As my records should show, my performance ratings have been consistently superior and my supervisors reported that I was due for a promotion in 3 months. My decision to leave is based on my pay.

I recognize that my pay package appears very large compared to the one I had in the States. Yet, it was very expensive to support my family and myself here in Madrid. I wanted to be able to provide my family everything they had in the States. I should be able to do that. My family should not suffer just because I accepted an assignment in Madrid.

I was also made to feel very uncomfortable at work. Most of the other workers there were Spanish. While they didn't really know the amount I was making, I always felt they had a good idea. They made considerably less than I did, even though they were doing the same job I was. I felt they resented me, primarily because of the differences in compensation. This made it difficult to work with them.

Finally, it was not very clear what my role would be when I returned to the States. I may not have my old job waiting for me when I return.

Just for your information, here are some comparative prices. Note the size of the allowance required to offset the differences in costs.

Tuition at an English speaking private school comparable to home country education

Madrid	1,400,000 pesetas per year	$10,000 per year
United States		7,000 per year
	Required allowance: $3,000	

3 bedroom, 2 bath duplex with community pool and tennis facilities

Madrid	23,800,000 pesetas	$170,000
United States		160,000
	Required allowance: $10,000	

2,000 sq ft single dwelling home with full yard

Madrid	42,000,000 pesetas	$300,000
Provo		260,000
	Required allowance: $40,000	

These data make my point about Medico's low expatriate allowances. My current salary is $80,000 (including my $2,000 profit sharing bonus). My housing allowance is only $7,000 and the foreign service premium is only $5,000. Just my children's school and my housing exceeds this $12,000 allowance by $1,000. A comparison:

	Actual Cost	*Medico Allowance*
Children's schooling	$ 3,000	$ 5,000 (total FS premium)
Housing in duplex	10,000	7,000
	$13,000	$12,000

A thousand dollar shortfall just on these two items! I had to pay for the opportunity to work in Spain!

Some Definitions

Foreign Service Premium Financial incentive to induce an employee to take an assignment overseas. In this period of globalization, many companies have abandoned this premium, theorizing that employees should be pleased to have the chance to work abroad.

Hardship Premium Financial incentive to induce an employee to take an assignment in difficult or dangerous living conditions. Usually between 10 and 25 percent of base salary, it is sometimes referred to as hazard pay.

Housing Allowance Set sum of money used for accommodations, or in very lengthy assignments (3 years+), buy a place to live.

Tax Protection The company agrees to pay taxes for any amount over what the employee paid in the home country. If the tax amount is less than the employee paid at home, employee usually gets to keep the windfall.

Tax Equalization The company deducts what the employee used to pay in taxes from base salary and agrees to pay all taxes and fees while the employee is on assignment abroad.

Questions

Prepare a memo that includes the following:

1. Your preliminary evaluation and analysis of expatriate pay at Medico. Critical problems to address in Medico's expat pay plan include: Should Medico provide some hardship premium for all assignments? Should Medico match its competitors' policies? What is the primary objective of the Medico expat plan: Motivate volunteers for foreign assignments? Make foreign assignments a "great deal"? Encourage a small contingent of employees to become permanent foreign workers?
2. Your recommendations. For example, would you recommend increasing the emphasis on base pay, short-term, or long-term incentives? What is your rationale?
3. What additional information do you recommend Medico collects before making its final decision? How would you use this information? Please be specific.

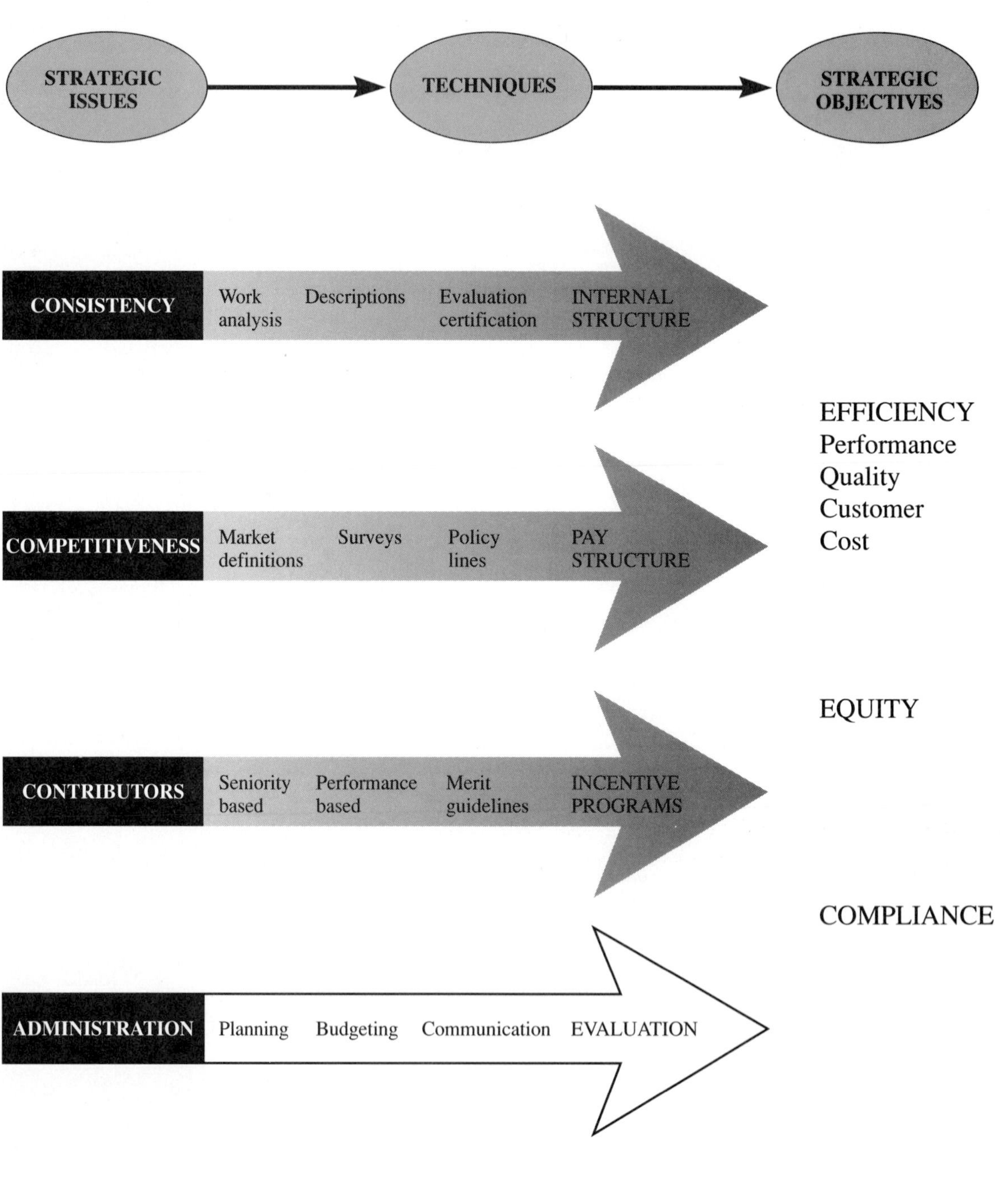

STRATEGIC ISSUES
TECHNIQUES
STRATEGIC OBJECTIVES
CONSISTENCY
Work analysis
Descriptions
Evaluation certification
INTERNAL STRUCTURE
COMPETITIVENESS
Market definitions
Surveys
Policy lines
PAY STRUCTURE
CONTRIBUTORS
Seniority based
Performance based
Merit guidelines
INCENTIVE PROGRAMS
ADMINISTRATION
Planning
Budgeting
Communication
EVALUATION
EFFICIENCY
Performance
Quality
Customer
Cost
EQUITY
COMPLIANCE

Managing the System

The last policy in our pay model is Administration. We have touched on aspects of administration already—the use of budgets in merit increase programs, the "message" that employees receive from their variable pay bonuses, communication and cost control in benefits, and the importance of employee involvement in designing the entire compensation system.

Several important issues remain. The first is the significant role that government and legislation play in managing compensation. Laws and regulations are the most obvious government intervention. As Chapter 17 points out, minimum wage legislation, the Equal Pay Act, and Title VII of the Civil Rights Act, among others, regulate pay decisions.

Government is more than a source of laws and regulations, however. As a major employer, as a consumer of goods and services, and through its fiscal and monetary policies, government affects the demand for labor. It affects the supply of labor by setting licensing standards, appropriating funds for education and training programs that affect skills, and by competing for human resources directly.

Another management issue is costs. In fact, one of the key reasons for being systematic about pay decisions is to control costs. What are the labor costs associated with pay decisions being considered? How can these costs be managed? As Chapter 18 will show, a compensation *system* is really a device for allocating money (expenses) consistent with the organization's objectives—systematic allocation of expenses.

A crucial issue confronting all organizations is how to manage changes in the way people are paid. Any system will founder if it is ineffectively implemented and managed. What will be communicated to whom is an important, ongoing issue. In addition to communication, the system must be constantly evaluated to judge its effectiveness. Is it helping the organization achieve the objectives? What information can help us make these judgments?

Chapter 18 also discusses how to organize the compensation department. Which activities should be done in-house and which may be candidates for reengineering and outsourcing are among the issues discussed.

CHAPTER 17 The Government's Role in Compensation

Chapter Outline

> The . . . wage curve . . . is not the same for women as for men because of the more transient character of the former, the relative shortness of their activity in industry, the differences in environment required, the extra services that must be provided, overtime limitations, extra help needed for the occasional heavy work, and the general sociological factors not requiring discussion herein. Basically then we have another wage curve . . . for women below and not parallel with the men's curve. [Excerpt from a 1939 pay policy handbook.][1]

Legislation seeking to change the thinking reflected in that policy has revolutionized the American workplace. Newspaper help-wanted ads specifying "perky gal-Fridays," whites-only local unions, and the pay practice described above are all part of the past. However, women still earn only 81 cents for every dollar earned by men on an hourly basis, up 15 cents since 1963.

Legislation does not always achieve what it intends. (Nor does it always intend what it achieves.) In addition, intentions change as new problems are identified and legislation to address them is passed. Consequently, compliance is an important objective of managing compensation.

In any society, the legislative procedure is the same. A problem is identified (not all citizens are receiving fair treatment in the workplace) and corrective legislation is proposed (the Civil Rights Act, Americans with Disabilities Act). If enough support develops, often as a result of compromises and trade-offs, the proposed legislation becomes law. Employers, along with other stakeholders, all attempt to influence the form any legislation will take.

Once passed, laws are enforced by agencies through rulings, regulations, inspections, and investigations. Companies respond to legislation by auditing and perhaps altering their practices, and perhaps again lobby for legislative change. Consequently, the regulatory climate—the laws and regulations issued by governmental agencies created to enforce the laws—represents a significant influence on compensation decisions throughout the world.

GOVERNMENT INFLUENCES ON THE IMPLICIT SOCIAL CONTRACT

In Chapter 16, we discussed government's role as a third party to the employment relationship. The exact role government should play in the contemporary workplace de-

---

[1] The job evaluation manual was introduced as evidence in *Electrical Workers (IUE) v. Westinghouse Electric Corp.*, 632 F.2d 1094, 23 FEP Cases 588 (3rd Cir. 1980), cert. denied, 452 U.S. 967, 25 FEP Cases 1835 (1981).

pends in part on one's political ideology. Some call for organizations and the government to act in concert to carry out a public policy that protects the interests of employees.[2] Others believe the constant reconfiguring that is inherent in market-based economies is vital to society's well-being; the economy ought to be allowed to adapt and transform, undistorted by government actions.[3] Countries throughout the world address these issues. However, no two countries arrive at precisely the same answers.

Different countries and cultures have different perspectives on the role the government should play in the social contract. As noted in Chapter 1, government is a key stakeholder in decision making about compensation. Governments' usual interest are whether procedures for determining pay are fair (e.g., pay discrimination), safety nets for the unemployed and disadvantaged are sufficient (e.g., minimum wage, unemployment compensation), and employees are protected (e.g., overtime pay, child labor). Consequently, pay in the workplace influences national debates on minimum wage, health care, the security and portability of pensions, even the quality of public education and the availability of training. So in addition to individuals and employers, government is a key third party to the implicit social contract. Compensation managers need to understand the importance of the implicit social contract as well as government's rightful role in it.

Government policy decisions also have an indirect effect on compensation, through the impact of policy in supply and demand for people.

Supply Legislation aimed at protecting specific groups also tends to restrict that group's participation in the labor market. For example, compulsory schooling law restrict the supply of children available to sell hamburgers or to assemble soccer balls. Licensing requirements for certain occupations (plumbers, cosmetologists, psychologists) restrict the number of people who can legally offer a service.

Demand Government affects demand for labor most directly as a major employer. In the United States, 18 million people are employed by local, state, and federal government units. A government also indirectly affects labor demand through its purchases (military aircraft, computer systems, paperclips) as well as its public policy decisions. For example, lowering interest rates generally boosts consumption and consequently manufacturing and construction of everything from cars to condominiums. Increased business activity translates into increased demand for labor, and upward pressure on wages. Government's effects on wages goes beyond specific legislation.

To see how regulations reflect a society, look at the U.S. compensation regulations in Exhibit 17.1. The pattern shows an early emphasis on basic protection: child labor was prohibited, and overtime wage provisions were specified in the Fair Labor Standards Act. Prevailing wage laws (Davis-Bacon and Walsh-Healey) specified government's obligations as an employer. While the minimum wage has been periodically increased ever since its initial passage, and additional prevailing wage legislation was passed in the 1960s, the main thrust of legislation shifted in the 1960s to a greater emphasis on civil rights, and an ever-increasing scope of that legislation.

---

[2] Bruce Kaufman, ed. *Government Regulation of the Employment Relationship* (Ithaca, NY: Cornell University Press, 1998).

[3] *Keeping America Competitive* (Washington, DC: Employment Policy Foundation, 1994).

EXHIBIT 17.1 The Evolving Nature of United States Federal Pay Laws

1931	Davis–Bacon Act	Requires that mechanics and laborers on public construction projects be paid the "prevailing wage" in an area.
1936	Walsh–Healey Public Contracts Act	Extends prevailing wage concept to manufacturers or suppliers of goods for government contracts.
1938	Fair Labor Standards Act	Sets minimum wage, hours of work, and prohibits child labor.
1963	Equal Pay Act	Equal pay required for men and women doing "substantially similar" work in terms of skill, effort, responsibility and working conditions.
1964	Title VII of Civil Rights Act	Prohibits discrimination in all employment practices on basis of race, sex, color, religion, origin, or pregnancy.
1967	Age Discrimination Act	Protects employees age 40 and over against age discrimination.
1978	Pregnancy Discrimination Act	Pregnancy must be covered to same extent that other medical conditions are covered.
1990	Americans with Disabilities Act	Requires that "essential elements" of a job be called out. If a person with a disability can perform these essential elements, reasonable accommodations must be provided. Essential elements are specified as part of job evaluation.
1991	Civil Rights Act	Makes filing a lawsuit easier and more attractive.
1993	Family and Medical Leave	Requires employers to provide up to 12 weeks unpaid leave for family and medical emergencies.
1997	Mental Health Act	Mental illness must be covered to same extent that other medical conditions are covered.

This chapter will examine the most important U.S. regulations concerning wages. Because our society continues to wrestle with the issue of discrimination, we will go into some depth on how pay discrimination has been defined and the continuing earnings gap between men and women and among racial groups.

FAIR LABOR STANDARDS ACT OF 1938

The Fair Labor Standards Act (FLSA) of 1938 covers all employees (with some exceptions discussed later) of companies engaged in interstate commerce or in production of goods for interstate commerce. FLSA has three major provisions:

1. Minimum wage
2. Hours of work
3. Child labor

Minimum Wage

Minimum wage legislation is intended to provide an income floor for workers in society's lowest paid and least productive jobs. When first enacted in 1938, the minimum wage was 25 cents an hour. It has been raised periodically; in 1997, a new minimum of $5.15 took effect. Almost all states have their own minimum wage to cover jobs

EXHIBIT 17.2

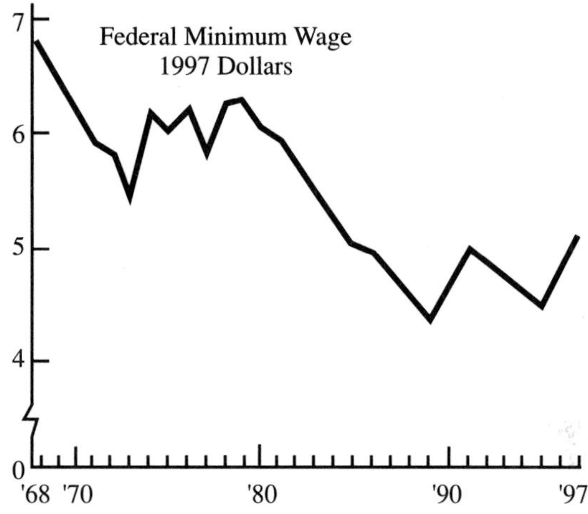

Source: Employment Policy Institute

omitted from federal legislation. Exhibit 17.2 shows the federal minimum wage in real terms (adjusted to match the consumer price index for November 1994). The graph of real wages translates into purchasing power, which has not kept pace with inflation. Consequently, someone earning the minimum wage today may not enjoy the same standard of living as someone earning the minimum wage in 1967, when costs of goods were much lower.

While we all immediately think of teenage employees of fast-food restaurants when we think of a minimum wage earner, in fact only one-third of the minimum-wage earners are teenagers.[4] The rest are adults over 25. An additional 5 percent of the work force receive wages within 50 cents of the minimum.[5] As legislation forces pay rates at the lowest end of the scale to move up, pay rates above the minimum often increase in order to maintain differentials. This shift in pay structure does not affect all industries equally. For example, the lowest rates paid in the steel, chemical, oil, and pharmaceutical industries are already well above minimum; any legislative change would have little direct impact on employers in these industries. However, retailing and service firms tend to pay at or near minimum wage to many clerks and sales personnel. When legislation results in substantially higher labor costs for these firms, they may consider substituting capital for jobs (e.g., automated inventory control systems, prepacked frozen french fries) or reducing the number of jobs available.

---

[4] Louis Uchitelle, "Minimum Wage and Jobs," *The New York Times*, January 12, 1995, pp. D1, D19.

[5] Judith Hellerstein and David Neumark, "Are Earnings Profiles Steeper than Productivity Profiles?" *Journal of Human Resources*, Winter 1995, pp. 89–112.

Conventional economic theory says that this job loss falls most heavily on inexperienced and unskilled workers, that is, their perceived value does not equal their actual cost. The high rate of unemployment among teenagers supports this theory. However, a number of recent studies cast doubt on this belief. A decade ago most studies concluded that 1 percent or more of all minimum wage workers lost their jobs for each 10 percent increase in the minimum wage.[6] But more recent studies declare the job loss to be minimal.[7]

The difference is mainly the result of the prolonged expansion of the U.S. economy. Fast-food restaurants and retail establishments, the traditional employers of minimum-wage workers, have been forced to pay above the minimum for quite some time, in order to attract sufficient employees during a period of record low unemployment levels. Consequently, legislation has been introduced to lift the minimum wage even further. Recall from Exhibit 17.2 that even with the 1996 and 1997 hikes, minimum wage workers still are not back to the inflation-adjusted levels they enjoyed in the 1960s and 1970s.

Minimum wage discussion is also tied up in the social good of the people who are not faring well in the market economy. Some make the case that continuing a low minimum wage permits the continuation of boring, dead-end jobs that ought to be modernized. Many employers won't bother doing the necessary upgrading and training of employees if they can get by at low pay. A higher minimum wage will make it more attractive to people to leave welfare or other government assistance and join the labor market.

Marriot for example, boasts of helping its low-wage cleaning staff apply for federal earned income tax credits. However, others consider this scenario as taxpayers being forced to subsidize Marriot's low wages. Marriot and others can get by paying minimum wages because all these other government benefit programs exist. Taxpayers are in effect compensating Marriot's low pay.

So the topic stirs endless debate. What is certain is that people working at or near the minimum wage who continue to work definitely do benefit from mandated minimum wage increases, and other workers in higher-level jobs in those same companies may also benefit. Yet as labor costs increase, fewer workers will be hired or hours will be cut if the increased costs cannot be passed on to consumers or offset by increased productivity.

Hours of Work

The overtime provision of the FLSA is aimed at sharing available work. It seeks to make hiring more workers a less costly option than scheduling overtime for current employ-

---

[6] Finis Welch, Donald Deere, and Kevin Murphy, "Estimates of Job Loss with Increasing Minimum Wage," Presentation at 1995 American Economic Association, Washington, DC; David Neumark and William Wascher, "Employment Effects of Minimum and Subminimum Wages: Panel Data on State Minimum Wage Laws," *Industrial and Labor Relations Review* 46, no. 1 (October 1992), pp. 55–81.

[7] David Card and Alan Krueger, "Minimum Wages and Employment: A Case Study of the Fast Food Industry in New Jersey and Pennsylvania," *American Economic Review*, September 1994, pp. 772–93; Lawrence F. Katz and Alan B. Krueger, "The Effect of the Minimum Wage on the Fast-Food Industry," *Industrial and Labor Relations Review* 46, no. 1 (October 1992), pp. 6–21.

ees by requiring payment at one-and-a-half times the standard for working more than 40 hours per week.

But the workplace has changed a lot since the law was passed. For current employers, overtime pay is often the least costly option. This is due to (1) an increasingly skilled work force with higher training costs per employee and (2) higher fringe benefits, the bulk of which are fixed per employee. These factors have lowered the breakeven point at which it pays employers to schedule longer hours and pay the overtime premium, rather than hire, train, and pay fringes for more employees.

Several amendments to increase the overtime penalty have been proposed over the years. These typically seek to increase the penalty, reduce the standard workweek to less than 40 hours, or repeal some of the exemptions.

Who Is Covered? Only about 58 percent of all employees are covered by the overtime provision. Determining which jobs are exempt is the most complex part of the act. Some of the exemptions are shown in Exhibit 17.3. Professional, executive, and administrative jobs are exempt. So are many jobs in the transportation industry.

Some exemptions suspend only certain provisions of the act; others suspend all provisions. Some apply to all employees of certain businesses, others to only certain employees. To compound the confusion, exemptions may overlap. Repeated amendments to the act have made the distinction between exempt and nonexempt difficult to determine. One writer observed, "As soon as the distinction between exempt and nonexempt begins to emerge clearly from court cases, the act is amended, setting off a new round of court cases."[8]

Many states have their own web pages that include their compensation legislation. (New York's wage data website, for example, is **http://www.labor.state.ny.us/wages**). What information is available from your state? Compare the extent of regulation in different regions of the United States. Are there any unique characteristics of your state that are addressed by state compensation legislation (e.g., unique industries, extent of unionization, etc.)?

The Wage-Hour Division of the Department of Labor, which is charged with enforcement of the FLSA, provides strict criteria that must be met in order for jobs to be considered professional and exempt from minimum wage and overtime provisions. Professionals must

Do work requiring knowledge generally acquired by prolonged, specialized study, or engage in original and creative activity in a recognized artistic field.
Consistently exercise discretion or judgment.
Do work that is primarily intellectual and nonroutine.
Devote at least 80 percent of their work hours to such activities.

[8] James Ledvinka, *Federal Regulation of Personnel and Human Resource Management* (Boston: Kent Publishing Company, 1982).

Exhibit 17.3 Some Exemptions to the Minimum Wage and Overtime Provisions of the Fair Labor Standards Act

Section 13(a)(1)	Outside salesmen, professional executive, and administrative personnel ("including any employee employed in the capacity of academic administrative personnel or teacher in elementary or secondary schools").
Section 13(a)(3)	Employees of certain seasonal amusements or recreational establishments.
Section 13(a)(5)	Fishing and fish processing at sea employees.
Section 13(a)(6)	Agricultural employees employed by farms utilizing fewer than 500 man-days of agricultural labor, employed by a member of their immediate family, certain local seasonal harvest laborers and seasonal hand harvest laborers 16 years of age or under, and employees principally engaged in the range production of livestock.
Section 13(a)(15)	Babysitters employed on a casual basis and persons employed to provide companion services.
Section 7(i)	Certain commissioned salespeople in retail or service establishments.
Section 13(b)(1)	Motor carrier employees
Section 13(b)(3)	Airline employees.
Section 13(b)(15)	Maple sap employees.

However, contemporary workplace trends that increase employee discretion and omit specific details on duties blur the distinction between exempt and nonexempt. In one case, a *Washington Post* reporter claimed that the newspaper owed him more than $100,000 in overtime accumulated during the six years he covered Washington politics. He said his job merely "required creativity" but did not "depend primarily" on it. But the judge ruled that the job required "invention, imagination, and talent," and thus fell into the category of artistic work and was, therefore, exempt from coverage.[9]

There are also criteria for exempt status for executives. Executives must

Primarily undertake management duties.
Supervise two or more employees.
Have control (or at least great influence) over hiring, firing, and promotion.
Exercise discretionary powers.
Devote at least 80 percent of their work hours to such activities.

In the 1980s, some fast-food chains were found guilty of giving too many people the title of manager and not paying overtime, even though the work of these "managers" differed only slightly from their coworkers.

What Time Is Covered? Sometimes counting the hours of work becomes a contest. Exhibit 17.4 details what we mean.

[9] Milo Geyelin, "*Washington Post* Wins Overtime Case by Ex-Reporter," *The Wall Street Journal*, January 5, 1995, p. B1.

EXHIBIT 17.4 There's No Such Thing as a Free . . . (Item posted to Internet by D. Shniad)

Gainers Workers Must Pay to Use Bathroom

EDMONTON—Employees at Gainers Inc. are now docked pay for every bathroom break visit made outside of breaks and lunch hour under regulations brought in last week by company owner Burns Meats Ltd.

A notice posted in the meat-packing plant tells employees that abusing washroom visits has lowered productivity. If employees need to use the bathroom outside of breaks, they must report to a supervisor, who records the time of departure and return. The time is tabulated at the end of the week and pay cheques are deducted based on an employee's hourly wage.

"How can they charge you for going to the washroom?" asked one angry employee.

The man said one worker at the plant had a kidney transplant and has to use the washroom often.

"Because of this system, he had to hold it in [between breaks] for a whole week. He went once for three minutes and was charged 43 cents."

Such washroom rules are rare but there is nothing in the Alberta employment standards code that requires a person to be paid when they don't work, said Kathy Lazowski, a public affairs officer with Alberta Labour.

—Canadian Press

Tallying the hours of work is not a piddling matter. In 1993, Iowa Beef Processors was hit with a multimillion dollar bill to cover the overtime wages due to slaughterhouse employees for walking to and from the knife room, waiting to have their knives sharpened, and time spent cleaning equipment. The issue is, When does the workday begin? The Portal-to-Portal Act, passed in 1947 as a result of earlier interpretations and lawsuits surrounding the definition of work time, provides that time spent on activities before beginning the "principal activity" is generally not compensable. In the case of Iowa Beef Processors, the court ruled that the time spent changing into and out of work clothes did not qualify. However, those employees required to wear special protective gear should be compensated for the time it takes to put on the gear as well as for the time spent cleaning tools and protective equipment.

A newer issue is the increased use of "on-call employees" who make themselves available to respond 24 hours a day.[10] Firefighters and other emergency personnel are traditional examples. But with more businesses relying on 24-hour service from their computer systems, telecommunications and software services personnel must respond quickly to problems outside their regularly scheduled workday. Sometimes a flat rate is paid for the added inconvenience of being on call. These payments must be included when computing overtime pay.

Gifts or special occasion bonuses do not need to be included, because they are at the employer's discretion. When a pay form is promised to employees if certain conditions are met, then those payments must be included as part of an employee's regular rate on which overtime is based.

[10] *1994–95 Survey of Exempt and Non-Exempt On-Call Practices: Job Site vs. Home-Based* (Dublin, OH: N. E. Fried and Associates, 1994).

Compensatory Time Off. The changing nature of the workplace and of pay systems has led to calls to reform FLSA to allow for more flexible scheduling and easier administration of variable pay plans.

In 1997 federal legislation was proposed that would give employees and employers the option of trading overtime for time off. Rather than paying overtime after 8 hours for a 10 hour workday, an employee would have the option of taking two or more hours off at another time. The employee would get more scheduling flexibility to attend to personal matters , and the employer would save money. Some public employees already get 1 1/2 hours off for every hour overtime worked. Legislation to extend this option to the private sector has been considered at both federal and state level. However, unions tend to oppose the legislation, who charge that the arrangement not only takes money away from employees, it also subjects them to manipulation and pressure from an employer who is loathe to pay overtime to which the employee was legally entitled.

Child Labor

Generally, persons under 18 cannot work in hazardous jobs such as meatpacking and logging; persons under 16 cannot be employed in jobs involving interstate commerce except for nonhazardous work for a parent or guardian. Additional exceptions and limitations also exist. While the intent of the law is straightforward, violations have soared in recent years as the supply of older teenagers dwindles and the service sector of the economy expands. The dramatic increase in violations has caused many states to reexamine child labor legislation.

The union movement in the United States has taken a leading role in publicizing the extent of child labor outside the United States, producing goods destined for the U.S. consumer.[11] While the contrast between the life led by television personality Kathie Lee Gifford and the children in Guatemala who sew the clothes licensed by Ms. Gifford is notable, Guatemalan authorities maintain that its population needs such jobs in order to improve its economy and bring down unemployment. They point to less savory options available to young Guatemalan females. Unfortunately, a lot of child labor around the world is still in dirty, dangerous jobs. A Your Turn exercise at the end of this chapter explores some of the issues surrounding child labor outside the United States.

The next group of laws set pay for work done to produce goods and services contracted by the federal government. These are called "prevailing wage" laws.

PREVAILING WAGE LAWS

A government-defined prevailing wage is the minimum wage that must be paid for work done on covered government projects or purchases. The original purpose was to prevent the government from undercutting local workers. For example, if a government project of the magnitude of Hoover Dam were to pay low wages to construction workers, the

---

[11] Douglas Kruse, "Estimates of Child Labor in the United States," (Working Paper, Rutgers University, 1998).

sheer size of the project could drive down the entire wage structure in the area. So the government requires that surveys identify the prevailing wage in an area. That prevailing wage then becomes the mandated minimum wage on the government-financed project.

Contractors object to this requirement because it frequently means that they have to match a wage rate that only a minority of area workers are receiving. Many taxpayers also object because they believe it drives up the cost of government.

A number of laws contain prevailing wage provisions. They vary on the government expenditures they target for coverage. The main prevailing wage laws, cited in Exhibit 17.1, include Davis–Bacon, the Walsh–Healey Public Contracts Act, the Service Contract Act, and the National Foundation for the Arts and Humanities Act.

Much of the legislation discussed so far was originally passed in the 1930s and 1940s in response to social issues of that time. In the 1960s, the equal rights movements pushed different social problems to the forefront. The Equal Pay Act and the Civil Rights Act were passed. Because of their substantial impact on human resource management and compensation, they are discussed at length

PAY DISCRIMINATION: WHAT IS IT?

Before we look at specific pay discrimination laws, let us address the more general question of how to legally define discrimination. The law recognizes two types of discrimination: access discrimination and valuation discrimination. The charges of discrimination/reverse discrimination that most often make the news involve *access discrimination.* Access discrimination denies particular jobs, promotions, or training opportunities to qualified women or minorities. The University of Michigan, for example, has been accused of access discrimination by using differential standards among different racial groups to determine who is "qualified" for admission.

A second legally recognized interpretation of discrimination is *valuation discrimination*, which looks at the pay women and minorities receive for the jobs they perform. The Equal Pay Act makes it clear that it is discriminatory to pay minorities or women less than males when performing equal work (i.e., working side by side, in the same plant, doing the same work, producing the same results). This definition of pay discrimination hinges on the standard of equal pay for equal work.

But many believe that this definition does not go far enough.[12] They believe that valuation discrimination can also occur when men and women hold entirely different jobs. For example, office and clerical jobs are typically staffed by women, and craft jobs (electricians, welders) are typically staffed by men. Is it illegal to pay employees in one job group less than employees in the other, if the two job groups contain work that is not equal in content or results, but is in some sense of comparable worth to the employer?

---

[12] Paula England, *Comparable Worth: Theories and Evidence* (New York: Aldine deGruyter, 1992); H. J. Aaron and C. M. Lougy, *The Comparable Worth Controversy* (Washington, DC: Brookings Institution, 1986).

In this case, the proposed definition of pay discrimination hinges on the standard of equal pay for work of comparable worth. Existing federal laws do not support this standard. However, several states have enacted laws that require a comparable worth standard for state and local government employees. The province of Ontario, Canada, has extended such legislation to the private sector.

So two standards for defining valuation discrimination need to be considered: the already legally established standard of equal pay for equal work, and the more stringent standard of equal pay for work of comparable worth. For an understanding of the legal foundations of each, let us turn to the legislation and key court cases.

THE EQUAL PAY ACT

The Equal Pay Act (EPA) of 1963 forbids wage discrimination on the basis of gender when

- Employees perform equal work in the same establishment.
- Employees perform jobs requiring equal skill, effort, and responsibility under similar working conditions.

Pay differences between equal jobs can be justified by an *affirmative defense*. Differences in pay between men and women doing equal work are legal if these differences are based on

- Seniority.
- Merit or quality of performance.
- Quality or quantity of production.
- Some factor other than sex.

These terms for comparison and permitted defenses seem deceptively simple. Yet numerous court cases have been required to clarify the act's provisions, particularly its definition of equal.

Definition of Equal

The Supreme Court established guidelines to define equal work in the *Schultz v. Wheaton Glass* case in 1970. Wheaton Glass Company maintained two job classifications for selector-packers in its production department, male and female. The female job class carried a pay rate 10 percent below that of the male job class. The company claimed that the male job class included additional tasks such as shoveling broken glass, opening warehouse doors, doing heavy lifting and the like that justified the pay differential. The plaintiff claimed that the extra tasks were infrequently performed, and not all men did them. Further, these extra tasks performed by some of the men were regularly performed by employees in another classification ("snap-up boys"), and these employees were paid only 2 cents an hour more than the women. Did the additional tasks performed by some members of one job class render the jobs unequal?

The court decided they did not. It ruled that the equal work standard required only that jobs be *substantially* equal, not identical. Additionally, in several cases where the duties employees actually performed were different from those in the job descriptions, the courts held that the *actual work performed* must be used to decide if jobs are substantially equal.

Skill, Effort, Responsibility, Working Conditions: Definitions

The Department of Labor provides these definitions of the four factors.

1. Skill: Experience, training, education, and ability as measured by the performance requirements of a particular job.
2. Effort: Mental or physical. The amount of degree of effort (not type of effort) actually expended in the performance of a job.
3. Responsibility: The degree of accountability required in the performance of a job.
4. Working conditions: The physical surroundings and hazards of a job including dimensions such as inside versus outside work, heat, cold, and poor ventilation.

Guidelines to clarify these definitions have evolved through court decisions. For an employer to support a claim of *unequal* work, the following conditions must be met:

1. The effort/skill/responsibility must be substantially greater in one of the jobs compared.
2. The tasks involving the extra effort/skill/responsibility must consume a *significant amount* of time for *all* employees whose additional wages are in question.
3. The extra effort/skill/responsibility must have a *value commensurate* with the questioned pay differential (as determined by the employer's own evaluation).
4. Time of day does not constitute dissimilar working conditions. However, if a differential for working at night is paid, it must be separated from the base wage for the job.

Factors Other than Sex

Unequal pay for equal work may be justified through the four affirmative defenses: seniority, merit, performance-based incentive system, or a factor other than sex. Factors other than sex include shift differentials; temporary assignments; bona fide training programs; differences based on ability, training, or experience; and other reasons of "business necessity." A practice will not automatically be prohibited simply because wage differentials result. Rather, the practice must be evaluated for its business necessity, and whether reasonable alternatives exist.

Factors other than sex have been interpreted as a broad exception that may include business reasons advanced by the employer. In *Kouba v. Allstate*, Allstate Insurance

Company paid its new sales representatives a minimum salary during their training period. After completing the training, the sales reps received a minimum salary or their earned sales commissions, whichever was higher. The minimum salary paid during training needed to be high enough to attract prospective agents to enter the training program, yet not so high as to lessen the incentive to earn sales commissions after training. Allstate maintained that the minimum salary needed to be calculated individually for each trainee, and the trainee's past salary was a necessary factor used in the calculation. But Allstate's approach resulted in women trainees generally being paid less than male trainees, because women had held lower paying jobs before entering the program. Allstate maintained the pay difference resulted from acceptable business reasons, a factor other than sex.

Lola Kouba didn't buy Allstate's arguments. She argued that acceptable business reasons were limited to "those that measure the value of an employee's job performance to his or her employer." But the court rejected Kouba's argument. It said that Allstate's business reasons for a practice must be evaluated for reasonableness. A practice will not automatically be prohibited simply because wage differences between men and women result.

The court did not say that Allstate's "business" reasons were justified. It did say that Allstate's argument could not be rejected *solely because the practice perpetuated historical differences in pay.* Rather, Allstate needed to justify the business relatedness of the practice.

The case was settled out of court, so no legal clarification of Allstate's rationale was ever provided. Thus, the definition of "factor other than sex" remains somewhat murky. It does seem that pay differences for equal work can be justified for demonstrably business-related reasons. But what is and is not demonstrably business related has not yet been cataloged.

Reverse Discrimination

Several cases deal with the important issue of reverse discrimination against men when pay for women is adjusted. In these cases, men have claimed that they were paid less than women doing similar work, simply because they were men. In one case, the University of Nebraska created a model to calculate salaries based on estimated values for a faculty member's education, field of specialization, years of direct experience, years of related experience, and merit.[13] Based on these qualifications, the university granted raises to 33 women whose salaries were less than the amount computed by the model. However, the university gave no such increases to 92 males whose salaries were also below the amount the model set for them based on their qualifications. The court found this system a violation of the Equal Pay Act. It held that, in effect, the university was using a new system to determine a salary schedule, based on specific criteria. To refuse to pay employees of one sex the minimum required by these criteria was illegal.

---

[13] G. Luna, "Understanding Gender-Based Wage Discrimination: Legal Interpretation and Trends of Pay Equity in Higher Education," *Journal of Law & Education* 19, no. 3 (1990), pp. 371–84; Marcia L. Bellas, "Comparable Worth in Academia: The Effects on Faculty Salaries of the Sex Composition and Labor-Market Conditions of Academic Disciplines," *American Sociological Review,* December 1994, pp. 807–21.

So what does this have to do with compensation management? Viewed collectively, the courts have provided reasonably clear directions. The design of pay systems must incorporate a policy of equal pay for substantially equal work. The determination of substantially equal work must be based on the actual work performed (the job content) and must reflect the skill, effort, and responsibility required, and the working conditions. It is legal to pay men and women who perform substantially equal work differently if the pay system is designed to recognize differences in performance, seniority, quality and quantity of results, or certain factors other than sex, in a nondiscriminatory manner. Further, if a new pay system is designed, it must be equally applied to all employees.

But what does this tell us about discrimination on jobs that are *not substantially equal*—dissimilar jobs? Fifty-eight percent of all working women are not in substantially equal jobs as men, so they are not covered by the Equal Pay Act. Title VII of the Civil Rights Act extends protection to them.

The legality of giving preferences to members of one group in order to overcome the effects of historic discrimination against other members of that group continues to be a divisive issue in the United States. Many lawyers believe it is only a matter of time before cases on preferences reach the Supreme Court. You can track legal issues and read transcripts of Supreme Court decisions at **http://www.law.cornell.edu/**

TITLE VII OF THE CIVIL RIGHTS ACT OF 1964, CIVIL RIGHTS ACT OF 1991

Title VII prohibits discrimination on the basis of sex, race, color, religion, or national origin in any employment condition, including hiring, firing, promotion, transfer, compensation, and admission to training programs.[14] Title VII was amended in 1972 and 1978. The 1972 amendments strengthened enforcement and expanded coverage to include employees of government and educational institutions, as well as private employers of more than 15 persons. The pregnancy amendment of 1978 made it illegal to discriminate based on pregnancy, childbirth, or related conditions.

Title VII court cases have established two theories of discrimination behavior under Title VII: (1) disparate treatment and (2) disparate impact. Exhibit 17.5 contrasts the two theories.

Disparate Treatment Disparate or unequal treatment applies different standards to different employees: For example, asking women but not men if they planned to have children. The mere fact of unequal treatment may be taken as evidence of the employer's intention to discriminate.

---

[14] 29 U.S.C. § 206 (d) (1) (1970). Its coverage is broader, also. Employers, employment agencies, labor organizations, and training programs involving 15 or more employees and some 120,000 educational institutions fall under its jurisdictions.

EXHIBIT 17.5 Discriminatory Behavior

Disparate Treatment	*Disparate Impact*
1. Different standards for different individuals or groups.	1. Same standards have differing consequences.
2. Intent to discriminate may be inferred by behaviors.	2. Discrimination shown by general statistical impact; discriminatory intent need not be present.
3. Employer can justify actions by absence of discriminatory intent and exercise of reasonable business judgment.	3. Employer can justify pay differences through business necessity.

Disparate Impact Practices that have a differential *effect* on members of protected groups are illegal, unless the differences are work related. The major case that established this interpretation of Title VII is *Griggs v. Duke Power Co.,* which struck down employment tests and educational requirements that screened out a higher proportion of blacks than whites. Even though the practices were applied equally—both blacks and whites had to pass the tests—they were prohibited because (1) they had the consequence of excluding a protected group (blacks) disproportionately and (2) the tests were not related to the jobs in question.

Under disparate impact, whether or not the employer intended to discriminate is irrelevant. A personnel decision can, on its face, seem neutral, but if its results are unequal, the employer must demonstrate that the decision is work related.

The Civil Rights Act of 1991 reinforced the two standards of discrimination—disparate treatment and disparate impact. However, the two standards remain difficult to apply to pay issues, since pay differences are legal for dissimilar work. It is still not clear what constitutes pay discrimination in dissimilar jobs.

PAY DISCRIMINATION AND DISSIMILAR JOBS

In 1981, the Supreme Court, in *Gunther v. County of Washington*, determined that pay differences for dissimilar jobs may reflect discrimination. In this case, four jail matrons in Washington County, Oregon, claimed that their work was comparable to that performed by male guards. The matrons also were assigned clerical duties, because guarding the smaller number of female prisoners did not occupy all of the work time.

Lower courts refused to consider the matrons' charge of discrimination on the grounds that their evidence did not meet the equal work requirement of the Equal Pay Act. But the Supreme Court stated that a Title VII pay case was not bound by the definitions of equal work or the affirmative defenses of the Equal Pay Act, ruling that "to hold that sex-based wage discrimination violates Title VII only if it also violates the EPA would be denying relief to victims of discrimination who did not hold the same jobs as a higher paid man." (The case was returned to a lower court for additional evidence of discrimination, and was eventually settled out of court.)

Although the *Gunther* case established that charges of pay discrimination on dissimilar (not equal) jobs could be brought under Title VII, it did not consider what might constitute pay discrimination in dissimilar jobs under Title VII.

Examples include the pay rates for nurses versus tree trimmers or nurses versus sanitarians or even professors of nursing versus professors of business administration. But if jobs are dissimilar and if no pattern of discrimination in hiring, promotion, or other personnel decisions exists, then what constitutes pay discrimination? Courts have ruled the use of market data (external competitiveness) as well as the use of job evaluation (internal consistency).

Proof of Discrimination: Use of Market Data

In a landmark case regarding the use of market data, Denver nurse Mary Lemons claimed that her job, held predominantly by women, was illegally paid less than the city and county of Denver paid jobs held predominantly by men (tree trimmers, sign painters, tire servicemen, etc.). Lemons claimed that the nursing job required more education and skill. Therefore, to pay the male jobs more than the nurses' jobs simply because the male jobs commanded higher rates in the local labor market was discriminatory. She argued that the market reflected historical underpayment of "women's work."

The court disagreed. The situation identified by *Lemons*—pay differences in dissimilar jobs—did not by itself constitute proof of intent to discriminate.

In fact, the courts have continually upheld employers' use of market data to justify pay differences for different jobs. *Spaulding v. University of Washington* developed the argument in greatest detail. In this case, the predominantly female faculty members of the Department of Nursing claimed that they were illegally paid less than faculty in other departments. They presented a model of faculty pay comparisons in "comparable" departments that controlled for the effects of level of education, job tenure, and other factors. They asserted that any pay difference not accounted for in their model was discrimination.[15]

But the courts have been dubious of statistics. As the late Carl Sagan used to say, "Just because it's a light doesn't make it a spaceship." Far better to define discrimination directly, rather than concluding that it is "whatever is left." The judge in the Spaulding case criticized the statistical model presented, saying it "unrealistically assumed the equality of all master's degrees, ignored job experience prior to university employment, and ignored detailed analysis of day-to-day responsibilities." Without such data, "we have no meaningful way of determining just how much of the proposed wage differential was due to sex and how much was due to academic discipline." "Market prices," according to the judge, "are inherently job-related."[16]

---

[15] Orley Ashenfelter and Ronald Oaxaca, "The Economics of Discrimination: Economists Enter the Courtroom," *American Economic Review*, May 1987, pp. 321–25; Victor Fuchs, *Women's Quest for Economic Equality* (Cambridge, MA. Harvard University Press, 1988).

[16] Sara L. Rynes and George T. Milkovich, "Wage Surveys: Dispelling Some Myths about the 'Market Wage,'" *Personnel Psychology*, Spring 1986, pp. 71–90; Marlene Kim, "Employers' Estimates of Market Wages: Implications for Wage Discrimination," (Working paper, Rutgers University, 1998); and Marlene Kim, "Salary Surveys: Theory, Practice, and the Influence of Power," (Working Paper, Rutgers University, 1997).

Is There a "Market Policy"? We wish we had as much confidence in "the market" as the judge. As you recall from Chapter 8, a lot of judgment goes into the wage survey process. Which employers constitute the "relevant market"? Does the relevant market vary by occupation? Do different market definitions yield different wage patterns? Clearly, judgment is involved in answering these questions. Yet the courts have thus far neglected to examine those judgments for possible bias.

Proof of Discrimination: Jobs of "Comparable Worth"

A second approach to determining pay discrimination on jobs of dissimilar content hinges on finding a standard by which to compare the value of jobs. The standard must be two things. First, it must permit jobs with dissimilar content to be declared equal or "in some sense comparable."[17] Second, it must permit pay differences for dissimilar jobs that are not comparable. Job evaluation has been proposed as that standard.[18] If an employer's own job evaluation study shows jobs of dissimilar content to be of equal value to the employer, then isn't failure to pay them equally proof of intent to discriminate? That is the issue considered in *AFSCME v. State of Washington.*

The state of Washington commissioned a study of the concept of comparable worth (discussed later in this chapter) and its projected effect on the state's pay system. The study concluded that by basing wages on the external market, the state was paying women approximately 20 percent less than it was paying men in jobs deemed of comparable value to the state. The state took no action on this finding, alleging it could not afford to do so, so the American Federation of State, County, and Municipal Employees (AFSCME) sued to force implementation of a compensation system based on comparable worth as outlined in the study. The union alleged that since the state was aware of the adverse effect of its present policy, failure to change it constituted discrimination.

But an appeals court ruled that the state was not obligated to correct the disparity. An employer's merely being aware of adverse consequences for a protected group did not constitute discrimination. "Job evaluation studies and comparable worth statistics alone are insufficient to establish the requisite inference of discriminatory motive. . . The plaintiff must show the employer chose the particular policy because of its effect on members of the protected class."[19]

AFSCME v. State of Washington differs from previous cases that considered the use of market data in that it is the first case in which the evidence that the jobs were in any sense "equal" was developed by the employer. But even though the state had commis-

---

[17] B. F. Reskin and H. I. Hartmann, eds. *Women's Work, Men's Work: Segregation on the Job* (Washington, DC: National Academy Press, 1986).

[18] *Job Evaluation: A Tool for Pay Equity* (Washington, DC: National Committee on Pay Equity, November 1987); Sara L. Rynes, Caroline L. Weber, and George T. Milkovich, "The Effects of Market Survey Rates, Job Evaluation, and Job Gender on Job Pay," *Journal of Applied Psychology* 74, no. 1 (1989), pp. 114–23.

[19] Jerald Greenberg and Claire L. McCarty, "Comparable Worth: A Matter of Justice," in *Research in Personnel and Human Resources Management*, vol. 8, ed. K. M. Rowland and G. R. Ferris (Greenwich, CT: JAI Press, 1990); Clauda Goldin, *Understanding the Gender Gap* (New York: Oxford University Press, 1990).

sioned the study, it had not agreed to implement the study's results. Therefore, the employer had not, in the court's view, admitted that the jobs were equal or established a pay system that purported to pay on the basis of "comparable worth" rather than markets. Rather than appeal, the parties settled out of court. The state revamped its pay system and agreed to make more than $100 million in "pay equity" adjustments.

So where does this leave us? Clearly, Title VII prohibits intentional discrimination in compensation if it is based on sex or other proscribed factors, whether or not the employees in question hold the same or different jobs. Discrimination may be proved by direct evidence of an employer's intent (e.g., an overall pattern of behavior that demonstrates disparate treatment).

Title VII rulings make it clear that pay discrimination is not limited only to equal jobs; it may also occur in setting different rates for different jobs. It is also clear that the use of external market rates is not illegal. Consequently, simply demonstrating pay differences on jobs that are not equal is insufficient to prove discrimination.

What additional implications for the design and administration of pay systems can be drawn? These court decisions imply that pay differentials between dissimilar jobs will not be prohibited under Title VII if the differences can be shown to be based on the content of the work, its value to the organization's objectives, and the employer's ability to attract and retain employees in competitive external labor markets. The courts appear to recognize that "the value of a particular job to an employer is but one factor influencing the rate of compensation for a job."[20] Absent new legislation, comparable worth is *not* the law of the land.

THE EARNINGS GAP

According to the Bureau of Labor Statistics, white women working full time in 1996 had a median weekly wage equal to 75 percent of the weekly wage earned by white men. The ratio for African-American males was 73 percent, for African-American females and Hispanic males about 60 percent, and for Hispanic females 54 percent. Exhibit 17.6 shows how the wage gap has persisted over time. Although the size of the differences has fluctuated, it has been extremely persistent, and always to the advantage of white males.

Women of all races have enjoyed significant gains in a wide range of traditionally male-dominated jobs. In 1995, women accounted for 48 percent of managers and professionals—occupations that pay higher-than-average wages and generally require a college degree. Two decades earlier, they were only 35 percent.[21] However, in the late 1990s, the wage gap began to increase again. Does that mean discrimination is increasing? What do we know about why that gap exists?

---

[20] *American Federation of State, County, and Municipal Employees v. State of Washington*, 578 F. Supp. 846 (W.D. Wash. 1983).

[21] Francine D. Blau and Lawrence M. Kahn, "Swimming Upstream: Trends in the Gender Wage Differentials," *Journal of Labor Economics*, 15, 1, 1997, pp. 1–42.

Exhibit 17.6 Changes in the Wage Gap, 1979–1996: Median Weekly Earnings as Percent of White Male Earnings

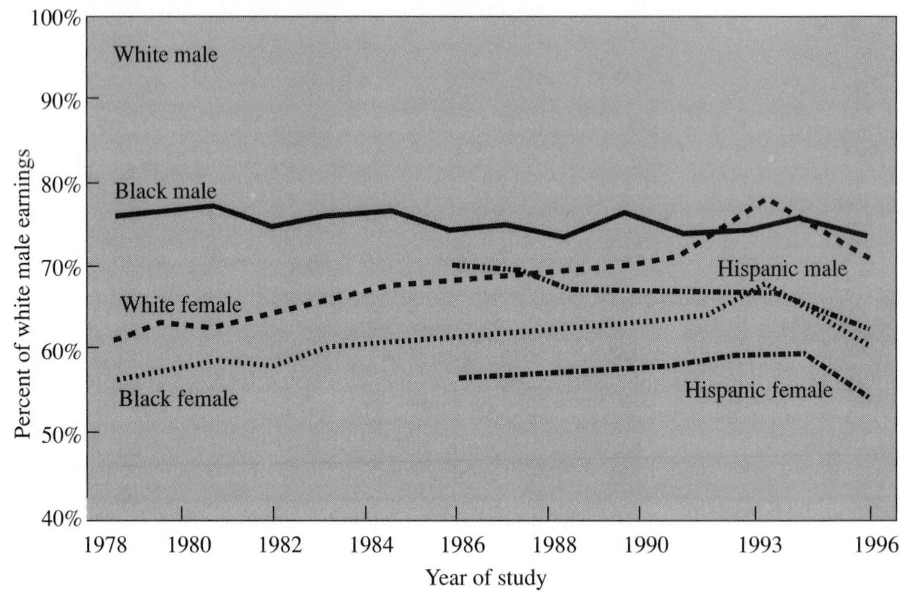

Source: U.S. Department of Labor, Bureau of Labor Statistics, Employment and Earnings (Washington, DC, January 1998).

Some of the more important factors, shown in Exhibit 17.7, include the following:

1. Differences in the occupational attainment and the jobs held by men and women.
2. Differences in personal work-related characteristics and work behaviors.
3. Differences among industries and firms.
4. Differences in union membership.
5. The presence of discrimination.

First let us examine some data, then some conflicting beliefs.

Differences in Occupational Attainment

One of the most important factors that accounts for much of the remaining gap is differences in jobs held by men and women. A variety of data illustrate these differences.

The Bureau of Labor Statistics reports that half of all working women in the United States are employed in only 20 percent of the 427 occupations. In addition, among the 427 occupational classes, 80 percent of women work in classes in which at least 70 percent of employees are women. Forty percent of Canadian women work in just 10 job

EXHIBIT 17.7 Possible Determinants of Pay Differences

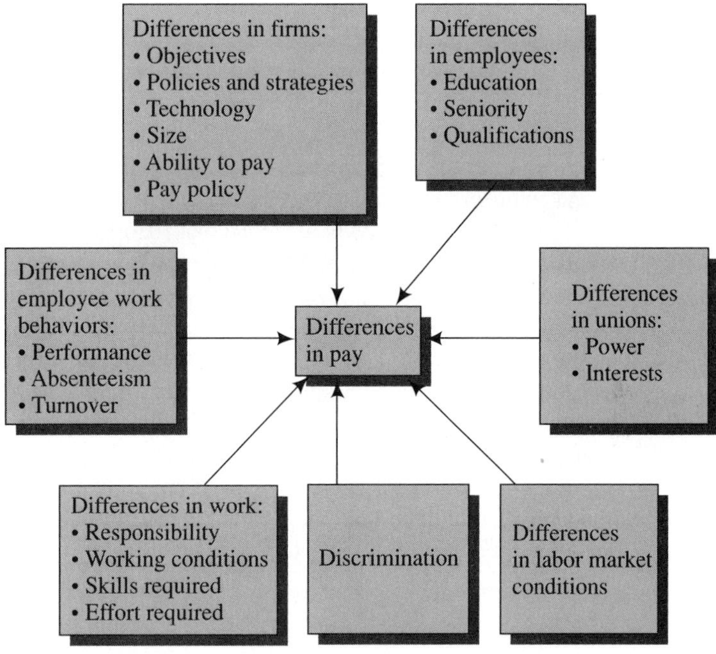

Source: George T. Milkovich, "The Emerging Debate," in *Comparable Worth: Issues and Alternatives,* ed. E. Robert Livernash (Washington, DC: Equal Employment Advisory Council, 1980).

categories. The difference in occupational attainment is the major factor accounting for the earnings gap.[22]

Recent data indicate that these occupational patterns are changing. Women are gaining access to a wider array of occupations. Those occupations with the biggest changes tend to be the ones that are growing the fastest. When a strong demand for employees exists, fewer barriers to women's entry exist. Both the wage gap and occupational segregation diminish.[23]

On the other hand, changing welfare regulations have meant an influx of poorly trained, low-skilled women into the labor force. Their employment in substantial numbers may increase both occupational segregation and the earnings gap until they acquire

[22] Linda Subich, Gerald Barrett, Dennis Doverspike, and Ralph Alexander , "The Effects of Sex Role-Related Factors on Occupational Choice and Salary," *Pay Equity: Empirical Inquiries* (Washington, DC: National Academy of Science, 1989); Randall K. Filer, "Occupational Segration, Compensating Differentials and Comparable Worth," *Pay Equity: Empirical Inquiries*; and Elaine Sorensen, "The Crowding Hypothesis and Comparable Worth," *Journal of Human Resources* 25, no. 1, pp. 55–89.

[23] Judith Fields and Edward Wolff, "The Decline of Sex Segregation and the Wage Gap, 1970–80," *Journal of Human Resources* 26, no. 4, pp. 608–22.

the skills and experience to move into more productive (and more highly paid) jobs. So future progress in reducing the gap will reflect two contradictory trends: the growing ranks of female college graduates, and the increased labor force participation of poorly educated women at the bottom of the income scale.[24]

Additionally, recent research concludes that a wave of women entering an occupation does not wash away problems. A study of women in science and engineering professions finds that even though they have already cleared the hurdles of misguided high school guidance counselors and/or lack of peer support or role models, women scientists and engineers are almost twice as likely to leave these occupations as males.[25]

Another study of M.B.A.s found that 10 to 15 years after receiving their degree, in addition to a pay gap there is also a gender-based chasm in such subjective measures as career satisfaction, boss appreciation, and feeling of discrimination.[26] Fully 46 percent of the women said they had experienced discrimination; only 9 percent of the men said they had. The most common problem women reported was that less qualified men were chosen for promotions over them. Additionally, they felt that discrimination has become more subtle and harder to prove. Clearly, many professional women and minorities believe they operate in less supportive work environments than their white male colleagues.[27]

Compensation systems are not self correcting. If no review and possible adjustment occurs, they will continue to perpetuate undervaluation of the work performed by minorities and women. This is part of the reason that the wage gap narrows so slowly.

Differences in Personal Work-Related Characteristics

Differences in employee attributes and behaviors help explain part of the earnings gap. Work-related differences include experience and seniority within a firm, continuous time in the work force, education, and the like. Personal characteristics of questionable work-relatedness include obesity and beauty. Yet empirical studies have found both of these factors related to pay differences.[28] Plain people earn less than average-looking people, who earn less than the good-looking. The "plainness penalty" is 5 to 10 percent.

Experience and Seniority. Consider experience and seniority differences among full-time workers. On average, men work 6 percent more hours per week than women. By the time men and women have been out of school for 6 years, women on average have worked 1.6 years, or 30 percent less than men. After 16 years out of school, women

---

[24] Fran D. Blau, Marianne A. Farber, and Ann E. Winkler, *The Economics of Women, Men, and Work* 3rd ed. (Simon and Schuster, 1998).

[25] Anne E. Preston, "Why Have All the Women Gone? A Study of Exit of Women from the Science and Engineering Professions," *American Economic Review*, December 1994, pp. 1446–62.

[26] Joy A. Schneer and Frieda Reitman, "The Importance of Gender in Mid-Career: A Longitudinal Study of MBAs," *Journal of Organizational Behavior* 15 (1994), pp. 199–207.

[27] Alison M. Konrad and Kathy Cannings, "Of Mommy Tracks and Glass Ceilings: A Case Study of Men's and Women's Careers in Management," *Relations Industrielles* 49, no. 2 (1994), pp. 303–33.

[28] Daniel S. Hamermesh and Jeff E. Biddle, "Beauty and the Labor Market," *The American Economic Review*, December 1994, pp. 1174–94; Susan Averett and Sanders Korenman, "The Economic Reality of 'The Beauty Myth' " (Working paper, Nationl Bureau of Economic Research 1993).

average half as much labor market experience as men.[29] But these patterns are changing and are likely to continue to change.

Education. Currently, men and women graduate from college in nearly equal numbers. However, they tend to choose different majors. And college major is the strongest factor affecting income of college graduates.[30]

In a study of middle-aged law school grads, the women lawyers did work fewer hours—about 91 percent as long as men.[31] But they were paid substantially (not proportionately) less; they earned only 61 percent of what men earned. Even with differences in work history accounted for, male lawyers continue to enjoy a considerable earnings advantage as well as a higher rate of growth earnings.

Combining Factors. Although many researchers studied the effects of differences in jobs and occupations and personal characteristics such as experience and education, few studies have looked at their effects on pay differences *over time*. One study controlled for education degree, college major, and prior experience. Males had a 12 percent *higher* starting salary than females. Among college graduates, college major was a key determinant of gender differences in starting salaries. When all the variables were included, the current salary differential among male college graduates and female college graduates was less than 3 percent. The implication is that women received greater pay increases after they were hired than men did, but differences in starting salary remain important and persistent contributors to gender-related pay differences.[32]

Differences in Industries and Firms

Other factors affecting earnings differences between men and women are the industry and the firms in which they are employed. There is some evidence that within the same occupations, industries that employ higher percentages of women (e.g., retail, insurance) tend to pay a lower average wage than those firms in industries employing higher percentages of men. In other words, office and clerical workers, most likely women, tend to be paid less in retailing than in manufacturing or chemicals.

Differences in the firm's compensation policies and objectives within a specific industry is another factor that accounts for some of the earnings gap. As noted in Chapters 7 and 8, some firms within an industry adopt pay strategies that place them among the leaders in their industry; other firms adopt policies that may offer more employment

---

[29] Fuchs, *Women's Quest for Economic Equality.*

[30] Francine Blau and Marianne Ferber, "Career Plans and Expectations of Young Women and Men," *Journal of Human Resources* 26 no. 4, pp. 581–607; Estelle James, N. Absalam, J. Conaty, and Duc-le To, "College Quality and Future Earnings." (Working Paper, Department of Economics, SUNY Stony Brook, Stony Brook, NY, 1989).

[31] Robert G. Wood, Mary E. Corcoran, and Paul N. Courant, "Pay Differences among the Highly Paid: The Male-Female Earnings Gap in Lawyers' Salaries," *Journal of Labor Economics* 11, no. 3 (1993), pp. 417–41.

[32] Barry A. Gerhart and George T. Milkovich, "Salaries, Salary Growth, and Promotions of Men and Women in a Large, Private Firm," *Pay Equity: Empirical Inquiries.*

security coupled with bonuses and gain-sharing schemes. The issue here is whether *within an industry* some firms are more likely to employ women than other firms and whether that likelihood leads to earnings differences.

Within a firm, differences in policies for different jobs may even exist. For example, many firms tie pay for secretaries to the pay for the manager to which the secretary is assigned. The rationale is that the secretary and the manager function as a team. When the manager gets promoted, the secretary also takes on additional responsibilities and therefore also gets a raise. However, this traditional approach breaks down when layers of management are cut. In 1995, IBM announced pay cuts of up to 36 percent for secretaries who had been assigned to managerial levels that no longer existed. IBM justified the cuts by saying the rates were way above the market. Prior to the reduction, the highest base salary for a senior executive secretary was $70,000 plus overtime.[33]

We also know that the size of a firm is systematically related to differences in wages. Female employment is more heavily concentrated in small firms. Wages of men in large firms are 54 percent higher than wages of men in small firms. That gap was only 37 percent for women in small versus large firms. The study of middle-aged lawyers revealed large sex differences in job setting. Men were much more likely than women to be in private practice, and they were twice as likely to practice in large firms (over 50 lawyers). Clearly, these differences are related to pay: the most highly paid legal positions are in private practice law firms, and the larger the law firm, the greater is the average rate of pay.

In contrast, men are much *less* likely than the women to be in the relatively low-paying areas of government and legal services. Other studies report that employees in some jobs can get about a 20 percent pay increase simply by switching industries in the same geographic area while performing basically similar jobs.[34]

To the extent that these differences in job setting are the result of an individual's preference or disposition, they are not evidence of discrimination. To the extent that these differences are the result of industry and firm practices that steer women and minorities into certain occupations and industries, or lower-paying parts of a profession, they may reflect discrimination. At the minimum, they require thoughtful exploration.

Differences in Contingent Pay

Recently, a new and interesting approach was used to examine the gender earnings differential. Total pay was divided into base pay and contingent pay that varies with job performance. After controlling for individual characteristics (e.g., education and experience), occupation, and job level, approximately 34 percent of the unexplained pay gap

---

[33] Laurie Hays, "IBM Plans to Slash Secretaries' Salaries in Sweeping Review," *The Wall Street Journal,* May 18, 1995, pp. A3, A7.

[34] Reuben Gronau, "Sex-Related Wage Differentials and Women's Interrupted Labor Careers—the Chicken or the Egg," *Journal of Labor Economics* 6, no. 31 (1988), pp. 277–301; Barry Gerhart and Nabil El Cheikh, "Earnings and Percentage Female: A Longitudinal Study" (Working Paper 89–04, Center for Advanced Human Resource Studies, Cornell University).

was due to gender differences in performance-based pay.[35] If these differences occur *within* a firm, several possible explanations exist. Perhaps firms are not offering men and women equal opportunities to earn contingent pay; perhaps men and women are treated differently in the evaluations used to determine contingent pay; perhaps men and women differ substantially on performance.

However, if the differences are *across* firms, then perhaps women prefer less pay risk and choose those occupations and firms with less variable pay. While their sample size did not permit the authors to say if the differences were within or across firms, if the pay gap is the result of the way people select their occupations and employers, then we need to understand how pay practices influence those choices.

Differences in Union Membership

Finally, we also know that belonging to a union will affect differences in earnings. Belonging to a union in the public sector seems to raise female wages more than it raises male wages. Little research has been devoted to studying the gender effect of union membership in the private sector.

Presence of Discrimination

So we know that many factors affect pay; discrimination may possibly be one of them.[36] But we are not in agreement as to what constitutes evidence of discrimination. Although the earnings gap is the most frequently cited example, closer inspection reveals the weaknesses in this statistic. Unfortunately, many studies of the earnings gap have little relevance to understanding discrimination in pay-setting practices.

Some studies use aggregated data, for instance treating all bachelor's degrees as the same, or defining an occupation incorrectly (e.g., the U.S. Department of Labor categorizes Michael Jordan as well as the basketball game timekeeper in the same occupation—"sports professional").

Another problem is that mere possession of a qualification or skill does not mean it is work related. Examples of cab drivers, secretaries, and house painters with college degrees are numerous, depending on the overall economic conditions.

A standard statistical approach for determining whether discrimination explains part of the gap is to try to relate pay differences to the factors just discussed above (e.g., occupation, type of work, experience, education, and the like). The procedure typically used is to regress some measure of earnings on those factors thought to legitimately influence

---

[35] Keith W. Chauvin and Ronald A. Ash, "Gender Earning Differentials in Total Pay, Base Pay, and Contingent Pay," *Industrial and Labor Relations Review*, July 1994, pp. 634–49.

[36] Donald J. Treiman and H. J. Hartmann, eds., *Women, Work and Wages* (Washington, DC: National Academy Press, 1981); James P. Gander, "Gender-Based Faculty-Pay Differences in Academe: A Reduced-Form Approach," *Journal of Labor Research*, Summer 1997, pp. 451–461; Gregory Attiyeh and Richard Attiyeh, "Testing for Bias in Graduate School Admissions," *Journal of Human Resources* 32, no. 3, pp. 524–548.

earnings. If the average wage of men with a given set of values for these factors is significantly different from the average wage of women with equal factors, then the standard statistical approach is to interpret the residual portion of the gap as discrimination.

Unfortunately, in a sample limited to white males, such an approach explained only 60 to 70 percent of their earnings. So statistical studies, by themselves, are not sufficient evidence.[37] Nevertheless, a recent study using this approach arrived at a ratio of women's to men's wages of 88 percent in data from 1988, a year in which the Bureau of the Census reported a 70 pecent ratio.[38]

On the other hand, even if legitimate factors fully explain pay differences between men and women, discrimination still could have occurred. First, the factors themselves may be tainted by discrimination. For example, past discrimination against women in the admission to engineering schools may have affected their earnings. Or women may be better qualified on some factors that were omitted in the analysis.

In sum, statistical analysis needs to be treated as part of a pattern of evidence and needs to reflect the wage behaviors of specific firms. As one reviewer has written, "It is not the quantity of studies that is lacking; it is the quality."[39]

COMPARABLE WORTH

Why are jobs held predominantly by women, almost without exception, paid less than jobs held predominantly by men? Do job evaluation systems give adequate recognition to job-related contributions in those jobs held primarily by women? The state of Washington conducted a study that concluded that the job of a licensed practical nurse required skill, effort, and responsibility equal to that of a campus police officer. The state paid the licensed practical nurse, on average, $739 a month. The campus police officer was paid, on average, $1,070 a month. These salary differences were not related to productivity-related job content characteristics included in the study.[40]

It is this type of wage difference (e.g., nurses' versus police officers' wages) that is controversial. The notion of comparable worth says that if jobs require comparable skill, effort, and responsibility, the pay must be comparable, no matter how dissimilar the job content may be.

---

[37] "Avoiding the Courtroom: Legal Strategies in Compensation," ed. L. Bennett, special issue of *Compensation and Benefits Review* July–August 1996.

[38] June O'Neill and Solomon Polachek, "Why the Gender Gap in Wages Narrowed in the 1980s," *Journal of Labor Economics* 11, no. 1 (1993), pp. 205–28; Francine Blau and Lawrence Kahn, "The Impact of Wage Structure on Trends in U.S. Gender Wage Differentials: 1975–87" (Working Paper no. 4748, National Bureau of Economic Research, May 1994).

[39] Donald P. Schwab, "Using Job Evaluation to Obtain Pay Equity," in *Comparable Worth: Issue for the 80's,* vol. 1.

[40] Sharon Toffey Shepela and Ann T. Viviano, "Some Psychological Factors Affecting Job Segregation and Wages," in *Comparable Worth and Wage Discrimination*, ed. H. Remick (Philadelphia: Temple University Press, 1984); Helen Remick, "Beyond Equal Pay for Equal Work: Comparable Worth in the State of Washington," in *Equal Employment Policy for Women*, ed. Ronnie Steinberg-Ratner (Philadelphia: Temple University Press, 1980), pp. 405–48.

Comparable worth has been debated off and on since World War II. Proponents continue to lobby for either new legislation or voluntary action on the part of employers that would include the comparable worth standard. Most of this political activity is occurring in state and local governments. Almost half the states have considered "pay equity adjustments" for state civil service employees. Over half of all women in the workforce are employed in the public sector.

The Mechanics

Establishing a comparable worth plan typically involves the following four basic steps:

1. *Adopt a single job evaluation plan for all jobs within a unit.* If employees are unionized, separate plans can be prepared for each bargaining unit and take precedence over previous agreements. The key to a comparable worth system is a single job evaluation plan for jobs with dissimilar content.
2. *All jobs with equal job evaluation results should be paid the same.* Although each factor in the job evaluation may not be equal, if the total points are equal, the wage rates must also be equal.
3. *Identify general representation (percentage male and female employees) in each job group.* A job group is all positions with similar duties and responsibilities, requires similar qualifications, is filled by similar recruiting procedures, and is paid under the same pay schedule. Typically, a female-dominated job class is defined as 60 percent or more female incumbents; a male-dominated job class has 70 percent or more male incumbents.
4. *The wage-to-job evaluation point ratio should be based on the wages paid for male-dominated jobs* since they are presumed to be free of pay discrimination.

These steps are based on the state of Minnesota's law that mandates comparable worth for all public sector employees (e.g., the state, cities, school districts, libraries).

To understand the mechanics more clearly, consider Exhibit 17.8. The solid dots represent jobs held predominantly by women (i.e., female representation greater than or equal to 60 percent). The circles represent jobs held predominantly by men (i.e., greater than or equal to 70 percent men). The policy line (solid) for the women's jobs is below and less than the policy line for men's jobs (dotted line). A comparable worth policy would use the results of the single job evaluation plan and price all jobs as if they were male-dominated jobs (dotted line). Thus, all jobs with 100 job points would receive $600, all those with 200 points would receive $800, and so on.

Market rates for male-dominated jobs would be used to convert the job evaluation points to salaries. The point-to-salaries ratio of male-dominated jobs is then applied to female-dominated jobs.

However, a mandated job evaluation approach that specifies a hierarchy of jobs seems counter to the direction that most organizations are moving today. A partner of Hay Associates observed:

> We, ourselves, do not know of a single case where a large and diverse organization in the private sector concluded that a single job evaluation method, with the same

EXHIBIT 17.8 Job Evaluation Points and Salary

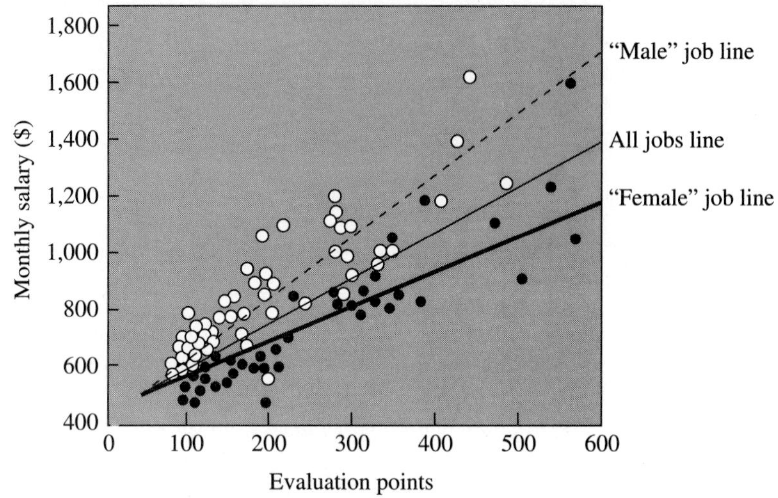

● Female-dominated jobs.
○ Male-dominated jobs.

compensable factors and weightings, was appropriate for its factory, office, professional, management, technical, and executive personnel in all profit center divisions and all staff departments.[41]

People who advocate job evaluation as a vehicle for comparable worth credit the technique with more explanatory power than it possesses.

Union Developments

The amount of union support for comparable worth appears to be related to its effects on the union's membership. AFSCME and the Communication Workers of America (CWA) actively support comparable worth and have negotiated comparable worth-based pay increases, lobbied for legislation, filed legal suits, and attempted to educate their members and the public about comparable worth.

The public sector faces little competition for its services and is frequently better able to absorb a wage increase, since public employees are in a better position to pressure lawmakers than are taxpayers.[42] This probably accounts for the relative success of

[41] Alvin O. Bellak, "Comparable Worth: A Practitioner's View," in *Comparable Worth: Issue for the 80's*, vol. 1.

[42] June O'Neill, Michael Brien, and James Cunningham, "Effect of Comparable Worth Policy: Evidence from Washington State," *American Economic Association Papers and Proceedings*, May 1989, pp. 305–9.

public employees' unions in bargaining comparable worth pay adjustments. But trade-offs between higher wages and fewer jobs make unions in industries facing stiff foreign competition (e.g., International Ladies' Garment Workers' Union and the United Steel Workers) reluctant to aggressively support comparable worth. The beauty of "equity adjustments," from a union's perspective, is that because they are a separate budget item, they do not appear to come at the expense of overall pay increases for all union members. Collective bargaining has produced more comparable worth pay increases than any other approach.

A PROACTIVE APPROACH

Compliance with laws and regulations can be a constraint and/or an opportunity for a compensation manager. The regulatory environment certainly constrains the decisions that can be made. Once laws are passed and regulations published, employers must comply. But a proactive compensation manager can influence the nature of regulations and their interpretation. Astute professionals must be aware of legislative and judicial currents to protect both employers' and employees' interests, and to ensure that compensation practices conform to judicial interpretation.

How can a compensation manager best undertake these efforts? First, join professional associations to stay informed on emerging issues and to act in concert to inform and influence public and legislative opinion. Second, constantly review compensation practices and the results of their applications. The equitable treatment of all employees is the goal of a good pay system, and that is that same goal of legislation. When interpretations of equitable treatment differ, informed public discussion is required. Such discussion cannot occur without the input of informed compensation managers.

Summary

Governments around the world play varying roles in the workplace. Legislation in any society reflects people's expectations about the role of government. Beyond direct regulation, government affects compensation through policies and purchases that affect supply and demand for labor.

In the United States, legislation reflects the changing nature of work and the workforce. In the 1930s, legislation was concerned with correcting the harsh conditions and arbitrary treatment facing employees, including children. In the 1960s, legislation turned to the issue of equal rights. Such legislation has had a profound impact on all of U.S. society. Nevertheless, discrimination in the workplace, including pay discrimination, remains an unresolved issue.

Pay discrimination laws require special attention for several reasons. First, these laws regulate the design and administration of pay systems. Second, the definition of pay discrimination, and thus the approaches used to defend pay practices, are in a state of flux. Many of the provisions of these laws simply require sound pay practices that should have been employed in the first place. And sound practices are those with three basic features:

1. They are work related.
2. They are related to the mission of the enterprise.
3. They include an appeals process for employees who disagree with the results.

Achieving compliance with these laws rests in large measure on the shoulders of compensation managers. It is their responsibility to ensure that the pay system is properly designed and managed.

Should comparable worth be legally mandated? Not surprisingly, opinions vary. But how much, if any, comparable worth policy will diminish the earnings differential remains an unanswered question. The earnings differential is attributable to many factors. Discrimination, whether it be access or valuation, is but one factor. Others include market force, industry and employer differences, and union bargaining priorities. Compensation managers need to examine critically traditional pay practices to ensure that they are complying with regulations. Certainly, the focus needs to be on pay discrimination.

Is all this detail on interpretation of pay discrimination really necessary? Yes. Without understanding the interpretation of pay discrimination legislation, compensation managers risk violating the law, exposing their employers to considerable liability and expense, and lose the confidence and respect of all employees when a few are forced to turn to the courts to gain nondiscriminatory treatment.

Review Questions

1. What is the nature of government's role in compensation?
2. Explain why changes in minimum wage can affect higher-paid employees as well.
3. What is the difference between access discrimination and valuation discrimination?
4. Consider contemporary practices such as skill/competency-based plans, broadbanding, market pricing, and pay-for-performance plans. Discuss how they may affect the pay discrimination debate.
5. What factors help account for the pay gap?
6. What kinds of proactive activities can an employer undertake to enhance the regulatory environment?
7. Could the pay objective of regulatory compliance ever conflict with other objectives? Could it conflict with the employer's notion of consistency or competitiveness? An employee's notion of equity? If so, how would you deal with such situations?

YOUR TURN

LEVI STRAUSS

Levi Strauss uses contractors around the world to produce its popular jeans. In 1992, Levi Strauss established operating guidelines that detail everything from environmental requirements to health and safety issues. To implement the guidelines, Levi Strauss audited its contractors and discovered that two contractors in Bangladesh were using workers in the factories who appeared to be underage. International standards have set a reasonable working age at 14. When the company brought it to the attention of the factory owners, the owners turned it back to ask Levi Strauss what it wanted the factory to do. There were no birth certificates so there was no way to know exactly how old these children were. Also, even if the children were younger than 14, they would very likely be a significant contributor to the family income and probably would be forced into other ways of making a living that would be more inhumane than working in a factory, such as prostitution or begging.

What should Levi Strauss recommend to the subcontractor?

YOUR TURN

WAYZATA POLICE OFFICERS

Background

The following information is based on an actual arbitration case in Wayzata, Minnesota. The parties to the case are the city of Wayzata and the Law Enforcement Union, which represents police officers.

The union requests a 5 percent increase in each of the two years of the contract. It bases its proposal on wage comparisons with police departments in Wayzata's geographic district and with other cities that are demographically comparable, that is, as wealthy as Wayzata. These market comparisons justify the union's salary request.

The city proposes a wage freeze in order to comply with Minnesota's comparable worth legislation, which downgrades the use of market rates. However, the legislation says that any arbitrator award should not exceed the 3.25 percent already granted to the public works employees.

Much of the debate centers around the comparable worth law, which states:

1. Every political subdivision shall establish equitable compensation relationships between female-dominated, male-dominated, and balanced classes of employees.

2. The arbitrator shall consider those compensation relationships, job evaluation studies, any employee objections to those studies, and any other standards appropriate to the arbitration.

3. The relationships shall be equitable if

a. The compensation for positions that require comparable skill, effort, responsibility, working conditions, and other relevant work-related criteria is comparable.

b. The compensation for positions that require differing skill, effort, responsibility, working conditions, and other relevant work-related criteria is proportional to the skill, effort, responsibility, working conditions, and other relevant work-related criteria required.

Additional Information

1. Wayzata uses a quantitative job analysis system to support its job evaluation.

2. The dots on Exhibit 1 show the ratios for job evaluation points to wages for a number of jobs in Wayzata's system. The ratio for police officers is extremely high.

3. The lines on Exhibit 1 show a market line generated using regression analysis. Two additional lines show 90 percent of the market and 110 percent of the market.

4. The job of patrol officer is male dominated.

5. The CPI increased by 3 percent last year and is projected to increase by a smaller rate next year.

Discussion

Divide the class into thirds. One-third is the union team and presents the union arguments. One-third presents the city's position. The final third of the class makes up the arbitration panel that issues a decision.

Issues for the Union

1. Evaluate the usefulness of job evaluation for the job of police officer. Do not focus on Wayzata's particular system; rather, focus on quantitative job evaluation per se and whether it can really "measure" a wide range of jobs.

2. Justify the high points/dollars ratio for police officers. What do these ratios mean?

3. Justify your market comparisons with other police departments.

Issues for the City

1. How do you respond to criticisms of quantitative job evaluation as applied to the police officers' job?

2. Is the city's financial condition relevant?

3. How should the market data be handled? What are relevant comparisons?

Issues for the Arbitrator

As the arbitrator, you have the legal duty to decide how to weight the usefulness of the job evaluation system against the legislative intent of comparable worth. What conclusions might the legislation lead you to in terms of relevance of market data for determining compensation relationships? What types of data might constitute "other standards" appropriate to interest arbitration? How will your decision about police officers' wages impact the wages of female-dominated professions valued comparably? Should police officers receive awards greater than those for comparable jobs outside law enforcement? Should the financial burden to the city of raising wages for female-dominated classes be a consideration in your decision about police officers' wages? Does the projected rise in price levels as indicated by the CPI make a difference?

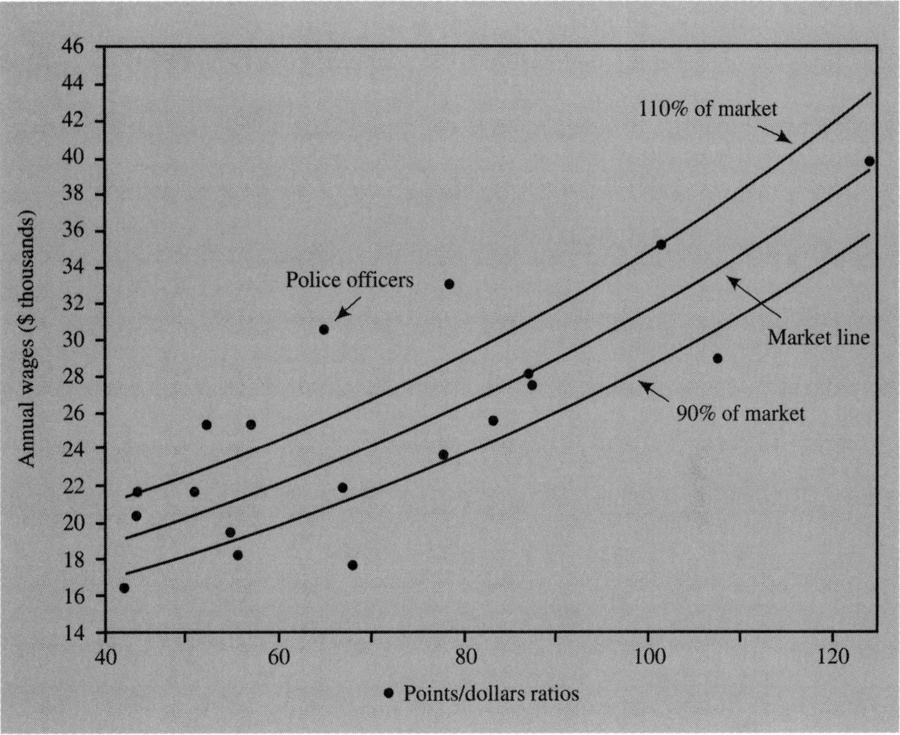

Annual wages ($ thousands)
46
44
42
40
38
36
34
32
30
28
26
24
22
20
18
16
14
40
60
80
100
120
110% of market
Police officers
Market line
90% of market
• Points/dollars ratios

CHAPTER 18

Budgets and Administration

Chapter Outline

John Russell, former American Compensation Association Board member, was approached by his Missouri community to develop a salary plan for the city. He worked on it diligently and submitted the plan.

Subsequently, he decided to run for the position of alderman on the city council and was elected. His salary program was then brought before the council for a vote. Mr. Russell voted against his own program. He explained his behavior by commenting, "I never realized how tight the budget was!"

Today, managers of compensation should not share Mr. Russell's dilemma. They are business partners. The financial status of the organization, the competitive pressures it faces, and budgeting are integral to managing compensation. The cost implications of decisions such as updating the pay structure, merit increases, or gain-sharing proposals are critical for making sound decisions. Consequently, budgets are an important part of managing compensation: they are also part of managing human resources and the total organization.[1]

Creating a compensation budget involves trade-offs among the basic pay policies—how much of the increase in external market rates should be budgeted according to employee contributions to the organization's success compared to automatic across-the-board increases. Trade-offs also occur over short- versus long-term incentives, over pay increases contingent on performance versus seniority, and over direct pay (cash) compared to benefits. Budgeting also involves trade-offs between how much to emphasize compensation compared to other aspects of human resource management.

Managers must decide the financial resources to deploy toward compensation compared to staffing (e.g., work force size and job security) compared to training (e.g., work force skills) and so on. The human resource budget implicitly reflects the organization's human resource strategies; it becomes an important part of the human resource plan. Finally, budgeting in the total organization involves allocating financial resources to human resources and/or technology, capital improvements, and the like. So from the perspective of a member of the city council, John Russell ended up making different resource allocation decisions than he might have made from the perspective of the compensation manager. Today's managers of compensation need to demonstrate how compensation decisions help achieve organization success while treating employees fairly.

How the pay systems are used by managers involves the administration of pay.

---

[1] Robert H. Meehan, "Analyzing Compensation Program Costs," in *Compensation Guide*, ed. William Caldwell (Boston, MA: Warren Gorham and Lamont, 1994); Michael Guthman, "Managing Total Labor Costs," *Compensation and Benefits Review*, November–December 1991, pp. 52–60.

ADMINISTRATION AND THE PAY MODEL

Consider making pay decisions without a formal system. Under such an arrangement, each manager would have total flexibility to pay whatever seemed to work at the moment. Total decentralization of compensation decision making, carried to a ridiculous extreme, would result in a chaotic array of rates. Employees could be treated inconsistently and unfairly. Managers would use pay to motivate behaviors that achieved their own objectives, not necessarily those of the overall organization.

This was the situation at the beginning of this century, where the "contract system" set up highly skilled workers as managers as well as workers. The employer agreed to provide the "contractor" with floor space, light, power, and the necessary raw or semi-finished materials. The contractor both hired and paid labor. Bethlehem Steel operated under such a contract system. Skilled workers and plant captains had wide discretion; pay inconsistencies for the same work were common. Some contractors demanded kick-backs from employees' pay checks; many hired their relatives and friends. Dissatisfaction and grievances became widespread, resulting in legislation and an increased interest in unions.

Lest we pass the contract system off as ancient history dredged up by overzealous compensation professors, read on. Some contemporary experts at the end of the century are promoting network organizations such as Benetton and Apple Computer, which rely on networks of independent parties to perform the essential functions of their businesses. Networking is linked to the concept of outsourcing. *Outsourcing* means that organizations secure a growing range of services and supplies from independent, external vendors. Ultimately, some see outsourcing driven to its logical extreme as a network of individual contractors or small teams. "All individual workers will be self-employed business units."[2] Look back to the turn of the century, replace the term *contract system* with *outsourcing*, and the contemporary similarities emerge. Will dissatisfaction, unfair treatment, cost sharing, and risk shifting to employees again be the result?

To avoid this result, any management system, including the compensation system, needs to be goal directed. Compensation is managed to achieve the three pay model objectives: efficiency, equity, and compliance. Properly designed pay techniques help managers achieve these objectives. Rather than goal-directed tools, however, pay systems often degenerate into bureaucratic burdens or blindly follow the fads and fashions of the day. Techniques become ends in themselves rather than focusing on objectives. Operating managers may complain that pay techniques are more a hindrance than a help, and these managers are frequently correct. So any discussion of administration must again raise the questions: What does this technique do for us? How does it help us better achieve our objectives? Are employees fairly treated? Although it is possible to design a system that includes internal consistency, external competitiveness, and employee contributions, the system will not achieve its objectives without competent administration.

---

[2] "The New World of Work," and "Sixty-Five Years of Work in America," *Business Week*, October 17, 1994, pp. 76–148; Richard Huber, "How Continental Bank Outsourced its Crowned Jewels," *Harvard Business Review*, January–February 1993, pp. 121–29.

EXHIBIT 18.1 Managing Labor Costs

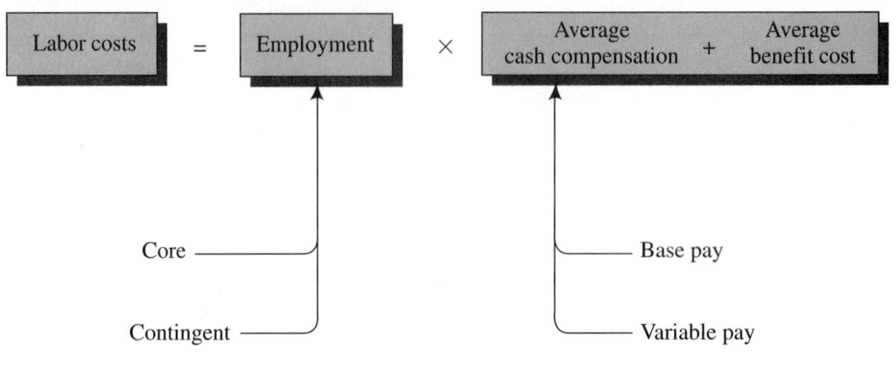

Although many pay administration issues have been discussed throughout the book, a few remain to be called out explicitly. Therefore, this chapter covers a variety of compensation administration issues, including (1) managing labor costs, (2) variable pay as a cost control, (3) inherent controls, (4) communication, and (5) structuring the compensation function.

MANAGING LABOR COSTS

You already know many of the factors that affect labor costs. As shown in Exhibit 18.1,

$$\text{Labor costs} = \text{Employment} \times \left(\begin{matrix}\text{Average cash}\\\text{compensation}\end{matrix} + \begin{matrix}\text{Average benefit}\\\text{cost}\end{matrix}\right)$$

Using this model, there are three main factors to control in order to manage labor costs: employment (e.g., number of employees and the hours they work), average cash compensation (e.g., wages, bonuses), and average benefit costs (e.g., health and life insurance, pensions). The cash and benefits factors are this book's focus. However, if our objective is to better manage labor costs, it should be clear that all three factors need attention. Controlling benefit costs were discussed at length in Chapters 12 and 13. Here we concentrate on controlling employment and the average salary.

Controlling Employment: Head Count and Hours

Managing the number of employees (head count) and/or the hours worked is the most obvious and perhaps most common approach to managing labor costs. Obviously, paying the same to fewer employees is less expensive.

There is some evidence that announcement of layoffs and plant closings have favorable effects on stock prices because the stock market reacts positively to events designed to improve cash flow and control costs. However, other evidence suggests that the adverse effects of work force reduction, such as loss of trained employees and

EXHIBIT 18.2 Core and Contingent Employees

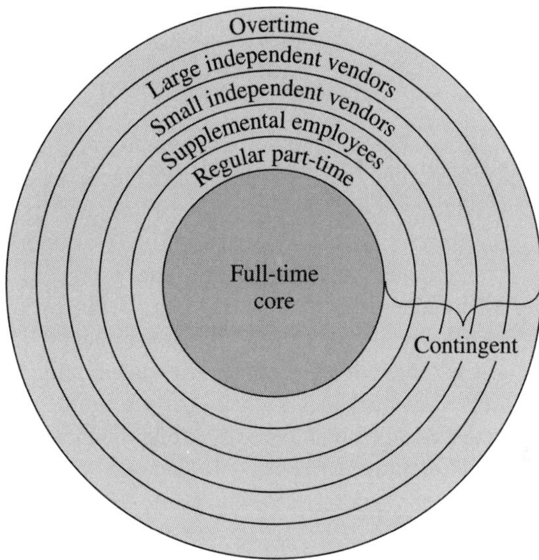

unrealized productivity, often causes the financial gains of the reductions to be less than anticipated.[3]

To manage labor costs better, many employers attempt to buffer themselves and employees by establishing different relationships with different groups of employees. As Exhibit 18.2 depicts, the two groups are commonly referred to as *core employees*, with whom a strong and long-term relationship is desired, and *contingent workers*, whose employment agreements may cover only short, specific time periods.[4] Rather than expand/contract the core work force, many employers achieve flexibility and control labor costs by expanding/contracting the contingent work force.[5] Hence, the fixed portion of labor costs becomes smaller and the variable portion longer. And one can expand/contract the variable portion more easily than the core.

---

[3]K. P. DeMeuse, P. A. Vanderheiden, and T. J. Bergmann, "Announced Layoffs: Their Effect on Corporate Financial Performance," *Human Resource Management* 33, no. 4 (1994), pp. 509–30; W. F. Cascio, "Downsizing: What Do We Know? What Have We Learned?" *Academy of Management Executive* 7, no. 1 (1993), pp. 95–104; Max Aquilera-Hellweg, "Getting Beyond Downsizing," *Fortune*, January 10, 1994, pp. 58–63.

[4]A. E. Polivka, "Contingent and Alternative Work Arrangements, Defined," *Monthly Labor Review*, October 1996, pp. 3–9; E. A. Lenz, "Flexible Employment: Positive Work Strategies for the 21st Century," *Journal of Labor Research* XVII, no. 4 (1996), pp. 555–65.

[5]Janet H. Marler, George T. Milkovich, and Melissa Barringer, "Boundaryless Organizations and Boundaryless Careers: A New Market for High-Skilled Temporary Work," (Ithaca, New York: Center for Advanced Human Resource Studies working paper #98-01, 1998); P. S. Tolbert, "Occupations, Organizations, and Boundaryless Careers," In *Boundaryless Careers*, ed. M. Arthur & D. M. Rousseau (pp. 331–349). (New York: Oxford University Press, 1996).

Contingent workers, as we discussed in Chapter 14, have many and varied compensation packages. It is common to pay more cash (base) but no benefits. Hence, contractors tend to be less expensive. So in the labor cost model, contingent workers' average salary may be greater, but there may be no additional benefits, which can run one-third or more of total compensation costs.[6]

Hours. Rather than defining employment in terms of number of employees, hours of work is often used. For nonexempt employees, hours over 40 per week are more expensive (1.5 × regular wage). Hence, another approach to managing labor costs is to examine overtime hours versus adding to the work force.

Note that the three factors—employment, cash compensation, and benefits costs—are not independent. Overtime hours require higher wages, but avoid the benefits cost of hiring a new employee. Other examples of interdependence are the apparent lower wages (and lack of benefits) for some contingent workers, or a program that sweetens retirement packages to make early retirement attractive. Sweetened retirements drive head count down and usually affect the most expensive head count: older, more experienced employees. Hence, the average wage and health care costs for the remaining (younger) work force will probably be lowered too.[7]

Controlling Average Cash Compensation

Controlling the average cash compensation, as shown in Exhibit 18.1, includes managing average salary level as well as variable compensation payments such as annual bonuses, gain-sharing, or profit sharing. A wide variety of approaches help manage adjustments to average salary level. Here we discuss two basic approaches: (1) *top down*, in which upper management determines pay and allocates it "down" to each subunit and to individual employees for the plan year, and (2) *bottom up*, in which individual employees' pay for the next plan year is forecasted and summed to create an organization salary budget.

CONTROL SALARY LEVEL: TOP DOWN

Top down, unit level budgeting involves estimating the pay increase budget for an entire organization unit. Once the total budget is determined, it is then allocated to each manager, who plans how to distribute it among subordinates. There are many approaches to unit level budgeting in use. A typical one, controlling the planned pay-level rise, will be considered. A planned pay-level rise is simply the percentage increase in average pay for the unit that is planned to occur.

---

[6]L. M. Segal and D. G. Sullivan, "The Growth of Temporary Services Work," *Journal of Economic Perspectives* 11, no. 2 (1997), pp. 117–136; M. W. Barringer and M. Sturman, "Exploring The Effects of Variable Work Arrangements on the Organizational Commitment of Contingent Workers," (Working Paper, University of Massachusetts, Amherst, 1998); Scott Lever, "An Analysis of Managerial Motivations behind Outsourcing Practices in Human Resources," *Human Resource Planning* 20, no. 2 (1997), pp. 37–47.

[7]M. Carnoy, M. Castells, and C. Benner, "Labour Markets and Employment Practices in the Age of Flexibility: A Case Study of Silicon Valley," *International Labour Review* 136, no. 1 (1997), pp. 27–48.

EXHIBIT 18.3 What Drives Level Rise?

Current year's rise Ability to pay Competitive market Turnover effects Cost of living	}	Percentage increase in average pay in plan year

As shown in Exhibit 18.3, several factors influence the decision about how much to increase the average pay level for the next period: how much the average level was increased this period, ability to pay, competitive market pressures, turnover effects, and cost of living.

Current Year's Rise

This is the percentage by which the average wage changed in the past year; mathematically:

Percent level rise =

$$100 \times \frac{\text{Average pay at year end} - \text{Average pay at year beginning}}{\text{Average pay at the beginning of the year}}$$

Ability to Pay

The decision regarding how much to increase the average pay level is in part a function of financial circumstances. Financially healthy employers may wish to maintain their competitive positions in the labor market, and some may even share outstanding financial success through bonuses and profit sharing.

Conversely, financially troubled employers may not be able to maintain competitive market positions. The conventional response in these circumstances has been to reduce employment. However, other options are to reduce the rate of increase in average pay by controlling adjustments in base pay and/or variable pay.

Competitive Market

In Chapter 8, we discussed how managers determine an organization's competitive position in relation to its competitors. Recall that a distribution of market rates for benchmark jobs was collected and analyzed into a single average wage for each benchmark. This "average market wage" became the "going market rate." It then was compared to the average wage paid by the organization for its benchmark jobs.[8] The market rates adjust differently each year in response to a variety of pressures.

[8]S. Snell and M.A. Youndt, "Human Resource Management and Firm Performance: Testing a Contingency Model of Executive Controls," *Journal of Management* issue 4, 1995.

Turnover Effects

Variously referred to as *churn* or *slippage*, the turnover effect recognizes the fact that when people leave (through layoffs, quitting, retiring), they typically are replaced by workers earning a lower wage. Depending on the degree of turnover, the effect can be substantial. Turnover effect can be calculated as annual turnover × planned average increase. For example, an organization whose labor costs equal $1 million a year has a turnover rate of 15 percent and a planned average increase of 6 percent. The turnover effect is 0.9 percent, or $9,000 (0.009 × $1,000,000). So instead of budgeting $60,000 to fund a 6 percent increase, only $51,000 is needed.

The lower average pay will also reduce those benefit costs linked to base pay, such as pensions. So the turnover effect influences both average pay and benefits costs in the total labor cost equation.

Cost of Living

Although there is little research to support it, employees undoubtedly compare their pay increases to changes in their costs of living, and unions consistently argue that increasing living costs justify adjustments in pay.[9]

A Distinction. It is important to distinguish among three related concepts: the cost of living, changes in prices in the product and service markets, and changes in wages in labor markets. As Exhibit 18.4 shows, changes in *wages* in labor markets are measured through pay surveys. These changes are incorporated into the system through market adjustments in the budget and updating the policy line and range structure. *Price changes for goods and services* in the product and service markets are measured by several government indexes, one of which is the Consumer Price Index. The third concept, *the cost of living*, refers to the expenditure patterns of individuals for goods and services. The cost of living is more difficult to measure because employees' expenditures depend on many things: marital status, number of dependents and ages, personal preferences, and so on. Different employees experience different costs of living, and the only accurate way to measure them is to examine the personal expenditures of each employee.

The three concepts are interrelated. Wages in the labor market are part of the cost of producing goods and services, and changes in wages create pressures on prices. Similarly, changes in the prices of goods and services create needs for increased wages in order to maintain the same lifestyle.

The Consumer Price Index (CPI). Many people refer to the CPI as a "cost of living" index, and many employers choose, as a matter of pay policy or in response to union pressures, to tie wages to it. But in doing so, employers are confounding the concepts of living costs and labor market costs. The CPI does not necessarily reflect an individual employee's cost of living.

---

[9]J. Barney, "Organizational Economics: Understanding the Relationship Between Organizations and Economic Analysis," in *Handbook of Organization Studies*, ed. S. Clegg, C. Hardy, and W. Nord (London: Sage Publishers, 1997), pp. 115–147.

EXHIBIT 18.4 Three Distinct but Related Concepts and Their Measures

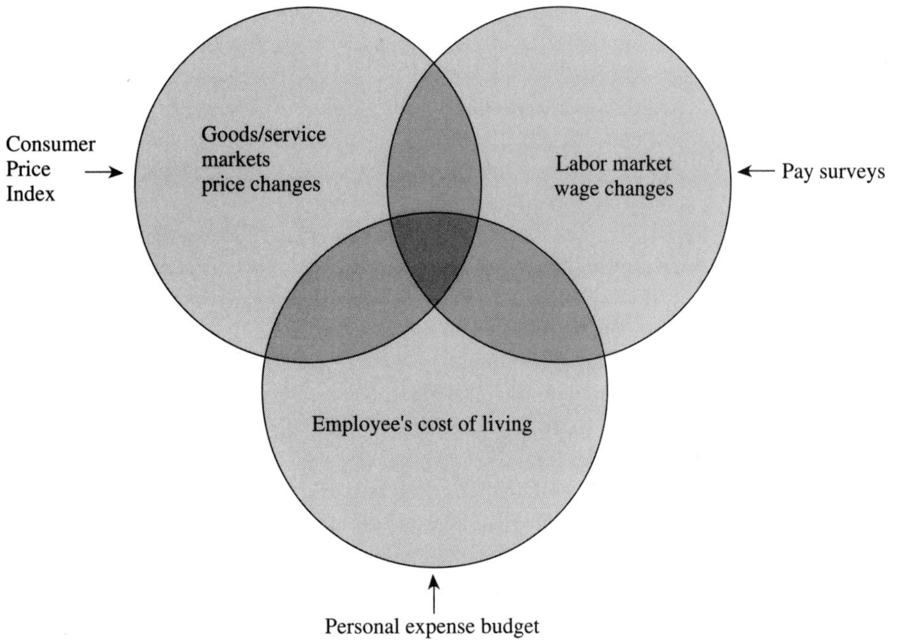

The CPI measures changes over time in prices of a hypothetical market basket of goods and services.[10] The present index is based on a 1993–1995 survey of the actual buying habits of urban Americans. Categories of major expenditures were derived, and weights were assigned based on each category's percentage of total expenditures. For example, the index gives a weighting of 5.02 percent to auto purchases. This means that of the total money spent by all the people in the study, 5.02 percent of it was spent to buy new cars. This weighting plan measures both the price of cars and the frequency of new car purchases. To determine the new car component for today's CPI, today's price of a new car identically equipped to the one purchased in 1993–95 is multiplied by the factor weight of 5.02 percent. The result is called today's *market basket price* of a new car.

The CPI is the subject of public interest because changes in it trigger changes in labor contracts, social security payments, federal and military pensions, and food stamp eligibility, as well as employers' pay budgets. Tying budgets or payouts to the CPI is called *indexing*. Note that the cost of living is one of the factors shown in Exhibit 18.3 that influences the percentage increase of average salary level. It also may affect cost of benefits faced by employers either through health insurance coverage or pension costs.

[10]For information on the CPI, contact the Bureau of Labor Statistics, Consumer Prices and Indexes: (202) 606-7000, or see their web page: **http://stats.bls.gov:80/datahome.htm**.

One of the main criticisms of the CPI is that the rigid "market basket" bears less and less resemblance to real world purchasing behavior. For example, the index includes the price of Macintosh apples, but if prices for Macintoshes escalate, I switch varieties to golden delicious or crispens. I've even been known to substitute an orange or a banana. Substitutes are not easily handled in the CPI. Another criticism of the index is that it is difficult to include discount prices. Thus, a trip to the car dealer, which the Bureau of Labor Statistics makes, does not really capture the difference between sticker and real prices. And pricing services, especially medical care, is difficult in light of the rapidly changing types and quality of service.

To cope with these issues, a revised CPI was introduced in January 1998. That revision included reselected geographic areas to reflect demographic changes, and new systems for data collecting and processing.[11] This change is part of a six-year revision plan. The January 1999 index rebases the CPI to 1993-95 = 100.

Most governments calculate some kind of consumer price index for their country. The web page for the United States Bureau of Labor Statistics provides many of these indexes (**http://stats.bls.gov**). They vary on how realistically they capture actual changes in prices.

Outside of government channels, there are other variations on the CPI There is even an index for those readers who plan to lead the good life. The annual Moet index tracks price changes for a dozen upper crust items. In a recent index, the biggest increase of all was in the price of a Rolls Royce Corniche IV convertible, up 7 percent from the previous year to $269,000. Other items on the Moet index include a Rolex Oyster watch for $13,950, up 5 percent, and a bottle of Dom Perignon, up 4.8 percent to $87. But not to worry; the overall increase in the Moet Luxury Index was only 2.3 percent.

A quicker way to compare living costs is to use the "relocation salary calculator" at **http://www.homefair.com**

Enter your salary, current city, and potential new city to see what salary you need in the new city based on cost-of-living differences.

How accurate do you think this website's information is?

Geographic Differentials. In addition to the national CPI, separate indexes are calculated monthly for five metropolitan areas and bimonthly for 23 other metropolitan areas and various regions. These local CPIs typically are more variable than the national indexes. They do not, as some mistakenly believe, indicate whether prices are absolutely higher in a particular area. Changes in the CPI indicate only whether prices have increased more or less rapidly in an area since the base period. For example, a CPI of 110 in Chicago and 140 in Atlanta does not necessarily mean that it costs more to live in

[11]John S. Greenlees and Charles C. Mason, "Overview of the 1998 Revision of the Consumer Price Index," *Monthly Labor Review*, December 1996, pp. 3–9 (also available on the BLS web site: (**http://stats.bls.gov**).

Atlanta. It does mean that prices have risen faster in Atlanta since the base year than they have in Chicago, since both cities started with bases of 100.

Rolling It All Together

Let us assume that the managers take into account all these factors—current year's rise, ability to pay, market adjustments, turnover effects, changes in the cost of living, and geographic differentials—and decide that the planned rise in average salary for the next period is 6.3 percent. This means that the organization has set a target of 6.3 percent as the increase in average salary that will occur in the next budget period. It does not mean that everyone's increase will be 6.3 percent. It means that at the end of the budget year, the average salary calculated to include all employees will be 6.3 percent higher than it is now.

The next question is, How do we distribute that 6.3 percent budget in a way that accomplishes management's objectives for the pay system and meets the organization's goals?

Distributing the Budget to Subunits. A variety of methods to determine what percentage of the salary budget each manager should receive exists. Some use a uniform percentage, in which each manager gets an equal percentage of the budget based on the salaries of each subunit's employees. Others vary the percentage allocated to each manager based on pay-related problems, such as turnover or performance, which have been identified in that subunit.

Once salary budgets are allocated to each subunit manager, they become a constraint: a limited fund of money that each manager has to allocate to subordinates. Typically, merit increase guidelines are used to help managers make these allocation decisions.

Merit increase grids help ensure that different managers grant consistent increases to employees with similar performance ratings and in the same position in their ranges. Additionally, grids help control costs. Examples of grids are included in Chapter 11.

One compensation manager reports having a great deal of difficulty with an employee who used the homefair web site **http://www.homefair.com** to determine that he should receive a 30 percent pay differential to accompany his transfer from one office to another. In contrast, the manager's information showed a differential of around 12 to 15 percent. How can you judge the accuracy of information obtained on the web?

How would you deal with the dissatisfied employee?

CONTROL SALARY LEVEL: BOTTOM UP

Bottom-up budgeting requires managers to forecast the pay increases they will recommend during the upcoming plan year. Exhibit 18.5 shows an example of the process involved. Each of the steps within this compensation forecasting cycle is described here.

1. *Instruct managers in compensation policies and techniques.* Train managers in the concepts of a sound pay-for-performance policy and in standard company compensation techniques such as the use of pay increase guidelines and budgeting techniques. Also communicate the salary ranges and market data.

2. *Distribute forecasting instructions and worksheets.* Furnish managers with the forms and instructions necessary to preplan increases. Exhibit 18.6 is an example of the forecasting worksheets that might be provided. In this exhibit, we see Sarah Ross's performance rating history, past raises, and timing of these raises.

Some argue that providing such detailed data and recommendations to operating managers makes the system too mechanical. How would you like your present instructor to look at your overall G.P.A. before giving you a grade in this course? Pay histories ensure that managers are at least aware of this information and that pay increases for any one period are part of a continuing message to individual employees, not some ad hoc response to short-term changes.

3. *Provide consultation to managers.* Offer advice and salary information services to managers upon request.

4. *Check data and compile reports.* Audit the increases forecasted to ensure that they do not exceed the pay guidelines and are consistent with appropriate ranges. Then use the data to feed back the outcomes of pay forecasts and budgets.

5. *Analyze forecasts.* Examine each manager's forecast and recommend changes based on noted inequities among different managers.

EXHIBIT 18.5 Compensation Forecasting and Budgeting Cycle

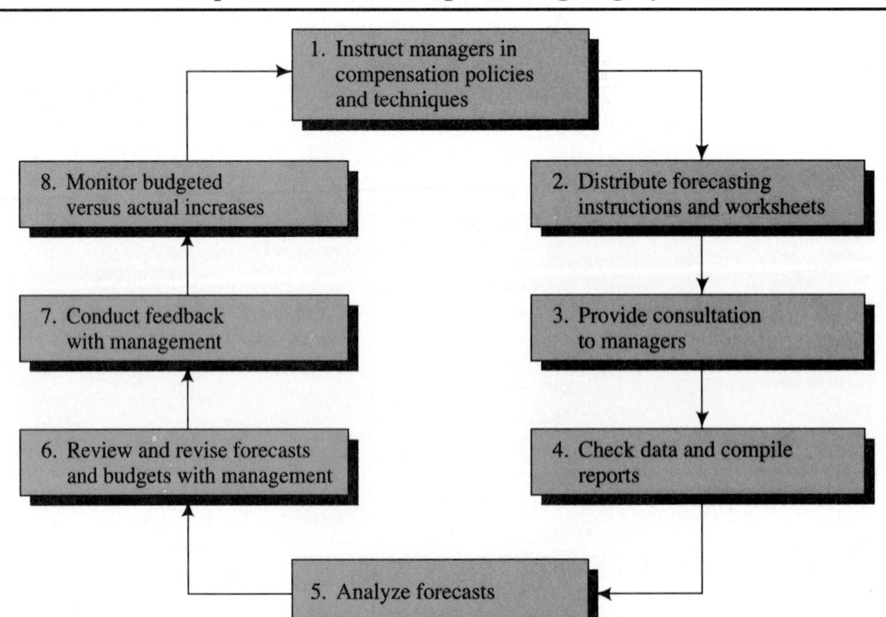

6. *Review and revise forecasts and budgets with management.* Consult with managers regarding the analysis and recommended changes. Obtain top-management approval of forecasts.
7. *Conduct feedback with management.* Present statistical summaries of the forecasting data by department and establish unit goals.
8. *Monitor budgeted versus actual increases.* Control the forecasted increases versus the actual increases by tracking and reporting periodic status to management.

The result of the forecasting cycle is a budget for the upcoming plan year for each organization's unit as well as estimated pay treatment for each employee. The budget does not lock in the manager to the exact pay change recommended for each employee. Rather, it represents a plan, and deviations due to unforeseen changes such as performance improvements, unanticipated promotions, and the like are common.

This approach to pay budgeting requires managers to plan the pay treatment for each of their employees. It places the responsibility for pay management on the managers. The compensation manager takes on the role of advisor to operating management's use of the system.[12]

INHERENT CONTROLS

Pay systems have two basic processes that serve to control pay decision making: (1) those inherent in the design of the techniques and (2) the formal budgeting process.

EXHIBIT 18.6 A Pay History Used for Forecasting

Name	YEAR END EXPERIENCE	EMPLOYMENT DATE	YEAR AND SERVICE	YEAR FIRST DEGREE	HIGHEST DEGREE	HIGHEST DISCIPLINE	SOC SEC NO
Sarah Ross	2	08-22-96	21/04	1996	BS	Acctg.	458-56-5332

Position	CLASSIF LEVEL	EMPL MO LEVEL	DATE ASSIGNED TO POSITION	DATE ASSIGNED TO CLASS LEVEL OF POSITION	
Accountant	26		08-22-96	08-22-96	

Previous Salary Change

DATE	PERFORMANCE RATING	AMOUNT	%	MONTHS INTERVAL	ANNUAL VALUE	FIC	SALARY	SALARY RANGE: UPPER BAND OR RANGE MAX	BAND MIDPOINT	LOWER BAND OR RANGE MIN
02 01 97	2.0						23040			
12 01 97	3.0	1920	8.3	10	10		24960			

Forecast Salary Change

DATE	PERFORMANCE RATING	AMOUNT	%	MONTHS INTERVAL	ANNUAL VALUE	FIC	SALARY	UPPER BAND OR RANGE MAX	BAND MIDPOINT	LOWER BAND OR RANGE MIN
09 01 98		2496	10.0	10	12		27456	30018	28016	25214

[12]Bruce Ellig, "The Compensation Professional in the New Business Environment," *Compensation and Benefits Management*, Autumn 1993, pp. 41–45; Ronald T. Albright and Bridge R. Compton, *Internal Consulting Basics* (Scottsdale, AZ: American Compensation Association, 1996).

Think back to the many techniques already discussed: job analysis and evaluation, skill/competency-based plans, policy lines, range minimums and maximums, bands, performance evaluation, gain-sharing, and salary increase guidelines. In addition to their primary purposes, these techniques also regulate managers' pay decisions by guiding what managers do. Controls are imbedded in the design of these techniques to ensure that decisions are directed toward the pay system's objectives. A few of these controls are examined below.

Range Maximums and Minimums

These ranges set the maximum and minimum dollars to be paid for specific work. The maximum is an important cost control. Ideally, it represents the highest value the organization places on the output of the work. Under job-based structures, skills and knowledge possessed by employees may be more valuable in another job, but the range maximum represents all that the work produced in a particular job is worth to the organization. For example, the job of airline flight attendant is in a pay range with a maximum that is the highest an airline will pay a flight attendant, no matter how well the attendant performs the job.

Pressures to pay above the range maximum occur for a number of reasons—for example, when employees with high seniority reach the maximum or when promotion opportunities are scarce. If employees are paid above the range maximum, these rates are called *red circle rates*. Most employers "freeze" red circle rates until the ranges are shifted upward by market update adjustments so that the rate is back within the range again. If red circle rates become common throughout an organization, then the design of the ranges and the evaluation of the jobs should be reexamined.

Range minimums are just that: the minimum value placed on the work. Often rates below the minimum are used for trainees. Rates below minimum may also occur if outstanding employees receive a number of rapid promotions and rate adjustments have not kept up.

Compa-Ratios

Range midpoints reflect the pay policy line of the employer in relationship to external competition. To assess how managers actually pay employees in relation to the midpoint, an index called a *compa-ratio* is often calculated.

$$\text{Compa-ratio} = \frac{\text{Average rates actually paid}}{\text{Range midpoint}}$$

A compa-ratio of less than 1.00 means that, on average, employees in that range are paid below the midpoint. Translated, this means that managers are paying less than the intended policy. There may be several valid reasons for such a situation. The majority of employees may be new or recent hires; they may be poor performers; or promotion may be so rapid that few employees stay in the job long enough to get into the high end of the range.

A compa-ratio greater than 1.00 means that, on average, the rates exceed the intended policy. The reasons for this are the reverse of those mentioned above: a majority of workers with high seniority, high performance, low turnover, few new hires, or low promotion rates. Compa-ratios may be calculated for individual employees, for each range, for organization units, or for functions.

Other examples of controls designed into the pay techniques include the mutual signoffs on job descriptions required of supervisors and subordinates. Another is slotting new jobs into the pay structure via job evaluation, which helps ensure that jobs are compared on the same factors.

Similarly, an organizationwide performance management system is intended to ensure that all employees are evaluated on similar factors.

Variable Pay

Variable pay depends on performance and is *not* "rolled into" (added to) employees' base pay. Thus, the compounding effects of merit pay and across-the-board increases do not occur. Variable pay takes many forms. The essence of variable pay is that it must be reearned each period, in contrast to conventional merit pay increases or across-the-board increases that are added to base pay each year and that increase the base on which the following year's increase is calculated.

Increases added into base pay have compounding effects on costs, and these costs are significant. For example, a $15 a week take-home pay added onto a $40,000 base compounds into $503,116 over 10 years. Here is another chance to use the *compound* key on your pocket calculator. If an employee earns $40,000 this year and receives a 5 percent increase every year, after 10 years the new salary is $62,000. The *total cash outflow* to this employee over 10 years is $503,116. In addition, costs for some benefits also increase. By comparison, the organization could keep base pay at $40,000 a year and pay a 26.8 percent bonus every single year for about the same $503,000. That 5 percent increase amounts to only $38 per week before taxes—probably about $15 a week more in take-home pay.

So from a labor cost perspective, conventional increases impact not only the average pay level but also the costs of all benefits contingent on base pay (e.g., pensions). Consequently, the greater the ratio of variable pay to base pay, the more variable (flexible) the organization's labor costs. Reconsider the general labor cost model in Exhibit 18.1; note that the greater the ratio of contingent to core workers and variable to base pay, the greater the variable component of labor costs, and the greater the options available to managers to control these costs.

Although variability in pay and employment may be an advantage for managing labor costs, it may be less appealing from the standpoint of managing equitable treatment of employees. The inherent financial insecurity built into variable plans may adversely affect employees' financial well-being and subsequently affect their behaviors at work and attitudes toward their employers. Managing labor costs is only one objective for managing compensation; other objectives in the pay model include sustaining competitive advantage (productivity, total quality, customer service, and costs) and equitable treatment of employees.

Analyzing Costs

Costing out wage proposals is commonly done prior to recommending pay increases. It is also used in preparation for collective bargaining. For example, it is useful to bear in mind the dollar impact of a 1 cent per hour wage change or a 1 percent change in payroll as one goes into bargaining. Knowing these figures, negotiators can quickly compute the impact of a request for a 9 percent wage increase.

Using Computers. If you've been thinking to yourself during these various budgetary calculations that "there's got to be an easier way," you're right. Commercial computer software can analyze almost every aspect of compensation information.

Computers can provide analysis and data that will improve the administration of the pay system. For example, computers can easily compare past estimates to what actually occurred (e.g., the percentage of employees that actually did receive a merit increase and the amount). Spreadsheet programs can simulate alternate wage proposals and compare their potential effects.

But computers have wider applications to compensation administration besides costing, for example, computerized job analysis and job evaluation. Software can also evaluate salary survey data and simulate the cost impact of incentive and gain-sharing options. However, trained compensation decision makers are still required to ensure the usefulness of the results.

COMPENSATION: MANAGING THE MESSAGE

Compensation communicates. It signals what is important and what is not. If you receive a pay increase for one more year of experience on your job—then one more year was important. If the pay increase is equal to any change in the CPI, then cost of living is important. If the increase is for moving to a bigger job or for outstanding performance, then a bigger job, or outstanding performance is important. Pay sends a powerful message about what matters. Therefore, managing that message is important.

Earlier in this book, we stressed that employees must believe that the pay system is fair. Employees' perceptions about the pay system are shaped through the treatment they receive by managers, formal communication programs about their pay and performance, and participation in the design of the system.

Pay delivers a strong message. Considerable resources have been devoted to designing a system that is intended to motivate effective performance and encourage productivity. For the pay system to influence work behaviors and attitudes, managers and employees must understand it.

The American Compensation Association recommends a six-stage process of communication, shown in Exhibit 18.7.[13]

Step one is, not surprisingly, defining the objectives of the communication program. Perhaps the objective is to ensure that employees fully understand all the compo-

---

[13]John A. Rubino, *Communicating Compensation Programs* (Scottsdale, AZ: American Compensation Association, 1997).

EXHIBIT 18.7 The Compensation Communication Cycle

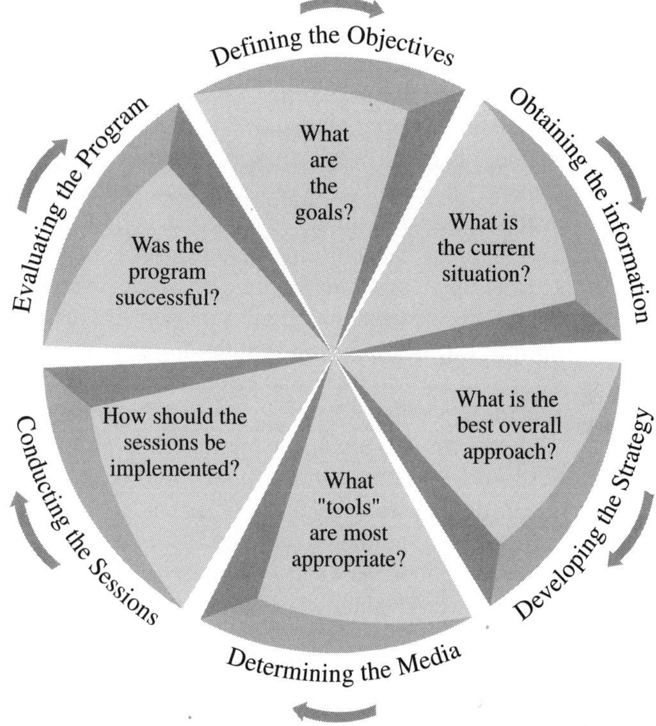

Source: Reprinted from ACA Building Block #4, "Communicating Compensation Programs, An Approach to Providing Information to Employees," by John A. Rubino, CCP with permission from the American Compensation Association (ACA), 14040 N. Northsight Blvd., Scottsdale, AZ U.S.A. 85260; telephone (602) 951-9191, fax: (602) 483-8352. © ACA.

nents of the compensation system; perhaps it is to change expectations, or to better capitalize on the motivational aspects built into the compensation systems. While specifying objectives as a first step seems obvious, it is often overlooked in the rush to design an attractive brochure.

Step two is to collect information from executives, managers and employees concerning their current perceptions, attitudes, and understanding of the compensation programs in effect. Information may be gathered through opinion survey questionnaires, focus groups, or formal or informal interviews. Some research concludes that employees misperceive the pay system. They tend to overestimate the pay of those with lower level jobs and to underestimate the pay of those in higher level jobs. If differentials are underestimated, their motivational value is diminished.

Further, there is some evidence to suggest that the goodwill engendered by the act of being open about pay may also affect employees' attitudes toward pay. Interestingly, the research also shows that employees in companies with open pay communication policies are as inaccurate in estimating pay differentials as those in companies in which pay secrecy prevails. However, employees under open pay policies tend to express higher satisfaction with their pay and with the pay system.

After the information on current attitudes and perceptions is analyzed, **step three** is to develop a communication strategy that will accomplish the original objectives. There is no standard approach on what to communicate to individuals about their own pay or that of their colleagues.

Some organizations have adopted a *marketing* approach. Similar to selling products to consumers, the pay system is a product, and employees and managers are the customers. Marketing approaches include consumer attitude surveys about the product, snappy advertising about the pay policies, and elaborate videotapes expounding policies and strengths. The objective is to manage expectations and attitudes about pay. In contrast, the *communication* approach tends to provide technical details. The marketing approach focuses on the quality and advantages of overall policies and is silent on specifics such as range maximums, increase guides, and the like.

Steps four and **five** of the communication process are to determine the most effective media, in light of the message and the audience, and conduct the campaign. Exhibit 18.8 recommends tuning the message in terms of detail and emphasis, depending on the audience. Executives, for example, will be interested on how the compensation programs fit the business strategy (Chapter 2). Managers will need to know how to use the development and motivation aspects of the compensation program for the people they supervise. Employees may want to know the process and policy (procedural justice) as well as specifics about how their pay is determined.

Intended and Unintended Consequences. **Step six** of the communication process suggests that the program be evaluated. Did it accomplish its goals? Pay communication can have unintended consequences. For example, providing accurate pay information may cause some initial short-term concerns among employees. Over the years, employees may have rationalized a set of relationships between their pay and the perceived pay and efforts of others. Receiving accurate data may require those perceptions to be adjusted.

Say What?

If the pay system is not based on work-related or business-related logic, then the wisest course is probably to avoid formal communication until the system is put in order. However, avoiding *formal* communication is not synonymous with avoiding communication. Employees are constantly getting intended and unintended messages through the pay treatment they receive.

Many employers communicate the range for an incumbent's present job and for all the jobs in a typical career path or progression to which employees can logically aspire.

In addition to ranges, some employers communicate the typical pay increases that can be expected for poor, satisfactory, and top performance. The rationale given is that employees exchange data (not always factual) and/or guess at normal treatment, and the rumor mills are probably incorrect. Providing accurate data may have a positive effect on employee work attitudes and behaviors.

EXHIBIT 18.8 Conducting Formal Communication Sessions for Various Audiences

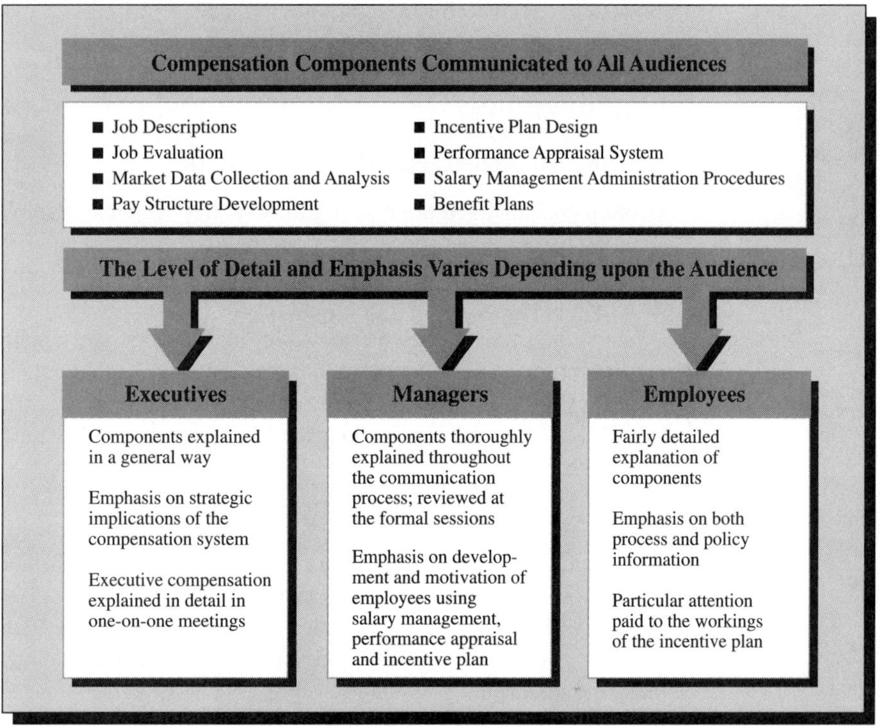

Source: Reprinted from ACA Building Block #4, "Communicating Compensation Programs, An Approach to Providing Information to Employees," by John A. Rubino, CCP with permission from the American Compensation Association (ACA), 14040 N. Northsight Blvd., Scottsdale, AZ U.S.A. 85260; telephone (602) 951-9191, fax: (602) 483-8352, © ACA.

One potential danger in divulging increase schedule data is the inability to maintain that schedule in the future for reasons outside the control of the compensation department (e.g., economic or product market conditions). Nevertheless, pay increase data, coupled with performance expectations, should enhance employee motivation, which is a prime objective of the pay system.

Opening the Books. There are some who advocate sharing all financial information with employees. All of it. For 10 years, employees at Springfield Remanufacturing, a rebuilder of engines, have been given weekly peeks at everything from revenues to labor costs. The employees, who own 31 percent of the company stock, and others argue that this "open book" approach results in high commitment and an understanding of how to maintain competitiveness. Many employers don't share information with such gusto, but they are increasingly disclosing more to their employees. Some are even providing basic business and financial training to help employees better understand the information.

Devotees of opening the books and financial training believe these methods will improve attitudes and performance, but there is no research to support them.

At the minimum, perhaps the most important information to be communicated is the work-related and business-related rationale on which pay systems are based. Some employees may not agree with these rationales or the results, but at least it will be clear that pay is determined by something other than the whims or biases of their supervisors.

Participation: Beliefs, Payoffs, and Practices

An often unchallenged premise in this book has been that employee (and manager) participation in the design and administration of pay systems pays off through increased understanding and commitment. As you might expect, research on the effects of employee participation in general shows mixed results.[14] Overall, the evidence suggests that participation does have positive effects, but they are not overwhelming.[15] A recent survey reports employees have no input into the design or implementation in 54 percent of the *Fortune* 500. Generally, employees seem to have input into aspects that are directly related to them (i.e., job descriptions), but not into overall policies, structure, or competitor salary surveys.[16]

The National Labor Relations Board (NLRB) and the Department of Labor have determined that employee committees formed to advise companies on issues such as pay, benefits and other conditions of work constitute unfair labor practices. In an important case, Electromation employee teams helped revise a bonus plan that had been discontinued because of wide employee dissatisfaction. The NLRB determined that the teams constituted a company-dominated labor organization because management facilitated and controlled committee discussions. This decision has effectively thrown up a major legal obstacle to formal employee participation (except through certified unions) in the design of pay systems.

PAY: CHANGE AGENT IN RESTRUCTURING

Compensation often plays a singular role when organizations restructure. Strategic changes in the business strategy mean the compensation strategy must be realigned as well.[17] Pay is a powerful signal of change; changing people's pay captures their attention.

Pay changes can play two roles in any restructuring. Pay can be a *leading catalyst* for change, or a *follower* of the change. Shifts from conventional across-the-board annual increases to profit sharing or from narrow job descriptions and ranges to broad roles and bands signal major change to employees. To signal yet another of AT&T's

[14]John Wagner III, "Participation's Effects on Performance and Satisfaction: A Reconsideration of Research Evidence," *Academy of Management Review* 19, no. 2 (1994), pp. 312–30.

[15]Barry Bluestone, *Negotiating the Future* (New York: Basic Books, 1992).

[16]Janice Stanger and J. Stephen Heinen, "Alternatives to Employee Task Forces," *Employee Benefits Journal*, June 1994, pp. 18–22.

[17]Dave Ulrich, "A New Mandate for Human Resources," *Harvard Business Review*, January–February 1998, pp. 125–134.

major restructurings, the company shifted its bonus plan measures from 25 percent based on corporate earnings and 75 percent on individual performance, to 75 percent on corporate earnings and 25 percent on individual performance. AT&T managers now "understand" that they need to focus on improving AT&T performance.

Whether pay is a **leading catalyst** for change or a **follower of change**, compensation managers need to learn how to implement change. Not only do they need to know the strategic and technical aspects of compensation, they also need to learn how to bargain, resolve disputes, empower employees, and develop teams.

STRUCTURING THE COMPENSATION FUNCTION

Compensation professionals seem to be constantly reevaluating where within the organization the responsibility for the design and administration of pay systems should be located. The organizational arrangements of the compensation function vary widely.

Centralization–Decentralization

An important issue related to structuring the function revolves around the degree of decentralization (or centralization) in the overall organization structure. *Decentralized* refers to a management strategy of giving separate organization units the responsibility to design and administer their own systems. This contrasts with a *centralized* strategy, which locates the design and administration responsibility in a single corporate unit.

Some firms, such as AT&T and Pacific Gas and Electric, have relatively large corporate staffs whose responsibility it is to formulate pay policies and design the systems. Administration of these policies and systems falls to those working in various units, who often are personnel generalists. Such an arrangement runs the risk of formulating policies and practices that are well tuned to overall corporate needs but less well tuned to each unit's particular needs and circumstances. The use of task forces, with members drawn from the generalists in the affected units, to design new policies and techniques helps diminish this potential problem.

Other more decentralized organizations, such as TRW and GE, have relatively small corporate compensation staffs (three or four professionals). Their primary responsibility is to manage the systems by which executives and the corporate staff are paid. These professionals operate in a purely advisory capacity to other organization subunits. The subunits, in turn, may employ compensation specialists. Or the subunits may choose to employ only personnel generalists rather than compensation specialists, and may turn to outside compensation consultants to purchase the expertise required on specific compensation issues.

Decentralizing certain aspects of pay design and administration has considerable appeal. Pushing these responsibilities (and expenses) close to the units, managers, and employees affected by them may help ensure that decisions are business related. However, decentralization is not without dilemmas. For example, it may be difficult to transfer employees from one business unit to another. Problems of designing pay systems that support a subunit's objectives but run counter to the overall corporate objectives crop up. So, too, does the potential for pay discrimination.

Flexibility within Corporatewide Principles

The answer to these and related problems of decentralization can be found in developing a set of corporatewide principles or guidelines that all must meet. Those principles may differ for each major pay technique. For example, IBM's business units worldwide have the flexibility to design incentive plans tailored to each unique business unit's strategies and cultures. The only guidance is to ensure that the plans adhere to IBM's basic beliefs, improve financial and business objectives, and maintain or enhance IBM's reputation.

Keep in mind that the pay system is one of many management systems used in the organization. Consequently, it must be congruent with these other systems. For example, it may be appealing, on paper at least, to decentralize some of the compensation functions. However, if financial data and other management systems are not also decentralized, the pay system may not fit and may even be at odds with other systems.

Reengineering and Outsourcing

Reengineering the compensation function involves changing the process of paying people. It means reshaping the compensation function to make it more client or customer focused. Clients probably include employees, managers, owners, and perhaps even real customers of the organization. The basic question asked during reengineering is, "Does each specific activity (technique) directly contribute to our objectives (i.e., to our competitive advantage)?" If some added value isn't apparent, then the technique should be dropped. The next question, directed at those pay activities that do contribute to achieving objectives is, "Should we be doing the specific activity in-house, or can others do it more effectively? That is, should we outsource it?"

Outsourcing is becoming a viable alternative in the compensation (and benefits) field as organizations struggle to cease doing activities that do not directly contribute to objectives. Employee benefits is a major candidate for outsourcing.[18] In a recent survey, about 33 percent of over 1,000 firms reported that they already outsourced major responsibilities for their pay (e.g., market surveys and structure design) and benefits administration.

Cost savings is the apparent major short-term advantage of outsourcing. All those compensation wonks can be laid off or retrained. Major disadvantages of outsourcing include less responsiveness to unique and specific employee–manager problems, less control over decisions that are often critical to all employees (i.e., their pay), and information leaks to rivals and competitors.[19]

---

[18] Brian Hackett, *Transforming the Benefit Function* (New York: The Conference Board, 1995); *Outsourcing HR Services* (New York: The Conference Board, 1994).

[19] Robert M. Dodd and Barbara M. Renterghem, "Increasing Benefit Plan Value Through Outsourcing," *Benefits Quarterly*, First Quarter 1997, pp. 14–19.

CONTROLS AS GUIDELINES: LET (THOUGHTFUL) MANAGERS BE FREE

One of the major attacks on traditional compensation plans is that they often degenerate into bureaucratic nightmares that interfere with the organization's ability to respond to competitive pressures. Some recommend reducing the controls and guidelines inherent in any pay plan. Hence, banding eliminates or at least reduces the impact of range maximums and minimums. Replacing merit grids with awards and bonuses eliminates the link between the pay increase and the employees' salary position in the range and performance rating. Replacing job evaluation with skill-based plans opens up the freedom to assign employees to a wider variety of work, regardless of their pay and the value of the work they perform.

Such approaches are consistent with the oft-heard plea that managers should be free to manage pay. Or, as some more bluntly claim, pay decisions are too important to be left to compensation professionals. There is a ring of truth to all this. Our experience with many companies is that their pay systems are managed like the worst bureaucratic nightmares in Kafka's *Trial*.

Yet permitting managers to be free to pay employees as they judge best rests on a basic premise: Managers will use pay to achieve the organization's objectives—efficiency, equity, and compliance with regulations—rather than their own objectives. Clearly, some balance between hidebound controls and chaos is required to ensure that pay decisions are directed at the organization goals, yet permit sufficient flexibility for managers and employees to respond to unique situations. Achieving the balance becomes part of the art of managing compensation.

A final issue related to pay design and administration involves the skills and competencies required in compensation managers. The grandest strategy and structure may seem well designed, well thought out in the abstract, but could be a disaster if people qualified to carry it out are not part of the staff.

In view of the importance of a well-trained staff, both the American Compensation Association (ACA) and the Society of Human Resource Managers (SHRM) have professional development programs to entice readers into the compensation field.[20] In addition, the web sites in the Appendix provide a lot more information.

Summary

We have now completed the discussion of the pay administration process. Administration includes control: control of the way managers decide individual employees' pay as well as control of overall costs of labor. As we noted, some controls are designed into the fabric of the pay system (inherent controls, range maximums and minimums, etc.).

[20]Schedules and course registration information are available from American Compensation Association, 14040 N. Northsight Blvd., Scottsdale, AZ 85260 (**http://www.acaonline.org**), and from Society of Human Resource Managers, 606 N. Washington Street, Alexandria, VA, 22314 (**http://www.shrm.org**).

The salary budgeting and forecasting processes impose additional controls. The formal budgeting process focuses on controlling labor costs and generating the financial plan for the pay system. The budget sets the limits within which the rest of the system operates.

Other aspects of administration we examined in this chapter included the fair treatment of employees in communications and participation. The basic point was that pay systems are tools, and like any tools, they need to be evaluated in terms of usefulness in achieving an organization's objectives.

Review Questions

1. How can employers control labor costs?
2. How does the administration of the pay system affect the pay objectives?
3. Why is the structure of the compensation function important?
4. Give some examples of how employers use inherent controls.
5. What activities in administering the pay system are likely candidates to be outsourced? Why?
6. Explain how employee communications and participation influence the effectiveness of the pay system.

Appendix

Compensation Web Sites

Consulting Firms

Many of the websites related to compensation and benefits, and many of the listings uncovered in a conventional search, are one- or two-page ads for consulting firms or software companies. These provide little actual information on compensation and benefit practices. However, a number of consulting firms provide publications and press releases on their web pages, and some of these are well worth reading.

Consulting Firms	*WWW Address*	*What does web site offer?*
Frederic W. Cook	http://www.fredericwcook.com	• Alert letter includes items on executive compensation issues and legislation • New publications ads

Consulting Firms	*WWW Address*	*What does web site offer?*
Hay Group	http://haygroup.com http://haypaynet.com	• News releases, legislative and regulatory updates, and survey data • Hay PayNet allows organization to tap into Hay's customized compensation databases
Hewitt Associates	http://www.hewitt.com	• Provides press releases, full text articles, brief items on laws and regulations and Federal agency activities
KPMG Peat Marwick	http://www.kpmg.com http://www.us.kpmg.com	• Summaries of developments in benefits laws and short reports on KPMG survey results
Runzheimer International	http://www.runzheimer.com	• A Wisconsin-based management consulting firm that developed standards for the IRS • Information on salary differentials, living costs, and travel and moving benefits
Sibson & Company	http://www.sibson.com	• Case studies drawn from client experiences • Items on compensation design, organization development, etc.
Towers Perrin	http://www.towersperrin.com	• Information on international pay and benefits • New legislation, regulations, and new issues in major countries
Watson Wyatt Worldwide	http://www.watsonwyatt.com	• Global news service, including reports and surveys from all over the world from two-tier pay systems in Spain to performance pay in China and Vietnam • Choice of five languages
William M. Mercer	http://www.mercer.com	• User can stop at Mercer's home page or go directly to its "Rewarding Employees" site with press releases, publications • Surveys on salaries, performance pay, assessment, compensation committees, and executive pay

Executive Compensation

A number of sites provide information focusing on executive compensation.

Executive Compensation	*WWW Address*	*What does web site offer?*
Business Week	http://www.businessweek.com	• Information on executive pay and corporate performance
Securities and Exchange Commission	http://www.sec.gov	• Executives' salaries and some executives' employment contracts

Broad Listing for Compensation

Workers' Compensation	*WWW Address*	*What does web site offer?*
American Compensation Association (ACA)	http://www.acaonline.org	• Information on ACA seminars and certification programs • Listings of ACA publications
American Management Association	http://www.amanet.org	• Information about AMA's training programs, publication and other resources
BLS Covered Employment and Wages	http://stats.bls.gov/cewhome.htm	• Leads to large files for timeseries data, all of which are downloadable
BLS Occupational Compensation Survey	http://stats.bls.gov/ocshome.htm	• Leads to large files for timeseries data, all of which are downloadable
BLS Economy at a Glance	http://stats.bls.gov/eag.table.html	• The latest data for employment, hours, earnings, productivity, the CPI, and the employment cost index
Bureau of Labor Statistics (BLS)	http://www.bls.gov	• The single largest source of data on salaries and wages, labor costs, employment, labor markets, benefits, workplace safety and health statistics, prices, and working conditions • All data are free and downloadable
Cornell University/HR Executive	http://www.ilr.cornell.edu http://www.workindex.com	• Performs more targeted searches than Yahoo and Alta Vista • Compensation-related site listings include: benefits, compensation, economic and business statistics, etc.
Institute of Management and Administration (IOMA)	http://www.ioma.com	• Launched a Report on Salary Surveys Compensation Discussion Group • Compensation and benefit professionals can post questions and offer comments • Extensive business directory with links to more than 400 websites, including a section on HR, compensation, and benefits
Society for HR Management	http://www.shrm.org	• HR news and wide range of links, including compensation and benefits • A number of links to private consulting firms and publishers
U.S. Chamber of Commerce	http://www.uschamber.org	• Lists local chambers, publications, policy papers, and searchable databases, plus new releases on compensation and benefit issues

Compensation Laws and Regulations

Compensation Laws and Regulations	*WWW Address*	*What does web site offer?*
Family Medical Leave Act	http://www.dol.gov/dol/esa/fmla.htm	• This is DOL site for FMLA regulations • Guidance on compliance issues and 800 # for assistance
National Labor Relations Board (NLRB)	http://www.nlrb.gov	• Weekly summaries, NLRB decisions, rules and regulations, and other information on labor relations issues
State Labor Department	e.g. website for New York State: http://www.labor.state.ny.us/wages/man.htm	• A number of states have websites for their labor department or employment agency with information on minimum wage, labor markets, and local wages
U.S. Department of Labor (DOL)	http://www.dol.gov	• Press releases, reports, forms, and compliance guidance

Benefits

Benefits	*WWW Address*	*What does web site offer?*
American Medical Association	http://www.ama-assn.org	• Information of relevance to benefit professionals—details on medical savings account programs • Reports on federal and state health insurance reforms, federal laws, and managed care issues
BenefitsLink	http://benefitslink.com	• Links to number of benefit topics, plus legal updates on pensions, retirement plans, and ERISA, and a forum for benefits professionals to post questions and offer comments • References for benefits-related official federal government documents and a list of service providers
Blair Mill Administration, Inc.	http://www.blairmill.com	• Information for organizations that self-insure their health benefits
Employease	http://www.eease.com	• Benefits bookstore • Lists of healthcare providers and links to other benefits and business websites

Benefits	WWW Address	What does web site offer?
Employee Benefit Research Institute (EBRI)	http://www.ebri.org	• A list of links to other benefits sources on the web • EBRI reports on benefit issues
Health and Human Services Department	http://www.healthfinder.gov	• Links to more than 500 health information websites, plus news, publications, on-line journals, and toll-free numbers (from private and public sources)
Health Insurance Association of America	http://www.hiaa.org	• Press releases on healthcare legislation and a list of HIAA publications • Extensive collection of statistics on health insurance and healthcare
International Foundation of Employee Benefit Plans	http://www.ifebp.org	• Industry news • Reports on benefit issues • Full listing of IFEBP services and resources
National Committee for Quality Assurance	http://www.ncqa.org	• The NCQA is the major accreditation organization for managed care providers • Allows user to select a provider or a location and view the provider's performance ratings

Pensions and Retirement

Pensions and Retirement	WWW Address	What does web site offer?
Association of Private Pension and Welfare Plans	http://www.appwp.org/appwp	• Information on legislation affecting pensions • Updates on current issues • Links to other websites
Pension Benefit Guarantee Corporation (PBGC)	http://www.pbgc.gov	• Information on pensions and ERISA, PBGC regulations, compliance guidance, and lists of underfunded pension plans
Social Security Administration	http://www.ssa.gov	• Basic social security and Medicare information for employers and employees
Thomas	http://thomas.loc.gov	• Legislative information for Congress

YOUR TURN:

TWO HARBORS TEACHERS

Public school teachers typically are paid according to salary schedules that include

1. "Steps" that pay for accumulating experience.
2. "Lanes" that pay for extra college credits.

Steps and lanes operate to boost pay even if the local school board does not grant any across-the-board or cost of living increases.

Critics of such schedules say that they guarantee steadily climbing costs, even in times when a district's finances do not permit increases.

Exhibit 1 shows a simplified salary schedule at Two Harbors, a district that employs 100 teachers and whose enrollment is growing at about 3 percent a year.

A. Calculate the change in salary in year 2 under the following conditions.
   1. Six teachers earning an average salary of $43,444 resign.
   2. Nine teachers are hired at an average of $25,666.

EXHIBIT 1 Two Harbors Salary Schedule Showing Distribution of 100 Teachers

Year One

Total salaries for 100 teachers ________ $3,110,000
Average salary ________ 31,100

	B.A. degree	*B.A. and credits*	*M.A. degree*	*M.A. and credits*
Step 5	7 teachers $29,000	18 teachers $33,000	14 teachers $36,000	11 teachers $41,000
Step 4	4 teachers $27,000	6 teachers $30,000	5 teachers $34,000	1 teacher $38,000
Step 3	6 teachers $25,000	4 teachers $28,000	3 teachers $31,000	1 teacher $35,000
Step 2	6 teachers $23,000	2 teachers $26,000	2 teachers $28,000	0 teachers $32,000
Step 1	8 teachers $22,000	1 teacher $24,000	1 teacher $26,000	0 teachers $28,000

Each step represents four years of service; the vertical columns show levels of college credits. In year 2, the faculty moves from an average of 3.86 steps to 3.93 and the proportion of teachers with master's degrees increases from 38 to 39 percent.

3. Ninety-four teachers get raises averaging $851 as they move up and to the right because of more experience and training.
4. One hundred three teachers are on staff for the year.
5. There are no changes to the salary schedule.

What is the average salary for year 2, and what is the change from the previous year?

B. From year 1 to year 2, the percentage of teachers with master's degrees went from 38 to 39 percent; they also went from an average step ranking of 3.86 to 3.93. How do the results change if the assumptions change? For example,
   1. What happens if enrollment declines by 3 percent a year?
   2. What happens if the district starts to grow at 6 percent a year?
   3. What happens if a nearby college opens an offsite facility that will make it easier for teachers to earn additional credits?
   4. What happens if the district increases its entire salary schedule by 5 percent for each of the next two years of its teachers' contract?

C. Take the role of superintendent of the Two Harbors school district. Money is tight, as always. The district is about to launch an expensive technology program to give all classrooms Internet access. A vocal group of parents have taken the lead in demanding the district get "on-line." The teachers are mixed in their support. Some are enthusiastic advocates, others believe it is a waste of resources, a few are personally uncomfortable with the technology. In addition to the equipment, extensive (and expensive) training will be required. Nevertheless, the school board supports the move and wants it to be successful. At the same time, they have stressed the need to hold the line on other expenses in order to support this new foray.

   Make the case that the district's ability to pay precludes any adjustments in the salary schedule for the next several years.

D. Take the role of president of the teachers negotiating committee. Make the case that the present salary schedule means that for the majority of teachers, their salaries will not even keep up with inflation. Yet the district is asking them to take on additional tasks without a pay increase. Because training in the new technology will be given within the district and will not receive college credit, it will not change teachers' positions in the schedule.

   Make the case that in addition to salary schedule adjustments to help the district remain competitive with comparable school districts, a new way of reimbursing teachers for their new skills is also required.

Internet Sites for Human Resources

Prepared by Suzanne Cohen and Deborah Joseph, Reference Librarians at the Martin P. Catherwood Library, School of Industrial and Labor Relations at Cornell University, September 1997.

PROFESSIONAL ASSOCIATIONS AND ORGANIZATIONS

Society for Human Resource Management
http://www.shrm.org/
This is a great place to start for human resources information. Nice table of contents and keyword searching capability. Membership information. Buyer's Guide. HR job openings. Government Affairs page monitors current legislation affecting HR. *HR Magazine* and other news online. Conferences. Also has a fantastic directory to Internet Resources divided by subject (Choose HR Links). Some pages are only open to SHRM members.

American Arbitration Association Home Page
http://www.adr.org
Membership information. Guides to developing alternative dispute resolution (ADR) programs. ADR law. Selected articles from *Dispute Resolution Journal* and *Dispute Resolution Times.* Labor arbitration rules. Can also download a complete Dispute Resolution package from the site.

IHRIM–The International Association for Human Resource Information Management
http://www.ihrim.org/
Membership information. Conference information. Management Resources Center with information on intranets, job descriptions, salaries. White papers. Buyer's Guide. Links to other Internet resources. Keyword searching ability is forthcoming. Not as extensive as the SHRM site, but it looks like they are working towards that with many areas "under construction."

International Personnel Management Association
http://www.ipma~hr.org/
Issues important to public sector managers and employees. Center for Personnel Research provides sample policies and other guidance to members, but non-members can view samples such as "NYS Internet Acceptable Use." Government Affairs, Training, and Global HR are among other topics.

IPMAAC Online!
http://ipmaac.org/
Home page of the International Personnel Management Association Assessment Council. Site would be most valuable to members, but for those interested in personnel assessment there is a Library of Internet Resources.

WARIA–Workflow And Reeingineering International Association
http://www.waria.com/
Useful to those interested in workflow issues and those in the process of reengineering their organization. Membership information, conferences, links to relevant web sites, job exchange, lists of vendors and consultants, bookstore.

IRRA Home Page
http://www.ilr.cornell.edu/irra/
The Industrial Relations Research Association. Announcements, Membership and Chapter information. Conferences. "Dialogues" by professionals on various issues. Publication titled "Perspectives on Work" which requires Adobe's Acrobat Reader.

American Compensation Association
http://www.acaonline.org/
Information and News section has bookstore and current news. Membership and certification information. 1997–1998 Total Salary Increase Budget Survey Results. Conferences and Events.

Academy of Management
http://www.aom.pace.edu/
Choose "Human Resource Management" from Divisions and Interest Groups. Membership information. Links to other Internet resources.

American Society for Training and Development
http://www.astd.org/
Legislative updates. Selected full text from *Training and Development Magazine.* Buyer's Guide with training suppliers and vendors in alphabetical order. Membership information. Hot topics page. Large list of training and performance links to other Internet resources.

Foundation for Enterprise Development
http://www.fed.org/
Nonprofit organization provides information about equity compensation, employee ownership and involvement, and other business strategies. More than 250 online documents.

American Society for Payroll Management
http://www.aspm.org/
Provides information on payroll industry best practices, payroll technology, federal and state legislative actions affecting payroll. Membership information. Links to other payroll resources on the Internet. Vendors. Events. Sign up to get a free issue of the monthly newsletter.

National Center for Employee Ownership
http://www.nceo.org/
Provides information on employee stock ownership plans (ESOPs), employee stock options, and other forms of employee ownership. Online library of articles. Excerpts from publications and ordering information. Membership information. Events. Links to other Internet resources. Bulletin Board online forum for discussion.

GOVERNMENT

Social Security Administration
http://www.ssa.gov/
Official web site of the Social Security Administration. Reference Guide for employers. Online publications including "Social Security Handbook," Welfare Reform updates, and "Factors in Evaluating Disability." Download Social Security forms. Request your Personal Earnings and Benefit Estimate Statement.

U.S. Census Bureau
http://www.census.gov/
Impressive site for social, demographic, and economic information. Search the site by keyword, place name, pointing and clicking on a map or use the alphabetical subject index from A–Z.

Bureau of Labor Statistics
http://stats.bls.gov/
Excellent source for labor statistics. Employment cost trends, Labor force statistics from the current population survey. Safety and health statistics. Online news releases on hot topics (i.e. "Expenditures for health care plans by employers and employees"). Both national and regional data. Keyword searching available.

U.S. Office of Personnel Management
http://www.opm.gov/
The Federal Government's Human Resources agency. Wealth of information about Federal employment, including job openings, salary tables, benefits. Information on alternative work schedules. Veterans information. Online forms.

National Labor Relations Board
http://www.nlrb.gov/
Weekly summary of cases. Search index of past decisions and orders. NLRB rules and regulations. Directory of Headquarters and Field Offices.

U.S. Department of Labor
http://www.dol.gov/
Starting point for accessing home pages of Department of Labor agencies. Media Releases. Statutory and Regulatory information. Links to labor-related data. Grant and Contract information. Download Department of Labor posters.

THOMAS Legislative Information on the Internet
http://thomas.loc.gov/
Search for Congressional Bills by title, number, sponsor, topic, or date. View the Congressional Record online. Committee information. Historical documents. View summaries of Congressional floor activity for the current week.

Employment and Training Administration
http://www.doleta.gov/
Home page is designed to accommodate different users—Click on "For Individuals," "For Employers," or "For Employment/Training Community." Electronic Reading Room for statutes, regulations, directives, and press releases. Welfare-to-Work resources.

Occupational Safety and Health Administration
http://www.osha.gov/
View or download safety and health online publications valuable to employees and employers. Ergonomics. Statistics & Data. Useful FAQ page. Agency information. Links to other safety and health Internet sites. Download interactive software to aid in compliance with OSHA standards.

Small Business Administration
http:/www.sba.gov/
Guidance for starting and running a small business. National and State information. Searchable 8(a) Contractor listing by state. Information on Women's Business Center Program. Link to more than 2,000 other business sites arranged by subject or keyword search.

Equal Employment Opportunity Commission
http://www.eeoc.gov
Summary of laws enforced by the agency. Fact sheets. Press releases on hot topics. Information on technical assistance and training programs offered by the EEOC.

Above are listed only government sites most directly related to Human Resources. The sites below are starting points for all Government information on the Internet.

LSU Libraries' Federal Government Agencies Page
http://www.lib.lsu.edu/gov/fedgov.html#exec
Searchable list of government agencies, including Boards, Commissions and Committees and Independent agencies. When I looked at this site, it had been updated that same day.

Fedworld
http://www.fedworld.gov
Search a comprehensive inventory of information disseminated by the federal government. Also includes information on purchasing government documents.

Selected State Departments of Labor

State of New York Department of Labor	**http://www.labor.state.ny.us/**
State of Connecticut Department of Labor	**http://www.ctdol.state.ct.us/**
New Jersey Department of Labor	**http://www.state.nj.us/labor/**
Pennsylvania Dept. of Labor and Industry	**http://www.li.state.pa.us**

OCCUPATIONAL SAFETY AND HEALTH

OSHWEB–Index of Occupational Safety and Health Resources
http://turva.me.tut.fi/~oshweb
A subject index of websites collected by Teuvo Uusitalo of the Institute of Occupational Safety Engineering. Site is up to date and international in scope. Subfields include risk management, government agencies, construction safety. and professional organizations. Search capabilities included.

The Occupational Safety & Health Administration Home Page
http://www.osha.gov
View or download safety and health online publications valuable to employees and employers. Ergonomics. Statistics & Data. Useful FAQ page. Agency information. Links to other safety and health Internet sites. Download interactive software to aid in compliance with OSHA standards.

National Institute for Safety and Health (NIOSH) Home Page
http://www.cdc.gov/niosh/homepage.html
Various information on NIOSH including the organization's directory, toll free number, background of what NIOSH does, information on NIOSH's activities throughout the U.S. Info on publications, workshops, extramural classes. Health hazards evaluation program.

CTDNews–Ergonomics and Workplace Safety
http://ctdnews.com
In its 5th year, this monthly online newsletter is published by the Center for Workplace Health. Provides summaries of current and back issues CTD symptoms. and preventions, ergonomic resources. Also covers special subjects such as fraud and abuse in workers' compensation. Product evaluations also available.

U.S. Workers Compensation Law
http://www.law.cornell.edu/topics/workers_compensation.html
Part of the Legal Information Institute at Cornell University's Law School, this site is a searchable database of Workers Compensation law material. In addition to Federal and State materials, the website also has links to other references such as the Occupational Safety and Health Administration, other employment law topics, and accident and injury compensation and prevention topics.

New York State Workers' Compensation Board
http://www.wcb.state.ny.us
Background Information about the Board. Important Phone Numbers and Directions to Hearing Points. New Laws, Rules and Regulations. Press Releases. Site also includes information on Workers' Compensation Law, Self Insurance programs, managed care pilot programs, and preferred provider programs.

IAIABC Homepage
http://www.iaiabc.org
Homepage of The International Association of Industrial Accident Boards and Commissions (IAIABC), an organization of workers' compensation specialists from a number of disciplines including Government officials and regulators, business and labor leaders, medical providers, law firms, insurance carriers, rehabilitation and safety experts. The organization "serves the needs of the workers compensation system through promoting efficient and far sighted regulation and administration of the law." A repository for workers' compensation information, this site also has a page of Workers' Compensation related links.

Safety Online
http://www.safetyonline.net
Features OSHA standards, EPA rulings and new developments in the safety industry with direct links to OSHA, EPA, and other sources of information. Also provides information on sources for safety products, training, and consultation.

Center for Office Technology
http://www.cot.org
Website for a national coalition of employers, manufacturers and associations "dedicated to improving the office working environment and to promoting informed approaches to comfort and well-being issues associated with computers and office technology." Site includes information on membership to the organization as well as facts on computer emissions, ergonomics, cumulative stress disorder and more.

Human Factors and Ergonomics Home Page
http://www.tc.cornell.edu:80/~hedge/
Created by Alan Hedge, Professor of Human Factors in the Department of Design and Environmental Analysis at Cornell University. Links to many studies in the field—some multimedia.

NIEHS–National Institute of Environmental Health Sciences
http://www.niehs.nih.gov
NIEHS, the National Institutes of Health's institute for basic research on environment-related diseases. Website gives introduction to NIEHS and briefly outlines its history and research highlights, as well as provides contact and visiting information. Access to the NIEHS Clearinghouse, a source of free information on environmental health effects of lead, radon, emf, specific chemicals, etc. News and Publications available from this site includes press releases about scientific discoveries such as the effects of asbestos exposure, the developmental impairment of children exposed to lead, and the health effects of urban pollution.

TRAINING AND DEVELOPMENT

American Society for Training and Development
http://www.astd.org
Legislative updates. Selected full text from Training and Development Magazine. Buyer's Guide with training suppliers and vendors in alphabetical order. Membership information. Hot topics page. Large list of training and performance links to other Internet resources.

International Federation of Trade and Development Organizations
http://www.iftdo.org
IFTDO is an accredited Non-Government Organization to the United Nations in New York and the UN's International Labour Organisation in Geneva. Its diversified network of human resource management and development organisations links HR professionals in HR societies,, corporations. universities, consultancies, government organizations and non-profit enterprises in order to identify, develop, and transfer knowledge, skills and technology to enhance personal and organizational growth, human performance, productivity, and sustainable development.

Training and Development Resource Center
http://www.tcm.com/trdev
Created by Canadian company TCM. Site includes HR Bookshop. training links, FAQ, newsgroups and listservs, an acronyms glossary and conference sites.

Training Forum
http://www.trainingforum.com
Offers training products and services featuring information from associations, conference organizers, and professional speakers and consultants. Training Forum also publishes CD-ROM training products.

Training Technology Resource Center
http://www.ttrc.doleta.gov
The Training Technology Resource Center (TTRC) was established in 1991 by the United States Department of Labor (USDOL), Employment and Training Administration (ETA) as part of an effort to create a system that delivers employment and training services. In addition the Center serves as an electronic point of access to a wide range of workforce development information and enables information sharing throughout the Employment and Training Community. Website includes information on School-to-work, job training programs, skill standards, and Welfare-to-Work programs. Users can link to guides on how to train and retrain new employees, etc. Good source for government information.

Human Resource Development (HRD)–Training Performance
http://www.nwlink.com/~donclark/hrd.html
Site includes training materials, including an on-line guide to implementing a training program, book reviews, links to training and learning information, news on training, and Human Resource development, and leadership guides.

Training Information Source
http://www.training-info.com
Database of training and development resources covering a range of professional topics, from Career Development to International Management. This site allows user to locate, review, and register for training resources selected as best-in-class by Fortune 500 companies. Included are: Seminars Video conferences Satellite down-links Customized services Train-the-trainer search engine will allow you to search by training topics, provider name, location, and type. You can search by all the categories or just a few. Other features include a "bookstore" and an "Ask the Expert" column.

Seminar Finder
http://www.seminarfinder.com
Page allows user to locate professional seminars and continuing education courses, on a variety of topics, in cities throughout the United States and Canada. Updated regularly. User can browse by seminar location or topic. Also offers "Seminar Express" service whereby user can register for free to receive e-mail announcements of relevant seminars.

BENEFITS AND COMPENSATION

BenefitsLink(tm)–The Employee Benefits Web Site
http://www.benefitslink.com/
Questions and Answers about Section 125, COBRA, HIPAA, and more. Comprehensive index of Internet resources alphabetically by topic. Job openings and Jobs wanted. Keyword search capability. Opportunity to communicate with people with similar benefits interests and experiences.

Benefits and Compensation Solutions Magazine
http://www.bcsolutionsmag.com/
Issues online starting with May 1997. July/August is a special Internet issue.

Integrated Benefits Institute
http://www.ibiweb.org/
Information about the mission of the Institute and its current members. Overview of publications and ordering information. Some articles on benefits topics.

Compensation and Benefits
http://www.us.kpmg.com/compben/
Compensation and Benefits analysis from KPMG Peat Marwick. Summary of Employee Benefits Law changes in 1997. Guides to health insurance portability and ERISA. Annual survey of employer-provided health plans.

Employee Benefit Research Institute
http://www.ebri.org/
Nonprofit organization committed to original public policy research and education on economic security and employee benefits. Currency of the site is proven by research here on the Teamsters-UPS strike. Fact sheets. Membership information. Ordering information for EBRI publications. EBRI testimony and presentations.

International Foundation of Employee Benefit Plans (IFEBP)
http://www.ifebp.org/
Nonprofit educational organization. Membership information and descriptions of services. Job postings. Hot topics with summaries of related articles. Details about the Employee Benefits INFOSOURCE database and document delivery service. Links to other Internet resources.

American Compensation Association
http://www.acaonline.org/
Information and News section has bookstore and current news. Membership and certification information. 1997–1998 Total Salary Increase Budget Survey Results. Conferences and Events.

The Pension Research Council Home Page
http://prc.wharton.upenn.edu/prc/prc.html
From the Wharton School of the University of Pennsylvania. Information and research on pensions and other employee benefits. Publications, working papers, symposium, and an online newsletter. Most information needs to be ordered and cannot be accessed online.

Social Security Administration On-Line
http://www.ssa.gov/
Official web site of the Social Security Administration. Reference Guide for employers. Online publications including "Social Security Handbook," Welfare Reform updates, and "Factors in Evaluating Disability." Download Social Security Forms. Request your Personal Earnings and Benefit Estimate Statement.

Wageweb
http://www.wageweb.com
Non-members may view national salary data for a variety of job descriptions. Includes mean, minimum, maximum, and percent bonus eligible. Members may also view data by geography, size of organization or industry.

Pencom-Interactive Salary Survey
http://www.pencomsi.com/industry.html
Salary survey for computer professionals. Enter location, industry, years of experience and skills to get results.

Homebuyer's Fair
http://homefair.com/home
Compare the cost of living in hundreds of U.S. and International cities. Provides state tax tables. Crime indexes for 500 cities. Interstate moving costs. Insurance premium estimates. Mortgage recommendations. Compute loan amount for which you may qualify. Plan your move with a custom timeline. Other interesting information for planning a move.

Compensation Strategies
http://www.fed.org/library.html#comp
Full-text articles written by human resource professionals and experts.

Yahoo's index to salary information
http://www.yahoo.com/Business_and_Economy/Employment/Salary_Information/
Links to online sources of salary data as well as companies who provide this information.

Salary Information
http://jobsmart.org/tools/salary/index.htm
Links to salary surveys organized by profession and negotiation strategies. Surveys come from several kinds of sources. Evaluate the information in terms of currency, geographic coverage and application to individual situations.

RETIREMENT INFORMATION

PWBA List of Publications
http://www.dol.gov/pwba/public/pubs/main.htm
Retirement pamphlets online from the U.S. Pension and Welfare Benefit Administration. For example, "Simple Retirement Solutions for Small Business" and "What You Should Know About Your Pension Rights."

Retirement Planning
http://www.fidelityatwork.com/
Divided into sections for employees of private, nonprofit and government organizations. Features online calculators and worksheets. FAQs provide basic information on investment options.

Retirement Guide
http://www.aetna.com/financial/investment/game/retirement_guide.html
Worksheets. Investment basics. Model portfolios. Definitions.

EMPLOYMENT AND LABOR LAW

Employment Law materials from Cornell's Legal Information Institute
http://www.law.cornell.edu/topics/employment.html
Well organized starting point for employment and labor law. Provides overviews of the law in collective bargaining, employment discrimination, unemployment compensation, pensions, workplace safety, and worker's compensation. Links to federal and state laws, regulations, and judicial decisions in each of the above areas.

Law Journal Extra site devoted to Labor and Employment Law
http://www.ljextra.com/practice/laboremployment/index.html
Provides text of court decisions from employment-related cases around the country. Provides analysis of state and federal labor laws and weighs their impact on employers. View the Top 10 Wacky Employment Cases of 1996!

U.S. House of Representatives Internet Law Library
http://law.house.gov/100.htm
Created for Congress, but available to the general public. Links to significant court decisions. State and federal employment statutes. Links to memos and online articles.

Yahoo's Index to Employment Law sites
http://www.yahoo.com/Government/Law/Employment_Law/
Yahoo's directory of employment law sites is a great starting point. Choose from their list of sites or do a keyword search to find what you're looking for. Also lists companies and firms who work in this area.

Employee relations web picks, published by New York Public Employment Reports
http://www.nyper.com/
Covers national issues on public employment with an emphasis on New York State.

Internet Legal Resources for Labor Law
http://www.findlaw.com/01topics/27labor/index.html
Good keyword searching capability. Divides sites into primary materials: laws and government documents, Publications: Journals, newsletters, and articles. Mailing list and usenet groups. Government agencies, Outlines. and Software. Or choose from the alphabetical list.

Labor Law Updates
http://www.perc_net/Law.html
Provided by PERC (Public Employee Relations Council). Articles relating to legal developments of interest to human resource managers. Examples of company policies.

WashLaw Web
http://lawlib.wuacc.edu/washlaw/searchlaw.html
Provided by Washburn University's Law School, allows users to search appellate court decisions by circuit. Links to other searchable legislative and judicial materials.

LawCrawler
http://www.lawcrawler.com/
Search the entire Internet for court findings as well as articles on legal topics. Useful for international law because search can be focused on a specific country.

Human Resource Management Law Page
http://www.hrmgt.com/hrmlaw.html
From California State University–Stanislaus. Special areas of focus include independent contractor law, wrongful discharge, employment-at-will, sexual harassment and age discrimination.

Ross Runkel's Labor and Employment Law Page
http://www.willamette.edu/law/laborlaw/
Updated frequently. Summaries of current cases and developments in arbitration, employment discrimination, employment and labor law. Professor Runkel has created "unofficial" pages for agencies such as the NLRB and EEOC to try and make the information more accessible.

DIVERSITY IN EMPLOYMENT

Dept. of Justice ADA Homepage
http://www.usdoj.gov/crt/ada
Government information from the Department of Justice including ADA technical assistance materials, settlement information and agreements, new or proposed regulations, IRS tax credits and deductions, telephone contact numbers, information on building codes and more. Also included are locations for ADA mediators and a link to other sites.

EEOC Homepage
http://www.eeoc.gov
The U.S. Equal Employment Opportunity Commission's homepage offers information on employment discrimination, filing charges, enforcement and litigation, technical assistance programs, and general information on the Commission including press releases and telephone contact points.

Disability Forum
http://www.employease.com/disability
Sponsored by the Fortis Benefits Insurance Company. Information on this site is obtained from both published and unpublished sources, and from contributions of the visitors to the Forum. The Disability Forum contains both factual information and opinions. It was designed to provide a meeting place for employees, employers, human resource administrators, and insurance specialists.

American Institute for Managing Diversity
http://www.aimd.org
The American Institute for Managing Diversity, Inc. (AIMD) is a nonprofit organization dedicated to education and research in the field of diversity management. Site gives information on the Institute with links to their Research department, Advocacy Services (designed to help organizations think through decision making questions). Also has links to various introductory resources on managing diversity including planning and implementation, measurement theory and methods, business rationale, and the organizational impact of managing diversity.

Workplace Diversity Network
http://www.ilr.cornell.edu/depts/WDN
Co-founded by the Cornell University School of Industrial and Labor Relations and The National Conference, The Workplace Diversity Network was created to extend "diversity learning" across organizations and work sector by breaking practitioner isolation. Network participants come from corporations, unions, small businesses, schools, community service agencies and government offices. The Network facilitates the exchange of strategies and best practices for creating effective, productive workplace environments where people can be different and still be respected and given opportunity to develop their talents. The website has registration information and link to Network Newsletter.

Employment Standards Administration
Office of Federal Contract Compliance Programs
http://www.dol.gov/dol/esa/public/ofcp_org.htm
Web site from the Dept. of Labor has search engine and "what's new" section with EEO poster in both and English and Spanish as well as general information on the Office. Media releases, special reports, statutory, regulatory and compliance information, and a public domain availability list are also available.

SEXUAL HARASSMENT IN THE WORKPLACE

Sexual Harassment Prevention
http://www.bna.com/bnac/docsex.html
A list of training program videos and manuals from BNA Communications, Inc. Site gives description of each program and information on renting or purchasing material. Topics include: Clarifying Appropriate Workplace Behavior and Reducing Litigation Risk, Preventing Costly Sexual Harassment Complaints and Lawsuits in Manufacturing and Service Industries, Training Managers and Employees to Recognize and Resolve Subtle Sexual Harassment, Preventing Sexual Harassment in Hotel, Restaurant, and Service Industries.

U.S. Employment Discrimination Law
http://www.law.cornell.edu/topics/employment_discrimination.html
Part of the Legal Information Institute at Cornell University's Law School, this site is a searchable database of Employment Discrimination law material. In addition to Federal and State materials including links to text of The Civil Rights Act of 1964, The Rehabilitation Act, The Black Lung Act, and The Age Discrimination in Employment, the website also has links to other relevant sites such as the U.S. Dept. of Labor.

Sexual Harassment—What is Sexual Harassment
http://www.altosnet.com/Sampler/harass.htm
The Altos Education Network offers business courses and training for managers, professionals and entrepreneurs on the Internet. This site is a sampler of their course on sexual harassment taught by trial court judge Frances Lynch. Included in the sampler are types of sexual harassment claims, EEOC claims, and a multiple choice sample exam.

RECRUITMENT AND JOB SEARCHING

Recruiting links
http://members.aol.com/hrmbasics/recruit.htm
Alphabetical list of recruiting web sites. Information on discussion groups about career development.

Jobtrak
http://www.jobtrak.com/
"With over 250,000 page views per day and 2,400 new job openings daily, JOBTRAK is one of the largest and most popular employment sites on the internet." There is a fee to post jobs here, but Jobtrak has formed partnerships with over 600 college and university career centers, MBA programs, and alumni associations so the audience is large. Job seekers (students or alumni) must obtain a password from their University career center.

Descriptions Now! Direct from Knowledge Point
http://www.jobdescription.com/
Thousands of ADA-compliant job descriptions that users can download and tailor to their own needs for a fee. Updated monthly to reflect new job titles, as well as new laws and rulings that affect how job descriptions are written. At time of writing, fees are $7.95 per description downloaded or $49 for 6-months unlimited use or $89 for 12-months unlimited use.

Employee Management Association
http://www.shrm.org/ema/
Professional Association affiliated with the Society for Human Resource Management. Recruitment and employment advertising are two areas of special interest. Link to job advertisements for the position of "recruiter" from around the country.

Recruitment Extra
http://recruitmentextra.com/
This site is divided into categories of layoffs, job and career fairs, salary surveys, unemployment figures, newspaper opportunities, magazine opportunities, lead sheet, recruitment on TV, rankings, and professional organizations. Helpful information for recruiters.

The Riley Guide
http://www.dbm.com/jobguide/
Great starting point. Job listings by occupation, place, population (i.e. women), or general listings. Find help with career and company research. Online resume databases. Margaret Riley writes, "All services and resources included in this guide must provide free and open access to the job listings they host or to significant other information, services, and/or resources of benefit to the job seeker . . . Some sites which charge for their services may be included since the information or service they offer is unique or the field or industry is not otherwise represented online."

American Job Bank
http://www.ajb.dni.us/
This site provides job listings for job seekers and also allows postings by employers. Search for jobs by keyword or using a menu or by occupational code. Post jobs free of charge after registering with the service. There is a good "Frequently Asked Questions" section to help job seekers or employers use this site. Also has links to job market information on the Internet and guides such as "Preparing your resume for the Internet."

Career Information
http://w3.one.net/~denek/Employ/emp496.htm
Job listings, recruiters, company profiles, interactive atlas, human resource information center. I'm not sure who Dennis Kaiser (the producer of the site) is but this page is good starting point.

Employment Resource Center
http://hubcap.clemson.edu/management/employ.html
From Clemson University's Department of Management. The professors who maintain this page have evaluated the job search engines for criteria such as cost to user, resume posting ability. keyword searching ability. Has links to job postings at major companies. Business directories for company research. Career guidance.

Yahoo's Employment Links
http://www.yahoo.com/Business/Employment/
Great starting point with indexes to web sites for jobs, resumes, salary information, telecommuting, career planning, women's career resources and more.

ARBITRATION AND MEDIATION

American Arbitration Association
http://www.adr.org
Provides up to the minute information about mediation, arbitration, and other alternative dispute resolution techniques. This site covers ADR laws, information on training programs, links to other educational resources, bibliographies. etc.

Conflict Resolution Consortium
http://www.colorado.edu/conflict/
From University of Colorado. Includes online conflict resolution course. Collection of 44 full-text case studies. Free online searching. Links to more than 650 conflict related web sources including such topics as peace research and environmental disputes. Information about education and training programs offered by the Consortium and others. Full text copies of more than 100 working papers.

Prevention & Early Resolution of Conflict (PERC)
http://www2.conflictresolution.org/perc/index.html
Founded by Theodore W. Keel, the Cornell/PERC Institute on Conflict Resolution endeavors to educate practitioners, users, teachers, and students in the field of conflict resolution. Homepage has links to PERC Bulletin, distance learning course in conflict resolution, access to roundtable of discussion in the area of conflict resolution and information on PERC projects.

Society of Professionals in Dispute Resolution
http://www.igc.apc.org/spidr
3,200 member professional association of mediators, arbitrators, dispute resolution professionals. Homepage has membership information and chapter location, publications and current programs.

CPR Institute for Dispute Resolution
http://www.cpradr.org
Nonprofit initiative of global corporations, law firms and law teachers developing new uses of alternative dispute resolution for business and public disputes. Search engine, International coverage. Offers practice tools such as Mediation Model Procedure. Full page of ADR in Industry and Practice areas including CPR publications in the areas of construction, food industry, employment, and antitrust.

IGC: ConflictNet
http://www.igc.org/igc/conflictnet
Maintained by the Institute of Global Communications, ConflictNet is one of five online communities of activists and organizations (the others being PeaceNet, EcoNet, LaborNet, and WomanNet). A gateway of articles, headlines, features and weblinks highlighting the work of practitioners and organizations.

SELECTED UNIONS

International Confederation of Free Trade Unions
http://www.icftu.org
Official site of The ICFTU, a confederation of national trade union centers, each of which groups together the trade unions of that particular country. The ICFTU has 195 affiliates in 137 countries on all five continents, with a membership of some 124 million. Site has policies and procedures of the ICFTU, links to member unions. and a press bulletin board.

Jobs with Justice
Cyber Picket Line
http://www.cf.ac.uk/ccin/union
Comprehensive directory of labor on the Web. British based but global coverage. Very comprehensive World Directory of trade unions with over 1200 links to sites all over the world. Timely strike coverage in Britain and abroad.

Union Ring
http://www.geocities.com/CapitolHill/5202/unionring.html
Privately maintained labor website based in Edmonton, Alberta. Trade union websites can register and place their homepages in this "ring" thus giving their site a wider exposure. Mostly Canadian and U.S. in scope.

AFL-CIO Home Page
http://www.aflcio.org
Information about AFL-CIO. Policy statements, boycott list. Information about organizing institute. Working Women's Department. Many links to related sites.

AFSCME–the American Federation of State, County, and Municipal Employees
http://www.afscme.org
Homepage of the nation's largest public employee and health care workers union, with more than 1.3 million members. Page has organizational structure and background information, links to relevant policy and legislation, news releases and links to other sites.

Union Resource Network
http://www.unions.org
Organized under the Communication Workers of America, the Union Resource Network (URN) is a comprehensive index of Union Websites on the Internet. Currently, approximately 10% of all union websites in the world are hosted on the URN server and arranged by state or country. Search by keyword, local number or acronym of union.

LABOR

IGC: LaborNet Directory
http://www.igc.org/igc/ln/bg/unions.html
Labor news articles, jump off sites for various labor related issues, unions and labor organizations. Strike page. Good starting point for further information.

Laborlink
http://www.laborlink.simplenet.com
Gateway to reference sources in organized labor and labor relations. Numerous employment law links.

U.S. Dept. of Labor
http://www.dol.gov
Starting point for accessing home pages of Department of Labor agencies. Media Releases. Statutory and Regulatory information. Links to labor-related data. Grant and Contract information. Download Department of Labor posters.

NYS Dept. of Labor
http://www.labor.state.ny.us
In addition to departmental information such as directories, press releases, etc. this site also provides job and career resources, information for employers, law affecting employees and employers and unemployment insurance information.

Guide to Labor-Oriented Internet Labor Resources
http://www.lib.berkeley.edu/IIRL/iirlnet.html
From Institute of Industrial Relations Library at UC Berkeley. Well organized jump off sites to national and international labor resources.

National Labor Relations Board
http://www.nlrb.gov
Weekly summary of cases. Search index of past decisions and orders. NLRB rules and regulations. Directory of Headquarters and Field Offices.

STATISTICAL SITES

U.S. Bureau of Labor Statistics
http://stats.bls.gov/
Excellent source for labor statistics. Employment cost trends. Labor force statistics from the current population survey. Safety and health statistics. Online news releases on hot topics (i.e., "Expenditures for health care plans by employers and employees"). Both national and regional data. Keyword searching available.

FedStats
http://www.fedstats.gov/
More than 70 agencies in the United States Federal Government produce statistics of interest to the public. The Federal Interagency Council on Statistical Policy maintains this site to provide easy access to the full range of statistics and information produced by these agencies for public use.

Economic Statistics Briefing Room
http://www.whitehouse.gov/fsbr/esbr.html
Easy access to statistics an production, sales, orders, inventories, income, expenditures, wealth, employment, unemployment, earnings, prices, money, credit, interest, transportation, international.

Social Statistics Briefing Room
http://www.whitehouse.gov/fsbr/ssbr.html
Easy access to statistics on crime, demographics, education, and health.

County and City Data Books
http://www.lib.virginia.edu/socsci/ccdb/
Provides Web access to the electronic versions of the 1988 and 1994 County and City Data Books. Provides the opportunity to create custom printouts and/or customized data subsets. Great for local information.

Demographic Data Viewer
http://plue.sedac.ciesin.org/plue/ddviewer/
Create maps and calculate statistics for 220 demographic variables from the 1990 U.S. Census. DDViewer will map counties, county subdivisions, census tracts, or block groups. Definitely check this site out!

Council of Professional Associations on Federal Statistics
http://members.aol.com/copafs/
Current news about developments in federal statistics and links to all federal statistical agencies.

Statistical Office of the European Communities
http://europa.eu.int/en/comm/eurostat/
Choose Dutch, English, or French. Choose "Online statistical publications and indicators" for statistics about European Union countries. View press releases, statistical news, and on-line catalogues. Find out about the statistical information service provided.

Statistics Canada
http://www.statcan.ca/start.html
Easy to use site for Canadian statistics. Includes free data from the 1996 census.

COMPANY INFORMATION

Hoover's Online
http://www.hoovers.com
Hoover's, Inc. is a company information publisher that distributes information through a wide variety of online media and on Web sites. Covers more than 11,000 U.S. and foreign companies, both public and private, with information including a description of the company, address, officers, sales and employment figures and links to more information such as financial reports and stock quotes. Some of the search engines are free of charge, others require a subscription. Search for historical financial information and job listings by company.

EDGAR Database
http://www.sec.gov/edgarhp.htm
EDGAR, the Electronic Data Gathering, Analysis, and Retrieval system, performs automated collection, validation, indexing, acceptance, and forwarding of submissions by companies and others who are required by law to file forms with the U.S. Securities and Exchange Commission (SEC). Not all documents filed with the Commission by public companies will be available on EDGAR. Filings are posted 24 hours after date of filing. User can search small business information, SEC filings, and current events analysis among others. Search by keyword, company name and ticker symbol.

Wall Street Research Net
http://www.wsrn.com
Wall Street Research Net consists of over 250,000 links to help professional and private investors perform fundamental research on actively traded companies and mutual funds and locate important economic data that moves markets. Search engines allow users to research a company (both U.S. and Canadian) by name of stock symbol. Can also research the economy, markets, business news and research publications, as well as searching information from the Dept. of Commerce, Federal Reserve sites, U. S. Courts, and international research.

Reuters MoneyNet.com
http://www.moneynet.com
Provides up to the minute business news and stock information. Users can customize stock reports and even create their own tickertape.

Companies Online Search
http://www.companiesonline.com
Free registration allows user to search over 100,000 public and private companies by name, stock symbol, url, and industry. Weekly featured companies have information on annual sales, company size, ownership structure, website and email addresses, and more.

HR AND RELATED ONLINE MAGAZINES

SHRM—HRMagazine
http://www.shrm.org/docs/HRmagazine.html
Published by the Society for Human Resource Management. Most recent issue online along with a search engine of back issues by keyword or topic. Articles have links to other sites. Subscription information available.

Industrial and Labor Relations Review
http://www.ilr.cornell.edu/depts/ILRrev
From the Industrial and Labor Relations School at Cornell University. Gives abstracts of articles from July 1994 to present. Also has information on research currently underway at other universities. Information on article submission and subscriptions also available.

Industrial Relations: A Journal of Economy and Society
http://violet.berkeley.edu/~iir/indrel/indrel.htm
Academic journal of the Institute of Industrial Relations at the University of California at Berkeley. Published quarterly. Each issue includes research articles, notes, and symposia on all aspects of employment relations and the labor market. Website gives abstracts for the two latest issues.

The Labor Center Reporter
http://violet.berkeley.edu/~iir/clre/lcr/lcr.html
A publication produced by graduate students, faculty, and Labor Center staff. Covering labor and employment data, technical advice and commentary for labor union staff, members and libraries. The more recent articles have covered diverse topics: NAFTA, unions and democracy, the health insurance crisis, bargaining and the family, defense conversion, and the Diamond Walnut strike. Full text of articles online. Subscription and submission information also available.

GENERAL NEWS SITES

CNN Interactive
http://www.cnn.com
Up to the minute. No registration required. Includes video and audio clips. Specialized "custom news" service.

New York Times
http://www.nyt.com
Free subscription online. Selected full-text. Tour for newcomers. Audio and video clips. Links to related articles. Search engine.

The Wall Street Journal
http://www.wsj.com
By subscription only. $49.00 a year. Free tour and two week trial period. Search engines include specialized searching for business and company information.

USA Today
http://www.usatoday.com
No subscription necessary. Updated several times a day. Feedback and interactive polls.

Washington Post
http://www.washingtonpost.com
Supplies image of daily front page. Search capability on most pages. Heavy on political news. Selected full text.

HR BOOKSTORES

Employee Benefits Books
http://www.benefitslink.com/benefits-bin/amazon.cgi
Benefit Link's List of Employee Benefits books from Amazon.com. Large list in alphabetical order, also has links author bibliographies from each book summary. Available for ordering online.

HR Bookstore
http://www.tcm.com/hr-books/
A link off of the Training and Development Resource Center. Subject divisions such as hiring/selection, intranets, performance management, teams, training and development. Links to author bibliographies and available for ordering online.

HR Publications
http://www.ihrim.org
Choose *HR Publications*, and then choose *HR Books & Publications*. This site is a link on the IHRIM home page. Publication orders are fulfilled by Business Outreach Books (www.bizoutreach.com/), and IHRIM members get a discount.

ILR Press
http://www.ilr.cornell.edu/depts/ilrpress/
From this home page, you may access the 1997 ILR Press Catalog from Cornell University.

SELECTED CONSULTANTS

Cornell University and the Earth Pledge Foundation do not endorse the following consultants. The sites are given as examples of consultants' home pages on the Web.

Hewitt Associates
http://www.hewittassoc.com
Hewitt Associates "help organizations gain a competitive advantage by . . . using methods ranging from long-term management strategies to day-to-day administration and delivery of human resource services." Press releases and news articles about Hewitt are available on the site.

Towers Perrin
http://www.towersperrin.com
"Our primary aim is to help organizations undergoing change improve their performance through people. Our consultants focus on business strategy as it relates to organizational change, effectiveness and the alignment of total rewards, organization communications, human resource (HR) policies and the other factors that help foster peak performance." Fields includes general management and HR services, employee benefits services, and integrated healthsystems consulting.

Aon Home Page
http://www.alexalex.com
"Aon Corporation is a family of insurance brokerage, consulting and consumer insurance companies serving clients and policyholders through global distribution networks owned by Aon subsidiary companies." Corporate and financial information included, along with 1996 annual report.

Nardoni Associates Inc. (NAI)
http://www.nardoni.com
"NAI is a world leader in competency-based succession planning and management development systems. With a worldwide Fortune 500 clientele, NAI has assisted companies in the design and implementation of effective processes and systems to manage their critical human resources." NAI offers a variety of software products and consulting services. Product information and links to HR sites are available on website.

Sierra Systems Consultants Inc.
http://www.sierrasys.com
"One of North America's most experienced and successful Information Technology professional services organizations, we've been giving clients practical advice and helping them develop cost-effective Information Technology-based business solutions since 1966." Site has "Human Resources Information Center" with articles on human resources and related subjects, Ask the Experts section and HR links.

Caras & Associates, Inc.
http://www.carasadr.com
Specializing in field of Alternative Dispute Resolution systems throughout the United States, Mexico, and Canada. "Specifically, our company has become a world leader in Alternative Dispute Resolution (ADR) systems through the implementation of a procedure known as Peer Review. Peer Review utilizes a fair and just process for resolving day-to-day workplace disagreements." Site includes video clips and client list.

INTRANET

The Complete Intranet Resource
http://www.intrack.com/intranet
Developed by Smart Infortech, Ltd., this webpage is a searchable index of sites concerning Intranet development including the latest events, mailing lists, online demos, news and jobs. Provides information on planning, designing, and implementing intranets through articles, case studies, software packages and more. Other features include "An Introduction to Extranets" and the site's selections for Intranet Application of the Week. Updated weekly.

The Intranet Journal
http://www.intranetjournal.com
Owned by Brill Editorial Services. Features include news, conferencing tools, training-related sites, newsgroups, search tools, information on shareware and freeware (including free downloading) and evaluations of new software. Other features include a calendar of upcoming intranet and extranet-related seminars and other events. Site also has its own intranet newsgroup.

Intranet Resources
http://www.strom.com/pubwork/intranet.html
Site maintained by David Strom Inc., a networking and communications consulting firm specializing in Internet-related product testing. Along with some of the features listed in the above intranet sites, this webpage offers links intranet information from Netscape, Microsoft and Lotus.

HTML

NCSA–A Beginner's Guide to HTML Home Page
http://www.ncsa.uiuc.edu/General/Internet/WWW/HTMLPrimer.html
Designed by The National Center for Supercomputing Applications, this guide, which is available for downloading, is used to start to understand the hypertext markup language (HTML) used on the World Wide Web. It is an introduction and does not pretend to offer instructions on every aspect of HTML. Links to additional Web-based resources about HTML and other related aspects of preparing files are provided at the end of the guide. There is also a link to Access Online. a NCSA publication.

Glossary of Web and HTML Terms
http://www.library.cornell.edu/design/dsigngloss.html
Designed by staff of the Cornell University Library system. A good starting point for understanding the terminology of HTML. In some cases, glossary has links to fuller definitions.

Introduction to HTML (Case Western University)
http://www.cwru.edu/help/introHTML/toc.html
From Case Western University. Very thorough, well laid out tutorial cover all aspects the beginner wanting an understanding of HTML. Includes glossary, index, and Frequently Asked Questions (FAQ).

Glossary of Terms

Ability Refers to an individual's capability to engage in a specific behavior.

Ability to Pay The ability of a firm to meet employee wage demands while remaining profitable; a frequent issue in contract negotiations with unions. A firm's ability to pay is constrained by its ability to compete in its product market.

Access Discrimination Focuses on the staffing and allocation decisions made by employers. It denies particular jobs, promotions, or training opportunities to qualified women or minorities. This type of discrimination is illegal under Title VII of the Civil Rights Act of 1964.

Across-the-Board Increases A general adjustment that provides equal increases to all employees.

Adjective Checklist An individual (or job) rating technique. In its simplest form, it is a set of adjectives or descriptive statements. If the employee (job) possesses a trait listed, the item is checked. A rating score from the checklist equals the number of statements checked.

Age Discrimination in Employment Act (ADEA) of 1967 (Amended 1978, 1986, and 1990) Makes nonfederal employees age 40 and over a protected class relative to their treatment in pay, benefits, and other personnel actions. The 1990 amendment is called the *Older Workers Benefit Protection Act.*

Agency Theory A theory of motivation that depicts exchange relationships in terms of two parties: agents and principals. According to this theory, both sides of the exchange will seek the most favorable exchange possible and will act opportunistically if given a chance. As applied to executive compensation, agency theory would place part of the executive's pay at risk, to motivate the executive (agent) to act in the best interests of the shareholders (principals) rather than in the executive's own self-interests.

All-Salaried Work Force Both exempt employees (exempt from provisions of the Fair Labor Standards Act), who traditionally are paid a salary rather than an hourly rate, and nonexempt employees receive a prescribed amount of money each pay period that does not primarily depend on the number of hours worked.

Alternation Ranking A job evaluation method that involves ordering the job description alternately at each extreme. All the jobs are considered. Agreement is reached on which is the most valuable, then the least valuable. Evaluators alternate between the next most valued and next least valued and so on until the jobs have been ordered.

American Compensation Association (ACA) A nonprofit organization for training compensation professionals.

Appeals Procedures Mechanism created to handle pay disagreements. They provide a forum for employees and managers to voice their complaints and receive a hearing.

Balance Sheet A method for compensating expatriates based upon the belief that the employee not suffer financially for accepting a foreign-based assignment. The expatriate's pay is adjusted so that the amounts of the financial responsibilities the expatriate had prior to the assignment are kept at about the same level while on assignment—the company pays for the difference.

Base Pay *See* Base Wage.

Base Wage The basic cash compensation that an employer pays for the work performed. Tends to reflect the value of the work itself and ignore differences in individual contributions.

Basic Pay Policies Include decisions on the relative importance of (1) internal consistency, (2) external competitiveness, (3) employee contributions, and (4) the administration of the pay system. These policies form the foundation for the design and administration of pay systems and serve as guidelines for managing pay to accomplish the system's objectives.

Bedeaux Plan Individual incentive plan that provides a variation on straight piecework and standard hour plans. Instead of timing an entire task, a Bedeaux plan requires determination of the time required to complete each simple action of a task. Workers receive a wage incentive for completing a task in less than a standard time.

Behaviorally Anchored Rating Scales (BARS) Variants on standard rating scales in which the various scale levels are anchored with behavioral descriptions directly applicable to jobs being evaluated.

Benchmark Conversion Matching survey jobs by applying the employer's plan to the external jobs and then comparing the worth of the external job with its internal "match."

Benchmark (or Key) Jobs A prototypical job, or group of jobs, used as reference points for making pay comparisons within or without the organization. Benchmark jobs have well-known and stable contents; their current pay rates are generally acceptable, and the pay differentials among them are relatively stable. A group of benchmark jobs, taken together, contains the entire range of compensable factors and is accepted in the external labor market for setting wages.

Benefit Ceiling A maximum payout for specific benefit claims (e.g., limiting liability for extended hospital stays to $150,000).

Benefit Cutbacks Similar to wage concessions, negotiations by some employers with employees to eliminate or reduce employer contributions to selected benefits options.

Best Pay Practices Compensation practices that allow employers to gain preferential access to superior human resource talent and competencies (i.e., valued assets), which in turn influence the strategies the organization adopts.

BLS *See* Bureau of Labor Statistics.

Bonus A lump-sum payment to an employee in recognition of goal achievement.

Bottom Up Approach to Pay Budgeting Under this approach individual employees' pay rates for the next plan year are forecasted and summed to create an organization's total budget.

Broadbanding Collapsing a number of salary grades into a smaller number of broad grades with wide ranges.

Budget A plan within which managers operate and a standard against which managers' actual expenditures are evaluated.

Bureau of Labor Statistics A major source of publicly available pay data. It also publishes the Consumer Price Index.

Cafeteria (Flexible) Benefit Plan A benefit plan in which employees have a choice as to the benefits they receive within some dollar limit. Usually a common core benefit package is required (e.g., specific minimum levels of health, disability, retirement, and death benefit) plus elective programs from which the employee may select a set dollar amount. Additional coverage may be available through employee contributions.

Capital Appreciation Plans *See* Long-Term Incentives.

Career Paths Refers to the progression of jobs within an organization.

Central Tendency A midpoint in a group of measures.

Central Tendency Error A rating error that occurs when a rater consistently rates a group of employees at or close to the midpoint of a scale irrespective of true score performance of ratees. Avoiding extremes (both high and low) in ratings across employees.

Churn *See* Turnover Effect.

Civil Rights Act Title VII of the Civil Rights Act of 1964 prohibits discrimination in terms and conditions of employment (including benefits) that is based on race, color, religion, sex, or national origin.

Civil Rights Act of 1991 Reestablishes the standards for proving discrimination that had been in general use before the 1989 Supreme Court rulings. Allows jury trials and damage awards.

Claims Processing Begins when employee asserts that a specific event (e.g., disablement, hospitalization, unemployment) has occurred and demands that the employer fulfill a promise for payment. As such, a claims processor must first determine whether the act has, in fact, occurred.

Classification Job evaluation method that involves slotting job descriptions into a series of classes or grades that cover the range of jobs and that serve as a standard against which the job descriptions are compared.

Clone Error Giving better ratings to individuals who are like the rater in behavior or personality.

Coinsurance Employees share in the cost of a benefit provided to them.

Commission Payment tied directly to achievement of performance standards. Commissions are directly tied to a profit index (sales, production level) and employee costs; thus, they rise and fall in line with revenues.

Comparable Worth A doctrine that maintains that women performing jobs judged to be equal on some measure of inherent worth should be paid the same as men, excepting allowable differences, such as seniority, merit, and production-based pay plans, and other non-sex-related factors. Objective is to eliminate use of market in setting wages for jobs held by women.

Compa-Ratio An index that helps assess how managers actually pay employees in relation to the midpoint of the pay range established for jobs. It estimates how well actual practices correspond to intended policy. Calculated as the following ratio:

$$\text{Compa-Ratio} = \frac{\text{Average rates actually paid}}{\text{Range midpoint}}$$

Comparators Used in Ontario, Canada's, pay equity legislation. Refers to jobs deemed appropriate for wage comparisons between male- and female-dominated job classifications.

Compensable Factors Job attributes that provide the basis for evaluating the relative worth of jobs inside an organization. A compensable factor must be work related, business related, and acceptable to the parties involved.

Compensating Differentials Economic theory that attributes the variety of pay rates in the external labor market to differences in attractive as well as negative characteristics in jobs. Pay differences must overcome negative characteristics to attract employees.

Compensation All forms of financial returns and tangible services and benefits employees receive as part of an employment relationship.

Compensation Budgeting A part of the organization's planning process; helps to ensure that future financial expenditures are coordinated and controlled. It involves forecasting the total expenditures required by the pay system during the next period as well as the amount of the pay increases. Bottom up and top down are the two typical approaches to the process.

Compensation Differentials Differentials in pay among jobs across and within organizations, and among individuals in the same job in an organization.

Compensation Objectives The desired results of the pay system. The basic pay objectives include efficiency, equity, and compliance with laws and regulations. Objectives shape the design of the pay system and serve as the standard against which the success of the pay system is evaluated.

Compensation at Risk *See* Earnings at Risk.

Compensation System Controls Basic processes that serve to control pay decision making. They include (1) controls inherent in the design of the pay techniques (e.g., increase guidelines, range maximums and minimums), and (2) budgetary controls.

Competency Basic units of knowledge and abilities employees must acquire or demonstrate in a competency-based plan in order to successfully perform the work, satisfy customers, and achieve business objectives.

Competency Based Links pay to the depth and scope of competencies that are relevant to doing the work. Typically used in managerial and professional work where what is accomplished may be difficult to identify.

Competency Analysis A systematic process to identify and collect information about the competencies required for the person and the organization to be successful.

Competitive Objective The midpoints for each pay range. The pay policy line that connects the midpoints becomes a control device: compensation must be managed to conform to these midpoints if the organization is to maintain the pay policy it has specified.

Competitive Position The comparison of the compensation offered by one employer relative to that paid by its competitors.

Compression Very narrow pay differentials among jobs at different organization levels as a result of wages for jobs filled from the outside (frequently these are entry-level jobs) increasing faster than the internal pay structure.

Congruency The degree of consistency or "fit" between the compensation system and other organizational components such as the strategy, product-market stage, culture and values, employee needs, union status.

Consolidated Omnibus Budget Reconciliation Act (COBRA) Employees who resign or are laid off through no fault of their own are eligible to continue receiving health coverage under employer's plan at a cost borne by the employee.

Consumer Price Index (CPI) Published by the Bureau of Labor Statistics, U.S. Department of Labor, it measures the changes in prices of a fixed market basket of goods and services purchased by a hypothetical average family.

Content Theories Motivation theories that focus on *what* motivates people rather than on *how* people are motivated. Maslow's need hierarchy theory and Herzberg's two-factor theory fall in this category.

Contingency Work Force A growing work force that includes flexible workers, temporaries, part-time employees, and independent contractors. The pay and benefits of contingent workers tend to be about half the pay and benefits of noncontingent workers.

Contingent Employees Workers whose employment is of a limited duration (part-time or temporary).

Contributory Benefit Financing Plans Costs shared between employer and employee.

Contributory Financing Refers to an employee benefit that is partially paid for by the employee.

Conventional Job Analysis Methods Methods (e.g., functional job analysis) that typically involve an analyst using a questionnaire in conjunction with structured interviews of job incumbents and supervisors. The methods place considerable reliance on analysts' ability to understand the work performed and to accurately describe it.

Cooperative Wage Study (CWS) A study undertaken by 12 steel companies and the United Steel Workers to design an industrywide point plan (the Steel Plan) for clerical and technical personnel.

Coordination of Benefits. Efforts to ensure that employer coverage of an employee does not "double pay" because of identical protection offered by the government (private pension and social security coordination) or a spouse's employer.

Core Employees Workers with whom a long-term full-time work relationship is anticipated.

Cost Containment Attempts made by organizations to contain benefits costs, such as imposing deductibles and coinsurance on health benefits or replacing defined benefit pension plans with defined contribution plans.

Cost of Living Actual individual expenditures on goods and services. The only way to measure it accurately is to examine the expense budget of each employee.

Cost of Living Adjustments (COLAs) Across-the-board wage and salary increases or supplemental payments based on changes in some index of prices, usually the Consumer Price Index (CPI). If included in a union contract, COLAs are designed to increase wages automatically during the life of the contract as a function of changes in the Consumer Price Index (CPI).

Cost of Living Increase *See* Cost of Living Adjustments.

Cost Savings Plans Group incentive plans that focus on cost savings rather than on profit increases as the standard of group incentive (e.g., Scanlon, Rucker, Improshare).

CPI *See* Consumer Price Index

Culture The informal rules, rituals, and value systems of an organization that influence the way employees behave.

Davis-Bacon Act of 1931 Requires most federal contractors to pay wage rates prevailing in the area.

Deductibles Employer cost-saving tool by which the employee pays first x number of dollars when a benefit is used (e.g., hospitalization). The employer pays subsequent costs up to some predetermined maximum.

Deferred Compensation Program Provide income to an employee at some future time as a compensation for work performed now. Types of deferred compensation programs include stock option plans and pension plans.

Defined Benefits Plan A benefits option or package in which the employer agrees to give the specified benefit without regard to cost maximum. Opposite of defined contribution plan.

Defined Contribution Plan A benefits option or package in which the employer negotiates a dollar maximum payout. Any change in benefits costs over time reduces the amount of coverage unless new dollar limits are negotiated.

Differentials Pay differences among levels within the organization, such as the difference in pay between adjacent levels in a career path, between supervisors and subordinates, between union and nonunion employees, and between executives and regular employees.

Differentiating Competencies Factors that distinguish superior performance from average performance.

Direct Compensation Pay received directly in the form of cash (e.g., wages, bonuses, incentives).

Disparate (Unequal) Impact Standard Outlaws the application of pay practices that may appear to be neutral but have a negative effect on females or minorities, unless those practices can be shown to be business related.

Disparate (Unequal) Treatment Standard Outlaws the application of different standards to different classes of employees unless they can be shown to be business related.

Dispersion Distribution of rates around a measure of central tendency.

Distributive Justice Fairness in the amount of reward distributed to employees.

DOLs Original Department of Labor methodology of job analysis. It categorized data to be collected as (1) actual work performed and (2) work traits or characteristics. Actual work performed is further refined into three categories: worker functions (what the worker does), work fields (the methods and techniques employed), and products and services (output).

Double-Track System A framework for professional employees in an organization whereby at least two general tracks of ascending compensation steps are available: (1) a managerial track to be ascended through increasing responsibility for supervision of people and (2) a professional track to be ascended through increasing contributions of a professional nature.

Drive Theory A motivational theory that assumes that all behavior is induced by drives (i.e., energizers such as thirst, hunger, sex), and that present behavior is based in large part on the consequences or rewards of past behavior.

Dual Career Ladders Two different ways to progress in an organization, each reflecting different types of contribution to the organization's mission. The managerial ladder ascends through increasing responsibility for supervision or direction of people. The professional track ascends through increasing contributions of a professional nature that do not mainly entail the supervision of employees.

Dual Coverage In families in which both spouses work, dual coverage refers to coverage of specific claims from each spouse's employment benefit package. Employers cut costs by specifying payment limitations under such conditions.

Earnings-at-Risk Plans *See* Risk Sharing.

Efficiency Pay Objective Involves (1) improving productivity and (2) controlling labor costs.

Efficiency Wage Theory A theory to explain why firms are rational in offering higher than necessary wages.

Employee Benefits That part of the total compensation package, other than pay for time worked, provided to employees in whole or in part by employer payments (e.g., life insurance, pension, workers' compensation, vacation).

Employee Contributions Refers to comparisons among individuals doing the same job for the same organization.

Employee Equity *See* Employee Contributions.

Employee-Pay-All Financing Refers to an employee benefit that is fully paid for by the employee.

Employee Retirement Income Security Act of 1974 (ERISA) An act regulating private employer pension and welfare programs. The act has provisions that cover eligibility for participation, reporting, and disclosure requirements, establish fiduciary standards for the financial management of retirement funds, set up tax incentives for funding pension plans, and establish the Pension Benefit Guaranty Corporation to insure pension plans against financial failures.

Employee Services and Benefits Programs that include a wide array of alternative pay forms ranging from payments for time not worked (vacations, jury duty) through services (drug counseling, financial planning, cafeteria support) to protection (medical care, life insurance, and pensions).

Employer of Choice The view that a firm's external wage competitiveness is just one facet of its overall human resource policy, and competitiveness is more properly judged on overall policies. So challenging work, high calibre colleagues, or an organization's prestige must be factored into an overall consideration of attractiveness.

Entitlement Employee belief that returns and/or rewards are due regardless of individual or company performance.

Entry Jobs Jobs that are filled from the external labor market and whose pay tends to reflect external economic factors rather than an organization's culture and traditions.

Equal Employment Opportunity Commission (EEOC) A commission of the federal government charged with enforcing the provisions of the Civil Rights Act of 1964 and the EPA of 1963 as it pertains to sex discrimination in pay.

Equalization Component As a part of an expatriate compensation package, equalization is one form of equity designed to "keep the worker whole" (i.e., maintain real income or purchasing power of base pay). This equalization typically comes in the form of tax equalization, housing allowances, and other allowances and premiums.

Equal Pay Act (EPA) of 1963 An amendment to the Fair Labor Standards Act of 1938 prohibiting pay differentials on jobs which are substantially equal in terms of skills, efforts, responsibility, and working conditions, except when they are the result of bona fide seniority, merit, or production-based systems, or any other job-related factor other than sex.

Equity Absolute or relative justice or "fairness" in an exchange such as the employment contract. Absolute fairness is evaluated against a universally accepted criterion of equity, while relative fairness is assessed against a criterion that may vary according to the individuals involved in the exchange, the nature of what is exchanged, and the context of the exchange.

Equity Pay Objective Fair pay treatment for all the participants in the employment relationship. Focuses attention on pay systems that recognize employee contributions as well as employee needs.

Equity Theory A theory proposing that in an exchange relationship (such as employment) the equality of outcome/input ratios between a person and a comparison other (a standard or relevant person/group) will determine fairness or equity. If the ratios diverge from each other, the person will experience reactions of unfairness and inequity.

ESOP (Employee Stock Ownership Plan) A plan in which a company borrows money from a financial institution using its stock as a collateral for the loan. Principal and interest loan repayment are tax deductible. With each loan repayment, the lending institution releases a certain amount of stock being held as security. The stock is then placed into an Employee Stock Ownership Trust (ESOT) for distribution at no cost to all employees. The employees receive the stock upon retirement or separation from the company. TRASOPs and PAYSOPs are variants of ESOPs.

Essay An open-ended performance appraisal format. The descriptors used could range from comparisons with other employees through adjectives, behaviors, and goal accomplishment.

Exchange Value The price of labor (the wage) determined in a competitive market; in other words, labor's worth (the price) is whatever the buyer and seller agree upon.

Executive Perquisites (Perks) Special benefits made available to top executives (and sometimes other managerial employees). May be taxable income to the receiver. Company-related perks may include luxury office, special parking, and company-paid membership in clubs/associations, hotels, resorts. Personal perks include such things as low-cost loans, personal and legal counseling, free home repairs and improvements, and so on. Since 1978, various tax and agency rulings have slowly been requiring companies to place a value on perks, thus increasing the taxable income of executives.

Exempt Jobs Jobs not subject to provisions of the Fair Labor Standards Act with respect to minimum wage and overtime. Exempt employees include most executives, administrators, professionals, and outside sales representatives.

Expatriate Colony Sections of large cities where expatriates tend to locate and form a ghetto-like community that takes on some of the cultural flavor of the expatriates' home countries. An example of an expatriate colony would be the Roppongi section of Tokyo, where many Americans live while working in Japan.

Expatriates Employees assigned outside their base country for any period of time in excess of one year.

Expectancies Beliefs (or subjective probability climates) individuals have that particular actions on their part will lead to certain outcomes or goals.

Expectancy (VIE) Theory A motivation theory that proposes that individuals will select an alternative based on how this choice relates to outcomes such as rewards. The choice made is based on the strength or value of the outcome and on the perceived probability that this choice will lead to the desired outcome.

Experience Rating Insurance premiums vary directly with the number of claims filed. Experience rating is applied to Unemployment Insurance and Workers' Compensation, and may be applied to commercial health insurance premiums.

External Competitiveness Refers to the pay relationships among organizations and focuses attention on the competitive positions reflected in these relationships.

External Equity Fairness in relation to the amount paid in the relevant external market.

Extrinsic Rewards Rewards that a person receives from sources other than the job itself. They include compensation, supervision, promotions, vacations, friendships, and all other important outcomes apart from the job itself.

Face Validity The determination of the relevance of a measuring device on "appearance" only.

Factor Comparison A job evaluation method in which jobs are assessed on the basis of two criteria: (1) a set of compensable factors and (2) wages for a selected set of jobs.

Factor Scales Reflect different degrees within each compensable factor. Most commonly five to seven degrees are defined. Each degree may also be anchored by the typical skills, tasks and behaviors, or key job titles.

Factor Weights Indicate the importance of each compensable factor in a job evaluation system. Weights can be derived either through a committee judgment or statistical analysis.

Fair Labor Standards Act of 1938 (FLSA) A federal law governing minimum wage, overtime pay, equal pay for men and women in the same types of jobs, child labor, and recordkeeping requirements.

Family and Medical Leave Act of 1993 Entitles eligible employees to receive unpaid leave up to 12 weeks per year for specified family or medical reasons, such as caring for ill family members or adopting a child.

Fat Grades The wide range of flexibility permitted in broadband pay structures in defining job responsibilities. Fat grades support redesigned, downsized, or seamless organizations that have eliminated layers of managerial jobs. Employees may move laterally across a band in order to gain depth of experience.

Federal Employee Pay Comparability Act of 1990 (FEPCA) Seeks to close any pay gap between federal employees and employees of local and state government as well as private industry. The act phases in wedge adjustments when rates differ from local market rates by more than 5 percent.

Federal Insurance Contribution Act (FICA) The source of social security contribution withholding requirements. The FICA deduction is paid by both employer and employee.

First Impression Error Developing a negative (positive) opinion of an employee early in the review period and allowing that to negatively (positively) color all subsequent perceptions of performance.

Flat Rates A single rate, rather than a range of rates, for all individuals performing each job. Ignores seniority and performance differences.

Flexible Benefits *See* Cafeteria (Flexible) Benefit Plan.

Flexible Benefits Plan Benefits package in which employees are given a core of critical benefits (necessary for minimum security) and permitted to expend the remainder of their benefits allotment on options that they find most attractive.

Flexible Compensation The allocation of employee compensation in a variety of forms tailored to organization pay objectives and/or the needs of individual employees.

Forms of Compensation Pay may be received directly in the form of cash (e.g., wages, bonuses, incentives) or indirectly through series and benefits (e.g., pensions, health insurance, vacations). This definition excludes other forms of rewards or returns that employees may receive, such as promotion, recognition for outstanding work behavior, and the like.

Forms of Pay *See* Forms of Compensation.

Functional Job Analysis (FJA) A conventional approach to job analysis that is followed by the U.S. Department of Labor. Five categories of data are collected: what the worker does; the methodologies and techniques employed; the machines, tools, and equipment used; the products and services that result; and the traits required of the worker. FJA constitutes a modification of DOLs methodology and is widely used in the public sector.

Gain-Sharing or Group Incentive Plans Incentive plans that are based on some measure of group performance rather than individual performance. Taking data on a past year as a base, group incentive plans may focus on cost savings (e.g., the Scanlon, Rucker, and Improshare plans) or on profit increases (profit sharing plans) as the standard to distribute a portion of the accrued funds among relevant employees.

Gantt Plan Individual incentive plan that provides for variable incentives as a function of a standard expressed as time period per unit of production. Under this plan, a standard time for a task is purposely set at a level requiring high effort to complete.

General Schedule (GS) A job evaluation plan used by the U.S. Office of Personnel Management for white collar employees. It has 18 "grades" (classes). Most jobs are in 15 grades; the top three are combined into a "supergrade" that covers senior executives.

Generic Job Analysis Generalized, less detailed data collection at a level used to write a broad job description that covers a large number of related tasks. The result is that two people doing the same broadly defined job could be doing entirely different, yet related, tasks.

Geographic Differentials *See* Locality Pay.

Glass Ceiling A subtle barrier that keeps women and minorities out of the very highest executive positions.

Global Approach Substitutes a particular skill and experience level for job descriptions in determining external market rates. Includes rates for all individuals who possess that skill.

Group Incentive Plans *See* Gain-Sharing or Group Incentive Plans.

Halo Error An appraiser gives favorable ratings to all job duties based on impressive performance in just one job function. For example, a rater who hates tardiness rates a prompt subordinate high across all performance dimensions exclusively because of this one characteristic.

Halsey 50-50 Method Individual incentive method that provides for variable incentives as a function of a standard expressed as time period per unit of production. This plan derives its name from the shared split between worker and employer of any savings in direct costs.

Hay System A point factor system that evaluates jobs with respect to know-how, problem solving, and accountability. It is used primarily for exempt (managerial/professional) jobs.

Health Maintenance Act Requires employers to offer alternative health coverage options (e.g., Health Maintenance Organizations) to employees.

Health Maintenance Organization (HMO) A nontraditional health care delivery system. HMOs offer comprehensive benefits and outpatient services, as well as hospital coverages, for a fixed monthly prepaid fee.

Hierarchies (or Job Structures) Jobs ordered according to their relative content and/or value.

High-Commitment Practices Prescribes high base pay, sharing successes only (not risks), guaranteed employment security, promotions from within, training and skill development, employee ownership, and long-term perspective. High-commitment practices are believed to attract and retain a high-committed workforce that will become the source of competitive advantage.

Hit Rate The ability of a job evaluation plan to replicate a predetermined, agreed-upon job structure.

Horn Error The opposite of a halo error; downgrading an employee across all performance dimensions exclusively because of poor performance on one dimension.

Human Capital Theory An economic theory proposing that the investment one is willing to make to enter an occupation is related to the returns one expects to earn over time in the form of compensation.

Hybrid Policy Pay plan that includes base pay set at or below competitive market rates *plus* performance-based bonuses that vary with the unit's profitability.

Integrated Manufacturing Strategies Organization strategies designed to gain competitive advantage such as just-in-time manufacturing, statistical quality control, and advanced technologies.

Implicit Employment Contract An unwritten understanding between employers and employees over the reciprocal obligations and returns; employees contribute to achieving the goals of the employer in exchange for returns given by the employer and valued by the employee.

Implicit Social Contract The beliefs and expectations held by a person of the inputs they are expected to make to society, and the outputs they are expected to get in return.

Improshare (IMproved PROductivity through SHARing) A gain-sharing plan in which a standard is developed to identify the expected hours required to produce an acceptable level of output. Any savings arising from production of agreed-upon output in fewer than expected hours are shared by the firm and the worker.

Incentive Inducement offered in advance to influence future performance (e.g., sales commissions).

Incentive Stock Options (ISOs) A form of deferred compensation designed to influence long-term performance. Gives an executive the right to pay today's market price for a block of shares in the company at a future time. No tax is due until the shares are sold.

Increase Guidelines Inherent compensation system controls. They specify amount and timing of pay increases on an organizationwide basis.

Indirect Compensation Pay received through services and benefits (e.g., pensions, health insurance, vacations).

Individual-Based Systems They focus on employee rather than job characteristics. Pay is based on the highest work-related skills employees possess rather than on the specific job performed.

Individual Incentive Plans Incentive compensation that is tied directly to objective measures of individual production (e.g., sales commissions).

Institutional Theory Theory that organizations base their practices to a large extent on what other organizations are doing.

Instrumentality The perceived contingency that an outcome (performing well) has another outcome (a reward such as pay).

Internal Consistency Refers to the pay relationships among jobs or skill levels within a single organization and focuses attention on employee and management acceptance of those relationships. It involves establishing equal pay for jobs of equal worth and acceptable pay differentials for jobs of unequal worth.

Internal Equity *See* Internal Consistency.

Internal Labor Markets The rules or procedures that regulate the allocation of employees among different jobs within a single organization.

Internal Pricing Pricing jobs in relationship to what other jobs within the organization are paid.

Interrater Reliability The extent of agreement among raters rating the same individual, group, or phenomena.

Inventories Questionnaires in which tasks, behaviors, and abilities are tested. The core of all quantitative job analysis.

Job Analysis The systematic process of collecting and making certain judgments about all of the important information related to the nature of a specific job. It provides the knowledge needed to define jobs and conduct job evaluation.

Job-Based Systems Focus on jobs as the basic unit of analysis to determine the pay structure; hence, job analysis is required.

Job Classes or Grades Each represents a grouping of jobs that are considered substantially similar for pay purposes.

Job Cluster A series of jobs grouped for job evaluation and wage and salary administration purposes on the basis of common skills, occupational qualifications, technology, licensing, working conditions, union jurisdiction, workplace, career paths, and organizational tradition.

Job Competition Theory Economic theory that postulates a "quoted" wage for a job irrespective of an individual's qualifications. Because the most qualified applicants will be hired first, later hires will be more costly because they will require more training or will be less productive.

Job Content Information that describes a job. May include responsibility assumed and/or the tasks performed.

Job Description A summary of the most important features of the job as it is performed. It identifies the job and describes the general nature of the work, specific task responsibilities, outcomes, and employee characteristics required to perform the job.

Job Evaluation A systematic procedure designed to aid in establishing pay differentials among jobs within a single employer. It includes classification, comparison of the relative worth of jobs, blending internal and external market forces, measurement, negotiation, and judgment.

Job Evaluation Committee Usually having a membership representing all important constituencies within the organization. It may be charged with the responsibility of (1) selecting a job evaluation system, (2) carrying out or at least supervising the process of job evaluation, and (3) evaluating the success with which the job evaluation has been conducted. Its role may vary among organizations.

Job Evaluation Manual Contains information on the job evaluation plan and is used as a "yardstick" to evaluate jobs. It includes a description of the job evaluation method used, descriptions of all jobs, if relevant, a description of compensable factors, numerical degree scales, and weights. May also contain a description of available review or appeals procedure.

Job Family Jobs involving work of the same nature but requiring different skill and responsibility levels (e.g., computing and account-recording is a job family; bookkeeper, accounting clerk, tellers are jobs within that family).

Job Grade *See* Pay Grade.

Job Hierarchy A grouping of jobs based on their job-related similarities and differences and on their value to the organization's objectives.

Job Pricing The process of assigning pay to jobs, based on thorough job analysis and job evaluation.

Job Structure Relationships among jobs inside an organization, based on work content and the job's relative contribution to achieving organization's objectives.

Job-to-Job Comparison Method of pay equity adjustment prescribed by Ontario, Canada's, pay equity legislation. Looks at working conditions, knowledge, and skills needed to perform the job regardless of gender. The relative worth of the job is compared to that of others in determining pay. Removes use of market data for setting pay.

Just Wage Doctrine A theory of job value that posited a "just" or equitable wage for any occupation based on that occupation's place in the larger social hierarchy. According to this doctrine, pay structures should be designed and justified on the basis of societal norms, custom, and tradition, not on the basis of economic and market forces.

Key Jobs *See* Benchmark (or Key) Jobs.

Knowledge Analysis The systematic collection of information about the knowledge or skills required to perform work in an organization.

Knowledge Blocks The different type of knowledge or competencies required to perform work.

Knowledge Systems Linking pay to additional knowledge related to the same job (depth) (e.g., scientists and teachers) or to a number of different jobs (breadth) (e.g., technician).

Labor Demand In economic models, the demand for labor is a curve that indicates how the desired level of employment varies with changes in the price of labor when other factors are held constant. The shape of the labor demand curve is downward sloping. Thus, an increase in the wage rate will reduce the demand for labor in both the short and long run.

Labor Supply In economic models, the supply of labor is a curve or schedule representing the average pay required to attract different numbers of employees. The shape of the labor supply curve varies depending on the assumptions. In perfectly competitive markets, an individual firm faces a horizontal (elastic) supply of labor curve.

Lag Pay Level Policy Setting a wage structure to match market rates at the beginning of plan year only. The rest of the plan year, internal rates will lag behind market rates. Its objective is to offset labor costs, but it may hinder a firm's ability to attract and retain quality employees.

Lead Pay Level Policy Setting a wage structure to lead the market throughout the plan year. Its aim is to maximize a firm's ability to attract and retain quality employees and to minimize employee dissatisfaction with pay.

Least Squares Line In regression analysis, the line fitted to a scatterplot of coordinates that minimizes the squared deviations of coordinates around the line. This line is known as the *best fit line*.

Legally Required Benefits Benefits that are required by statutory law: workers' compensation, social security, and unemployment compensation are required in the United States. Required benefits vary among countries. Companies operating in foreign countries must comply with host country compensation and benefits mandates.

Leniency Error Consistently rating someone higher than is deserved.

Leveling Weighting market survey data according to the closeness of the job matches.

Level of Aggregation Refers to the size of the work unit for which performance is measured (e.g., individual work group, department, plan, or organization) and to which rewards are distributed.

Level Rise The percentage increase in the average wage rate paid.

Percent level rise =

$$100 \times \frac{\text{Avg. pay year end} - \text{Avg. pay year beginning}}{\text{Avg. pay at the beginning of the year}}$$

Lifetime Employment Most prevalent in Japanese companies, this refers to the notion of an employee staying with the same company for their entire career, despite possible poor performance on the part of either the employee or the company.

Linear Regression A statistical technique that allows an analyst to build a model of a relationship between variables that are assumed to be linearly related.

Line of Sight Refers to an employee's ability to see how individual performance affects incentive payout. Employees on a straight piecework pay system have a clear line of sight—their pay is a direct function of the number of units they produce; employees covered by profit sharing have a fuzzier line of sight—their payouts are a function of many forces, only one of which is individual performance.

Local Country Nationals (LCNs) Citizens of a country in which a U.S. foreign subsidiary is located. LCNs' compensation is tied either to local wage rates or to the rates of U.S. expatriates performing the same job. Each practice has different equity implications.

Locality Pay Adjusting pay rates for employees in a specific geographic area to account for local conditions such as labor shortages, housing cost differentials, and so on.

Long-Term Disability (LTD) Plan An insurance plan that provides payments to replace income lost through an inability to work that is not covered by other legally required disability income plans.

Long-Term Incentives Inducements offered in advance to influence longer rate (multiyear) results. Usually offered to top managers and professionals to focus on long-term organization objectives.

Low-High Approach Using the lowest- and highest-paid benchmark job in the external market to anchor an entire skill-based structure.

Lump-Sum Award Payment of entire increase (typically merit based) at one time. Amount is not factored into base pay so any benefits tied to base pay also don't increase.

Lump-Sum Bonus *See* Lump-Sum Award.

Managed Care Refers to steps taken to contain health care and Workers' Compensation costs, such as switching to preferred provider organizations for health care delivery, utilization-review procedures and medical bill audits.

Management by Objectives (MBO) An employee planning, development, and appraisal procedure in which a supervisor and a subordinate, or group of subordinates, jointly identify and establish common performance goals. Employee performance on the absolute standards is evaluated at the end of the specified period.

Marginal Product of Labor The additional output associated with the employment of one additional human resources unit, with other factors held constant.

Marginal Productivity Theory (MPT) By contrast with Marxist "surplus value" theory, MPT focuses on labor demand rather than supply and argues that employers will pay a wage to a unit of labor that equals that unit's use (not exchange) value. That is, work is compensated in proportion to its contribution to the organization's production objectives.

Marginal Revenue of Labor The additional revenue generated when the firm employs one additional unit of human resources, with other factors held constant.

Market Pay Lines Summarize the distribution of market rates for the benchmark jobs under consideration. Several methods to construct the lines can be used: a single line connecting the distributions' midpoints (means or medians), or the 25th, 50th, and 75th percentiles. Often the lines are fitted to the data through a statistical procedure, such as regression analysis.

Market Pricing Setting pay structures almost exclusively through matching pay for a very large percentage of jobs with rates paid in the external market.

Maturity Curves A plot of the empirical relationship between current pay and years since a professional has last received a degree (YSLD), thus allowing organizations to determine a competitive wage level for specific professional employees with varying levels of experience.

Merit Pay A reward that recognizes outstanding past performance. It can be given in the form of lump-sum payments or as increments to the base pay. Merit programs are commonly designed to pay different amounts (often at different times) depending on the level of performance.

Merit Pay Increase Guidelines Tie pay increases to performance. They may take one of two forms: The simplest version specifies pay increases permissible for different levels of performance. More complex guidelines tie pay not only to performance but also to position in the pay range.

Merrick Plan Individual incentive plan that provides for variable incentives as a function of units of production per time period. It works like the Taylor plan, but three piece-work rates are set: (1) high—for production exceeding 100 percent of standard; (2) medium—for production between 83 percent and 100 percent of standard; and (3) low—for production less than 83 percent of standard.

Middle and Top Management Employees above the supervisory level who have technical and administrative training and whose major duties entail the direction of people and the organization. They can be classified as special groups to the extent the organization devises special compensation programs to attract and retain these relatively scarce human resources. By this definition, not all managers above the supervisory level qualify for consideration as a special group.

Minimum Wage A minimum wage level for most Americans established by Congress as part of the FLSA of 1938.

Motivation An individual's willingness to engage in some behavior. Primarily concerned with (1) what energizes human behavior, (2) what directs or channels such behavior, and (3) how this behavior is maintained or sustained.

Multiskill Systems Link pay to the number of *different jobs* (breadth) an employee is certified to do, regardless of the specific job he or she is doing.

Mutual Commitment Compensation A pay strategy that combines high wages with an emphasis on quality, innovation, and customer service. Based on the belief that high wages are essential to reinforce cooperation and participation and will provide a better living standard for all employees.

National Electrical Manufacturing Association (NEMA) A point factor job evaluation system that evolved into the National Position Evaluation Plan sponsored by NMTA associates.

National Metal Trades Association Plan (NMTA) A point factor job evaluation plan for production, maintenance, and service personnel.

National Position Evaluation Plan A point factor job evaluation system that evolved from the former plan. Today, the plan is sponsored by 11 management/manufacturing associations and is offered under the umbrella group, NMTA associates.

Need Theories Motivation theories that focus on internally generated needs that induce behaviors designed to reduce these needs.

Noncontributory Financing An employee benefit that is fully paid for by the employer.

Nonexempt Employees Employees who are subject to the provisions of the Fair Labor Standards Act.

Nonqualified Deferred Compensation Plans A plan does not qualify for tax exemption if an employer who pays high levels of deferred compensation to executives does not make proportionate contributions to lower level employees.

Nonqualified Stock Options Gives an executive the right to purchase stock at a stipulated price; the excess over fair market value is taxed as ordinary income.

Objective Performance-Based Pay Systems Focus on objective performance standards (e.g., counting output) derived from organizational objectives and a thorough analysis of the job (e.g., incentive and gain-sharing plans).

Occupational Diseases Diseases that arise out of the course of employment, not including "ordinary diseases of life," for which Workers' Compensation claims can be filed.

Occupational Safety and Health Act (OSHA) of 1970 Designed to improve working conditions in industry, thereby reducing worker accidents and job-related illnesses.

On-Call Employees Employees who must respond to work-related assignments/problems 24 hours a day. Firefighters, SPCA humane officers, and other emergency personnel are traditional examples. Increasingly, this group includes technical workers such as software service personnel.

Organizational Culture The composite of shared values, symbols, and cognitive schemes that ties people together in the organization.

Organizational Values Shared norms and beliefs regarding what is socially, organizationally, and individually right, worthy, or desirable. The composite of values contributes to form a common organizational culture.

Outlier An extreme value that may distort some measures of central tendency.

Outsourcing The practice of hiring outside vendors to perform functions that do not directly contribute to business objectives and in which the organization does not have comparative advantage.

Paired Comparison A ranking job evaluation method that involves comparing all possible pairs of jobs under study.

Pay Bands Combining separate job classifications into a smaller number of divisions, called *bands*. Created to increase flexibility.

Pay Discrimination It is usually defined to include (1) access discrimination that occurs when qualified women and minorities are denied access to particular jobs, promotions, or training opportunities and (2) valuation discrimination that takes place when minorities or women are paid less than white males for performing substantially equal work. Both types of discrimination are illegal under Title VII of the Civil Rights Act of 1964. Others argue that valuation discrimination can also occur when men and women hold entirely different jobs (in content or results) that are of comparable worth to the employer. Existing federal laws do not support the "equal pay for work of comparable worth" standard.

Pay Equity *See* Comparable Worth.

Pay-for-Knowledge System A compensation practice whereby employees are paid for the number of different jobs they can adequately perform or the amount of knowledge they possess.

Pay-for-Performance Plans Pay that varies with some measure of individual or organizational performance, such as merit pay, lump-sum bonus plans, skill-based pay, incentive plans, variable pay plans, risk sharing, and success sharing.

Pay Grade One of the classes, levels, or groups into which jobs of the same or similar values are grouped for compensation purposes. All jobs in a pay grade have the same pay range—maximum, minimum, and midpoint.

Pay Increase Guidelines The mechanism through which performance levels are translated into pay increases and, therefore, dictate the size and time of the pay reward for good performance.

Pay Level An average of the array of rates paid by an employer.

Pay Level Policies Decisions concerning a firm's level of pay vis-à-vis product and labor market competitors. There are three classes of pay level policies: to lead, to match, or to follow competition.

Pay Mix Relative emphasis among compensation compotents such as base pay, merit, incentives, and benefits.

Pay Objectives *See* Compensation Objectives.

Pay Plan Design A process to identify pay levels, components, and timing that best match individual needs and organizational requirements.

Pay Policy Line Represents the organization's pay-level policy relative to what competitors pay for similar jobs.

Pay Ranges The range of pay rates from minimum to maximum set for a pay grade or class. They put limits on the rates an employer will pay for a particular job.

Pay Satisfaction A function of the discrepancy between employee perceptions of how much pay they *should* receive and how much pay they *do* receive. If these perceptions are equal, an employee is said to experience pay satisfaction.

PAYSOPs (Payroll-Based Tax Credit Employee Stock Ownership Plans) A form of TRASOP in which the tax credit allotted to plan sponsors who permit and match voluntary employee contributions is payroll based, not investment based.

Pay Structures The array of pay rates for different jobs within a single organization; they focus attention on differential compensation paid for work of unequal worth.

Pay Techniques Mechanisms or technologies of compensation management, such as job analysis, job descriptions, market surveys, job evaluation, and the like, that tie the four basic pay policies to the pay objectives.

Pay with Competition Policy This policy tries to ensure that a firm's labor costs are approximately equal to those of its competitors. It seeks to avoid placing an employer at a disadvantage in pricing products or in maintaining a qualified work force.

Pension Benefit Guaranty Corporation To protect individuals from bankrupt companies (and pension plans!), employers are required to pay insurance premiums to this agency. In turn, the PBGC guarantees payment of vested benefits to employees formerly covered by terminated pension plans.

Pension Plan A form of deferred compensation. All pension plans usually have four common characteristics: (1) they involve deferred payments to a former employee (or surviving spouse) for past services rendered; they all specify (2) a normal retirement age at which time benefits begin to accrue to the employee, (3) a formula employed to calculate benefits, and (4) integration with social security benefits.

Percentage Pay Range Overlap *See* Range Overlap.

Performance-Based Pay *See* Pay-for-Performance Plans.

Performance Dimension Training Training performance appraisers about the performance dimensions on which to evaluate employee performance.

Performance Evaluation (or Performance Appraisal) A process to determine correspondence between worker behavior/task outcomes and employer expectations (performance standards).

Performance Ranking The simplest, fastest, easiest to understand, and least expensive performance appraisal technique. Orders employees from highest to lowest in performance.

Performance Share/Unit Plans Cash or stock awards earned through achieving specific goals.

Performance Standard An explicit statement of what work output is expected from employees in exchange for compensation.

Performance Standard Training Training that gives performance appraisers a frame of reference for making ratee appraisals.

Perquisite Also known as a "perk"; the extras bestowed on top management, such as private dining rooms, company cars, first class airfare.

Phantom Stock Plan Stock plan in which an increase in stock price at a fixed future date determines the cash or stock award. These are called phantom plans because the organization in question is not publicly traded. Stock price, therefore, is an illusion. The "phantom price" is derived from standard financial accounting procedures.

Planned Compa-Ratio Budgeting A form of top-down budgeting in which a planned compa-ratio rather than a planned level rise is established to control pay costs.

Planned Level Rise The percentage increase in average pay that is planned to occur after considering such factors as anticipated rates of change in market data, changes in cost of living, the employer's ability to pay, and the efforts of turnover and promotions. This index may be used in top-down budgeting to control compensation costs.

Planned Level Rise Budgeting A form of top-down budgeting under which a planned level rise rather than a planned compa-ratio is established as the target to control pay costs.

Point (Factor) Method A job evaluation method that employs (1) compensable factors, (2) factor degrees numerically scaled, and (3) weights reflecting the relative importance of each factor. Once scaled degrees and weights are established for each factor, each job is measured against each compensable factor and a total score is calculated for each job. The total points assigned to a job determine the job's relative value and hence its location in the pay structure.

Policy Capturing Approach to Factor Selection *See* Statistical Approach to Factor Selection.

Policy Line A pay line that reflects the organization's policy with respect to the external labor market.

Portability Transferability of pension benefits for employees moving to a new organization; ERISA does not require mandatory portability of private pensions. On a voluntary basis, the employer may agree to let an employee's pension benefit transfer to an individual retirement account (IRA), or, in a reciprocating arrangement, to the new employer.

Position Analysis Questionnaire (PAQ) A structured job analysis technique that classifies job information into seven basic factors: information input, mental processes, work output, relationships with other persons, job context, other job characteristics, and general dimensions. The PAQ analyzes jobs in terms of worker-oriented data.

Position Description Questionnaire (PDQ) A quantitative job analysis technique.

Preferred Provider Organization (PPO) Health care delivery system in which there is a direct contractual relationship between and among employers, health care providers, and third-party payers. An employer is able to select providers (e.g., selected doctors) who agree to provide price discounts and submit to strict utilization controls.

Pregnancy Discrimination Act of 1978 An amendment to Title VII of the Civil Rights Act. It requires employers to extend to pregnant employees or spouses the same disability and medical benefits provided other employees or spouses of employees.

Prevailing Wage Laws A government-defined prevailing wage is the minimum wage that must be paid for work done on covered government projects or purchases. In practice, these prevailing rates have been union rates paid in various geographic areas. The main prevailing wage laws are (1) Davis-Bacon (1931), (2) Walsh-Healey Public Contracts Act (1936), and (3) McNamara-O'Hara Service Contract Act (1965).

Procedural Equity Concerned with the process used to make and implement decisions about pay. It suggests that the way pay decisions are made and implemented may be as important to employees as the results of the decisions.

Procedural Justice Fairness in the procedures used to determine the amount of reward employees will receive.

Process Theories Motivation theories that focus on *how* people are motivated rather than on *what* motivates people (e.g., drive, expectancy, and equity theories).

Product Market The market (or market segments) in which a firm competes to sell products or services.

Professional Employee An employee who has specialized training of a scientific or intellectual nature and whose major duties do not entail the supervision of people.

Profit Sharing Plan Focus on profitability as the standard for group incentive. These plans typically involve one of three distributions: (1) cash or current distribution plans provide full payment to participants soon after profits have been determined (quarterly or annually); (2) deferred plans have a portion of current profits credited to employee accounts, with cash payments made at time of retirement, disability, severance, or death; and (3) combination plans incorporate aspects of both current and deferred options.

Progression through the Pay Ranges Three strategies to move employees through the pay ranges: (1) automatic or seniority-based progression, which is most appropriate when the necessary job skills are within the grasp of most employees; (2) merit progression, which is more appropriate when jobs allow variations in performance; and (3) a combination of automatic and merit progression. For example, employers may grant automatic increases up to the midpoint of the range and permit subsequent increases only when merited on the basis of performance appraisal.

Proportional Value Method of pay equity adjustment prescribed by Ontario, Canada's, pay equity legislation. Can be used to make equity adjustments for female workers when no male-dominated job class exists in the same workplace. An employer examines the relationship or pattern between pay and value for all the male job classes to determine if a pay equity adjustment is required.

Proxy Comparison Method of pay equity adjustment used only in the public sector in Ontario, Canada. Predominately female workplaces (e.g., libraries, day care centers) borrow job information on similar female jobs in other public sector settings that have male comparators.

Psychological Contract Perceptions and beliefs on the part of individuals regarding the terms and conditions of the employment relationship. Psychological contracts differ from implied contracts insofar as they describe individual perceptions of mutual obligation not necessarily observable and verifiable by others.

Purchasing Power The ability to buy goods and services in a certain currency, determined by exchange rates and availability of goods. Companies must determine purchasing power when allocating allowances to expatriates.

Qualified Deferred Compensation Plan To qualify for tax exemption, a deferred compensation program must provide contributions or benefits for employees other than executives that are proportionate in compensation terms to contributions provided to executives.

Quantitative Job Analysis (QJA) Job analysis method that relies on scaled questionnaires and inventories that produce job-related data that are documentable, can be statistically analyzed, and may be more objective than other analysis.

Range Maximums The maximum values to be paid for a job grade, representing the top value the organization places on the output of the work.

Range Midpoint The salary midway between the minimum and maximum rates of a salary range. The midpoint rate for each range is usually set to correspond to the pay policy line and represents the rate paid for satisfactory performance on the job.

Range Minimums The minimum values to be paid for a job grade, representing the minimum value the organization places on the work. Often rates below the minimum are used for trainees.

Range Overlap The degree of overlap between adjoining grade ranges is determined by the differences in midpoints among ranges and the range spread. A high degree of overlap and narrow midpoint differentials indicate small differences in the value of jobs in the adjoining grades and permit promotions without much change in the rates paid. By contrast, a small degree of overlap and wide midpoint differentials allow the manager to reinforce a promotion with a large salary increase. Usually calculated as

$$\text{Percentage overlap} = 100 \times \frac{\text{Maximum rate for lower pay grade} - \text{Minimum rate for higher pay grade}}{\text{Maximum rate for lower pay grade} - \text{Minimum rate for lower pay grade}}$$

Ranges *See* Pay Ranges.

Range Width or Spread The range maximum and minimum are usually based on what other employers are doing and some judgment about how the range spread fits the organization, including the amount of individual discretion in the work. Usually calculated as

$$\frac{\text{Range maximum} - \text{Range minimum}}{\text{Range minimum}}$$

Ranking A simple job evaluation method that involves ordering the job descriptions from highest to lowest in value.

Ranking Format A type of performance appraisal format that requires the rater to compare employees against each other to determine the relative ordering of the group on some performance measure.

Rater Error Training Training performance appraisers to identify and suppress psychometric errors such as leniency, severity, central tendency, and halo errors when evaluating employee performance.

Rating Errors Errors in judgment that occur in a systematic manner when an individual observes and evaluates a person, group, or phenomenon. The most frequently described rating errors include halo, leniency, severity, and central tendency errors.

Rating Formats A type of performance appraisal format that requires raters to evaluate employees on absolute measurement scales that indicate varying levels of performance.

Recency Error The opposite of first impression error. Performance (either good or bad) at the end of the review period plays too large a role in determining an employee's rating for the entire period.

Red Circle Rates Pay rates that are above the maximum rate for a job or pay range for a grade.

Reengineering Changes in the way work is designed to include external customer focus. Usually includes organizational de-layering and job restructuring.

Regression A statistical technique for relating present pay differentials to some criterion, that is, pay rates in the external market, rates for jobs held predominantly by men, or factor weights that duplicate present rates for all jobs in the organization.

Reinforcement Theories Theories such as expectancy and operant conditioning theory grant a prominent role to rewards (e.g., compensation) in motivating behavior. They argue that pay motivates behavior to the extent merit increases and other work-related rewards are allocated on the basis of performance.

Relational Returns The nonquantifiable returns employees get from employment, such as social satisfaction, friendship, feeling of belonging, or accomplishment.

Relative Value of Jobs Refers to their relative contribution to organizational goals, to their external market rates, or to some other agreed-upon rates.

Relevant Markets Those employers with whom an organization competes for skills and products/services. Three factors commonly used to determine the relevant markets are: the occupation or skills required, the geography (willingness to relocate and/or commute), and the other employers involved (particularly those who compete in the product market).

Reliability The consistency of the results obtained. That is, the extent to which any measuring procedure yields the same results on repeated trials. Reliable job information does not mean that it is accurate (valid), comprehensive, or free from bias.

Reopener Clause A provision in an employment contract that specifies that wages, and sometimes such nonwage items as pension/benefits, will be renegotiated under certain conditions (changes in cost of living, organization, profitability, and so on).

Reservation Wage A theoretical minimum standard below which a job seeker will not accept an offer, no matter how attractive the other job attributes.

Resource Dependency The theory that internal pay structures are based on the differential control jobs exert over critical resources.

Responsibility-Oriented Job descriptions that focus on outcomes. Recognizes broad accountability for the accomplishment of results that help the organization attain its objectives.

Restricted Stock Plan Grants stock at a reduced price with condition that it not be sold before a specified date.

Revenue Act of 1978 Primarily simplified pension plans, added tax incentives for individual retirement accounts (IRAs), and adjusted requirements for ESOPs. The act also provided that cafeteria benefit plans need not be included in gross income and reaffirmed the legality of deferring compensation and taxes due on it for an employee.

Revenue Reconciliation Act of 1993 Limits employer deductions for executive compensation to $1 million and caps the amount of executive compensation used to compute contributions to and benefits from qualified retirement plans.

Reward System The composite of all organizational mechanisms and strategies used to formally acknowledge employee behaviors and performance. It includes all forms of compensation, promotions, and assignments; nonmonetary awards and recognitions; training opportunities; job design and analysis; organizational design and working conditions; the supervisor; social networks; performance standards and reward criteria; performance evaluation; and the like.

Risk Sharing An incentive plan in which employee base wages are set below a specified level (e.g., 80 percent of the market wage) and incentive earnings are used to raise wages above the base. In good years an employee's incentive pay will more than make up for the 20 percent shortfall, giving the employee a pay premium. Because employees assume some of the risk, risk sharing plans pay more generously than success sharing plans in good years.

Rowan Plan Individual incentive plan that provides for variable incentives as a function of a standard expressed as time period per unit of production. It is similar to the Halsey plan, but in this plan a worker's bonus increases as the time required to complete the task decreases.

Rucker Plan A group cost savings plan in which cost reductions due to employee efforts are shared with the employees. It involves a somewhat more complex formula than a Scanlon plan for determining employee incentive bonuses.

Salary Pay given to employees who are exempt from regulations of the Fair Labor Standards Act, and hence do not receive overtime pay (e.g., managers and professionals). "Exempts" pay is calculated at an annual or monthly rate rather than hourly.

Salary Continuation Plans Benefit options that provide some form of protection for disability. Some are legally required, such as Workers' Compensation provisions for work-related disability and Social Security disability income provisions for those who qualify.

Salary Sales Compensation Plan Under this plan, the sales force is paid a fixed income not dependent on sales volume.

Sales Compensation Any form of compensation paid to sales representatives. Sales compensation formulas usually attempt to establish direct incentives for sales outcomes.

Scaling Determining the intervals on a measurement instrument.

Scanlon Plan A group cost savings plan designed to lower labor costs without lowering the level of a firm's activity. Incentives are derived as the ratio between labor costs and sales values of production (SVOP).

Self-Insurance An organization funding its own insurance claims, for either health or life insurance or Workers' Compensation.

Seniority Increases These tie pay increases to a progression pattern based on seniority. To the extent performance improves with time on the job, this method has the rudiments of paying for performance.

Severity Error The opposite of leniency error. Rating someone consistently lower than is deserved.

Shirking Behavior The propensity of employees to allow the marginal revenue product of their labor to be less than its marginal cost; to be lax. One measure of shirking is the number of disciplinary layoffs.

Short-Term Disability *See* Workers' Compensation.

Short-Term Incentives Inducements offered in advance to influence future short-range (annual) results. Usually very specific performance standards are established.

Short-Term Income Protection *See* Unemployment Insurance.

Sick Leave Paid time when not working due to illness or injury.

Signaling The notion that an employer's pay policy communicates to both prospective and current employees what kinds of behaviors are sought. Applicants may signal their likely performance to potential employees through their personal credentials such as experience or educational degrees.

Simplified Employee Pension (SEP) A retirement income arrangement intended to markedly reduce the paperwork for regular pension plans.

Single Rate Pay System A compensation policy under which all employees in a given job are paid at the same rate instead of being placed in a pay grade. Generally applies to situations in which there is little room for variation in job performance, such as an assembly line.

Skill Analysis A systematic process to identify and collect information about skills required to perform work in an organization.

Skill Based Links pay to the depth and/or breadth of the skills, abilities, and knowledge a person acquires/demonstrates that are relevant to the work. Typically applies to operators, technicians, and office workers where the work is relatively specific and defined. The criterion chosen can influence employee behaviors by describing what is required to get higher pay.

Skill-Based/Global Approach to Wage Survey This approach does not emphasize comparison of pay for specific jobs. Instead, it recognizes that employers usually tailor jobs to the organization or individual employee. Therefore, the rates paid to every individual employee in an entire skill group or function are included in the salary survey and become the reference point to design pay levels and structures.

Skill-Based Pay System *See* Pay-for-Knowledge System.

Skill Blocks Basic units of knowledge employees must master to perform the work, satisfy customers, and achieve business objectives.

Skill Requirement Includes experience, training, and ability as measured by the performance requirements of a particular job.

Slippage *See* Turnover Effect.

Social Contract Reciprocal understandings involving a critical third party to the employment exchange (e.g., the government). Public policies such as minimum wages, tax laws, social security, and union-management regulations play a significant role in the employment exchange.

Social Information Processing Theory (SIP) Counters need theory by focusing on external factors that motivate performance. According to SIP theorists, workers pay attention to environmental cues (e.g., inputs/outputs of coworkers) and process this information in a way that may alter personal work goals, expectations, and perceptions of equity. In turn, this influences job attitudes, behavior, and performance.

Social Security The Social Security Act of 1935 established what has become the federal old-age, survivors, disability, and health insurance system. The beneficiaries are workers that participate in the social security program, their spouses, dependent parents, and dependent children. Benefits vary according to (1) earnings of the worker, (2) length of time in the program, (3) age when benefits start, (4) age and number of recipients other than the worker, and (5) state of health of recipients other than the worker.

Special Groups Employee groups for whom compensation practices diverge from typical company procedures (e.g., supervisors, middle and upper management, nonsupervisory professionals, sales, and personnel in foreign subsidiaries).

Spillover Effect This phenomenon refers to the fact that improvements obtained in unionized firms "spill over" to nonunion firms seeking ways to lessen workers' incentives for organizing a union.

Spillover Error Continuing to downgrade an employee for performance errors in prior rating periods.

Spot Award One-time award for exceptional performance; also called a Spot Bonus.

Standard Hour Plan Individual incentive plan in which rate determination is based on time period per unit of production, and wages vary directly as a constant function of product level. In this context, the incentive rate in standard hour plans is set based on completion of a task in some expected time period.

Standard Rating Scales Characterized by (1) one or more performance standards being developed and defined for the appraiser and (2) each performance standard having a measurement scale indicating varying levels of performance on that dimension. Appraisers rate the appraisee by checking the point on the scale that best represents the appraisee's performance level. Rating scales vary in the extent to which anchors along the scale are defined.

Statistical Approach to Factor Selection A method that uses a variety of statistical procedures to derive factors from data collected through quantitative job analysis from a sample of jobs that represent the range of the work employees (or an employee group) perform in the company. It is often labeled as *policy capturing* to contrast it with the committee judgment approach.

Stock Appreciation Rights (SARs) SARs permit an executive all the potential capital gain of a stock incentive option (ISO) without requiring the purchase of stock and, thus, reduce an executive's cash commitment. Payment is provided on demand for the difference between the stock option price and current market price.

Stock Purchase Plan (Nonqualified) A plan that is, in effect, a management stock purchase plan. It allows senior management or other key personnel to buy stock in the business. This plan has certain restrictions: (1) the stockholder must be employed for a certain period of time, (2) the business has the right to buy back the stock, and (3) stockholders cannot sell the stock for a defined period.

Stock Purchase Plan (Qualified) A program under which employees buy shares in the company's stock, with the company contributing a specific amount for each unit of employee contribution. Also, stock may be offered at a fixed price (usually below market) and paid for in full by the employees.

Straight Piecework System Individual incentive plan in which rate determination is based on units of production per time period; wages vary directly as a constant function of production level.

Straight Ranking Procedure A type of performance appraisal format that requires the rater to compare or rank each employee relative to each other employee.

Strategic Issues Critical considerations in compensation design such as congruency between the pay system and the strategy, the organization's culture and values, employee needs, and the nature of the union relationships.

Strategy The fundamental direction of the organization. It guides the deployment of all resources, including compensation.

Subjective Performance-Based Pay Systems Focus on subjective performance standards (e.g., achievement of agreed-upon objectives) derived from organizational objectives and a thorough analysis of the job.

Substantive Equity In contrast with procedural equity, refers to the equity of the outcomes (results such as pay level, structure, and employee differentials) of the pay system.

Success Sharing An incentive plan (e.g., profit sharing or gain-sharing) in which an employee's base wage is constant (e.g., set as 100 percent of market wage) and variable pay adds on during successful years. Because base pay is not reduced in bad years, employees bear little risk; their total pay will likely be less than it would be under a risk sharing plan in good years.

Supplemental Unemployment Benefits (SUB) Plan Employer-funded plan that supplements state unemployment insurance payments to workers during temporary periods of layoffs. Largely concentrated in the automobile, steel, and related industries.

Surplus Value The difference between labor's use and exchange value. According to Marx, under capitalism wages are based on labor's exchange value—which is lower than its use value—and, thus, provide only a subsistence wage.

SVOP (Sales Value of Production) This concept includes sales revenue and the value of goods in inventory.

Task Oriented Job descriptions that describe individual jobs in detail based on a prescribed set of duties.

Tax Equalization Allowances A method whereby an expatriate pays neither more nor less tax than the assumed home-country tax on base remuneration. The employer usually deducts the assumed home-country tax from monthly salary and reimburses the employee for all taxes paid in the country of assignment and any actual home-country tax on company remuneration only.

Taylor Plan Individual incentive plan that provides for variable incentives as a function of units of production per time period. It provides two piecework rates that are established for production above (or below) standard, and these rates are higher (or lower) than the regular wage incentive level.

Team Incentive Group incentive restricted to team members with payout usually based on improvements in productivity, customer satisfaction, financial performance, or quality of goods and services directly attributable to the team.

Third Country Nationals (TCNs) Employees of a U.S. foreign subsidiary who maintain citizenship in a country other than the United States or the host country. TCNs' compensation is tied to comparative wages in the local country, the United States, or the country of citizenship. Each approach has different equity implications.

Thrift Savings Plans The typical thrift plan is designed to help American workers in meeting savings goals. The most common plan involves a 50 percent employer match on employee contributions up to a maximum of 6 percent of pay.

Title VII of the Civil Rights Act of 1964 A major piece of legislation prohibiting pay discrimination. It is much broader in intent than the EPA, forbidding discrimination on the basis of race, color, religion, sex, pregnancy, or national origin.

Top-Down Approach to Pay Budgeting Also known as unit-level budgeting. Under this approach, a total pay budget for the organization (or unit) is determined and allocated "down" to individual employees during the plan year. There are many approaches to unit-level budgeting. They differ in the type of financial index used as a control measure. Controlling to planned level rise and controlling to a planned compa-ratio are two typical approaches.

Topping Out When employees in a skill-based compensation plan attain the top pay rate in a job category by accumulating and/or becoming certified for the top-paid skill block(s).

Total Compensation The complete pay package for employees including all forms of money, benefits, services, and in-kind payments.

Total Reward System Includes financial compensation, benefits, opportunities for social interaction, security, status and recognition, work variety, appropriate work load, importance of work, authority/control/autonomy, advancement opportunities, feedback, hazard-free working conditions, and opportunities for personal and professional development. An effective compensation system will utilize many of these rewards.

Tournament Theory The notion that larger differences in pay are more motivating than smaller differences. Like prize awards in a golf tournament, pay increases should get successively greater as one moves up the job hierarchy. Differences between the top job and second highest job should be the largest.

Transactional Returns Cash and benefit forms, as contrasted with relational returns, which emphasize the socio-psychological returns.

TRASOP (Tax Reduction Act Employee Stock Ownership Plan) A form of Employee Stock Ownership Plan (ESOP) that meets specific requirements of the Tax Reform Act of 1975, as amended.

Turnover Effect The downward pressure on average wage that results from the replacement of high-wage-earning employees with workers earning a lower wage.

Two-Tier Pay Plans Wage structures that differentiate pay for the same jobs based on hiring date. A contract is negotiated that specifies that employees hired after a stated day will receive lower wages than their higher seniority peers working on the same or similar jobs.

Unemployment Benefits *See* Unemployment Insurance.

Unemployment Compensation *See* Unemployment Insurance.

Unemployment Insurance (UI) State-administered programs that provide financial security for workers during periods of joblessness. These plans are wholly financed by employers except in Alabama, Alaska, and New Jersey, where there are provisions for relatively small employee contributions.

Unequal Impact *See* Disparate (Unequal) Impact Standard.

Unequal Treatment *See* Disparate (Unequal) Treatment Standard.

U.S. Expatriates (USEs) American citizens working for a U.S. subsidiary in a foreign country. Main compensation concerns are to "keep the expatriates whole" relative to U.S.-based counterparts and to provide expatriates with an incentive wage for accepting the foreign assignment.

Universal Job Factors Factors that could theoretically be used to evaluate all jobs in all organizations.

Use Value The value or price ascribed to the use or consumption of labor in the production of goods or services.

Valence The amount of positive or negative value placed on specific outcomes by an individual.

Validity The accuracy of the results obtained. That is, the extent to which any measuring device measures what it purports to measure.

Valuation Discrimination Focuses on the pay women and minorities receive for the work they perform. Discrimination occurs when members of these groups are paid less than white males for performing substantially equal work. This definition of pay discrimination is based on the standard of "equal pay for equal work." Many believe that this definition is limited. In their view, valuation discrimination can also occur when men and women hold entirely different jobs (in content or results) that are of comparable worth to the employer. Existing federal laws do not support the "equal pay for work of comparable worth" standard.

Variable Pay Tying pay to productivity or some measure that can vary with the firm's profitability.

Vesting A benefit plan provision that guarantees that participants will, after meeting certain requirements, retain a right to the benefits they have accrued, or some portion of them, even if employment under their plan terminates before retirement.

VIE Theory *See* Expectancy (VIE) Theory.

Wage Pay given the employees who are covered by overtime and reporting provisions of the Fair Labor Standards Act. "Nonexempts" usually have their pay calculated at an hourly rate rather than a monthly or annual rate.

Wage Adjustment Provisions Clauses in a multilayer union contract that specify the types of wage adjustments that have to be implemented during the life of the contract. These adjustments might be specified in three major ways: (1) deferred wage increases—negotiated at the time of contract negotiation with the time and amount specified in the contract, (2) cost-of-living adjustments (COLAs) or escalator clauses, and (3) reopener clauses.

Wage and Price Controls Government regulations that aim at maintaining low inflation and low levels of unemployment. They frequently focus on "cost push" inflation, limiting the size of the pay raises and the rate of increases in the prices charged for goods and services. Used for limited time periods only.

Wage Survey The systematic process of collecting information and making judgments about the compensation paid by other employers. Wage survey data are useful to design pay levels and structures.

Walsh-Healey Public Contracts Act of 1936 A federal law requiring certain employers holding federal contracts for the manufacture or provision of materials, supplies, and equipment to pay industry-prevailing wage rates.

Work or Task Data Involve the elemental units of work (tasks), with emphasis on the purpose of each task, collected for job analysis. Work data describe the job in terms of actual tasks performed and their output.

Worker or Behavioral Data Include the behaviors required by the job. Used in job analysis.

Workers' Compensation An insurance program, paid for by the employer, designed to protect employees from expenses incurred for a work-related injury or disease. Each state has its own workers' compensation law.

YSLD Years since a professional has last received a degree.

Zones Ranges of pay used as controls or guidelines within pay bands that can keep the system more structurally intact. Maximums, midpoints, and minimums provide guides to appropriate pay for certain levels of work. Without zones employees may float to the maximum pay, which for many jobs in the band is higher than market value.

COMPANY INDEX

SUBJECT INDEX